*Major Problems in
American History Since 1945*

MAJOR PROBLEMS IN AMERICAN HISTORY SERIES

GENERAL EDITOR

THOMAS G. PATERSON

Major Problems in American History Since 1945

DOCUMENTS AND ESSAYS

THIRD EDITION

EDITED BY

ROBERT GRIFFITH

AMERICAN UNIVERSITY

PAULA BAKER

OHIO STATE UNIVERSITY

HOUGHTON MIFFLIN COMPANY
Boston   New York

For Our Students

Publisher: Patricia Coryell
Senior Consulting Editor: Jean Woy
Senior Development Editor: Jeffrey Greene
Project Editor: Aimee Chevrette
Editorial Assistant: Katherine Leahey
Senior Art and Design Coordinator: Jill Haber Atkins
Photo Editor: Michael Farmer
Cover Design Manager: Anne S. Katzeff
Composition Buyer: Chuck Dutton
Associate Manufacturing Buyer: Susan Brooks
Senior Marketing Manager: Katherine Bates
Marketing Assistant: Lauren Bussard

Cover image: © Diana Ong / SuperStock

Printed in the U.S.A.

Library of Congress Control Number: 2006928406

Instructor's exam copy
ISBN-13: 978-0-618-73159-6
ISBN-10: 0-618-73159-8

For orders, use student text ISBNs:
ISBN-13: 978-0-618-55006-7
ISBN-10: 0-618-55006-2

3456789-MV-10 09 08

Contents

Preface   **xiii**

C H A P T E R   1
The Origins of Postwar America
Page 1

E S S A Y S

Thomas G. Paterson • The Origins of the Postwar International System   **3**

Alan Brinkley • The Legacies of World War II   **16**

Byron E. Shafer • The Puzzle of Postwar Politics   **24**

F U R T H E R   R E A D I N G   **34**

C H A P T E R   2
The Origins of the Cold War
Page 36

D O C U M E N T S

1. President Harry S Truman Discusses the Atom Bomb at Potsdam, July 1945
   38

2. George F. Kennan's "Long Telegram," 1946   **39**

3. Secretary of Commerce Henry A. Wallace Urges a Conciliatory Approach,
   July 1946   **42**

4. Soviet Ambassador Nikolai Novikov Reports on the U.S. Drive for World
   Supremacy, September 1946   **43**

5. The Truman Doctrine, March 1947   **46**

6. Senator Joseph McCarthy Charges the Democrats Are "Soft on Communism,"
   1950   **49**

7. The President's Advisers Urge Military Expansion (NSC-68), April 1950   **51**

E S S A Y S

Arnold A. Offner • President Harry S Truman and the Origins of the Cold War   **55**

John Lewis Gaddis • Two Cold War Empires   **63**

F U R T H E R   R E A D I N G   **79**

CHAPTER 3
The Consumer's Republic: The 1950s and the Emergence of a New Economy of Mass Consumption
Page 81

DOCUMENTS

1. U.S. Business Celebrates the "Miracle of America," 1948   **82**

2. A Report on the Baby Boom, 1954   **84**

3. *Newsweek* Decries the Problem of Dangerous Teens, 1955   **85**

4. *Life* Magazine Identifies the New Teen-age Market, 1959   **88**

5. *U.S. News and World Report* Assesses the Perils of Mass Culture and the Evils of Television, 1955   **90**

6. Vance Packard Warns Against the "Hidden Persuaders," 1957   **94**

ESSAYS

Roland Marchand • Visions of Classlessness   **97**

Kelly Schrum • Making the American Girl   **109**

FURTHER READING   **124**

CHAPTER 4
John F. Kennedy, the Cuban Revolution, and the Cold War
Page 125

DOCUMENTS

1. Fidel Castro Denounces U.S. Policy Toward Cuba, 1960   **127**

2. President John F. Kennedy Calls for an Alliance for Progress, 1961   **130**

3. A Board of Inquiry Reports on the Bay of Pigs, 1961   **131**

4. A Senate Committee Investigates U.S. Plots to Assassinate Castro, 1960–1965 (1975)   **134**

5. President Kennedy and His Advisers Debate Options in the Missile Crisis, October 16, 1962   **136**

6. Soviet Premier Nikita Khrushchev Appeals to President Kennedy, October 26, 1962   **144**

7. Soviet Ambassador Anatoly I. Dobrynin Reports on His Meeting with Robert Kennedy, October 28, 1962   **147**

ESSAYS

Thomas G. Paterson • Spinning Out of Control: Kennedy's War Against Cuba and the Missile Crisis   **148**

Ernest R. May and Philip D. Zelikow • Aftermath   **159**

FURTHER READING   **171**

CHAPTER 5
The African American Struggle for Equality
Page 173

DOCUMENTS

1. The *New York Times* Reports a Murder in Georgia, 1946   **175**

2. African American Parents Petition the Clarendon, S.C., School Board, 1949   **176**

3. A South African Novelist Examines the Plight of "The Negro in the North," 1954   **178**

4. Franklin McCain Remembers the First Sit-in, 1960   **180**

5. Martin Luther King Jr., "I Have a Dream," 1963   **182**

6. Stokely Carmichael Explains "Black Power," 1967   **185**

7. A Senate Committee Reports on the FBI's Campaign Against Martin Luther King, 1963–1968 (1976)   **187**

8. Police and Fire Department Logs Record an Urban Riot, 1967   **189**

ESSAYS

Charles M. Payne • The View from the Trenches   **193**

Thomas J. Sugrue • The Continuing Racial Crisis   **203**

FURTHER READING   **209**

CHAPTER 6
The Great Society and the Politics of Liberal Reform
Page 212

DOCUMENTS

1. President Lyndon B. Johnson Declares War on Poverty, 1964   **214**

2. Congress Strikes Down Segregation in Public Accommodations: The Civil Rights Act of 1964, Title II (1964)   **216**

3. Ronald Reagan Warns of the Dangers of the Welfare State, 1964   **217**

4. Two White House Aides Report the Achievements of the Great Society, 1966   **218**

5. A Conservative Strategist Hails an "Emerging Republican Majority," 1969   **220**

6. Earth Day, 1970   **224**

ESSAYS

James T. Patterson • The Rise of "Rights Consciousness"   **226**

Matthew D. Lassiter • Suburban Politics and the Limits of the Great Society   **233**

FURTHER READING   **242**

C H A P T E R   7
The New Radicalism: Politics and Culture in the 1960s
Page 244

D O C U M E N T S

1. Students for a Democratic Society Issue the Port Huron Statement, 1962   **245**
2. Jerry Rubin Declares Himself a "Child of Amerika," 1970   **250**
3. Radicals Proclaim: "You Don't Need a Weatherman to Know Which Way the Wind Blows," 1969   **251**
4. The FBI's Secret Campaign Against the New Left, 1968–1971 (1976)   **252**
5. Raymond Mungo Searches for a New Age at Total Loss Farm, 1970   **255**
6. A Pollster Reports on "The Big Chill," 1974   **258**

E S S A Y S

Maurice Isserman and Michael Kazin • The Contradictory Legacy of the Sixties   **260**

Hugh Heclo • The Sixties and the Origins of "Postmodern" America   **270**

F U R T H E R   R E A D I N G   **278**

C H A P T E R   8
From the Feminine Mystique to "Second Wave" Feminism
Page 280

D O C U M E N T S

1. Betty Friedan on "The Problem That Has No Name," 1963   **281**
2. NOW Statement of Purpose, 1966   **284**
3. Redstockings Manifesto, 1970   **286**
4. Welfare Is a Women's Issue, 1972   **288**
5. A *Redbook* Magazine Reader Discovers Consciousness-Raising, 1973   **290**
6. The Supreme Court Rules on Abortion: *Roe v. Wade,* 1973   **292**
7. Equal Rights Amendment, 1972   **295**
8. Phyllis Schlafly Proclaims the Power of the Positive Woman, 1977   **295**

E S S A Y S

Alice Echols • Women's Liberation and Sixties Radicalism   **298**

Beth Bailey • Women at Work   **310**

F U R T H E R   R E A D I N G   **322**

C H A P T E R   9
Vietnam and the Crisis of American Empire
Page 324

D O C U M E N T S

1. The Vietnamese Declare Their Independence, 1945   **325**
2. President Dwight D. Eisenhower Explains the Domino Theory, 1954   **327**

3. Final Declaration of the Geneva Conference on Indochina, 1954   **328**

4. A South Vietnamese Peasant Explains Why He Joined the Vietcong, 1961 (1986)   **330**

5. The Gulf of Tonkin Resolution, 1964   **331**

6. President Lyndon Johnson's Advisers Debate Expanding the War, 1965   **332**

7. A "Tunnel Rat" Testifies About the My Lai Massacre, 1969   **334**

8. The Paris Accords, 1973   **336**

E S S A Y S

Michael H. Hunt • The Wages of War   **338**

Arnold R. Isaacs • Competing Memories   **342**

F U R T H E R   R E A D I N G   **347**

C H A P T E R   1 0
Ronald Reagan and the Transformation of America
Page 350

D O C U M E N T S

1. President Jimmy Carter and the Crisis of the American Spirit, 1979   **353**

2. Presidential Candidate Ronald Reagan Calls for New Economic Policies, 1980   **355**

3. A New Right Activist Explains Conservative Success, 1980   **356**

4. President Ronald Reagan Proclaims America's "Spiritual Reawakening," 1983   **360**

5. A Congressional Committee Reports on "Irangate," 1987   **361**

6. An Environmentalist Attacks the Administration's Record, 1988   **366**

7. Surgeon General C. Everett Koop Recalls the Administration's Response to the AIDS Crisis, 1981–1988 (2001)   **369**

E S S A Y S

Benjamin Ginsberg and Martin Shefter • The Republicans Take Control   **372**

Jules Tygiel • A Disputed Legacy   **382**

F U R T H E R   R E A D I N G   **392**

C H A P T E R   1 1
The Promises and Perils of a New Economy
Page 394

D O C U M E N T S

1. "New Democrats" Hail the New Economy, 1998   **395**

2. A Federal Reserve Report Extols "Mass Customization," 1998   **397**

3. *Money* Magazine Asks of Wal-Mart, "How Big Can It Get?" 1999   **403**

4. A Critic Assails the Influence of Wal-Mart, 1999   **405**

5. A Columnist Decries "Outsourcing" in the New Global Economy, 2004   **408**

6. Americans for Democratic Action Reports Growing Poverty and Inequality, 2004   **409**

7. A Research Firm "Segments" the American Market, 2000   **411**

ESSAYS

Barbara Ehrenreich • Working at Wal-Mart   **413**

Michael J. Weiss • The Fragmenting of America   **423**

FURTHER READING   **434**

CHAPTER 12
E Pluribus Unum: *Race and Ethnicity in a Changing World*
Page 435

DOCUMENTS

1. Coming to America, 1900–2002   **437**

2. Proposition 187: Californians Seek to Close the Door to Undocumented Immigrants, 1994   **438**

3. Two Reporters Describe Los Angeles's Racial Tensions, 1995   **439**

4. Social Scientists Report on the "New Americans," 1997   **442**

5. An African American Novelist Decries "Race Talk," 1993   **446**

6. Richard Rodriguez Ponders What It Means to Be "Brown," 2002   **448**

7. Americans Express Support for Both Unity and Diversity, 2003   **450**

ESSAYS

George J. Sanchez • Race, Immigration and Nativism   **452**

Thomas C. Holt • Race, Nation, and the Global Economy   **459**

FURTHER READING   **468**

CHAPTER 13
Politics and Political Culture in "Postmodern" America
Page 471

DOCUMENTS

1. Presidential Candidate Bill Clinton Promises a "New Covenant," 1992   **473**

2. "Gays in the Military" Prompts Mobilization of Conservatives, 1993   **475**

3. The Republican "Contract with America," 1994   **478**

4. President Bill Clinton Ends "Welfare as We Know It," 1996   **480**

5. Special Prosecutor Kenneth Starr's Indictment of President Bill Clinton, 1998   **482**

6. Who Voted for Whom in 2000: A Chart   **484**

7. A Columnist Reports on How the Nation's Agenda Is Set, 2000   **485**

ESSAYS

Bruce Miroff • Bill Clinton and the Postmodern Presidency   **488**

Matthew A. Crenson and Benjamin Ginsberg • The Imperial Presidency Redivivus
501

FURTHER READING   **507**

CHAPTER 14
New World Order
Page 509

DOCUMENTS

1. Presidential George H. W. Bush Announces a New World Order, 1990   **511**

2. One World: An American Diplomat Hails the Opportunities of a New Era,
   1995   **512**

3. Osama Bin Laden Declares Jihad Against America, 1998   **514**

4. The *New York Times* Reports Last Words from the World Trade Center, 2001
   516

5. President George W. Bush Announces a New National Security Strategy,
   2002   **519**

6. Senator Robert C. Byrd Charges "The Emperor Has No Clothes," 2003   **522**

7. An Army Officer Ponders How America Is Losing Hearts and Minds in Iraq,
   2004   **524**

ESSAYS

John Lewis Gaddis • Setting Right a Dangerous World   **527**

Michael H. Hunt • In the Wake of September 11   **534**

FURTHER READING   **542**

Preface

If historians interpret the past through the prism of their own times, they do so especially when they try to understand America's recent past. Consider how the world has changed since the second edition of this book appeared in early 2001. The euphoria and triumphalism that accompanied the sudden and unexpected end of the Cold War have given way to new fears and insecurities following the September 11, 2001, terrorist attacks on the World Trade Center and Pentagon, and the U.S.-launched wars in Afghanistan and Iraq. The collapse of the "dot.com" boom of the 1990s and revelations of widespread scandal and corruption in many U.S. businesses have chastened the exuberance expressed earlier by so many apostles of the "new economy." The arrival of new immigrants has continued to reconfigure the nation's demographics, prompting worried, sometimes nativist-tinged debates over the security of U.S. borders and the future of American national identity. Here, as in so many other areas, Americans continue to struggle with the economic, political, and cultural impact of globalization. The revolution in new information technologies continues to reshape commerce and culture, sometimes in unexpected ways, as when companies outsource programming jobs or when computer viruses attack on a global scale. The "rights revolution" continues to rework the contours of American culture and politics, as evidenced most recently by court decisions regarding gay marriage.

The third edition of *Major Problems in American History Since 1945* is designed to address both the new issues that Americans face in the wake of September 11, as well as changing interpretations of long-standing issues. The present volume addresses new developments both in American life and in the work of historians, social scientists, and other commentators since the last edition. Three-quarters of the essays and more than half of the documents are new for this edition, as are the last four chapters.

Like earlier editions, this edition addresses classic issues raised by America's rise as a global economic and military power in the wake of World War II. The introductory chapter includes a sweeping new essay on postwar politics by political scientist Byron E. Shafer. Chapter 2, on the origins of the Cold War, adds a new and highly critical essay by Arnold A. Offner on President Harry Truman, drawn from his presidential address to the Society for the History of American Foreign Relations. Chapter 3 focuses on the emergence in the 1940s and 1950s of a "mixed economy" based on high levels of mass consumption and offers a new excerpt from Vance Packard's 1957 exposé, *The Hidden Persuaders*. A lively new article by Kelly Schrum on *Seventeen Magazine* and the culture of American girls nicely complements Roland Marchand's classic essay on American popular culture in the 1950s. Our chapter on the Cuban missile crisis (Chapter 4) presents a new transcript of the riveting "ExComm" debate edited by Ernest R. May and Philip D. Zelikow, as well as a concluding essay drawn from the newest edition of their book. Chapter 5, on the Civil Rights movement, includes new documents on the origins of *Brown v. Board of Education* and on the condition of African Americans in the urban north, as well as an essay from the newest edition of Steven F. Lawson and Charles Payne's book, *Debating the Civil Rights Movement, 1945–1968.*

Chapter 6, which focuses on the liberal politics of the "Great Society," includes new documents on the Civil Rights Act of 1964 and the organization of conservative opposition. It also includes two new essays: one by James T. Patterson on the rise of "rights consciousness," and another by Matthew D. Lassiter, which situates the rise of conservatism within the social dynamics of postwar suburbanization. Chapter 7 combines such classic documents as the Port Huron Statement and a proclamation by the "Weathermen" with pollster Daniel Yankelovich's revealing portrait of the changing cultural climate of the early 1970s. Chapter 8, on "second wave" feminism, combines iconic documents (from Betty Friedan to Phyllis Schlafly) with an essay from our second edition by Alice Echols and a new essay by Beth Bailey on women and work in the 1970s. Chapter 9, on Vietnam, includes a powerful new eyewitness account of the My Lai massacre and two new essays. In the first, diplomatic historian Michael Hunt offers an unflinchingly critical examination of the war; in the second, Arnold R. Isaacs explores the meaning of the war in American memory.

The closing chapters, all new, focus on the last decades of the twentieth century and the first years of the twenty-first: on the dramatic changes in American politics and political economy identified with the "Reagan revolution" and on the "post-liberal" world of Presidents Bill Clinton and George W. Bush; on the challenges to foreign policy in a new era marked not only by the end of the Cold War but also by the opportunities and dangers of a world in which national boundaries seem to matter less and less and stateless terrorism threatens international order. Chapter 10, on the Reagan years, includes mostly new documents, as well as recently published essays by Benjamin Ginsberg and Martin Shefter and by Jules Tygiel. Chapter 11 examines the changes and continuities that accompanied the so-called "new economy" of the 1990s. Its documents reflect the impact of new technologies on patterns of work and consumption, including mass customization, as well as the growing inequality that characterized late twentieth century America. Two of the documents offer contrasting views of Wal-Mart, which embodies many aspects of the new economy. The first essay, by Barbara Ehrenreich, describes what it is like to work at Wal-Mart. The second, by Michael J. Weiss, traces the growing role of market segmentation, a process with broad implications for how Americans construct their identities and communities. Chapter 12 explores the complicated interplay of race and ethnicity. We have selected documents that reveal an America still coming to terms with the consequences of the civil rights struggles of the 1960s and 1970s, while also confronting the changes introduced by globalization and the resumption of large scale immigration. The chapter's first essay, by George J. Sanchez, investigates the rise of nativism in the late twentieth century; the second, by Thomas C. Holt, explores the changing role of race in the global economy. Chapter 13 focuses on politics in the late twentieth and early twenty-first centuries. Its documents explore the bitter social issues that have divided Americans, as well as the growing role of lobbyists, campaign contributors, and consultants in the increasingly media-saturated world of

American politics. Its first essay, by Bruce Miroff, focuses on the role of polling and political reinvention during the presidency of Bill Clinton; the second, by Matthew A. Crenson and Benjamin Ginsberg, examines the increase in presidential power during the post-9/11 presidency of George W. Bush. Our last chapter (Chapter 14) examines the interrelated issues of globalization and empire. Its documents include speeches and policies by American leaders, a fatwah issued by Al-Qaeda leader Osama Bin Laden, and a moving excerpt of voices from inside the World Trade Center just before its collapse. The chapter ends with a nuanced defense of American empire by John Lewis Gaddis and a sharply critical appraisal by Michael Hunt.

Like other volumes in this series, *Major Problems in American History Since 1945* approaches its subject in two ways: documents introduce historical problems and highlight key issues under debate at the time, while the essays reveal how scholars can draw different interpretations from reading the same documents or observing the same phenomena. We invite readers to analyze the diversity of viewpoints and approaches on critical issues and arrive at their own conclusions. The chapter introductions and headnotes to the documents and the essays place the readings in historical and interpretive perspective. Suggestions for further reading at the end of each chapter provide additional resources for students who want to continue their study of particular historical problems.

We would like to thank again the many readers who provided helpful suggestions and comments on the first two editions: Numan V. Barley, Laura A. Belmonte, Roger Biles, William Brinker, Mark S. Byrnes, Rodney Carlisle, Frank C. Costigliola, John D'Emilio, Gregory Field, Richard M. Fried, Cheryl Greenberg, Samuel Hand, Susan Hartmann, Norman Markowitz, Gary May, Philip I. Mitterling, Mary Beth Norton, Chester Pach, Thomas G. Ryan, David F. Schmitz, John Sharpless, Philip W. Warken, and Theodore A. Wilson. We would also like to thank the following reviewers who gave us helpful suggestions and comments for the third edition: Jeff Charles, California State University San Marcos; James Hilty, Temple University; Caroline Hoefferle, Wingate University; and Pam Pennock, University of Michigan-Dearborn. And we wish to thank all those with whom we have worked at Houghton Mifflin: Thomas G. Paterson, the General Editor of the Major Problems in American History series; Jean Woy, Senior Consulting Editor; Terri Wise, Development Editor; Mary Dalton-Hoffman, Permissions Editor; and Aimee Chevrette, Project Editor. We owe a special word of thanks to Phillip Calderwood, whose keen editorial eye and diligent work contributed to a greatly improved final manuscript. We are indebted to colleagues at the various institutions at which we have taught and to our many students, to whom this new edition is again dedicated. As with the earlier editions, we look forward to hearing suggestions as to what should or should not be included in future editions, and invite students and teachers alike to write us in care of our respective institutions: bgriff@american.edu; baker.973@osu.edu.

R. G.
P. B.

The Origins of Postwar America

In the spring of 1945, the new president of the United States, Harry S Truman, anxiously surveyed a world in turmoil and transition. In Europe more than three decades of economic crisis and violent upheaval not only had inflicted an enormous toll in lives and material but had irreparably weakened the old, European-led world system that had organized international affairs for more than a century. Germany, which had dominated the continent economically and militarily during much of the twentieth century, now faced virtual annihilation as Allied armies closed in on Berlin from east and west. France and Great Britain, once mighty imperial nations and now ostensibly victorious, were only a little better off than the vanquished. By contrast, the Soviet Union had emerged from the war a battered but nevertheless major new world power. In Asia the imminent defeat of Japan promised to alter the balance of power in the Pacific radically. Throughout the colonial world of Asia, Africa, and the Middle East, the collapse of imperial Europe released powerful revolutionary stirrings among peoples seeking self-determination and economic development.

The United States, which alone of the great powers had escaped the war's physical destruction, was now the strongest nation in the world. In victory, however, Americans and their leaders confronted many difficult questions involving how, toward what ends, and in whose interest their enormous resources would be deployed. What would be the character of America's postwar relations with its allies, especially the Soviet Union; with its vanquished enemies, Germany and Japan; with the war-devastated nations of Europe; and with the peoples of Latin America, Africa, Asia, and the Middle East? What role would the United States play in the recovery of shattered foreign nations and in the reconstruction of a stable postwar system of international relations? How would the costs and burdens of that role be distributed, and with what consequences at home and abroad?

In domestic affairs, President Truman and other Americans faced an equally daunting set of problems. The decade of depression that had preceded World War II had produced enormous, if piecemeal and at times contradictory, changes in U.S. politics and the American political economy. The New Deal had sought to impose social discipline on American capitalism, to protect individuals from arbitrary and impersonally inflicted deprivation, and to mobilize ordinary men and women in pursuit of a more democratic social and economic order. But the New Deal had also aroused fierce opposition from U.S. business leaders, who were determined if not to destroy reform, then at least to turn it to their own purposes. The power and reach of the federal government had grown enormously during the depression and war, but questions of how and in whose interest that power would be used remained largely unanswered. Could the American economy be harnessed to democratic and egalitarian goals, or would it serve as a great engine of inequality and special privilege? Would the New Deal's supporters succeed in constraining the autonomy of private property through progressive taxation, vigorous pro-consumer regulation, and public ownership? Or would government be used instead to secure and defend patterns of privilege? Would the federal government seek to redistribute power by encouraging the organization of the powerless, or would its authority now be used to restrain organized workers, farmers, and urban minorities?

Beyond politics and foreign affairs, Americans faced still other challenges in their day-to-day lives. A great metamorphosis in American society was under way as the continued spread of industrial organization, mass consumption, mass communication, and secular values transformed the nation from a patchwork of local village cultures into an increasingly interdependent, national culture. Both the Great Depression and the Second World War, moreover, powerfully reshaped American lives. "The great knife of the depression . . . cut down through the entire population, cleaving open the lives of rich as well as poor," wrote Robert and Helen Lynd upon their return in the 1930s to "Middletown," the Midwestern city of Muncie, Indiana, which they had studied a decade earlier. "The experience has been more nearly universal than any prolonged recent emotional experience in the city's history; it has approached in its elemental shock the primary experiences of birth and death." The impact of war was equally profound and far-reaching. More than 12 million men and women had entered the armed forces, nearly a million of whom had been killed or wounded. More than 15 million others had taken work in the humming defense industries. The war accelerated many changes in American life: urban migration, unionization, the entry of women and African Americans into the industrial workplace, and the covert emergence of homosexual communities all created patterns of change that would play out, at times dramatically, in the years that followed.

In 1945, as the war drew to a close and the nation began its conversion to peacetime, Americans anxiously faced a future over which they had only partial control. Would they secure jobs in the transformed postwar society, and if so, on what terms? Would they find decent housing, and if so, where and at what costs? How would Americans confront the deep and potentially explosive divisions of race, class, and gender? What would be the character of relationships between husbands and wives, parents and children, friends and neighbors? How would balances be struck between private and public consumption, between development and preservation, between competition and community?

The way in which all these questions—foreign and domestic, political and economic, social and cultural—were answered; the way in which the conflicts of nations and classes and interests were resolved or institutionalized; the myriad compromises, arrangements, accommodations, bargains, and truces that were struck; and the balances of power that resulted, all would mark the emergence in the late 1940s of a fundamentally new era in American and world history. The essays that follow explore the origins of this new postwar era.

✦ E S S A Y S

In the first essay, diplomatic historian Thomas G. Paterson of the University of Connecticut examines the impact of World War II on world politics and the early efforts of U.S. leaders to shape the emerging postwar international system. In the second essay, Alan Brinkley of Columbia University traces the complicated legacies of World War II that would help shape the lives of ordinary Americans in the years that followed. In the final essay, Byron E. Shafer of Oxford University traces the shifting politics of the "late New Deal" era.

The Origins of the Postwar International System

THOMAS G. PATERSON

Winston S. Churchill wore his usual bulldog visage. The ever-present cigar and hunched gait, other familiar trademarks of the British prime minister, also drew the crowd's attention on that very hot day of July 16, 1945. He was surveying the dusty remains of the Nazi capital—"That rubble heap near Potsdam," murmured one Berliner. This time a preoccupied Churchill evinced little interest in his curious onlookers. What captured Churchill's attention in Berlin was the grisly aftermath of heavy Allied bombing and artillery fire and stout German resistance. He and the passengers in his motorcade grew sick, utterly stunned by the stark display of carnage in the humbled German city.

The prime minister entered what was left of Adolf Hitler's Chancellery. The Führer's marble-topped desk lay in a thousand pieces. Iron Crosses, military ribbons, and papers littered the floor. The British visitors picked up souvenirs; one pocketed a fragment of Hitler's world map. The descent into the damp hideaway carried great moment for Churchill, who uncharacteristically, said little. Shaken by what he saw, General H. L. Ismay hurried away to his villa to take a hot bath and a strong drink. That night Churchill finally talked about his visit to the Chancellery. "It was from there that Hitler planned to govern the world," he mused. "A good many have tried that; all failed." Savoring the Allied victory, the prime minister smiled contentedly and went to bed.

The president of the United States, Harry S Truman, surveyed Berlin that same day. After reviewing the American Second Armored Division, the president led his entourage down the Wilhelmstrasse to the Chancellery of the Third Reich, all the while growing more awestruck by the destruction of the city. "That's what happens," he remarked, "when a man overreaches himself." For two hours Truman rode through Berlin's streets. "I was thankful," he noted later, "that the United States had been spared the unbelievable devastation of this war."

At the time 65 to 75 percent of Berlin was leveled or damaged. General Lucius Clay, who was soon to become the military governor of the American zone, found that "the streets were piled high with debris which left in many places only a narrow

From *On Every Front: The Making and Unmaking of the Cold War,* Revised Edition by Thomas G. Paterson. Copyright © 1992, 1979 by W. W. Norton & Company, Inc. Used by permission of W. W. Norton & Company, Inc.

one-way passage between mounds of rubble, and frequent detours had to be made where bridges and viaducts were destroyed. . . . It was like a city of the dead." The once-prized chariot of victory on the Brandenburg Gate had been reduced to a gnarled mass of molten metal, the Reichstag to a hollow shell. Some "Nicht Für Juden" signs remained, ugly reminders of the Nazi extermination of European Jews. Factories that had escaped bombing raids now stood hull-like, stripped as war booty by the conquering Soviets, who tore industrial equipment from their foundations.

"There is nothing to do here," sighed a dispirited Berliner. Old men, women, and children trudged along, aimlessly pushing wheelbarrows. More than a million people lived in cellars, ruins, and makeshift suburban shacks, trading what they could for precious scraps of food to support their meager diets. In the western zones of Germany alone, two million crippled people hobbled about. Thirty-four percent of the Germans born in 1924 were badly mutilated in some way by 1945. "The people seem so whipped," wrote an American official to a friend back home, "that you can never believe that they had nursed Storm Troopers among them." Partially buried corpses lay rotting in the sun. As Berliners, under the stern guidance of Soviet and other Allied soldiers, began to stack bricks and shovel ashes, thousands of bodies were unearthed. The American diplomat Robert Murphy smelled "the odor of death" everywhere. Indeed, "the canals were choked with bodies and refuse." Lord Moran, who traveled with Churchill through Berlin, "felt a sense of nausea." Worse, "it was like the first time I saw a surgeon open a belly and the intestines gushed out."

From urban center to rural village, Germany looked charred and ravaged. Bomb-gutted Cologne and Nuremberg were hardly recognizable. Ninety-three percent of the houses in Düsseldorf were totally destroyed. Hamburg, Stuttgart, and Dresden had been laid waste by fire bombs and fire storms. In Dresden mounds of bodies had to be bulldozed into mass graves or burned on huge makeshift grills, so great was the toll and the fear of epidemic disease. An American army air corpsman flying low over the country at the end of the war could not spot streets or homes in Mannheim—only tossed dirt. "Aachen," he observed, "lay bleaching in the sun like bones on a desert." A disbelieving companion gazed at the pulverized land below and asked, "Where do the people live?" . . .

In Churchill's once-mighty island nation the war also claimed a frightful toll. Some observers after V-E Day grimly observed that the Germans looked better fed and less ragged than many British. The air blitz, which struck London, Coventry, and other cities in 1940–1941, and then subsided, began anew in 1944 with German V-1 and V-2 rockets that indiscriminately pounded buildings and people. Major districts of London were badly mangled, turning that regal city into a shabby, battered replica of itself. The Foreign Office building lost most of its windows and doors, and the prime minister's residence at No. 10 Downing Street looked racked as well. After one attack it took workmen six hours to free a woman from a tumbled row house on Stepney High Street. The rescuers asked if she had a husband. "Yes," she snapped. "He's at the front, the dirty coward."

Few Europeans escaped the marauding armies and death-dealing bombers of the Second World War. In Greece in 1945 a million people were homeless; one-quarter of the nation's buildings were damaged or destroyed. . . .

In neighboring Yugoslavia the retreating Germans had devastated the country-side, causing starvation in some regions. Upon liberation only one of Yugoslavia's seven large power stations was operating, and the rails running through the Danube Valley, which linked the nation to other European states, were inoperable. In the Hungarian capital of Budapest, the splendor of the Hapsburgs had given way inelegantly to the specter of death. All the bridges over the Danube were demolished, houses were flattened, and the 860-room royal palace of Maria Theresa and Franz Josef survived only as a maze of walls. During the winter of 1944–1945, near the war's end, the cold, hungry people of Budapest huddled in basements as Soviet bombs pummeled suspected German positions. One citizen described his apartment as a "ghostly castle, inhabited by a few scarcely living shadows." In Austria, German fires and Allied bombs had gutted 70 percent of the center of Vienna, not even sparing the seven-hundred-year-old St. Stephen's Cathedral. Women searched for sticks in the Vienna Woods, there being no coal for fuel. Elderly Viennese men and women looked pallid; listless young people begged for GI rations.

In Czechoslovakia and Italy, Prague and Rome had mercifully escaped large-scale devastation, but such blessings were rare in those otherwise-trampled nations. Italy's agricultural production was down 50 percent, and the government lacked foreign currency to pay for essential imports of food and raw materials. People in Naples clawed like cats through garbage cans for tidbits of food. Before abandoning that city, the Germans had wrecked the gas, electric, and water systems and put the torch to the university. In the Netherlands, 540,000 acres were flooded and Rotterdam was battered. As for France, Paris had largely been spared, but almost 20 percent of the buildings in the entire country were destroyed—twice the number demolished in the First World War. As many as 90 percent of French trucks were out of action, and much of the French fleet rested on the bottom of the harbor at Toulon. . . .

To the east, the Union of Soviet Socialist Republics tallied the greatest losses of all. More than 21 million soldiers and civilians had died—one-ninth of the total population. More than 30,000 industrial plants and 40,000 miles of railroad track were destroyed. Thousands of towns and cities had been leveled. Agricultural production was half of what it had been in 1940. Coal mines were flooded; bridges were down. The oil industry suffered shortages of steel pipe. As if the war had not done damage enough, a killer drought struck farming regions in 1946. The Ukraine ranked high in the gruesome record of war losses. Before the war a mainstay of the Soviet economy with its large production of coal, pig iron, steel, and manganese, as well as farm goods, the region now lay denuded by the Soviet scorched earth policy and the German rampage. Mines were blown up and flooded, the Dnieper Dam blasted, whole farm villages razed, tractors wrecked, and livestock massacred or driven off. The modern Zaporozhal steel plant near the Dnieper Dam was reduced to acres and acres of tangled debris. Famine and starvation hit the Brovary district, where 12,099 out of 16,000 prewar farm buildings were destroyed. The Soviet Socialist Republic of Byelorussia fared no better. Outside Minsk, thirty-four pits held the corpses of 150,000 people murdered and buried by the Germans. The much fought-over province of Vitebsk counted 300,000 dead.

Elsewhere in the Soviet Union, correspondent Harrison Salisbury called Sevastopol "a city of the dead." Of the city's fifteen thousand houses, only five hundred remained standing after the German retreat. "If a room has three walls and a ceiling," the mayor told Salisbury, "we count it in good shape." As for Stalingrad, American Ambassador W. Averell Harriman viewed "a desert of broken brick and rubble, the survivors huddling in cellars or tar-paper shanties." Another reporter, Alexander Werth, passed through Istra, west of Moscow, and saw nothing but a "forest of chimneystacks." The people of Moscow looked haggard as they piled their rubble. Shortly after the war British visitors entered a Moscow trade school and began asking students about their economic problems. Did their homes have heat and water? The school's director interrupted. There were more important questions. He asked pupils who had lost fathers at the front to stand up. All but one rose. The lone student who remained seated explained that his father had also fought against the Germans but had lost both his legs rather than his life.

The Second World War claimed the lives of some 55 million—*55 million*—people, and at least 35 million of them were Europeans. The grisly statistical gallery ranked the Soviet Union an uncontested first. The exact numbers are not known, but Poland and Germany (and Austria) shared second place with about 6 million dead each; Yugoslavia lost at least 1.6 million; France, 600,000; Rumania, 460,000; Hungary, 430,000; Czechoslovakia, 415,000; Italy, 410,000; Britain, 400,000; and the Netherlands, 280,000. . . .

As for the living, they had to endure food shortages, closed factories, idle fields, cold stoves, currency inflation, festering wounds. Displaced persons (DPs) provided another picture. "The wind will tell you what has come to us; / It rolls our brittle bones from pole to pole," went "The Refugees' Testament." Many dazed refugees wandered helplessly through Europe, searching for relatives, for friends, for a livelihood, for a ride home. . . .

Asia had its own sobering chronicle of the living and the dead. As the imperial Japanese went down to stubborn defeat, they took other Asians down with them. The lush vegetation of the Philippines and numerous Pacific islands was singed and burned, whole jungles disappearing. Some 120,000 Filipinos died, and Manila lay in ruins. Nobody counted exactly, but probably 4 million Indonesians died under Japanese occupation. In 1945, 1 million Vietnamese died of starvation; the war also took the lives of 150,000 natives of Okinawa, 70,000 Koreans, 40,000 Indians, and 30,000 Australians.

China had known population pressure, hunger, and epidemics before the war. But Japanese plunder, destruction of cities, and disruption of vital agricultural production increased the burdens that the Chinese had to bear in the postwar period. The provinces of Hunan, Guangxi, and Guangdong, like others, were visited by famine; millions suffered malnutrition and outright starvation. Cholera, plague, tuberculosis, smallpox, and malaria struck a population that had only twelve thousand physicians—one for every forty thousand people. In 1938 the Japanese had blown up the key dikes along the Huang Ho (Yellow) River—"China's Sorrow"—killing thousands and flooding three million acres of fertile land. China's rivers now rampaged in the spring and summer through vulnerable villages. Manchuria's industrial plants were destroyed or dismantled, and China's small railroad network hardly functioned.

The Chinese counted ten million war dead, many of them in 1945–1946 from starvation or disease caused by Japan's end-of-the-war devastation of rice-producing areas. People in Harbin suffered a peculiar calamity: in 1947 thirty thousand of them died from bubonic plague; two years earlier, at war's end, Japanese military researchers experimenting with germ warfare techniques had released infected rats into the city. . . .

For defeated Japan, the bitter results of imperial dreams could be measured in the loss of 2.5 million lives. American planes had dropped napalm-filled bombs on Tokyo, engulfing residential districts in fire storms which generated intense temperatures that reached 1,800° F. The odor of burning flesh drifted upward, sickening the pilots who delivered the horrible punishment. After a savage March 1945 raid that killed 84,000 people in what observers described as a mass burning, a Japanese reporter wrote that Tokyo was "like a desert, in a drab and monotonous panorama of hopelessness." The fifteen-mile stretch between Yokohama and Tokyo, remarked an American officer who accompanied American General Douglas MacArthur to Japan, had become a "wilderness of rubble." A light dust hung in the air, staining visitors' clothing. Wood and paper houses had been reduced to powdered ashes, factories to twisted metal. A shantytown of rusted, corrugated sheets and other junk ringed the capital city, its inhabitants reminding some observers of the Okies who trekked to California during the Great Depression—except that the Japanese scene was more shocking. One of the first American naval officers to arrive in Tokyo wrote to a friend that "I feel like a tramp who has become used to sleeping in a graveyard."

Hiroshima and Nagasaki became special cases, sharing and enduring a special fate, giving unique meaning to the most familiar postwar word: "rubble." Hiroshima was Japan's eighth-largest city, a residential, commercial center of 250,000 people. But until 8:15 A.M. on August 6, 1945, Hiroshima had not witnessed large-scale American bombing raids. On that cloudless day the crew of the *Enola Gay,* a custom-outfitted B-29, unleashed "Little Boy," an atomic device packing the power of twenty thousand tons of TNT. The bomb fell for fifty seconds and exploded about two thousand feet aboveground. A blinding streak of light raced across the sky; a tremendous boom punctuated the air. Then a huge purplish cloud of dust, smoke, and debris shot forty thousand feet into the atmosphere. At ground level the heat became suffocating, the winds violent. Buildings instantly disintegrated. Shadows were etched in stone. Trees were stripped of their leaves. Fires erupted everywhere, and the sky grew dark. Survivors staggered toward water to quench their intense thirst. Skin peeled from burned bodies. A maimed resident, Dr. Michihiko Hachiya, noted that "no one talked, and the ominous silence was relieved only by a subdued rustle among so many people, restless, in pain, anxious, and afraid, waiting for something else to happen."

The toll: 140,000 dead, tens of thousands wounded, and 81 percent of the city's buildings destroyed. Three days later the nightmare was repeated in Nagasaki, where at least 70,000 died. Two weeks before the slaughter President Truman told his diary that the atomic bomb "seems to be the most terrible thing ever discovered, but it can be made the most useful." Upon hearing of the success of the world's first nuclear destruction of a city inhabited by "savages," as the president had recently called the Japanese, he allowed that "this is the greatest thing in history." Truman's words did not necessarily mean that he was pleased that so many Japanese civilians had been killed but rather that he was marveling over the new, spectacularly deadly weapon in America's possession—a weapon that might bring the long war to a close and boost U.S. power in the postwar era.

The Hiroshima tragedy was but one chapter in the story of massive, war-induced destruction. This story, with all its horrid details, must be recounted not because it shocks or sensationalizes but because it illustrates how massive and daunting were the problems of the postwar world, how shaky the scaffolding of the international order. Hitler had once said about his warmongering pursuits that "we may be destroyed, but if we are, we shall drag a world with us—a world in flames." Because he largely satisfied his prophecy, the Second World War, like any war of substantial duration, served as an agent of conspicuous international changes. The conflagration of 1939–1945 was so wrenching, so total, so profound, that a world was overturned— not simply a material world of crops, buildings, and rails, not simply a human world of healthy and productive laborers, farmers, merchants, financiers, and intellectuals, not simply a secure world of close-knit families and communities, not simply a military world of Nazi storm troopers and Japanese kamikazes, but all that and more. The war also unhinged the world of stable politics, inherited wisdom, traditions, institutions, alliances, loyalties, commerce, and classes. . . .

Leaders of all political persuasions, as they witnessed the immensity of the destruction, spoke of a new age without knowing its dimensions. "The world was fluid and about to be remade," remembered the American journalist Theodore H. White. The normal way of doing things now seemed inappropriate, although as creatures of the past the survivors remained attached to ideas and institutions that seemed to provide security through familiarity. They sensed the seriousness and the enormity of the tasks of cleaning up the rubble, of putting the broken world back together again, of shaping an orderly international system. But imponderables abounded. Would peoples in the long-restive colonized countries, for example, rebel against their foreign masters at the very time that the once-mighty imperial nations themselves suffered internal political upheavals? Few people could say with confidence that they knew the configuration of the postwar world. What lay ahead was a tortuous time of experimenting, of trial and error, of stumbling and striving, of realized and dashed hopes, of contests among competing formulas for a stable world order.

Few nations or individuals had the material resources, talent, and desire—the sheer energy, guts, and money—to mold a brave new world out of the discredited and crumbled old. If the reconstruction tasks seemed Herculean, however, the opportunities appeared boundless for the ambitious, the hearty, and the caring. One vigorous, optimistic, well-intentioned, competitive voice sounded above the rubble that constituted London, Berlin, Warsaw, Minsk, and Tokyo. That voice echoed with power from the United States, the wartime "arsenal of democracy."

At war's end President Truman declared a two-day national holiday. Horns, bells, and makeshift noisemakers sounded across the nation. Paraders in Los Angeles played leapfrog on Hollywood Boulevard; farther north, jubilant sailors broke windows along San Francisco's Market Street. In New York City office workers tossed tons of paper from the windows of skyscrapers on cheering crowds below. Stock market prices shot up. A five-year-old boy recorded the August 1945 moment: "This is the best year. The war is over. Two wars are over. Everyone is happy. Tins cans are rolling. Everything is confused. And little pieces of paper." Not only had the dying subsided, but also the United States had emerged from the global conflict in the unique position of an unscathed belligerent. No bombs had fallen on American cities. No armies had ravaged the countryside. No American boundaries had been redrawn. Factories stood in place, producing goods at an impressive rate. In August, at the

General Motors plant in Moraine, Ohio, shiny new Frigidaire refrigerators and airplane propeller blades moved along parallel assembly lines. Farm fields were rich in crops, and full employment during the war years had buoyed family savings. "The American people," remarked the director of the Office of War Mobilization and Reconversion, "are in the pleasant predicament of having to learn to live 50 percent better than they have ever lived before."

Whereas much of Europe and Asia confronted a massive task of "reconstruction," the United States faced "reconversion"—adjusting the huge war machine to peacetime purposes. Automobile plants had to convert production from tanks to cars, a delightful prospect for auto manufacturers, who knew that Americans were eager to spend their wartime earnings on consumer goods once again. With great pride Americans applauded their good fortune. They were different. They had no rubble to clear. The Soviets knew, said Joseph Stalin in a grand understatement, that "things are not bad in the United States."

Actually Americans had worries. Some feared that the sparkling prosperity of the war years would dissipate in a postwar economic disaster. They remembered that military production, not Franklin D. Roosevelt's New Deal reform program, had pulled the United States out of the Great Depression of the 1930s. Would there be enough jobs for the returning GIs? Americans also suffered temporary shortages of many goods, sugar and gasoline among them, and resented the rationing that limited their economic freedom. "Hey, don'tcha know there's a war on?" said clerks to anxious consumers. There were not enough houses to meet the needs of an expanding and mobile American population, which grew from 131 million to 140 million during the war years and was entering a "baby boom" period. The national debt skyrocketed from $37 billion to $269 billion. The war cost the federal government $664 billion. Inflation threatened economic stability. At least 10 million American families still lived in poverty in this land of plenty. Although these national pains aroused grumbles, they seemed bearable and soluble, were played down, or were ignored. As *Fortune* magazine commented two months after V-J Day: "August 14, 1945, marked not only the war's end but the beginning of the greatest peacetime industrial boom in the world's history."

Americans read charts brimming with impressive data that justified such enthusiasm. The gross national product of the United States expanded from $90.5 billion (1939) to $211.9 billion (1945). Steel production jumped from fifty-three million tons in 1939 to eighty million tons at the close of the war. Cut off from rubber imports from the Dutch East Indies during the war, Americans developed synthetic rubber, launching a new industry. New aluminum plants went up, and the aircraft industry, in infancy when Germany attacked Poland, became a major new business as well. In 1939 only 5,856 military and civil airplanes were turned out; but in 1945 the figure reached 48,912, a decline from the peak of over 95,000 in 1944. All told, over 300,000 aircraft rolled from American factories during the war—a figure far surpassing that of any other nation, including Germany and Japan combined. Employment in the aircraft industry swelled 1,600 percent. With its numerous aircraft factories, Southern California bustled, becoming a mecca for dreamers of wealth and adventure. During the war 444,000 people moved to Los Angeles.

Workers' wages kept up with inflation during the war years. Women took jobs once held by men who were called to military duty. Unable to spend their abundant incomes on the shrinking supply of consumer items during the war, many Americans visited their banks. Total personal savings increased from $6.85 billion to $36.41 billion. Americans continued to spend for pleasure as well. The baseball World Series played on, and films whirred at local theaters. Beaches beckoned vacationers. In the summer of 1944, as Europe and Asia reeled from the blasts of war, Americans flocked to resorts and racetracks. Betting on horse racing totalled a record-breaking $1.4 billion in 1945, even though the tracks were closed from January to May. Farmers enjoyed some of their best years of the twentieth century. Whereas in 1939 they counted sixty-six million head of cattle, by 1945 that figure reached eighty-three million. Agricultural output rose 15 percent. American universities also made wartime advances. Government contracts for scientific research went to the California Institute of Technology for rocket studies; Princeton University received grants for ballistics research. In mid-1945 the Massachusetts Institute of Technology held government contracts worth $117 million. The GI Bill, which offered money to veterans for their college educatiohs, promised higher enrollments. Wartime musicals like *Oklahoma!* and *Carousel* caught the optimistic mood, and sluggers Joe DiMaggio and Ted Williams were heading home to reclaim their baseball fame. Despite uncertainties about the future, life looked good to Americans, and after the hardships and setbacks of the depression decade, "the old self-confident America is coming into its stride again."

When foreign delegates journeyed to San Francisco for the United Nations Conference in April of 1945, many crossed the territorial United States and could not help but notice the stark contrast with war-torn Europe and Asia. Soviet Foreign Minister V. M. Molotov once referred to statistics in the *World Almanac* to remind Americans about their uniqueness as prosperous survivors of the Second World War. During a conversation with Stalin in 1944, the president of the United States Chamber of Commerce, Eric A. Johnston, citing the American example, lectured the Kremlin leader on the need for a better distribution of goods in the Soviet Union. No doubt wondering how so knowledgeable a man as Johnston could be misreading reality, Stalin replied that in order to distribute, there must be something to distribute." Months before, at the Teheran Conference, Stalin had toasted the United States as a "country of machines," applauding its great productive capacity for delivering victory to the Allies. Truman's words also bear repeating: "I was thankful that the United States had been spared the unbelievable devastation of this war." Even the death count for Americans in uniform, about four hundred thousand, appeared merciful when compared with staggering figures elsewhere. Indeed, the *Saturday Evening Post* editorialized in 1945 that "we Americans can boast that we are not as other men are." The war had overturned a world, and many Americans believed that they were now on top of it. A new international system for the postwar era was in the making, and the United States intended to be its primary architect. . . .

Two nations with quite different ideologies emerged from the rubble of World War II to claim high rank. The United States and the Soviet Union, eager to realize their universalist visions of the postwar world and to seize opportunities for extending their respective influence, tried to fill vacuums of power. With the old barriers to American and Soviet expansion gone, Washington and Moscow clashed over occupation policies in German, Italy, Japan, Austria, and Korea. They squabbled over which political groups should replace the Nazi regimes in Eastern Europe.

The competitive interaction between the United States and the Soviet Union—"like two big dogs chewing on a bone," said Senator J. William Fulbright—shaped the bipolarism or bipolarity of the immediate postwar years. "Not since Rome and Carthage," Dean Acheson claimed, "had there been such a polarization of power on this earth." This new bipolar structure replaced the multipolar system of the 1930s, wherein at least six nations had been active, influential participants. By the late 1940s decisions made in the imperial capitals of Washington and Moscow often determined whether people in other nations voted, where they could travel, how much they ate, and what they could print.

To say that the world was bipolar, however, is not to suggest that the two poles were equal in power. They were not. An asymmetry—not a balance—of power existed. In fact, the United States held preponderant power and flexed its multidimensional muscle to build even more power. As the only major nation not devastated by the war, the United States so outdistanced other nations in almost every measurement of power—from industrial production to domestic political stability—that it enjoyed hegemony. Hegemony exists when one nation possesses superior economic, military, and political power in the world system. The first ingredient is a prerequisite for the other two. No nation can aspire to hegemony or achieve that Olympian status unless its economy is strong—and stronger than any other's. More than statistics established American supremacy. World conditions did so. The United States was powerful because almost every other nation was war-weakened.

Both the United States and the Soviet Union emerged from the war as powers, but only one at that time was a superpower—the United States. The Soviet Union was certainly not weak. Although handicapped by its economic wreckage, the huge nation held predominant postwar power over its neighbors in Eastern Europe. Still, the Soviet Union was a regional, not a global, power before the early 1950s. The characteristic of hegemony meant that the United States had more opportunities and resources than other nations to shape the postwar system. By exercising their preponderant global power—through military occupations, foreign aid and loans, and domination of the World Bank and United Nations Organization, for example—U.S. officials pushed the world toward the American postwar goal of a nonradical, capitalist, free trade international order in the mold of domestic America. . . .

Another prominent characteristic of the international system that unleashed conflict was the destruction of economies in many parts of the world. The war cut an ugly scar across Europe and Asia. "If Hitler succeeds in nothing else," mused Office of Strategic Services officer Allen Dulles, "like Samson, he may pull down the pillars of the temple and leave a long and hard road of reconstruction." The postwar task was forbidding. Not only did cities have to be rebuilt, factories opened, people put back to work, rails repaired, rivers and roads made passable, and crop yields increased, but the flow of international commerce and finance had to be reestablished if nations were to raise through exports the money needed to buy the imports required for recovery. Many old commercial and financial patterns had been broken, and given the obstacle of economic disarray, new exchanges were difficult to establish. Where would Germany's vital coal and steel go? Would industrial Western Europe and agricultural Eastern Europe re-create old commercial ties? Would the restrictive trade practices of the 1930s, especially the tariff barriers, continue into the 1940s? Would colonies continue to provide raw materials to their imperial lords? Could international cooperation and organizations like the General Agreement on Tariffs and Trade (1948) curb economic nationalism? Would trade be conducted on a multilateral, "open door" basis, as the United States preferred, or by bilateral or preferential methods, as many others, such as Britain and the Soviet Union, practiced? Would the economic disorders spawned by the Great Depression be repeated to produce political chaos, aggression, and war?

The answers to these questions helped define the international system of the post-1945 era. The new international system, it was hoped, would enjoy stable economic conditions to ensure pacific international relations. Yet the very effort to reconstruct economies and create economic order engendered conflict because different models and formulas—Communist? socialist? capitalist? mixed economy?—competed to define the future. At the same time the asymmetrical distribution of power persuaded weaker nations that they faced the danger of economic coercion.

The Second World War also bequeathed domestic political turmoil to the new international system. The governments of the 1930s, now discredited, vied with insurgent groups for governing power in many states. Socialists, Communists, and other varieties of the political left, many of whom had fought in the underground resistance movements and had thus earned some popular respect and following, challenged the more entrenched, conservative elites, many of whom had escaped into exile when the German armies goose-stepped into their countries. In Poland the Communist, Soviet-sponsored Lublin Poles successfully undercut the political authority of the Poles who had fled to London. The conservative Dutch government-in-exile watched warily as leftist resistance groups gradually rallied political support. Political confusion in the Netherlands was heightened by the wartime loss of voting lists. In Greece a coalition of leftists in the National Liberation Front (EAM) fought the return to power of a British-created government and the unpopular Greek monarchy of King George. The civil war that rocked Greece until fall 1949 claimed some 158,000 lives and ended in an American-backed conservative government. In France Charles de Gaulle gained ascendancy after vying for power with the Communists. The Chinese civil war, which had raged for years between the Communists of Mao Zedong and the Nationalists of Jiang Jieshi (Chiang Kai-shek), flared up again at the close of the war. That internecine struggle ended in a Communist victory in 1949. Yugoslavia was also the scene of political battle between Josip Borz Tito's ultimately successful Partisans and a group headed by Dr. Ivan Šubašić of the London émigré government, which in turn suffered strained ties with King Peter. In the occupied nations of Germany, Austria, and Korea, moreover, the victors created competitive zones, postponing the formation of central governments. In the defeated countries of Japan and Italy, American officials decided who would rule, whereas in parts of Eastern Europe, Soviet officials placed Communists in strategic positions of power.

The major powers, in short, intervened abroad to exploit the political opportunities created by the destructive scythe of World War II. The stakes seemed high. A change in a nation's political orientation might presage a change in its international alignment. The great powers tended to ignore local conditions, especially nationalism, which might and often did mitigate against alignment with an outside power. Americans nonetheless feared that a leftist or Communist Greece would look to the East and permit menacing Soviet bases on Greek territory or open the door to a Soviet naval presence in the Mediterranean. Moscow dreaded a conservative anti-Soviet Polish government led by the London faction, for it might prove so weak and so hostile to Moscow as to permit a revived Germany to send storm troopers once again through the Polish corridor into the heart of Russia or block the Soviet Union's efforts to contain a resurgent Germany. A Communist China, thought Americans, might align with the Soviet Union; a Nationalist China would remain in the American camp. All in all, the rearranging of political structures within nations drew the major powers into competition, accentuating the conflict inherent in the postwar international system.

Just as the war threw politics into chaos, it also hastened the disintegration of empires. The Japanese movement into French Indochina and drive for Dutch East Indies oil had led to Pearl Harbor in 1941. The initially successful Japanese expansion demonstrated to many Asian nationalists that their white imperial masters could be defeated. In a spirit of Pan-Asianism, some nationalists collaborated with Tokyo during the war. The Japanese, in need of administrators to manage occupied areas, trained and armed some indigenous leaders. Japan granted Burma considerable autonomy in 1942, for example, and after the war the Burmese became determined to push the British out. Other nationalists gained organizational unity, élan, and experience by battling the Japanese invaders. At the end of the war the European powers, exhausted and financially hobbled, had to struggle to reestablish mastery over rebellious colonies. The appeal of the self-determination principle, still echoing from the days of Woodrow Wilson and given new emphasis by the Atlantic Charter (1941) and the United Nations Charter (1945), became far-reaching. The long process of "regime collapse" in what became known as the Third World gained momentum. "There are many peoples who are clamoring for freedom from the colonial powers," American Undersecretary of State Sumner Welles remarked during the war. He predicted "trouble" unless these peoples got what they wanted. Failure to plan for the transfer of power to them, he warned "would be like failing to install a safety valve and then waiting for the boiler to blow up." There were too many boilers and too few safety valves.

No empire was immune to decolonization. The United States granted the Philippines independence in 1946, but that new nation became a client state where U.S. officials helped the government resist a peasant revolt led by the Huks. The British, worn low by the war and by the challenges of nationalist groups demanding independence, retreated in 1947 from India, which then descended into civil war between Hindus and Muslims. The two new nations of India and Pakistan were thus born amid massacres and a massive uprooting of people. The following year Britain also relinquished Burma (Myanmar) and Ceylon (Sri Lanka). Israel, carved out of British-governed Palestine, became a new independent state in 1948. The British also found it difficult to maintain their sphere of influence in Iran, Greece, and Egypt and began retreats from those politically unsteady states. The French clung to Indochina, where nationalist forces led by Ho Chi Minh had declared an independent Vietnam by quoting the American Declaration of Independence. "If those gooks want a fight," boasted French General Étienne Valluy, "they'll get it." Bloody battle ensued, ultimately forcing French withdrawal in 1954. The French empire also came under siege in Africa; in early 1947 Malagasy insurgents in the island colony of Madagascar rebelled. Ninety thousand people died as French troops crushed the insurrection the next year (France finally granted the Malagasy Republic independence in 1960). The Dutch also decided to fight, but after four debilitating years of combat they pulled out of Indonesia in 1949. The defeated Japanese were forced to give up their claims to Formosa and Korea, as well as to Pacific island groups. Italy departed from Ethiopia and lost its African colonies of Tripolitania (Libya) and Eritrea. In the Middle East, Lebanon, Syria, and Jordan, areas once managed by Europeans, gained independence in 1943, 1944, and 1946, respectively.

The world map, as after World War I, was redrawn. The emergence of so many new states, and the instability associated with the transfer of authority, shook the very foundations of the international system. Power was being redistributed. In varying degrees, the United States and Soviet Union competed for the allegiance of the new governments, meddled in colonial rebellions, and generally sought to exploit opportunities for an extension of their influence. In the case of Vietnam the powers supported different sides: Washington, without relish, backed the ruling French, and Moscow endorsed the Vietminh insurgency. The stakes seemed high. President Roosevelt told an adviser near the end of the war that more than one billion "brown people" yearned for independence—and "1,100,000,000 potential enemies are dangerous." The emerging nations could serve as strategic bases, markets for exports, sources of vital raw materials, sites for investments, and votes in international organizations; conversely, they could deny powerful nations such assets. As a Central Intelligence Agency report emphasized, the resource-rich Third World and the reconstruction of hobbled Western Europe were intricately linked: "The continuance of unsettled conditions [in colonial or former colonial areas] hinders economic recovery and causes a diversion of European strength into efforts to maintain or reimpose control by force."

To the angry frustration of the great powers, some new nations, like India, chose nonalignment in the developing Cold War. Asian countries, asserted Indian nationalist leader Jawaharlal Nehru, "can no longer be used as pawns by others; they are bound to have their own policies in world affairs. . . . We do not intend to be the playthings of others." To U.S. officials, neutralism meant not only that some nations were not with them but also that they stood against them—that the nonaligned countries were forming "a power bloc against us," as the American ambassador to Burma put it. Indeed, Americans feared that Nehru championed a "third force" that, if it developed to the stage of a bloc of like-minded states, could shift the world from bipolar to tripolar form. Avowedly neutral states thus ultimately became targets for Cold War conversion through American and Soviet foreign aid, subversion, and propaganda campaigns.

As one U.S. government study noted, the disintegration of empires, especially the withdrawal of the British from their once-vast domain, created an "over-all situation of near chaos" in the international system. In some areas, such as Southeast Asia, it meant a "new balance of power." The upheaval was fundamental: "Old values are being changed and new ones sought. New friendships are being formed." The international system creaked and swayed under this unsettled burden.

Conflict over and within the new United Nations Organization also disturbed the system. At the Dumbarton Oaks Conference in 1944 the Allies initiated plans for a United Nations Organization to replace the defunct League of Nations. The United States, Britain, and Soviet Union became its chief architects, and the institution they created at the San Francisco Conference of April–June 1945 reflected their insistence on big-power domination. They instituted a veto power for the five "permanent members" of the Security Council (the United States, Britain, U.S.S.R., France, and China) and assigned the General Assembly, the forum for smaller nations, a subordinate status. Because each member recognized that the new international body could become an instrument, through bloc voting, of one nation's foreign policy, they feuded. Churchill crudely complained that China, hardly a "great" power, would be a "faggot vote on the side of the United States," and the Soviets protested that France would simply represent a British vote. "China was a joke," remarked State Department veteran John Hickerson, "a FDR joke." For a time Roosevelt pushed Brazil as a veto power member; Brazil, he said, was "a card up his sleeve." Because Britain could marshall the votes of several of its Commonwealth countries and the United States could muster most of the Latin American nations, the conferees at the Yalta Conference of early 1945 acknowledged the glaring imbalance by granting the Soviet Union three votes in the General Assembly.

At the San Francisco Conference membership applications from Argentina and Poland produced heated differences. Against vehement Soviet objections, Argentina, which had declared war against Germany only at the last minute and which some critics considered a "fascist" nation, gained membership after the United States backed its application and the nations of the Western Hemisphere voted yes as a bloc. Yet when Lublin-led Poland, not yet reorganized according to the American interpretation of the Yalta accords, applied for entry, the United States voted no, and the conference denied Poland a seat. Moscow railed at this rebuff, charging a double standard. The United Nations Organization, which held its first session in January 1946, thus made its debut amid controversy. Rather than serve as a stabilizing force in the postwar international system, the largely U.S.-dominated United Nations early became a source of conflict, a competitive arena of power brokers, a verbal battleground for the allegiance of world opinion, a vehicle for condemnatory resolutions, a graveyard for idealistic hopes—in short, part of a "masquerade peace."

The new atomic bomb and the ensuing nuclear arms race further destabilized the postwar international system. As the two bickering major powers groped for ways to deal with "the bomb" and spurred their atomic development programs, people everywhere held their breaths, harboring thoughts about doomsday. Nuclear weapons were not simply dangerous to enemies; they threatened apocalypse for humankind. Cartoonists sketched pictures of uncontrollable monsters that the scientists had created. "All the scientists are frightened—frightened for their lives—and frightened for *your* life," a Nobel Prize-winning chemist wrote in early 1946 in a popular magazine. About the same time a French radio station broadcast a make-believe story about an atomic storm engulfing the earth after radioactive atoms had escaped from a U.S. research laboratory. Many Parisians thought they heard truth and panicked. One observer suggested that a Soviet-American war "might not end with *one* Rome but with *two* Carthages."

The atomic bomb, uncontrolled, envied, copied, and brandished, became a major obstacle to a peaceful postwar international system. The "most terrible weapon ever known in human history," Secretary of War Henry L. Stimson quietly told the president, unsettled the world community, for it was an agent of massive human destruction, and "in a world atmosphere already extremely sensitive to power, the introduction of this weapon has profoundly affected political considerations in all sections of the globe." Nations that possessed *the* bomb seemed to hold an advantage in international politics, for it could serve as a deterrent against an adversary as well as a means to annihilate an enemy. When combined with air power and a long-range delivery capability, the atomic bomb also hurdled geographical boundaries, rendering them useless as protective elements in a nation's security shield. With the perfecting of air warfare in World War II, "the roof blew off the territorial state."

The question that dogged the peacemakers was: How were they to control the development, spread, and use of atomic energy? There had been arms races before, and disarmament conferences in the 1920s and 1930s, but the postwar nuclear race moved at a far different and more dangerous level. The atomic bomb was the "absolute weapon," not only more violent but also capable of speedy delivery, rapid retaliation, immediate cataclysm, and lingering death-dealing radioactivity. Americans worried that they would lose their monopoly—that nuclear proliferation would leave them vulnerable, too. Such fears intensified when the Soviet Union successfully produced its own bomb in 1949. While from the start some people appealed for a world government to put the atomic genie back in the bottle—"world state or world doom"—others began to marvel over the new armament's potential value as a diplomatic weapon to pry concessions from adversaries or as a deterrent to keep them at bay. . . .

Such was the postwar international system—with its opportunities and constraints, with its many characteristics that generated conflict. The makers of the postwar order grappled with immense, new problems, and they strove to reduce the systemic instability. Their decisions, however, exacerbated conflict. The reason why the leaders of the postwar world made bad conditions worse is clear: Sensing danger from the volatile international system to their domestic systems, they sought to build their nations' power, to enlarge their spheres of influence. The conflict inherent in any international system, especially one struggling to make the transition from full-scale war to postwar peace, hardened into a four-decade-long Cold War.

The Legacies of World War II

ALAN BRINKLEY

"The great majority of Americans," Archibald MacLeish said in 1943, "understand very well that this war is not a war only, but an end and a beginning—an end to things known and a beginning of things unknown. We have smelled the wind in the streets that changes weather. We know that whatever the world will be when the war ends, the world will be different."

Almost everyone who looked ahead to the postwar era realized, as MacLeish did, that the war had unleashed large forces that would produce a new world and a

Excerpt from *Liberalism and Its Discontents* by Alan Brinkley (Harvard University Press: 1998). Excerpt previously published in different forms in the *New York Times* and in *The War in American Culture*, edited by Erenberg & Hirsch (University of Chicago Press: 1995). Reprinted by permission of University of Chicago Press and the author.

new American society. But Americans greeted the prospects for change in many different ways. MacLeish—a liberal, a New Dealer, and an administrator in the wartime government—welcomed change and believed it could be harnessed (through the efforts of an enlightened government) to the goal of creating a better and more just society. Others viewed the future with trepidation, many of them hoping to preserve the patterns of power and wealth that had shaped the world they had known before the war. The social and cultural legacy of World War II was the product of broad social forces that no individuals or institutions could ultimately control. But it was also the result of many visions of the postwar world among many groups of Americans—almost all of them certain that the war validated their often sharply different, and even conflicting, expectations.

In the prologue to *Six Armies in Normandy,* his classic portrait of the 1944 Allied invasion of France, the historian John Keegan captured one critical aspect of how the war affected the United States. He wrote of his own wartime experiences as a child in the English countryside when, a few months before D-Day, the Americans arrived. Almost overnight, he recalls, his "backwater" town filled with GIs. "How different they looked from our own jumble-sale champions, beautifully clothed in smooth khaki, as fine in cut and quality as a British officer's—an American private, we confided to each other at school, was paid as much as a British captain, major, colonel." The British army traveled about in "a sad collection of underpowered makeshifts." The Americans rode in "magnificent, gleaming . . . four-wheel-drive juggernauts." For a few months—before they vanished suddenly one night in early June—they dominated the countryside, dazzling girls, overwhelming roads, shops, and pubs, distributing largesse. "Thus" Keegan recalled, "I made my first encounter with the bottomless riches of the American economy."

Even as a child, Keegan had understood the role of abundance in American life and the role of World War II in producing it. The war ended the Depression and made the nation rich again. It created expectations of abundance that would survive for more than a generation. And it removed what had in the 1930s been deep doubts about the ability of the capitalist economy ever again to experience substantial growth. By 1944, as Keegan suggests, American abundance was already capturing the global imagination and firing the hopes of the American people themselves. The vast productive power of the United States supplied both its own armed forces and those of its allies with airplanes, ships, tanks, and ammunition. It fed, clothed, and housed the American people, who experienced only modest privations, and it helped feed, clothe, and house much of the rest of the world as well. Alone among the major nations, the United States faced the future in 1945 with an intact and thriving industrial economy poised to sustain a long period of prosperity and growth. The Gross National Product in the war years rose from $91 billion to $166 billion; 15 million new jobs were created, and the most enduring problem of the Depression—massive unemployment—came to an end; industrial production doubled; personal incomes rose (depending on the location) by as much as 200 percent.

Abundance created a striking buoyancy in American life in the early 1940s that the war itself only partially counterbalanced. Suddenly, people had money to spend again and—despite the many shortages of consumer goods—at least some things to spend it on. The theater and movie industries did record business. Resort hotels, casinos, and race tracks were jammed with customers. Advertisers, and at times even the government, exhorted Americans to support the war effort to ensure a future of material comfort and consumer choice for themselves and their children. "Your people are giving their lives in useless sacrifice," the *Saturday Evening Post* wrote in a mock letter to the leaders of wartime Japan. "Ours are fighting for a glorious future of mass employment, mass production, and mass distribution and ownership." Even troops at the front seemed at times to justify their efforts with reference to the comforts of home more than to the character of the enemy or the ideals America claimed to be defending. "They are fighting for home," John Hersey once wrote from Guadalcanal (with at least a trace of dismay), because "Home is where the good things are—the generosity, the good pay, the comforts, the democracy, the pie."

One legacy of World War II, therefore, was the return of abundance, and with it the relegitimation of capitalism. Another was a rising popular expectation of economic security and material comfort—of what was already becoming known as "the American dream," a dream that rested on visions of increasing consumption. But abundance also helped strengthen other hopes for change. As Hersey's statement suggests, to some the "American dream" meant more than apple pie alone. Democracy, he said, was part of the mix—not as an alternative to visions of material comfort, but as both a precondition for and a result of them. Defining what democracy meant, mediating among the very different visions the word inspired among Americans, created some of the great struggles of both wartime and the postwar era.

One of the first such conflicts emerged over the political implications of abundance itself, and of the "democratic" initiatives it spawned. Archibald MacLeish and many other liberals eager to see the survival and expansion of the New Deal interpreted the return of economic growth as a mandate to pursue their emerging goal of "full employment" through purposeful government action. A broad coalition of Keynesian economists, union leaders, agricultural activists, consumer groups, and many others rallied in 1944 and 1945 behind what ultimately became the Employment Act of 1946, but which they at first called the "Full Employment" bill—a bill that, had it been passed in its original form, would have committed the government to using Keynesian tools to stimulate economic growth to levels that would ensure very low joblessness. Other liberals rallied around the related proposals that had emerged during the war from the National Resources Planning Board, the New Deal's only real planning agency, which called for, among other things, a major expansion of the welfare programs the New Deal had launched and (in the spirit of full employment) an expansion as well of public works planning to provide the stimuli they believed the post-war economy would often need.

Out of the confluence of abundance and democracy, in other words, had come a vision of an expanded liberal state. Freed from the immediate pressures of the Great Depression, convinced by the wartime growth that the economy was not as irretrievably stagnant as they once had feared, liberals seized on abundance as the basis for an ambitious social and economic agenda that would, if successful, greatly expand the role of the state in ensuring prosperity and protecting the beleaguered.

But to many other Americans, and to the conservative Republicans and Democrats who already by 1943 were coming to dominate the United States Congress, abundance had a very different impact—and the idea of postwar democracy took a very different form. To them the end of the Depression removed whatever justification there had been for the New Deal interventions into the economy and mandated a return to a less regulated market, a less profligate government, and a less expansive welfare state. One by one, in 1943 and 1944, Congress reduced or eliminated New Deal programs that economic growth seemed to have obviated: the Works Progress Administration, the Civilian Conservation Corps, the National Youth Administration, and many others. It abolished the National Resources Planning Board, in retribution for its ambitious and—to conservatives—alarming proposals. It began efforts, which would culminate in 1948, to weaken the Wagner Act. Abundance, they argued, was proof that there was no longer any need for the "socialism" of the New Deal, that it was time to return to what they considered true democracy—a regime of untrammeled economic freedom and minimal government.

Politics was only one of many realms in which the war—the abundance it produced and the hopes for democracy it inspired—provided conflicting lessons and divided legacies. Nowhere was that clearer than in the experiences of African Americans in the 1940s. Prosperity transformed the material circumstances of many black men and women; the war against fascism—and its democratic rationale—transformed their expectations. But the war also reinforced opposition to their hopes.

Two million African Americans left the rural South in the 1940s, more than the total number of migrants in the three decades before (decades that included what is still known as the Great Migration before and during World War I). They moved for many reasons, some of them unrelated to the war. The mechanization of agriculture (and of cotton picking in particular) eliminated the demand for the labor of many black farmers in the South. The sharecropping system, already weakened by the Depression and by New Deal farm subsidies that often made it more profitable for landowners to leave their property fallow than to let it out to tenants, all but disintegrated during the war. Many African Americans also moved because the war created economic opportunities in industrial cities. With millions of men leaving the workforce to join the military, traditional barriers that had kept blacks out of some factories collapsed, at least for a time. The number of blacks employed in manufacturing more than doubled during the war; and there were major increases in the number of African Americans employed as skilled craftsmen or enrolled in unions. There was a substantial movement of black women out of domestic work and into the factory and the shop.

The wartime migration also helped carry the question of race out of the countryside and into the city, out of the South and into the North. The growing concentration of black populations in urban areas made organization and collective action easier and more likely. It made African Americans more important politically. Now that many of them lived in the North, where they could vote more or less at will, they became an increasingly significant force in the Democratic party (to which virtually all African Americans had become committed during the 1930s, in response to the New Deal). Demographic changes, in short, laid the groundwork for the political mobilization of American blacks both during and after the war. There was growing membership and increasing activism in the Urban League, the NAACP, and other existing civil rights organizations. A new and more militant organization emerged: the Congress of Racial Equality—more outspoken, less accommodationist than most older ones. And already during World War II, in Washington, D.C., Detroit, and other cities, there were demonstrations against racial discrimination—picketing, sit-ins, occasionally violence—that anticipated the civil rights movement of a decade and more later.

Black Americans who attempted to explain these modest but significant political stirrings did so by pointing to the nature of the war itself. In North Carolina one African American told a visiting journalist: "No clear thinking Negro can afford to ignore our Hitlers here in America. As long as you have men like [Governor Eugene] Talmadge in Georgia [an outspoken white supremacist] we have to think of the home front whether we want to or not." Many black men and women talked openly of the "Double V," which stood for simultaneous victory over the Axis abroad and over racism at home. "If we could not believe in the realization of democratic freedom for ourselves," one black journalist wrote, "certainly no one could ask us to die for the preservation of that ideal for others." To engage in the struggle for freedom in the world while ignoring the struggle for freedom at home was to make a mockery of both.

Some white Americans were beginning to make that connection too. *Fortune* magazine published an article in June 1942 entitled "The Negro's War," which suggested the slow shift in thinking among many whites about the nation's "racial question." The essay catalogued the long list of legitimate grievances African Americans were raising against their country, and it argued, in effect, that the war required America to do something about them. It cited with alarm Japanese propaganda about racial injustice in America, describing a recent race riot in Detroit as "a boon to the Japanese and . . . the German . . . propagandists." And it argued, in terms that clearly resonated with the larger sense of mission that the war had aroused (and that Henry Luce, *Fortune*'s publisher, had endorsed with notable enthusiasm), that

> . . . this is a war in which ideas . . . are sometimes substitutes for armies. The Negro's fate in the U.S. affects the fate of white American soldiers in the Philippines, in the Caribbean, in Africa; bears on the solidity of our alliance with 800 million colored people in China and India; influences the feelings of countless neighbors in South America. In this shrunken world of ours, a fracas in Detroit has an echo in Aden, and what a southern Congressman considers to be a small home-town affair can actually interfere with grand strategy.

This growing awareness of the nation's racial burdens forced many liberals, even if slowly and incompletely, to reconsider one of the staples of New Deal thought: that the principal goal of public life was to confront economic, not racial or cultural, issues. Perhaps, some liberals began now to think, the problems of the modern world were not purely economic. Perhaps class was not the only, or even the best, concept with which to analyze social problems. Perhaps race, ethnicity, religion, and culture—the divisive, "irrational" issues that had so damaged the Democratic party in the 1920s and from which white liberals had taken pains to distance themselves in the 1930s—were, in fact, essential to understanding America after all. "One of the greatest problems of democratic civilization," the great liberal theologian Reinhold Niebuhr wrote in 1944, "is how to integrate the life of its various subordinate ethnic, religious and economic groups in the community in such a way that the richness and harmony of the whole community will be enhanced and not destroyed by them." Niebuhr dismissed the smug liberal confidence of the 1920s that had anticipated what he called a "frictionless harmony of ethnic groups" and the capacity of economic progess alone to achieve "their eventual assimilation in one racial unity." Instead, he called on "democratic society" to use "every strategem of education and every resource of religion" to fight the influence of racial bigotry— a bigotry that would not wither away simply as a result of material prosperity.

Early in 1944 an explosive event helped galvanize this growing but still murky sense of urgency: the publication of Gunnar Myrdal's *An American Dilemma*. Myrdal, an eminent Swedish sociologist whom the Carnegie Foundation had commissioned in the late 1930s to supervise a major examination of America's "race problem," described the "American dilemma" in part as an economic problem— the failure of American society to extend its riches to its black citizens. But it was also a moral dilemma—a problem in the hearts and minds of white Americans, a problem born of the impossible attempt to reconcile a commitment to freedom and democracy with the effort to deny one group of citizens a set of basic rights guaranteed to everyone else. In the shadow of Nazi tyranny, such a contradiction seemed to Myrdal—and to many readers of his book—especially glaring as he made clear in his powerful concluding chapter:

> The three great wars of this country have been fought for the ideals of liberty and equality to which the nation was pledged. . . . Now America is again in a life-and-death struggle for liberty and equality, and the American Negro is again watching for signs of what war and victory will mean in terms of opportunity and rights for him in his native land. To the white American, too, the Negro problem has taken on a significance greater than it has ever had since the Civil War. . . . The world conflict and America's exposed position as the defender of the democratic faith is thus accelerating an ideological process which was well under way.

An American Dilemma became one of those rare books that help define a moment in history, and its reputation grew rapidly over the next several years. That Myrdal was a European and a distinguished scholar; that he couched his findings in the presumably objective language of social science; that a respected, nonpartisan foundation had sponsored the project; that a large number of prominent academics had collaborated with Myrdal on it; that the book itself was nearly 1,500 pages long, with mountains of data and over 500 pages of footnotes, lending it an air of profound scholarly authority: all helped make its findings seem almost unassailable. It was a "study to end all studies," something close to a definitive analysis of the problem.

And yet it would be a mistake to exaggerate the impact of the war on the willingness of Americans to confront the nation's "race problem." For the war did not simply inspire those who believed in racial equality to reconsider the nation's customs and institutions. It also inspired those who defended white supremacy with renewed ardor. Among white Americans, and among white southerners in particular, there were many who considered the war not a challenge to but a confirmation of their commitment to preserving the old racial order. To them democracy meant their right to order their society as they pleased and to sustain the customs and institutions they had always known. This interpretation of democracy was visible, for example, in the Congress, where southern members led by the notorious John Rankin of Mississippi sought to obstruct the GI Bill of Rights until they could feel certain it would not threaten white supremacy. It was evident in the redoubled commitment of many white veterans when they returned home to the South to protect the world they knew. And because much of what they sought to protect was their idealized vision of white women, a vision much romanticized during the war, segregation assumed a specially heightened importance for many of them. In much of the country the World War II generation—the young men who returned from the war fired with determination to make a better world—produced dynamic young leaders impatient with old structures and injustices. In much of the South the new generation of leaders emerging from the war became especially militant defenders of the region's racial institutions.

World War II changed America's racial geography economically, spatially, and ideologically. It ensured that the system of segregation and oppression that had enjoyed a dismal stability for more than half a century would never be entirely stable again. But it ensured, too, that the defenders of that system would confront the new challenges to it with a continued and even strengthened commitment.

In much the same ambiguous, incomplete way the war challenged traditional notions of the role of women in America. Nearly six million women joined the paid workforce during World War II (raising the total number of working women by 60 percent). The new workers were much more likely to be married than earlier female workers had been. They were more likely to have young children. And they were more likely to work in jobs—including some heavy industrial jobs—that had previously been reserved for men (who were now in short supply). Hence the famous image of "Rosie the Riveter." Some women found the experience transforming. In the absence of fathers, brothers, husbands, and boyfriends, many women lived, worked, and traveled alone for the first time in their lives. Some joined unions. Others wore uniforms—as members of the WAACs and WAVEs and other female military organizations.

For many it was an experience of unprecedent freedom; and as a female aircraft worker later recalled, "It really opened up another viewpoint on life." The popular folklore of the time described "Rosie the Riveter" as someone pitching in to win the war but eager to return to home and family. In fact most working women came to the end of the war determined not to return to a purely domestic life. Some lost their jobs when peace arrived and the men came home, but most of those who did looked for work somewhere else. The number of females in the paid workforce never declined to its prewar levels, and it continued to grow throughout the 1950s and beyond.

And yet while the war (and the economic opportunities it opened up) was creating new expectations among many women, it was confirming more traditional expectations among many men. At the front, fighter pilots gave their planes female names and painted bathing beauties on their nosecones. Sailors pasted pin-ups inside their lockers, and infantrymen carried them (along with pictures of wives, mothers, and girlfriends) in their knapsacks. The most popular female icon was Betty Grable, whose picture found its way into the hands of over 5 million fighting men by the end of the war. She was a mildly erotic figure to be sure, but she was not a sex goddess; in her films, she generally played wholesome, innocent young women, the kind any guy would want to marry. And she became a model at the front for the modest, genteel girlfriend or wife many servicemen dreamed of finding on their return. In

1943, when she married the bandleader Harry James and had a child, her popularity actually grew—as if the image of domesticity had enhanced, rather than diminished, her appeal. Thousands of servicemen sent letters to her, suggesting how central her image had become to their own notion of the meaning of the war. . . . When John Hersey compiled his list of comfortable images that he claimed motivated GIs to fight ("generosity, good pay . . . pie"), he might well have added another vision of the kind of world men were hoping to return to: a world of healthy, heterosexual love, a world in which supportive, nurturing women were waiting to welcome their men back and make a home for them.

For the servicemen who remained in America during the war, and for soldiers and sailors in cities far from home in particular, the company of friendly, "wholesome" women was, the military believed, critical to maintaining morale. USOs recruited thousands of young women to serve as hostesses in their clubs—women who were expected to dress nicely, dance well, and chat happily with lonely men. Other women joined "dance brigades" and traveled by bus to military bases for social evenings with servicemen. They, too, were expected to be pretty, to dress attractively (and conservatively), and to interact comfortably with men they had never met before and would likely never see again. Neither the USO hostesses nor the members of the "dance brigades" were supposed to offer anything more than chaste companionship. The USO actually forbade women to have dates with soldiers after parties in the clubs, and the members of the "dance brigades" were expected to have no contact with servicemen except during the dances. The military sent chaperones to most social events and established clear "rules" for both servicemen and the women who sought to entertain them. Clearly, such regulations were sometimes violated. But while the military took elaborate measures to root out homosexuals and lesbians from their ranks (unceremoniously dismissing many of them with undesirable discharges), it quietly tolerated other relationships. "Healthy" heterosexuality was more important than chastity.

But there was a dark counter-image to this official view of women as wholesome nurturing companions. It was the image of brassy independent, and hence dangerous women who—in the fluid social atmosphere of the war years—were becoming more numerous, more visible, and more mobile. One result of that anxiety was a new war agency: the Social Protection Division (SPD) of the Office of Community War Services. Its job was, in essence, to protect men from women. Originally, that meant getting rid of the red-light districts that had sprung up around military bases around the country, districts that military leaders feared would expose servicemen to venereal diseases. But before long the SPD was engaged in a more general effort to round up "promiscuous" females (which often meant single women who seemed in any way "loose" or provocative). A battle against venereal disease had quickly escalated to become a larger attack on independent, sexually active women.

For the rest of the war the SPD engaged in something like a witch-hunt, searching out "suspicious" women, or women of "low character" in the vicinity of military bases; enlisting local police and even hotel detectives to spy on suspected women and arrest them if they were found alone anywhere with a serviceman; encouraging citizens to offer anonymous tips. The government was, in effect, waging war on promiscuous women. Servicemen, the SPD implicitly argued, were simply acting out natural urges; they were the victims. The women were the aggressors—"throwing themselves at the soldiers," one official noted, luring presumably helpless men into sin and possibly disease. In enforcing these new directives, the SPD gradually came not to worry very much about whether supposedly "loose" women were, in fact, infected with VD. Any "promiscuous" woman could *become* a carrier, even if she was not yet one. Men needed to be protected from them all. State and local governments were pressured to change their own laws, and in some places there were quite extraordinary measures to restrict the freedom of movement of single, unescorted women, of whom there were, of course, a great many during the war. Some women were summarily arrested and quarantined for weeks, even months, if found to be infected. Some women were detained for many days even without any evidence of infection if there was other evidence that they might be of "loose" morals.

There is an apparent contradiction in American social history in the first decade or so after the war. On one side was the new reality of women moving in unprecedented numbers into the paid workforce. On the other side was the growing power of a more traditional image of women as wives, mothers, and homemakers. But that postwar paradox is simply a continuation of the contrary experiences of women and men during the war itself: for many women, the exhilarating discovery of new freedoms and opportunities; for many men, a fear of independent women and a strengthened expectation of traditional family life.

The Puzzle of Postwar Politics

BYRON E. SHAFER

In their own time, the surface upheavals of American politics during the immediate postwar years might reasonably have suggested a major political shift, the coming of a new political era with different issue contents and different supporting arrangements. Yet with hindsight, the immediate postwar period, for all its undeniable fluctuations, still appears politically of a piece with the ongoing New Deal era. Elite partisan combatants of the day variously hoped or feared that 1956 would mark an effective end to this era. The election of 1956 would instead confirm its continuation, albeit in a form modified from its substantive and structural heyday. Participants could not know that the central substantive concerns of that era had a full postwar generation to run, nor that its central structural supports had a full postwar generation in which to be key shaping influences. But it *would* be a full generation from the end of the Second World War before evident and dramatic issue shifts came together with glacial but irresistible social changes, explosively, to demand a different political dynamic.

Similarly, when that explosion finally arrived in the late 1960s, few participants could be confident that it represented lasting change. Both the fearful and the hopeful were naturally inclined to focus on surface manifestations of disruption that almost could not, in principle, form the underpinnings of an extended era. Few observers at the time failed to notice the extensive anomalies of the 1968 election—anomalies,

Bryon E. Shafer, "The Two Majorities and the Puzzle of Modern American Politics," in Byron E. Shafer and Anthony J. Badger, eds., *Contesting Democracy: Substance and Structure in American Political History, 1775–2000* (Lawrence, KS: University Press of Kansas, 2001), 225–237. Copyright © 2001 by University Press of Kansas. Reprinted by permission of the University Press of Kansas.

that is, when viewed within the confines of the New Deal order. None missed the fact that these led to Richard Nixon's narrow victory as president, while the Democratic Party retained solid control of both houses of Congress. Yet none could know that the latter was to become the diagnostic partisan outcome for a new political era. And none could know that the surface anomalies of 1968 were best seen not as idiosyncratic events in their own right but as crystallizing vehicles for the emergent issues and long-term forces that would terminate the late New Deal.

None of this seemed inevitable when the postwar era began. Indeed, a reasonable reading of immediate postwar politics would have suggested that some new era was already in the process of being born. In the first fully postwar election, that of 1946, the chaos of economic and social reconversion produced the first Republican Congress since 1928. Harry S Truman then spiked hopes (or fears) that the New Deal era had been just a Roosevelt interregnum when Truman held the presidency in his own right in 1948 and regained control of Congress. But the Republicans were back in 1952, in control of both the presidency and Congress this time, making that a potential turning point in their hopes for a new political order. By 1956, however, what Dwight D. Eisenhower, his voters, and Americans in general were entitled to deduce from all this superficial upheaval was only that they were living in a modified extension of the existing political world, in what can rightfully be called the "late New Deal era."

Afterward, the world of the 1950s would be widely understood as an extension of the political world of Franklin D. Roosevelt and the New Deal. The great and dominating substantive concern of both ends of this era was social welfare, as befitted an agenda called into being by economic catastrophe. By the time an Eisenhower presidency was under serious discussion, the policy content of this dominant economic-welfare dimension included all the hallmark programs of the Rooseveltian New Deal: unemployment compensation, Social Security, industrial recovery, farm price supports, labor-management regulation, rural electrification, and so on. By the time Eisenhower was actually president, the policy content of the same dimension had expanded to include full employment plus the "missing pieces" of the original New Deal agenda: health care, housing assistance, poverty amelioration, higher education, and, last but not least, civil rights. The staying power of these programs, as items for partisan conflict, would prove remarkable.

The great and dominating secondary concern of this period was foreign affairs, again befitting an era forced within a painfully few years to confront the catastrophe of total war. In the years when Eisenhower was becoming both an international leader and a household name, this major secondary focus involved proper pursuit of World War II, through a huge buildup of defense manpower and industry. In the years of his full celebrity, it involved proper pursuit of a cold war, with its mixture of international alliances, military support, and conventional foreign aid. The United States had been drawn reluctantly into the worldwide conflicts capped by the Second World War; it was to be a principal architect of the succeeding international environment, so that this environment would remain an ever-present substantive concern.

Lest such continuity seem dependent on simple substantive interpretation, it is worth noting that it was accompanied by—was part and parcel of—a parallel extension of key structural influences. Thus there were social coalitions to go with these programmatic directions, coalitions that were in fact integral to them. By 1946, two of these, robustly constructed, dominated the political landscape. Both were built principally on social class, unlike the geographic basis of the previous political world, albeit with important ethnic and regional twists. The larger was a blue-collar coalition, aligned with the national Democratic Party, that featured working-class Americans generally, a few key multiclass minorities (especially Jews), and the entire (the "solid") South. The smaller was a white-collar coalition, aligned with the national Republican Party and essentially reliant on middle-class Americans. Truman confirmed the incentives for racial minorities (especially blacks) to shift toward the Democratic coalition. After his reelection, as the urban orientation of the Democratic Party was also confirmed and as the role of organized labor in party councils increased, farmers as a group and rural areas generally, outside the South, shifted in turn toward the Republican coalition.

These social coalitions were buttressed by organized interests of a highly partisan sort in which labor-management divisions were critical. There were some undeniable ironies to this divide. From one side, industrial recovery as fostered by the Democrats, along with a wartime boom, had restored profitability to corporate business. From the other side, corporate gigantism was especially good at producing organizational gains for union labor. But regardless, organized labor became an increasingly important adjunct to the Democratic Party in legislative and then in electoral politics, to the point where it actually substituted for the party in more and more places. By contrast, although corporate management provided some funding and the occasional "blue-ribbon" candidate for the Republicans, it was really small business—the Chamber of Commerce, not the National Association of Manufacturers—that carried the load for the minority party among the interest groups.

Policy positions and social coalitions were then knit together and connected to the institutions of national government by the political parties. By 1956, however, these were not just mirror images within a two-party system; they had become parties that were different in organizational kind. The Democrats were an amalgam of urban machines in the North, courthouse rings in the South, and volunteer activist branches scattered throughout the country. New Deal programs had actually helped extend the life of the organized (the "regular") Democratic Party within this mix. The Republicans, still paying a high price for incumbency when the Great Depression hit, had already moved to become the kind of organizationally amorphous, activist-based political party that both would become in the second postwar era, relying on ideology and issues to motivate party workers. For them, this was not so much modernization as simple survival. Although they retained some rural rings in the North, New Deal programs had essentially wiped out the Republican machines present in the pre-depression years.

There was, in consequence, a diagnostic partisan dynamic to this mix of policy conflicts, social coalitions, and organized intermediaries—a distinctive character to political competition in the late New Deal era. Seen by way of ongoing policy conflicts, the party on the Left, the Democrats, was widely perceived as more in tune with public preferences on social welfare. By contrast, the party on the Right, the Republicans, was widely perceived as more in tune with public preferences on foreign affairs. The crucial fact was that the public ordinarily gave a much higher priority to social welfare. Seen by way of ongoing social coalitions instead, the dominant fact about partisan politicking from 1932 through 1968 was that the unity and vitality of the Democratic coalition remained the central story of electoral and institutional politics. The election of 1946 had signaled an adjustment to this dominant fact. Before, Democrats won, full stop. Afterward, Republicans could win if Democratic policy assets were devalued, as they were in 1946, or if Republicans had special assets of their own, as they would in 1952. But this was still an adjustment, not a change.

As happened so often in American history, the basic institutional structure of American government channeled this partisan dynamic in important ways. Because president and Congress were separately elected, there had to be, in effect, *four* institutional parties within the American two-party system: a presidential and a congressional Democratic and Republican Party. But here, it was the response of the minority Republicans that was most revealing. In a presidential contest, all those state Republican Parties that found themselves in either competitive or Democratic states—at that time, the Republican Parties of states representing the majority of Americans— needed an economic moderate as their nominee. And for more than a generation, they got one: Wendell Willkie in 1940, Thomas Dewey in 1944, Dewey again in 1948, Dwight Eisenhower in 1952, Eisenhower again in 1956, and Richard Nixon in 1960. Which is to say, the presidential Republican Party did accept the social welfare consensus.

In congressional contests, however, the situation—with its incentive structure— was strikingly different. Many seats remained reliably Republican and thus had no need for social welfare accommodation. Many of the rest were reliably Democratic, such that accommodation (or not) was irrelevant. Lacking much incentive, then, few successful Republican Parties moderated at the congressional level. Moreover, just to make the partisan picture more stark (and Republican problems more severe), it should be noted that an institutional arrangement that helped hobble a minority Republican response to party competition presented no counterpart difficulties for the majority Democrats. For them, differing presidential and congressional parties, both dominant, could comfortably go their separate ways under the Democratic label. If they needed to reconcile for policy purposes, they could always do so in government, in Washington.

Those facts made the Eisenhower interlude especially good at showing the political dynamic of the late New Deal in its full complexity. Eisenhower, the Republican presidential candidate in 1952, was the most popular living American. If Roosevelt had beaten the depression, "Ike" had won the war—and Roosevelt was dead. Yet Eisenhower largely accepted the strategic imperatives that FDR had bequeathed him, featuring foreign policy issues but emphasizing that he was a "modern Republican," at home with popular social welfare programs. This was sufficient not just to earn him the presidency but also to draw a Republican congressional majority into office with him. His fellow officeholders, however, those Republican beneficiaries of his presidential coattails, had not begun to make their peace with the New Deal. Accordingly, the public threw them out at its first opportunity, in the midterm elections of 1954, and even Eisenhower could not drag them back with him when he was reelected (by a landslide) in 1956.

More lastingly, Eisenhower would accomplish one great partisan task and fail at another, and the two together would influence party competition until after 1968. In the first, Eisenhower ended the Korean War while simultaneously cementing his fellow Republicans into the cold war consensus. This was one policy realm about which he really cared, and he would be lastingly successful in it. What he failed to do was bring the Republican congressional party into the social welfare consensus too. Indeed, Eisenhower himself actually moved closer to Republican dissidence on these issues as his administration aged. As a result, the human icon could still be comfortably reelected; there was no counterpart figure on the political landscape. But his party, despite the fact that it increasingly *was* his party, could not.

The year 1956 was noteworthy for a much less obvious fact about American society, albeit a fact with substantial implications for American politics. This was the first year in American history that the Census Bureau declared a white-collar majority for the nation as a whole. The political implications of this massive subterranean fact were indirect and complex. Indeed, the next round of elections, the congressional elections of 1958, would bring one of the largest *Democratic* gains of the postwar years; it would be almost two generations before the Democratic Party gave these back. Yet American society was changing in glacial but irresistible ways that were utterly uncharacteristic of the world of the depression and the Second World War, and hence unlikely to underpin a continuing New Deal order.

The great if undifferentiated engine for this change was the postwar economic boom. From the late 1940s through the mid 1960s, the American economy provided explosive growth. Appearing all the more remarkable from the viewpoint of the other developed nations, each more seriously damaged by the Second World War, economic growth in postwar America remained remarkable in its own right, and it represented a complex of further changes. It was not just total income—and median income and average income—that grew apace in the postwar years. Such wealth was the product of a hugely different economy, in which a long-term trend away from agriculture became a huge movement into manufacturing and industry and then eventually into service provision and information technology. A different structure to the economy also meant, by definition, a different occupational structure for American society. And a different occupational structure meant a different *class* structure as well.

The partisan implications of this change, as it moved closer to an impact on politics and public policy, were not straightforward. The great decline in national economic fortunes of the late 1920s and 1930s *had* shifted the social base for American politics from a geographical to a class alignment. By the end of the Second World War, there was one party rooted in the working class, facing another party rooted in the middle class, with many cross-currents but with a clear societal majority for the former. Had these sharpened class lines held in anything like their mid-century incarnation, the implication of postwar economic change would have been obvious: as the middle class grew, so should the Republicans. Yet the hidden breakpoint of 1956 was early evidence that this was not to be the case. The middle-class majority had already arrived; Republican prospects continued to lag. Indeed, the share of society identified with the Democratic rather than the Republican Party actually continued to grow. And very little of this further partisan drift resulted from any additional working-class increment to the Democrats.

What was happening instead was a major change in the class base of both parties, but especially of the Democrats, with powerful implications for subsequent politics. By inexorable extension, the Democrats too were becoming a more middle-class party. One implication of this change, in turn, was that a growing segment of the party would be less concerned with the old redistributional issues that had underpinned the New Deal Democratic coalition and more concerned with an aggregate of social, cultural, and behavioral issues—less with the "quantity of life" and more with the "quality of life" instead. Middle-class Democrats, representing the more liberal elements of the American middle class, would never turn their backs on the social welfare gains of the New Deal, and this fact would remain important. But new priorities almost had to follow from their new and growing partisan presence.

Because the Republicans would remain the minority party throughout the ensuing generation, their story was less consequential to American politics as a whole. Once, they would have acquired the liberal middle class by means of class identifications. If they no longer did, then this party too was becoming a very different social coalition (and ideological vehicle) just under the surface. If anything, its commitment to economic and welfare conservatism was being strengthened. But so was the potential for a newly fashioned conservatism on those quality-of-life issues. This particular subterranean fact would be masked for another generation, while the liberal Republicans of the Northeast, the industrial Midwest, and the West Coast remained an important minority faction within the minority party. But by 1956, these liberal Republicans were already, had they known it, an endangered species.

Such grand and gross partisan transitions were hardly the end of the roster of political impacts from economic development. The major interest groups of American politics were being reshaped as well, again indirectly but forcefully. One of the great stories of the New Deal era had been the rise of organized labor generally and then its integration into the Democratic coalition. Economic decline and resurgent class conflict would have been stimuli toward union resurgence on their own. But this time, the government had been actively supportive of labor organization, union recognition, and collective bargaining, and this legislative support was a powerful contributor to the explosive growth of the labor movement in the immediate postwar years. Unlike earlier periods of union growth, however, organized labor this time came quickly to establish a huge overhead agency, the AFL-CIO, and to affiliate it, informally but effectively, with the national Democratic Party. The result was important for keeping social welfare issues at the center of American politics and for forging the policy link between welfare liberalism and cold war anti-communism.

There had been a parallel development on the other side of the organizational aisle, for the immediate postwar years were also the heyday of the giant corporations, massive corporate entities characteristic of a booming postwar economy. The form itself had emerged by the 1920s, before the Great Depression had choked off its spread. Its growth merely resumed in the immediate postwar years. Yet this was to be the era of corporate gigantism, and that fact too had implications for the New Deal order. Much more than small business, big business was prepared to make its peace both with union labor as an organized interest and with the main policy substance of the New Deal. This remained a practical, not a principled, peace; the great corporations would hardly become another element of the Democratic coalition. Yet they did accept labor-management relations as a normal part of economic life. Moreover, because they tended to be concentrated in states where big labor was also particularly strong, corporate Republicans came to accept basic social welfare programs as a normal element—that is, a normal imperative—of the political landscape.

The postwar economic boom then undermined both these developments, which is to say, in undermining both these great organized interests, economic change undermined their policy contribution as well. The membership of organized labor peaked in the early 1950s and declined gradually from then on. It peaked as the sectors of the economy that were most easily unionized—those same great corporate manufacturing sectors—peaked themselves as a share of the economy. Thereafter it declined, as manufacturing gave way to service provision as the growth sector of the economy. Labor remained a crucial element of the Democratic coalition, in triumph through the mid-1960s and in adversity thereafter. But it would never again walk the halls of Congress, much less the corridors of the White House, with the confidence it had in the 1950s and early 1960s.

Once more, there were parallel developments on the other side of the labor-management divide, for corporate gigantism also peaked in the 1950s. Ironically, just when social thinkers were beginning to set out the character of an organizational world built around these giant economic units, they began to recede. This too was a response to the growth of the service and knowledge sectors of the economy, as opposed to the industrial and manufacturing sectors. It meant that a number of other social phenomena associated with the rise of what Eisenhower designated "modern Republicanism"—accepting of organized labor, at ease with social welfare—also began to change. Eventually, this more liberal wing of the Republican Party would be folded into the regular party structure.

These economic changes, in their final indirect contribution to politics, naturally began to affect the structure of the political parties. Among Democrats, the result was huge policy tensions within the dominant Democratic coalition, followed by extensive procedural reform. The key impetus to both was the explosive rise in the share of college-educated Democratic identifiers. At the end of the Second World War, although there was an unavoidable "intellectual wing" to the Democratic coalition, the share of college graduates was minuscule. During the 1950s, courtesy of the economic boom generally but also of the GI Bill as a conscious policy intervention, not only the share of college-educated Americans but also the share of college-educated Democrats grew apace.

There were problems as well as prospects in this growth. The new (middle-class, college-educated) Democrats were not normally members of the main organized constituency groups of the national Democratic Party—namely, organized labor and the growing civil rights organizations. They resided in areas where the orthodox party organization, the "regular" Democratic Party, was frequently enfeebled—namely, the burgeoning suburbs. They were also equipped and inclined to participate in politics as independent actors, often motivated by specific causes, rather than as devoted members of basically partisan organizations. Eventually, they would have their way through a stream of participatory procedural reforms, from extending the reach of primary elections into presidential politics to extending a bill of rights for individual members of Congress.

The Republican version of this story was inevitably related, though with the main elements reversed. The Republican Party had long since achieved the organizational character that the Democrats were only just approaching, courtesy of the death of the old Republican machines and the debilitating effect of protracted minority status. More to the practical point, as the New Deal era aged and as the Democratic

Party grew but became more internally divided, the Republicans at first appeared to shrink and become more homogeneous. Liberal Republicans, the main dissident faction, had always been heavily dependent on deference from the regular party. When corporate gigantism receded and the party structure became more skeletal and hence more dependent on the Old Guard, this more liberal faction just disappeared into the regular party structure.

As the liberal middle class also became more Democratic, there was a more evidently homogeneous social base, a more socially but especially a more economically conservative social base, left to be reflected in this more skeletal Republican Party structure. What prevented this from becoming a long-running extension of the old order was a different and even more indirect fallout from economic growth, capped by a conscious elite reaction to developments inside the Democratic Party. Said differently, as educated Democrats began to secure their policy wishes within the Democratic Party, a less-educated segment of society, reacting against these policies, became increasingly available to the Republicans. And this development brought both counterpart opportunities and counterpart tensions to the other side of the partisan aisle.

This new target population was the evangelical—the pietistic—Protestants, and they were strong conservatives on the very cultural and national questions that were central to the rise of middle-class Democrats. Economic development contributed to their leadership too, producing new seminaries that paid special attention to the latest technology for reaching their followers. It was these leaders who would forge an informal but strong relationship to the Republican Party. As with the coming of corporate Republicans in an earlier era, however, this potential for numerical gain came at the cost of increased intraparty tensions. From one side, the evangelicals were much more socially conservative than the remainder of the party. From the other, they were much less economically conservative, resting well inside the national social welfare consensus.

The issue substance of American politics was likewise undergoing an evolution during the late New Deal years. But here, the surface manifestations of change were insistent, even intrusive. Each great underlying dimension to public policy—social welfare and foreign affairs—generated a dramatic and extended substantive conflict. Although both these conflicts were inevitably shaped by the changing contours of the society in which they occurred, neither was directly a product of these changes. Rather, both grew logically out of the policy positions and social coalitions of the New Deal era. By the time they played out, however—and both were not just dramatic but also long running—they had helped refashion the entire nature of substantive conflict in American politics.

The greatest and most dramatic of these new issues was civil rights, culminating in a veritable civil rights revolution. In playing his part in constructing the New Deal order, Franklin Roosevelt had consciously avoided this issue area. For him, a central task in building a liberal coalition behind the social welfare programs of the New Deal had been attracting and then holding southern Democrats. The problem was that they were both numerically essential and the most conservative elements in this aspiring coalition. What made the American South "solid" in the Democratic coalition, despite this instinctive conservatism, was a multiclass white majority united by racial segregation as public policy. Roosevelt recognized that civil rights as a policy priority would challenge this arrangement, stress his coalition, and thus potentially imperil his economic and welfare gains. He chose social welfare and allowed civil rights to languish.

In partisan terms, not much changed with the passing of Roosevelt. A focus on civil rights still seemed likely to reduce the policy advantage that the national Democratic Party derived from economic and welfare issues, perhaps in a major way. Nevertheless, liberal activists in the postwar years set about redressing this otherwise curious hole in their overall policy program, a move in which they were powerfully reinforced by an increasingly aggressive and mobilized civil rights movement. The Civil Rights Act of 1957 and then the far more consequential Civil Rights Act of 1964 and Voting Rights Act of 1965 were the main substantive products. Huge new constituencies for the Democratic Party were their most immediate structural result, in the form of newly mobilized black voters in the South but also in the North. Huge new stresses in the northern Democratic coalition and major cracks in its southern counterpart also followed.

The other great, partially autonomous, substantive contribution of the late New Deal era, one that had a curious parallel to that of civil rights, involved what was to become the Vietnam War. There had been an earlier attempt to draw the United States into combat in Southeast Asia, when the French were defeated at Dien Bien Phu and Vietnam was partitioned. But President Eisenhower, with Korea as a powerful recent analogy—that is, mindful of the fact that *ending* the Korean War remained a major policy asset for the Republican Party—failed to respond. By contrast, John F. Kennedy, an orthodox product of a Democratic coalition that melded pursuit of social welfare with prosecution of the cold war, and needing personally to neutralize foreign policy issues by appearing no less firm than his Republican opponents, took the opposite tack.

Lyndon Johnson then brought both aspects of the Democratic policy inheritance from the New Deal to their postwar zenith. He launched the Great Society, including Medicare, Head Start, and the War on Poverty. And he escalated the war in Vietnam by means of a manpower draft that ultimately reached into the collegiate middle class. The partisan consequences, by way of stresses inside the Democratic coalition, were cataclysmic. The new college-educated Democrats were not stressed by the Great Society; it was not what principally motivated them, but they were supportive. They were, however, deeply unhappy with the Vietnam War, and the baby-boom generation, in college at the time, would provide them with expressive "shock troops" for their unhappiness. In the process, dramatic public protests also elevated the issue realm of foreign affairs in the public mind, a realm where Republicans retained the policy advantage.

These two issue areas, separately and together, were to draw an array of others onto the substantive agenda of American politics. The violent aftermath of the civil rights revolution, along with the extensiveness of student protest, fueled an associated concern with public order. More tellingly, so did an explosion of crime in general within American society. Murder, robbery, burglary, rape, and assault all jumped alarmingly in the 1960s, most with the greatest decadal increase since statistics were collected. If legal desegregation was the most intensive substantive development of the time, and if student protest was the most symbolically dramatic, increased criminal activity was both more extensive than the former and more tangible than the latter. No party would be able to seize any continuing advantage from being better able to handle crime, but the perception of being tolerant of it would thereafter always be extremely harmful.

A cluster of other, lesser concerns also claimed their place on the policy agenda, and if most of these had been seen before, in earlier historical incarnations, they inevitably reappeared in a manner appropriate to the structural character of contemporary politics. Thus the natural environment came back as a matter for political debate, but in a way that reflected the postwar boom and the new social composition of the political parties. Historically it had been the more middle-class Republican Party that was the vehicle for conservation and environmental concern, while the Democrats focused on redistribution and concrete benefits. Now, it was the middle-class wing of the Democratic Party—the liberal middle class—that focused on conservation and environmental activism. Feminism moved onto the agenda as well, with the same social and partisan relationships. Historically, feminism had fit most comfortably with the Progressivism of the Republican Party. Now, it fit most comfortably in the college-graduate wing of the Democratic Party instead.

It jumps ahead of the story to note that all these latter concerns—Richard Nixon would first summarize them simply as "permissiveness"—fueled a backlash by Protestant evangelicals to what they viewed as inescapable evidence of moral and cultural decline. But what was already much in evidence by the early 1960s was the role of one particular *institution* of American national government in further propelling and then holding these cultural and social concerns at the center of the American policy agenda. That role was to be large and recurrent. It was also a particularly good example of the way in which partially autonomous (and thoroughly unintended) structural changes could shape the substantive content of a national policy agenda.

This institution was, of course, the U.S. Supreme Court. The Court under Chief Justice Earl Warren had already, in the 1950s, been a critical actor in vastly upweighting the importance of civil rights as a policy realm. Beginning in the 1960s, the Court then turned to a string of essentially cultural conflicts, once more elevating their public importance as it did so. Moreover, the Warren Court—ending an era in which economic regulation dominated the agenda of the Court and beginning an era characterized by civil liberties instead—reliably offered one side, the progressive position, on cultural issues such as busing, school prayer, abortion, capital punishment, criminal justice, homosexual rights, and so on, often in clear contraposition to public preferences.

The key point, however, did not involve the individual substance of any of these issues, great or small. The key point instead was that civil rights as a new twist on social welfare, along with Vietnam as the latest twist on foreign affairs, was only the flash point, however dramatic, for a much larger evolution in the central substance of American politics. There are many ways to distinguish the substantive core of the new era. But at bottom, the old political world had featured partisan division and issue conflict over the (re)distribution of material goods, around economics and social welfare. The new political world added—and often featured—partisan division and issue conflict over the character of national life, over the behavior operationalizing a national culture, from the family hearth to the international stage.

This first set of concerns was essentially distributional, involving the proper share of divisible goods allocated to various sectors of society. The second set was essentially valuational, involving the proper behavioral norms within which social life should proceed. The older economic-welfare concerns hardly went away, and their continuing presence remained central to the substantive character of the new era. But they were joined by the new cultural-national concerns on secondary, equal, or superior footing, depending on the context of the day. In that sense, the key substantive characteristic of this successor era was the vigorous presence of *two* great (and, as we shall see, cross-cutting) dimensions to political conflict.

Given that its substantive and structural foundations were shifting—crumbling over much of the postwar period—the New Deal era managed to last and last. Nevertheless, it could not last forever, and it came apart, with an explosion, in one disruptive year. At the time, it was possible to chalk up the disruptions of 1968 to peculiar—horrible—acts of fortune, such as the assassination of Robert Kennedy, or to dramatic but idiosyncratic personalities, such as the quixotic emergence of George Wallace. For some years afterward, it was still possible to chalk up the presidency of Richard Nixon to the specific events of 1968, events disastrous enough to bring a defeated former vice president to power with only a plurality vote, and an exceedingly narrow one at that. In such a context, it was still reasonable to believe that the American political sequence might feature a Nixon interregnum, as it had earlier featured an Eisenhower interregnum, followed by restoration of unified Democratic control of national government.

Yet with hindsight, what those disastrous events did was to crystallize a set of long-running developments, developments that had been undermining the late New Deal Era since at least the mid-1950s. The crystallizing events would, of course, go away. Their underlying developments would not. Said differently, the constituent elements of a new political era, in both its substance and its structure, were all incipiently present by the time of the 1968 election. It may have *seemed* that some simple strategic correction could neutralize that fact. But when political orders shift, this is a common (temporary) misperception. In the nature of politics, the passage of time is required for a new political dynamic, appropriate to these substantive and structural contours, to be consolidated. And this dynamic necessarily acquires its operational impact through the details of politicking on particular events. But all that would not just occur. It was effectively prefigured by 1968.

◈ *F U R T H E R   R E A D I N G*

Acuna, Rodolfo. *Occupied America: A History of Chicanos* (1981).
Anderson, Karen Tucker. *Wartime Women: Sex Roles, Family Relations, and the Status of Women During World War II* (1981).
Berube, Allen. *Coming Out Under Fire: The History of Gay Men and Women in World War Two* (1990).
Blum, John Morton. *V Was for Victory: Politics and American Culture During World War II* (1976).
Brinkley, Alan. *Liberalism and Its Discontents* (1998).
Campbell, D'Ann Mae. *Women at War with America: Private Lives in a Patriotic America* (1984).
Capeci, Dominic J. *The Harlem Riot of 1943* (1977).
Costello, John. *Virtue Under Fire: How World War II Changed Our Social and Sexual Attitudes* (1985).

Dalfiume, Richard M. *Desegregation in the United States Armed Forces: Fighting on Two Fronts: 1939–1953* (1969).

Daniels, Roger. *Concentration Camps USA: Japanese Americans and World War II* (1971).

Divine, Robert A. *Roosevelt and World War II* (1969).

Erenberg. Lewis A., and Susan E. Hirsh. *The War in American Culture* (1996).

Evans, Peter B., Dietrich Rueschemeyer, and Theda Skocpol, eds. *Bringing the State Back In* (1985).

Funigiello, Philip J. *The Challenge to Urban Liberalism* (1978).

Fussell, Paul. *Wartime: Understanding and Behavior in the Second World War* (1989).

Gluck, Sherna Berger. *Rosie the Riveter Revisited: Women, the War, and Social Change* (1987).

Graham, Otis L., Jr. *Toward a Planned Society: From Roosevelt to Nixon* (1976).

Harris, Mark Jonathan, Franklin D. Mitchell, and Stephen Schechter, eds. *Homefront: America During World War II* (1984).

Hartmann, Susan. *The Home Front and Beyond* (1982).

Hill, Robert A., ed. *The FBI's RACON: Racial Conditions in the United States During World War II* (1995).

Hobsbawm, Eric. *The Age of Extremes* (1994).

Honey, Maureen. *Creating Rosie the Riveter: Class, Gender, and Propaganda During World War II* (1984).

Hooks, Gregory Michael. *Forging the Military Industrial Complex* (1991).

Irons, Peter. *Justice at War* (1983).

Jeffries, John W. *Wartime America: The World War II Home Front* (1996).

Kaledin, Eugenia. *Daily Life in the United States, 1940–1959* (2000).

Kennedy, David M. *Freedom from Fear* (1999).

Kersten, Andrew E. *Fighting for Fair Employment: The FEPC in the Midwest, 1941–1946* (2000).

Koppes, Clayton R., and Gregory D. Black. *Hollywood Goes to War* (1987).

Leigh, Michael. *Mobilizing Consent: Public Opinion and American Foreign Policy, 1937–1947* (1986).

Lichtenstein, Nelson. *Labor's War at Home: The CIO in World War II* (1982).

Lipsitz, George. *Rainbow at Midnight: Labor and Culture in the 1940s* (1994).

Milkman, Ruth. *Gender at Work: The Dynamics of Job Segregation by Sex During World War II* (1988).

O'Brien, Kenneth Paul, and Lyn Hudson Parsons, eds. *The Home-Front War* (1995).

Okihiro, Gary Y. *Whispered Silences: Japanese Americans and World War II* (1996).

O'Neill, William L. *A Democracy at War* (1993).

Perrett, Geoffrey. *Days of Sadness, Years of Triumph: The American People, 1939–1945* (1973).

Pfeffer, Paula E. *A. Philip Randolph* (1990).

Polenberg, Richard. *War and Society: The United States, 1941–1945* (1972).

Reed, Merle E. *Seedtime for the Modern Civil Rights Movement* (1991).

Roeder, George H., Jr. *The Censored War* (1993).

Samuel, Lawrence R. *Pledging Allegiance* (1997).

Sears, Steven W., ed. *World War II* (1991).

Sherry, Michael S. *In the Shadow of War* (1995).

Sparrow, Bartholomew H. *From the Outside In: World War II and the American State* (1996).

Terkel, Studs. *"The Good War": An Oral History of World War II* (1984).

Tuttle, William M. *Daddy's Gone to War* (1993).

Waddell, Brian. *The War Against the New Deal* (2001).

Winkler, Allan J. *Home Front U.S.A,*. 2nd ed. (2000).

Wyman, David S. *The Abandonment of the Jews: America and the Holocaust, 1941–1945* (1984).

CHAPTER
2

The Origins of
the Cold War

*Germany's final defeat in the spring of 1945 ended an era in which European nations
had dominated world politics through their vast colonial empires and commercial
networks. The United States and the Soviet Union would take the lead in the new
era. The United States, which alone among the great powers had escaped the
devastation of war on its own soil, was in 1945 unquestionably the most powerful
nation in the world, and the prospect of a new American-led world—what magazine
publisher Henry Luce had called an American century—seemed realistic. The
U.S.S.R., although it had suffered enormous losses during the war, remained the
most powerful military presence on the European continent, and propelled by its
own history and ideology, soon challenged American leadership. The conflict between
these two powerful nations, what came to be called the Cold War, not only would
shape international relations for the next forty-five years but would deeply affect
both nations' political, economic, and cultural life. The Cold War would ultimately
embrace much of the Third World (comprising Africa, Asia, Latin America, and
the Middle East), where it often transformed local struggles into "hot" proxy wars
between the superpowers. Yet the Cold War began in Europe, just as it would
end there more than four decades later with the fall of the Berlin Wall. It was here
that the U.S. vision of a postwar world of American-led nations ran up against the
Soviet Union's fears for its own security and its determination to refashion much
of Eastern Europe in its own image.*

*There is an enormous amount of historical literature on the Cold War, filled
with conflicting interpretations. Was conflict precipitated by an aggressive and expansionist U.S.S.R., as most early "orthodox" interpretations of the Cold War insisted?
Or, as later generations of "revisionist" historians have argued, was the United
States, in its efforts to create a postwar world that reflected its own interests, also
responsible? What were the sources of U.S. policy: domestic politics? A need to secure
foreign markets? Strategic and geopolitical considerations? What role did misperception play in shaping U.S. and Soviet responses? To what extent did allies
and clients successfully maneuver the great powers? Could the Cold War have been
avoided, or its enormous costs in lost lives, distorted priorities, and political regression
somehow minimized? Or will the new dangers that have accompanied the end of
the Cold War make some now yearn for the lost stability of the "long peace"?*

✦ D O C U M E N T S

The United States' decision to drop atomic bombs on the Japanese cities of Hiroshima and Nagasaki on August 6 and 9, 1945, was a pivotal event in world history, marking both the end of World War II and foreshadowing a new Cold War that would shape international affairs for the next forty years. As Document 1 reveals, the bomb was much on President Harry S Truman's mind as he met with Soviet leader Joseph Stalin and British Prime Minister Winston Churchill at Potsdam, the last of the allied wartime conferences. In turn, the dropping of the atomic bomb played an important role in shaping the emerging "cold war" between the United States and the Soviet Union. So did conflicting goals over the future of Germany and Eastern Europe. On February 22, 1946, U.S. attaché George F. Kennan voiced the concerns of a growing number of senior U.S. officials in what would come to be known as the "Long Telegram" (Document 2). Later published anonymously in the journal *Foreign Affairs,* Kennan's analysis quickly became the basis for the emerging U.S. policy of containment. Ironically, Kennan himself would become a critic of containment when U.S. policy was expanded and militarized following the Korean War in 1950. Not everyone agreed with Kennan. In July 1946, Secretary of Commerce and former Vice President Henry A. Wallace would appeal to Truman (Document 3) to reverse what Wallace believed was the warlike drift of U.S. policy. When Wallace delivered a speech that same month, repeating the points he had made earlier in his letter, Truman unceremoniously fired him. Meanwhile, the Soviets were reaching conclusions that mirrored those of American leaders, as in the September 27, 1946, report by Soviet Ambassador Nikolai Novikov, excerpts from which are printed as Document 4. On March 12, 1947, Truman publicly announced the Truman Doctrine, calling for economic and military assistance to suppress a rebellion in Greece and promising to support "free peoples" throughout the world (Document 5). The Truman Doctrine marked a major departure in the history of American foreign relations, committing the United States to an expansive new diplomacy. Though couched in the defensive language of "containment," it projected U.S. power around the world on a scale unprecedented in American history. The implementation of the Truman Doctrine was quickly followed by a bold program to aid the economic reconstruction of Europe—the Marshall Plan—and then in 1949 by the North Atlantic Treaty Organization (NATO).

The new diplomacy was accompanied by a strident new policy of anti-communism in which Republican conservatives such as Senator Joseph McCarthy (Document 6) accused the Truman administration of being "soft on communism." It also led to a series of sweeping governmental reorganizations that included, among other things, the creation of the Department of Defense, the National Security Council, the Central Intelligence Agency, the Atomic Energy Commission, and the National Security Agency. The new diplomacy also required a massive expansion of U.S. military programs, as the president's national security advisers would argue in NSC-68, an April 1950 report (Document 7). The result was an enormous network of government agencies, private corporations, local communities, and solicitous congressional committees that President Dwight D. Eisenhower would later call "the military industrial complex." The North Korean invasion of South Korea, on June 25, 1950, marked the final act in the evolution of the early Cold War. The Korean War, which followed the communist revolution in China, the Soviet Union's explosion of its first atomic bomb, and the emergence of McCarthyism, thus became the linchpin of the Cold War, shaping in turn the politics, culture, and foreign policies of the United States for decades to come.

1. President Harry S Truman Discusses the Atom Bomb at Potsdam, July 1945

[Potsdam]
July 17, [19]45

Just spent a couple of hours with Stalin. Joe Davies called on Maiski and made the date last night for noon today. Promptly a few minutes before twelve I looked up from the desk and there stood Stalin in the doorway. I got to my feet and advanced to meet him. He put out his hand and smiled. I did the same[,] we shook[,] I greeted Molotov and the interpreter, and we sat down. After the usual polite remarks we got down to business. I told Stalin that I am no diplomat but usually said yes & no to questions after hearing all the argument [*sic*]. It pleased him. I asked him if he had the agenda for the meeting. He said he had and that he had some more questions to present. I told him to fire away. He did and it is dynamite—but I have some dynamite too which I am not exploding now. He wants to fire [Generalissimo Francisco] Franco [the Spanish fascist dictator], to which I wouldn't object and divide up the Italian colonies, and other mandates, some no doubt that the British have. Then he got on the Chinese situation[,] told us what agreements had been reached and what was in abeyance. Most of the big points are settled. He'll be in the Jap War on August 15th. Fini Japs when that comes about. We had lunch[,] talked socially[,] put on a real show drinking toasts to everyone, then had pictures made in the back yard. I can deal with Stalin. He's honest—but smart as hell.

[Potsdam]
July 18, [19]45

At breakfast with nephew Harry, a sergeant in the Field Artillery [in which Truman had served as a Captain during World War I]. He is a good soldier and a nice boy. They took him off [the troopship] Queen Elizabeth at Glasco [Glasgow] and flew him here. Sending him home Friday. Went to lunch with P.M. [British Prime Minister Winston Churchill] at 1:30 walked around to British Hqrs [Headquarters]. Met at the gate by Mr. Churchill. Guard of honor drawn up. Fine body of men Scottish Guards Band played the Star Spangled Banner. Inspected Guard and went in for lunch. P.M. & I ate alone. Discussed Manhattan [Project] (it is a success). Decided to tell Stalin about it. Stalin had told P.M. of telegram from Jap Emperor asking for peace. Stalin also read his answer to me. It was satisfactory. Believe Japs will fold up before Russia comes in.

   I am sure they will when Manhattan appears over their homeland. I shall inform Stalin about it at an opportune time. Stalin's luncheon was a most satisfactory meeting. I invited him to come to the U.S. Told him I'd send the Battleship Missouri for him if he'd come. He said he wanted to cooperate with U.S. in peace as we had cooperated in War but it would be harder. Said he was grossly misunderstood in the U.S. and I was misunderstood in Russia. I told him that we each could help to remedy that situation in our home countries and that I intended to try with all I had

---

Harry S Truman diary, July 17, 18, and 25, 1945, President's Secretary's Files, Papers of the President, Harry S Truman Library, Independence, Mo.

to do my part at home. He gave me a most cordial smile and said he would do as much in Russia.

We then went to the conference and it was my job to present the Ministers' proposed agenda. There were three proposals and I banged them through in short order, much to the surprise of Mr. Churchill. Stalin was very much pleased. Churchill was too after he had recovered. I'm not going to stay around this terrible place all summer just to listen to speeches. I'll go home to the Senate for that.

[Potsdam]
July 25, 1945

We met at 11 A.M. today. That is Stalin, Churchill and the U.S. President. But I had a most important session with Lord Mountbatten & General Marshall before that. We have discovered the most terrible bomb in the history of the world. It may be the fire destruction prophesied in the Euphrates Valley Era, after Noah and his fabulous Ark.

Anyway we "think" we have found the way to cause a disintegration of the atom. An experiment in the New Mexico desert was startling—to put it mildly. Thirteen pounds of the explosive caused the complete disintegration of a steel tower 60 feet high, created a crater 6 feet deep and 1,200 feet in diameter, knocked over a steel tower 1/2 mile away and knocked men down 10,000 yards away. The explosion was visible for more than 200 miles and audible for 40 miles and more.

This weapon is to be used against Japan between now and August 10th. I have told the Sec[retary]. of War, Mr. [Henry] Stimson to use so that military objectives and soldiers and sailors are the target and not women and children. Even if the Japs are savages, ruthless, merciless, and fanatic, we as the leader of the world for the common welfare cannot drop this terrible bomb on the old Capital [Kyoto] or the new [Tokyo].

He & I are in accord. The target will be a purely military one and we will issue a warning statement asking the Japs to surrender and save lives. I'm sure they will not do that, but we will have given them the chance. It is certainly a good thing for the world that Hitler's crowd or Stalin's did not discover this atomic bomb. It seems to me to be the most terrible thing ever discovered, but it can be made the most useful.

2. George F. Kennan's "Long Telegram," 1946

At bottom of Kremlin's neurotic view of world affairs is traditional and instinctive Russian sense of insecurity. Originally, this was insecurity of a peaceful agricultural people trying to live on vast exposed plain in neighborhood of fierce nomadic peoples. To this was added, as Russia came into contact with economically advanced West, fear of more competent, more powerful, more highly organized societies in that area. But this latter type of insecurity was one which afflicted rather Russian rulers than Russian people; for Russian rulers have invariably sensed that their rule was relatively archaic in form, fragile and artificial in its psychological foundation,

---

This document can be found in U.S. Department of State, *Foreign Relations of the United States, 1946, Eastern Europe: The Soviet Union* (Washington, D.C.: Government Printing Office, 1969), VI, 699–701, 706–707.

unable to stand comparison or contact with political systems of Western countries. For this reason they have always feared foreign penetration, feared direct contact between Western world and their own, feared what would happen if Russians learned truth about world without or if foreigners learned truth about world within. And they had learned to seek security only in patient but deadly struggle for total destruction of rival power, never in compacts and compromises with it.

It was no coincidence that Marxism, which had smouldered ineffectively for half a century in Western Europe, caught hold and blazed for first time in Russia. Only in this land which had never known a friendly neighbor or indeed any tolerant equilibrium of separate powers, either internal or international, could a doctrine thrive which viewed economic conflicts of society as insoluble by peaceful means. After establishment of Bolshevist regime, Marxist dogma, rendered even more truculent and intolerant by Lenin's interpretation, became a perfect vehicle for sense of insecurity with which Bolsheviks, even more than previous Russian rulers, were afflicted. In this dogma, with its basic altruism of purpose, they found justification for their instinctive fear of outside world, for the dictatorship without which they did not know how to rule, for cruelties they did not dare not to inflict, for sacrifices they felt bound to demand. In the name of Marxism they sacrificed every single ethical value in their methods and tactics. Today they cannot dispense with it. It is fig leaf of their moral and intellectual respectability. Without it they would stand before history, at best, as only the last of that long succession of cruel and wasteful Russian rulers who have relentlessly forced country on to ever new heights of military power in order to guarantee external security of their internally weak regimes. This is why Soviet purposes must always be solemnly clothed in trappings of Marxism, and why no one should underrate importance of dogma in Soviet affairs. Thus Soviet leaders are driven [by?] necessities of their own past and present position to put forward a dogma which [apparent omission] outside world as evil, hostile and menacing, but as bearing within itself germs of creeping disease and destined to be wracked with growing internal convulsions until it is given final *coup de grace* by rising power of socialism and yields to new and better world. This thesis provides justification for the increase of military and police power of Russian state, for that isolation of Russian population from outside world, and for that fluid and constant pressure to extend limits of Russian police power which are together the natural and instinctive urges of Russian rulers. Basically this is only the steady advance of uneasy Russian nationalism, a centuries old movement in which conceptions of offense and defense are inextricably confused. But in new guise of international Marxism, with its honeyed promises to a desperate and war torn outside world, it is more dangerous and insidious than ever before.

It should not be thought from above that Soviet party line is necessarily disingenuous and insincere on part of all those who put it forward. Many of them are too ignorant of outside world and mentally too dependent to question [apparent omission] self-hypnotism, and who have no difficulty making themselves believe what they find it comforting and convenient to believe. Finally we have the unsolved mystery as to who, if anyone, in this great land actually receives accurate and unbiased information about outside world. In atmosphere of oriental secretiveness and conspiracy which pervades this Government, possibilities for distorting or poisoning sources and currents of information are infinite. The very disrespect of Russians for objective truth—indeed, their disbelief in its existence—leads them to view all stated facts as instruments for furtherance of one ulterior purpose or another. There is good reason to suspect that this Government is actually a conspiracy within a conspiracy; and I for one am reluctant to believe that Stalin himself receives anything like an objective picture of outside world. Here there is ample scope for the type of subtle intrigue at which Russians are past masters. Inability of foreign governments to place their case squarely before Russian policy makers—extent to which they are delivered up in their relations with Russia to good graces of obscure and unknown advisers who they never see and cannot influence—this to my mind is most disquieting feature of diplomacy in Moscow, and one which Western statesmen would do well to keep in mind if they would understand nature of difficulties encountered here. . . .

In summary, we have here a political force committed fanatically to the belief that with US there can be no permanent modus vivendi, that it is desirable and necessary that the internal harmony of our society be disrupted, our traditional way of life be destroyed, the international authority of our state be broken, if Soviet power is to be secure. This political force has complete power of disposition over energies of one of world's greatest peoples and resources of world's richest national territory, and is borne along by deep and powerful currents of Russian nationalism. In addition, it has an elaborate and far flung apparatus for exertion of its influence in other countries, an apparatus of amazing flexibility and versatility, managed by people whose experience and skill in underground methods are presumably without parallel in history. Finally, it is seemingly inaccessible to considerations of reality in its basic reactions. For it, the vast fund of objective fact about human society is not, as with us, the measure against which outlook is constantly being tested and reformed, but a grab bag from which individual items are selected arbitrarily and tendenciously to bolster an outlook already preconceived. This is admittedly not a pleasant picture. Problem of how to cope with this force [is] undoubtedly greatest task our diplomacy has ever faced and probably greatest it will ever have to face. It should be point of departure from which our political general staff work at present juncture should proceed. It should be approached with same thoroughness and care as solution of major strategic problem in war, and if necessary, with no smaller outlay in planning effort. I cannot attempt to suggest all answers here. But I would like to record my conviction that problem is within our power to solve—and that without recourse to any general military conflict. And in support of this conviction there are certain observations of a more encouraging nature I should like to make:

1. Soviet power, unlike that of Hitlerite Germany, is neither schematic nor adventuristic. It does not work by fixed plans. It does not take unnecessary risks. Impervious to logic of reason, and it is highly sensitive to logic of force. For this reason it can easily withdraw—and usually does—when strong resistance is encountered at any point. Thus, if the adversary has sufficient force and makes clear his readiness to use it, he rarely has to do so. If situations are properly handled there need be no prestige-engaging showdowns.
2. Gauged against Western World as a whole, Soviets are still by far the weaker force. Thus, their success will really depend on degree of cohesion, firmness and vigor which Western World can muster. And this is factor which it is within our power to influence.
3. Success of Soviet system, as form of internal power, is not yet finally proven. It has yet to be demonstrated that it can survive supreme test of successive transfer

of power from one individual or group to another. Lenin's death was first such transfer, and its effects wracked Soviet state for 15 years. After Stalin's death or retirement will be second. But even this will not be final test. Soviet internal system will now be subjected, by virtue of recent territorial expansions, to series of additional strains which once proved severe tax on Tsardom. We here are convinced that never since termination of civil war have mass of Russian people been emotionally farther removed from doctrines of Communist Party than they are today. In Russia, party has now become a great and—for the moment— highly successful apparatus of dictatorial administration, but it has ceased to be a source of emotional inspiration. Thus, internal soundness and permanence of movement need not yet be regarded as assured.

4. All Soviet propaganda beyond Soviet security sphere is basically negative and destructive. It should therefore be relatively easy to combat it by any intelligent and really constructive program.

3. Secretary of Commerce Henry A. Wallace Urges a Conciliatory Approach, July 1946

My dear Mr. President:

I hope you will excuse this long letter. Personally I hate to write long letters, and I hate to receive them.

My only excuse is that this subject is a very important one—probably the most important in the world today. I checked with you about this last Thursday and you suggested after Cabinet meeting on Friday that you would like to have my views.

I have been increasingly disturbed about the trend of international affairs since the end of the war, and I am even more troubled by the apparently growing feeling among the American people that another war is coming and the only way that we can head it off is to arm ourselves to the teeth. Yet all of past history indicates that an armaments race does not lead to peace but to war. The months just ahead may well be the crucial period which will decide whether the civilized world will go down in destruction after the five or ten years needed for several nations to arm themselves with atomic bombs. Therefore I want to give you my views on how the present trend toward conflict might be averted.

How do American actions since V-J Day appear to other nations? I mean by actions the concrete things like $13 billion for the War and Navy Departments, the Bikini tests of the atomic bomb and continued production of bombs, the plan to arm Latin America with our weapons, production of B-29s and planned production of B-36s, and the effort to secure air bases spread over half the globe from which the other half of the globe can be bombed. I cannot but feel that these actions must make it look to the rest of the world as if we were only paying lip service to peace at the conference table. These facts rather make it appear either (1) that we are preparing ourselves to win the war which we regard as inevitable or (2) that we are trying to build up a predominance of force to intimidate the rest of mankind. How would it

Wallace to Truman, July 1946, Truman Papers, Harry S Truman Library, Independence, Mo.

look to us if Russia had the atomic bomb and we did not, if Russia had 10,000-mile bombers and air bases within a thousand miles of our coast lines and we did not? . . .

Other Problems of American-Russian Relationships

I believe that for the United States and Russia to live together in peace is the most important single problem facing the world today. Many people, in view of the relatively satisfactory outcome of the recent Paris Conference, feel that good progress is being made on the problem of working out relations between the Anglo-Saxon powers and Russia. This feeling seems to me to be resting on superficial appearances more productive of a temporary truce than of final peace. On the whole, as we look beneath the surface in late July of 1946, our actions and those of the western powers in general carry with them the ultimate danger of a third world war—this time an atomic world war. As the strongest single nation, and the nation whose leadership is followed by the entire world with the exception of Russia and a few weak neighboring countries in Eastern Europe, I believe that we have the opportunity to lead the world to peace.

4. Soviet Ambassador Nikolai Novikov Reports on the U.S. Drive for World Supremacy, September 1946

The foreign policy of the United States, which reflects the imperialist tendencies of American monopolistic capital, is characterized in the postwar period by a striving for world supremacy. This is the real meaning of the many statements by President Truman and other representatives of American ruling circles: that the United States has the right to lead the world. All the forces of American diplomacy—the army, the air force, the navy, industry, and science—are enlisted in the service of this foreign policy. For this purpose broad plans for expansion have been developed and are being implemented through diplomacy and the establishment of a system of naval and air bases stretching far beyond the boundaries of the United States, through the arms race, and through the creation of ever newer types of weapons. . . .

Europe has come out of the war with a completely dislocated economy, and the economic devastation that occurred in the course of the war cannot be overcome in a short time. All of the countries of Europe and Asia are experiencing a colossal need for consumer goods, industrial and transportation equipment, etc. Such a situation provides American monopolistic capital with prospects for enormous shipments of goods and the importation of capital into these countries—a circumstance that would permit it to infiltrate their national economies.

Such a development would mean serious strengthening of the economic position of the United States in the whole world and would be a stage on the road to world domination by the United States. . . .

The foreign policy of the United States is not determined at present by the circles in the Democratic party that (as was the case during Roosevelt's lifetime) strive to

From Nikolai Novikov, *Origins of the Cold War: The Novikov, Kennan and Roberts "Long Telegrams" of 1946,* ed. Kenneth M. Jensen; trans. Kenneth M. Jensen and John Glad. Copyright © by the Endowment of the United States Institute of Peace, 1991. Used with permission by the United States Institute of Peace, Washington, D.C.

strengthen the cooperation of the three great powers that constituted the basis of the anti-Hitler coalition during the war. The ascendance to power of President Truman, a politically unstable person but with certain conservative tendencies, and the subsequent appointment of [James F.] Byrnes as Secretary of State meant a strengthening of the influence on U.S. foreign policy of the most reactionary circles of the Democratic party. The constantly increasing reactionary nature of the foreign policy course of the United States, which consequently approached the policy advocated by the Republican party, laid the groundwork for close cooperation in this field between the far right wing of the Democratic party and the Republican party. . . .

At the same time, there has been a decline in the influence on foreign policy of those who follow Roosevelt's course for cooperation among peace-loving countries. Such persons in the government, in Congress, and in the leadership of the Democratic party are being pushed farther and farther into the background. The contradictions in the field of foreign policy existing between the followers of [Henry] Wallace and [Claude] Pepper, on the one hand, and the adherents of the reactionary "bi-partisan" policy, on the other, were manifested with great clarity recently in the speech by Wallace that led to his resignation from the post of Secretary of Commerce. Wallace's resignation means the victory of the reactionary course that Byrnes is conducting in cooperation with [Senator Arthur] Vandenberg and [Senator Robert] Taft.

Obvious indications of the U.S. effort to establish world dominance are also to be found in the increases in military potential in peacetime and in the establishment of a large number of naval air bases both in the United States and beyond its borders.

In the summer of 1946, for the first time in the history of the country, Congress passed a law on the establishment of a peacetime army, not on a volunteer basis but on the basis of universal military service. The size of the army, which is supposed to amount to about one million persons as of July 1, 1947, was also increased significantly. The size of the navy at the conclusion of the war decreased quite insignificantly in comparison with wartime. At the present time, the American navy occupies first place in the world, leaving England's navy far behind, to say nothing of those of other countries.

Expenditures on the army and navy have risen colossally, amounting to 13 billion dollars according to the budget for 1946–47 (about 40 percent of the total budget of 36 billion dollars). This is more than ten times greater than corresponding expenditures in the budget for 1938, which did not amount to even one billion dollars.

Along with maintaining a large army, navy, and air force, the budget provides that these enormous amounts also will be spent on establishing a very extensive system of naval and air bases in the Atlantic and Pacific oceans. According to existing official plans, in the course of the next few years 228 bases, points of support, and radio stations are to be constructed in the Atlantic Ocean and 258 in the Pacific. . . .

The establishment of American bases on the islands that are often 10,000 to 12,000 kilometers from the territory of the United States and are on the other side of the Atlantic and Pacific oceans clearly indicates the offensive nature of the strategic concepts of the commands of the U.S. army and navy. This interpretation is also confirmed by the fact that the American navy is intensively studying the naval approaches to the boundaries of Europe. For this purpose, American naval vessels in the course of 1946 visited the ports of Norway, Denmark, Sweden, Turkey, and Greece. In addition, the American navy is constantly operating in the Mediterranean Sea.

All of these facts show clearly that a decisive role in the realization of plans for world dominance by the United States is played by its armed forces.

One of the stages in the achievement of dominance over the world by the United States is its understanding with England concerning the partial division of the world on the basis of mutual concessions. The basic lines of the secret agreement between the United States and England regarding the division of the world consist, as shown by facts, in their agreement on the inclusion of Japan and China in the sphere of influence of the United States in the Far East, while the United States, for its part, has agreed not to hinder England either in resolving the Indian problem or in strengthening its influence in Siam and Indonesia.

In connection with this division, the United States at the present time is in control of China and Japan without any interference from England. . . .

In recent years American capital has penetrated very intensively into the economy of the Near Eastern countries, in particular into the oil industry. At present there are American oil concessions in all of the Near Eastern countries that have oil deposits (Iraq, Bahrain, Kuwait, Egypt, and Saudi Arabia). American capital, which made its first appearance in the oil industry of the Near East only in 1927, now controls about 42 percent of all proven reserves in the Near East, excluding Iran. Of the total proven reserves of 26.8 billion barrels, over 11 billion barrels are owned by U.S. concessions. Striving to ensure further development of their concessions in different countries (which are often very large—Saudi Arabia, for example), the American oil companies plan to build a trans-Arabian pipeline to transport oil from the American concession in Saudi Arabia and in other countries on the southeastern shore of the Mediterranean Sea to ports in Palestine and Egypt. . . .

The "hard-line" policy with regard to the U.S.S.R. announced by [Secretary of State James F.] Byrnes after the rapprochement of the reactionary Democrats with the Republicans is at present the main obstacle on the road to cooperation of the Great Powers. It consists mainly of the fact that in the postwar period the United States no longer follows a policy of strengthening cooperation among the Big Three (or Four) but rather has striven to undermine the unity of these countries. The objective has been to impose the will of other countries on the Soviet Union. This is precisely the tenor of the policy of certain countries, which is being carried out with the blessing of the United States, to undermine or completely abolish the principle of the veto in the Security Council of the United Nations. This would give the United States opportunities to form among the Great Powers narrow groupings and blocs directed primarily against the Soviet Union, and thus to split the United Nations. Rejection of the veto by the Great Powers would transform the United Nations into an Anglo-Saxon domain in which the United States would play the leading role.

The present policy of the American government with regard to the U.S.S.R. is also directed at limiting or dislodging the influence of the Soviet Union from neighboring countries. In implementing this policy in former enemy or Allied countries adjacent to the U.S.S.R., the United States attempts, at various international conferences or directly in these countries themselves, to support reactionary forces with the purpose of creating obstacles to the process of democratization of these countries. In so doing, it also attempts to secure positions for the penetration of American capital into their economies. . . .

One of the most important elements in the general policy of the United States, which is directed toward limiting the international role of the U.S.S.R. in the postwar world, is the policy with regard to Germany. In Germany, the United States is taking measures to strengthen reactionary forces for the purpose of opposing democratic re-construction. Furthermore, it displays special insistence on accompanying this policy with completely inadequate measures for the demilitarization of Germany.

The American occupation policy does not have the objective of eliminating the remnants of German Fascism and rebuilding German political life on a democratic basis, so that Germany might cease to exist as an aggressive force. The United States is not taking measures to eliminate the monopolistic associations of German indus-trialists on which German Fascism depended in preparing aggression and waging war. Neither is any agrarian reform being conducted to eliminate large landholders, who were also a reliable support for the Hitlerites. Instead, the United States is con-sidering the possibility of terminating the Allied occupation of German territory before the main tasks of the occupation—the demilitarization and democratization of Germany—have been implemented. This would create the prerequisites for the revival of an imperialist Germany, which the United States plans to use in a future war on its side. One cannot help seeing that such a policy has a clearly outlined anti-Soviet edge and constitutes a serious danger to the cause of peace. . . .

5. The Truman Doctrine, March 1947

Mr. President, Mr. Speaker, Members of the Congress of the United States:

The gravity of the situation which confronts the world today necessitates my appearance before a joint session of the Congress.

The foreign policy and the national security of this country are involved.

One aspect of the present situation, which I present to you at this time for your consideration and decision, concerns Greece and Turkey.

The United States has received from the Greek Government an urgent appeal for financial and economic assistance. Preliminary reports from the American Economic Mission now in Greece and reports from the American Ambassador in Greece cor-roborate the statement of the Greek Government that assistance is imperative if Greece is to survive as a free nation.

I do not believe that the American people and the Congress wish to turn a deaf ear to the appeal of the Greek Government.

Greece is not a rich country. Lack of sufficient natural resources has always forced the Greek people to work hard to make both ends meet. Since 1940, this industrious, peace loving country has suffered invasion, four years of cruel enemy occupation, and bitter internal strife.

When forces of liberation entered Greece they found that the retreating Germans had destroyed virtually all the railways, roads, port facilities, communications, and merchant marine. More than a thousand villages had been burned. Eighty-five per-cent of the children were tubercular. Livestock, poultry, and draft animals had almost disappeared. Inflation had wiped out practically all savings.

Public Papers of the Presidents of the United States: Harry S Truman, 1945–53 (Washington, D.C.: GPO, 1963), 176–180.

As a result of these tragic conditions, a militant minority, exploiting human want and misery, was able to create political chaos which, until now, has made economic recovery impossible. . . .

The very existence of the Greek state is today threatened by the terrorist activities of several thousand armed men, led by Communists, who defy the government's authority at a number of points, particularly along the northern boundaries. A Commission appointed by the United Nations Security Council is at present investigating disturbed conditions in northern Greece and alleged border violations along the frontier between Greece on the one hand and Albania, Bulgaria, and Yugoslavia on the other.

Meanwhile, the Greek Government is unable to cope with the situation. The Greek army is small and poorly equipped. It needs supplies and equipment if it is to restore authority to the government throughout Greek territory.

Greece must have assistance if it is to become a self-supporting and self-respecting democracy. . . .

No government is perfect. One of the chief virtues of a democracy, however, is that its defects are always visible and under democratic processes can be pointed out and corrected. The government of Greece is not perfect. Nevertheless it represents 85 percent of the members of the Greek Parliament who were chosen in an election last year. Foreign observers, including 692 Americans, considered this election to be a fair expression of the views of the Greek people.

The Greek Government has been operating in an atmosphere of chaos and extremism. It has made mistakes. The extension of aid by this country does not mean that the United States condones everything that the Greek Government has done or will do. We have condemned in the past, and we condemn now, extremist measures of the right or the left. We have in the past advised tolerance, and we advise tolerance now.

Greece's neighbor, Turkey, also deserves our attention.

The future of Turkey as an independent and economically sound state is clearly no less important to the freedom-loving peoples of the world than the future of Greece. The circumstances in which Turkey finds itself today are considerably different from those of Greece. Turkey has been spared the disasters that have beset Greece. And during the war, the United States and Great Britain furnished Turkey with material aid.

Nevertheless, Turkey now needs our support.

Since the war Turkey has sought additional financial assistance from Great Britain and the United States for the purpose of effecting that modernization necessary for the maintenance of its national integrity.

That integrity is essential to the preservation of order in the Middle East.

The British Government has informed us that, owing to its own difficulties, it can no longer extend financial or economic aid to Turkey.

As in the case of Greece, if Turkey is to have the assistance it needs, the United States must supply it. We are the only country able to provide that help.

I am fully aware of the broad implications involved if the United States extends assistance to Greece and Turkey, and I shall discuss these implications with you at this time.

One of the primary objectives of the foreign policy of the United States is the creation of conditions in which we and other nations will be able to work out a way of life free from coercion. This was a fundamental issue in the war with Germany and Japan. Our victory was won over countries which sought to impose their will, and their way of life, upon other nations.

To ensure the peaceful development of nations, free from coercion, the United States has taken a leading part in establishing the United Nations. The United Nations is designed to make possible lasting freedom and independence for all its members. We shall not realize our objectives, however, unless we are willing to help free peoples to maintain their free institutions and their national integrity against aggressive movements that seek to impose upon them totalitarian regimes. This is no more than a frank recognition that totalitarian regimes imposed upon free peoples, by direct or indirect aggression, undermine the foundations of international peace and hence the security of the United States.

The peoples of a number of countries of the world have recently had totalitarian regimes forced upon them against their will. The Government of the United States has made frequent protests against coercion and intimidation, in violation of the Yalta agreement, in Poland, Rumania, and Bulgaria. I must also state that in a number of other countries there have been similar developments.

At the present moment in world history nearly every nation must choose between alternative ways of life. The choice is too often not a free one.

One way of life is based upon the will of the majority, and is distinguished by free institutions, representative government, free elections, guarantees of individual liberty, freedom of speech and religion, and freedom from political oppression.

The second way of life is based upon the will of a minority forcibly imposed upon the majority. It relies upon terror and oppression, a controlled press and radio, fixed elections, and the suppression of personal freedoms.

I believe that it must be the policy of the United States to support free peoples who are resisting attempted subjugation by armed minorities or by outside pressures.

I believe that we must assist free peoples to work out their own destinies in their own way.

I believe that our help should be primarily through economic and financial aid which is essential to economic stability and orderly political processes.

The world is not static, and the *status quo* is not sacred. But we cannot allow changes in the *status quo* in violation of the Charter of the United Nations by such methods as coercion, or by such subterfuges as political infiltration. In helping free and independent nations to maintain their freedom, the United States will be giving effect to the principles of the Charter of the United Nations.

It is necessary only to glance at a map to realize that the survival and integrity of the Greek nation are of grave importance in a much wider situation. If Greece should fall under the control of an armed minority, the effect upon its neighbor, Turkey, would be immediate and serious. Confusion and disorder might well spread throughout the entire Middle East.

Moreover, the disappearance of Greece as an independent state would have a profound effect upon those countries in Europe whose peoples are struggling against great difficulties to maintain their freedoms and their independence while they repair the damages of war.

It would be an unspeakable tragedy if these countries, which have struggled so long against overwhelming odds, should lose that victory for which they sacrificed so much. Collapse of free institutions and loss of independence would be disastrous not only for them but for the world. Discouragement and possibly failure would quickly be the lot of neighboring peoples striving to maintain their freedom and independence.

Should we fail to aid Greece and Turkey in this fateful hour, the effect will be far reaching to the West as well as to the East. . . .

6. Senator Joseph McCarthy Charges the Democrats Are "Soft on Communism," 1950

The great difference between our western Christian world and the atheistic Communist world is not political, gentlemen, it is moral. For instance, the Marxian idea of confiscating the land and factories and running the entire economy as a single enterprise is momentous. Likewise, Lenin's invention of the one-party police state as a way to make Marx's idea work is hardly less momentous.

Stalin's resolute putting across of these two ideas, of course, did much to divide the world. With only these differences, however, the east and west could most certainly still live in peace.

The real, basic difference, however, lies in the religion of immoralism—invented by Marx, preached feverishly by Lenin, and carried to unimaginable extremes by Stalin. This religion of immoralism, if the Red half of the world triumphs—and well it may, gentlemen—this religion of immoralism will more deeply wound and damage mankind than any conceivable economic or political system.

Karl Marx dismissed God as a hoax, and Lenin and Stalin have added in clear-cut, unmistakable language their resolve that no nation, no people who believe in a god, can exist side by side with their communistic state.

Karl Marx, for example, expelled people from his Communist Party for mentioning such things as love, justice, humanity[,] or morality. He called this "soulful ravings" and "sloppy sentimentality."

While Lincoln was a relatively young man in his late thirties, Karl Marx boasted that the Communist specter was haunting Europe. Since that time, hundreds of millions of people and vast areas of the world have come under Communist domination. Today, less than 100 years after Lincoln's death, Stalin brags that this Communist specter is not only haunting the world, but is about to completely subjugate it.

Today we are engaged in a final all-out battle between communistic atheism and Christianity. The modern champions of communism have selected this as the time, and ladies and gentlemen, the chips are down—they are truly down.

Lest there be any doubt that the time has been chosen, let us go directly to the leader of communism today—Joseph Stalin. Here is what he said—not back in 1928, not before the war, not during the war—but 2 years after the last war was ended: "To think that the Communist revolution can be carried out peacefully, within the framework of a Christian democracy, means one has either gone out of one's mind and lost all normal understanding, or has grossly and openly repudiated the Communist revolution."

Congressional Record, 81st Cong., 2d sess. (February 20, 1950), 1953–1980.

This is what was said by Lenin in 1919—and quoted with approval by Stalin in 1947:

"We are living," says Lenin, "not merely in a state, but in a system of states, and the existence of the Soviet Republic side by side with Christian states for a long time is unthinkable—one or the other must triumph in the end. And that before that end supervenes, a series of frightful collisions between the Soviet Republic and the bourgeois states will be inevitable."

Ladies and gentlemen, can there by anyone tonight who is so blind as to say that the war is not on? Can there be anyone who fails to realize that the Communist world has said the time is now—that this is the time for the slowdown between the democratic Christian world and the communistic atheistic world?

Unless we face this fact, we shall pay the price that must be paid by those who wait too long.

Six years ago, at the time of the first conference to map out the peace, there was within the Soviet orbit, 180,000,000 people. Lined up on the anti-totalitarian side there were in the world at that time, roughly 1,625,000,000 people. Today, only 6 years later, there are 80,000,000,000 [*sic*] people under the absolute domination of Soviet Russia—an increase of over 400 percent. On our side, the figure has shrunk to around 500,000 [*sic*]. In other words, in less than 6 years the odds have changed from 9 to 1 in our favor to 8 to 1 against us.

This indicates the swiftness of the tempo of Communist victories and American defeats in the cold war. As one of our outstanding historical figures once said, "When a great democracy is destroyed, it will not be from enemies without, but rather because of enemies within."

The truth of this statement is becoming terrifyingly clear as we see this country each day losing on every front.

At war's end we were physically the strongest nation on earth—and at least potentially the most powerful intellectually and morally. Ours could have been the honor of being a beacon in the desert of destruction—shining proof that civilization was not yet ready to destroy itself. Unfortunately, we have failed miserably and tragically to arise to the opportunity.

The reason why we find ourselves in a position of impotency is not because our only powerful potential enemy has sent men to invade our shores—but rather because of the traitorous actions of those who have been treated so well by this Nation. It has not been the less fortunate, or members of minority groups who have been traitorous to this Nation—but rather those who have had all the benefits that the wealthiest Nation on earth has had to offer—the finest homes, the finest college education and the finest jobs in government we can give.

This is glaringly true in the State Department. There the bright young men who are born with silver spoons in their mouths are the ones who have been most traitorous. . . . And, ladies and gentlemen, while I cannot take the time to name all the men in the State Department who have been named as active members of the Communist Party and members of a spy ring, I have here in my hand a list of 205—a list of names that were made known to the Secretary of State [Dean Acheson] as being members of the Communist Party and who nevertheless are still working and shaping policy in the State Department.

One thing to remember in discussing the Communists in our Government is that we are not dealing with spies who get 30 pieces of silver to steal the blueprints of a new weapon. We are dealing with a far more sinister type of activity because it permits the enemy to guide and shape our policy.

7. The President's Advisers Urge Military Expansion (NSC-68), April 1950

Within the past thirty-five years the world has experienced two global wars of tremendous violence. It has witnessed two revolutions—the Russian and the Chinese—of extreme scope and intensity. It has also seen the collapse of five empires—the Ottoman, the Austro-Hungarian, German, Italian, and Japanese— and the drastic decline of two major imperial systems, the British and the French. During the span of one generation, the international distribution of power has been fundamentally altered. For several centuries it had proved impossible for any one nation to gain such preponderant strength that a coalition of other nations could not in time face it with greater strength. The international scene was marked by recurring periods of violence and war, but a system of sovereign and independent states was maintained, over which no state was able to achieve hegemony.

Two complex sets of factors have now basically altered this historical distribution of power. First, the defeat of Germany and Japan and the decline of the British and French Empires have interacted with the development of the United States and the Soviet Union in such a way that power has increasingly gravitated to these two centers. Second, the Soviet Union, unlike previous aspirants to hegemony, is animated by a new fanatic faith, antithetical to our own, and seeks to impose its absolute authority over the rest of the world. Conflict has, therefore, become endemic and is waged, on the part of the Soviet Union, by violent or non-violent methods in accordance with the dictates of expediency. With the development of increasingly terrifying weapons of mass destruction, every individual faces the ever-present possibility of annihilation should the conflict enter the phase of total war.

On the one hand, the people of the world yearn for relief from the anxiety arising from the risk of atomic war. On the other hand, any substantial further extension of the area under the domination of the Kremlin would raise the possibility that no coalition adequate to confront the Kremlin with greater strength could be assembled. It is in this context that this Republic and its citizens in the ascendancy of their strength stand in their deepest peril.

The issues that face us are momentous, involving the fulfillment or destruction not only of this Republic but of civilization itself. They are issues which will not await our deliberations. With conscience and resolution this Government and the people it represents must now take new and fateful decisions. . . .

Our overall policy at the present time may be described as one designed to foster a world environment in which the American system can survive and flourish. It therefore rejects the concept of isolation and affirms the necessity of our positive participation in the world community.

This broad intention embraces two subsidiary policies. One is a policy which we would probably pursue even if there were no Soviet threat. It is a policy of attempting

---

Excerpts from "NSC-68: A Report to the National Security Council," April 14, 1950, from *The Naval War College Review* 27/6, May/June 1975, pp. 51–108. Reprinted by permission of the Naval War College Review.

to develop a healthy international community. The other is the policy of "containing" the Soviet system. These two policies are closely interrelated and interact on one another. Nevertheless, the distinction between them is basically valid and contributes to a clearer understanding of what we are trying to do.

The policy of striving to develop a healthy international community is the long-term constructive effort which we are engaged in. It was this policy which gave rise to our vigorous sponsorship of the United Nations. It is of course the principal reason for our long continuing endeavors to create and now develop the Inter-American system. It, as much as containment, underlay our efforts to rehabilitate Western Europe. Most of our international economic activities can likewise be explained in terms of this policy.

In a world of polarized power, the policies designed to develop a healthy international community are more than ever necessary to our own strength. . . .

A comprehensive and decisive program to win the peace and frustrate the Kremlin design should be so designed that it can be sustained for as long as necessary to achieve our national objectives. It would probably involve:

1. The development of an adequate political and economic framework for the achievement of our long-range objectives.
2. A substantial increase in expenditures for military purposes adequate to meet the requirements for the tasks listed in Section D-1.
3. A substantial increase in military assistance programs, designed to foster cooperative efforts, which will adequately and efficiently meet the requirements of our allies for the tasks referred to in Section D-1-*e*.
4. Some increase in economic assistance programs and recognition of the need to continue these programs until their purposes have been accomplished.
5. A concerted attack on the problem of the United States balance of payments, along the lines already approved by the President.
6. Development of programs designed to build and maintain confidence among other peoples in our strength and resolution, and to wage overt psychological warfare calculated to encourage mass defections from Soviet allegiance and to frustrate the Kremlin design in other ways.
7. Intensification of affirmative and timely measures and operations by covert means in the fields of economic warfare and political psychological warfare with a view to fomenting and supporting unrest and revolt in selected strategic satellite countries.
8. Development of internal security and civilian defense programs.
9. Improvement and intensification of intelligence activities.
10. Reduction of Federal expenditures for purposes other than defense and foreign assistance, if necessary by the deferment of certain desirable programs.
11. Increased taxes. . . .

Conclusions and Recommendations

The foregoing analysis indicates that the probable fission bomb capability and possible thermonuclear bomb capability of the Soviet Union have greatly intensified the Soviet threat to the security of the United States. This threat is of the same character as that described in NSC 20/4 (approved by the President on November 24, 1948) but is more immediate than had previously been estimated. In particular, the United States now faces the contingency that within the next four or five years the Soviet Union will possess the military capability of delivering a surprise atomic attack of such weight that the United States must have substantially increased general air, ground, and sea strength, atomic capabilities, and air and civilian defenses to deter war and to provide reasonable assurance, in the event of war, that it could survive the initial blow and go on to the eventual attainment of its objectives. In turn, this contingency requires the intensification of our efforts in the fields of intelligence and research and development. . . .

In the light of present and prospective Soviet atomic capabilities, the action which can be taken under present programs and plans, however, becomes dangerously inadequate, in both timing and scope, to accomplish the rapid progress toward the attainment of the United States' political, economic, and military objectives which is now imperative.

A continuation of present trends would result in a serious decline in the strength of the free world relative to the Soviet Union and its satellites. This unfavorable trend arises from the inadequacy of current programs and plans rather than from any error in our objectives and aims. These trends lead in the direction of isolation, not by deliberate decision but by lack of the necessary basis for a vigorous initiative in the conflict with the Soviet Union.

Our position as the center of power in the free world places a heavy responsibility upon the United States for leadership. We must organize and enlist the energies and resources of the free world in a positive program for peace which will frustrate the Kremlin design for world domination by creating a situation in the free world to which the Kremlin will be compelled to adjust. Without such a cooperative effort, led by the United States, we will have to make gradual withdrawals under pressure until we discovered one day that we have sacrificed positions of vital interest.

It is imperative that this trend be reversed by a much more rapid and concerted build-up of the actual strength of both the United States and the other nations of the free world. The analysis shows that this will be costly and will involve significant domestic financial and economic adjustments.

The execution of such a build-up, however, requires that the United States have an affirmative program beyond the solely defensive one of countering the threat posed by the Soviet Union. This program must light the path to peace and order among nations in a system based on freedom and justice, as contemplated in the Charter of the United Nations. Further, it must envisage the political and economic measures with which and the military shield behind which the free world can work to frustrate the Kremlin design by the strategy of the cold war; for every consideration of devotion to our fundamental values and to our national security demands that we achieve our objectives by the strategy of the cold war, building up our military strength in order that it may not have to be used. The only sure victory lies in the frustration of the Kremlin design by the steady development of the moral and material strength of the free world and its projection into the Soviet world in such a way as to bring about an internal change in the Soviet system. Such a positive program—harmonious with our fundamental national purpose and our objectives—is necessary if we are to regain and retain the initiative and to win and hold the necessary popular support and cooperation in the United States and the rest of the free world.

This program should include a plan for negotiation with the Soviet Union, developed and agreed with our allies and which is consonant with our objectives. The United States and its allies, particularly the United Kingdom and France, should always be ready to negotiate with the Soviet Union on terms consistent with our objectives. The present world situation, however, is one which militates against successful negotiations with the Kremlin—for the terms of agreements on important pending issues would reflect present realities and would therefore be unacceptable, if not disastrous, to the United States and the rest of the free world. After a decision and a start on building up the strength of the free world has been made, it might then be desirable for the United States to take an initiative in seeking negotiations in the hope that it might facilitate the process of accommodation by the Kremlin to the new situation. Failing that, the unwillingness of the Kremlin to accept equitable terms or its bad faith in observing them would assist in consolidating popular opinion in the free world in support of the measures necessary to sustain the build-up.

In summary, we must, by means of a rapid and sustained build-up of the political, economic, and military strength of the free world, and by means of an affirmative program intended to wrest the initiative from the Soviet Union, confront it with convincing evidence of the determination and ability of the free world to frustrate the Kremlin design of a world dominated by its will. Such evidence is the only means short of war which eventually may force the Kremlin to abandon its present course of action and to negotiate acceptable agreements on issues of major importance.

The whole success of the proposed program hangs ultimately on recognition by this Government, the American people, and all free peoples, that the cold war is in fact a real war in which the survival of the free world is at stake. Essential prerequisites to success are consultations with Congressional leaders designed to make the program the object of non-partisan legislative support, and a presentation to the public of a full explanation of the facts and implications of the present international situation. The prosecution of the program will require of us all the ingenuity, sacrifice, and unity demanded by the vital importance of the issue and the tenacity to persevere until our national objectives have been attained.

✦ E S S A Y S

Early histories described the Cold War in ways scarcely distinguishable from the speeches of American leaders, as a war thrust upon a virtuous republic by a malevolent and evil empire. American dreams for a postwar peace were rudely shattered, wrote leading diplomatic historian Thomas Bailey, when "the Kremlin brutally slapped outside the outstretched American hand." Writing of the Truman administration, historian John Spanier concluded that "history had once more shown that when a great and democratic people is given decisive and courageous leadership, the people will respond quickly and wisely." In the late 1960s, however, the war in Vietnam prompted a critical reappraisal of U.S. policies, focusing on the expansiveness of America's postwar goals and assigning a much greater degree of responsibility for the Cold War to the United States and its leaders. For almost two decades, such "revisionist" interpretations dominated Cold War scholarship. By the 1980s, however, revisionist studies of the Cold War were increasingly challenged by newer, "post-revisionist" accounts. Post-revisionism, like revisionism itself, was a slippery term that embraced a variety of approaches and interpretations. For some, post-revisionism meant exploring newly opened archives in the Soviet Union, Eastern Europe, and elsewhere, recasting the history of the Cold War in a broader, multi-national framework. For others, post-revisionism was part of the broader, conservative reconstitution of American thought and culture that accompanied the presidency of Ronald Reagan and the collapse of the Soviet Union.

In the first essay, from his 1999 presidential address to the Society for the History of American Foreign Relations, diplomatic historian Arnold A. Offner sharply challenges post-revisionist accounts of the Cold War, arguing that Truman's personal insecurity, inexperience, and reflexive nationalism led him to exacerbate tensions with the Soviet Union. In the second essay, Yale historian John Lewis Gaddis, the preeminent post-revisionist historian of the Cold War, argues the case for Soviet responsibility, empha-sizing the fusion of traditional Russian expansionism and Marxist ideology and stressing the brutal repressiveness of post-World War II Soviet actions.

President Harry S Truman and the Origins of the Cold War

ARNOLD A. OFFNER

As the twenty-first century nears, Present Harry S Truman's reputation stands high. his is especially true regarding his stewardship of foreign policy although, ironically, he entered the Oval Office in 1945 untutored in world affairs, and during his last year in the White House Republicans accused his administration of having surrendered fifteen countries and five hundred million people to communism and sending twenty thousand Americans to their "burial ground" in Korea. Near the end of his term, Truman's public "favorable" rating had plummeted to 23 percent.

Within a decade, however, historians rated Truman a "near great" president, crediting his administration with reconstructing Western Europe and Japan, resist-ing Soviet or Communist aggression from Greece to Korea, and forging collective security through NATO. In the 1970s the "plain speaking" Truman became a popular culture hero. Recently, biographers have depicted him as the allegory of American life, an ordinary man whose extraordinary character led him to triumph over adver-sity from childhood through the presidency, and even posited a symbiotic relation-ship between "His Odyssey" from Independence to the White House and America's rise to triumphant superpower status. . . .

The collapse of the Soviet Union and Europe's other Communist states, whose archives have confirmed Truman's belief in 1945 that their regimes governed largely by "clubs, pistols and concentration camps," has further raised the former president's standing. This has encouraged John Lewis Gaddis and others to shift their focus to Stalin's murderous domestic rule as the key determinant of Soviet foreign policy and the Cold War. As Gaddis has contended, Stalin was heir to Ivan the Terrible and Peter the Great, responsible for more state-sanctioned murders than Adolf Hitler, and

From Arnold A. Offner, " 'Another Such Victory': President Truman, American Foreign Policy, and the Cold War," *Diplomatic History* 23:2 (Spring 1999). Reprinted by permission of Blackwell Publishing Ltd.

treated world politics as an extension of domestic politics: a zero sum game in which his gaining security meant depriving all others of it. For Gaddis and others, that is largely the answer to the question of whether Stalin sought or caused the Cold War.

But as Walter LaFeber has said, to dismiss Stalin's policies as the work of a paranoid is greatly to oversimplify the Cold War. Indeed, historians of Stalin's era seem to be of the preponderant view that he pursued a cautious but brutal realpolitik. He aimed to restore Russia's 1941 boundaries, establish a sphere of influence in border states, provide security against a recovered Germany or Japan or hostile capitalist states, and gain compensation, notably reparations, for the ravages of war. Stalin calculated forces, recognized America's superior industrial and military power, put Soviet state interests ahead of Marxist-Leninist ideology, and pursued pragmatic or opportunistic policies in critical areas such as Germany, China, and Korea.

Thus, the time seems ripe, given our increased knowledge of Soviet policies, to reconsider President Truman's role in the Cold War. As Thomas G. Paterson has written, the president stands as the pinnacle of the diplomatic-military establishment, has great capacity to set the foreign policy agenda and to mold public opinion, and his importance, especially in Truman's case, cannot be denied. But contrary to prevailing views, I believe that his policymaking was shaped by his parochial and nationalistic heritage. This was reflected in his uncritical belief in the superiority of American values and political-economic interests and his conviction that the Soviet Union and communism were the root cause of international strife. Truman's parochialism also caused him to disregard contrary views, to engage in simplistic analogizing, and to show little ability to comprehend the basis for other nations' policies. Consequently, his foreign policy leadership intensified Soviet-American conflict, hastened the division of Europe, and brought tragic intervention in Asian civil wars. . . .

Truman's parochialism and nationalism, and significant insecurity, were rooted in his background, despite his claim to have had a bucolic childhood of happy family, farm life, and Baptist religiosity. In fact, young Harry's poor eyesight, extended illness, and "sissy" piano playing alienated him from both his peers and his feisty father and fostered ambivalence in him toward powerful men. On the one hand, Truman deferred to "Boss" Thomas Pendergast, his dishonest political benefactor, and to Secretaries of State George Marshall and Dean Acheson, whose manner and firm viewpoints he found reassuring. On the other hand, he denounced those whose style or ways of thinking were unfamiliar. This included the State Department's "striped pants boys," the military's "brass hats" and "prima donnas," political "fakirs" [*sic*] such as Teddy and Franklin Roosevelt, and "professional liberals." For Truman, Charles de Gaulle, Josef Stalin, Ernest Bevin, and Douglas MacArthur were each, at one time or another, a "son of a bitch." . . .

Truman's self-tutelage in history derived largely from didactic biographies of "great men" and empires. This enhanced his vision of the globe but provided little sense of complexity or ambiguity and instilled exaggerated belief that current events had exact historical analogues that provided the key to contemporary policy. The new president was "amazed" that the Yalta accords were so "hazy" and fraught with "new meanings" at every reading, which probably contributed to his "lackluster" adherence to them. Shortly, Truman uncritically applied analogues about 1930s appeasement of Nazi Germany to diplomacy with the Soviet Union and crises in Iran, Greece, Turkey, and Korea.

Further, young Harry's Bible reading and church going did not inspire an abiding religiosity or system of morals so much as a conviction that the world was filled with "liars and hypocrites," terms he readily applied to his presidential critics, and a stern belief, as he wrote in 1945, that "punishment always followed transgression," a maxim that he applied to North Korea and the People's Republic of China (PRC).

Truman's early writings disdained non-Americans and minorities ("Chink doctor," "dago," "nigger," "Jew clerk," and "bohunks and Rooshans"), and in 1940 he proposed to deport "disloyal inhabitants." As president in 1945 he questioned the loyalty of "hyphenate" Americans, and in 1947 he signed Executive Order 9835, creating an unprecedented "loyalty" program that jettisoned basic legal procedural safeguards and virtually included a presumption of guilt.

Truman's command of men and bravery under fire in World War I were exemplary but not broadening. He deplored Europe's politics, mores, and food and sought only to return to "God's country." He intended never to revisit Europe: "I've nearly promised old Miss Liberty that she'll have to turn around to see me again," he wrote in 1918, and in 1945 he went reluctantly to Potsdam to his first and only European summit.

Nonetheless, Truman identified with Wilsonian internationalism, especially the League of Nations, and as a senator he supported President Franklin Roosevelt on the World Court, neutrality revision, rearmament, and Lend Lease for Britain and Russia. He rightfully said "I am no appeaser." But his internationalism reflected unquestioned faith in American moral superiority, and his foreign policy proposals largely comprised military preparedness. He was indifferent to the plight of Republican Spain and too quickly blamed international conflict on "outlaws," "savages," and "totalitarians." After Germany invaded the Soviet Union in 1941, he hastily remarked that they should be left to destroy one another—although he opposed Germany's winning—and he likened Russian leaders to "Hitler and Al Capone" and soon inveighed against the "twin blights—atheism and communism." Hence, while Truman supported the fledgling United Nations and the liberalization of world trade, the man who became president in April 1945 was less an incipient internationalist than a parochial nationalist given to excessive fear that appeasement, lack of preparedness, and enemies at home and abroad would thwart America's mission (the "Lord's will") to "win the peace" on its terms.

President Truman inherited an expedient wartime alliance that stood on shaky ground at Yalta in February 1945 and grew more strained over Soviet control in Romania and Poland and U.S. surrender talks with German officials at Bern that aroused Stalin's fears of a separate peace. Truman lamented that "they didn't tell me anything about what was going on." He also had to depend on advisers whose views ranged from Ambassador Averell Harriman's belief that it was time to halt the Russians' "barbarian invasion" of Europe to counsel from FDR emissaries Joseph Davies and Harry Hopkins to try to preserve long-term accord. Truman's desire to appear decisive by making quick decisions and his instinct to be "tough" spurred his belief that he could get "85 percent" from the Russians on important matters and that they could go along or "go to hell."

Initially, the president's abrupt style and conflicting advice produced inconsistent policy. His mid-April call for a "new" government in Poland and his "one-two to the jaw" interview with [Soviet Foreign Minister Vyacheslav] Molotov brought only a sharp reply from Stalin, after which the United States recognized a predominantly Communist Polish government. In May, Truman approved "getting tough" with the Russians by suddenly curtailing Lend Lease shipments, but Anglo-Soviet protests caused him to countermand the cutoffs. He then refused Prime Minister Winston Churchill's proposal to keep Anglo-American troops advanced beyond their agreed occupation zones to bargain in Germany and soon wrote that he was "anxious to keep all my engagements with the Russians because they are touchy and suspicious of us."

Still, Truman determined to have his way with the Russians, especially in Germany. Tutored in part by Secretary of War Henry L. Stimson, he embraced the emergent War-State Department position that Germany was key to the balance of power in Europe and required some reconstruction because a "poor house" standard of living there meant the same for Europe, and might cause a repeat of the tragic Treaty of Versailles history. Truman replaced Roosevelt's reparations negotiator, Isador Lubin, with conservative oil entrepreneur Edwin Pauley, who brushed off both Soviet claims to Yalta's $20 billion in reparations and State Department estimates that Germany could pay $12–14 billion. Truman also said that when he met with Churchill and Stalin he wanted "all the bargaining power—all the cards in my hands, and the plan on Germany is one of them."

The other card was the atomic bomb, which inspired Truman and [Secretary of State] Byrnes to think that they could win their way in Europe and Asia. Byrnes told the president in April that the bomb might allow them to "dictate our terms" at the war's end and in May indicated his belief that it would make the Russians more "manageable." Stimson counseled Truman that America's industrial strength and unique weapon comprised a "royal straight flush and we mustn't be a fool about how we play it," that it would be "dominant" in any dispute with Russia over Manchuria, and a "weapon" or "master card" in America's hand in its "big stakes" diplomacy with the Russians. . . .

After meeting Stalin [at Potsdam, Germany,] on 17 July Truman wrote that he was unfazed by the Russian's "dynamite" agenda because "I have some dynamite too which I'm not exploding now." The following day he asserted that the "Japs will fold up" before Russia entered the Pacific war, specifically "when Manhattan appears over their homeland." Truman agreed with Byrnes that use of the bomb would permit them to "out maneuver Stalin on China," that is, negate the Yalta concessions in Manchuria and guarantee that Russia would "not get in so much on the kill" of Japan or its occupation. . . .

News of the bomb's power also greatly reinforced Truman's confidence to allow Byrnes to press European negotiations to impasse by refusing the Russians access to the Ruhr, rejecting even their low bid for $4 billion in industrial reparations, and withdrawing the Yalta accords. Convinced that the New Mexico atomic test would allow the United States to "control" events, Byrnes pushed his famous 30 July tripartite ultimatum on German zonal reparations [limiting Soviet reparations mainly to the Soviet occupational zone and reducing the amounts discussed by FDR and Stalin at Yalta], Poland's de facto control over its new western border (including Silesia) with Germany, and Italy's membership in the UN. "Mr. Stalin is stallin'," Truman wrote hours before the American-set deadline on 31 July, but that was useless because "I have an ace in the hole and another one showing," aces that he knew would soon fall upon Japan.

Truman won his hand, as Stalin acceded to zonal reparations. But Truman's victory was fraught with more long-term consequences than he envisioned. He had not only equated his desire to prevent use of taxpayer dollars to help sustain occupied Germany with the Russians' vital need for reparations but also given them reason to think, as Norman Naimark has written, that the Americans were deaf to their question for a "paltry" $10 billion or less to compensate for Germany's having ravaged their nation. Further, America's insistence on zonal reparations would have impeded development of common economic policy for all of Germany and increase likelihood of its East-West division. . . .

Truman backed Byrnes's [hard-headed] diplomacy at the London CFM [Council of Foreign Ministers], which deadlocked over Russian control in Eastern Europe and American control in Japan. Truman told Byrnes to "stick to his guns" and tell the Russians "to go to hell." The president then agreed with "ultranationalist" advisers who opposed international atomic accord by drawing misleading analogies about interwar disarmament and "appeasement" and by insisting that America's technological-industrial genius assured permanent atomic supremacy. Truman held that America was the world's atomic "trustee"; that it had to preserve the bomb's "secret"; and that no nation would give up the "locks and bolts" necessary to protect its "house" from "outlaws." The atomic arms race was on, he said in the fall of 1945, and other nations had to "catch up on their own hook."

In the spring of 1946, Truman undercut the Dean Acheson-David Lilienthal plan for international control and development of atomic resources by appointing as chief negotiator Bernard Baruch, whose emphasis on close inspections, sanctions, no veto, and indefinite American atomic monopoly virtually assured Russian refusal. Despite Acheson's protests, Truman analogized that "if Harry Stimson had been back up in Manchuria [in 1931] there would have been no war." And as deadlock neared in July 1946, the president told Baruch to "stand pat."

Ultimately the UN commission weighing the Baruch Plan approved it on 31 December 1946. But the prospect of a Soviet veto in the Security Council precluded its adoption. Admittedly, Stalin's belief that he could not deal with the United States on an equal basis until he had the bomb and Soviet insistence on retention of their veto power and national control of resources and facilities may have precluded atomic accord in 1946. Still, Baruch insisted that the United States could get its way because it had an atomic monopoly, and American military officials sought to preserve a nuclear monopoly as long as possible and to develop a strategy based on air power and atomic weapons. . . .

Meanwhile, Byrnes's diplomacy in Moscow in December 1945 had produced Yalta-style accords on a European peace treaty process, Russian predominance in Bulgaria and Romania and American primacy in China and Japan, and compromise over Korea, with Soviet disputes with Iran and Turkey set aside. But conservative critics cried "appeasement," and in his famous but disputed letter of 5 January 1946, an anxious president charged that Byrnes had kept him "completely in the dark"; denounced Russian "outrage[s]" in the Baltic, Germany, Poland, and Iran and intent to invade Turkey; and said that the Russians understood only an "iron fist" and "divisions" and that he was tired of "babying" them. In fact, Truman knew of most of Byrnes's positions; they had hardly "babied" Russia since Potsdam; and no Russian attack was imminent. The letter reflected Truman's new "get tough" policy, or personal cold war declaration, which, it must be emphasized, came six weeks before George Kennan's Long Telegram and Churchill's Iron Curtain speech.

Strong American protests in 1946 caused the Russians to withdraw their troops from Iran and their claims to joint defense of the Turkish Straits. In the latter case, Truman said he was ready to follow his policy of military response "to the end" to determine if Russia intended "world conquest." Once again he had taken an exaggerated, nationalist stance. No one expected a Russian military advance; America's action rested on its plans to integrate Turkey into its strategic planning and to use it as a base of operations against Russia in event of war. And in September Truman approved announcement of a Mediterranean command that led to the United States becoming the dominant naval power there by year's end.

Meanwhile, Truman ignored Secretary of Commerce Henry Wallace's lengthy memoranda during March–September 1946 that sought to promote economic ties with Russia and questioned America's atomic policies and global military expansiveness. The president then fired Wallace after he publicly challenged Byrnes's speech on 6 September in Stuttgart propounding West German reconstruction and continued American military presence there. The firing was reasonable, but not the rage at Wallace as "a real Commy" and at "parlor pinks and soprano-voiced men" as a "national danger" and "sabotage front" for Stalin.

Equally without reason was Truman's face value acceptance of White House special counsel Clark Clifford's "Russian Report" of September 1946 and accompanying "Last Will of Peter the Great." Clifford's report rested on a hasty compilation of apocalyptic projections of Soviet aim to conquer the world by military force and subversion, and he argued that the United States had to prepare for total war. He wrote in the "black and white" terms that he knew Truman would like and aimed to justify a vast global military upgrade and silence political critics on the left and right. Tsar Peter's will was an old forgery purporting to show that he had a similar design to conquer Eurasia. Truman may have found the report so "hot" that he confined it to his White House safe, but he believed the report and the will and soon was persisting that the governments of the czars, Stalin, and Hitler were all the same. Later he told a mild critic of American policy to read Tsar Peter's will to learn where Russian leaders got their "fixed ideas."

It was a short step, Clifford recalled, from the Russian Report to Truman's epochal request in March 1947 for military aid to Greece and Turkey to help "free peoples" fight totalitarianism. Truman vastly overstated the global-ideological aspects of Soviet-American conflict. Perhaps he sought to fire "the opening gun" to rouse the public and a fiscally conservative Republican Congress to national security expenditures. But he also said that this was "only the beginning" of the "U.S. going into European politics," that the Russians had broken every agreement since Potsdam and would now get only "one language" from him. He added in the fall of 1947 that "if Russia gets Greece and Turkey," it would get Italy and France, the iron curtain would extend to western Ireland, and the United States would have to "come home and prepare for war."

Truman's fears were excessive. Stalin never challenged the Truman Doctrine or Western primacy in Turkey, now under U.S. military tutelage, and Greece. He provided almost no aid to the Greek rebels and told Yugoslavia's leaders in early 1948 to halt their aid because the United States would never allow the Greek Communists to win and break Anglo-American control in the Mediterranean. When Marshal Josip Broz Tito balked, Stalin withdrew his advisers from Yugoslavia and expelled that nation from the Cominform. Tito finally closed his borders to the Greek rebels in July 1949.

Perhaps U.S. officials feared that Britain's retreat from Greece might allow Russia to penetrate the Mediterranean, or that if Greek Communists overthrew the reactionary Greek regime (Turkey was not threatened) they might align Athens with Moscow. Still, the Truman administration's costly policy never addressed the causes of Greece's civil war; instead, it substituted military "annihilation of the enemy for the reform of the social and economic conditions" that had brought civil war. Equally important, Truman's rhetorical division of the world into "free" versus "totalitarian" states . . . created . . . an unfortunate model for later interventions, such as in Korea— "the Greece of the Far East," as Truman would say—and in French Indochina.

The Truman Doctrine led to the Marshall Plan in June 1947, but they were not "two halves of the same walnut," as Truman claimed. State Department officials who drew up the European Recovery Plan (ERP) differentiated it from what they viewed as his doctrine's implications for "economic and ultimately military warfare." The Soviets likened the Truman Doctrine to retail purchase of separate nations and the Marshall Plan to wholesale purchase of Europe.

The Soviet view was narrow, although initially they had interest in participating and perhaps even harbored dreams that the United States would proffer a generous Lend Lease-style arrangement. But as the British quickly saw, Soviet participation was precluded by American-imposed financial and economic controls and, as Michael J. Hogan has written, by the integrated, continental approach to aid rather than a nation-by-nation basis that would have benefited war-devastated Russia. Indeed, in direct talks in Paris, U.S. officials refused concessions, focused on resources to come from Russia and East Europe, and insisted on German contributions to the ERP ahead of reparations payments or a peace treaty—and then expressed widespread relief when the Soviets rejected the ERP for themselves and East Europe.

The Marshall Plan proved to be a very successful geostrategic venture. It helped to spur American-European trade and Western European recovery, bring France into camp with Germany and satisfy French economic and security claims, and revive western Germany industrially without unleashing the 1930s-style "German colossus" that Truman's aides feared. The Marshall Plan was also intended to contain the Soviets economically, forestall German-Soviet bilateral deals, and provide America with access to its allies' domestic and colonial resources. Finally, as the British said, the Truman administration sought an integrated Europe resembling the United States, "God's own country."

The Marshall Plan's excellent return on investment, however, may have cost far more than the $13 billion expended. "The world is definitely split in two," Undersecretary of State Robert Lovett said in August 1947, while Kennan forewarned that for defensive reasons the Soviets would "clamp down completely on Czechoslovakia" to strengthen their hold on Eastern Europe. Indeed, the most recent evidence indicates that Stalin viewed the Marshall Plan as a "watershed" event, signaling an American effort to predominate over all of Europe. This spurred the Soviets into a comprehensive strategy shift. They now rigged the elections in Hungary, proffered [Politburo spokesman] Andrei Zhdanov's "two camps" approach to world policy, created the

Cominform, and blessed the Communist coup in Czechoslovakia in February 1948. Truman, in turn, concluded that the Western world confronted the same situation it had a decade earlier with Nazi Germany, and his bristling St. Patrick's Day speeches in March 1948 placed sole onus for the Cold War on the Soviet Union. Subsequently, Anglo-American talks at the Pentagon would culminate in NATO in April 1949.

·Meanwhile, The U.S. decision to make western Germany the cornerstone of the ERP virtually precluded negotiations to reunify the country. In fact, when Secretary of State Marshall proposed during a CFM meeting in the spring of 1947 to offer current production reparations to the Russians to induce agreement to unify Germany, the president sternly refused. Marshall complained of lack of "elbow room" to negotiate. But Truman would not yield, and by the time of the next CFM in late 1947 the secretary showed no interest in Russian reparations or Ruhr access. Despite America's public position, Ambassador to Moscow Walter Bedell Smith wrote, "we really do not want nor intend to accept German unification on any terms that the Russians might agree to, even though they seemed to meet most of our requirements."

The Americans were by then onto their London Conference program to create a West German state and, as Stalin said in February 1948, "The West will make Western Germany their own, and we shall turn Eastern Germany into our own state." In June the Soviet dictator initiated the Berlin blockade to try to forestall the West's program, but Truman determined to "stay period." He believed that to withdraw from Berlin would seriously undermine U.S. influence in Europe and the ERP and destroy his presidential standing, and he remained determined to avert military confrontation.

But Truman saw no connection between the London program and the blockade, as Carolyn Eisenberg has written. Further, his belief that "there is nothing to negotiate" and accord with General Lucius Clay's view that to withdraw from Berlin meant "we have lost everything we are fighting for" exaggerated the intent of Stalin's maneuver and diminished even slim chances for compromise on Germany, including Kennan's "Plan A" for a unified, neutralized state with American and Soviet forces withdrawn to its periphery. As Marshall said in August 1948, there would be "no abandonment of our position" on West Germany.

Eventually, Truman and the airlift prevailed over Stalin, who gave in to a face-saving CFM in May 1949 that ended the blockade, with nothing else agreed. The new secretary of state, Acheson, said that the United States intended to create a West German government "come hell or high water" and that Germany could be unified only by consolidating the East into the West on the basis of its incipient Bonn Constitution. Likewise Truman said in June 1949 that he would not sacrifice West Germany's basic freedoms to gain "nominal political unity." . . .

No one leader or nation caused the Cold War. The Second World War generated inevitable Soviet-American conflict as two nations with entirely different political-economic systems confronted each other on two war-torn continents. The Truman administration would seek to fashion a world order friendly to American political and economic interests, to achieve maximum national security by preventing any nation from severing U.S. ties to its traditional allies and vital areas of trade and resources, and to avoid 1930s-style "appeasement." Truman creditably favored creation of the UN, fostered foreign aid and reconstruction, and wished to avert war. . . .

Nonetheless, from the Potsdam Conference through the Korean War, the president contributed significantly to the growing Cold War and militarization of American foreign policy. He assumed that America's economic-military-moral superiority assured that he could order the world on its terms, and he ascribed only dark motives to nations or leaders who resisted America's will. . . .

It is clear that Truman's insecurity with regard to diplomacy and world politics led him to seek to give the appearance of acting decisively and reinforced his penchant to view conflict in black and white terms and to divide nations into free or totalitarian societies. He shied from weighing the complexities of historic national conflicts and local or regional politics. Instead, he attributed nearly every diplomatic crisis or civil war—in Germany, Iran, Turkey, Greece, and Czechoslovakia— to Soviet machination and insisted that the Russians had broken every agreement and were bent on "world conquest." To determine his response he was quick to reach for an analogy, usually the failure of the Western powers to resist Germany and Japan in the 1930s, and to conclude that henceforth he would speak to the Russians in the only language that he thought they understood: "divisions." This style of leadership and diplomacy closed off both advocates and prospects for more patiently negotiated and more nuanced or creative courses of action. . . .

In conclusion, it seems clear that despite Truman's pride in his knowledge of the past, he lacked insight into the history unfolding around him. He often could not see beyond his immediate decision or visualize alternatives, and he seemed oblivious to the implications of his words or actions. More often than not he narrowed rather than broadened the options that he presented to the American citizenry, the environment of American politics, and the channels through which Cold War politics flowed. Throughout his presidency, Truman remained a parochial nationalist who lacked the leadership to move America away from conflict and toward détente. Instead, he promoted an ideology and politics of Cold War confrontation that became the modus operandi of successor administrations and the United States for the next two generations.

Two Cold War Empires

JOHN LEWIS GADDIS

Leaders of both the United States and the Soviet Union would have bristled at having the appellation "imperial" affixed to what they were doing after 1945. But one need not send out ships, seize territories, and hoist flags to construct an empire: "informal" empires are considerably older than, and continued to exist alongside, the more "formal" ones Europeans imposed on so much of the rest of the world from the fifteenth through the nineteenth centuries. During the Cold War years Washington and Moscow took on much of the character, if never quite the charm, of old imperial capitals like London, Paris, and Vienna. And surely American and Soviet influence, throughout most of the second half of the twentieth century, was at least as ubiquitous as that of any earlier empire the world had ever seen.

From John Lewis Gaddis, *We Now Know: Rethinking Cold War History* (New York: Oxford University Press, 1997), pp. 27–46. © 1997 by John Lewis Gaddis. Reprinted by permission of Oxford University Press.

Ubiquity never ensured unchallenged authority, though, and that fact provides yet another reason for applying an imperial analogy to Cold War history. For contrary to popular impressions, empires have always involved a two-way flow of influence. Imperializers have never simply acted upon the imperialized; the imperialized have also had a surprising amount of influence over the imperializers. The Cold War was no exception to this pattern, and an awareness of it too will help us to see how that rivalry emerged, evolved, and eventually ended in the way that it did.

Let us begin with the structure of the Soviet empire, for the simple reason that it was, much more than the American, deliberately designed. It has long been clear that, in addition to having had an authoritarian vision, Stalin also had an imperial one, which he proceeded to implement in at least as single-minded a way. No comparably influential builder of empire came close to wielding power for so long, or with such striking results, on the Western side.

It was, of course, a matter of some awkwardness that Stalin came out of a revolutionary movement that had vowed to smash, not just tsarist imperialism, but all forms of imperialism throughout the world. The Soviet leader constructed his own logic, though, and throughout his career he devoted a surprising amount of attention to showing how a revolution and an empire might coexist. Bolsheviks could never be imperialists, Stalin acknowledged in one of his earliest public pronouncements on this subject, made in April 1917. But surely in a *revolutionary* Russia nine-tenths of the non-Russian nationalities would not *want* their independence. Few among those minorities found Stalin's reasoning persuasive after the Bolsheviks did seize power later that year, however, and one of the first problems Lenin's new government faced was a disintegration of the old Russian empire not unlike what happened to the Soviet Union after communist authority finally collapsed in 1991.

Whether because of Lenin's own opposition to imperialism or, just as plausibly, because of Soviet Russia's weakness at the time, Finns, Estonians, Latvians, Lithuanians, Poles, and Moldavians were allowed to depart. Others who tried to do so—Ukrainians, Belorussians, Caucasians, Central Asians—were not so fortunate, and in 1922 Stalin proposed incorporating these remaining (and reacquired) nationalities into the Russian republic, only to have Lenin as one of his last acts override this recommendation and establish the multi-ethnic Union of Soviet Socialist Republics. After Lenin died and Stalin took his place it quickly became clear, though, that whatever its founding principles the USSR was to be no federation of equals. Rather, it would function as an updated form of empire even more tightly centralized than that of the Russian tsars.

Lenin and Stalin differed most significantly, not over authoritarianism or even terror, but on the legitimacy of Great Russian nationalism. The founder of Bolshevism had warned with characteristic pungency of "that truly Russian man, the Great-Russian chauvinist," and of the dangers of sinking into a "sea of chauvinistic Great-Russian filth, like flies in milk." Such temptations, he insisted, might ruin the prospects of revolution spreading elsewhere in the world. But Stalin—the implied target of Lenin's invective—was himself a Great Russian nationalist, with all the intensity transplanted nationals can sometimes attain. "The leaders of the revolutionary workers of all countries are avidly studying the most instructive history of the working class of Russia, its past, the past of Russia," he would write in a revealing private letter in 1930, shortly after consolidating his position as Lenin's successor. "All this instills (cannot but instill!) in the hearts of the Russian workers a feeling of revolutionary national pride, capable of moving mountains and working miracles."

The "Stalin constitution" of 1936, which formally specified the right of non-Russian nationalities to secede from the Soviet Union, coincided with the great purges and an officially sanctioned upsurge in Russian nationalism that would persist as a prominent feature of Stalin's regime until his death. It was as if the great authoritarian had set out to validate his own flawed prediction of 1917 by creating a set of circumstances in which non-Russian nationalities would not even *think* of seceding, even though the hypothetical authority to do so remained. The pattern resembled that of the purge trials themselves: one maintained a framework of legality—even, within the non-Russian republics, a toleration of local languages and cultures considerably greater than under the tsars. But Stalin then went to extraordinary lengths to deter anyone from exercising these rights or promoting those cultures in such a way as to challenge his own rule. He appears to have concluded, from his own study of the Russian past, that it was not "reactionary" to seek territorial expansion. His principal ideological innovation may well have been to impose the ambitions of the old princes of Muscovy, especially their determination to "gather in" and dominate all of the lands that surrounded them, upon the anti-imperial spirit of proletarian internationalism that had emanated from, if not actually inspired, the Bolshevik Revolution.

Stalin's fusion of Marxist internationalism with tsarist imperialism could only reinforce his tendency, in place well before World War II, to equate the advance of world revolution with the expanding influence of the Soviet state. He applied that linkage quite impartially: a major benefit of the 1939 pact with Hitler had been that it regained territories lost as a result of the Bolshevik Revolution and the World War I settlement. But Stalin's conflation of imperialism with ideology also explains the importance he attached, following the German attack in 1941, to having his new Anglo-American allies confirm these arrangements. He had similar goals in East Asia when he insisted on bringing the Soviet Union back to the position Russia had occupied in Manchuria prior to the Russo-Japanese War: this he finally achieved at the 1945 Yalta Conference in return for promising to enter the war against Japan. "My task as minister of foreign affairs was to expand the borders of our Fatherland," Molotov recalled proudly many years later. "And it seems that Stalin and I coped with this task quite well."

From the West's standpoint, the critical question was how far Moscow's influence would extend *beyond* whatever Soviet frontiers turned out to be at the end of the war. Stalin had suggested to Milovan Djilas that the Soviet Union would impose its own social system as far as its armies could reach, but he was also very cautious. Keenly aware of the military power the United States and its allies had accumulated, Stalin was determined to do nothing that might involve the USSR in another devastating war until it had recovered sufficiently to be certain of winning it. "I do not wish to begin the Third World War over the Trieste question," he explained to disappointed Yugoslavs, whom he ordered to evacuate that territory in June 1945. Five years later, he would justify his decision not to intervene in the Korean War on the grounds that "the Second World War ended not long ago, and we are not ready for the Third World War." Just how far the expansion of Soviet influence would proceed depended, therefore, upon a careful balancing of opportunities against risks. "[W]e were on the offensive," Molotov acknowledged:

> They [presumably the West] certainly hardened their line against us, but we had to consolidate our conquests. We made our own socialist Germany out of our part of Germany, and restored order in Czechoslovakia, Poland, Hungary, and Yugoslavia, where the situations were fluid. To squeeze out capitalist order. This was the cold war.

But, "of course," Molotov added, "you had to know when to stop. I believe in this respect Stalin kept well within the limits."

Who or what was it, though, that set the limits? Did Stalin have a fixed list of countries he thought it necessary to dominate? Was he prepared to stop in the face of resistance within those countries to "squeezing out the capitalist order"? Or would expansion cease only when confronted with opposition from the remaining capitalist states, so that further advances risked war at a time when the Soviet Union was ill-prepared for it?

Stalin had been very precise about where he wanted Soviet boundaries changed; he was much less so on how far Moscow's sphere of influence was to extend. He insisted on having "friendly" countries around the periphery of the USSR, but he failed to specify how many would have to meet this standard. He called during the war for dismembering Germany, but by the end of it was denying that he had ever done so: that country would be temporarily divided, he told leading German communists in June 1945, and they themselves would eventually bring about its reunification. He never gave up on the idea of an eventual world revolution, but he expected this to result—as his comments to the Germans suggested—from an expansion of influence emanating from the Soviet Union itself. "[F]or the Kremlin," a well-placed spymaster recalled, "the mission of communism was primarily to consolidate the might of the Soviet state. Only military strength and domination of the countries on our borders could ensure us a superpower role."

But Stalin provided no indication—surely because he himself did not know—of how rapidly, or under what circumstances, this process would take place. He was certainly prepared to stop in the face of resistance from the West: at no point was he willing to challenge the Americans or even the British where they made their interests clear. Churchill acknowledged his scrupulous adherence to the famous 1944 "percentages" agreement confirming British authority in Greece, and Yugoslav sources have revealed Stalin's warnings that the United States and Great Britain would never allow their lines of communication in the Mediterranean to be broken. He quickly backed down when confronted with Anglo-American objections to his ambitions in Iran in the spring of 1946, as he did later that year after demanding Soviet bases in the Turkish Straits. This pattern of advance followed by retreat had shown up in the purges of the 1930s, which Stalin halted when the external threat from Germany became too great to ignore, and it would reappear with the Berlin Blockade and the Korean War, both situations in which the Soviet Union would show great caution after provoking an unexpectedly strong American response.

What all of this suggests, though, is not that Stalin had limited ambitions, only that he had no timetable for achieving them. Molotov retrospectively confirmed this: "Our ideology stands for offensive operations when possible, and if not, we wait." Given this combination of appetite with aversion to risk, one cannot help but wonder what would have happened had the West tried containment earlier. To the extent that it bears partial responsibility for the coming of the Cold War, the historian Vojtech Mastny has argued, that responsibility lies in its failure to do just that.

Where Western resistance was unlikely, as in Eastern Europe, Stalin would in time attempt to replicate the regime he had already established inside the Soviet Union. Authority extended out from Moscow by way of government and party structures whose officials had been selected for their obedience, then down within each of these countries through the management of the economy, social and political institutions, intellectuals, even family-relationships. The differentiation of public and private spheres that exists in most societies disappeared as all aspects of life were fused with, and then subordinated to, the interests of the Soviet Union as Stalin himself had determined them. Those who could not or would not go along encountered the same sequence of intimidation, terror, and ultimately even purges, show trials, and executions that his real and imagined domestic opponents had gone through during the 1930s. "Stalin's understanding of friendship with other countries was that the Soviet Union would lead and they would follow," Khrushchev recalled. "[He] waged the struggle against the enemies of the people there in the same way that he did in the Soviet Union. He had one demand: absolute subordination."

Stalin's policy, then, was one of imperial expansion and consolidation differing from that of earlier empires only in the determination with which he pursued it, in the instruments of coercion with which he maintained it, and in the ostensibly anti-imperial justifications he put forward in support of it. It is a testimony to his skill, if not to his morality, that he was able to achieve so many of his imperial ambitions at a time when the tides of history were running against the idea of imperial domination—as colonial offices in London, Paris, Lisbon, and The Hague were finding out—and when his own country was recovering from one of the most brutal invasions in recorded history. The fact that Stalin was able to *expand* his empire when others were contracting and while the Soviet Union was as weak as it was requires explanation. Why did opposition to this process, within and outside Europe, take so long to develop?

One reason was that the colossal sacrifices the Soviet Union had made during the war against the Axis had, in effect, "purified" its reputation: the USSR and its leader had "earned" the right to throw their weight around, or so it seemed. Western governments found it difficult to switch quickly from viewing the Soviet Union as a glorious wartime ally to portraying it as a new and dangerous adversary. President Harry S Truman and his future Secretary of State Dean Acheson—neither of them sympathetic in the slightest to communism—nonetheless tended to give the Soviet Union the benefit of the doubt well into the early postwar era. A similar pattern developed within the United States occupation zone in Germany, where General Lucius D. Clay worked out a cooperative relationship with his Soviet counterparts and resisted demands to "get tough" with the Russians, even after they had become commonplace in Washington.

Resistance to Stalin's imperialism also developed slowly because Marxism-Leninism at the time had such widespread appeal. It is difficult now to recapture the admiration revolutionaries outside the Soviet Union felt for that country before they came to know it well. "[Communism] was the most rational and most intoxicating, all-embracing ideology for me and for those in my disunited and desperate land who so desired to skip over centuries of slavery and backwardness and to bypass reality itself," Djilas recalled, in a comment that could have been echoed throughout much of what came to be called the "third world." Because the Bolsheviks themselves had overcome one empire and had made a career of condemning others, it would take decades for people who were struggling to overthrow British, French, Dutch, or Portuguese colonialism to see that there could also be such a thing as Soviet imperialism. European communists—notably the Yugoslavs—saw this much earlier, but even to most of them it had not been apparent at the end of the war.

Still another explanation for the initial lack of resistance to Soviet expansionism was the fact that its repressive character did not become immediately apparent to all who were subjected to it. With regimes on the left taking power in Eastern and Central Europe, groups long denied advancement could now expect it. For many who remembered the 1930s, autarchy within a Soviet bloc could seem preferable to exposure once again to international capitalism, with its periodic cycles of boom and bust. Nor did Moscow impose harsh controls everywhere at the same time. Simple administrative incompetence may partially account for this: one Russian historian has pointed out that "[d]isorganization, mismanagement and rivalry among many branches of the gigantic Stalinist state in Eastern Europe were enormous." But it is also possible, at least in some areas, that Stalin did not expect to *need* tight controls; that he anticipated no serious challenge and perhaps even spontaneous support. Why did he promise free elections after the war? Maybe he thought the communists would win them.

One has the impression that Stalin and the Eastern Europeans got to know one another only gradually. The Kremlin leader was slow to recognize that Soviet authority would not be welcomed everywhere beyond Soviet borders; but as he did come to see this he became all the more determined to impose it everywhere. The Eastern Europeans were slow to recognize how confining incorporation within a Soviet sphere was going to be; but as they did come to see this they became all the more determined to resist it, even if only by withholding, in a passive but sullen manner, the consent any regime needs to establish itself by means other than coercion. Stalin's efforts to consolidate his empire therefore made it at once more repressive and less secure. Meanwhile, an alternative vision of postwar Europe was emerging from the other great empire that established itself in the wake of World War II, that of the United States, and this too gave Stalin grounds for concern.

The first point worth noting, when comparing the American empire to its Soviet counterpart, is a striking reversal in the sequence of events. Stalin's determination to create his empire preceded by some years the conditions that made it possible: he had first to consolidate power at home and then defeat Nazi Germany, while at the same time seeing to it that his allies in that enterprise did not thwart his long-term objectives. With the United States, it was the other way around: the conditions for establishing an empire were in place long before there was any clear intention on the part of its leaders to do so. Even then, they required the support of a skeptical electorate, something that could never quite be taken for granted.

The United States had been poised for global hegemony at the end of World War I. Its military forces played a decisive role in bringing that conflict to an end. Its economic predominance was such that it could control both the manner and the rate of European recovery. Its ideology commanded enormous respect, as Woodrow Wilson found when he arrived on the Continent late in 1918 to a series of rapturous public receptions. The Versailles Treaty fell well short of Wilson's principles, to be sure, but the League of Nations followed closely his own design, providing an explicit legal basis for an international order that was to have drawn, as much as anything else, upon the example of the American constitution itself. If there was ever a point at which the world seemed receptive to an expansion of United States influence, this was it.

Americans themselves, however, were not receptive. The Senate's rejection of membership in the League reflected the public's distinct lack of enthusiasm for international peace-keeping responsibilities. Despite the interests certain business, labor, and agricultural groups had in seeking overseas markets and investment opportunities, most Americans saw few benefits to be derived from integrating their economy with that of the rest of the world. Efforts to rehabilitate Europe during the 1920s, therefore, could only take the form of private initiatives, quietly coordinated with the government. Protective tariffs hung on well into the 1930s—having actually increased with the onset of the Great Depression—and exports as a percentage of gross national product remained low in comparison to other nations, averaging only 4.2 per cent between 1921 and 1940. Investments abroad had doubled between 1914 and 1919 while foreign investment in the United States had been cut in half; but this shift was hardly sufficient to overcome old instincts within the majority of the public who held no investments at all that it was better to stand apart from, rather than to attempt to dominate, international politics outside of the Western hemisphere.

This isolationist consensus broke down only as Americans began to realize that a potentially hostile power was once again threatening Europe: even their own hemisphere, it appeared, might not escape the consequences this time around. After September 1939, the Roosevelt administration moved as quickly as public and Congressional opinion would allow to aid Great Britain and France by means short of war; it also chose to challenge the Japanese over their occupation of China and later French Indochina, thereby setting in motion a sequence of events that would lead to the attack on Pearl Harbor. Historians ever since have puzzled over this: why, after two decades of relative inactivity on the world scene, did the United States suddenly become hyperactive? Might the administration have realized that it would never generate public support for the empire American elites had long desired without a clear and present danger to national security, and did it not then proceed to generate one? Can one not understand the origins and evolution of the Cold War in similar terms?

There are several problems with such interpretations, one of which is that they confuse contingency with conspiracy. Even if Roosevelt had hoped to maneuver the Japanese into "firing the first shot," he could not have known that Hitler would seize this opportunity to declare war and thereby make possible American military intervention in Europe. The Pacific, where the United States would have deployed most of its strength in the absence of Hitler's declaration, would hardly have been the platform from which to mount a bid for global hegemony. These explanations also allow little room for the autonomy of others: they assume that Hitler and the Japanese militarists acted *only* in response to what the United States did, and that other possible motives for their behavior—personal, bureaucratic, cultural, ideological, geopolitical—were insignificant. Finally, these arguments fail to meet the test of proximate versus distant causation. The historian Marc Bloch once pointed out that one could, in principle, account for a climber's fall from a precipice by invoking physics and geology: had it not been for the law of gravity and the existence of the mountain, the accidents surely could not have occurred. But would it follow that all who ascend mountains must plummet from them? Just because Roosevelt *wanted* the United States to enter the war and to become a world power afterwards does not mean that his actions made these things happen.

A better explanation for the collapse of isolationism is a simpler one: it had to do with a resurgence of authoritarianism. Americans had begun to suspect, late in the nineteenth century, that the internal behavior of states determined their external behavior; certainly it is easy to see how the actions of Germany, Italy, and Japan during the 1930s could have caused this view to surface once again, much as it had in relations with tsarist Russia and imperial Germany during World War I. Once that happened, the Americans, not given to making subtle distinctions, began to oppose authoritarianism everywhere, and that could account for their sudden willingness to take on several authoritarians at once in 1941. But that interpretation, too, is not entirely adequate. It fails to explain how the United States could have coexisted as comfortably as it did with authoritarianism in the past—especially in Latin America—and as it would continue to do for some time to come. It certainly does not account for the American willingness during the war to embrace, as an ally, the greatest authoritarian of this century, Stalin himself.

The best explanation for the decline of isolationism and the rise of the American empire, I suspect, has to do with a distinction Americans tended to make— perhaps they were more subtle than one might think—between what we might call benign and malignant authoritarianism. Regimes like those of Somoza in Nicaragua or Trujillo in the Dominican Republic might be unsavory, but they fell into the benign category because they posed no serious threat to United States interests and in some cases even promoted them. Regimes like those of Nazi Germany and imperial Japan, because of their military capabilities, were quite another matter. Stalin's authoritarianism had appeared malignant when linked to that of Hitler, as it was between 1939 and 1941; but when directed against Hitler, it could come to appear quite benign. What it would look like once Germany had been defeated remained to be seen.

With all this, the possibility that even malignant authoritarianism might harm the United States remained hypothetical until 7 December 1941, when it suddenly became very real. Americans are only now, after more than half a century, getting over the shock: they became so accustomed to a Pearl Harbor mentality—to the idea that there really are deadly enemies out there—that they find it a strange new world, instead of an old familiar one, now that there are not. Pearl Harbor was, then, the defining event for the American empire, because it was only at this point that the most plausible potential justification for the United States becoming and remaining a global power as far as the American people were concerned—an endangered national security—became an actual one. Isolationism had thrived right up to this moment; but once it became apparent that isolationism could leave the nation open to military attack, it suffered a blow from which it never recovered. The critical date was not 1945, or 1947, but 1941.

It did not automatically follow, though, that the Soviet Union would inherit the title of "first enemy" once Germany and Japan had been defeated. A sense of vulnerability preceded the identification of a source of threat in the thinking of American strategists: innovations in military technology—long-range bombers, the prospect of even longer-range missiles—created visions of future Pearl Harbors before it had become clear from where such an attack might come. Neither in the military nor the political-economic planning that went on in Washington during the war was there consistent concern with the USSR as a potential future adversary. The threat, rather, appeared to arise from war itself, whoever might cause it, and the most likely candidates were thought to be resurgent enemies from World War II.

The preferred solution was to maintain preponderant power for the United States, which meant a substantial peacetime military establishment and a string of bases around the world from which to resist aggression if it should ever occur. But equally important, a revived international community would seek to remove the fundamental causes of war through the United Nations, a less ambitious version of Wilson's League, and through new economic institutions like the International Monetary Fund and the World Bank, whose task it would be to prevent another global depression and thereby ensure prosperity. The Americans and the British assumed that the Soviet Union would want to participate in these multilateral efforts to achieve military and economic security. The Cold War developed when it became clear that Stalin either could not or would not accept this framework.

Did the Americans attempt to impose their vision of the postwar world upon the USSR? No doubt it looked that way from Moscow: both the Roosevelt and Truman administrations stressed political self-determination and economic integration with sufficient persistence to arouse Stalin's suspicions—easily aroused, in any event—as to their ultimate intentions. But what the Soviet leader saw as a challenge to his hegemony the Americans meant as an effort to salvage multilateralism. At no point prior to 1947 did the United States and its Western European allies abandon the hope that the Russians might eventually come around; and indeed negotiations aimed at bringing them around would continue at the foreign ministers' level, without much hope of success, through the end of that year. The American attitude was less that of expecting to impose a system than one of puzzlement as to why its merits were not universally self-evident. It differed significantly, therefore, from Stalin's point of view, which allowed for the possibility that socialists in other countries might come to see the advantages of Marxism-Leninism as practiced in the Soviet Union, but never capitalists. They were there, in the end, to be overthrown, not convinced.

The emergence of an opposing great power bloc posed serious difficulties for the principle of multilateralism, based as it had been on the expectation of cooperation with Moscow. But with a good deal of ingenuity the Americans managed to *merge* their original vision of a single international order built around common security with a second and more hastily improvised concept that sought to counter the expanding power and influence of the Soviet Union. That concept was, of course, containment, and its chief instrument was the Marshall Plan.

The idea of containment proceeded from the proposition that if there was not to be one world, then there must not be another world war either. It would be necessary to keep the peace while preserving the balance of power: the gap that had developed during the 1930s between the perceived requirements of peace and power was not to happen again. If geopolitical stability could be restored in Europe, time would work against the Soviet Union and in favor of the Western democracies. Authoritarianism need not be the "wave of the future"; sooner or later even Kremlin authoritarians would realize this fact and change their policies. "[T]he Soviet leaders are prepared to recognize *situations,* if not arguments," George F. Kennan wrote in 1948. "If, therefore, situations can be created in which it is clearly not to the advantage of their power to emphasize the elements of conflict in their relations with the outside world, then their actions, and even the tenor of their propaganda to their own people, *can* be modified."

This idea of time being on the side of the West came—at least as far as Kennan was concerned—from studying the history of empires. Edward Gibbon had written in *The Decline and Fall of the Roman Empire* that "there is nothing more contrary to nature than the attempt to hold in obedience distant provinces," and few things Kennan ever read made a greater or more lasting impression on him. He had concluded during the early days of World War II that Hitler's empire could not last, and in the months after the war, he applied similar logic to the empire Stalin was setting out to construct in Easter Europe. The territorial acquisitions and spheres of influence the Soviet Union had obtained would ultimately become a source of *insecurity* for it, both because of the resistance to Moscow's control that was sure to grow within those regions and because of the outrage the nature of that control was certain to provoke in the rest of the world. "Soviet power, like the capitalist world of its own conception, bears within it the seeds of its own decay," Kennan insisted in the most famous of all Cold War texts, his anonymously published 1947 article on the "The Sources of Soviet Conduct." He added, "the sprouting of those seeds is well advanced."

All of this would do the Europeans little good, though, if the new and immediate Soviet presence in their midst should so intimidate them that their own morale collapsed. The danger here came not from the prospect that the Red Army would invade and occupy the rest of the continent, as Hitler had tried to do; rather, its demoralized and exhausted inhabitants might simply vote in communist parties who would then do Moscow's bidding. The initial steps in the strategy of containment—stopgap military and economic aid to Greece and Turkey, the more carefully designed and ambitious Marshall Plan—took place within this context: the idea was to produce instant intangible reassurance as well as eventual tangible reinforcement. Two things had to happen in order for intimidation to occur, Kennan liked to argue: the intimidator had to make the effort, but, equally important, the target of those efforts had to agree to be intimidated. The initiatives of 1947 sought to generate sufficient self-confidence to prevent such acquiescence in intimidation from taking place.

Some historians have asserted that these fears of collapse were exaggerated: that economic recovery on the continent was already underway, and that the Europeans themselves were never as psychologically demoralized as the Americans made them out to be. Others have added that the real crisis at the time was within an American economy that could hardly expect to function hegemonically if Europeans lacked the dollars to purchase its products. Still others have suggested that the Marshall Plan was the means by which American officials sought to project overseas the mutually-beneficial relationship between business, labor, and government they had worked out at home: the point was not to make Wilsonian values a model for the rest of the world, but rather the politics of productivity that had grown out of American corporate capitalism. All of these arguments have merit: at a minimum they have forced historians to place the Marshall Plan in a wider economic, social, and historical context; more broadly they suggest that the American empire had its own distinctive internal roots, and was not solely and simply a response to the Soviet external challenge.

At the same time, though, it is difficult to see how a strategy of containment could have developed—with the Marshall Plan as its centerpiece—had there been nothing to contain. One need only recall the early 1920s, when similar conditions of European demoralization, Anglo-French exhaustion, and American economic predominance had existed; yet no American empire arose as after World War II. The critical difference, of course, was national security: Pearl Harbor created an atmosphere of vulnerability Americans had not known since the earliest days of the republic, and the Soviet Union by 1947 had become the most plausible source of threat. The American empire arose *primarily,* therefore, not from internal causes, as had the Soviet empire, but from a perceived external danger powerful enough to overcome American isolationism.

Washington's wartime vision of a postwar international order had been premised on the concepts of political self-determination and economic integration. It was intended to work by assuming a set of *common* interests that would cause other countries to *want* to be affiliated with it rather than to resist it. The Marshall Plan, to a considerable extent, met those criteria: although it operated on a regional rather than a global scale, it did seek to promote democracy through an economic recovery that would proceed along international and not nationalist lines. Its purpose was to create an American sphere of influence, to be sure, but one that would allow those within it considerable freedom. The principles of democracy and open markets required nothing less, but there were two additional and more practical reasons for encouraging such autonomy. First, the United States itself lacked the capability to administer a large empire: the difficulties of running occupied Germany and Japan were proving daunting enough. Second, the idea of autonomy was implicit in the task of restoring Europeans self-confidence; for who, if not Europeans themselves, was to say when the self-confidence of Europeans had been restored?

Finally, it is worth noting that even though Kennan and the other early architects of containment made use of imperial analogies, they did not see themselves as creating an empire, but rather a restored balance of power. Painfully—perhaps excessively—aware of limited American resources, fearful that the domestic political consensus in favor of internationalism might not hold, they set out to reconstitute *independent* centers of power in Europe and Asia. These would be integrated into the world capitalist system, and as a result they would certainly fall under the influence of its new hegemonic manager, the United States. But there was no intention here of creating satellites in anything like the sense that Stalin understood that term; rather, the idea was that "third forces" would resist Soviet expansionism while preserving as much as possible of the multilateralist agenda American officials had framed during World War II. What the United States really wanted, State Department official John D. Hickerson commented in 1948, was "not merely an extension of US influence but a real European organization strong enough to say 'no' both to the Soviet Union and to the United States, if our actions should seem so to require."

The American empire, therefore, reflected little imperial consciousness or design. An anti-imperial tradition dating back to the American Revolution partially accounted for this: departures from that tradition, as in the Spanish–American War of 1898 and the Philippine insurrection that followed, had only reinforced its relevance—outside the Western hemisphere. So too did a constitutional structure that forced even imperially minded leaders like Wilson and the two Roosevelts to accommodate domestic attitudes that discouraged imperial behavior long after national capabilities had made it possible. And even as those internal constraints diminished dramatically in World War II—they never entirely dropped away—Americans still found it difficult to think of themselves as an imperial power. The idea of remaking the international system in such a way as to transcend empires altogether still lingered, but so too did doubts as to whether the United States was up to the task. In the end it was again external circumstances—the manner in which Stalin managed his own empire and the way in which this pushed Europeans into preferring its American alternative—that brought the self-confidence necessary to administer imperial responsibilities into line with Washington's awareness of their existence.

The test of any empire comes in administering it, for even the most repressive tyranny requires a certain amount of acquiescence among its subjects. Coercion and terror cannot everywhere and indefinitely prop up authority: sooner or later the social, economic, and psychological costs of such measures begin to outweigh the benefits. Empires that can accommodate dissent defuse it, and perhaps even reorient themselves to reflect certain aspects of it, are more likely to survive than those that simply try to suppress it. Resilience is as important as rigidity in designing buildings, bridges, and baseball bats: the world of politics is not all that different.

It is apparent now, even if it was not always at the time, that the Soviet Union did not manage its empire particularly well. Because of his personality and the structure of government he built around it, Stalin was—shall we say—less than receptive to the wishes of those nations that fell within the Soviet sphere. He viewed departures from his instructions with deep suspicion, but he also objected to manifestations of independent behavior where instructions had not yet been given. As a result, he put his European followers in an impossible position: they could satisfy him only by seeking his approval for whatever he had decided they should do—even, at times, before he had decided that they should do it.

An example occurred late in 1944 when the Yugoslavs—then the most powerful but also the most loyal of Stalin's East European allies—complained politely to Soviet commanders that their troops had been raping local women in the northern corner of the country through which they were passing. Stalin himself took note of this matter, accusing the Yugoslavs—at one point tearfully—of showing insufficient respect for Soviet military sacrifices and for failing to sympathize when "a soldier who has crossed thousands of kilometers through blood and fire and death has fun with a woman or takes some trifle." The issue was not an insignificant one: the Red Army's behavior was a problem throughout the territories it occupied, and did much to alienate those who lived there. Stalin's only concern, though, seems to have been that the Yugoslavs were failing to meet the standards of deference and obedience he expected from allies; for their part, the Yugoslavs began to wonder, apparently for the first time, just whose interests international communism as directed from Moscow was supposed to serve.

Similar questions arose regarding Yugoslav plans for a postwar Balkan federation. Stalin had initially supported this idea, perhaps as an excuse for removing

American and British military representatives from former enemy states like Romania, but he soon developed reservations. The Yugoslavs themselves might become too powerful; and their propensity for hot-headedness—evident in their claims to Trieste and their shooting down of two American Air Force planes in 1946—might provoke the West. Orders went out that the Yugoslavs were to proceed slowly in their plans to take over Albania, and were to stop assisting the Greek guerrillas altogether. Within the context of the Cold War, these actions reflected Stalin's caution about confronting the British and the Americans; to that extent, they defused tensions. But to the militant Yugoslavs, they suggested the arrogance of an imperial authority determined to subordinate their interests—which they had defined largely in ideological terms—to those of the Soviet state.

Stalin did little better managing Western European communists, despite the fact that they still regarded themselves as his loyal supporters. In May 1947, the French Communist Party voted no confidence in the government of Premier Paul Ramadier, only to have him expel their representatives from his cabinet. The Italians, with strong American encouragement, threw out their own communists later that month. Andrei Zhdanov, who managed the Soviet Communist Party's relations with its foreign counterparts, sharply reprimanded the French comrades for acting without Moscow's authorization and therefore arousing concerns in the minds of "Soviet workers." He then passed on this communication to all other European communist parties. The implication seemed to be that none of them should do anything without consulting Moscow first, a requirement that would obviously be difficult to meet for communists who had responsibilities within national governments and therefore some obligation to consider national interests.

The Americans' unexpected offer of Marshall Plan aid to the Soviet Union and Eastern Europe in June 1947, caused even greater difficulties for Stalin's management of empire—which is precisely what Kennan hoped for when he recommended making it. In one of the stranger illusions arising from their ideology, Soviet leaders had always anticipated United States economic assistance in some form. Lenin himself expected American capitalists, ever in search of foreign markets, to invest eagerly in the newly formed USSR, despite its official antipathy toward them. Stalin hoped for a massive American reconstruction loan after World War II, and even authorized Molotov early in 1945 to offer acceptance of such assistance in order to help the United States stave off the economic crisis that Marxist analysis showed must be approaching. When the Marshall Plan was announced Stalin's first reaction was that the capitalists must be desperate. He concluded, therefore, that the Soviet Union and its East European allies should indeed participate in the plan, and quickly dispatched Molotov and a large delegation of economic experts to Paris to take part in the conference that was to determine the nature and extent of European needs.

But then Stalin began to reconsider. His ambassador in Washington, Nikolai Novikov, warned that the American offer to the Soviet Union could not be sincere: "A careful analysis of the Marshall Plan shows that ultimately it comes down to forming a West European bloc as a tool of US policy. All the good wishes accompanying the plan are demagogic official propaganda serving as a smokescreen." Soviet intelligence picked up reports—accurate enough—that American Under-Secretary of State William Clayton had been conspiring with British officials on using the Marshall Plan to reintegrate Germany into the West European economy and to deny further reparations shipments to the Soviet Union. This information, together with indications at Paris that the Americans would require a coordinated European response, caused Stalin to change his mind and order his own representatives to walk out. "The Soviet delegation saw those claims as a bid to interfere in the internal affairs of European countries," Molotov explained lamely, "thus making the economies of these countries dependent on US interests."

Curiously, though, Stalin did not at first demand that the East Europeans follow the Soviet example. Instead he instructed their delegations to attend follow-up sessions of the Paris conference, but to "show . . . that the Anglo-French plan is unacceptable, prevent its unanimous approval and then . . . withdraw from the meeting, taking with them as many delegates of other countries as possible." These orders stood for only three days, however, because Stalin then considered again: what if the East Europeans—especially the Czechs, whose communists did not yet completely control the government—chose not to follow the script and proceeded to accept Marshall Plan aid? Accordingly, a new message went out stating awkwardly that the Soviet Communist Party Central Committee "proposes refusing to participate in the meeting, that is, sending no delegations to it. Each country may give the reasons for its refusal as it sees fit."

Unfortunately, the Czechs and the Poles, following the earlier instructions, had already announced their intention to attend. The Poles quickly changed their mind but the Czechs procrastinated, more because of confusion than determined resistance. Stalin responded by peremptorily summoning their leaders to Moscow. He had been persuaded "on the basis of material reasons," he told them, that the Americans were using the Marshall Plan to consolidate a Western coalition hostile to the Soviet Union:

> The Soviet government has therefore been surprised by your decision to accept this invitation. For us it is a matter of friendship. . . . If you go to Paris you shall demonstrate your will to cooperate in the action of isolating the Soviet Union. All the Slavonic states have refused, not even Albania feared to refuse, and therefore, we think you should reverse your decision.

Stalin's intentions were now clear to all including himself: there would be no East European participation in the Marshall Plan, or in any other American scheme for the rehabilitation of Europe. "I went to Moscow as the Foreign Minister of an independent sovereign state," Czech Foreign Minister Jan Masaryk commented bitterly. "I returned as a lackey of the Soviet government."

But the Kremlin boss too had shed some illusions. Marxist-Leninist analyses had long predicted, not just a postwar economic collapse in the West, but eventual conflict between the British and the Americans. In a September 1946 report from Washington which Molotov had carefully annotated, Ambassador Novikov had insisted that "the United States regards England as its greatest potential competitor." The Anglo-American relationship "despite the temporary attainment of agreements on very important questions, [is] plagued with great internal contradictions and cannot be lasting." By early 1947, Stalin was even offering the British a military alliance: as one report to Molotov put it, "Soviet diplomacy has in England practically unlimited possibilities." What the Marshall Plan showed was how wrong these assessments were. Capitalists, it now appeared, could indeed reconcile their differences; they considered the Soviet Union a greater threat to all than each posed to the other; time was not on Moscow's side. Ideology again had led Stalin into romanticism and away from reality. Once he realized this—in Europe at least—he never quite recovered from the shock.

The United States, in contrast, proved surprisingly adept at managing an empire. Having attained their authority through democratic processes, its leaders were experienced—as their counterparts in Moscow were not—in the arts of persuasion, negotiation and compromise. Applying domestic political insights to foreign policy could produce embarrassing results, as when President Truman likened Stalin to his old Kansas City political mentor, Tom Pendergast, or when Secretary of State James F. Byrnes compared the Russians to the US Senate: "You build a post office in their state, and they'll build a post office in our state." But the habits of democracy had served the nation well during World War II: its strategists had assumed that their ideas would have to reflect the interests and capabilities of allies; it was also possible for allies to advance proposals of their own and have them taken seriously. That same pattern of mutual accommodation persisted after the war, despite the fact that all sides acknowledged—as they had during most of the war itself—the disproportionate power the United States could ultimately bring to bear.

Americans so often deferred to the wishes of allies during the early Cold War that some historians have seen the Europeans—especially the British—as having managed *them.* The new Labour government in London did encourage the Truman administration to toughen its policy toward the Soviet Union; Churchill—by then out of office—was only reinforcing these efforts with his March 1946 "Iron Curtain" speech. The British were ahead of the Americans in pressing for a consolidation of Western occupation zones in Germany, even if this jeopardized prospects for an overall settlement with the Russians. Foreign Secretary Ernest Bevin determined the timing of the February 1947 crisis over Greece and Turkey when he ended British military and economic assistance to those countries, leaving the United States little choice but to involve itself in the eastern Mediterranean and providing the occasion for the Truman Doctrine. And it was the desperate economic plight of the West Europeans generally that persuaded newly appointed Secretary of State George C. Marshall, in June 1947, to announce the comprehensive program of American assistance that came to bear his name.

But one can easily make too much of this argument. Truman and his advisers were not babes in the woods. They knew what they were doing at each stage, and did it only because they were convinced their actions would advance American interests. They never left initiatives entirely up to the Europeans: they insisted on an integrated plan for economic recovery and quite forcefully reined in prospective recipients when it appeared that their requests would exceed what Congress would approve. "[I]n the end we would not *ask* them," Kennan noted, "we would just *tell* them, what they would get." The Americans were flexible enough, though, to accept and build upon ideas that came from allies; they also frequently let allies determine the timing of actions taken. As a consequence, the British, French, and other West Europeans came to feel that they had a stake in what Washington was doing, despite the fact that it amounted to their own incorporation within an American sphere of influence.

One might argue, to be sure, that European elites agreed to all of this for their own self-interested reasons; that the European "masses" were never consulted. It is worth remembering, however, that free elections ultimately ratified alignment with the United States in every country where that took place. The newly-formed Central Intelligence Agency, not always confident of such outcomes, did take it upon itself at times to manipulate democratic processes, most conspicuously in the Italian elections of April 1948. But these covert efforts—together with clandestine CIA support for anti-communist labor unions and intellectual organizations—could hardly have succeeded had there not already existed in Europe a widespread predisposition to see the Americans as the lesser of two evils, and perhaps even as a force for good. "I am entirely convinced," the French political theorist Raymond Aron insisted, "that for an anti-Stalinist there is no escape from the acceptance of American leadership." French peasants did not see it all that differently.

The habits of democracy were no less significant when it came to defeated adversaries. The Roosevelt administration had planned to treat Germany harshly after the war; and even after the President himself backed away from the punitive Morgenthau Plan in late 1944, its spirit lingered in the occupation directive for American forces, JCS 1067, which prohibited doing anything to advance economic rehabilitation beyond the minimum necessary to avoid disease or disorder. The American design for a postwar world based on economic integration and political self-determination seemed not to apply, or so at first it appeared, to occupied Germany.

Uneasiness about this inconsistency soon developed, though; and in any event Americans far from Washington customarily maintained a certain irreverence toward orders emanating from it. General Clay concluded almost at once that his instructions were unworkable and that he would either get them changed, sabotage them, or ignore them. Here he followed the lead of his own troops who, having found prohibitions against fraternizing with the Germans to be ridiculous, quickly devised ways of circumventing them. Confronted with inappropriate directives in a difficult situation, the American occupiers—with a breezy audacity that seems remarkable in retrospect—fell back upon domestic instincts and set about transplanting democracy into the part of Germany they controlled.

Soviet occupation authorities too, we now know, found themselves hampered by unclear directives ill-suited to the problems they faced; some of them managed to carve out a fair amount of autonomy, at times in defiance of Moscow's wishes. But it was what was done with autonomy that made the difference. The Red Army, repeating its practices elsewhere in Eastern Europe, indulged in looting and physical assaults on so massive a scale that the full extent of it is only now becoming known: reparations extractions removed about a third of the Soviet zone's industrial capacity and Russian troops raped as many as *two million* German women in 1945 and 1946. As the historian Norman Naimark has emphasized,

> women in the Eastern zone—both refugees from further east and inhabitants of the towns, villages, and cities of the Soviet zone—shared an experience for the most part unknown in the West, the ubiquitous threat and the reality of rape, over a prolonged period of time.

Whereas the American occupation authorities at first forbade fraternization but quickly reversed that policy, their Soviet counterparts initially encouraged such contacts but eventually had to prohibit them altogether because of the hostility they generated. Certainly the Russians did little to evolve practices or build institutions that promised Germans within their zone—apart from Communist Party functionaries— a stake in their success.

The United States could of course hold out the prospect of economic recovery and the Soviet Union could not: this certainly made the advantages of democracy more evident than they might otherwise have been. But democratization, under Clay's leadership, was well under way before there was any assurance that Germans would receive Marshall Plan aid or anything comparable. Authoritarianism, which was all Moscow would or could provide, was by far the less attractive alternative. "Soviet officers bolshevized their zone," Naimark has concluded, "not because there was a plan to do so, but because that was the only way they knew to organize society. . . . By their own actions, the Soviet authorities created enemies out of potential friends." Or, as General Clay recalled years afterwards: "We began to look like angels, not because we were angels, but we looked [like] that in comparison to what was going on in Eastern Europe."

The Americans simply did not find it necessary, in building a sphere of influence, to impose unrepresentative governments or brutal treatment upon the peoples that fell within it. Where repressive regimes already existed, as in Greece, Turkey, and Spain, serious doubts arose in Washington as to whether the United States should be supporting them at all, however useful they might be in containing Soviet expansionism. Nor, having constructed their empire, did Americans follow the ancient imperial practice of "divide and rule." Rather, they used economic leverage to overcome nationalist tendencies, thereby encouraging the Europeans' emergence as a "third force" whose obedience could not always be assumed. It was as if the Americans were projecting abroad a tradition they had long taken for granted at home: that civility made sense; that spontaneity, within a framework of minimal constraint, was the path to political and economic robustness; that to intimidate or to overmanage was to stifle. The contrast to Stalin's methods of imperial administration could hardly have been sharper.

✦ *F U R T H E R   R E A D I N G*

Anderson, Terry H. *The United States, Great Britain, and the Cold War, 1944–1947* (1981).
Blum, Robert M. *Drawing the Line: The Origins of American Containment Policy in East Asia* (1982).
Brands, H. W. *The Devil We Knew* (1993).
———. *Inside the Cold War: Loy Henderson and the Rise of the American Empire, 1918–1961* (1991).
Brinkley, Douglas. *Dean Acheson: The Cold War Years, 1952–1971* (1992).
Buhite, Russell D. *Decisions at Yalta: An Appraisal of Summit Diplomacy* (1986).
Callahan, David. *Dangerous Capabilities: Paul Nitze and the Cold War* (1990).
Davis, Lynn Etheridge. *The Cold War Begins: Soviet-American Conflict over Eastern Europe* (1974).
Eckes, Alfred E., Jr. *A Search for Solvency: Bretton Woods and the International Monetary System, 1941–1971* (1975).
Fried, Richard M. *Nightmare in Red* (1990).
Gaddis, John Lewis. *The Cold War: A New History* (2005).
———. *The Long Peace: Inquiries into the History of the Cold War* (1987).
———. *We Now Know: Rethinking Cold War History* (1997).
Gardner, Lloyd C. *Architects of Illusion: Men and Ideas in American Foreign Policy, 1941–1949* (1970).
Hamby, Alonzo L. *Man of the People: A Life of Harry S Truman* (1994).
Hersberg, James. *James B. Conant: Harvard to Hiroshima and the Making of the Nuclear Age* (1993).

Hogan, Michael J. *The Marshall Plan: America, Britain, and the Reconstruction of Western Europe, 1947–1952* (1987).
———, ed. *America in the World: The Historiography of American Foreign Relations Since 1941* (1995).
———, and Thomas G. Paterson, eds. *Explaining the History of American Foreign Relations* (1991).
Holloway, David. *Stalin and the Bomb* (1994).
Hoopes, Townsend, and Douglas Brinkley. *Driven Patriot: The Life and Times of James Forrestal* (1992).
Hunter, Allen, ed. *Rethinking the Cold War* (1998).
Iatrides, John O., and Linda Wrigley, eds. *Greece at the Crossroads: The Civil War and Its Legacy* (1995).
Isaacson, Walter, and Evan Thomas. *The Wise Men: Six Friends and the World They Made: Acheson, Bohlen, Harriman, Kennan, Lovett, McCloy* (1986).
Kofsky, Frank. *Harry S Truman and the War Scare of 1948: A Successful Campaign to Deceive the Nation* (1993).
Kolko, Gabriel. *The Politics of War: The World and United States Foreign Policy, 1943–1945* (1968).
Kolko, Joyce, and Gabriel Kolko. *The Limits of Power: The World and United States Foreign Policy, 1945–1954* (1972).
Kovrig, Bennett. *Of Walls and Bridges: The United States and Eastern Europe* (1991).
Kuniholin, Bruce R. *The Origins of the Cold War in the Near East: Great Power Conflict and Diplomacy in Iran, Turkey, and Greece* (1980).
Kuznick, Peter J., and James Gilbert, eds. *Rethinking Cold War Culture* (2001).
Leffler, Melvyn P. *A Preponderance of Power: National Security, the Truman Administration, and the Cold War* (1992).
Mastny, Vojtech. *The Cold War and Soviet Insecurity: The Stalin Years* (1996).
May, Ernest R. *American Cold War Strategy: Interpreting NSC 68* (1993).
McMahon, Robert J. *The Cold War: A Very Short Introduction* (2003).
Messer, Robert L. *The End of an Alliance: James F. Byrnes, Roosevelt, Truman, and the Origins of the Cold War* (1982).
Miller, James E. *The United States and Italy, 1940–1950* (1986).
Milward, Alan S. *The Reconstruction of Western Europe, 1945–51* (1984).
Montefiore, Simon Sebag. *Stalin: The Court of the Red Tsar* (2004).
Offner, Arnold. *Another Such Victory: President Truman and the Cold War, 1945–1953* (2002).
Painter, David S. *The Cold War: An International History* (2002).
Paterson, Thomas G. *Meeting the Communist Threat: Truman to Reagan* (1988).
———. *On Every Front: The Making of the Cold War* (1979).
Pollard, Robert. *Economic Security and the Origins of the Cold War, 1945–1950* (1980).
Raack, R. C. *Stalin's Drive to the West, 1938–1945: The Origins of the Cold War* (1995).
Schaller, Michael. *The American Occupation of Japan: The Origins of the Cold War in Asia* (1985).
Schrecker, Ellen. *Many Are the Crimes: McCarthyism in America* (1999).
Trachtenberg, Marc. *A Constructed Peace: The Making of the European Settlement, 1945–1963* (1991).
Walker, Martin. *The Cold War: A History* (1994).
Weinstein, Allen. *Perjury: The Hiss-Chambers Case* (1997).
———, and Vassiliev, Alexander. *The Haunted Wood: Soviet Espionage in America—The Stalin Era* (1999).
Whitfield, Stephen J. *The Culture of the Cold War*, 2nd ed. (1996).
Williams, William A. *The Tragedy of American Foreign Policy* (1962).
Yergin, Daniel. *Shattered Peace: The Origins of the Cold War and the National Security State* (1977).
Zubok, Vladislav, and Constantine Pleshakov. *Inside the Kremlin's Cold War: From Stalin to Khrushchev* (1996).

CHAPTER
3

The Consumer's Republic:
The 1950s and the Emergence
of a New Economy of
Mass Consumption

For most Americans, the 1950s were a decade of unprecedented prosperity, economic growth, high employment, and rapid if uneven spread of homesteads in suburbia. It was a decade marked not only by the mass production of consumer goods and services but also by the increasingly important role of advertising and mass communication in organizing consumption—in ensuring that what was produced was in fact consumed. It was a decade in which young "baby boomers" emerged as a market and a cultural force. It was a decade, finally, when all of the big ideological and political conflicts of the 1930s and 1940s seemed played out, leaving a contented if bland consensus in their wake.

 This vision was accurate to a point. Economic prosperity stood as a blessing and an achievement for a nation that had just emerged from depression and war; and it was understandable that some Americans smugly contrasted their own well-being with continued privation throughout much of war-ravaged Europe and Asia. Yet if the 1950s were an age of affluence, they were also an age of anxiety—over the Cold War, Korea, and McCarthyism; over the ominous threat of nuclear war; and over the growing bureaucratization and impersonality of mass society. Moreover, the experiences of countless people clashed with the decade's dominant imagery: for example, the millions of Americans who at decade's end remained mired in poverty; the millions of African Americans whose struggle for equality would soon ignite the civil rights movement; and the educated middle-class women whose quiet desperation Betty Friedan would later chronicle in The Feminine Mystique *(1963). Moreover, prosperity bred new anxieties: commentators—conservative, liberal, and those in between—worried about juvenile delinquency and the family. Some feared that comfort had made Americans soft, bereft of passion, and perhaps unable to respond to the challenges that remained ahead. Still others worried that modern social science and psychology had developed new tools for manipulating people's desires, or that advertising trickery might turn elections into vapid contests indistinguishable from campaigns to sell detergent. Thus, while a new "consumer's republic" promised to bring the good life within everyone's reach, many tensions remained—tensions reflecting both the limits of the new economy of abundance and an uneasiness about prosperity itself.*

✦ D O C U M E N T S

The years following World War II opened a great number of new opportunities to many Americans, the prospect of which was both welcome and a bit frightening. The following documents illustrate some of the complexities of American culture in the new postwar era. To begin with, prosperity itself was a relatively new phenomenon, especially for Americans who had just emerged from almost two decades of depression and war. Business leaders in particular feared that memories of the depression might fuel a postwar revival of New Deal reform, a prospect they sought to avoid by spending millions of dollars on campaigns to convince Americans of the benefits of the U.S. economic system. Document 1, an excerpt from a pamphlet titled "The Miracle of America," was part of a multimillion-dollar effort launched in 1948 by the Advertising Council, a trade association of advertising agencies, media outlets, and large corporate advertisers. Fueling the rapid economic growth of the 1950s were a sharp increase in the birthrate and a decline in the age at marriage, demographic phenomena considered in Document 2, a report on the baby boom. This large population cohort continued to shape American society, culture, and public policy, as the baby boomers successively entered schools, colleges, and the workforce; had children of their own; and assumed positions of economic, cultural, and political power. As the leading edge of the baby boom nears retirement age, concern mounts about the future of Social Security and Medicare. In the 1950s, the burgeoning youth population fueled fears of juvenile delinquency on the part of parents, politicians, and journalists (Document 3). As an article in *Life* magazine suggests (Document 4), by the late 1950s advertisers had identified teenagers as a newly emerging market, one that had to be approached with strategies different from those used to reach adults. While the hard direct-sell and classic appeals to insecurity ruled the industry in the 1950s, advertisers also began to target different markets, an early example of late twentieth-century market segmentation. Americans worried about new technologies of consumption, even as they hurried to embrace them. Document 5, from *U.S. News and World Report,* describes some of the fears that television inspired about Americans' apparently increasing passivity. In a similar vein, Vance Packard warns how advertisers sought to manipulate the public in his best-selling book *The Hidden Persuaders* (Document 6).

1. U.S. Business Celebrates the "Miracle of America," 1948

It all started . . . when Junior looked up from his homework:

"It says here America is great and powerful on account of the American economic system. What's our economic system, Dad?"

Dad put his paper down and appeared to be thinking hard.

"I'd like to know, too," Mother put in. "I think in these times *every* American ought to be informed about what makes up the American way of life."

"So do I," Sis added.

Excerpts from "The Miracle of America," a pamphlet prepared for the Advertising Council, Inc. (1948).

"Well, I could give you all sorts of answers," Dad said. "But maybe we ought to get the story straight from the one who knows it best."

"Who's that?" asked Junior.

"You'll recognize him all right," Dad said. "Let's go!"

So they did. . . .

Junior gasped. "Gee whiz—I know *him!*"

"Uncle Sam," Dad began, "my boy here wants to know what makes America great. You know—our economic system and all that. Fact is, I guess we all do." . . .

"In the early days, men and animals did most of our work.

"We even used the wind to run our machines.

"Then we began to use water power to turn millstones and run looms. But in some places no water power was to be had.

"We needed something better. Our inventors and business men kept testing and trying. There would be big rewards in our free market for reliable power that could be used *anywhere.*

"At last we had it—thanks to an ingenious Scotsman—James Watt. He invented an engine driven by steam made from coal!

"Later still Americans developed engines run by gasoline and electricity.

"Now we're looking for ways to use atomic power. . . .

"Americans are known as inventive people. Why? Because we have had the incentive to profit by making improvements—and backing them with our savings.

"When our people realized that they were free to shape their own destinies, they began to devise machines which multiplied each man's work power.

"In 1799, Eli Whitney, inventor of the cotton gin that did 50 men's work, made history with an order for muskets awarded by the U.S. Army. Instead of building each gun separately, he turned out standard parts which could be used interchangeably on *any* gun.

"Hearing of this, the clocksmith Eli Terry started to make clocks on the same principle. With all the laborious fitting eliminated, he found that he could sell clocks for $10 apiece instead of the regular $25. In three years, he and his partner, Seth Thomas sold 5,000.

"Eli Terry saw that if he cut his costs by mass production, and distributed a bigger volume more widely, he would benefit more people and make more money. And it worked out exactly that way!

"Pins had long been made by hand, selling as high as 20 cents each. Then a Connecticut man perfected machines to make *two million pins a week!*

"Down through the years, Americans invented hundreds of thousands of work-saving machines.

"Of course, it takes money to make and install those new, labor-saving machines in factories—more money than any one man could afford. A machine for one worker often costs thousands of dollars. So the owner took in many *partners*—thrifty men and women who received *stock* in exchange for their money. All these *partners* joined to form a *company* which they owned together. In order to make a profit in competition with other companies, they had to turn out better and less expensive products.

"The same new freedoms that made Americans ingenious and inventive made us better and better workers—no matter what our jobs.

"The planners and managers of industry found new and improved ways of designing factories and work flow—so that goods were turned out more quickly and cheaply.

"They found new and better ways to get those goods from the factories to the stores and into the homes. Advertising and selling opened up bigger markets by telling the story to millions.

"And the individual worker became steadily more skillful at his job. He realized that the more he could produce during the hours he worked, the more he would increase his own value. When many workers did that, it added up to national prosperity!

"Labor unions and collective bargaining strengthened the worker's sense of security and improved working conditions. The result is that America gradually developed the greatest group of skilled workers and technicians the world has ever seen. . . .

"It is because we Americans *produce* so much better for every hour we work that we *earn* more and can *buy* more. . . .

". . . and the end is not yet. We have learned that *in the long run, when output per hour goes up, prices drop, so more people can buy and all of us* gain.

"*But when output per hour goes down, prices rise, so fewer people can buy and all of us* lose.

"Of course, there are unusual periods when these principles don't seem to work—times when business is far above or far below normal. But over the long pull you'll find that these rules of productivity *do* apply.

"On the average, productivity has increased in the United States almost one-fifth every 10 years since 1850. We topped this in the 20 years 1920–1940, and we can do it again!"

"Can we keep right on doing it?" Dad asked.

"We certainly can!" Uncle Sam replied. "If everybody who plays a part in making things will team up to do it, we can raise productivity so far and so fast that we can share the benefits and have real security for *all* our people."

2. A Report on the Baby Boom, 1954

The trend toward larger families among married college graduates is still continuing, the Population Reference Bureau reports.

For the last eight years, since 1946, the number of babies per graduate has been going up. The increase is greater for men graduates than for women.

"There is even a possibility," says a report in the Population Bulletin, "that members of the class of 1944 will replace themselves in the new generation." Statisticians figure that each graduate must have an average of 2.1 children to be sure that one will live to grow up, marry and have children to carry on the chain unbroken.

The low was reached by men graduates in the class of 1922 with 1.70 children per graduate; by women in the class of 1926 with 1.18.

For many years in the United States the tendency among white women of childbearing age has been for those with the most education to have the fewest children. The figure in 1940 was 1.23 for college graduates as compared with 4.33 for women who had not gone beyond fourth grade.

"Baby Boom Continues Among College Grads," *Science News Letter,* June 19, 1954.

The institution leading in number of children per graduate, for men of both the class 1944 and the class 1929 and women for the class 1929, is Brigham Young University in Utah. But this university is outdistanced by the 1944 women graduates of St. Mary's College in Indiana.

The increasing fertility of recent college graduates is attributed to an improvement in economic conditions and to changing attitudes toward marriage. In the 20's and early 30's, marriage and birth rates were both low. People were marrying later in life.

Now that it is easier for young couples to set up their home and start families, they are marrying younger. Births are not deferred as often nor as long as they were 15 years ago.

3. *Newsweek* Decries the Problem of Dangerous Teens, 1955

Call him "Tarzan." That's what he calls himself.

His real name is Frank Santana and he looks like a malnourished mouse, but he thinks he's quite a guy—especially when he's carrying a gun.

A slim, dark, adenoidal kid of 17, he was strutting down a street in the Bronx last week with a dozen members of his gang, the Navajos. They were in uniform. They wore blue jeans and leather jackets, trimmed in yellow and emblazoned with the insigne of the gang, a portrait of a Plains Indian. And they were looking for Golden Guineas. The Golden Guineas are a gang of teen-agers, too. The day before a group of them had caught "Tarzan" and given him a pushing around. The Navajos wanted revenge.

Model

William Blankenship Jr., 15, came up the street. He wasn't a Navajo or a Golden Guinea. He wasn't a member of any gang. He was a model student in high school, the son of a research chemist who spent his spare time working to prevent juvenile delinquency.

"Tarzan" gave his gun, a .32-caliber Italian automatic, to a lieutenant to hold. He grabbed Blankenship and accused him of being a Golden Guinea. The lieutenant, Ralph Falcon, 16, "Superman," waved the gun menacingly.

"Don't point that gun at me," cried Blankenship.

"Superman" put the gun in his belt.

"Don't chicken out," then screamed "Tarzan" at "Superman."

He grabbed the gun and fired, killing Blankenship.

The Navajos scattered.

The cops found "Tarzan" at his apartment. They found the gun in the bathroom water tank. They also found a pair of brass knuckles.

"Why did you shoot the kid?" the policemen asked.

"Tarzan" looked at his fists.

"I didn't want to bang up these knuckles," he said. "I'm a boxer, you know. So I used a gun." He added with an air of apology: "I'm not very good at street fighting, anyway."

Jungle

It took a crime as senseless as the murder of young Blankenship last week to make Americans aware of a chilling fact: In several of the nation's cities, and particularly in New York and Chicago, juvenile delinquency is actually becoming organized gangsterism. The old Prohibition mobs are gone. Yet some of the cities remain jungles. Where the Prohibition mobsters prowled, teen-age hoodlums, organized like armies, have taken over. They are not just "bad kids." They are criminals. And they don't hesitate to kill. The Prohibition mobsters killed for a purpose. The teen-agers often will kill simply for the sake of killing or because, like Frank Santana, they don't want to "chicken out." . . .

Juvenile delinquents come from every class of society, but the teen-age gang is a phenomenon of the slums. And it is a phenomenon also of the so-called minority groups. Sociologists say the gangs give the youngsters a sense of status and a feeling of "belonging." The trouble is, they can become vicious.

Escaped

"Gangs," says Cook County Sheriff Joseph D. Lohman, a professional criminologist and a onetime professor of sociology at the University of Chicago, "attract youngsters because they fill a need that is lacking in society. They provide an escape from the boredom and distasteful conditions that parents and schools impose. There is excitement in gang conflict and action. There are new and challenging experiences. The gang solves a boy's problems by offering what parents and society fail to provide the restless, growing adolescent."

The gangs range in size from a dozen youngsters to 50 or 100 or even 250. All the members of each gang live in the same neighborhood; usually, they are from the same racial group. They give themselves names like the Navajos, the Golden Guineas, the Jolly Gents, the Baldies, the Redwings. And they call themselves social clubs or athletic clubs.

Trouble Makers

In New York, the police say, there are about 100 teen-age gangs. Of these, about 50 are listed by the cops as "active." This means they are trouble makers. They wage wars in the streets with other gangs and they commit crimes.

Like Frank Santana's Navajos, the gangs usually wear uniforms—in New York, blue jeans and leather jackets; in Chicago, pegged trousers and black Ike jackets. The Chicago teen-age hoods also affect ducktail haircuts.

The leaders are usually elected. And decisions usually are made by majority vote. The organization is rarely cohesive. Members come and go. They move out of the neighborhood; they go into the Army; they get married. Sometimes, gangs will disintegrate almost overnight. A few months later, a new gang will spring up, with many of the old members, but with a new name, a new insigne, and new leaders.

By and large, the gangs do not admit girls. Instead, they have girls' auxiliaries. In Chicago, for example, the Commanders have the Commandettes; the Hawks have the Squaws; the Mum-Checks have the Mum-Chicks. The girls also dress in uniform—in Chicago, blue jeans and jackets. Says one: "It's hard for girls to wear skirts when we sit on the corner with the guys. We'd get our skirts dirty."

Until last year, many of the Chicago gang girls wore their hair pony-tail style. Now they wear it bobbed.

Rumble

The girls often carry the weapons the boys use, since policemen hesitate to frisk a girl. And they are often the cause of gang wars—or rumbles, as the New York teen-agers call them. Members of two rival gangs will attend the same dance. A girl belonging to one gang will dance with a member of the other. The first gang's honor is hurt. So there will be a rumble. The hoods will fight out in the streets, sometimes with guns. And there will be casualties.

The gangs are as touchy as nations about their territories. When a gang from one neighborhood walks through another, that's considered an invasion and an act of war. . . .

Real guns are so easy to come by that few of the teen-age hoods bother with zip-guns now.

When boy and girl gang members start going steady, they exchange jackets or rings. In Chicago, the gang code demands that a boy seldom travel with his girl except in a car, called a "short." Frequently the boys steal the cars, in which case they are called "hot shorts."

At one suburban Chicago high school last winter, nearly 100 boys and girls crammed into fifteen shorts, most of them hot, and systemically raided and demolished a swanky North Shore dining place, causing damage that was estimated by police at nearly $250,000. "When they asked me to go along with them, I had to," a gang member explained. "If I didn't go along, they'd know I was chicken and I couldn't live around here any more."

One night last month, nearly 40 young toughs crashed a Delta Upsilon fraternity dance at the University of Chicago, hurled bottles, bricks, and clubs, stabbed a student in the back and beat up ten others. "They had it coming to them," a Mum-Check explained. "They always acted so superior. They thought they were better than us because they went to college. We felt it was about time to take care of them anyway."

Two weeks ago, after a rumor got around that one gang [member] was dating the girl friend of another gang's leader, the second gang grabbed baseball bats and raced through the city streets in two cars seeking revenge. They savagely slugged two boys, only to discover that neither boy was a member of the offending mob.

"Protection"

Steal-a-car clubs of six to eight teen-agers have become increasingly popular in Chicago. So has the practice of girl mobsters beating up other girls simply for laughs. The girl hoods also have adopted the practice of beating up motorists. One girl will play the part of a hitchhiker. When a car stops for her, the other girls will swarm out of hiding and start pummeling the driver.

In elementary and high schools in both New York and Chicago, the hoods frequently will force other students to pay them "protection money." Several youngsters who refused have been stabbed or slugged. Last year, one of the hoods was killed by three boys who got tired of paying him for "protection."

Says a thoughtful juvenile expert: "These street-corner group societies are organized on a system of values opposed to the values of their parents and society. We can't reach them through conventional means. The gangs are hostile to all organized help. They are systematically attacking society. It's not an individual problem but a group problem. Perhaps the viciousness of mankind in the past few decades has taken its ghastly toll on our youth."

What can be done about the teen-age gangs? Detroit helped to solve the problem by a get-tough policy. The police broke up the gangs. They established a curfew, and they enforce it.

What Answer?

Some jurists believe that police action is the only answer to the teen-age gangs. Others insist that beating up the teen-agers only makes them more antisocial. Officially, that is the attitude in New York. The city has established a Youth Board, which works with the gangs and attempts to direct them from antisocial to social ends.

This week, Henry Epstein, Deputy Mayor of New York, recommended to Mayor Robert F. Wagner that the work of the Youth Board be extended. And he recommended, also, that the city appropriate approximately $300,000 to private agencies working to prevent delinquency among youth.

4. *Life* Magazine Identifies the New Teen-age Market, 1959

To some people the vision of a leggy adolescent happily squealing over the latest fancy present from Daddy is just another example of the way teen-agers are spoiled to death these days. But to a growing number of businessmen the picture spells out the profitable fact that the American teen-agers have emerged as a big-time consumer in the U.S. economy. They are multiplying in numbers. They spend more and have more spent on them. And they have minds of their own about what they want.

The time is past when a boy's chief possession was his bike and a girl's party wardrobe consisted of a fancy dress worn with a string of dime-store pearls. What Depression-bred parents may still think of as luxuries are looked on as necessities by their offspring. Today teen-agers surround themselves with a fantastic array of garish and often expensive baubles and amusements. They own 10 million phonographs, over a million TV sets, 13 million cameras. Nobody knows how much parents spend on them for actual necessities nor to what extent teen-agers act as hidden persuaders on their parents' other buying habits. Counting only what is spent to satisfy

Excerpts from "A Young $10 Billion Power: The US Teen-age Consumer Has Become a Major Factor in the Nation's Economy," *Life*, August 31, 1959, 78–84. Courtesy of *Life* Magazine. Reprinted with permission.

their special teen-age demands, the youngsters and their parents will shell out about $10 billion this year, a billion more than the total sales of GM.

Until recently businessmen have largely ignored the teen-age market. But now they are spending millions on advertising and razzle-dazzle promotional stunts. Their efforts so far seem only to have scratched the surface of a rich lode. In 1970, when the teen-age population expands from its present 18 million to 28 million, the market may be worth $20 billion. If parents have any idea of organized revolt, it is already too late. Teen-age spending is so important that such action would send quivers through the entire national economy. . . .

At 17 Suzie Slattery of Van Nuys, Calif., fits any businessman's dream of the ideal teen-age consumer. The daughter of a reasonably well-to-do TV announcer, Suzie costs her parents close to $4,000 a year, far more than average for the country but not much more than many of the upper middle income families of her town. In an expanding economy more and more teen-agers will be moving up into Suzie's bracket or be influenced as consumers by her example.

Last year $1,500 was spent on Suzie's clothes and $550 for her entertainment. Her annual food bill comes to $900. She pays $4 every two weeks at the beauty parlor. She has her own telephone and even has her own soda fountain in the house. On summer vacation days she loves to wander with her mother through fashionable department stores, picking out frocks or furnishings for her room or silver and expensive crockery for the hope chest she has already started.

As a high school graduation present, Suzie was given a holiday cruise to Hawaii and is now in the midst of a new clothes-buying spree for college. Her parents' constant indulgence has not spoiled Suzie. She takes for granted all the luxuries that surround her because she has had them all her life. But she also has a good mind and some serious interests. A top student in her school, she is entering Occidental College this fall and will major in political science. . . .

Some Fascinating Facts About a Booming Market

FOOD: Teen-agers eat 20% more than adults. They down 3½ billion quarts of milk every year, almost four times as much as is drunk by the infant population under 1. Teen-agers are a main prop of the ice cream industry, gobble 145 million gallons a year.

BEAUTY CARE: Teen-agers spent $20 million on lipstick last year, $25 million on deodorants (a fifth of total sold), $9 million on home permanents. Male teen-agers own 2 million electric razors.

ENTERTAINMENT: Teen-agers lay out more than $1.5 billion a year for entertainment. They spend about $75 million on single pop records. Although they create new musical idols, they are staunchly faithful to the old. Elvis Presley, still their favorite, has sold 25 million copies of single records in four years, an all-time high.

HOMEMAKERS: Major items like furniture and silver are moving into the teen-age market because of growing number of teen-age marriages. One third of all 18- and 19-year-old girls are already married. More than 600,000 teen-agers will be married this year. Teen-agers are now starting hope chests at 15.

CREDIT RISKS: Some 800,000 teen-agers work at full-time jobs and can buy major items on credit.

5. *U.S. News and World Report* Assesses the Perils of Mass Culture and the Evils of Television, 1955

The biggest of the new forces in American life today is television. There has been nothing like it in the postwar decade, or in many decades before that—perhaps not since the invention of the printing press. Even radio, by contrast, was a placid experience.

The impact of TV on this country has been so massive that Americans are still wondering what hit them. Has the effect been good or bad? What permanent effects on the American way of life may be expected? These and other questions are considered in this survey.

Probably there are some people in the U.S. who have never seen a television program, but you would have to go into the hills to find them. Two out of three U.S. families now own their own sets, or are paying for them. In 32 million homes, TV dials are flicked on and off, from channel to channel, at least 100 million times between 8 A.M. and midnight.

Everywhere, children sit with eyes glued to screens—for three to four hours a day on the average. Their parents use up even more time mesmerized by this new marvel—or monster. They have spent 15 billion dollars to look since 1946.

Now, after nearly 10 years of TV, people are asking: "What hath TV wrought? What is this thing doing to us?"

Solid answers to this question are very hard to get. Pollsters, sociologists, doctors, teachers, the TV people themselves come up with more contradictions than conclusions whenever they start asking.

But almost everybody has an opinion and wants to air it.

What do these opinions add up to? People have strong views. Here are some widely held convictions, both against and for television:

That TV has kept people from going places and doing things, from reading, from thinking for themselves. Yet it is said also that TV has taken viewers vicariously into strange and fascinating spots and situations, brought distinguished and enchanting people into their living rooms, given them a new perspective.

That TV has interfered with schooling, kept children from learning to read and write, weakened their eyesight and softened their muscles. But there are those who hold that TV has made America's youngsters more "knowing" about life, more curious, given them a bigger vocabulary. Teaching by TV, educators say, is going to be a big thing in the future.

That TV arouses morbid emotions in children, glorifies violence, causes juvenile crime—that it starts domestic quarrels, tends to loosen morals and make people lazy and sodden. However, it keeps families together at home, provides a realm of cheap entertainment never before available, stimulates new lines of conversation.

That TV is giving the U.S. an almost primitive language, made up of grunts, whistles, standardized wisecracks and clichés—that it is turning the average American into a stereotype. Yet it is breaking down regional barriers and prejudices, ironing out accents, giving people in one part of the country a better understanding of people in other parts. That TV is making politics "a rich man's game," turning statesmanship into a circus, handing demagogues a new weapon. But it is giving Americans their first good look at the inside of their Government, letting them judge the people they elect by sight as well as by sound and fury.

That TV has distorted and debased Salesmanship, haunting people with singing "commercials" and slogans. However, because or in spite of TV, people are buying more and more things they never before thought they needed or wanted.

These are just some of the comments that people keep on making about TV. The experts say that it probably will be another generation before there is a firm basis of knowledge about television's impact on America.

Today's TV child, the boy or girl who was born with a TV set in his home, is too young to analyze his feelings. Older people, despite their frequent vehemence about TV, are still far from sure whether they have all Aladdin's lamp or hold a bear by the tail.

Goliath with Tubes

One thing you can be sure about. TV, a giant at 10, continues to grow like nobody's business. Here are some figures and comparisons: The 15 billion dollars that the U.S. people have invested in TV sets and repairs since the war is 15 per cent more than the country spent for new school and college buildings. About a billion more has gone into TV stations and equipment.

TV-viewing time is going *up,* not down, latest surveys show. This explodes the theory that people would taper off on television "once they got used to it."

"Pull" of popular TV programs is believed to be very effective. Pollsters report that three times as many people will leave a meal to answer questions at the door as will get up to abandon "Dragnet."

The number of families holding out against TV is declining to a small fraction. There still are 16 million families without sets, but most of these families either can't pay for sets or else live out of range of TV signals.

On an average evening, twice as many set owners will be watching TV as are engaged in any other form of entertainment or leisure activity, such as movie-going, card playing, or reading. Seven out of 10 American children watch TV between 6 and 8 o'clock most evenings.

Analysts are intrigued by the evidence that adults, not children, are the real television fans. The newest trend in viewing habits is a rise in the number of housewives who watch TV in the morning. One out of five with a set now watches a morning show with regularity.

What Is It?

Why do people want TV? A $67.50-per-week shoe repairman in San Francisco, puts it about as plainly as anyone can. "TV," he says, "is the only amusement I can afford." That was the reason he gave for paying four weeks' wages for his set.

The cobbler's comment explains TV's basic lure. It is free entertainment except for the cost of [the] set, and repairs and electricity. It becomes so absorbing that a broken set is a family catastrophe. People will pay to have the set fixed before they will pay the milk bill, if necessary.

What does TV do to people? What do people do with TV? The researchers are digging into these questions all the time. In general, they come to theories, rather than conclusions. There are three main theories:

THEORY "A": This is widely held by people whose professions bring them into close contact with juveniles—judges, district attorneys, police officers, ministers. It assumes that TV is bound to be affecting the American mind and character because it soaks up one to five hours a day or more that used to be spent in outdoor play, in games requiring reasoning and imagination, or in reading, talking, radio listening, or movie-going.

Even the more passive of these pursuits, the theory runs, required more exercise of brain than does TV watching. Then, too, many TV programs, the theorists say, are violent or in questionable taste.

Net effect, according to these people, is a wasting away or steady decline in certain basic skills among American youngsters. Children lose the ability to read, forfeit their physical dexterity, strength, and initiative.

Some see a definite connection between TV and juvenile delinquency. The Kefauver Subcommittee of the Senate Judiciary Committee has just explored this aspect. It stated:

"Members of the subcommittee share the concern of a large segment of the thinking public for the implications of the impact of this medium [television] . . . upon the ethical and cultural standards of the youth of America. It has been unable to gather proof of a direct casual relationship between the viewing of acts of crime and violence and the actual performance of criminal deeds. It has not, however, found irrefutable evidence that young people may not be negatively influenced in their present-day behavior by the saturated exposure they now receive to pictures and drama based on an underlying theme of lawlessness and crime which depict human violence."

THEORY "B": Mainly held by sociologists, communications economists, pollsters. This is that television is changing the American mind and character, although nobody knows for sure just how. The evidence is too fragmentary. The analysts are disturbed by some aspects of TV's effect on viewers. Some think TV is conditioning Americans to be "other directed," that is, getting the ideas from someone else. The early American, by contrast, is supposed to have been "inner directed," a man who thought things out for himself on the basis of his own reasoning.

A fancy name for this suspected effect of TV is "narcotic disfunction." This means that more and more men come home in the evening, drop into a chair in front of the TV set after supper and slip into a dream world of unreality.

However, the same researchers confess that TV can have a broadening influence, bringing to the masses a taste of the arts and sciences, a peek into government that they couldn't get any other way.

THEORY "C": This is what the TV people themselves like to think. It is that television is rapidly becoming "one more service" to the U.S. public, another medium such as newspapers, magazines, radio. Some people watch TV a lot, others very little. Most people want a set around, but some don't lean on it.

The TV people minimize the idea that TV is dominating American life. It is almost as if they were afraid their own baby is getting too big. What they usually say is that the people who allow their lives to be controlled by television were similarly dominated by radio and the movies—and that they are only a small minority.

The TV Habit

What do the theorists base their theories on? What have they found out about the place of the TV set in American life?

Many studies have been made of the "TV habit." Latest of these indicates that TV viewing reaches a peak just after a set enters a home, then falls off rather sharply. Next, viewing begins to rise again in the average home, building up, evidently, toward a new peak that is not yet measured.

The A. C. Nielsen Company, a market research organization that attaches mechanical recorders to sets in private homes, finds this: During the 12 months ended in April 1955, average use per day of TV sets was 4 hours and 50 minutes. That was up 4 per cent over the year before. . . .

Other studies indicate that women watch TV more than men do. Children, contrary to general impression, watch TV less than adults in the average home. Persons low in income, education, or job status as a rule spend more time in front of TV sets than those with more money and education.

What's on TV

What do people get on TV? What do they want? Three out of every four TV programs are entertainment shows. . . . In a typical week of the peak TV season, in January of last year, crime, comedy, variety, and Western shows accounted for 42.7 per cent of all TV program time on New York City screens. News accounted for 6.1 per cent of TV time—about the same share of time as was taken by quiz, stunt, and contest shows. Other informational types of TV shows, such as interviews, weather reports, travelogues, children's instructional programs, and cooking classes, got 16.2 per cent of the time.

Rating figures tend to show that people are getting just about what they want, in the opinion of the broadcasting industry. According to the "popularity" ratings of top shows, comedy and drama and straight entertainment are outpulling everything else.

What about information? The popularity cards seem to indicate the reaction is a stifled yawn. In a two-week period last June, when two comedy programs, the "George Gobel Show" and "I Love Lucy," were at the top of the list, each reaching more than 13 million homes, the top-ranking informational programs were way down the line. The "March of Medicine," for example, was No. 62, reaching 6.57 million homes; "Meet the Press" was No. 150, getting to 1.14 million families.

Studies also have been made of how long various programs hold their audiences. Love and adventure performances, it develops, will keep about 85 per cent of the audience to the end. By contrast, the most gripping historical sketches hold only 65 per cent, and many hold less than one third of their starting viewers. Informational programs, again, rank near the bottom in "holding power."

Television critics, who write about TV programs in newspapers and magazines, are frequently harsh in their remarks about violence, sadism, bad taste on the screen. However, Dallas W. Smythe, a professor of communications economics at the University of Illinois, analyzed New York City programs for 1955 and concludes that programs which critics liked best seldom drew the biggest audiences.

The public is fickle. Top rating is hard to hold. The viewers tire rapidly of a particular show unless the producers manage to come up with fresh material, new appeals.

6. Vance Packard Warns Against the "Hidden Persuaders," 1957

The use of mass psychoanalysis to guide campaigns of persuasion has become the basis of a multimillion-dollar industry. Professional persuaders have seized upon it in their groping for more effective ways to sell us their wares—whether products, ideas, attitudes, candidates, goals, or states of mind.

This depth approach to influencing our behavior is being used in many fields and is employing a variety of ingenious techniques. It is being used most extensively to affect our daily acts of consumption. The sale to us of billions of dollars' worth of United States products is being significantly affected, if not revolutionized, by this approach, which is still only barely out of its infancy. Two thirds of America's hundred largest advertisers have geared campaigns to this depth approach by using strategies inspired by what marketers call "motivation analysis."

Meanwhile, many of the nation's leading public-relations experts have been indoctrinating themselves in the lore of psychiatry and the social sciences in order to increase their skill at "engineering" our consent to their propositions. Fund raisers are turning to the depth approach to wring more money from us. A considerable and growing number of our industrial concerns (including some of the largest) are seeking to sift and mold the behavior of their personnel—particularly their own executives—by using psychiatric and psychological techniques. Finally, this depth approach is showing up nationally in the professional politicians' intensive use of symbol manipulation and reiteration on the voter, who more and more is treated like Pavlov's conditioned dog.

The efforts of the persuaders to probe our everyday habits for hidden meanings are often interesting purely for the flashes of revelation they offer us of ourselves. . . . The findings of the depth probers provide startling explanations for many of our daily habits and perversities. It seems that our subconscious can be pretty wild and unruly.

What the probers are looking for, of course, are the *whys* of our behavior, so that they can more effectively manipulate our habits and choices in their favor. This has led them to probe why we are afraid of banks; why we love those big fat cars; why we really buy homes; why men smoke cigars; why the kind of car we draw reveals the brand of gasoline we will buy; why housewives typically fall into a hypnoidal trance when they get into a supermarket; why men are drawn into auto showrooms by convertibles but end up buying sedans; why junior loves cereal that pops, snaps, and crackles.

Excerpts from Vance Packard, *The Hidden Persuaders* (New York: David McKay, 1957), 3–10. Reprinted by permission of the Estate of Vance Packard.

We move . . . into the chilling world of George Orwell and his Big Brother, however, as we explore some of the extreme attempts at probing and manipulating now going on.

Certain of the probers, for example, are systematically feeling out our hidden weaknesses and frailties in the hope that they can more efficiently influence our behavior. At one of the largest advertising agencies in America psychologists on the staff are probing sample humans in an attempt to find how to identify, and beam messages to, people of high anxiety, body consciousness, hostility, passiveness, and so on. A Chicago advertising agency has been studying the housewife's menstrual cycle and its psychological concomitants in order to find the appeals that will be more effective in selling her certain food products.

Seemingly, in the probing and manipulating nothing is immune or sacred. The same Chicago ad agency has used psychiatric probing techniques on little girls. Public-relations experts are advising churchmen how they can become more effective manipulators of their congregations. In some cases these persuaders even choose our friends for us, as at a large "community of tomorrow" in Florida. Friends are furnished along with the linen by the management in offering the homes for sale. Everything comes in one big, glossy package.

Somber examples of the new persuaders in action are appearing not only in merchandising but in politics and industrial relations. The national chairman of a political party indicated his merchandising approach to the election of 1956 by talking of his candidates as products to sell. In many industrial concerns now the administrative personnel are psycho-tested, and their futures are charted, by trained outside experts. And then there is the trade school in California that boasts to employers that it socially engineers its graduates so that they are, to use the phrase of an admiring trade journal, "custom-built men" guaranteed to have the right attitudes from the employer's standpoint.

What the persuaders are trying to do in many cases was well summed up by one of their leaders, the president of the Public Relations Society of America, when he said in an address to members: "The stuff with which we work is the fabric of men's minds." In many of their attempts to work over the fabric of our minds the professional persuaders are receiving direct help and guidance from respected social scientists. Several social-science professors at Columbia University, for example, took part in a seminar at the university attended by dozens of New York public-relations experts. In the seminar one professor, in a sort of chalk talk, showed these manipulators precisely the types of mental manipulation they could attempt with most likelihood of success.

All this probing and manipulation has its constructive and its amusing aspects; but also, I think it fair to say, it has seriously antihumanistic implications. Much of it seems to represent regress rather than progress for man in his long struggle to become a rational and self-guiding being. Something new, in fact, appears to be entering the pattern of American life with the growing power of our persuaders.

In the imagery of print, film, and air wave the typical American citizen is commonly depicted as an uncommonly shrewd person. He or she is dramatized as a thoughtful voter, rugged individualist, and, above all, as a careful hardheaded consumer of the wondrous products of American enterprise. He is, in short, the following of twentieth-century progress and enlightenment.

Most of us like to fit ourselves into this picture, and some of us surely are justified in doing so. The men and women who hold up these glowing images, particularly the professional persuaders, typically do so, however, with tongue in cheek. The way these persuaders—who often refer to themselves good-naturedly as "symbol manipulators"—see us in the quiet of their interoffice memos, trade journals, and shop talk is frequently far less flattering, if more interesting. Typically they see us as bundles of daydreams, misty hidden yearnings, guilt complexes, irrational emotional blockages. We are image movers given to impulsive and compulsive acts. We annoy them with our seemingly senseless quirks, but we please them with our growing docility in responding to their manipulation of symbols that stir us to action. They have found the supporting evidence for this view persuasive enough to encourage them to turn to depth channels on a large scale in their efforts to influence our behavior.

The symbol manipulators and their research advisers have developed their depth views of us by sitting at the feet of psychiatrists and social scientists (particularly psychologists and sociologists) who have been hiring themselves out as "practical" consultants or setting up their own research firms. Gone are the days when these scientists confined themselves to classifying manic depressives, fitting round pegs in round holes, or studying the artifacts and mating habits of Solomon Islanders. These new experts, with training of varying thoroughness, typically refer to themselves as "motivation analysts" or "motivation researchers." The head of a Chicago research firm that conducts psychoanalytically oriented studies for merchandisers, Louis Cheskin, sums up what he is doing in these candid terms:

"Motivation research is the type of research that seeks to learn what motivates people in making choices. It employs techniques designed to reach the unconscious or subconscious mind because preferences generally are determined by factors of which the individual is not conscious. . . . Actually in the buying situation the consumer generally acts emotionally and compulsively, unconsciously reacting to the images and designs which in the subconscious are associated with the product." Mr. Cheskin's clients include many of America's leading producers of consumer goods.

These motivational analysts, in working with the symbol manipulators, are adding depth to the selling of ideas and products. They are learning, for example, to offer us considerably more than the actual item involved. A Milwaukee advertising executive commented to colleagues in print on the fact that women will pay two dollars and a half for skin cream but no more than twenty-five cents for a cake of soap. Why? Soap, he explained, only promises to make them clean. The cream promises to make them beautiful. (Soaps have now started promising beauty as well as cleanness.) This executive added, "The women are buying a promise." Then he went on to say: "The cosmetic manufacturers are not selling lanolin, they are selling hope. . . . We no longer buy oranges, we buy vitality. We do not buy just an auto, we buy prestige."

The reason why I mention merchandisers more frequently than the other types of persuader in this exploration is that they have more billions of dollars immediately at stake and so have been pouring more effort into pioneering the depth approach. But the others—including publicists, fund raisers, politicians, and industrial personnel experts—are getting into the field rapidly, and others with anything to promote will presumably follow. . . .

The motivational analyst and symbol manipulator pooling their talents, and with millions of dollars at their disposal, make a fascinating and at times disturbing team. Results of their maneuvers indicate they are still quite a way from being infallible. Many of them are quick to admit their techniques are still not precise. But startling beginnings are being made.

These depth manipulators are, in their operations beneath the surface of American life, starting to acquire a power of persuasion that is becoming a matter of justifiable public scrutiny and concern.

⟐ E S S A Y S

Historians have found that reading the "texts" of mass culture—films, popular novels, magazines, popular music, even vernacular architecture—is a fruitful way to understand some of the cultural and social tensions of the 1950s. In the first essay, the late Roland Marchand, a prominent historian of advertising, examines a wide range of cultural artifacts and explores their connection to race relations, youth culture, and politics. In the second essay, George Mason University historian Kelly Schrum uses *Seventeen* magazine to explore the emergence of segmented advertising and its impact on young women's lives in the 1950s.

Visions of Classlessness

ROLAND MARCHAND

The constraints and sacrifices of World War II did not prepare Americans to meet the realities of the postwar era with equanimity.* Expectations ran high, despite underlying anxieties about atomic perils and the possibility of a postwar depression. Wartime discourse resonated with acclamations of equality and promises of the coming of a better, technologically wondrous life for all. The common man, idealized in nostalgic imagery, would carve out a future of unobstructed independence. Centralized controls, bureaucratic complexities, diminished autonomy for the individual— these were largely dismissed as the temporary conditions of war. Postwar popular culture reflected these expectations, expressing complacent satisfaction in the realization of some and providing vicarious compensations for the intense disappointment of others.

World War II came closer than any other twentieth-century phenomenon to enacting the drama of the melting pot in the United States, as disparate groups and values seemed to fuse into a composite national culture. Four years of war brought unprecedented national consolidation. Vast wartime migrations—to the armed forces and to war industries and boomtowns—undermined regional loyalties and broadened provincial horizons. Class barriers, and even some of the outward identifying

"Visions of Classlessness, Quests for Dominion: American Popular Culture," by Roland Marchand, from *Reshaping America: Society and Institutions, 1945–1960,* ed. Robert H. Bremner and Gary W. Reichard (Ohio State University Press: 1982). Reprinted by permission of the Estate of Roland Marchand.

*I am indebted to the students in my fall 1979 undergraduate seminar, and to David Brody, Eckard Toy, and James Lapsley, for their criticism of ideas contained in an initial version of this essay.

marks of class, seemed to disappear. The nation's dramatists of popular culture, its persuaders and performers, enlisted in the task of uniting the nation behind common assumptions.

The explicitly democratic themes of wartime popular culture promoted unity. Morale-builders stressed the idea of equal sacrifices and personalized the war through such democratic figures as G. I. Joe, Rosie the Riverter, Norman Rockwell's everyman figure in the "Freedom of Speech" poster, and Rockwell's Willie Gillis (the common man as G.I.). The war years also prolonged the modest redistribution of income from rich to poor that had begun during the 1930s. Although this process was to come to a standstill in the late 1940s, Americans emerged from the war confident of a snowballing trend toward economic democratization and a classless culture.

Meanwhile, in what Frank Fox has characterized as "World of Tomorrow" advertising, business interests painted stirring images of the technological future. Wartime research, when applied to consumer products, would bring new power and comfort to the common man in a "thermoplastic, aerodynamic, supersonic, electronic, gadgetonic" postwar world. Popular anticipation of a precise watershed moment—when the war would end and the "future" begin—took on a millennial cast. In style these wartime visions paralleled themes of the General Motors Futurama at the 1939 World's Fair. The message was one of man's technological dominion over nature, of machines as social solutions. Yet another wartime message, infused in advertising and other forms of popular culture, promised that victory would restore a cherished version of the true American way of life, based on the small town, the corner drugstore, and the close-knit family—an image aptly described as "American Pastoral."

Instead, the postwar world brought bureaucratic complexity, cold war insecurity, and a shrunken sense of individual mastery. It produced a technology of atomic peril as well as material comfort. Inspired by the sweeping democratic promises of wartime ideology and a hunger for security and stability, Americans welcomed the notion of classless prosperity. Enticed by expectations of increased power and control, they reacted with dismay as they found themselves slipping into a condition of greater vulnerability and dependency. In response they embraced popular culture reveries that seemed to enhance their sense of personal dominion.

The postwar period saw the emergence of a popular culture more homogeneous than Americans had previously known, as the cold war reinforced the trend toward consolidation. This greater homogeneity also reflected changes in demography, increasingly centralized production of popular culture images and artifacts, and more effective dissemination of popular culture by the media.

One measure of increasing homogeneity was a decline in competition from ethnic cultures. By the time of World War II, unrestricted immigration had been cut off for a full generation. Between 1940 and 1960 the percentage of foreign-born declined from 8.8 percent to 5.4 percent, and the percentage of Americans with at least one parent of foreign birth fell from 17 percent to 13.5 percent. A decline in carriers of ethnic culture such as foreign-language newspapers, theaters, musical organizations, and social halls reflected these demographic changes. Commercial entertainment increasingly outrivaled the attractions of ethnic folk culture and filled the new increments of leisure time. Network radio expanded its nationalizing and homogenizing influence, and radio sets in use increased right up to the advent of an even more powerful agent of common popular culture—television. Between 1940 and 1950 the "big four" popular periodicals, *Life, Reader's Digest, Look,* and *Saturday Evening Post,* increased their combined total circulation by 105 percent. Although some groups did maintain "taste subcultures," more and more Americans read, heard, and saw the same popular fare.

Another measure of homogeneity was the decline of class and regional differences in clothing and recreation. During the late 1940s sales of traditional work clothes fell precipitously, with the production of men's casual pants and shirts rising almost as rapidly. More workers wore casual clothes on the job, and off work men of different classes seemed indistinguishable on the street. *Life* referred matter-of-factly in 1949 to blue jeans as part of a national teenage "uniform." By the 1950s these classless, vaguely "western" progeny of democratic G.I. dungarees had come to symbolize the triumph of denim as an equalizing casual wear for virtually all Americans. Steady increases in the length of paid vacations for workers had also begun to equalize the distribution of formal leisure time. The Bureau of Labor Statistics even argued that by 1950 the earlier, distinctively "working class" patterns of spare-time activities and expenditures had almost disappeared among urban workers.

Signs of a national culture abounded. In the early 1950s, as journalist Russell Lynes remarked, Sears, Roebuck ceased publication of regional catalogs on the grounds that tastes in furniture had become identical throughout the country. *Fortune* reported that tastes in food were "flattening" regionally. Merchandising consultants began to talk about a "standard middle-majority package," a laundry list of home furnishings and other consumer goods that should be marketable to all families. One suburb looked pretty much like another; what Louise Huxtable has characterized as "Pop Architecture" dominated the landscape everywhere. Local bowling palaces, motels, and auto showrooms quickly copied the flash, glitter, and eccentric shapes of Las Vegas's "architecture of the road." Even where franchised chains did not proliferate, the designers of shopping centers and the entrepreneurs of a thousand "miracle miles" created uniform visual imagery.

The leveling of styles was in many ways a leveling *down*—a fact that did not escape the champions of high culture. In their search for the culprits of cultural debasement, they excoriated first the threats to literacy, order, and good taste coming from the comic book industry, and then the affronts to high culture by the new monster, TV. No previous mass medium, not even radio, expanded its audience so explosively as television. Households with TV sets mounted from fewer than one million in 1949 to more than 46 million in 1960, at which point 90 percent of all American homes were consuming TV programming at an average rate of five hours per day. The convenience of TV and the national standards of performance it set were devastating to provincial commercial entertainment and much of ethnic culture.

The 1950s would later seem a golden age of diversity and cultural quality on TV. But, fixing their gaze on Hopalong Cassidy, Milton Berle, wrestling matches, and formula westerns, contemporary critics denounced the new medium as an attack on culture and literacy. With the advance of TV, homogenized franchise operations, and organizational bureaucracy, a major debate erupted among intellectuals over the prospects and perils of mass culture. Even political concerns seemed to fade before the social menace of mass culture. Did a debased mass culture involve passivity, conformity, and a stifling of creativity in the audience and a formulaic, manipulative, whatever-will-sell attitude by the producer? Then TV seemed to its critics to have unquestionably triumphed as *the* mass culture medium.

Actually, TV probably served more to nationalize and homogenize than either to uplift or degrade. Television advertising embedded slogans, brand names, and affective imagery into the national consciousness with a new intensity, creating symbols for a more uniform national language. Television also helped promote the "common language" functions of national sports spectatorship. Together with convenient air travel, TV made attractive the nationalizing of the professional sports leagues. Minor league baseball declined as did a multitude of more significant local institutions—ethnic clubs, local union meetings, local political clubs—contributing, in Martin Mayer's view, to individual feelings of anomie and powerlessness.

Manufacturers of TV sets fought this negative interpretation of the social impact of TV. Their ads nostalgically depicted warm family scenes in which the connective links of the old family circle were restored in the harmony of the family semicircle plus TV. However specious the implied claims that TV would keep the kids home and the generations together, TV did serve the momentarily unifying function of making children more frequent participants in (or cospectators of) their parents' entertainment. . . .

The dream of suburban comfort and microcosmic control was a striking instance of upper-middle-class myopia. "Everybody" was *not* moving to the suburbs, despite impressions conveyed by Sunday supplements, TV advertisements, and popular sociology. Most housing developments were priced out of the range of those below the median income. The migration that inundated the suburbs came primarily from those among the top 40 percent in family income, especially those of the professional and technological elites who made impressive gains in income after 1945. Moreover, the most highly publicized sociological studies of suburbia focused on areas that were even more affluent than average—thus exaggerating "typical" suburban prosperity. Since writers, academics, and advertising executives came from the very segment of society making the most rapid gains, they found it easy to believe everyone was riding the same wave of prosperity. The idea of a consummated classlessness struck them with the force of a revelation.

The celebration of this "classless prosperity" permeated the popular culture that other Americans of the era consumed. Russell Lynes helped popularize the new "obsolescence" of class with his essay "High-brow, Low-brow, Middle-brow" in 1949. *Life* magazine's version carried a striking two-page chart depicting the cultural tastes of Lynes's various "brows" in ten categories ranging from furniture to entertainment. Economic classes were obsolete, Lynes insisted; people now chose their pleasures and consumer goods strictly on the basis of individual taste. Sociologist William Whyte noted the "displacement of the old class criterion" by "the impulse to 'culture' and 'good taste.'" Values were "coming together," he concluded, and the suburbs had become the "second great melting pot."

"The distinction between economic levels in the ownership of tangibles is diminishing," the Bureau of Labor Statistics noted, thus "breaking down the barriers of community and class." Sportswriters celebrated the supposed democratization of golf: "Class lines are eliminated," they argued, "when the nation wears sports clothes." Producers of the big-money TV quiz shows nurtured popular enthusiasm for illusions of equality by creating such folk heroes as the "cop who knew Shakespeare." The sponsor of "The $64,000 Question" explained: "We're trying to show

the country that the little people are really very intelligent. . . ." Winners were prototypes of the common man and woman, symbols of democratized intelligence.
Advertisers now cast affluent suburban families not only as models of appropriate
consumer styles but also as realistic portrayals of *average* Americans. In the 1920s
and 1930s, Americans had known that they were seeing explicit models of high
society "smartness" in many ads. Now they were encouraged to see the advertising
models as mirrors of themselves.

Such images and perceptions of classlessness eventually found expression in
the language itself. The 1961 *Webster's International Dictionary* acknowledged the
existence of a new word not recognized in earlier editions: *life-style.* This new term,
which gradually replaced the older phrase "way of life," conveyed nuances of
classlessness. The phrase "way of life," had been fully compatible with a recognition
of important economic class distinctions. Although people might be described as
seeking to *choose* or *achieve* a certain "way of life," they could also easily be thought
of as having inherited a particular way of life along with their class standing. But a
"life-style" was less likely to seem class-determined or inherited. the word *style*
suggested free choice, the uninhibited search for what looked and felt right. It might
also connote a particular consumer-consciousness, a notion of choosing among
various ensembles or "packages" of goods that represented a style consistency, i.e.,
that "went well together." Behind the rise of the word *life-style* lay the assumption
that increases in real income, the equalizing qualities of new synthetic fabrics and
suburban amenities, and the expansion of automobile and appliance ownership had
created a totally middle-class society in which all significant differences were simply
free expressions of personal tastes.

This vision reflected some real changes in American society. During the 1950s
the average income of all families and individuals rose 26 percent in real dollars, and
increased installment buying allowed many families to raise their living standard at
an even greater rate. Still, as Richard Parker has pointed out, "among those who
called themselves middle class, perhaps a majority have always lacked the money to
be in fact what they believe they are." It was those of high income, as ever, who consumed the bulk of popular culture products and services—whether sports event admissions, frozen foods, cars, or hi-fi components. And the gains that *were* achieved
by median and marginal sectors of the society did not represent gains in relative
wealth or power. In fact, those below the top 40 percent remained stationary in their
proportion of national income during the 1950s, and all but the wealthiest lost in
relative power. Despite the National Advertising Council's puffery about "people's
capitalism," corporate assets were more narrowly held in 1960 than in 1945.

Americans appreciated their new material comforts, but many no doubt sensed
an erosion of independence and control as large organizations in media, government,
and business overshadowed or preempted their spheres of competence and power. It
fell to popular culture to exorcise these demons and provide compensating, vicarious
adventures in potency and dominion.

Enter the Shmoo and Mike Hammer! Best described as a "snow-white ham with
legs," the Shmoo appeared in cartoonist Al Capp's 1948 parable on the quandaries
of prosperity. Lured musically into that consumer's paradise, the "Valley of the
Shmoon," Capp's hero Li'l Abner recognized the Shmoo as utopia incarnate. The accommodating little creature, so eager to please that it would die of sheer happiness
from one hungry look, provided for nearly all material needs. It laid eggs (in cartons)

and gave milk (bottled). Broiled, it made the finest steak; roasted, it resembled pork; fried, it came out chicken. And Shmoos reproduced at a remarkable rate.

A national favorite, the Shmoo recapitulated wartime promises. It offered families in Capp's Dogpatch lifelong control over the necessities of life, just as Americans had been led to dream of a technological utopia. In another sense the Shmoo, endlessly and identically reproduced, conjured up intimations of conformity, of boring and emotionless satiety. So dull was this prospect that Capp eventually had his obliging and well-merchandised progeny commit "Shmooicide." Although the spirit of the Shmoo lived on in such tangible forms as the energy consumption binge, the national credit card, and the Playboy bunny, Capp found its appropriate cartoon replacement in the Kigmy, who loved to be kicked. Americans of the era, Capp implied, sought a target for the release of aggression as keenly as they yearned for the security of the Shmoo.

Mike Hammer's phenomenal success as a popular culture hero seemed to confirm that notion. First appearing in 1947 in Mickey Spillane's *I, the Jury,* detective Mike Hammer rewrote the history of American best-sellers with his escapades of vengeance. His self-righteous vigilantism breathed contempt for established institutions and authorities. He worried that prosperity would make Americans soft and weak. And he banished the specters of impotence and conformity by acting remorselessly and alone:

> . . . I killed more people tonight than I have fingers on my hands. I shot them in cold blood and enjoyed every minute of it. . . . They were Commies, Lee. They were red sons-of-bitches who should have died long ago. . . . I just walked into that room with a tommy gun and shot their guts out. They never thought that there were people like me in this country. They figured us all to be soft as horse manure. . . .

For Americans beginning to suffer from a vague closed-in feeling, a restless frustration stemming from Russian threats abroad and the restraints and manipulations of large organizations at home, Mike Hammer represented recovery of a lost dominion. In postwar popular culture the defense of traditional masculinity was difficult to separate from this search for renewed dominion. John Cawelti aptly describes Spillane's "love" scenes as stripteases, many of them unconsummated sexual provocations that led ultimately to "fulfillment in violence." Contempt for women, expressed in frequent violence and sadism by Mike Hammer and in manipulative detachment by such mutant successors as James Bond and the Hugh Hefner Playboy, may have expressed fears of feminine power that went beyond insecure resentments of fancied sexual teasing. Modern society seemed to place "feminine" restraints on man's dominion. In large organizations the executive as well as the worker had to "subdue his personality to another's . . . to act like a good old-fashioned wife." One response in the popular culture was to reassert a compensating image of masculinity that conceded nothing to feminine limitations. . . .

As if in reaction to the blurring of sexual stereotypes during the war, popular culture accentuated women's strictly "feminine" roles. With the home symbolizing the security and stability recently thwarted by war and depression, the paramount role was homemaker. Pert, streamlined housewives dominated the ads. Although married women were employed outside the home in greater numbers than ever before, the popular media romanticized domesticity and elevated it to the status of a national purpose.

Less "feminine" roles for women were disparaged. "Woman driver" jokes reached a peak, and advertisements helped reassert masculine roles. Whereas automobile advertisements in the late 1920s and early 1930s had portrayed nearly as many women as men behind the wheel, those of the mid-1950s depicted far more men than women drivers. The occasional strong, independent female movie roles of the late 1930s disappeared by the 1950s. The older film seductresses who had projected poise, self-assurance, and a sense of challenge were superseded, most strikingly, by Marilyn Monroe, queen of the sexual Shmoos. Her salient qualities were availability and vulnerability. In their contribution to popular psychology, *Modern Woman: The Lost Sex,* Ferdinand Lundberg and Marynia Farnham reinforced notions of the mutual exclusiveness of feminine and masculine qualities. Women's aspirations to masculine achievement lay at the base of modern confusions and anxieties, they warned; only a return to total femininity could avert psychological disaster. In case children should fail to learn absolute gender distinctions from other forms of socialization, Cliff May's *Western Ranch Houses* described how dark wood paneling could be used to given the son's room a "strongly masculine air" and the daughter's room would be designed with "built-in femininity."

The emphasis on traditional masculinity may have stemmed in part from the fear that increasing leisure would tempt Americans to become soft—perhaps to lose their competitive drive and their will to resist communism. Another part may have arisen from the loss of a sense of achievement and mastery within the workplace and from indignities experienced in lives constrained by the actions of faceless organizations. The increased collective power that had subdued nature with vast highways and massive expenditures of electrical energy did not enhance the power of individuals in their increasingly complex interactions with other people. The traditional gender of the word *mastery* in American culture had been unequivocally male. Fears of powerlessness in the midst of mass society had unsurprisingly triggered ritual efforts to reaffirm the masculine.

Americans of the postwar era also sought solace from anxieties and frustrations by turning their search for dominion inward. Both religion and popular psychology flourished in the postwar era, as did hybrids of the two.

Church membership advanced steadily during the late 1940s and early 1950s until it reached the unprecedented level of 63 percent of all Americans. Works on religion, from the Revised Standard Bible to Catherine Marshall's *A Man Called Peter,* were nonfiction best-sellers. The religious novels of Lloyd Douglas and Sholem Asch gained a comparable place in popular fiction. Billy Graham, using every modern device from the card file to the television set, built upon his 1949 triumph in a Los Angeles evangelical crusade to gain a place among America's ten most-admired men by the mid-1950s. Monsignor Fulton J. Sheen adapted his theatrical style to the new media, and in 1953 was named television's man of the year. Church construction advanced at record rates, and the appearance of drive-in churches seemed to augur the assimilation of religion to a car culture that had already produced the drive-in restaurant and the drive-in movie.

In the atmosphere of a cold war against "atheistic" communism, religion tended to merge with patriotism. In the mid-1950s Congress sought to formalize the union by adding "under God" to the pledge of allegiance and establishing a prayer room in the Capitol. The physical mobility of the 1940s also enhanced the church's role as social anchor in the midst of social disruption, a place where new residents in a community might make social contacts. Theologian Will Herberg concluded that the three major faiths, Protestantism, Catholicism, and Judaism, had come to serve as a new American "triple melting pot" for third-generation immigrants as ethnic subcultures declined. But Herberg and other religious leaders also worried about the quality of the new "religious awakening." What could one make of an enthusiasm for faith in which 86 percent of all Americans declared the Bible to be the word of God, yet 53 percent could not name a single one of the four Gospels? Perhaps the answer lay in a 1957 Gallup poll in which 81 percent affirmed their expectation that "religion can answer all or most of today's problems."

Postwar piety was paralleled by a surge of psychology. The prewar decades had witnessed a considerable popularization of the concepts of psychology and psychiatry, especially among the well-educated. World War II increased popular awareness of applied psychology and its contributions to personnel selection and "adjustment." Familiarity with psychological jargon—neurosis, inferiority complex, schizophrenia, maladjustment—was already widespread. But in the postwar years, psychology became a popular mania. Publishers responded to a thirst for self-analysis quizzes, how-to-do-it manuals, and psychological advice. A typical issue of *Reader's Digest* contained at least two articles of the "What's Your Personality?" and "Do You Think like a Man or a Woman?" variety.

Among books and films one could almost predict that if it was "serious," it was also psychological. Even the durable western tended to become a stage setting for the playing out of psychological dramas. Advertisers threw themselves headlong into motivation research and "depth interviews" in a search for those "deep-lying habits, feelings, aversions, inner compulsions, and complexes" that might inhibit the buying impulse. Artzybasheff included in his fanciful cartoon of "Improved Design for Modern Man" for *Life* in 1951 a hole in the side of the modern woman's head labeled "Aperture for easy access to brain compartment by psycho-analyst." When Lucy set up her "Psychiatric Help—5¢" booth in Charles Schulz's popular "Peanuts" comic strip, it simply marked with mild satire a logical conclusion to the trend toward universal dissemination of popular psychology.

The craze for the psychological explanation did not reflect unequivocal acceptance of psychological techniques. True, psychologists were much in demand to provide explanations of juvenile delinquency, rock 'n' roll music, marriage problems, personal aptitudes, and college panty raids. Even the Kinsey Reports on sexual practices were accepted as useful by a majority of Americans. But the frequency with which psychology and psychoanalysis served as topics for humor attested to deep ambivalence about psychology's "contributions." Although psychology promised a kind of control, an opportunity to reshape one's personality or gain a form of dominion by understanding and manipulating others, it also awakened fears that one might be the *object* rather than the *agent* of manipulation.

In *The Hidden Persuaders* (1957), Vance Packard found a large audience for his warnings about dangers embedded in motivation research and subliminal suggestion by advertisers. Americans might have been more alarmed if they had been fully aware of such new psychological "machines" and techniques as the "People

Machine," Galvanic Skin Response, "Simulmatics," and "aroma mood music," to which some ad agencies were giving curious, if skeptical, attention. William Whyte, in *The Organization Man,* described the pressures toward conformity embodied in the proliferating personality tests given by business organizations. Whyte even appended a subversive chapter on "How to Cheat on Personality Tests" as his meager contribution to the preservation of personal dominion. Americans worried about "brain-washing," and 1950s science fiction movies were sometimes as concerned with loss of personal control, with invasion or infiltration by some alien force, as they were with the specter of atomic warfare. As the autonomy of the individual seemed to shrink, psychology, for all its fascination, still did not offer unequivocal assurance of gaining dominion over self.

Millions of Americans, however, hopefully sought such assurance from a fusion of psychology and religion. A major element in postwar popular culture was the "cult of reassurance," promoted most effectively by the Presbyterian minister Norman Vincent Peale. An amalgam of psychology and religion, the cult gained its initial postwar impulse from Rabbi Joshua Liebman's prescriptions for the cure of inner tensions in *Peace of Mind* (1946). Liebman's book topped the best-seller list in 1947 and eventually sold a million copies. Peale advanced the movement's momentum with his best-selling *A Guide to Confident Living* (1949) and then with *The Power of Positive Thinking* (1952), which dominated the nonfiction best-seller charts from 1952 to 1955, soon surpassing two million copies. . . .

A popular culture of reassurance was not everybody's answer to powerlessness. It was true that certain consolidating tendencies—the influences of network television and the common language and repetitive visual landscapes of national advertising, pop architecture, and restaurant and motel chains—worked to reinforce the "adjustment" theme of applied psychology. And it was true also that the "packaging" craze in popular culture, from shopping centers to entertainment "worlds" like Disneyland, helped push forward the process of homogenization by offering convenience and relief from individual decision-making. In fact, the whole Disney empire, from the "disneyfication" of children's classics to TV's Mickey Mouse Club and the Davy Crockett craze, strikingly epitomized the trend toward uniformity. But consolidation in popular culture did not advance undisturbed. As regional, ethnic, and visible class divergences began to fade, new fissures appeared. Some pursued the quest for dominion not through adjustment and reassurance but rather through excitement, diversity, and vicarious rebellion.

The most obvious, and to contemporaries the most shocking, new breach in society was an apparently increasing division based on age. Juvenile delinquency had appeared to rise during World War II and afterward. The striking increase in disposable income and free time among teen-agers in the late 1940s stamped adolescence as a social phenomenon rather than simply a stage in individual development. "The brute fact of today," Dr. Robert Linder warned a Los Angeles audience in 1954, "is that our youth is no longer in rebellion but in a condition of downright active and hostile mutiny." In "a profound and terrifying change," youth now acted out its "inner turmoil."

Psychological analyses of juveniles, both delinquent and normal, abounded. The film industry, reacting to the loss of its mass audience to television, began to produce specialized films for minority audiences—one of which was teen-agers.

Radio followed the same pattern. Advertisers soon recognized the existence of a massive teen-age market. Eugene Gilbert built a large marketing business by providing advertisers with inside information on teen-age consumers. His trick was spectacularly simple: employ teen-agers themselves to quiz other teen-agers about their wants and needs. Eventually *Life* confirmed the discovery of a teen-age market in an article entitled "A New $10 Billion Power: The U.S. Teen-age Consumer." *Life* personalized the story by featuring pictures of the loot accumulated by "the businessman's dream of the ideal teen-ager," Suzie Slattery from (where else?) California.

Attempts by the media to explore the rebellious aspects of the teen-age culture created new fissures in popular culture. In the movie *Rebel without a Cause* (1955), the plot and dialogue comprise a virtual textbook of popular psychology. The police lieutenant is an amateur psychologist; the hero's mother, a castrating female. The father's multiple complexes make him a complete buffoon. The hero's friend is a self-destructive neurotic, abandoned by his parents; and the heroine's father panics at her emerging sexuality and treats her with alternating rage and condescension. *Rebel without a Cause* was a "lesson" movie for parents: be careful and understanding, or this (rebellion) could happen to you. But James Dean's portrayal of the teen-age hero, his most influential acting role, diverted attention to the style and mannerisms of the misunderstood "rebel." Youths made the movie theirs. Vicarious rebels adopted the James Dean image as an expression of contempt for the satiated and challengeless life of middle-aged suburban America.

The evolution of popular music revealed even more vividly the process of disruption, the fraying of social nerves by age conflicts. Before the 1950s producers of popular music had largely ignored age differences, and the songs of adults and teen-agers were the same. As late as 1951 Gallup polls on favorite vocalists showed little variation among age groups. Far more significantly, the pollsters did not record responses for persons under 21. Yet teen-agers were already a major buying public for records, and the average age of purchasers continued to fall during the 1950s. With the rise of the 45 rpm record (cheap, unbreakable, easy to transport and change) and the transformation of radio in the early 1950s, the weight of teen-age preferences tipped the scales toward diversity in this form of popular culture.

Even earlier, fragmentation had begun to appear within the popular music industry. A boycott by radio stations in the early 1940s had broken the monopoly of the "big three" record companies. Radio disc jockeys gained new power, and technological advances meant that production of quality recordings was no longer confined to a handful of studios in New York, Chicago, and Los Angeles. Independent companies, the primary producers of "race" and "hillbilly" music, gained new opportunities. Still, the resulting tremors in the industry were relatively minor. From 1946 to 1953 the six dominant recording companies—Decca, Columbia, Victor, Capitol, MGM, and Mercury—recorded all but 5 of the 163 records that sold over a million copies.

Radio, in reaction to the abrupt abduction of its general audience by TV, cast about for minority tastes to satisfy. One market for subcultural programming was teen-agers. Specialized radio stations now gave them a medium of their own. Some argue that teen-age audiences created "rock 'n' roll." Others explain that TV, that powerful consolidating force in popular culture, was also, inadvertently, the cause of this vehicle of dissent and fragmentation. Both are largely correct; together these two forces set the stage for a popular culture explosion.

By 1953 certain ingredients of rock 'n' roll had been fermenting for several years. Migrations out of the South had increased national familiarity with "hillbilly" and black styles in music. In the late 1940s *Billboard* magazine, the arbiter of pop music, bolstered the respectability of both styles by rechristening the "hillbilly" category as "country and western" and race music" as "rhythm and blues." Elements of each style began to appear in pop hits. Meanwhile, with the postwar demise of the big bands, the individual singer gained prominence. Frank Sinatra epitomized the trend, winning the adulation of young "bobby-soxers" in the early 1940s and sustaining his popularity by projecting qualities of sincerity and involvement. Meanwhile, country singers Roy Acuff and then Hank Williams won huge followings with their sincere, emotional styles.

Against the backdrop of a pallid, taken-for-granted prosperity and cold war perils about which youth could do little, a thirst arose among the young for forms of popular culture that would permit expressions of highly personalized emotion. Frankie Laine ("Jezebel," "Your Cheatin' Heart," "I Believe") "sold Emotion . . . with a capital E" even more explicitly than did Sinatra. In 1951 Johnnie Ray stirred up a riotous teen-age response and set new standards for emotion and involvement in his popular hit "Cry." Ray, unlike Sinatra, was neither smooth nor controlled. He exposed an emotional vulnerability as he abandoned himself to the song's despair, "quivering, sobbing, crying and finally collapsing on the floor." Here were intimations not only of the impending rock 'n' roll performer as oracle of unconcealed emotion but also of the sensitive hero as victim.

It was in 1953 that Cleveland disc jockey Alan Freed, intrigued by his discovery that white adolescents were increasingly buying "rhythm and blues" records, initiated his "Moondog's Rock and Roll Party," playing records by black singers for a largely white teen-age radio audience. *Billboard* noted Freed's success. Record companies rushed to find white performers to "cover" (copy) up-tempo, heavy beat, rhythm and blues hits. Bill Haley and His Comets made the national pop charts with "Crazy Man Crazy" in 1953. The next year Haley's cover of "Shake, Rattle, and Roll" ranked in the top ten for twelve weeks, followed by an even longer run for "Rock around the Clock," the theme song from the popular film on juvenile delinquency *Blackboard Jungle.*

A mystique emerged that fused elements of Marlon Brando's role in *The Wild One,* James Dean's portrayal in *Rebel without a Cause,* J. D. Salinger's Holden Caulfield in *Catcher in the Rye,* the rebels of *Blackboard Jungle,* and the driving energy and aggressive sexuality of the new heroes of rock 'n' roll into a single image. The mystique emphasized a hunger for authenticity and sensitivity. In emotional expressiveness it ranged from moody insecurity to fierce independence with nuances of sexuality, pain, and violence. Raucous, exhibitionist rock 'n' roll singers disdained the "cool" of James Dean, but both expressed a contempt for hypocrisy and conventionality and used body language to convey emotion.

In 1956 the polarizing assault by rock 'n' roll on popular music (and on American culture generally) culminated. A black original, Little Richard's strident "Long Tall Sally," outsold Pat Boone's bland cover version. With his frantic movements and raucous shouts, Little Richard, in Charlie Gillett's words, was "coarse, uncultured, and uncontrolled, in every way hard for the musical establishment to take." The lines were being drawn largely on the basis of age, although the preference of many white teen-agers for "black" music added another dimension to the rift.

Critics of the new music and of the mixed-up, misunderstood hero decried the new mystique. The tough, self-pitying "sad-bad-boy" figures represented an "apotheosis of the immature." Rock 'n' roll used a jungle strain" to provoke a "wave of adolescent riot." How could a prosperous, middle-class nation find satisfaction in such moronic lyrics and "quivering adolescents"? *Time* compared rock 'n' roll concerts to Hitler's mass meetings, and other critics denounced the new music as nauseating and degenerate, an appeal to "vulgarism and animality." Could a consolidating popular culture even begin to bridge the gap suggested by such reactions?

Extreme views would remain irreconcilable. But 1955 elevated to stardom a versatile performer who brought the rock 'n' roll movement to a climax yet ultimately helped partially to reconcile rock with mainstream popular culture. Elvis Presley, the "hillbilly cat," as Greil Marcus writes, "deeply absorbed black music, and transformed it. . . ." The style of his early singles was "rockabilly"—"the only style of early rock 'n' roll that proved white boys could do it all—that they could be as strange, as exciting, as scary, and as free as the black men who were suddenly walking America's airwaves. . . ." Even as Elvis moved up to RCA and national fame in 1955 and 1956 with "Heartbreak Hotel" and "You Ain't Nuthin' But a Hound Dog," he continued to evoke sexuality, exhibitionism, and a defiance of restraint. Elvis projected emotional involvement; he encompassed the prized qualities of both toughness and vulnerability.

But Elvis not only fulfilled the image of frustrated, sensitive, rebellious hero for the new teen-age generation; he was also "hellbent on the mainstream." By the end of the 1950s, he had achieved hits with gospel songs and sentimental ballads. Eventually, one of his best-selling albums was "Blue Hawaii." His style encompassed schmaltz as well as rebellion, Las Vegas as well as Memphis. Along with Pat Boone, Bobby Darin, Bobby Rydell, Paul Anka, Ricky Nelson, and a host of new teen-age crooners, and with the added influence of Dick Clark's "American Bandstand" on TV, Elvis eased rock 'n' roll's way into the mainstream. The aura of challenge and threat in rock was overshadowed by the sentimentalities of teen-age love. By 1960 the popular music industry was fragmented. The venerable and consensus-based "Your Hit Parade" had expired after a period of senility, spurred on by rock 'n' roll. More concerned with the style of performance than with the song itself, the new rock audience was bored by interpretations of hit rock numbers by "Hit Parade" regulars. But, thus far, the fissure created in American popular culture by rock 'n' roll and generational stress had proved to be a crevice rather than a chasm.

Teen culture and rock 'n' roll, however, were not the only signs in the late 1950s of a possible countermarch in popular culture away from homogeneity toward segmentation. In reaction to the severe inroads of TV, movie-makers had sought specialized audiences that included intellectuals as well as teen-agers. Radio had fully adopted specialty programming. Gated, exclusive suburban developments gained in popularity. Portents of a difficult future for the great mass-circulation, general-audience magazines began to appear, as both *Life* and *Saturday Evening Post* lost advertising. Despite the "whitewardly mobile" messages of middle-class black magazines like *Ebony,* inklings could be found in the eventual movement of blacks to a more protective, conserving attitude toward the distinctive qualities of their own culture. On top of everything, enclaves of "beatniks" now flaunted a lifestyle even more irreconcilable with mainstream popular culture than that associated with rock 'n' roll.

One prospect for popular culture at the end of the 1950s was fragmentation, with increasing specialization in production and participation. But in one significant way, the consolidating process in American popular culture continued to move ahead. The history of modern popular culture is more characteristically an aspect of the history of business than an aspect of the histories of art, literature, music, or architecture. And the business interests that determined the available choices for *most* popular culture consumers had not been verging toward fragmentation or diversity. The "popular culture establishment"—in the form of CBS, NBC, and ABC, or General motors, Walt Disney Enterprises, MGM, and *Time-Life,* or the J. Walter Thompson, Young and Rubicam, and other great advertising agencies—certainly wielded a more extensive control over the range of products and images available to the public in 1960 than in 1945. These giants, like most of the small popular culture entrepreneurs, watched the sales figures, the Nielsen ratings, and the audience surveys and produced what would sell itself or sell the sponsor's goods. . . .

Beset by cold war fears and organizational complexities, Americans found solace in a popular culture that provided hopeful visions of an emerging classlessness and vicarious compensations for a hedged-in, manipulated feeling. Popular culture provided the fantasies, evasions, material artifacts, and vicarious experiences through which Americans tried to recapture a sense of dominion.

Making the American Girl

KELLY SCHRUM

Seventeen magazine made its debut in September 1944 amidst economic, social, cultural, and institutional changes that provided the basis for an emerging concept of the "teenage girl." The magazine's editors and publishers invested substantial resources in interpreting and promoting their definition of the prototypical teenager girl, "Teena." Slogans such as "Teena means business" had multiple interpretations: Teena meant advertising revenues for *Seventeen* as well as sales and profits for businesses that marketed to her, but she also had a future as a thoughtful, determined person with a mind of her own. *Seventeen* magazine was instrumental in developing the image of the teenage girl as a consumer of the magazine and the products advertised within its covers, but also as a member of society. It invested the teenage girl with two separate, yet related, identities: the image of a consumer for manufacturers, businessmen, and advertisers, and the image of a teenage girl for girls themselves. This essay begins by exploring the broader societal changes that led to the rise of teenage culture and *Seventeen*'s place within that culture. Deepening our understanding of consumer culture by focusing on the formation of an age- and gender-segmented market, it then analyzes *Seventeen*'s role in developing images of teenage girls through promotional materials, relationships with advertisers, and editorial content.

Seventeen magazine built on late nineteenth- and early twentieth-century developments in publishing. By the late nineteenth century, popular magazines had become commercial products that effectively blended editorial and advertising content. By

the twentieth century, magazines catered to a world in which the reader was perpet-
ually enticed and unfulfilled as advertisers began to focus on creating and appealing to consumer anxiety. The multiple roles of magazines blurred further through
design techniques such as ad-stripping and editorial advertisements. *Seventeen* used
both techniques while professing to teach teenage girls fashion sense and consumer
skills. To be effective, these strategies relied on a magazine's ability to target an increasingly homogeneous readership whose members were likely to purchase similar
products. Teenage girls proved to be such a group.

Why media devoted attention to teenage girls during World War II—a time of
instability, international insecurity, and mass destruction—must be addressed within
the larger context of the national emergence of teenage consumer culture. The most
noticeable change was economic growth. After the lean years of the 1930s, the United
States economy leaped into wartime production as federal expenditures rose from
$8.8 billion in 1939 to almost $100 billion in 1945. Although production of civilian
goods had slowed in 1942, supplies remained, and by spring 1944, when shortages
were most apparent, the peak of wartime production had passed. Even during shortages, retail sales increased because employment opportunities and real wages rose
and translated into consumer buying power for men, women, and children.

Advertising also did not suffer unduly, during the war or after. Throughout
Seventeen's early years, consumer goods and advertising budgets multiplied. Between 1939 and 1956, the number of national advertisers and brands merchandised
grew rapidly, as did advertising expenditures. Rather than risk accusations of un-
patriotic behavior during rationing, advertisers attempted to funnel consumer desire
into postwar purchases. One advertisement explained that consumers could not
lose: "Lucky gals may find some Featherknits at their favorite shops. Plucky gals will
be glad to wait for Victory." Such appeals were successful in both respects as sales
and profits remained high during the war and climbed even higher after its end. By
1945, Americans consumed many more goods than before the war. These conditions
opened the doors for *Seventeen*.

Economic prosperity translated into consumer power for teenagers as well as
adults and provided the material base for an evolving teen consumer culture. With
rising incomes and limited durable goods, more money was available for amenities.
Through increased allowances and work, teenagers secured more spending money
collectively than in previous years and as a poll in the mid-1940s found, the vast
majority of youth felt satisfied with the size of their discretionary spending budgets.
Business Week wrote in 1946 that the teenage market was undoubtedly accelerated
by the wartime economy and exclaimed, "Teen-age Market: It's 'Terrif'."

But economic prosperity and teenagers' enhanced buying power alone cannot
explain the emergence of a defined teenage culture. Other factors include teenagers'
decreasing presence in the full-time work force and greater high school attendance.
These trends enhanced the separation of teenagers from the adult world and increased
the potential for a distinct age-specific identity dependent on peers. In the decades
preceding World War II, the number of adolescents who worked full-time declined
due to mechanization, efforts of child labor reformers, and the Depression. Although
government officials, educators, and social scientists watched the rise in youth employment during the war with alarm, the long-term decline resumed after 1945. Combined with compulsory education laws, this led to greater high school enrollment.

The remarkable growth of high school attendance affected the formation of teenage culture as the proportion of fourteen- to seventeen-year-olds who attended high school grew from 11 percent in 1900, about 630,000 students, to almost 80 percent in 1940, over seven million students. Enrollment for girls roughly equaled that of boys. By the 1940s, the majority of American teenagers attended high school and a shrinking minority worked full-time. High school, although regulated and supervised by adults, was the central meeting place for teenagers, an arena for teenage interaction and peer influence. Advertisers and mass media helped create, and profited from, this group and the subculture developing around it.

The influence of school and peers, combined with the growing prominence throughout the early twentieth century of professionals who advised on family life and child-rearing practices, decreased parental authority. Social critics bemoaned these changes and castigated teenage culture and juvenile delinquency as their consequences. They also blamed these developments on the rising number of women in the work force, although mothers of *Seventeen* readers usually did not work.

Even when family life was not radically altered, teenagers began to rely more heavily on their peers and on commercial popular culture, such as movies and music, for guidance and entertainment. Teen canteens, teen- and community-organized places to dance and socialize, became popular during the war and, like music and movies, contributed to the teenager's designated role as consumer. *Seventeen* encouraged all these habits through monthly movie and music columns, as well as articles about popular teen canteens and how to start one. Soft drink companies heavily promoted teen canteens as well in order to enhance business. Academics and others involved with youth noted this growth of mass-produced, group-oriented entertainment popular among teenagers and worried over the loss of creative, individual entertainment.

While these teenagers were not the first youth to evoke adult concern, they were younger than those previously studied. "Youth," aged eighteen to twenty-four emerged in the 1920s as a distinct cultural entity, recognized in part by their trend-setting fashions. Estelle Ellis, the first promotional director at *Seventeen* magazine, noted, "They're growing older, younger," and by the late 1930s and early 1940s, the emerging image of the teenager, between the ages of thirteen and eighteen, embodied the new youth. In the early years of teenage consumer culture, advertisers and clothing manufacturers experimented with a wide variety of appellations for this group including "teenster" and "Petiteen." This attention to teenagers and interest in their sobriquets and habits marked the consumer-oriented transition from youth to teenager. The word "teenager" described a group defined by high school attendance. In the 1940s, however, this definition expanded, along with teenagers' growing economic power, to include participation in specific leisure activities, styles, and fashions that attracted national media and business attention, *Seventeen* capitalized on this attention in promoting teenage girls as a subculture.

Studying this subculture serves to balance a gender bias common in the literature about youth and youth culture. While recent work, such as Grace Palladino's *Teenagers,* addresses the lives of teenage girls as well as boys, much of the literature does not. Joseph Kett acknowledged in his innovative 1977 history of adolescence in the United States that his primary focus on males reflected his attempt to trace past discussions of youth, which were historically of boys. In the 1950s, as teenage culture became a widespread, national obsession, scholars and media continued to write predominantly about males, as reflected in James Gilbert's work on societal response to juvenile delinquency and male youth culture. Rock and roll, drag racing, and rebellion were the territory of boys.

As in Kett's book, most twentieth-century literature on boys emphasized education, work, independence, rebellion, and financial responsibility. The scant literature on female adolescents addressed issues of behavior, appearance, and relationships and idealized teenage girls for their domesticity and dependence on consumer goods to alleviate feelings of inferiority. These anxieties deepened as teenage girls were identified and targeted as a viable consumer group by *Seventeen* and its advertisers who depended on those insecurities and used them to help shape the teenager's consumer identity. The magazine cultivated concern about appearance, grooming, clothes, posture, figure, and weight, and offered products and advice as remedies.

Seventeen was not the first publication to notice teenage girls. Magazines such as *Parent's, Ladies' Home Journal,* and *Good Housekeeping* started monthly columns about, and sometimes for, teenage girls in the late 1930s. With names like "Sub-Deb" and "Teens of our Times," these columns recognized the teenage audience, but were confined to adult magazines. Although they spread information about teen social life and contributed to the definition of teenagers as a separate social category, these publications did not speak specifically to teenagers.

It was not until *Parent's* magazine attempted to reach this market in July 1941, with *Calling All Girls,* that an entire magazine focused on "girls and sub-debs." The magazine offered thirty-two pages of "girl comics" and a distinct tone, clearly articulated in its initial editorial message, "Well, girls, at last we have a magazine of comics, and stories and things that [are] published just for us! . . . Don't you think we should all get together to boost our own magazine? We want all the girls we know to read it too, don't we?" . . . The magazine addressed dating, beauty, fashion, and manners in addition to the comics, and circulation eventually reached a respectable 500,000. But the average age of readers was thirteen and the magazine never gained readership among high school girls. *American Girl,* the Girl Scout magazine, did not attract the general population of teenagers either and its circulation hovered around 200,000.

In comparison, *Seventeen* reached the teenage market far more successfully. The first issue in September 1944 sold out quickly—400,00 copies in six days. Circulation exceeded one million copies by February 1947 and two-and-a-half million by July 1949. *Seventeen* declared that through copies shared with friends and family, it reached over half of the six million teenage girls in the United States. The magazine's readers were mostly white middle- and upper-middle-class; 63 percent of their fathers worked as business executives, owners, professionals, or in other white-collar occupations and an additional 19 percent earned their living as skilled workers. This reader cohort was more heterogeneous than the very exclusive band of debutantes who had previously received sole media attention, but it still did not represent the entire population of teenage girls in the 1940s. In spite of this demographic reality, *Seventeen* claimed to be the voice of the aggregate population of teenage girls and declared itself the cultural mediator between the "American teenage girl" and advertisers, manufacturers, and mass media in general.

Those who did read *Seventeen* liked the magazine because it attempted to make its readers better teenagers rather than instant adults. Helen Valentine, *Seventeen's* first editor-in-chief, envisioned a magazine that would treat teenage girls seriously and respect what she perceived to be their emotional and intellectual needs. In addition to helping the teenage girl negotiate her way through the market and choose her first lipstick, Valentine wanted to teach her a "concern for how we are as persons, for how we relate to family and friends, how we present ourselves. But also a deep concern for what's happening in the world politically and socially. As women, as full human beings, to be part of the greater human struggle." Many teenage girls appreciated this effort. One teenager wrote to *Seventeen* exclaiming, "Congratulations for being smart enough to realize that we can take a dose of seriousness along with the more pleasurable fashions, beauty articles, etc." One admirer particularly appreciated the age-appropriateness, "Puleez, *Seventeen,* always stay seventeen. That is, some of these so-called magazines for the high school crowd we pick up either have us in the Fifth Grade having our pigtails pulled or seated at a bar in some swanky nightclub, fluttering eyelashes at some Navy lieutenant." This comment captures part of *Seventeen*'s successful formula and illustrates the degree to which teenage girls saw their age group as socially and culturally distinct.

Physically larger than today's magazine, *Seventeen* was initially 10⅜ by 13⅛ inches, printed on quality, thirty-five pound paper. The reader, first attracted to the colorful cover that promised "Young fashions and beauty, movies and music, ideas and people," would pause to view either a head-and-shoulder or full-body photograph of an innocent-looking, neatly dressed, young, white model, occasionally accompanied by a similar male or female model. The cover model and background promoted each month's theme and advertised clothing and accessories. The reader then turned past two full-page advertisements to find the contents and store locations of the cover fashions. She also found section headings, dividing the entire magazine into well-defined categories such as "What You Wear," "How You Look and Feel," "Getting Along in the World," "Your Mind," and "Having Fun." Whether the girl then turned straight to a seductive article or slowly wandered through the magazine's collage of images, colors, and words, she entered a world of advertising and advice, shopping and responsibility. Advice appeared in the voice of a big sister or aunt—older and experienced, yet friendly and concerned. For only fifteen cents, *Seventeen* offered moments of enjoyment for the curious and many hours of thorough reading for the dedicated.

The staff of *Seventeen* carefully shaped the public image of the teenage girl as her perceived power as a consumer increased and competition for the money she spent intensified. Among those charged with helping define and harness the teenage girl's consumer identity was a recent college graduate who, through a chance meeting with Valentine, began a career in promotion that continued for over fifty years. Estelle Ellis explained her prime responsibility as *Seventeen*'s promotional director as one of translation: to translate *Seventeen*'s editorial message, readers, and readers' buying power for the advertising industry, business, and retailers. "Of course the emphasis was on consumption—the buying power of this age group," she reflected, "to prove that this magazine had marketing power because it could move people to believe in it enough to want to buy the products that were in that magazine, whether it was editorial content or ads." The significant amount of money Triangle Publications spent to create and distribute its image, attract advertising, and strengthen the teenage market attests to their seriousness in achieving this goal.

Ellis's promotional materials from the first six years of *Seventeen*'s history, 1944–1950, provide a unique glimpse of this transition during the formation of the teenage girl's consumer identity. She designed these materials to convince the business community to invest money in the magazine and in marketing to teenage girls, and she always emphasized girls' value as consumers—how many there were, how much money they spent annually on clothes, shoes, hats, cosmetics, and shampoo, and how to reach them. She also presented the teenage girl as responsible, a future voting, consuming citizen with a family to shop for and an eye on world politics.

Ellis based the "ideal teenage girl" on her own personal impressions and experiences. It was over a year after the initial planning meetings and six months after *Seventeen*'s first publication that the magazine undertook its first substantial market research in 1945 entitled *Life with Teena: A Seventeen Magazine Survey* to study, personalize, and package the teenage girl as a consumer. *Seventeen* embodied the results in a prototypical teenage girl they created and named "Teena." As with contemporary sociological and psychological studies of girls, market researchers assumed that teenage girls invested substantial time and energy in commercial self-improvement by purchasing fashion and beauty products. The survey examined Teena's family, educational background, future plans, and favorite types of entertainment, but focused primarily on clothes, cosmetics, and personal grooming items. The most detailed section surveyed recent purchases and brand preferences. A follow-up study in June 1946, *Life with Teena, Volume II—Food,* expanded to include teenage girls who did not read *Seventeen* and surveyed teenagers' food consumption habits, specifically focusing on name brand recognition of, and preferences for, packaged food.

Many of the promotional materials *Seventeen* sent to retailers, advertising agencies, and manufacturers or published in advertising trade journals emphasized the teenage girl's decision-making and purchasing power. Ellis combined slogans with census and consumer information on the six million girls between the ages of thirteen and eighteen who spent two billion dollars annually on food, clothing, cosmetics, and entertainment. One sales pitch read, "Teena is a good listener. . . . Tell her your sales story! Teena, the high school girl has a mind of her own—but it's open to suggestions. . . . At a fast-growing fashion-conscious age, Teena and her teen-mates comprise a market . . . that is strong in its buying power and positive in its brand preferences."

In the promotional materials, Ellis also emphasized *Seventeen*'s success with the teenage reader, both as a magazine through editorial content and as a venue for distributing advertising messages. A 1946 campaign contained "love letters" written to *Seventeen* primarily from manufacturers, retailers, and advertising agencies. The letters applauded the magazine's marketing success: "The ad we ran in *Seventeen* made mail order history for Neiman-Marcus." These testimonials were sent out to convince other advertisers of teenage girls' buying power and of *Seventeen*'s role as the appropriate avenue for reaching their pocketbooks. . . .

Ellis's promotional materials repeatedly emphasized readers' devotion to the magazine and belief in what they read there: "A dress is a dress is a dress until you see it in *Seventeen!*" because "naturally, Teena finds the answer to her needs and wants in the magazine she reads and believes—*Seventeen*." But this message had to be carefully constructed. *Seventeen* strove to persuade the advertisers that Teena could be convinced to buy almost anything, but had to avoid the dangers in promoting the image of purely irrational, silly girls. When it came to the magazine, therefore, *Seventeen* claimed, "There's nothing fickle about our girl Teena. . . . She's sold on *Seventeen*—sold solid on everything in it." It connected Teena as an individual to Teena as a generic member of a broader category and magnified each teenage girl's individual buying power through her collective strength.

Promotional materials emphasized girls' independence from adults and children as well as their dependence on peers and group pressure. Ellis always implied, and often explicitly stated, that teenage girls bought as a group—an advertisement strategically placed between its covers would sell not just one girl, but the whole crowd. If Teena liked it, all six million teenage girls would. "Teena is a copycat—what a break for you!" The copy continued, "She and her teen-mates speak the same language . . . wear the same clothes . . . use the same brand of lipstick." When addressing advertisers, *Seventeen* therefore highlighted the developing intensity of peer groups, especially in the high school, and the increasing role friends played in behavior and consumer decisions.

At the same time the magazine depended on advertisers' belief in the reliability of teenage girls as a unified market, it strove to combat negative stereotypes of swooning bobby-soxers. In an attempt to develop positive images of the teenage girl as a valuable member of society, Ellis highlighted one of *Seventeen*'s editorial messages—that the teenage girl cared about her world and would one day be a responsible citizen and therefore a responsible consumer. A March 1946 promotion emphasized that "Seventeeners are intensely curious about the place in the world they're slated to inherit. Adult-level articles on politics, civics and world affairs are featured regularly." In combination, these promotional materials represented the identity *Seventeen* magazine presented to the advertising and business world: an intelligent yet impressionable, consumption-oriented, economically powerful, peer-dependent, teenage female consumer.

Beyond selling the teenage girl as consumer to attract advertising, *Seventeen* had a vested interest in shaping her image in the advertising content. To further its vision, as well as attract revenue, the magazine created an advertising advisory board to encourage age-appropriate advertisements and unite advertising and editorial content into a seamless product. The magazine tried to build a wholesome image and quickly earned a reputation for strict standards regarding advertisements and products. This was not easy in the beginning, but *Seventeen* worked quickly to replace advertisements it considered inappropriate. Success in this area was significant because the promotion department convinced advertisers to create special images and copy for *Seventeen* and the teenage market that required substantial investment of money and resources. Willingness to make such an investment demonstrated advertisers' considerable interest in the female teenage market.

To help advertisers create the advertising *Seventeen* desired, the advisory board produced a booklet entitled "Who Is Teena? Judy Jeckyll or Formalda Hyde?" that recommended ways to bridge the gap between editorial and advertising content. The cover pictured a girl split in half. One half was Teena, the ideal *Seventeen* teenager in a sweater and skirt with long, straight hair and no make-up. The other half depicted her opposite—a girl in a slinky evening gown and fishnet stockings with lipstick, rouge, big earrings, and hair piled on her head. The booklet asked why advertisers tried to attract the teenage girl with slang or sell her on "glamour girls who piled on the warpaint . . . wore bird nest hair-do's and sprouted claw-y fingernails." *Seventeen* preferred a "wholesome" teenage girl, neither her mother nor her younger sister, who dressed neatly and conservatively for high school and dates. This idealized, wholesome girl, who was always white, quiet, and virginal, excluded many real-life teenage girls who were nevertheless supposed to identify with, and aspire to, this image.

One of *Seventeen*'s primary concerns in constructing this image was the negotiation and control of teenage girls' sexuality. Girls were supposed to think about being attractive and highlighting their feminine qualities, but not about wearing fishnet stockings or big earrings. General fear of conspicuous sexuality, combined with the wartime panic over female sex delinquents, led the magazine to be even more cautious in shaping Teena's sexuality. The magazine tried to manage her sexuality without compromising sexual allure. The sweater and skirt implied white, middle- to upper-middle-class girls who controlled their sexuality, used it only to attract men, and then safely tucked it away for the postnuptial bedroom.

These efforts to encourage a more homogenous, sexually attractive but controlled teenage image were fairly successful. Teen cosmetics and back-to-school dresses replaced movie fan magazine holdovers, such as sexy make-up and blond hair dye, in *Seventeen*'s advertising pages. Slang use and advertisements for older women appeared less frequently. Advertisements for shoes with four-inch spiked heels, like the one named "Jr. Skyscraper[,]" gradually gave way to ones for flat or low-heeled shoes, such as the "American Revolution" in low heels. The switch to low heels further symbolized Teena's conservative, controlled sexuality, never flashy or loud.

To further ensure controlled sexuality, perfume advertisements quickly toned down their appeal from Varva perfume's 1944 slogan, "She's Varvacious. Her presence is dynamic . . . her attraction undeniable . . . her impression unforgettable," accompanied by a sexy woman wearing an evening dress and long gloves, to Beau Catcher Perfume. The teenager in the 1945 Beau Catcher advertisement was still trying to lasso a man (literally), but wearing a short polka dot skirt and a pony tail; the copy read, "It's the saucy scent that won't take 'no' for an answer . . . fills your date book." Both were trying to catch men, but while the Beau Catcher wanted dates, the Varvacious woman was looking for a longer evening. Teena was undeniably the former, longing for a prom date who would admire and marry, but not kiss, her.

The promotion department accomplished many of its goals. Although some advertisers initially doubted the economic viability of the female teenage market, within two years advertisers purchased more ad lineage in *Seventeen* than in all other youth magazines combined. Estelle Ellis and her staff successfully encouraged advertisers not only to purchase space in *Seventeen*'s pages but to invest money into redesigning their advertisements or creating entirely new advertising campaigns. *Seventeen* controlled what products it would and would not accept, a formidable feat for a new publication, and worked to shape the image of teenage girls as consumers. While the teenage girl's identity, as displayed in advertisements, varied, it was consistently consumer-oriented. The editorial message was less uniformly and more subtly so.

As *Seventeen* negotiated with advertisers, it also negotiated with readers, responding to them but ultimately controlling the final product. In such a young publication with a newly defined market, boundaries were unclear and the editorial and advertising pages sometimes worked together and at other times offered multiple messages for broader appeal. Valentine and the editorial staff worked as hard to create an image of the teenage girl for readers and for society at large as the promotional staff did to attract advertisers. This editorial task was complicated by a desire to help girls forge their own way through their problems and the world, and, at the same time, a wish to communicate directly with girls as responsible young women.

Seventeen's relationship with its readers is difficult to assess. The magazine welcomed, even solicited, readers' comments and reactions to the magazine. In response to reader requests, the magazine added a fiction component and a section entitled "It's All Yours," with stories, poems, and pictures created by teenagers. Readers themselves often articulated both sides of the conflicting messages within the magazine and demonstrated the diversity of its audience. Their responses serve as a gauge of teenage girls' responses, a glimpse at how they consumed and reacted to *Seventeen* and how the magazine utilized or ignored their requests. The magazine listened to their compliments and complaints in shaping and reshaping the image of the teenage girl it displayed for reader consumption, even as it maintained control of that image.

Valentine envisioned a magazine that would speak to all female teenage readers, to the studious future doctor as well as the future homemaker—a magazine that combined "boys and books, clothes and current events, people and politics, cooking and careers." Inherent in such a vision was some degree of conflict—cooking and careers were not always compatible. On one level, *Seventeen* was primarily a fashion and beauty magazine that cultivated insecurity and the constant need for personal improvement, similar to its advertising content. But true to the editor's promise, *Seventeen* also recommended books on inflation and atomic energy, offered articles on politics and world affairs, and encouraged its readers to take responsibility for themselves and become active, questioning citizens. The result was a kind of civic consumerism, combining one's democratic role as [an] active citizen with one's duty as a responsible and active consumer. This discussion occurred within a sheltered, limited world, but even within it, not all was uniform. A close examination of *Seventeen*'s major themes—fashion and beauty, boys, education, and politics— reveals that the magazine did not attempt to portray teenage girls as solely one-dimensional or homogenous. To appeal to the interests of all its readers, the magazine offered a variety of messages that remained open to multiple interpretations.

In controlling that image, *Seventeen* was no exception to the general emphasis of women's magazines on fashion, beauty, health, and the continual need to improve oneself; its innovation was in the group of consumers it targeted. Cosmetics and the pursuit of beauty were commercial industries by the late nineteenth century and by 1921 were firmly rooted in American culture with the first Miss America beauty pageant. Also well established long before *Seventeen* was the notion that beauty was available for the price of hair products, deodorant, or cosmetics. The fashion industry depended on feelings of inadequacy and the potential for redemption through consumption. In *Seventeen*'s first issue, 70 percent of the total paid and editorial advertising pages were for bras, girdles, hair and nail products, make-up, or shoes. Within five years, that total soared to 88 percent. On the editorial side, *Seventeen* contained articles such as "Year-Round Beauty" that encouraged concern with personal beauty: "You want to be more attractive—you and every woman between the ages of four and eighty-eight! You want Tom to be pleased with the way you look, and Joe and Eric and Ted. And you want to be pleased with yourself! This isn't vanity. It's perfectly natural and we're all for it." The professed ultimate goal of this obsession—to free oneself from these petty worries and focus attention on others—was rather flimsy, given that once insecurity was cultivated, few could escape its lingering doubts. Sometimes *Seventeen* informed readers that all problems could be corrected or camouflaged through fashion tricks or commercial products, and other times it emphasized general health, cleanliness, and exercise. The overarching theme, however, was still concern with one's physical appearance, a message woven deeply into the magazine's editorial and advertising pages.

Teenagers responded in a variety of ways—some applauded, some criticized, but most accepted the critical importance of beauty. Many teenagers wrote that *Seventeen*'s advice had changed their habits forever: "Believe me—I decided maybe I'd better make some repairs on myself and I must admit they've helped." But not all teens accepted the fashion and beauty advice unquestioningly and one responded to an article on Christian Dior and the "New Look," "Nauseating! That's the only way to describe the replicas of the clothes our mothers wore twenty years ago." She was not questioning the desire for beauty, however, but the path toward attaining it, and the magazine continued the quest for beauty within its pages.

Seventeen did not always agree with its readers. A telling example of teenagers' resistance to *Seventeen*'s advertising and editorial message that did not elicit change involved girdles. *Seventeen*'s early market research showed that the majority of readers did not wear girdles; in fact 74 percent did not even own a girdle and another 19 percent owned only one. *Seventeen,* however, strongly encouraged wearing a girdle through articles and advertising. "A Fine Figger—Or Else" and "Wear a Girdle" reinforced the message that "Girdles help the adolescent silhouette take shape. . . . *Seventeen* feels strongly about this." Girdle advertising copy similarly tried to convince teenage girls that their figures, though young, required improvement: "Some of you may not have had to figure on your figure much as yet. . . . [But] even the youngest of us needs a kind but firm control to mould [*sic*] us and hold us in the way we should go."

Seventeen readers responded in a variety of ways. One mother wrote thanking *Seventeen* for her daughter's conversion, but more teenagers wrote in disagreement: "I definitely do not agree with your article, 'Wear a Girdle'. . . . I feel that there are many girls, including myself, who do not need one. . . . Hence I say: girdles . . . fooey!" Thus, fashion and beauty advice, prevalent throughout each issue and often fueling feelings of insecurity, was complex and questioned by readers. The number of manufacturers producing girdles for teenagers continued to rise in the late 1940s. Combined with the "New Look" that dictated a tiny waist and exaggerated female figure, girdle use probably increased among teenagers. But teenage girls were not passively accepting all fashion mandates, and even a magazine that continued to promote girdles had to register its readers' dissent.

Articles, advertisements, and letters on dating, kissing, and marriage continued the trend towards offering multiple messages on a topic. According to studies conducted in the late 1930s and early 1940s, teenage girls were deeply concerned about male-female relationships. *Seventeen* both fueled and countered this interest by encouraging dating but emphasizing tame sexuality. "Good" girls in the 1940s were advised to snare or catch a boyfriend or date, but always passively. *Seventeen* counseled girls to combine physical attractiveness with strong moral virtues. Starting in April 1945, the magazine devoted an annual issue to the theme "Boy meets Girl," in addition to articles on how to converse with and attract boys and the ubiquitous teenage romance fiction. *Seventeen* encouraged teenage girls to concentrate their energy on boys and to attract male attention, but strongly discouraged necking, petting, going steady, or early marriage.

Teenagers did not always agree. Again *Seventeen*'s editors allowed them an outlet to voice their dissent, but did not alter the magazine's message. A 1942 *Fortune* survey of teenagers' attitudes showed that although girls condemned necking on a moral basis more frequently than boys, they participated in roughly equal numbers, 71 percent for boys and 63 percent for girls. Teenagers expressed these feelings in letters to *Seventeen:* "In the gang I go with, the boys are really swell. At least I thought so until I read your article. We are actually wicked enough to believe in necking. And, hold your hat, I really enjoy it!" *Seventeen,* however, continued to discourage kissing in articles such as "No for an Answer" and "How to Say No Nicely."

The continual focus on boys advised girls not to talk too much, but rather to ask the boy about himself and to always sound interested. "How to Win Men and Influence Statistics," in April 1949, gave opposing advice. Ignore the statistics that college-educated women never marry, *Seventeen* warned, and never change just to attract a boy. A girl cannot please every man she meets, "So why not decide to suit yourself and be sure of pleasing one person at least?" In response to these and similar conflicting messages, one reader wrote, "A girl's life is not centered around boys all the time, just pleasing them and living for them."

Beyond dating and kissing, marriage dawned as an increasingly imminent prospect for teenagers. The median age at first marriage for females fell from 22.0 in 1890 to 21.5 in 1940 and 20.3 in 1950. The median age for males at first marriage also declined from 26.1 in 1890 to 24.3 in 1940 and 22.8 in 1950. *Seventeen*'s editorial message not to marry young was increasingly in conflict with its proliferation of wedding-related advertisements for engagement rings, hope chests, silver, linen, china, and carpets. Such advertisements always emphasized the wisdom of planning young, starting a hope chest and silver collection in preparation for the inevitable, much anticipated, heterosexual marriage.

Seventeen further complicated its messages in 1948 with a new "Food and Home Doings" section and articles on choosing silver patterns and filling hope chests, but it continued to encourage education over early marriage. Not only was seventeen too young to marry, *Seventeen* opined, but the magazine also urged readers to plan education and careers. As the debate regarding the validity of academic education versus domestic training for women raged, the magazine validated all options. *Seventeen* encouraged those with aptitude for college to continue their education and printed articles on choosing a college and financing higher education. Although career articles often highlighted traditional female jobs such as teaching, nursing, and secretarial work, some discussed new opportunities for women in publishing and banking. "So You Want to Be a Scientist?" informed readers that, "Women are discovering a 'new' industry for themselves." The article continued, "[W]omen have been showing themselves to be just as brightly intelligent about aerodynamics and isotopes, equations and Bunsen burners, as the next man." College bound or not, the message that work might be a necessity was also clearly stated: "A girl who plans to mark time in a job until marriage, or thinks a bridal veil cancels jobs forever, is flouting the statistics. Over a third of the women in America who are of working age work for a living." These messages reflected options open to some women and encouraged well-informed decisions, but the emphasis on college and professional careers reflected the experiences of Helen Valentine and the editorial staff. They were predominantly college-educated women who often continued to work after marriage and children. As a whole, however, career articles did not overshadow *Seventeen*'s emphasis on cleaning, decorating, shopping, cooking, or planning parties. But they did signify—and help legitimate—new opportunities for women.

The issue was further clouded by messages that reinforced good study habits and continued education, but projected negative images of smart women. In one Singer advertisement, " 'The Brain' learns an angle *not* in the geometry book. Carol is our Valedictorian and a math shark, but as my brother Boz remarked—'too bad she dresses like the square root of pi.' " After learning the secrets of Singer's teenage sewing course, Carol received the desired male attention. A comical rendition of prom disasters, "How Not to Get Another Prom Bid," however, rendered the bookworm with glasses doomed because of her intelligence: "Big books and words denote a brain / All beaux will fear to date again." The first girl ended up with dates *in spite* of her intelligence because she learned to dress well while the second lost out completely. *Seventeen* was both encouraging and discouraging regarding education and careers. It responded to requests for college and career advice, yet continued to project negative stereotypes of intelligent women. This attempt to appeal to a wider range of girls and expand their ideas of women's opportunities did not challenge the cultural norms that shaped women as consumers.

Beyond beauty, careers, and relationships, *Seventeen* attempted to bolster teenage girls' responsibility as individuals and citizens. "We expect you to run this world a lot more sensibly than we have," the editors declared in April 1945 as war in Europe approached an end. Such pronouncements can easily be dismissed as hypocritical cover for advertising and promotion of consumerism, but to assume that any women's magazine could only teach fashion denies *Seventeen*'s breadth and depth of coverage of world affairs and politics. It also assumes a disinterested reception on the part of readers. The New Year's editorial letter in January 1945 criticized the intolerant or those with a "terrific preoccupation with the way your hair curls" and declared, "Here is our world, sick and in need of healing. Here are you—the generation whose gigantic job it will be to bring us back into a balance of sanity. . . . Never for a moment think: I'm only a girl in my teens, what can *I* do? You can do plenty." This message criticized a sole preoccupation with curls if it precluded citizenship, but did not challenge the importance of fashion and beauty. It reflected the assumption that teenage girls needed encouragement to care about their world, as well as the belief that they could and should care.

The theme of personal responsibility resonated throughout the first six years of *Seventeen* among all the beauty and fashion, with the goal of cultivating responsible, democratic, consuming citizens. This theme was prevalent in American society throughout the war. It was every person's patriotic duty to purchase war bonds and to pay regulated prices. Hoarding goods or paying inflated prices was un-American and undemocratic. After the war, *Seventeen* continued to link the themes of responsibility with consumption and to encourage both separately. The proportions were unbalanced in favor of gratuitous consumerism, but to conclude that it was merely a token attempt to appear non-frivolous is to assume that the serious content meant nothing for the girls who read the magazine. In contrast, there is ample evidence that in addition to praise from national service organizations, teachers, and parents, many teenagers supported these efforts. The enormous growth and circulation figures attest to the popularity of the magazine as a whole, and readers' letters printed in the magazine were disproportionately in favor of teaching teenagers about the problems and complex issues of the world and in encouraging them to participate actively. Whether this imbalance demonstrates the actual proportion of letters received or an editorial bias in favor of these responses, it reflects at a minimum a strong editorial commitment to personal responsibility in national and world affairs and support among readers.

There were, of course, dissenting voices. Occasionally *Seventeen* printed letters complaining about the editorial content, "Why, oh why, must you print articles on world affairs in a magazine that a girl looks to for advice on clothes, charm and personality?" or "I think you should have more articles on dates and shyness. . . . Stories like those on Atomic Energy are *very* boring." *Seventeen* editors took this criticism seriously and replied, "If enough world citizens are similarly bored by atomic energy, we fear that teen-agers may find themselves with no dates left to worry about." But other teenage girls praised the effort: "Although I am thirteen, I feel that I am not too young to think seriously about the part I am to play in the great postwar world." Another reader agreed, "Seven out of ten teen-age girls don't know half as much as they should about world affairs. . . . *Seventeen* can and *must* create a teen-age interest in world affairs." These and similar letters attest that at least some teenage girls were serious, concerned individuals who wanted the magazine that claimed to represent them to reflect their values and discuss world issues. Few read only the serious articles; they could have read other magazines or newspapers if this was their sole desire. But *Seventeen* strove to attain a balance between fun and substantive material and most readers consumed the magazine for this combination, some asking for more, some less, of each.

The world in which *Seventeen* appeared was not comforting, but the magazine did not encourage its readers to ignore disturbing issues. The first issue was published eight months before the end of World War II in Europe and almost a year before the United States dropped an atomic bomb on Hiroshima. Although *Seventeen* readers themselves may not have been as affected by shortages and working mothers as other teens, the war's psychological impact was apparent in articles on postwar peace, dangers of wartime inflation, and war refugees. *Seventeen* readers responded with letters, donations, and volunteer work.

Atomic energy also captured public attention in 1945. The article "Atomic Energy . . . Fearful Miracle" explained how atomic energy was produced and discussed its potential uses, both destructive and beneficial. In May 1946, *Seventeen* recommended the book *One World or None: A Report to the Public on the Full Meaning of the Atomic Bomb.* Warning the reader to expect big words and scientific terms, the reviewer emphasized its importance: "This is a book you must read, think about and discuss. You've absolutely got to realize that the problems presented in it are your own, not those of other people. You are a citizen of the world; you must bear the responsibility." *Seventeen*'s editors always treated war issues seriously and encouraged education, individual responsibility, and action.

Stressing this theme of responsibility, *Seventeen* strongly encouraged political involvement and knowledge of current events. It advised young women to develop political acumen in preparation for their role as voting citizens: "You're not old enough to vote—but you certainly can *think!*" The article "Straw Vote" furthered the connection between good citizenship and good consumerism when it compared voting to dress shopping. With a five-point plan for choosing a candidate that advised teenagers to research important issues, study past records of candidates and party platforms, and analyze campaign speeches, a wise shopper could easily apply her skills to become a wise voter.

Voting and democracy, as well as pride in America and the right to buy goods, were common themes throughout this period, a reflection of both lingering war rhetoric and the beginning of the cold war. Discussions of tolerance and prejudice appeared throughout *Seventeen*'s first six years—a call for tolerance that encouraged cultural homogenization and often denied ethnic differences. But *Seventeen* did not interpret this declaration of equality as a challenge to its own pages that continued to picture only white models. T. F. in Chicago responded to the article "What Kind of World," "I'm a Negro, and my people are one of the many victims of prejudice. The article didn't exactly make 'life beautiful,' but it did help me to see through a lot." She then asked, "Could you have an article written on the part the colored boys are taking in this war? They're not all smiles the way pictures show them. They work hard. They sweat and shed blood, too. They give their lives, and above all, they're humans." This girl's poignant letter exemplified the complexity of racism and the ideals of tolerance versus acceptance. The writer simultaneously accepted the magazine's affirmative message and recognized the shallowness of such messages of harmony and unity.

So who were these consumers of *Seventeen* magazine and how did the magazine influence their lives? Their world was changing and increasingly reflected the role of high school and peers, as well as that of mass media like *Seventeen*. Although their family life may not have changed drastically during the war, they were still affected by the important issues of the day. They looked to their contemporaries for what to wear and how to behave, but also wanted advice from respected sources other than parents or teachers. Teenagers wanted guidance in fashion and dating etiquette, but also in becoming teenagers. *Seventeen* worked hard to address these issues and to communicate with teenagers seriously about the problems central to their lives. Although the advice was often similar to that given by teachers, parents, and professionals, its delivery in a teen-oriented package was both more acceptable and rooted in consumerism.

Seventeen magazine was a product of the 1940s. Manufacturers, advertisers, and businesses were interested in teenage girls and what they consumed. *Seventeen* actively recruited and shaped that energy and served as both creator of and vehicle for the teenage girl's consumer identity. It played a significant role in identifying and constructing teenage girls as a distinct group through negotiations among the magazine's staff and with advertisers over the teenage girl's identity. This discussion continued within its pages over how to appeal to a large audience's diverse interests and goals. The bulk of the magazine focused on fashion and beauty, but it was also a magazine designed to respect teenage girls' concerns and intelligence and to encourage their self-awareness as a group. While these intentions were occasionally inconsistent, *Seventeen* attempted to display them all.

Sometimes political messages merged with the dominant fashion and consumer-oriented aspects of the magazine and sometimes they simply appeared side-by-side. In one vivid example, an editorial Christmas letter expressed sorrow over the war while the editorial advertisement on the opposite page displayed a colorful holiday dress with the caption, 'As long as no one seems to be looking at the Christmas cards anyway, we might as well tell you that the bold-checked basque-bodice dress . . . is $14.95." What message the reader grasped from these two pages is difficult to assess—perhaps a message of peace, an idea for a party dress and new hair style, or a feeling that sadness existed but was potentially alleviated by pretty dresses. It is possible that the focus on good citizenship was simply a shallow attempt to fill pages and appear respectable, a façade over the desire to sell products. Or that the magazine was in transition, trying alternative approaches to create a successful, marketable product. Most likely, *Seventeen* offered myriad messages intending to appeal to readers with varying interests with the ultimate aim of cultivating consuming citizens who voted responsibly with their dollars and their ballots.

These possibilities are not mutually exclusive. *Seventeen* magazine helped shape a new market from 1944 to 1950 and therefore played the role of advertiser, translator, and advisor for their version of the teenage girl. It experimented with content and style and rarely offered a solid, unified image of the quintessential teenager for simple digestion. It was necessarily fluid in these attempts, experimenting with various voices in pursuit of a successful balance. It did not conclusively answer many of the questions it raised. Whether the hard work and intelligence that helped one achieve a dream of college and a science career would necessarily scare away dates, or why it was important to be beautiful and sexy to get dates, but not to kiss them, remained for the reader to decide. It also did not radically alter its message in response to readers' requests. This mixture was dominated by fashion, beauty, style, and the redemptive value of consumption, yet clear in its moral advice to vote, think, and participate as a responsible citizen.

Consumer culture for teenage girls was a primary beneficiary in this interchange. Manufacturers, retailers, and advertisers who targeted teenage girls reaped large profits and, although advertisements were increasingly age-appropriate, they never substantively adjusted their image of the teenage girl from a swooner to a serious individual. Their goal was to sell; their means were the creation and marketing of products designed specifically for teenage girls. It is difficult to know whether the girls themselves benefited from the attention—from clothes and products designed for their changing bodies or the magazine that claimed to represent and reach over half of them. What is clear is that *Seventeen*'s messages were significant for the millions and millions of teenage girls who continued to consume the magazine and praise its efforts. Teenagers read, however quickly or thoroughly, the medley of messages and learned something beyond style as they adapted new information to their changing value systems. They neither accepted nor rejected all. Through the process, manufacturers, advertisers, and *Seventeen* magazine capitalized on an enormous, wealthy, newly defined market and in turn helped define that market. They also articulated a complex, multifaceted set of identities of the teenage girl as consumer and citizen.

◆ *F U R T H E R   R E A D I N G*

Bailey, Beth L. *From Front Porch to Back Seat: Courtship in Twentieth-Century America* (1988).

Barson, Michael. *"Better Dead Than Red!"* (1992).

Biskind, Peter. *Seeing Is Believing: How Hollywood Taught Us to Stop Worrying and Love the Fifties* (1983).

Brandon, Barbara. *The Passion of Ayn Rand* (1986).

Byars, Jackie. *All That Hollywood Allows: Re-Reading Gender in 1950s Melodrama* (1991).

Carmichael, Virginia. *Framing History: The Rosenberg Story and the Cold War* (1993).

Carter, Paul. *Another Part of the Fifties* (1983).

Cohen, Lizabeth. *A Consumers' Republic: The Politics of Mass Consumption in Postwar America* (2003).

Coontz, Stephanie. *The Way We Never Were: American Families and the Nostalgia Trap* (1992).

Davis, Kenneth C. *Two-Bit Culture: The Paperbacking of America* (1984).

Diggins, John Patrick. *The Proud Decades: America in War and Peace, 1941–1960* (1988).

Doherty, Thomas. *Cold War, Cool Medium: Television, McCarthyism, and American Culture* (2003).

Englehardt, Tom. *The End of Victory Culture* (1995).

Fernlund, Kevin J., ed. *The Cold War American West, 1945–1989* (1998).

Foreman, Joel, ed. *The Other Fifties: Interrogating Midcentury American Icons* (1997).

Fox, Richard Wightman. *Reinhold Niebuhr: A Biography* (1986).

Fried, Richard M. *The Russians Are Coming! The Russians Are Coming!: Pageantry and Patriotism in Cold-War America* (1998).

Gilbert, James B. *A Cycle of Outrage: Juvenile Delinquency and the Mass Media* (1986).

———. *Men in the Middle: Searching for Masculinity in the 1950s* (2005).

Harvey, Brett. *The Fifties: A Woman's Oral History* (1993).

Haut, Woody. *Pulp Culture: Hardboiled Fiction and the Cold War* (1995).

Hendra, Tony. *Going Too Far* (1988).

Henriksen, Margot A. *Dr. Strangelove's America: Society and Culture in the Atomic Age* (1997).

Horowitz, Daniel, ed. *American Social Classes in the 1950s* (1995).

Hunner, Joe. *Inventing Los Alamos: The Growth of an Atomic Community* (2004).

Hurley, Andrew. *Diners, Bowling Alleys, and Trailer Parks: Chasing the American Dream in the Postwar Consumer Culture* (2001).

Inglis, Fred. *The Cruel Peace: Everyday Life and the Cold War* (1991).

Lhamon, W. T., Jr. *Deliberate Speed: The Origins of a Cultural Style in the American 1950s* (1990).

Lipsitz, George. *Class and Culture in Cold War America* (1982).

Marling, Karal Ann. *As Seen on TV: The Visual Culture of Everyday Life in the 1950s* (1994).

May, Elaine Tyler. *Homeward Bound: American Families in the Cold War Era* (1988).

Meyerowitz, Joanne, ed. *Not June Cleaver: Women and Gender in Postwar America, 1945–1960* (1994).

Oakes, Guy. *The Imaginary War: Civil Defense and American Cold War Culture* (1994).

Palladino, Grace. *Teenagers: An American History* (1996).

Rose, Lisle A. *The Cold War Comes to Main Street: America in 1950* (1999).

Silk, Mark. *Spiritual Politics* (1988).

Whitfield, Stephen J. *The Culture of the Cold War,* 2nd ed. (1996).

CHAPTER
4

John F. Kennedy,
the Cuban Revolution,
and the Cold War

To comprehend the nature of the United States' troubled relations with Cuba during the 1960s requires an understanding of at least three separate but inter-related topics: the history of U.S. relations with Latin America, especially the Caribbean; the response of the United States to social revolutions both in Latin America and throughout the Third World; and the United States' Cold War struggle with the Soviet Union. The history of relations between the United States and Cuba serves in turn to highlight patterns that were common to postwar U.S. policy throughout the Third World, including Southeast Asia and the Middle East.

Throughout the early twentieth century, the United States had exercised a dominant influence in Latin America and particularly in the Caribbean, featuring armed interventions in Cuba, Colombia (Panama), the Dominican Republic, Haiti, Nicaragua, and Mexico. The United States forswore such military actions in 1933 with Franklin D. Roosevelt's Good Neighbor Policy, but following World War II that policy was increasingly honored in the breach as the United States intervened directly or indirectly in Guatemala (under Eisenhower), Cuba (Kennedy), the Dominican Republic (Johnson), Chile (Nixon), Nicaragua (Reagan), Grenada (Reagan), Panama (George H. W. Bush), and Haiti (Clinton). Seen from this perspective, Kennedy's "fixation" with Cuba was simply part of a deeply rooted historical pattern.

U.S. leaders were especially troubled by the growth of social revolutions throughout Latin America, revolutions that they feared would threaten the nation's economic interests—property, investments, and markets—as well as its strategic control of the region. Cuban revolutionary Fidel Castro, whose forces overthrew the dictatorship of Fulgencio Batista in 1959, posed a special threat as a result of his seizure of industries owned by U.S. investors and his rapid rise as a popular symbol of resistance to the United States.

It was the Cold War with the Soviet Union, however, that helped revive historic patterns of U.S. intervention and served to heighten and rationalize growing fears of social revolution. In Latin America, as in Asia, the United States identified most revolutions with the foreign policies of the Soviet Union. Many Latin American revolutions were led by men and women who were socialists, if not communists; and the Soviet Union often supported such revolutions when it was in its interest to do so. American leaders compounded the problem, however, through their inability or unwillingness to distinguish between indigenous social change and foreign subversion. Reflexive opposition to social revolutions thus became a cardinal theme of the Cold War era.

In 1954, for example, the United States engineered the overthrow of the demo-cratically elected, reformist government of Guatemala. Established in 1944 following decades of dictatorship, the new Guatemalan government had introduced various reforms, including the nationalization of lands belonging to the powerful United Fruit Company. The protests of United Fruit, combined with (largely groundless) fears that Guatemala might become a beachhead of Soviet influence in the region, led the Eisenhower administration to launch a CIA-led coup that resulted in the over-throw of the Guatemalan government and the installation of a right-wing, pro-U.S. dictatorship. The success of the Guatemalan intervention served, in turn, as a model for the U.S. officials who planned the abortive 1961 Bay of Pigs landing in Cuba.

U.S.-Cuban relations were thus shaped by a long history of U.S. involvement in Cuban affairs, by strong opposition to the new economic programs of the Cuban revolution, and by a growing fear on the part of U.S. leaders that the victory of the Cuban revolutionaries would also become a Cold War victory for the Soviet Union. The process was dialectic: Castro was a dedicated revolutionary. Given the history of U.S.-Cuban relations, given also the extent of U.S. property and investments in the island, it was altogether likely that the revolution would evolve in ways antago-nistic to American interests. U.S. opposition, and especially its failed attempt to overthrow the new Cuban government, strongly reinforced the direction and pace of that evolution, helping to propel Castro and the Cubans into an ever tighter embrace of the Soviet Union. This development, in turn, tempted the Soviets to introduce nuclear weapons into Cuba, thus setting the stage for the Cuban missile crisis.

♦ D O C U M E N T S

By October 1960, relations between the United States and the new Cuban government had already deteriorated. In Document 1, a 1960 speech before the United Nations, the new Cuban leader, Fidel Castro, traces the history of U.S. relations with his nation, defends the Cuban revolution, denounces U.S. efforts to overthrow his government, and praises the Soviet Union. Castro's speech, which is excerpted from the *United Nations Review*, follows the UN practice of paraphrasing the speaker's remarks, rather than reporting them directly. On March 13, 1961, President John F. Kennedy announced the Alliance for Progress (Document 2), a boldly ambitious plan to stimulate economic development and democracy throughout Latin America while avoiding radical social revolutions of the Cuban variety. The alliance failed, partly because the Kennedy adminis-tration remained divided over the degree of support for social and economic reform versus military aid to right-wing (but pro-American) dictators, partly because Kennedy's successors weakened the program, and partly because many of Latin America's economic and political problems were simply beyond the ability of the United States to solve.

In 1961, in the same month in which Kennedy introduced the Alliance for Progress, he and his advisers put the finishing touches on their plan for a CIA-backed invasion of Cuba by pro-Batista Cuban exiles. In the wake of its failure, Kennedy appointed a top-secret board of inquiry under General Maxwell Taylor. Document 3 is excerpted from the board's report, dated June 13, 1961. U.S. efforts to overthrow Castro included numerous plots to assassinate the Cuban leader. In 1975, following Watergate, a select committee of the U.S. Senate, chaired by Senator Frank Church of Idaho, opened an investigation of these and other covert activities by U.S. intelligence agencies. Document 4 is excerpted from the Church committee's final report.

During the summer of 1962, the Soviet Union began to ship nuclear missiles to Cuba. Although the United States retained a huge lead in nuclear weapons (including those in Cuba), the discovery in October 1962 of the Soviet missiles precipitated the Cuban missile crisis. Document 5 is taken from the transcripts of two meetings on October 16, 1962, in which Kennedy and his top advisers first discussed possible responses to the crisis. Soviet Premier Nikita Khrushchev's initial response to Kennedy's action, dated October 26, 1962, is reprinted as Document 6. In the days that followed, the advice given to Kennedy ranged all the way from pursuing a purely diplomatic course to an attack on Cuba itself and the real possibility of a nuclear war with the Soviet Union. Denouncing the blockade, Khrushchev offered to remove the missiles in return for a U.S. pledge not to invade Cuba, emotionally appealing to Kennedy to help avoid "the catastrophe of thermonuclear war." Working behind the scenes, the president's brother, Attorney General Robert Kennedy, and Soviet Ambassador Anatoly I. Dobrynin worked out a cautious agreement that led to a resolution of the crisis (Document 7). The announcement that the Soviet Union would withdraw the missiles from Cuba was widely interpreted as a victory for Kennedy and the United States.

1. Fidel Castro Denounces U.S. Policy Toward Cuba, 1960

The Prime Minister of Cuba recalled to the Assembly that many speakers who had preceded him on the rostrum had quite correctly referred to the problem of Cuba as one of the problems facing the world. As far as the world is concerned, he said, the problem of Cuba had come to a head in the last two years, and as such it was a new problem. Before that, the world had few reasons for knowing that his country existed; for many it was an offshoot—in reality, a colony—of the United States.

He traced the history of Cuba and referred to the law passed by the United States Congress at the time of the American military occupation of Cuba during the war with Spain, which, he claimed, said that the Constitution of Cuba—which was then being drafted—must have a rider under which the United States would be granted the right to intervene in Cuba's political affairs and to lease certain parts of the country for naval bases or for their coal deposits. In other words, the right to intervene and to lease naval bases was imposed by force by the legislative body of another country, since Cuban senators were clearly told that if they did not accept, the occupation forces would not be withdrawn.

The colonization of Cuba, he asserted, began with the acquisition of the best land by United States firms, concessions of Cuban natural resources and public services—concessions of all kinds. Cuba eventually had to fight to attain its independence, which was finally achieved after seven bloody years of tyranny "of those in our country who were nothing but the cat's-paws of those who dominated the country economically." The Batista Government of Cuba was appropriate for the United States monopolies, but not for the Cuban people.

United Nations Review (November 1960), 46–47.

How could any system inimical to the interests of the people stay in power unless by force? These were the governments that the guiding circles of United States policy preferred, he said, and that was why governments of force still ruled in Latin America. . . .

Mr. Castro traced some of the conditions which he said the successful revolution in Cuba had uncovered. Public services, he alleged, all belonged to United States monopolies and a major portion of the banking business, importing business, oil refineries, sugar production, the lion's share of arable land, and the most important industries in all fields in Cuba belonged to North American companies. The balance of payments from 1950 to 1960 was favorable to the United States by one billion dollars.

What the Revolutionary Government had wanted to do was to devote itself to the settling of its own problems at home; to carry out a program for the betterment of its people. But when the Revolutionary Government began to pass laws to overcome the advantages obtained by the monopolies, difficulties arose. Then "we began to be called communists; then we began to be painted red," he said.

The first unfriendly act perpetrated by the Government of the United States, he said, was to throw open its doors to a gang of murderers, bloodthirsty criminals who had murdered hundreds of defenceless peasants, who had never tired of torturing prisoners for many, many years, who had killed right and left. These hordes were received by the United States with open arms. Why this unfriendly act on the part of the Government of the United States toward Cuba? At the time Cuba could not understand, but now saw the reason clearly. The policy was part of an attitude of the United States.

He also criticized and blamed the United States Government for the fact that bombs were dropped on the sugar fields of Cuba before the harvest was in, and he accused the United States Government for allowing the planes which dropped the bombs to leave United States territory.

But, he said, aerial incursions finally stopped. Then came economic aggression. It was said that agrarian reform would cause chaos in agricultural production. That was not the case. Had it been so, the United States would not have had to carry on its economic aggression. They could have trusted in the Revolutionary Government's ruining the country. Fortunately that did not happen. Cuba needed new markets for its products. Therefore it signed a trade treaty with the Soviet Union to sell it a million tons of sugar and to purchase a certain amount of Russian products. Surely no one could say that was incorrect.

What could Cuba do? Go to the United Nations and denounce this economic aggression? The United Nations has power to deal with these matters; but it sought an investigation to be carried out by the Organization of American States. As a result, the United States was not condemned. No, the Soviet Union was condemned. All the Soviet Union had said was that if there was military aggression against Cuba, it would support the victims with rockets. Since when was the support of a weak country, conditioned on attack by a powerful country, regarded as interference? If there were no possibility that Cuba would be attacked, then there was no possibility that there would be Soviet support.

"We, the small countries," he added, "do not as yet feel too secure about the preservation of our rights. That is why, when we decide to be free, we know full well that we become free at our own risk."

The Cuban revolution, he continued, was changing. What was yesterday a land [of] misery, a land of illiterates, was gradually becoming one of the most enlightened, advanced, and developed lands of the continent. Developing this theme, he gave figures about the building of schools, housing, and industries, told of the success of plans for conservation of natural resources, medical plans, and other advances since the revolution.

In view of the tremendous reality of underdevelopment, the United States Government, at Bogotá, had come out with a plan for economic development, but he criticized it, saying that the governments of Latin America were being offered not the resources for economic development but resources for social development: houses for people who have no work, schools to which children could not go, and hospitals that would be unnecessary if there were enough food to eat. Cuba was not included in this proposed assistance, but they were not going to get angry about that because the Cubans were solving their own problems.

The Government of Cuba, he said, had always been ready to discuss its problems with the Government of the United States, but the latter had not been willing to do so. He quoted notes which had been addressed to the United States in January and February last, and a reply which said that the United States could not accept the conditions for negotiation laid down in those notes. The Government and the people of Cuba, he said, were much concerned "at the aggressive turn in American policy regarding Cuba" and denounced the efforts of the United States to promote "the organization of subversive movements against the Revolutionary Government of Cuba."

He also said the United States had taken over "in a military manner" Honduran territory—*Islas Cisnes* (Swan Islands)—in violation of treaties, set up a powerful broadcasting station for subversive groups, and was promoting subversion and the landing of armed forces in Cuba.

Turning to the subject of the United States leased naval base in Cuba, Mr. Castro said there was fear and concern in Cuba "of a country that has followed an aggressive and warlike policy possessing a base in the very heart of our island, that turns our island into the possible victim of any international conflict. It forces us to run the risk of any atomic conflict without us having even the slightest intervention in the problem." . . .

The case of Cuba, continued Mr. Castro, was the case of all the underdeveloped colonial countries and the problems he had described in relation to Cuba applied perfectly well to the whole of Latin America, where, he alleged, the economic resources were controlled by the North American monopolies. There is a United Nations report, he said, which explains how even private capital, instead of going to the countries which need it most for setting up basic industries, is preferably being channelled to the more industrialized countries. The development of Latin America, he added, would have to be achieved through public investment, planned and granted unconditionally without any political strings attached. In this, the problems of Latin America were like the problems of Africa and Asia.

"The world," he declared, "has been divided among the monopolistic interests, which do not wish to see the development of peoples but to exploit the natural resources of the countries and to exploit the people."

2. President John F. Kennedy Calls for an Alliance for Progress, 1961

Common Ties Uniting the Republics

We meet together as firm and ancient friends, united by history and experience and by our determination to advance the values of American civilization. For this new world of ours is not merely an accident of geography. Our continents are bound together by a common history—the endless exploration of new frontiers. Our nations are the product of a common struggle—the revolt from colonial rule. And our people share a common heritage—the quest for the dignity and the freedom of man.

The revolutions which gave us birth ignited, in the words of Thomas Paine, "a spark never to be extinguished." And across vast, turbulent continents these American ideals still stir man's struggle for national independence and individual freedom. But as we welcome the spread of the American Revolution to other lands, we must also remember that our own struggle—the revolution which began in Philadelphia in 1776 and in Caracas in 1811—is not yet finished. Our hemisphere's mission is not yet completed. *For our unfulfilled task is to demonstrate to the entire world that man's unsatisfied aspiration for economic progress and social justice can best be achieved by free men working within a framework of democratic institutions.* If we can do this in our own hemisphere, and for our own people, we may yet realize the prophecy of the great Mexican patriot, Benito Juarez, that "democracy is the destiny of future humanity."

As a citizen of the United States let me be the first to admit that we North Americans have not always grasped the significance of this common mission, just as it is also true that many in your own countries have not fully understood the urgency of the need to lift people from poverty and ignorance and despair. But we must turn from these mistakes—from the failures and the misunderstandings of the past—to a future of peril but bright with hope.

Throughout Latin America—a continent rich in resources and in the spiritual and cultural achievements of its people—millions of men and women suffer the daily degradations of hunger and poverty. They lack decent shelter or protection from disease. Their children are deprived of the education or the jobs which are the gateway to a better life. And each day the problems grow more urgent. Population growth is outpacing economic growth, low living standards are even further endangered, and discontent—the discontent of a people who know that abundance and the tools of progress are at last within their reach—that discontent is growing. In the words of José Figueres, "once dormant peoples are struggling upward toward the sun, toward a better life."

If we are to meet a problem so staggering in its dimensions, our approach must itself be equally bold, an approach consistent with the majestic concept of Operation Pan America. Therefore I have called on all the people of the hemisphere to join in a new Alliance for Progress—*Alianza para Progreso*—a vast cooperative effort, unparalleled in magnitude and nobility of purpose, to satisfy the basic needs of the

Department of State Bulletin, XLIV, No. 1136 (April 3, 1961), pp. 471–474.

American people for homes, work and land, health and schools—*techo, trabajo y tierra, salud y escuela. . . .*

Let us once again transform the American Continent into a vast crucible of revolutionary ideas and efforts, a tribute to the power of the creative energies of free men and women, an example to all the world that liberty and progress walk hand in hand. Let us once again awaken our American revolution until it guides the struggles of people everywhere—not with an imperialism of force or fear but the rule of courage and freedom and hope for the future of man.

3. A Board of Inquiry Reports on the Bay of Pigs, 1961

1. Although the Cuban situation had been the subject of serious study in the Special Group [a senior oversight committee], Central Intelligence Agency [CIA], and other government agencies since 1958, this study takes as its point of departure the basic policy paper, "A Program of Covert Action Against the Castro Regime," approved by the President on 17 March 1960. . . . This document, developed by the Central Intelligence Agency and indorsed by the Special Group, provided a program divided into four parts to bring about the replacement of the Castro regime by covert means:

   a. The creation of a responsible and unified Cuban opposition to the Castro regime located outside of Cuba.
   b. The development of means for mass communication to the Cuban people as a part of a powerful propaganda offensive.
   c. The creation and development of a covert intelligence and action organization within Cuba which would be responsive to the orders and directions of the exile opposition.
   d. The development of a paramilitary force outside of Cuba for future guerrilla action.

2. Since the primary purpose of this study is to examine the paramilitary actions growing out of this program and its successive modifications, the paragraph referring to the paramilitary aspects of the plan is quoted in its entirety:

   "d. Preparations have already been made for the development of an adequate paramilitary force outside of Cuba, together with mechanisms for the necessary logistics support of covert military operations on the island. Initially a cadre of leaders will be recruited after careful screening and trained as paramilitary instructors. In a second phase a number of paramilitary cadres will be trained at secure locations outside of the United States so as to be available for immediate deployment into Cuba to organize, train, and lead resistance forces recruited there both before and after the establishment of one or more active centers of resistance. The creation of this capability

---

The Taylor Report on Limited War Programs, June 13, 1961, John Fitzgerald Kennedy Library. NSF. Box 61A. Taylor Report Part I. Memoranda 1–4, at Digital National Security Archive.

will require a minimum of six months and probably closer to eight. In the meanwhile, a limited air capability for resupply and for infiltration and exfiltration already exists under CIA control and can be rather easily expanded if and when the situation requires. Within two months it is hoped to parallel this with a small air supply capability under deep cover as a commercial operation in another country."

3. It is apparent from the above excerpt that at the time of approval of this document the concept of paramilitary action was limited to the recruitment of a cadre of leaders and the training of a number of paramilitary cadres for subsequent use as guerrillas in Cuba.

4. The CIA began at once to implement the decisions contained in the policy paper on 17 March 1960. A target of 300 men was set for the recruitment of guerrillas to be trained covertly outside the United States. "Radio Swan" was installed on Swan Island and ready for broadcasting on 17 May 1960. . . . Steps were taken to develop the FRD (*Frente Revolucionario Democrático*) as the Cuban front organization composed of a broad spectrum of Cuban political elements other than Communists and Batistianos. . . . On August 18th, a progress report was given to the President and the Cabinet, at which time a budget of some $13 million was approved, as well as the use of Department of Defense personnel and equipment. However, it was specified at this time that no United States military personnel were to be used in a combat status.

5. Sometime in the summer of 1960 the paramilitary concept for the operation began to change. It appears that leaders in the CIA Task Force set up in January 1960 to direct the project were the first to entertain the thought of a Cuban strike force to land on the Cuban coast in supplementation of the guerrilla action contemplated under the March 17, 1960, paper. These CIA officers began to consider the formation of a small force of infantry (200–300 men) for contingency employment in conjunction with other paramilitary operations, and in June began to form a small Cuban tactical air force. Eventually it was decided to equip this force with B-26 aircraft which had been widely distributed to foreign countries including countries in Latin America.

6. There were ample reasons for this new trend of thought. The air drops into Cuba were not proving effective. There were increasingly heavy shipments of Communist arms to Cuba, accompanied by evidence of increasingly effective control of the civilian population by Castro. The Special Group became aware of these adverse factors which were discussed repeatedly in the Committee meetings during the fall of 1960. The minutes of the conferences indicate a declining confidence in the effectiveness of guerrilla efforts alone to overthrow Castro.

7. In this atmosphere the CIA began to implement the new concept, increasing the size of the Cuban force in training and reorienting the training toward preparation for its use as an assault force on the Cuban coast. On November 4th, CIA in Washington dispatched a cable to the project officer in Guatemala describing what was wanted. . . . The cable directed a reduction of the guerrilla teams in training to 60 men and the introduction of conventional training for the remainder as an amphibious and airborne assault force. From that time on, the training emphasis was placed on the assault mission and there is no evidence that the members of the assault force received any further preparation for guerrilla-type

operations. The men became deeply imbued with the importance of the landing operation and its superiority over any form of guerrilla action to the point that it would have been difficult later to persuade them to return to a guerrilla-type mission. The final training of the Cubans was done by

[1½ lines deleted from transcript]

in Guatemala where 400–500 Cubans had been assembled. . . .

16. On November 18, 1960, President-elect [John F.] Kennedy had first learned of the existence of a plan for the overthrow of Castro through a call on him at Palm Beach by Mr. [Allen] Dulles [Central Intelligence Director] and Mr. [Richard] Bissell [Deputy Director of Central Intelligence for Plans]. He received his first briefing on the developing plan as President on January 28 at a meeting which included the Vice President [Lyndon B. Johnson], Secretary of State [Dean Rusk], Secretary of Defense [Robert McNamara], the Director of Central Intelligence [John McCone], the Chairman of the Joint Chiefs of Staff [General Maxwell Taylor], Assistant Secretary [of State Thomas] Mann, Assistant Secretary [of Defense Paul] Nitze, Mr. Tracy Barnes [Bissell's assistant], and Mr. McGeorge Bundy [the National Security Adviser]. . . . After considerable discussion, the President authorized the following:

a. A continuation and accentuation of current activities of the CIA, including increased propaganda, increased political action, and increased sabotage. Continued overflights of Cuba were specifically authorized.

b. The Defense Department was to review CIA proposals for the active deployment of anti-Castro Cuban forces on Cuban territory and the results of this analysis were to be promptly reported to the CIA.

c. The State Department was to prepare a concrete proposal for action with other Latin American countries to isolate the Castro regime and to bring against it the judgment of the Organization of American States. . . .

19. While the Joint Chiefs of Staff [JCS] supported the Trinidad Plan as one having "a fair chance of success" the plan encountered difficulties in other quarters. From its inception the plan had been developed under the ground rule that it must retain a covert character, that is, it should include no action which, if revealed, could not be plausibly denied by the United States and should look to the world as an operation exclusively conducted by Cubans. This ground rule meant, among other things, that no U.S. military forces or individuals could take part in combat operations. In due course it was extended to exclude pre-D-Day air strikes in support of the landing since such strikes could not have the appearance of being launched from Cuban soil before an airstrip had been seized by the landing force. This effort to treat as covert an operation which in reality could not be concealed or shielded from the presumption of U.S. involvement raised in due course many serious obstacles to the successful conduct of the operation which will be the subject of subsequent comment.

20. The President and his advisors were thoroughly aware of the difficulties of preserving the covert character of an operation as visible as a landing on a hostile shore and from the outset viewed the Trinidad Plan with caution. In particular,

the State Department representatives opposed features of the plan because of the difficulty of concealing U.S. participation and also because of their fear of adverse reactions to the United States in Latin American countries and in the United Nations. They objected in particular to the conduct of any tactical air operations unless these aircraft were either actually or ostensibly based on Cuban soil.

21. On the other hand, working to overcome this reluctance to approve the Trinidad Plan was the need to decide quickly what to do with the Cuban Expeditionary Force. The President was informed that this force must leave Guatemala within a limited time and that, further, it could not be held together long in the United States if it were moved there. If the decision were taken to disband the force, that fact would soon become known and would be interpreted asa renunciation by the U.S. of the effort to free Cuba from Castro. Faced with two unattractive alternatives, the President and his advisors asked the CIA to come up with various proposals for the use of this force as alternatives to Trinidad.

22. These proposals were the subject of detailed consideration on March 11th when the President and the National Security Council met to consider the various plans then being entertained for Cuba. Mr. Bissell of CIA presented a paper entitled, "Proposed Operation Against Cuba" which summarized the action to date and presented four alternative courses of action. . . . It concluded by recommending the Trinidad Plan which he described to be an operation in the form of an assault in force preceded by a diversionary landing as the action having the best chance of achieving the desired result. The assault in force was to consist of an amphibious/airborne assault with concurrent (but no prior) tactical air support, to seize a beachhead contiguous to terrain suitable for guerrilla operations. The provisional government would land as soon as the beachhead had been secured. If initial military operations were successful and especially if there were evidence of spreading disaffection against the Castro regime, the provisional government could be recognized and a legal basis provided for U.S. logistic support.

23. The military plan contemplated the holding of a perimeter around a beachhead area. It was believed that initial attacks by the Castro militia, even if conducted in considerable force, could be successfully resisted. The scale of the operation, a display of professional competence, and determination on the part of the assault force would, it was hoped, demoralize the Castro militia, cause defections therefrom, impair the morale of the Castro regime, and induce widespread rebellion. . . .

4. A Senate Committee Investigates U.S. Plots to Assassinate Castro, 1960–1965 (1975)

We have found concrete evidence of at least eight plots involving the CIA to assassinate Fidel Castro from 1960 to 1965. Although some of the assassination plots did not advance beyond the stage of planning and preparation, one plot, involving the use of underworld figures, reportedly twice progressed to the point of sending poison pills to Cuba and dispatching teams to commit the deed. Another plot involved furnishing

Excerpts from *Alleged Assassination Plots Involving Foreign Leaders: An Interim Report of the Select Committee to Study Government Operations with Respect to Intelligence Activities,* United States Senate, 94:1 (November 20, 1975), 71–82.

weapons and other assassination devices to a Cuban dissident. The proposed assassination devices ran the gamut from high-powered rifles to poison pills, poison pens, deadly bacterial powders, and other devices which strain the imagination.

The most ironic of these plots took place on November 22, 1963—the very day that President [John F.] Kennedy was shot in Dallas—when a CIA official offered a poison pen to a Cuban for use against Castro while at the same time an emissary from President Kennedy was meeting with Castro to explore the possibility of improved relations.

The following narrative sets forth the facts of assassination plots against Castro as established before the Committee by witnesses and documentary evidence. . . .

(a) Plots: Early 1960

(i) Plots to Destroy Castro's Public Image.   Efforts against Castro did not begin with assassination attempts.

From March through August 1960, during the last year of the Eisenhower Administration, the CIA considered plans to undermine Castro's charismatic appeal by sabotaging his speeches. According to the 1967 Report of the CIA's Inspector General, an official in the Technical Services Division (TSD) recalled discussing a scheme to spray Castro's broadcasting studio with a chemical which produced effects similar to LSD, but the scheme was rejected because the chemical was unreliable. During this period, TSD impregnated a box of cigars with a chemical which produced temporary disorientation, hoping to induce Castro to smoke one of the cigars before delivering a speech. The Inspector General also reported a plan to destroy Castro's image as "The Beard" by dusting his shoes with thallium salts, a strong depilatory that would cause his beard to fall out. The depilatory was to be administered during a trip outside Cuba, when it was anticipated Castro would leave his shoes outside the door of his hotel room to be shined. TSD procured the chemical and tested it on animals, but apparently abandoned the scheme because Castro cancelled his trip.

(ii) Accident Plot.   The first action against the life of a Cuban leader sponsored by the CIA of which the Committee is aware took place in 1960. A Cuban who had volunteered to assist the CIA in gathering intelligence informed his case officer in Havana that he would probably be in contact with Raul Castro [Fidel Castro's brother and Minister of Defense]. CIA Headquarters and field stations were requested to inform the Havana Station of any intelligence needs that the Cuban might fulfill. The case officer testified that he and the Cuban contemplated only acquiring intelligence information and that assassination was not proposed by them.

The cable from the Havana Station was received at Headquarters on the night of July 20. The duty officer, who was summoned to Headquarters from his home, contacted Tracy Barnes, Deputy to Richard Bissell, CIA's Deputy Director for Plans and the man in charge of CIA's covert action directorate. The duty officer also contacted J. C. King, Chief of the Western Hemisphere Division within the Directorate for Plans.

Following their instructions, he sent a cable to the Havana Station early in the morning of July 21, stating: "Possible removal top three leaders is receiving serious consideration at HQS." The cable inquired whether the Cuban was sufficiently motivated to risk "arranging an accident" involving Raul Castro and advised that the station could "at discretion contact subject to determine willingness to cooperate and his suggestions on details." Ten thousand dollars was authorized as payment "after successful completion," but no advance payment was permitted because of the possibility that the Cuban was a double agent. According to the case officer, this cable represented "quite a departure from the conventional activities we'd been asked to handle."

The case officer contacted the Cuban and told him of the proposal. The case officer avoided the word "assassinate" but made it clear that the CIA contemplated an "accident to neutralize this leader's [Raul's] influence." After being assured that his sons would be given a college education in the event of his death, the Cuban agreed to take a "calculated risk," limited to possibilities that might pass as accidental.

Immediately after returning to the station the case officer was told that a cable had just arrived stating: "Do not pursue ref. Would like to drop matter." This cable was signed by Tracy Barnes.

It was, of course, too late to "drop the matter" since the Cuban had already left to contact Raul Castro. When the Cuban returned, he told the case officer that he had not had an opportunity to arrange an accident.

(iii) Poison Cigars.   A notation in the records of the Operations Division, CIA's Office of Medical Services, indicates that on August 16, 1960, an official was given a box of Castro's favorite cigars with instructions to treat them with lethal poison. The cigars were contaminated with a botulinum toxin so potent that a person would die after putting one in his mouth. The official reported that the cigars were ready on October 7, 1960; TSD notes indicate that they were delivered to an unidentified person on February 13, 1961. The record does not disclose whether an attempt was made to pass the cigars to Castro. . . .

5. President Kennedy and His Advisers Debate Options in the Missile Crisis, October 16, 1962

11:50 a.m.: Meeting on the Cuban Missile Crisis

[Deputy CIA Director] Marshall Carter: This is the result of the photography taken Sunday, sir. There's a medium-range ballistic missile launch site and two new military encampments on the southern edge of the Sierra del Rosario in west-central Cuba. . . .

The launch site at one of the encampments contains a total of at least 14 canvas-covered missile trailers measuring 67 feet in length, 9 feet in width. The overall length of the trailers plus the tow bars is approximately 80 feet. The other encampment contains vehicles and tents but with no missile trailers.

[Arthur] Lundahl [head of the National Photographic Interpretation Center (NPIC)]: [quietly to President Kennedy] These are the launchers here. Each of these are places we discussed. In this instance the missile trailer is backing up to the

---

Excerpts from Ernest R. May and Philip D. Zelikow, eds., *The Kennedy Tapes: Inside the White House During the Cuban Missile Crisis* (W. W. Norton and Co., 2002), 32–69.

launching point. The launch point of this particular vehicle is here. This canvas-covered [*unclear*] is 67 feet long.

Carter: The site that you have there contains at least eight canvas-covered missile trailers. Four deployed probable missile erector launchers. These are unrevetted. The probable launch positions as indicated are approximately 850 feet, 700 feet, 450 feet—for a total distance of about 2,000 feet.

In Area Two, there are at least 6 canvas-covered missile trailers, about 75 vehicles, and about 18 tents. And in Area Number Three we have 35 vehicles, 15 large tents, 8 small tents, 7 buildings, and 1 building under construction. The critical one—do you see what I mean?—is this one.

Lundahl: [*quietly to President Kennedy*] There is a launcher right there, sir. The missile trailer is backing up to it at the moment. [*Unclear.*] And the missile trailer is here. Seven more have been enlarged here. Those canvas-covered objects on the trailers are 67 feet long, and there's a small building between the two of them. The eighth one is the one that's not on a particular trailer. [*Unclear*] backs up. That looks like the most-advanced one. And the other area is about 5 miles away. There are no launcher erectors on there, just missiles. . . .

President Kennedy: Is this ready to be fired?

[Sidney] Graybeal [NPIC]: No, sir.

President Kennedy: How long. . . ? We can't tell that can we, how long before it can be fired?

Graybeal: No, sir. That depends on how ready the GSC [ground support for the missile] [is], how—

President Kennedy: Where does it have to be fired from?

Graybeal: It would have to be fired from a stable, hard surface. This could be packed earth. It could be concrete, or asphalt. The surface has to be hard. Then you put a flame deflector plate on that to direct the missile.

[Secretary of Defense] Robert McNamara: Would you care to comment on the position of nuclear warheads? This is in relation to the question from the President—when can these be fired?

Graybeal: Sir, we've looked very hard. We can find nothing that would spell nuclear warhead in terms of any isolated area or unique security in this particular area. The mating of the nuclear warhead to the missile—from some of the other short-range missile data—[it] would take about a couple of hours to do this. . . .

[Secretary of State] Dean Rusk: Mr. President this is, of course, a very serious development. It's one that we, all of us, had not really believed the Soviets could carry this far. They seemed to be denying that they were going to establish bases of their own [in Cuba] and this one that we're looking at is a Soviet base. It doesn't do anything essential from a Cuban point of view. The Cubans couldn't do anything with it anyhow at this stage.

Now, I do think we have to set in motion a chain of events that will eliminate this base. I don't think we can sit still. The question then becomes whether we do it by a sudden, unannounced strike of some sort or we build up the crisis to the point where the other side has to consider very seriously about giving in, or even the Cubans themselves take some action on this.

The thing that I'm, of course, very conscious of is that there is no such thing, I think, as unilateral action by the United States. It's so intimately involved with

42 allies and confrontation in many places that any action that we take will greatly increase the risks of direct action involving our other alliances and our other forces in other parts of the world.

So I think we have to think very hard about *two* major courses of action as alternatives. One is the quick strike. The point where we think there is the overwhelming, overriding necessity to take all the risks that are involved in doing that. I don't think this in itself would require an invasion of Cuba. You can do it with or without such an invasion—in other words, if we make it clear that what we're doing is eliminating this particular base or any other such base that is established. We ourselves are not moved to general war. We're simply doing what we said we would do if they took certain action. Or we're going to decide that this is the time to eliminate the Cuban problem by action [*unclear*] the island.

The *other* would be, if we have a few days from the military point of view, if we have the little time, then I would think that there would be another course of action, a combination of things, that we might wish to consider. First, that we stimulate the OAS [Organization of American States] procedure immediately for prompt action to make it quite clear that the entire hemisphere considers that the Rio Pact has been violated, and [*unclear*] over the next few days, under the terms of the Rio Pact. . . .

I think also that we ought to consider getting some word to Castro, perhaps through the Canadian ambassador in Havana or through his representative at the UN. I think perhaps the Canadian ambassador would be the best, the better channel to get to Castro, get him apart privately and tell him that this is no longer support for Cuba, that Cuba is being victimized here, and that the Soviets are preparing Cuba for destruction, or *betrayal*. You saw the [*New York*] *Times* story yesterday morning that high Soviet officials were saying, "We'll trade Cuba for Berlin." This ought to be brought to Castro's attention. It ought to be said to Castro that this kind of a base is intolerable and not acceptable. The time has now come when he must, in the interests of the Cuban people, must now break clearly with the Soviet Union and prevent this missile base from becoming operational.

And I think there are certain military actions that we might well want to take straight away. First, to call up highly selected units, up to 150,000, unless we feel that it's better, more desirable, to go to a general national emergency so that we have complete freedom of action. If we announce, at the time that we announce this development—and I think we do have to announce this development some time this week—we announce that we are conducting a surveillance of Cuba, over Cuba, and we will enforce our right to do so. We reject the condition of secrecy in this hemisphere in a matter of this sort.

We reinforce our forces in Guantánamo. We reinforce our forces in the southeastern part of the United States, whatever is necessary from the military point of view, to be able to give, clearly, an overwhelming strike at any of these installations, including the SAM [surface-to-air missile] sites. And also to take care of any MiGs [Soviet jet fighters] or bombers that might make a pass at Miami or at the United States. Build up heavy forces, if those are not already in position.

We then would move more openly and vigorously into the guerrilla field and create maximum confusion on the island [of Cuba]. We won't be too squeamish at this point about the overt/covert character of what is being done. . . .

But I think that, by large, there are these two broad alternatives:

One, the quick strike.

The other, to alert our allies and Mr. Khrushchev that there is an utterly serious crisis in the making here, and that Mr. Khrushchev may not himself really understand that or believe that at this point.

I think we'll be facing a situation that could well lead to general war. . . .

McNamara: Mr. President, there are a number of unknowns in this situation I want to comment upon and, in relation to them, I would like to outline very briefly some possible military alternatives and ask General Taylor to expand upon them.

But before commenting on either the unknowns or outlining some military alternatives, there are two propositions I would suggest that we ought to accept as foundations for our further thinking. My first is that if we are to conduct an air strike against these installations, or against any part of Cuba, we must agree now that we will schedule that prior to the time these missile sites become operational. I'm not prepared to say when that will be. But I think it is extremely important that our talk and our discussion be founded on this premise: that any air strike will be planned to take place prior to the time they become operational. Because, *if* they become operational *before* the air strike, I do not believe we can state we can knock them out before they can be launched. And if they're launched there is almost certain to be chaos in part of the East Coast or the area in a radius of 600 to 1,000 miles from Cuba.

Secondly, I would submit the proposition that any air strike must be directed not solely against the missile sites, but against the missile sites plus the airfields, plus the aircraft which may not be on the airfields but hidden by that time, plus all potential nuclear storage sites. Now this is a fairly extensive air strike. It is not just a strike against the missile sites, and there would be associated with it potential casualties of Cubans, not of U.S. citizens, but potential casualties of Cubans in, at least, in the hundreds, more likely in the low thousands—say two or three thousand. It seems to me these two propositions should underlie our discussion.

Now, what kinds of military action are we capable of carrying out and what may be some of the consequences? We could carry out an air strike within a matter of days. We would be ready for the start of such an air strike within a matter of days. If it were absolutely essential, it could be done almost literally within a matter of hours. I believe the Chiefs would prefer that it be deferred for a matter of days. But we are prepared for that quickly.

The air strike could continue for a matter of days following the initial day, if necessary. Presumably there would be some political discussions taking place either just before the air strike or both before and during.

In any event, we would be prepared, following the air strike, for an invasion, both by air and by sea. Approximately seven days after the start of the air strike that would be possible, if the political environment made it desirable or necessary at that time.

Fine. Associated with this air strike undoubtedly should be some degree of mobilization. I would think of the mobilization coming not before the air strike but either concurrently with or somewhat following, say possibly five days afterwards, depending upon the possible invasion requirements. The character of the mobilization would be such that it could be carried out in its first phase at least within the limits of the authority granted by Congress. There might have to be a second phase, and then it would require a declaration of a national emergency.

Now this is very sketchily, the military capabilities, and I think you may wish to hear General Taylor outline his.

[General Maxwell] Taylor [chairman of the Joint Chiefs of Staff]: We're impressed, Mr. President, with the great importance of getting a strike with all the benefits of surprise, which would mean *ideally* that we would have all the missiles that are in Cuba above ground, where we can take them out.

That desire runs counter to the strong point the Secretary made, if the other optimum would be to get every missile before it could become operational. Practically, I think, our knowledge of the timing of the readiness is going to be so difficult that we'll never have the exact, perfect timing. What we'd like to do is to look at this new photography, I think, and take any additional, and try to get the layout of the targets in as near an optimum position as possible, and then take them out without any warning whatsoever. . . .

I would also mention among the military actions we should take, that once we have destroyed as many of these offensive weapons as possible, we should prevent any more coming in, which means a naval blockade. So I suppose that, and also, a reinforcement of Guantánamo and evacuation of dependents. . . .

Then the decision can be made as we're mobilizing, with the air strike, as to whether we invade or not. I think that's the hardest question militarily in the whole business, and one which we should look at very closely before we get our feet in that deep mud in Cuba. . . .

President Kennedy: What is the advantage? There must be some major reason for the Russians to set this up. It must be that they're not satisfied with their ICBMs [inter-continental ballistic missiles]. What'd be the reason that they would . . . ?

Taylor: What it'd give them is, primarily, it makes a launching base for short-range missiles against the United States to supplement their rather deceptive ICBM system, for example. That's one reason. . . .

Rusk: Mr. President, about why the Soviets are doing this, Mr. McCone [John A. McCone, director of the CIA] suggested some weeks ago that one thing Mr. Khrushchev may have in mind is that he knows that we have a substantial nuclear superiority, but he also knows that we don't really live under fear of his nuclear weapons to the extent that he has to live under fear of ours.

Also, we have nuclear weapons nearby, in Turkey and places like that.

President Kennedy: How many weapons do we have in Turkey?

Taylor: We have the Jupiter missiles.

[McGeorge] Bundy [assistant for National Security Affairs]: We have how many?

McNamara: About 15, I believe to be the figure. . . .

Rusk: . . . Mr. McCone expressed the view that Khrushchev may feel that it's important for us to learn about living under medium-range missiles, and he's doing that to sort of balance that political, psychological flank.

I think also that Berlin is very much involved in this. For the first time, I'm beginning really to wonder whether maybe Mr. Khrushchev is entirely rational about Berlin. [Acting UN Secretary-General] U Thant has talked about his obsession with it. And I think we have to keep our eye on that element.

But they may be thinking that they can either bargain Berlin and Cuba against each other, or that they could provoke us into a kind of action in Cuba which would give an umbrella for them to take action with respect to Berlin. In other words, like the Suez-Hungary combination [in 1956]. If they could provoke us into taking the first overt action, then the world would be confused and they would have what they would consider to be justification for making a move somewhere else.

But I must say I don't really see the rationality of the Soviets pushing it this far unless they grossly misunderstand the importance of Cuba to this country. . . .

President Kennedy: You have any thoughts, Mr. Vice President?

Vice President Johnson: . . . I think that we're committed at any time that we feel that there's a buildup that in any way endangers, to take whatever action we must take to assure our security. . . .

I'm fearful if we . . . I spent the weekend with the ambassadors of the Organization of American States. I think this organization is fine. But I don't think, I don't rely on them much for any strength in anything like this.

And I think that we're talking about our other allies, I take the position that Mr. Bundy says: "Well we've lived all these years [with missiles]. Why can't you? Why get your blood pressure up?" But the fact is the country's blood pressure *is* up, and they are fearful, and they're insecure, and we're getting divided, and I don't think that. . . .

President Kennedy: Well this is really talking about are two or three different potential operations.

One is the strike just on these three bases.

The second is the broader one that Secretary McNamara was talking about, which is on the airfields and on the SAM sites and on anything else connected with missiles.

Third is doing both of those things and also at the same time launching a blockade, which requires, really, the third and which is a larger step.

And then, as I take it, the fourth question is the degree of consultation. . . .

[Attorney General] Robert Kennedy: Mr. President?

President Kennedy: Yes?

Robert Kennedy: We have the fifth one, really, which is the invasion. I would say that you're dropping bombs all over Cuba if you do the second, air and the airports, knocking out their planes, dropping it on all their missiles. You're covering most of Cuba. You're going to kill an awful lot of people, and we're going to take an awful lot of heat on it. And then—you know the heat. Because you're going to announce the reason that you're doing it is because they're sending in these kinds of missiles.

Well, I would think it's almost incumbent upon the Russians then, to say, "Well, we're going to send them in again. And if you do it again, we're going to do the same thing to Turkey. And we're going to do the same thing to Iran."

President Kennedy: I don't believe it takes us, at least. . . . How long does it take to get in a position where we can invade Cuba? Almost a month? Two months?

McNamara: No, sir. No sir. It's a bare seven days after the air strike, assuming the air strike starts the first of next week. Now, if the air strike were to start today, it wouldn't necessarily be seven days after today, but I think you can basically consider seven days after the air strike. . . .

President Kennedy: I think, what we ought to do is, after this meeting this afternoon, we ought to meet tonight again at six, consider these various proposals.

In the meanwhile, we'll go ahead with this maximum, whatever is needed, from the flights. And, in addition, we will. . . .

I don't think we've got much time on these missiles. They may be. . . . So it may be that we just have to. . . . We can't wait two weeks while we're getting ready to roll. Maybe we just have to just take them out, and continue our other preparations if we decide to do that. That may be where we end up.

I think we ought to, beginning right now, be preparing to present what we're going to do *anyway.* We're certainly going to do [option] number one. We're going to take out these missiles.

The questions will be whether, what I would describe as number two, which would be a general air strike. That we're not ready to say, but we should be in preparation for it.

The third is the general invasion. At least we're going to do number one. So it seems to me that we don't have to wait very long. We ought to be making *those* preparations. . . .

[The meeting broke up just before 1:00 PM. The group reassembled at 6:30 PM. The excerpt picks up with a summary by Secretary of Defense McNamara.]

McNamara: Mr. President, could I outline three courses of action we have considered and speak very briefly on each one?

The first is what I would call the political course of action, in which we follow some of the possibilities that Secretary Rusk mentioned this morning by approaching Castro, by approaching Khrushchev, by discussing with our allies. An overt and open approach politically to the problem, attempting to solve it. This seemed to me likely to lead to no satisfactory result, and it almost stops subsequent military action. Because the danger of starting military action *after* they acquire a nuclear capability is so great, I believe we would decide against it, particularly if that nuclear capability included aircraft as well as missiles, as it well might at that point.

A second course of action we haven't discussed, but lies in between the military course we began discussing a moment ago and the political course of action, is a course of action that would involve declaration of open surveillance: A statement that we would immediately impose a blockade against offensive weapons entering Cuba in the future and an indication that, with our open surveillance reconnaissance which we would plan to maintain indefinitely into the future, we would be prepared to immediately attack the Soviet Union in the event that Cuba made any offensive move against this country. . . .

But the third course of action is any one of these variants of military action directed against Cuba, starting with an air attack against the missiles. The Chiefs are strongly opposed to so limited an air attack. But even so limited an air attack is a very extensive air attack. It is not 20 sorties or 50 sorties or 100 sorties, but probably several hundred sorties. We haven't worked out the details. It's very difficult to do so when we lack certain intelligence that we hope to have tomorrow or the next day. But it's a substantial air attack. And to move from that into the more extensive air attacks against the MiGs, against the airfields, against the potential nuclear storage sites, against the radar installations, against the SAM sites, means—as Max suggested—possibly 700 to 1,000 sorties per day for five days. This is the very, very rough plan that the Chiefs have outlined, and it is their judgment that that is the type of air attack that should be carried out.

To move beyond that, into an invasion following the air attack, means the application of tens of thousands, between 90 and over 150,000 men, to the invasion forces.

It seems to me almost certain that any one of these forms of direct military action will lead to a Soviet military response of some type, some place in the world. It may well be worth the price. Perhaps we should pay that. But I think we should recognize that possibility and, moreover, we must recognize it in a variety of ways. . . .

Rusk: I would not think that they would use a nuclear weapon unless they're prepared for general nuclear war. I just don't see that possibility.

Bundy: I would agree.

Rusk: That would mean that—you know we could be just utterly wrong—but we've never really believed that Khrushchev would take on a general nuclear war over Cuba. . . .

President Kennedy: We certainly have been wrong about what he's trying to do in Cuba. There isn't any doubt about that. Not many of us thought that he was going to put MRBMs [medium-range ballistic missiles] on Cuba. . . .

Bundy: But the question that I would like to ask is, quite aside from what we've said and we're very hard locked on to it, I know: What is the strategic impact on the position of the United States of MRBMs in Cuba? How gravely does this change the strategic balance?

McNamara: Mac, I asked the Chiefs that this afternoon, in effect. They said: "Substantially." My own personal view is: Not at all. . . .

President Kennedy: Right. Well, now, what is it, in the next 24 hours, what is it we need to do in order, if we're going to do, let's first say, one and two by Saturday or Sunday? You're doing everything that is. . . .

McNamara: Mr. President, we need to do two things, it seems to me.

First, we need to develop a specific strike plan limited to the missiles and the nuclear storage sites, which we have not done. This would be a part of the broader plan, but I think we ought to estimate the minimum number of sorties. Since you have indicated some interest in that possibility, we ought to provide you that option. We haven't done this.

President Kennedy: OK.

McNamara: But that's an easy job to do.

The second thing we ought to do, it seems to me, as a government, is to consider the consequences. I don't believe we have considered the consequences of any of these actions satisfactorily. And because we haven't considered the consequences, I'm not sure we're taking all the action we ought to take now to minimize those.

I don't know quite what kind of a world we live in after we have struck Cuba, and we've started it. . . .

Now after we've launched 50 to 100 sorties, what kind of a world do we live in? How do we stop at that point? I don't know the answer to this. I think tonight State and we ought to work on the consequences of any one of these courses of actions, consequences which I don't believe are entirely clear to any of us. . . .

President Kennedy: If it doesn't increase very much their strategic strength, why is it—can any Russian expert tell us—why they . . . ? After all Khrushchev demonstrated a sense of caution over Laos. Berlin, he's been cautious—I mean, he hasn't been. . . .

[George W.] Ball [Under-Secretary of State]: Several possibilities, Mr. President. One of them is that he has given us word now that he's coming over in November to the UN. He may be proceeding on the assumption, and this lack of a sense of apparent urgency would seem to support this, that this isn't going to be discovered at the moment and that, when he comes over, this is something he can do, a ploy—that here is Cuba armed against the United States.

Or possibly use it to try to trade something in Berlin, saying he'll disarm Cuba if we'll yield some of our interests in Berlin and some arrangement for it. I mean that—it's a trading ploy. . . .

President Kennedy: Why does he put these in there, though? . . . [W]hat is the advantage of that? It's just as if we suddenly began to put a major number of MRBMs in Turkey. Now that'd be goddamn dangerous, I would think.

Bundy: Well, we did, Mr. President.

[Under-Secretary for Political Affairs] Alexis Johnson: We did it. We did it in England.

President Kennedy: Yeah, but that was five years ago.

Alexis Johnson: That's when we were short. We put them in England too when we were short of ICBMs.

President Kennedy: But that was during a different period then.

Alexis Johnson: But doesn't he realize he has a deficiency of ICBMs vis-à-vis our capacity perhaps? In view of that he's got lots of MRBMs and this is a way to balance it out a bit. . . .

Robert Kennedy: Well, I want to say, can I say that one other thing is whether we should also think of whether there is some other way we can get involved in this, through Guantánamo Bay or something. Or whether there's some ship that . . . you know, sink the *Maine* again or something.

President Kennedy: Well it's a goddamn mystery to me. I don't know enough about the Soviet Union, but if anybody can tell me any other time since the Berlin blockade where the Russians have given us so clear a provocation, I don't know when it's been. Because they've been awfully cautious, really. The Russians . . . I've never. . . .

Now, maybe our mistake was in not saying some time before this summer, that if they do this we're going to act. . . .

6. Soviet Premier Nikita Khrushchev Appeals to President Kennedy, October 26, 1962

[Moscow]

Dear Mr. President:

I have received your letter of October 25. From your letter, I got the feeling that you have some understanding of the situation which has developed and (some) sense of responsibility. I value this.

Now we have already publicly exchanged our evaluations of the events around Cuba and each of us has set forth his explanation and his understanding of these

Department of State Bulletin, vol. 69 (November 19, 1973), pp. 640–643.

events. Consequently, I would judge that, apparently, a continuation of an exchange of opinions at such a distance, even in the form of secret letters, will hardly add anything to that which one side has already said to the other.

I think you will understand me correctly if you are really concerned about the welfare of the world. Everyone needs peace: both capitalists, if they have not lost their reason, and, still more, communists, people who know how to value not only their own lives, but, more than anything, the lives of the peoples. We, communists, are against all wars between states in general and have been defending the cause of peace since we came into the world. We have always regarded war as a calamity, and not as a game nor as a means of the attainment of definite goals, nor, all the more, as a goal in itself. Our goals are clear, and the means to attain them is labor. War is our enemy and a calamity for all the peoples.

It is thus that we, Soviet people, and, together with us, other peoples as well, understand the questions of war and peace. I can, in any case, firmly say this for the peoples of the socialist countries, as well as for all progressive people who want peace, happiness, and friendship among peoples.

I see, Mr. President, that you too are not devoid of a sense of anxiety for the fate of the world, of understanding, and of what war entails. What would a war give you? You are threatening us with war. But you well know that the very least which you would receive in reply would be that you would experience the same consequences as those which you sent us. And that must be clear to us, people invested with authority, trust, and responsibility. We must not succumb to intoxication and petty passions, regardless of whether elections are impending in this or that country, or not impending. These are all transient things, but if indeed war should break out, then it would not be in our power to stop it, for such is the logic of war. I have participated in two wars and know that war ends when it has rolled through cities and villages, everywhere sowing death and destruction.

In the name of the Soviet Government and the Soviet people, I assure you that your conclusions regarding offensive weapons on Cuba are groundless. It is apparent from what you have written me that our conceptions are different on this score, or rather, we have different estimates of these or those military means. Indeed, in reality, the same forms of weapons can have different interpretations.

You are a military man and, I hope, will understand me. Let us take for example a simple cannon. What sort of means is this: offensive or defensive? A cannon is a defensive means if it is set up to defend boundaries or a fortified area. But if one concentrates artillery, and adds to it the necessary number of troops, then the same cannons do become an offensive means, because they prepare and clear the way for infantry to attack. The same happens with missile-nuclear weapons as well, with any type of this weapon. . . .

I believe that you have no basis to think this way. You can regard us with distrust, but, in any case, you can be calm in this regard, that we are of sound mind and understand perfectly well that if we attack you, you will respond the same way. But you too will receive the same that you hurl against us. And I think that you also understand this. My conversation with you in Vienna gives me the right to talk to you this way.

This indicates that we are normal people, that we correctly understand and correctly evaluate the situation. Consequently, how can we permit the incorrect actions which you ascribe to us? Only lunatics or suicides, who themselves want to perish and to destroy the whole world before they die, could do this. We, however, want to live and do not at all want to destroy your country. We want something quite different: to compete with your country on a peaceful basis. We quarrel with you, we have differences on ideological questions. But our view of the world consists in this, that ideological questions, as well as economic problems, should be solved not by military means, they must be solved on the basis of peaceful competition, i.e., as this is understood in capitalist society, on the basis of competition. We have proceeded and are proceeding from the fact that the peaceful coexistence of the two different social-political systems, now existing in the world, is necessary, that it is necessary to assure a stable peace. That is the sort of principle we hold. . . .

Let us normalize relations. We have received an appeal from the Acting Secretary General of the UN, U Thant, with his proposals. I have already answered him. His proposals come to this, that our side should not transport armaments of any kind to Cuba during a certain period of time, while negotiations are being conducted—and we are ready to enter such negotiations—and the other side should not undertake any sort of piratical actions against vessels engaged in navigation on the high seas. I consider these proposals reasonable. This would be a way out of the situation which has been created, which would give the peoples the possibility of breathing calmly. You have asked what happened, what evoked the delivery of weapons to Cuba? You have spoken about this to our Minister of Foreign Affairs. I will tell you frankly, Mr. President, what evoked it.

We were very grieved by the fact—I spoke about it in Vienna—that a landing took place, that an attack on Cuba was committed, as a result of which many Cubans perished. You yourself told me then that this had been a mistake. . . .

Why have we proceeded to assist Cuba with military and economic aid? The answer is: we have proceeded to do so only for reasons of humanitarianism. At one time, our people itself had a revolution, when Russia was still a backward country. We were attacked then. We were the target of attack by many countries. The USA participated in that adventure. . . .

You once said that the United States was not preparing an invasion. But you also declared that you sympathized with the Cuban counterrevolutionary emigrants, that you support them and would help them to realize their plans against the present government of Cuba. It is also not a secret to anyone that the threat of armed attack, aggression, has constantly hung, and continues to hang over Cuba. It was only this which impelled us to respond to the request of the Cuban government to furnish it aid for the strengthening of the defensive capacity of this country.

If assurances were given by the President and the government of the United States that the USA itself would not participate in an attack on Cuba and would restrain others from actions of this sort, if you would recall your fleet, this would immediately change everything. I am not speaking for Fidel Castro, but I think that he and the government of Cuba, evidently would declare demobilization and would appeal to the people to get down to peaceful labor. Then, too, the question of armaments would disappear, since, if there is no threat, then armaments are a burden for every people. Then, too, the question of the destruction, not only of the armaments which you call offensive, but of all other armaments as well, would look different. . . .

Let us therefore show statesmanlike wisdom. I propose: we, for our part, will declare that our ships, bound for Cuba, will not carry any kind of armaments. You would declare that the United States will not invade Cuba with its forces and will not support any sort of forces which might intend to carry out an invasion of Cuba. Then the necessity for the presence of our military specialists in Cuba would disappear.

Mr. President, I appeal to you to weigh well the aggressive, piratical actions, which you have declared the USA intends to carry out in international waters, would lead to. You yourself know that any sensible man simply cannot agree with this, cannot recognize your right to such actions.

If you did this as the first step towards the unleashing of war, well then, it is evident that nothing else is left to us but to accept this challenge of yours. If, however, you have not lost your self-control and sensibly conceive what this might lead to, then, Mr. President, we and you ought not now to pull on the ends of the rope in which you have tied the knot of war, because the more the two of us pull, the tighter that knot will be tied. And a moment may come when that knot will be tied so tight that even he who tied it will not have the strength to untie it, and then it will be necessary to cut that knot. And what that would mean is not for me to explain to you, because you yourself understand perfectly of what terrible forces our countries dispose.

Consequently, if there is no intention to tighten that knot and thereby to doom the world to the catastrophe of thermonuclear war, then let us not only relax the forces pulling on the ends of the rope, let us take measures to untie that knot. We are ready for this. . . .

These thoughts are dictated by a sincere desire to relieve the situation, to remove the threat of war.

Respectfully yours,

N. Khrushchev

7. Soviet Ambassador Anatoly I. Dobrynin Reports on His Meeting with Robert Kennedy, October 28, 1962

R. Kennedy, with whom I met, listened very attentively to N. S. Khrushchev's response. Expressing thanks for the report, he said that he would quickly return to the White House in order to inform the President about the "important response" of the head of the Soviet government. "This is a great relief," R. Kennedy added further, and it was evident that he expressed his words somehow involuntarily. "I," said R. Kennedy, "today will finally be able to see my kids, for I have been entirely absent from home."

According to everything it was evident that R. Kennedy with satisfaction, it is necessary to say, really with great relief met the report about N. S. Khrushchev's response.

Russian and East European Archival Documents Database (READD/RADD), Collection of the National Security Archive, George Washington University. Translation by Mark H. Doctoroff.

In parting, R. Kennedy once again requested that strict secrecy be maintained about the agreement with Turkey. "Especially so that the correspondents don't find out. At our place for the time being even [Press Secretary Pierre] Salinger does not know about it" (it was not entirely clear why he considered it necessary to mention his name, but he did it).

I responded that in the Embassy no one besides me knows about the conversation with him yesterday. R. Kennedy said that in addition to the current correspondence and future exchange of opinions via diplomatic channels, on important questions he will maintain contact with me directly, avoiding any intermediaries.

Before departing, R. Kennedy once again gave thanks for N. S. Khrushchev's quick and effective response.

Your instructions arrived here 1.5 hours after the announcement via radio about the essence of N. S. Khrushchev's response. I explained to R. Kennedy that the tardiness was caused by a delay of telegrams at the telegraph station.

◆ *E S S A Y S*

In the first essay, diplomatic historian Thomas G. Paterson of the University of Connecticut places John F. Kennedy's policies toward Cuba in a broad perspective, linking U.S. attempts to overthrow the Castro government with the subsequent missile crisis. A prominent critic of U.S. Cold War policies, Paterson suggests that Kennedy was responsible for the failure of U.S. policy toward Cuba, a program that posed a real risk of nuclear war and left as its legacy a bitter hostility that continues even today to shape U.S.-Cuban relations. In the second essay, Harvard diplomatic historian Ernest R. May and political scientist Philip D. Zelikow, now director of the Miller Center of Public Affairs at the University of Virginia, review the Cuban missile crisis itself. May and Zelikow draw on both the transcripts of deliberations within the White House from their edited work, *The Kennedy Tapes: Inside the White House During the Cuban Missile Crisis* (2002), and on recently released Soviet documents.

Spinning Out of Control: Kennedy's War Against Cuba and the Missile Crisis

THOMAS G. PATERSON

"My God," muttered Richard Helms of the Central Intelligence Agency, "these Kennedys keep the pressure on about [Fidel] Castro." Another CIA officer heard it straight from John F. and Robert F. Kennedy: "Get off your ass about Cuba." Defense Secretary Robert McNamara remembered that "we were hysterical about Castro at the time of the Bay of Pigs and thereafter." When White House assistant Arthur

This essay is based on Thomas G. Paterson, "Fixation with Cuba: The Bay of Pigs, Missile Crisis, and Covert War Against Castro," in Thomas G. Paterson, ed., *Kennedy's Quest for Victory: American Foreign Policy, 1961–1963* (New York: Oxford University Press, 1989), 123–155, 343–352; Thomas G. Paterson, "The Defense-of-Cuba Theme and the Missile Crisis," *Diplomatic History,* XIV (Spring 1990), 249–256; and Thomas G. Paterson, *Contesting Castro: The United States and the Triumph of the Cuban Revolution* (New York: Oxford Univeristy Press, 1994); and documents declassified and studies published since the publication of these works.

Schlesinger, Jr., returned from an early 1962 overseas trip, he told the president that people abroad thought that the administration was "obsessed with Cuba." President Kennedy himself acknowledged during the missile crisis that "most allies regard [Cuba] as a fixation of the United States."

This essay seeks, first, to explain the U.S. "fixation" with Cuba in the early 1960s, identifying the sources and negative consequences of the Kennedy administration's multitrack war against Cuba. Second, to demonstrate the considerable American responsibility for the onset of the dangerous missile crisis of fall 1962. Third, to explore Kennedy's handling of the crisis, questioning the thesis of deft, cautious management. And, last, to illustrate the persistence of the "fixation" by studying the aftermath of the missile crisis, when the revitalization of the U.S. war against Castro's government set Cuban-American relations on a collision course for decades.

A knowledgeable and engaged President Kennedy spent as much or more time on Cuba as on any other foreign-policy problem. Cuba stood at the center of his administration's greatest failure, the Bay of Pigs, and its alleged greatest success, the missile crisis. Why did President Kennedy and his chief advisers indulge such an obsession with Cuba and direct so many U.S. resources to an unrelenting campaign to monitor, harass, isolate, and ultimately destroy Havana's radical regime? One answer springs from a candid remark by the president's brother, Robert F. Kennedy, who later wondered "if we did not pay a very great price for being more energetic than wise about a lot of things, especially Cuba." The Kennedys' famed eagerness for action became exaggerated in the case of Cuba. They always wanted to get moving on Cuba, and Castro dared them to try. The popular, intelligent, but erratic Cuban leader, who in January 1959 overthrew the U.S. ally Fulgencio Batista, hurled harsh words at Washington and defiantly challenged the Kennedy model of evolutionary, capitalist development so evident in the Alliance for Progress. As charismatic figures charting new frontiers, Kennedy and Castro often personalized the Cuban-American contest. To Kennedy's great annoyance, Castro could not be wheedled or beaten.

Kennedy's ardent war against *fidelismo* may also have stemmed from his feeling that Castro had double-crossed him. As a senator, Kennedy had initially joined many Americans in welcoming the Cuban Revolution as an advancement over the "oppressive" Batista dictatorship. Kennedy had urged a "patient attitude" toward the new government, which he did not see as Communist. Denying repeatedly that he was a Communist, Castro had in fact proclaimed his allegiance to democracy and private property. But in the process of legitimizing his revolution and resisting U.S. pressure, Castro turned more and more radical. Americans grew impatient with the regime's highly-charged anti-Yankeeism, postponement of elections, jailing of critics, and nationalization of property. . . .

Richard N. Goodwin, the young White House and State Department official, provided another explanation for the Kennedy "fixation" with Cuba. He remarked that "the entire history of the Cold War, its positions and assumptions, converged upon the 'problem of Cuba.'" The Cold War dominated international politics, and as Cuban-American relations steadily deteriorated, Cuban-Soviet relations gradually improved. Not only did Americans come to believe that a once-loyal ally had jilted them for the tawdry embrace of the Soviets; they also grew alarmed that Castro sneered at the Monroe Doctrine by inviting the Soviet military to the island. When Castro, in late 1961, declared himself a Marxist-Leninist, Americans who had long denounced him as a Communist then felt vindicated. . . .

American politics also influenced the administration's Cuba policy. In the 1960 presidential campaign, Kennedy had seized the Cuban issue to counter Richard Nixon's charge that the inexperienced Democratic candidate would abandon Zinmen (Quemoy) and Mazu (Matsu) to Communism and prove no match for the hard-nosed Khrushchev. "In 1952 the Republicans ran on a program of rolling back the Iron Curtain in Eastern Europe," Kennedy jabbed. "Today the Iron Curtain is 90 miles off the coast of the United States." He asked in private, "How would *we* have saved Cuba if we had [had] the power," but he nonetheless valued the political payback from his attack. "What the hell," he informed his aides, "they never told us how they would have saved China." Apparently unaware that President Dwight D. Eisenhower had initiated a clandestine CIA program to train Cuban exiles for an invasion of the island, candidate Kennedy bluntly called for just such a project. After exploiting the Cuban issue, Kennedy, upon becoming president, could not easily have retreated.

Overarching all explanations for Kennedy's obsession with Cuba is a major phenomenon of the second half of the twentieth century: the steady erosion of the authority of imperial powers, which had built systems of dependent, client, and colonial governments. The strong currents of decolonization, anti-imperialism, revolutionary nationalism, and social revolution, sometimes in combination, undermined the instruments the imperial nations had used to maintain control and order. The Cuban Revolution exemplified this process of breaking up and breaking away. American leaders reacted so hostilely to this revolution not simply because Castro and his 26th of July Movement taunted them or because domestic politics and the Cold War swayed them, but also because Cuba, as symbol and reality, challenged U.S. hegemony in Latin America. The specter of "another Cuba" haunted President Kennedy, not just because it would hurt him politically, but because "the game would be up through a good deal of Latin America," as Under Secretary of State George Ball put it. The Monroe Doctrine and the U.S. claim to political, economic, and military leadership in the hemisphere seemed at stake. As Castro once remarked, "the United States *had* to fight his revolution."

The Eisenhower Administration bequeathed to its successor an unproductive tit-for-tat process of confrontation with Cuba and a legacy of failure. In November 1959, President Eisenhower decided to encourage anti-Castro groups within Cuba to "replace" the revolutionary regime and thus end an anti-Americanism that was "having serious adverse effects on the United States position in Latin America and corresponding advantages for international Communism." In March 1960 Eisenhower ordered the CIA to train Cuban exiles for an invasion of their homeland—this shortly after Cuba signed a trade treaty with the Soviet Union. The CIA, as well, hatched assassination plots against Castro and staged hit-and-run attacks along the Cuban coast. As Cuba undertook land reform that struck at American interests and nationalized American-owned industries, the United States suspended Cuba's sugar quota and forbade American exports to the island, drastically cutting a once-flourishing commerce. On January 3, 1961, fearing an invasion and certain that the U.S. embassy was a "nest of spies" aligned with counterrevolutionaries who were burning cane fields and sabotaging buildings, Castro demanded that the embassy staff be greatly reduced. Washington promptly broke diplomatic relations with Havana. . . .

The plan to invade Cuba at the Bay of Pigs began to unravel from the start. As the brigade's old, slow freighters plowed their way to the island, B-26 airplanes took to the skies from Nicaragua. On April 15, D-Day-minus-2, the brigade pilots destroyed several parked planes of Castro's meager air force. That same day, as part of a pre-invasion ploy, a lone, artificially damaged B-26 flew directly to Miami, where its pilot claimed that he had defected from the Cuban military and had just bombed his country's airfields. But the cover story soon cracked. Snooping journalists noticed that the nose cone of the B-26 was metal; Cuban planes had plastic noses. They observed too that the aircraft's guns had not been fired. The American hand was being exposed. The president, still insistent upon hiding U.S. complicity, decided to cancel a second D-Day strike against the remnants of the Cuban air force.

Shortly after midnight on April 17, more than 1,400 commandoes motored in small boats to the beaches at Bahía de Cochinos. The invaders immediately tangled with Castro's militia. Some commandoes never made it, because their boats broke apart on razor-sharp coral reefs. In the air, Castro's marauding airplanes shot down two brigade B-26s and sank ships carrying essential communications equipment and ammunition. Fighting ferociously, the brigade nonetheless failed to establish a beachhead. Would Washington try to salvage the mission? Kennedy turned down desperate CIA appeals to dispatch planes from the nearby U.S.S. *Essex,* but he did permit some jets to provide air cover for a new B-26 attack from Nicaragua. Manned this time by American CIA pilots, the B-26s arrived an hour after the jets had come and gone. Cuban aircraft downed the B-26s, killing four Americans. With Castro's boasting that the *mercenarios* had been foiled, the final toll proved grim: 114 of the exile brigade dead and 1,189 captured. One hundred-and-fifty Cuban defenders died. . . .

The most controversial operational question remains the cancelled second D-day air strike. Post-crisis critics have complained that the president lost his nerve and made a decision that condemned the expedition to disaster. Cuban air supremacy did prove important to Cuba's triumph. But was it decisive? A preemptive strike on D-Day against the Cuban air force would not have delivered victory to the invaders. After the first air attack, Castro had dispersed his planes; the brigade's B-26s would have encountered considerable difficulty in locating and destroying them. And, even if a D-Day assault had disabled all of Castro's planes, then what? The brigade's 1,400 warriors would have had to face Castro's army of 25,000 and the nation's 200,000 militia. The commandoes most likely would not have survived the overwhelming power of the Cuban military. . . .

Critical to understanding the frightening missile crisis of fall 1962 is the relationship between post–Bay of Pigs U.S. activities and the Soviet/Cuban decisions to place on the island nuclear-tipped missiles that could strike the United States, endangering the lives of 92 million people. In late April, after hearing from Cuban leaders that they expected a direct U.S. invasion and sought Soviet help to resist an attack, and after protesting the deployment of U.S. intermediate-range Jupiter missiles in Turkey, Nikita Khrushchev began to think about a missile deployment in Cuba; in late May, after dismissing the skepticism of some key advisers who judged his plan provocative to the United States and therefore highly explosive, he made the offer of missiles to Fidel Castro, who quickly accepted them. . . . The plan called for the Soviets' installation on the island of forty-eight medium-range ballistic missiles (SS-4s with a range of 1,020 miles), thirty-two intermediate-range ballistic missiles (SS-5s with a range of 2,200 miles), 144 surface-to-air missiles (SAMs), theater-nuclear weapons (Lunas), forty-eight IL-28 light bombers (with a range of 600 miles), and 42,000 Soviet combat troops.

After the Bay of Pigs, the Kennedy administration launched a multitrack program of covert, economic, diplomatic, and propagandistic elements calculated to overthrow the Castro government. This multidimensional project prompted the Cuban/Soviet decisions of mid-1962. Secretary of Defense Robert McNamara said later: "If I had been in Moscow or Havana at that time [1961–1962], I would have believed the Americans were preparing for an invasion." Indeed, Havana had to fear a successful Bay of Pigs operation conducted by U.S. forces.

Encouraged by the White House, the CIA created a huge station in Miami called JMWAVE to recruit and organize Cuban exiles. In Washington, Robert Kennedy became a ramrod for action. At a November 4, 1961, White House meeting, the Attorney General insisted: "stir things up on the island with espionage, sabotage, general disorder. . . ." The president himself asked Colonel Edward Lansdale to direct Operation Mongoose—"to use our available assets . . . to help Cuba overthrow the Communist regime." Operation Mongoose and JMWAVE, although failing to unseat Castro, punished Cubans. CIA-handled saboteurs burned cane fields and blew up factories and oil storage tanks. In a December 1961 raid, for example, a seven-man team blasted a railroad bridge, derailed an approaching train, and torched a sugar warehouse. One group, Agrupacíon Montecristi, attacked a Cuban patrol boat off the northern coast of the island in May 1962. Directorio Revolucionario Estudiantil, another exile organization, used two boats to attack Cuba in August, hoping to hit a hotel where Castro was dining.

The CIA, meanwhile, devised new plots to kill Castro with poisonous cigars, pills, and needles. To no avail. Did the Kennedys know about these death schemes? In May 1961, Federal Bureau of Investigation Director J. Edgar Hoover informed Robert Kennedy that the CIA had hired mafia boss Sam Giancana to do some "dirty business" in Cuba. Kennedy noted on the margin of the Hoover memorandum that this information should be "followed up vigorously." A year later, the CIA briefed the attorney general about its use of mafia gangsters to assassinate Castro. If his brother Robert knew about these CIA assassination plots, the president surely did, for Robert was John's closest confidant. They kept little if anything from one another. President Kennedy apparently never directly ordered the assassination of Castro—at least no trail of documents leads to the White House. But, of course, nobody uttered the word "assassination" in the presence of the president or committed the word to paper, thereby honoring the principle of plausible deniability. Advisers instead simply mentioned the need to remove Castro. "And if killing him was one of the things that was to be done in this connection," assassination was attempted because "we felt we were acting within the guidelines," said the CIA's Richard Helms.

Intensified economic coercion joined these covert activities. The Kennedy administration, in February 1962, banned most imports of Cuban products. Washington also pressed its North Atlantic Treaty Organization allies to support the "economic isolation" of Cuba. The embargo hurt. Cuba had to pay higher freight costs, enlarge its foreign debt, and suffer innumerable factory shut-downs due to the lack of spare parts once bought in the United States. Cuba's economic woes also stemmed from the flight of technicians and managers, a decline in tourism, high workers' absenteeism rates, the drying up of foreign capital investment, hastily conceived policies to diversify the economy, and suffocating government controls. . . .

[A] contemporary document, this one from the chairman of the Joint Chiefs of Staff, General Maxwell Taylor, noted in spring 1962 that the Mongoose plan to overthrow the Cuban government would be undertaken largely by "indigenous resources," but "recognizes that final success will require decisive U.S. military intervention." Because the plan also required close cooperation with Cuban exiles, it is very likely that Castro's spies picked up from the Cuban community in Miami leaks that the U.S. military contemplated military action against Cuba. As CIA agents liked to joke, there were three ways to transmit information rapidly: telegraph, telephone, and tell-a-Cuban. Cuban officials have claimed, in fact, that their intelligence agency had infiltrated anti-Castro exile groups and had learned about some of the activities associated with Lansdale's scheme. Although they surely did not know the details of President Kennedy's National Security Action Memorandum No. 181 (NSAM-181), dated August 23, a directive to engineer an internal revolt that would be followed by U.S. military intervention, the Cubans no doubt began to observe accelerated U.S. actions to achieve that goal. . . .

By the late spring and early summer of 1962, then, when Havana and Moscow discussed defensive measures that included missiles with nuclear warheads, Cuba felt besieged from several quarters. The Soviet Union had become its trading partner, and the Soviets, after the Bay of Pigs, had begun military shipments of small arms, howitzers, machine guns, armored personnel carriers, patrol boats, tanks, and MiG jet fighters. Yet all of this weaponry had not deterred the United States. And, given the failure of Kennedy's multitrack program to unseat Castro, "were we right or wrong to fear direct invasion" next, asked Fidel Castro. As he said in mid-1962, shortly after striking the missile-deployment agreement with the Soviets: "We must prepare ourselves for that direct invasion."

Had there been no exile expedition at the Bay of Pigs, no destructive covert activities, no assassination plots, no military maneuvers and plans, and no economic and diplomatic steps to harass, isolate, and destroy the Castro government in Havana, there would not have been a Cuban missile crisis. The origins of the October 1962 crisis derived largely from the concerted U.S. campaign to quash the Cuban Revolution. To stress only the global dimension (Soviet-American competition in the nuclear arms race) is to slight the local origins of the conflict. To slight these sources by suggesting from very incomplete declassified Soviet records that the "thought of deterring a U.S. invasion figured only incidentally" in Moscow's calculations, as argued by Ernest R. May and Philip D. Zelikow, editors of the tape recordings that Kennedy made during the crisis, is to overlook the substantial evidence of Soviet (and Cuban) preoccupation with the defense of Cuba and is to miss the central point that Premier Nikita Khrushchev would never have had the opportunity to install dangerous missiles in the Caribbean if the United States had not been attempting to overthrow the Cuban government. This interpretation does not dismiss the view that the emplacement of nuclear missiles in Cuba also served the Soviet strategic goal of catching up in the nuclear arms race. Rather, the interpretation in this essay emphasizes that both Cuba and the Soviet Union calculated that their interests would be served by putting nuclear-capable rockets on the island. . . .

Why did the Cubans and Soviets decide on nuclear-tipped ballistic missiles instead of a military pact, conventional (non-nuclear) forces, or just the battlefield Lunas—in short, weapons that Washington could not label "offensive" because they could not reach the United States? The Cubans sought effective deterrence, or what the historian Mark White has called "the *ultimate* deterrent." One thinks here of similar American thinking, near the end of the Second World War, that the Japanese were so fanatical that only the threat of annihilation from atomic bombs would persuade them to surrender. The Cubans, in fact, looking for an immediate deterrent effect, had wanted to make the 1962 missile agreement public, but the Soviets, guessing that the deployment could be camouflaged until the missiles became operational, preferred secrecy.

On October 14, an American U-2 plane photographed missile sites in Cuba, thus providing the first "hard" evidence, as distinct from the "soft" reports of exiles, that the island was becoming a nuclear base. "He can't do that to me!" snapped Kennedy when he saw the pictures on the 16th. He had warned the Soviets that the United States would not suffer "offensive" weapons in Cuba, although the warnings had come after the Cuban-Soviet agreement of early summer. Shortly before noon on October 16, the president convened his top advisers (a group eventually called the Executive Committee, or ExComm). His first questions focused on the firing readiness of the missiles and the probability that they carried nuclear warheads. The advisers gave tentative answers. All agreed that the missiles could become operational in a brief time. Discussion of military options (invasion? air strike?) dominated this first meeting. Kennedy's immediate preference became clear: "We're certainly going . . . to take out these . . . missiles." Kennedy showed little interest in negotiations. Perhaps his initial tilt toward military action derived from his knowledge of the significant U.S. military plans, maneuvers, and movement of forces and equipment undertaken after he signed NSAM-181, thus making it possible for the United States to respond with military effectiveness.

At a second meeting on the 16th, Secretary of State Dean Rusk argued against the surprise air strike that General Taylor had bluntly advocated. Rusk recommended instead "a direct message to Castro." At the close of Rusk's remarks, Kennedy immediately asked: "Can we get a little idea about what the military thing *is?*" Bundy then asked: "How gravely does this change the strategic balance?" McNamara, for one, thought "not at all," but Taylor disputed him. Kennedy himself seemed uncertain, but he did complain that the missile emplacement in Cuba "makes them look like they're co-equal with us." And, added Treasury Secretary C. Douglas Dillon, who obviously knew the president's competitive personality, the presence of the missiles made it appear that "we're scared of the Cubans."

Then the rambling discussion turned to Khrushchev's motivation. The Soviet leader had been cautious on Berlin, Kennedy said. "It's just as if we suddenly began to put a major number of MRBMs [medium-range ballistic missiles] in Turkey," the President went on. "Now that'd be goddam[n] dangerous. . . ." Bundy jumped in: "Well, we *did,* Mr. President." Not liking the sound of a double standard, Kennedy lamely answered, "Yeah, but that was five years ago." Actually, the American Jupiter missiles in Turkey were IRBMs (intermediate-range ballistic missiles) which, under a 1959 agreement with Ankara, had gone into launch position in mid-1961—during the Kennedy administration—and were turned over to Turkish forces on October 22, 1962, the very day Kennedy informed Moscow that it must withdraw its missiles from Cuba.

For the next several days, ExComm met frequently in tight secrecy and discussed four policy options: "talk them out," "squeeze them out," "shoot them out," or "buy them out." In exhausting sessions marked by frank disagreement and changing minds, the president's advisers weighed the advantages and disadvantages of invasion, bombing, quarantine, and diplomacy. The president gradually moved with a majority of ExComm toward a quarantine or blockade of Cuba: incoming ships would be stopped and inspected for military cargo. When queried if an air strike would knock out all of the known missiles General Taylor said that "the best we can offer you is to destroy 90%. . . ." In other words, some missiles in Cuba would remain in place for firing against the United States. Robert Kennedy also worried that the Soviets might react unpredictably with military force, "which could be so serious as to lead to general nuclear war." In any case, the attorney general insisted, there would be no "Pearl Harbor type of attack" on his brother's record.

By October 22 the president had made two decisions. First, to quarantine Cuba to prevent further military shipments and to impress the Soviets with U.S. resolve to force the missiles out. If the Soviets balked, other, more drastic, measures would be undertaken. Second, Kennedy decided to inform the Soviets of U.S. policy through a television address rather than through diplomatic channels. Several advisers dubiously argued that a surprise public speech was necessary to rally world opinion behind U.S. policy and to prevent Khrushchev from issuing an ultimatum, but some ExComm participants recommended that negotiations be tried first. Former ambassador to the Soviet Union Charles Bohlen advised that Moscow would have to retaliate against the United States if its technicians died from American bombs. A stern letter to Khrushchev should be "tested" as a method to gain withdrawal of the missiles. "I don't see the urgency of military action," Bohlen told the president. And ambassador to the United Nations Adlai Stevenson appealed to an unreceptive Kennedy: "the existence of nuclear missile bases anywhere is negotiable before we start anything." Stevenson favored a trade: withdrawing the U.S. Jupiter missiles from Turkey and evacuating the Guantánamo naval base, turning it over to Cuba, in exchange for withdrawal of the Soviet missiles from Cuba. The president, according to the minutes of an October 20 ExComm meeting, "sharply rejected" Stevenson's proposal, especially on the issue of Guantánamo. . . .

In his evening television speech of October 22, Kennedy demanded that the Soviets dismantle the missiles in Cuba, and he announced the Caribbean quarantine as an "initial" step. Later that evening, in a telephone conversation, he told British prime minister Harold Macmillan that U.S. credibility was on the line; if he had not acted, America's resolve to defend Berlin might be questioned and Soviet success in deploying the missiles "would have unhinged us in all of Latin America." The missile crisis soon became an international war of nerves. More than sixty American ships began patrols to enforce the blockade. The Strategic Air Command went on nuclear alert, moving upward to Defense Condition (DEFCON) 2 for the first time ever (the next level is deployment for combat). B-52 bombers, loaded with nuclear weapons, stood ready, while men and equipment moved to the southeastern United States to prepare for an invasion. The Soviets did not mobilize or redeploy their huge military, nor did they take measures to make their strategic forces less vulnerable. The Soviets also refrained from testing the quarantine: Their ships turned around and went home. But what next? On the 26th, Kennedy and some ExComm members, thinking that the Soviets were stalling, soured on the quarantine. Sentiment for military action strengthened.

On the afternoon of the 26th, an intelligence officer attached to the Soviet embassy, Aleksandr Feklisov (alias Fomin), met with ABC television correspondent

John Scali and suggested a solution to the crisis: The Soviet Union would withdraw the missiles if the United States would promise not to invade Cuba. Scali scurried to Secretary of State Dean Rusk, who sent him back to Feklisov with the reply that American leaders were interested in discussing the proposal. As it turns out, and unbeknownst to American leaders, Feklisov was acting on his own and a report of his conversations with Scali did not reach the Soviet foreign secretary in Moscow until the late afternoon of October 27. Feklisov's independent intervention, in other words, did not influence the writing of the two critical letters that Khrushchev sent to Washington on the 26th and 27th, but ExComm thought the Feklisov initiative and Khrushchev's letters were linked, thus clearly signaling an earnest Soviet desire to settle.

Khrushchev's first letter, a rambling emotional private message that ruminated on the horrors of war, offered to withdraw the missiles if the United States pledged not to invade Cuba. The Soviet premier defended the initial installation of the missiles with the argument that the United States had been threatening the island. In the morning of October 27, another Khrushchev letter reached the president. Khrushchev now upped the stakes: He would trade the missiles in Cuba for the American missiles in Turkey. Kennedy felt boxed, because "we are now in the position of risking war in Cuba and in Berlin over missiles in Turkey which are of little military value." At first, Kennedy hesitated to accept a swap—because he did not want to appear to be giving up anything in the face of Soviet provocation; because he knew that the proud Turks would recoil from the appearance of being "traded off in order to appease an enemy"; and because acceptance of a missile trade would lend credence to charges that the United States all along had been applying a double standard. Kennedy told ExComm that Khrushchev's offer caused "embarrassment," for most people would think it "a very fair trade." Indeed, Moscow had played "a very good card."

In the afternoon of the 27th, more bad news rocked the White House. An American U-2 plane overflew the eastern part of the Soviet Union, probably because its equipment malfunctioned. "There is always some son of a bitch who doesn't get the word," the president remarked. Soviet fighters scrambled to intercept the U-2, and American fighter jets from Alaska, carrying Falcon missiles with nuclear warheads, took flight to protect the errant aircraft. Although the spy plane flew home without having sparked a dog fight, the incident carried the potential of sending the crisis to a more dangerous level.

Also on the 27th, a U-2 was shot down over Cuba and its pilot killed by a surface-to-air missile (SAM). The shoot-down constituted a serious escalation. A distressed McNamara, not knowing that the order to shoot was made independently by the Soviet air defense commander in Cuba without orders from Moscow, now thought "invasion had become almost inevitable." He urged that U.S. aircraft "go in and take out that SAM site." But Kennedy hesitated to retaliate, surely scared about taking a step in toward a nuclear nightmare. The president decided to ignore Khrushchev's second letter and answer the first. The evening of the 27th, he also dispatched his brother Robert to deliver an ultimatum to Soviet Ambassador Anatoly Dobrynin: Start pulling out the missiles within forty-eight hours or "we would remove them." After Dobrynin asked about the Jupiters in Turkey, Robert Kennedy presented an important American concession: They would be dismantled if the problem in Cuba were resolved. As the president had said in an ExComm meeting, "we can't very well invade Cuba with all its toil . . . when we could have gotten them out by making a deal on the same missiles in Turkey." But, should the Soviets leak word of a "deal," Robert Kennedy told the Soviet ambassador, the United States would disavow the offer. Dobrynin, who judged President Kennedy a "hot-tempered gambler," cabled an account of the meeting to Moscow, pointing out that the "very upset" president's brother insisted that "time is of the essence" and that if another U.S. plane were shot at, the United States would return fire and set off "a chain reaction" toward "a real war."

On October 28, faced with an ultimatum and a concession, and fearful that the Cubans might precipitate a greater Soviet-American conflagration, Khrushchev retreated and accepted the American offer: the Soviet Union would dismantle its missiles under United Nations supervision and the United States would pledge not to invade Cuba. The crisis had ended—just when the nuclear giants seemed about to stumble over the brink. . . .

Many analysts give John F. Kennedy high marks for his handling of the Cuban missile crisis, applauding a stunning success, noble statesmanship, and model of crisis management. Secretary Rusk lauded Kennedy for having "ice water in his veins." The journalist Hugh Sidey has gushed over "the serene leader who guides the nation away from nuclear conflict." Arthur Schlesinger, Jr., has effusively written that Kennedy's crisis leadership constituted a "combination of toughness and restraint, of will, nerve, and wisdom, so brilliantly controlled, so matchlessly calibrated." May and Zelikow celebrate Kennedy's "finest hours," sketching a "lucid" and "calm" president, who, in the end, steps back from the brink.

Kennedy's stewardship of policymaking during the crisis actually stands less as a supreme display of careful crisis management and more as a case of near misses, close calls, narrow squeaks, physical exhaustion, accidents, and guesses that together scared officials on both sides into a settlement, because, in the words of McGeorge Bundy, the crisis was "so near to spinning out of control." When McNamara recalled those weeks, he questioned the entire notion of crisis management because of "misinformation, miscalculation, misjudgment, and human fallibility." "We were in luck," Ambassador John Kenneth Galbraith ruminated, "but success in a lottery is no argument for lotteries." . . .

Danger lurked too in the way the commander of the Strategic Air Command issued DEFCON 2 alert instructions. He did so in the clear, instead of in code, because he wanted to impress the Soviets. Alerts serve to prepare American forces for war, but they may also provoke an adversary to think that the United States might launch a first strike. Under such circumstances, the adversary might be tempted to strike first. The Navy's antisubmarine warfare activities also carried the potential of escalating the crisis. Soviet submarines prowled near the quarantine line, and, following standing orders, Navy ships forced several of them to surface. In one case, a Navy commander exercised the high-risk option of dropping a depth charge on a Soviet submarine. As in so many of these examples, decisionmakers in Washington actually lost some control of the crisis to personnel at the operational level.

ExComm members represented considerable intellectual talent and experience, but a mythology of grandeur, illusion of control, and embellishment of performance have obscured the history of the committee. ExComm debated alternatives under "intense strain," often in a "state of anxiety and emotional exhaustion," recalled

Under Secretary Ball. McGeorge Bundy told Ball on October 24 that he (Bundy) was getting "groggy." Two advisers may have suffered such stress that they became less able to perform their responsibilities. An assistant to Adlai Stevenson recalled that he had had to become an ExComm "back-up" for the ambassador because, "while he could speak clearly, his memory wasn't very clear. . . ." Asked if failing health produced this condition, Vice Admiral Charles Wellborn answered that the "emotional state and nervous tension that was involved in it [missile crisis] had this effect." Stevenson was feeling "pretty frightened." So apparently was Dean Rusk. The president scratched on a notepad during an October 22 meeting: "Rusk rather quiet & somewhat fatigued." Robert Kennedy remembered that the secretary of state "had a virtually complete breakdown mentally and physically." Once, when Rusk's eyes swelled with tears, Dean Acheson barked at him: "Pull yourself together, . . . you're the only secretary of state we have." We cannot determine how stress affected the advice ExComm gave Kennedy, but at least we know that its members struggled against time, sleep, exhaustion, and themselves, and they did not always think clearheadedly at a time when the stakes were very high.

What about the president himself, gravely ill from Addison's disease and often in severe pain because of his ailing back? Dr. Max Jacobson, known as "Dr. Feelgood" by the Hollywood crowd that paid for his services, and a frequent visitor to the White House, administered amphetamines and steroids to President Kennedy during the first days of the missile crisis. Medical doctors have reported that the effect of these unorthodox injections might have been supreme confidence and belligerence. One might speculate that JFK's inclination toward a bold military response at the start of the crisis was influenced by the doses of potent drugs he was taking. . . .

As for the Soviets, they too worried about their decisionmaking process and the crisis spinning out of control. Khrushchev, of course, had miscalculated from the outset. He somehow thought that the Americans would not discover the missiles until after all of them had become operational. He had no fallback plan once they were photographed. Because he had never informed his own embassy in Washington that missiles were being placed in Cuba, he had cut himself off from critical advice— counsel that would have alerted him to the certain vigorous U.S. response to the emplacement. . . .

Add to these worries the Soviet premier's troubles with Fidel Castro, who demanded a bold Soviet response to U.S. actions and who might provoke an incident with the United States that could escalate the crisis. Castro pressed the Soviets to use nuclear weapons to save Cuba should the United States attack. Soviet leaders urged Castro not to "initiate provocations" and to practice "self-restraint." Such "adventurists," remarked a Soviet decisionmaker about the Cubans. Khrushchev sternly told his advisers: "You see how far things can go. We've got to get those missiles out of there before a real fire starts."

President Kennedy helped precipitate the missile crisis by harassing Cuba through his multitrack program. Then he reacted to the crisis by suspending diplomacy in favor of public confrontation. In the end, with the management of the crisis disintegrating, he frightened himself. In order to postpone doomsday, or at least to prevent a high-casualty invasion of Cuba, he moderated the American response and compromised. Khrushchev withdrew his mistake, while gaining what ExComm member Ambassador Llewellyn Thompson thought was the "important thing" all along for the Soviet leader: being able to say, "I saved Cuba. I stopped an invasion." . . .

After the missile imbroglio, the pre-crisis "fixation" reasserted itself. For example, the State Department's Policy Planning Council on November 7 urged a "maximal U.S. strategy" to eliminate the Castro regime. The messy ending to the crisis—no formal accord was reached, no formal document signed—also left the Kennedy administration room to hedge on the no-invasion promise. Using the argument that the United States had agreed not to invade the island only if the missiles were withdrawn under United Nations inspection and that Castro had blocked such inspection, Kennedy refused to give an unqualified no-invasion pledge. . . .

Kennedy's retreat to an ambiguous no-invasion promise reflected his administration's unrelenting determination to oust Castro. In early January 1963, the CIA director noted that "Cuba and the Communist China nuclear threat" were the two most prominent issues on Kennedy's foreign-policy agenda. Later that month, the president himself told the National Security Council that Cuba must become a U.S. hostage. "We must always be in a position to threaten Cuba as a possible riposte to Russian pressure against us in Berlin. We must always be ready to move immediately against Cuba" should the Soviets move against Berlin. "We can use Cuba to limit Soviet actions," he concluded. The administration set about once again to threaten Cuba, to "tighten the noose" around Cuba, although Kennedy grew impatient with exile attacks, because they did not deliver "any real blow at Castro."

In June 1963, the National Security Council approved a new sabotage program. The CIA quickly cranked up destructive plots and revitalized its assassination option by making contact with a traitorous Cuban official, Rolando Cubela. Codenamed AM/LASH, he plotted with CIA operatives to kill Fidel Castro. . . .

After President Kennedy's death, the new Johnson administration decided to put the "marginal" and "tenuous" Cuban-American contacts "on ice." President Johnson also instructed his advisers to avoid "high risk actions" toward Cuba. Throughout the 1960s, as the United States became hostage to the war in Vietnam, Cuba receded as a top priority. Fidel Castro may have been correct when he remarked a decade after the missile crisis that Cuba "was saved by Vietnam. Who can say whether the immense American drive that went into Vietnam . . . would not have been turned against Cuba?" Except for a thaw in the mid to late-1970s, U.S.-Cuba relations remained frozen in hostility. Kennedy's "fixation" with Cuba fixed itself on U.S.-Cuba policy for decades.

Aftermath

ERNEST R. MAY AND PHILIP D. ZELIKOW

Though anxiety gave way to euphoria after Khrushchev's broadcast of Sunday, October 28, the crisis was not over. Low-level reconnaissance on October 29 appeared to detect continuing construction. The Joint Chiefs suspected Khrushchev of simply trying to buy time. If Kennedy stopped aerial surveillance, as [acting Secretary-General of the United Nations] U Thant had requested, how would he know whether the Chiefs were right or wrong?

President Kennedy's position remained awkward through the last days of October. Led to believe that the crisis was essentially over, reporters expected evidence that the missiles were being pulled out. The government had no such evidence to release. Kennedy had little to go on except his own belief that Khrushchev was sincere, a belief reinforced by intelligence of Cuban and Chinese anger at what they seemed to regard as Soviet betrayal.

On October 28 Khrushchev sent a private message to President Kennedy, trying to nail down the deal on withdrawal of the Jupiter missiles. Khrushchev said he understood the need to handle this matter confidentially. He had respected that need in his public message agreeing to withdraw the missiles from Cuba. But the Soviet leader said his concessions "took into account" the U.S. agreement to resolve the Jupiter problem.

Dobrynin delivered this letter to Robert Kennedy on October 29. The next day Robert Kennedy called in Dobrynin and gave the letter back, refusing to accept it. Robert Kennedy's handwritten notes for this meeting say: "No quid pro quo as I told you. The letter makes it appear that there was." The missiles would leave Turkey; "you have my word on this & that is sufficient . . . ; if you should publish any document indicating a deal then it is off." Dobrynin said his government would never publish anything. Robert Kennedy reminded Dobrynin that his government had also said it would never put missiles in Cuba. Dobrynin took the letter back, and the U.S. government kept no record of the letter or its receipt.

On October 30 Khrushchev sent another private letter to President Kennedy congratulating them both on having "in the main liquidated" a "dangerous crisis"; but in the same letter he suggested immediate removal of the quarantine and U.S. abandonment of Guantánamo.

Not surprisingly, President Kennedy remained wary. He continued to review invasion plans, leaving in place forces to execute the air strike and invasion. Though McNamara and others predicted that nothing would come of U Thant's mission to Havana, Kennedy waited on its outcome.

When U Thant met with Castro in Havana on October 30, he found a Cuban leader whose fury covered all points of the compass. U Thant later told the Americans that Castro had been in an "impossible and intractable mood"—"extremely bitter" toward the Soviets, the Americans, and even U Thant himself, whom he seemed to regard as a lackey of the imperialists. U Thant said he had never had a more trying encounter in all his experience. Castro refused any cooperation in verification. Given Castro's mood, U.S. resumption of aerial reconnaissance involved the risk of further shoot-downs and further debates about appropriate forms of reprisal. Nonetheless, Kennedy authorized new U-2 and low-level reconnaissance flights. . . .

Covert harassment of the Castro government resumed, spurred by discoveries of new Cuban attempts to subvert the governments in Venezuela and other South American countries. By the summer of 1963 these operations had returned to about where they had been in the summer of 1962, before the Soviet arms shipments began. Washington was again back to a policy judged to have low risk and low return—petty harassment that was probably not enough to bring down Castro but also not enough to drag the United States into an open or direct intervention in Cuba.

Also left out of President Kennedy's November 20 press conference was any mention of the Jupiter missiles. The matter was not forgotten but was handled in broader reviews of NATO's nuclear force posture, including a meeting in Paris in December 1962 marked, as one delegate put it, by almost "intolerable serenity," spilling over from the satisfying outcome of the Cuban crisis. The Turks agreed to removal of the Jupiters. The missiles were dismantled by the end of April 1963. A Polaris missile submarine took up station in the Mediterranean.

Throughout the crisis, the Americans asked themselves repeatedly why the Soviets had decided to put missiles in Cuba despite Kennedy's explicit and repeated warnings. They differed in their guesses as to how the Soviets would react to U.S. statements and actions and why the Soviets did what they did. Why, for example, did most ships subject to Moscow's orders stop sailing for Cuba while some, particularly the *Grozny,* kept going? Why did Soviet SAM [surface-to-air missile] crews in Cuba do nothing about U-2 flights from October 14 through October 26, then shoot one down on October 27? Why did Khrushchev change his terms for withdrawing the missiles? In his long private message received by the United States late on October 26, he seemed to say his only condition was a U.S. promise not to invade Cuba. In his message publicly broadcast on the morning of October 27 (U.S. time), he called in addition for removal of U.S. "offensive means" from Turkey. Why? And why, having publicly adopted this position, did Khrushchev back down on October 28?

Owing to the passage of time, the publication of memoirs by Khrushchev and others, and a study of Aleksandr Fursenko and Timothy Naftali with access to Presidium and KGB files not yet accessible to other scholars, we have information on these questions well beyond that available to Kennedy and his circle. The two main findings are these. First, Kennedy and his advisers did not make any serious misjudgments about the Soviets. Most of what we know now confirms what was surmised by Kennedy's "demonologists," especially Thompson. Second, our best retrospective judgments about the Soviet side still entail guesswork; in all probability, no one will ever be able to answer with complete confidence *any* of the questions about the Soviets that bothered Kennedy and his advisers.

With these caveats, let us summarize what can now be said about each of the major puzzles, beginning with the question of why the Soviets put the missiles into Cuba and thus brought on the crisis. This separates, like a Russian doll, into several parts. Why did Khrushchev order in May 1962 that the Soviet Strategic Rocket Forces set up MRBM [medium-range ballistic missile] and IRBM [intermediate-range ballistic missile] launchers in Cuba, and why did he make such a secret of it? Had he announced his intentions or even told Kennedy privately that he planned to base IRBMs in Cuba, the crisis would have unfolded differently. Conceivably, there might have been no crisis at all. The tapes of the September 4 meetings show that Kennedy's public warning was crafted to give the appearance of firmness and head off a decision which he thought Khrushchev had not yet made but which some of Kennedy's advisers (including his brother) thought might tempt Khrushchev if the United States did not show a bit of steel. After the Soviet government then announced (on September 11) that no missiles would be sent, Kennedy himself was emboldened to repeat his warning two days later, again trying to show the public (and Congress) that he took Soviet moves in Cuba seriously but at seemingly little risk. It was the fact that Khrushchev lied to Kennedy and tried to surprise him that made the missile deployments such an excruciating test of Kennedy's mettle and the credibility of the United States. Why did Khrushchev not at least *consider* telling Kennedy what he had in mind?

Khrushchev had made his decision in May. But since the missiles were still only en route to Cuba when Kennedy issued his September 4 warning, why did Khrushchev not at least pause to reconsider what he was doing? Since the Soviets understood the U-2's capabilities and knew that the United States conducted reconnaissance over Cuba, what made any of them think the secret could be kept? What did they plan to do if the secret were not kept? And, if the secret were kept, what did they plan to do once the missiles were fully in place?

To explain the original Soviet decision, Kennedy and his advisers considered several hypotheses. Their favorite was that Khrushchev intended the missiles in Cuba as levers to loosen U.S. concessions regarding Berlin. A second hypothesis focused on the strategic balance. The Joint Chiefs of Staff, for example, presumed that Khrushchev had gambled as he did in order to get wider target coverage against the United States and offset the U.S. lead in ICBMs [inter-continental ballistic missiles]. A third hypothesis was that Khrushchev had acted in order to protect Cuba from invasion. Everyone knew this was Khrushchev's story; no one seemed to believe it. This was why, on October 18, Kennedy told visiting Soviet foreign minister Gromyko that the United States would be happy to promise not to invade Cuba and that the Soviet government could have had such a pledge for months. With this hyperbole he was daring the Soviet foreign minister to name this condition, which seemed quite trivial to Kennedy in comparison to what was at stake with Berlin. Kennedy does not appear to have been the least bit surprised that Gromyko ignored his offer. Thompson argued, in the afternoon meeting of October 27, that the Jupiters in Turkey were of secondary interest to the Soviets. "The important thing for Khrushchev . . . ," he said, "is to be able to say: I saved Cuba. I stopped an invasion." But Thompson was speaking then of how Khrushchev could save face. A fourth hypothesis presumed factional interplay in the Kremlin. Thus, whatever the motive or motives, they might not be Khrushchev's own. To account for the difference in content between Khrushchev's private letter and broadcast message, Bundy hazarded that the former was Khrushchev's, the latter that of "hard-nosed people overruling him."

Since 1962 no other hypotheses have been advanced to supplement the four voiced by Kennedy and his advisers. But the hypotheses have had different fates. Berlin, oddly, dropped from sight. Hardly anyone writing retrospectively about the crisis, except the participants, stresses Berlin as a possible primary factor in Soviet decisions. The strategic balance hypothesis has proved more hardy. Two RAND analysts wrote a book not long after the crisis, developing at length the strategic balance rationale for Khrushchev's actions. This argument has remained an important strain in writings about the crisis by historians and political scientists specializing in international relations or security studies. But the defense-of-Cuba hypothesis has proved the most robust and longest lived, especially among historians. This view has derived its strength and longevity not only from the United States's demonstrated "arrogance of power" (in Senator Fulbright's phrase) before, during, and since the Vietnam War but also from documentary revelations concerning Operation Mongoose and precrisis invasion planning, as well as the subsequent stories offered by Khrushchev and some other Russians.

Kennedy and his advisers understood the reasoning in the Kremlin better than have most scholars writing about the crisis in retrospect. While Khrushchev and his colleagues did indeed care a great deal about Cuba, the thought of deterring a U.S. invasion figured only incidentally in their discussions about the missile deployments. Calculations about the strategic nuclear balance were much more in evidence. Berlin was an omnipresent and dominating concern.

To summarize what we now know about Soviet deliberations in 1962 is not, however, to state a final verdict on the motives guiding Soviet behavior before and during the crisis. The more we learn about Soviet decision making in the Khrushchev era, the less confidence we can feel in any analyses that explain decisions in terms of a hierarchy of interest calculations.

To interpret Soviet decisions is to interpret Khrushchev. He alone decided on policy. Other members of the Soviet elite who favored other policies could have their way only when Khrushchev was not around or not paying attention. No one could overrule him—yet.

Khrushchev made decisions largely on his own. Now and then, he would talk over a question with a fellow member of the Politburo or someone from the bureaucracy, but he did not systematically seek even advice, let alone policy analysis. He looked on other members of the Politburo as potential enemies. He may have had some respect for military leaders; he treasured memories of working with generals on the Ukrainian front in World War II. But he probably heeded military men only with regard to narrowly military issues. Khrushchev never obtained advice and analysis such as Kennedy obtained from his Executive Committee and, given the quality of the rest of the Soviet leadership, he could not have got it if he had tried.

Khrushchev acted more from instinct than from calculation. Whether Berlin or the strategic balance or concern about Cuba was uppermost in his mind at the time he ordered the missiles sent to Cuba, he himself could probably not have said. Having made a decision, however, he tended not to entertain second thoughts unless and until he had no choice. In both foreign and domestic affairs, he behaved like a roulette player who chooses a number and puts chips on the number until it produces a big payoff or the stack of chips has disappeared. Searching for the right adjective with which to characterize him, Fyodor Burlatsky and Georgi Shaknazarov, who had been aides to Khrushchev, agreed on the word *azartnyi,* which means, in Russian, "reckless" or "hotheaded." . . .

A few years later, as he dictated his memoirs, Khrushchev remembered that during an official visit to Bulgaria, From May 14 to 20, 1962, "[O]ne thought kept hammering at my brain: what will happen if we lose Cuba?" Soviet-Cuban relations were deeper and much more complex than Americans realized. The Soviets had begun providing covert assistance to the Castro government in the spring of 1959 and secretly arranged the first sales of arms that fall, before the U.S. government had decided whether Castro would be a friend or a foe. Some Americans and many Cubans suspected that the Castro regime harbored a secret radical agenda, that the security ministries were being brought under the control of pro-Soviet Communists in order to pursue this revolutionary agenda at home and abroad, and that this faction included Fidel Castro's brother, Raul, and Che Guevara, if not Fidel himself. Evidence from Soviet files shows that these suspicions were well founded.

From 1960 onward Castro repeatedly predicted horrific scenarios involving U.S. action against him, then took actions that made his prophecies self-fulfilling. In March 1960, blaming U.S. agents for the catastrophic explosion of a ship carrying arms into Havana from Belgium (there is no evidence of any U.S. involvement in the event), he denounced Washington and tightened his relations with Moscow. In anticipation of nationalizing U.S. property and liquidating his domestic opponents, he sought further Soviet military, economic, and intelligence assistance to contend with the U.S. intervention that he asserted would surely follow. The Kremlin obliged with a "blank check to buy whatever he needed," including direct cash payments to Fidel. Though Washington did not know all this, Castro's March 1960 attacks did catalyze the Eisenhower administration's decision to begin preparing covert operations to overthrow the Cuban leader.

In June 1960 Castro nationalized U.S. oil refineries (which had refused to refine Soviet crude oil) and again told the Soviets that an invasion was imminent. At about the same time Khrushchev received an intelligence report from a Soviet spy at NATO that the "chiefs at the Pentagon" were hoping to launch a preventive strike against the Soviet Union (the report was untrue). Apparently this report was taken seriously, for in early July Khrushchev gave a speech stressing Soviet capabilities for nuclear attack on the United States. In his best Suez crisis vein, Khrushchev threatened that Soviet rockets might fly if Washington chose to invade Cuba. The speech delighted the Cuban leader, who told the Soviets they had deterred an U.S. attack. Castro then publicized his closer friendship with Moscow.

There was another invasion scare in October 1960, Fursenko and Naftali discovered, based on rumors that Cuban exiles were being trained by the CIA in Guatemala. (Such training was in fact taking place, but the force was still months from being ready.) The Soviet and Cuban governments, genuinely believing an attack to be imminent, mobilized troops and sounded loud public alarms. Moscow again threatened use of its nuclear missiles. When the invasion did not come, the Cubans again believed the Soviet threats had deterred it. In early November, in a private address heard by Cuban Communists and the Soviet KGB resident, Castro extolled Marxism, professed always to have been a Marxist, and said again and again: "Moscow is our brain and our great leader, and we must pay attention to its voice."

Both the Cubans and the Soviets were caught by surprise when the Cuban exiles actually did invade, in April 1961. Khrushchev again thundered support for Castro and warnings to Washington, adding this time the threat that the flames ignited in Cuba could touch off a chain reaction of conflict across the globe. Again the Soviets took credit for deterring Kennedy from providing the military support that might have made the invasion succeed. And the Americans still failed to grasp that the Soviets and Cubans credited Soviet missiles for an apparent series of deterrent successes.

Increasingly, Khrushchev and the Soviet government linked their prestige with Castro's. They held out Cuba as the prime example of success in their newly announced global strategy of undermining capitalism through wars of national liberation in the developing world. It offered the chief proof that the Soviet Union, not China, remained the vanguard of world revolution. . . .

. . . Khrushchev broached his idea [of placing ballistic missiles in Cuba] to Defense Minister Rodion Malinovsky, who instantly became an enthusiastic supporter.

Knowing not only that the Soviet Union was far behind the United States in ICBMs but also that the existing ICBMs (SS-6s) were monstrous weapons of doubtful reliability and that successor models (SS-7s and SS-8s) were stalled in the two missile design bureaus, Malinovsky recognized in Khrushchev's proposal a way of shortcutting the time required to even the strategic balance. And Khrushchev was apparently enthusiastic. "Why not throw a hedgehog at Uncle Sam's pants?" he asked Malinovsky.

The Americans did not fully grasp how deeply, in the spring of 1962, Khrushchev and his colleagues felt that, in Malinovsky's words, "our inferior position was impossible to us." The United States touched the Soviets on this raw nerve by completing the long-delayed deployment of 15 Jupiter IRBMs at five launch sites in Turkey in early 1962. The Soviets had known all about the planned deployment for years. The plan was publicly announced by NATO in 1957, and Moscow had complained loudly, especially during 1958 and 1959. Although there is no evidence that Soviet planners attached any particular strategic significance to these obsolete systems or even to the nuclear-armed U.S. aircraft based in Turkey, which were the more worrisome weapons militarily, the deployment may have made it easier for Khrushchev and others to rationalize the decision concerning the missiles in Cuba.

In March and April 1962 the aspect of the nuclear standoff that most fully engaged both the Soviets and the Americans was their intense negotiations in Geneva about banning further test explosions of nuclear weapons. The Soviets had resumed aboveground testing with a dramatic series of detonations in September 1961. Under constant pressure to reciprocate in kind, Kennedy had held back. The key issue was the verification of a ban. Rusk and Gromyko wrangled over the issue in Geneva and got nowhere. On April 25 the United States resumed test explosions in the Pacific. This was when Khrushchev began privately exploring with Mikoyan and Malinovsky the idea of deploying missiles to Cuba.

Together, the Jupiter deployments and the resumption of testing irritated Khrushchev. He recalled later thinking that "it was high time America learned what it feels like to have her own land and her own people threatened." Since the United States was already threatened by Russian bombers and ICBMs, few or primitive though they might be, Khrushchev was surely thinking of the more visceral sense of threat created by missiles just across one's borders. Yuri Andropov, then a senior adviser to Khrushchev, privately told his boss that the Soviet deployment of missiles to Cuba was a way to "sight them at the soft underbelly of the Americans." Kennedy certainly felt it just that way. "A thing stuck right in our guts," was the metaphor he used to the Joint Chiefs of Staff on the morning of October 19. . . .

In July 1962 Raul Castro visited Moscow bringing a question for Khrushchev from Fidel: What would happen if the operation was discovered while in progress? Khrushchev answered that there was nothing to worry about; if there were trouble, he would send out the Baltic fleet as a show of support. Castro later acknowledged that the Cubans "did not think that it was the Baltic fleet that would solve the problem. What we were thinking about was Soviet will and determination, about Soviet strength. And we got the statement of the top leader of the Soviet Union that there was nothing to worry about, that he would not allow it. So what was really protecting us was the global strategic might of the USSR, not the rockets here." Castro was presuming that Khrushchev had thought through how he would handle a nuclear confrontation if the missile deployment was discovered before it was complete. As Castro himself later realized, there is no evidence that Khrushchev ever seriously considered this question.

Khrushchev did have an image of what would happen if he succeeded in presenting the United States with his planned fait accompli. The Kennedy administration, he believed, would "swallow this bitter pill. . . . I knew that the United States could knock out some of our installations, but not all of them. If a quarter or even a tenth of our missiles survived—even if only one or two big ones were left—we could still hit New York, and there wouldn't be much of New York left." Viewing Kennedy as a young, inexperienced intellectual presiding over a dangerously bellicose military establishment, Khrushchev apparently thought that Kennedy would let him get away with trickery and that he would end up with both the Soviet Union and Cuba better protected against the "chiefs in the Pentagon."

Khrushchev did not ask whether his ambassador in Washington or any other experts shared his estimate of the United States. Gromyko claimed later that he had warned Khrushchev privately "putting our missiles in Cuba would cause a political explosion in the United States" but that Khrushchev was unmoved by this advice. Commenting that Khrushchev "grossly misunderstood the psychology of his opponents," Ambassador Anatoly Dobrynin complained later: "Had he asked the embassy beforehand, we could have predicted the violent American reaction to his adventure once it became known. It is worth noting that Castro understood this. . . . But Khrushchev wanted to spring a surprise on Washington; it was he who got the surprise in the end when his secret plan was uncovered."

On May 12, on the eve of the key decisions about sending missiles to Cuba, Khrushchev spent about 14 hours with Kennedy's press aide, Pierre Salinger, then visiting Moscow. He barely mentioned Cuba. The central issue, Khrushchev said, was Berlin. Dobrynin, who took up his post at this time, remembered that "Germany and Berlin overshadowed everything." Describing what he expected to be his position when negotiations on Berlin resumed, Khrushchev had written to Kennedy in November 1961: "You have to understand, I have no ground to retreat further, there is a precipice behind."

The expression "precipice behind" vividly conveys the value Khrushchev now attached to success on Berlin. In another letter to Kennedy, Khrushchev protested that Washington's willingness to threaten a nuclear war to protect Berlin "can rest, excuse my harsh judgments, only on the megalomania, on an intention to act from the position of strength." In March 1962 he promised Kennedy that "one way or another" he would force the Western troops out. In late April the negotiations in Geneva between Gromyko and Rusk had reached a stalemate over Berlin. Angering his West German allies, Kennedy was willing to offer a modus vivendi that might allow the status quo to continue. But this had not been good enough for the Soviet government, which denounced the failure of the talks at the end of April.

Thus in late April and early May 1962, when Khrushchev was in the final stages of his decision to send missiles to Cuba, Berlin clearly had a large place in his thinking. Having issued ultimatums in 1958 and again in 1961, demanding Western departure from Berlin by specified deadlines, and having let those deadlines pass with the promise that negotiations would attain this goal, he was being forced to acknowledge failure publicly. East Germans were demanding a tougher

Soviet policy. The Americans, relying on their nuclear superiority, were pursuing a "policy of strength." In March 1962 Khrushchev told Dobrynin, just before the new ambassador left for Washington, that Berlin was the principal issue in U.S.-Soviet relations, said the U.S. was acting "particularly arrogant" about their nuclear deterrent, and concluded, "It's high time their long arms were cut shorter." He liked Kennedy and considered him a man of character, yet he also clearly believed "that putting pressure on Kennedy might bring us some success." . . .

Moscow was caught completely off guard by the U.S. discovery of the missiles and by Kennedy's simultaneous unveiling of both the discovery and the blockade. The reasons for their surprise puzzled U.S. officials at the time and remains puzzling to this day.

To provide a defense against U-2 surveillance, Khrushchev had suggested in July that the SA-2 air defense missiles go in first so they could shoot down U-2s and thwart detection of the missile installation. The vast plan for the shipments was reorganized accordingly, and the SA-2 missiles were in place and operational by late September. The U.S. fears of a U-2 shoot-down had, after some argument, deterred Washington from flying directly over Cuba for more than a month, but the overflights resumed in mid-October.

Soviet troops in Cuba seem to have tracked the U-2 overflights of October 14, 15, and 17. Their standing orders appear to have granted them authority to fire. We do not know why they did not. We can speculate that, with the U.S. warnings in the air, the central authorities in Moscow informally let commanders in Cuba know that they did not want any clash or gave other orders we do not know about. The Soviet forces in Cuba realized at the time of the overflights that the missile sites and IL-28s could well have been discovered. Fingers were pointed about adequate camouflage, though the construction of such complex sites for such large missiles was inherently hard to conceal. Yet, in a further mystery, there is no evidence that the commanders in Cuba ever dared to tell Moscow that the missile sites had been overflown and that the Americans probably knew about the missiles.

The Kremlin plunged into its own crisis deliberations on October 22, with news of the impending Kennedy speech. Unlike Kennedy, Khrushchev continued his usual foreign policy process, consulting a small group of Presidium members aided by the defense and foreign ministers and the leading international expert from the Communist Party's Central Committee. When a formal decision was needed, Khrushchev convened the full Presidium. At this point the 36 MRBMs (for 24 launchers) were in Cuba, with their nuclear warheads. So were nearly 100 other nuclear warheads for the coastal defense missiles, short-range rockets, and IL-28 bombers. Nuclear warheads to be carried on the IRBMs (for the 18 launch sites still under construction) were also in Cuba. The IRBMs themselves were still at sea.

Khrushchev was now very worried that the Americans would attack Cuba. He considered turning the nuclear weapons over to the Cubans and letting them respond. But he assured his colleagues he would not let Castro use the MRBMs against the United States. Perhaps, he wondered, the Cubans could deter an invasion simply by threatening use of the short-range tactical nuclear weapons against an invading force. In such a case, of course, a U.S. air strike, by itself, would in effect be uncontested.

The Presidium first decided that Malinovsky should cable General Issa Pliyev, the commander of Soviet troops in Cuba, ordering him to bring his troops to combat readiness and to use all Cuban and Soviet forces, except the nuclear arms, to meet an attack. Then, changing its mind, it considered a message authorizing use of the tactical nuclear weapons but not the ballistic missiles. Malinovsky was uneasy about this instruction, worrying that the Americans might intercept it and use it as a pretext for striking with their own nuclear weapons. So the Kremlin sent the first draft, withholding final authorization to use the nuclear weapons.

News of Kennedy's speech announcing the quarantine was greeted with relief when it arrived in Moscow in the early morning of October 23. The Americans were not going to attack. Reports also arrived from Soviet envoys. Dobrynin characterized the U.S. move as a general effort to reverse a decline in its world power, partly as a result of fears about Berlin. He warned that the Americans were preparing for a real test of strength, and then recommended that Moscow threaten a move against Berlin, starting with a ground blockade and "leaving out for the time being air routes so as not to give grounds for a quick confrontation." Yet Dobrynin added that Moscow should not be in a hurry to implement a blockade "since an extreme aggravation of the situation, it goes without saying, would not be in our interests." [Former intelligence agent and now Soviet Ambassador to Cuba Aleksandr] Alekseev meanwhile reported from Havana that the Cubans had mobilized, would not fire on U.S. planes unless the Americans fired first, would await the Soviet response, "and are placing their hopes on the wisdom of our decisions."

Considering the U.S. imposition of a blockade a weaker response that left room for political maneuver, the Kremlin issued its flat, tough response of October 23. Khrushchev and his Presidium did decide to halt most of the 30 ships en route to Cuba, but they directed that the 4 carrying IRBMs and a fifth, loaded with nuclear warheads for these missiles, continue on course. They ordered that the nuclear-armed submarines headed for Cuba also keep going. When [Soviet Deputy Minister of Foreign Affairs Vasily V.] Kuznetsov echoed Dobrynin's suggestion of countering the blockade with pressure against West Berlin, Khrushchev answered sharply that he could "do without such advice. . . . [W]e had no intention to add fuel to the conflict." Thus, General Curtis LeMay may have been right when he told Kennedy on October 19 that U.S. nuclear might would continue to safeguard Berlin. Nevertheless, some Soviet officials were ready to consider the option.

Tension increased on October 24. That morning brought Kennedy's brief unyielding demand for strict Soviet observance of the OAS [Organization of American States] quarantine. It also brought Dobrynin's cable reporting Robert Kennedy's flat statement that "We intend to stop your ships." Replying defiantly to Kennedy, Khrushchev declared that Soviet captains would run the blockade. At the same time, however, the Presidium decision of the previous day was apparently reversed. As McCone reported in the taped meeting on October 24, a fresh burst of signals had gone out to Soviet ships at sea in midmorning (Moscow time). The ships carrying the IRBMs now halted. A few ships with more innocent cargoes, including the *Bucharest* and *Grozny,* became the ones sailing ahead to test the quarantine. (The ship carrying the nuclear warheads for the IRBMs had already made it to a Cuban port.) Since it is extremely unlikely that the IRBM ships acted without Khrushchev's knowledge, it is possible that he was not candid with his own colleagues when he spoke at the Presidium of October 25 as if the missile ships were continuing on their way. Actual Soviet behavior justified Rusk's conclusion that, in the face of American firmness, Khrushchev "blinked." . . .

On the morning of October 25 the Soviet leadership had received Kennedy's tough, terse reply to Khrushchev's message. Khrushchev reconvened the Presidium. He told them he did not want to trade "caustic remarks" any longer with Kennedy. Instead he wanted to turn around four ships that were still carrying IRBMs to Cuba and try to resolve the crisis. (Again a puzzle, was Khrushchev only now revealing to his colleagues that he had ordered these ships to turn around the previous day?) Conciliation supplanted the previous day's defiance. Khrushchev announced to the Presidium his readiness to "dismantle the missiles to make Cuba into a zone of peace." He suggested sending a message including the words, "Give us a pledge not to invade Cuba, and we will remove the missiles." He would allow U.N. inspection of the missile sites. First, though, he wanted to be able to "look around" and be sure Kennedy really would not yield. . . .

Khrushchev promptly made several moves. He sent instructions to accept U Thant's proposal for avoiding a confrontation at the quarantine line, thereby promising to keep Soviet ships away from this line. He also dictated the long letter to Kennedy suggesting a peaceful resolution of the crisis: if the US promised not to invade Cuba, "the necessity for the presence of our military specialists in Cuba would disappear." . . .

With his October 26 letter to Kennedy, Khrushchev had moved to defuse the threat of an imminent invasion, but he had still not conceded anything concrete. Moreover, by keeping the correspondence private, he had hidden his tentative move from Castro. The frantic Soviet military activity in Cuba continued. By the next morning, October 27, Khrushchev came to a judgment, for reasons that are still obscure, that the Americans could be pushed harder. Perhaps, as some Americans had feared he might, he interpreted the selective U.S. enforcement of the quarantine as a sign of weakness. In direct contrast to Castro, whose relaxed attitude about a U.S. invasion had switched to alarm on October 26, Khrushchev had switched from alarm on October 26 to a more relaxed attitude on October 27.

The Soviet commander in Cuba, General Issa Pliyev, reported to the Defense Ministry that the Cubans had concluded that a U.S. air strike would begin that night or at dawn on October 27. Castro had ordered air defense units to fire at U.S. aircraft if there was an attack. Pliyev said that he had dispersed nuclear warheads closer to their launchers. The Soviet leaders endorsed Pliyev's plans.

Nevertheless, when Khrushchev convened the Presidium he told them that the United States would not dare to attack Cuba. Five days had passed since Kennedy's speech, and nothing had happened. "To my mind they are not ready to do it now." Since, however, there was no guarantee against a U.S. attack, Khrushchev would make another, more concrete offer that both acknowledged the presence of missiles in Cuba and added the U.S. missiles in Turkey to the bargain. With that, he said, "we would win."

Just as there is little evidence to explain why Khrushchev reversed his assessment of U.S. intentions, there is little evidence to explain why he now chose to add the Turkish missiles as a bargaining point. The missiles in Turkey had not been an important topic in any of the previous Presidium discussions during the crisis. . . .

Events during October 27 dispelled Khrushchev's complacent mood. A message from Castro, sent from Cuba on October 26, announced that a massive U.S. air strike, and possibly also an invasion, was "almost inevitable" in the next 24 to 72 hours. In the event of invasion, Castro urged Khrushchev to consider the "elimination of such a danger," plainly referring to the use of Soviet nuclear weapons against the United States. "However difficult and horrifying this decision may be," Castro wrote, "there is, I believe, no other recourse."

The same day brought news about the incursion of the U.S. U-2 into Siberian airspace. Aside from a reproach in his October 28 letter to Kennedy, we have no evidence about how Khrushchev viewed that episode.

Then the Cubans shot at unarmed U.S. low-level reconnaissance aircraft. On October 26 Castro had given the order to fire on any aircraft entering Cuban airspace. Alexeev had reported this intention on October 25, but Moscow seems not to have noticed. Castro discussed his order with Soviet commanders on October 26; this fact may have been reported to Moscow too. On October 27 Khrushchev sent instructions to Alexeev to suggest that Castro rescind the order; but by then, of course, it was too late, even if Castro had wished to heed the advice.

When the U-2 came over, it too was apparently, and falsely, perceived as posing a threat. Authority to fire had been delegated in the event of U.S. attack, and the local Soviet commanders (below Pliyev himself, who was temporarily unavailable) chose to interpret their instructions liberally in order to aid their excited Cuban comrades. Although a Soviet missile actually downed the plane, Khrushchev seems not to have fully grasped this fact until some time later.

Late in the afternoon of October 27 Khrushchev would have heard that the Americans had immediately rejected his public proposal with a press statement of their own. Alexeev reported telling Castro that "in the present circumstances it would not be fitting to aggravate the situation and initiate provocations." He said Castro understood, but "considering the rise in the army's martial spirit and the Americans' warning, our friends were compelled to take such a step."

Shaken by the shoot-down of the U-2, Khrushchev was also unnerved by Castro's urging him to prepare for using nuclear weapons against the United States. A few days later, in another message to Castro, Khrushchev referred to this "very alarming" message in which "you proposed that we be the first to carry out a nuclear strike against the enemy's territory." "Naturally," Khrushchev added, "you understand where that would lead us. It would not be a simple strike, but the start of a thermonuclear world war."

Kennedy's message to Khrushchev arrived late that evening, laying out the deal that would entail the verified withdrawal of Soviet "offensive weapons" in exchange for the noninvasion pledge. Khrushchev opened the Presidium session on the morning of October 28 with a very different assessment from the day before. He warned his colleagues that they were "face to face with the danger of war and of nuclear catastrophe, with the possible result of destroying the human race." He went on: "In order to save the world, we must retreat."

The new assessment was *not* apparently based on news of Robert Kennedy's latest (October 27) conversation with Dobrynin, but the news reinforced it. *After* Khrushchev made his declaration to the Politburo, word came in of the cable from Dobrynin reporting on the discussion in bleak, ominous terms. A summary of the cable was read to the Presidium. One of Khrushchev's staff recalled that the "entire tenor of the words by the President's brother, as they were relayed by Anatoly Dobrynin, prompted the conclusion that the time of reckoning had come." Khrushchev later told Castro that his warning of an imminent U.S. attack had been confirmed by other sources and that he had hurried to prevent it.

Khrushchev's resolve to yield was reinforced by Robert Kennedy's reported warning and by his assurance that Jupiters would eventually be withdrawn from Turkey. Reportedly only Khrushchev, Gromyko, and Mikoyan had much to say at this Presidium session. "Others preferred to keep silent as if hinting to Khrushchev that since he had made his bed, he could sleep on it." . . .

There was no time to consult with Castro. He learned of Khrushchev's decision from the radio, along with the rest of the world.

After the missile crisis was over, in January 1963, Khrushchev began walking away from his failed Berlin policy, by simply declaring victory. He began to argue that he had really won because in 1961 he had forced the West to accept the construction of the Berlin Wall and live with a divided Berlin. This had not, of course, been his position in 1962.

Khrushchev still could not stop wondering whether the Americans would really have gone to nuclear war over Berlin. Surely the Americans would not make such a threat unless they were incredibly complacent about their nuclear superiority. His Cuban deployment would have punctured that complacency. It would have vividly demonstrated the vulnerability he wanted the Americans to feel, the vulnerability that he thought would restrain them. After the Cuban venture failed, even after he had then also abandoned his 1962 plan of action on Berlin, Khrushchev still wanted to know: Had Washington been bluffing: In August 1963 Khrushchev asked Rusk point-blank: "Why should I believe that you Americans would fight a nuclear war over Berlin?" Rusk remembered, "That was quite a question. . . . So I stared back at him and said, 'Mr. Chairman, you will have to take into account the possibility that we Americans are just goddamn fools.' We glared at each other, unblinking and then he changed the subject and gave me three gold watches to take home to my children."

In November 1963 President Kennedy was murdered by a gunman who had long harbored grievances about Kennedy's hostility toward Castro's Cuba. In October 1964 Khrushchev was ousted from power by his Presidium colleagues. "You insisted that we deploy our missiles in Cuba," one of his Presidium accusers thundered. "This provoked the deepest crisis, carried the world to the brink of nuclear war, and even frightened terribly the organizer of this very danger." . . .

✦ F U R T H E R   R E A D I N G

Acosta, Tomas Diez. *October 1962: The "Missile" Crisis as Seen from Cuba* (2002).
Allison, Graham T. *Essence of Decision: Explaining the Cuban Missile Crisis* (1971).
Beschloss, Michael R. *The Crisis Years: Kennedy and Khrushchev, 1960–1963* (1991).
Betts, Richard K. *Nuclear Blackmail and Nuclear Balance* (1987).
Bissell, Richard M., Jr., with Jonathan E. Lewis and Frances T. Pudlow. *Reflections of a Cold Warrior: From Yalta to the Bay of Pigs* (1996).
Blaisier, Cole. *The Hovering Giant: U.S. Responses to Revolutionary Change in Latin America* (1975).

Blight, James G., Bruce J. Allyn, and David A. Welch. *Cuba on the Brink: Castro, the Missile Crisis, and the Soviet Collapse* (1993).

————, and David A. Welch. *On the Brink: Americans and Soviets Reexamine the Cuban Missile Crisis* (1989).

————, and Philip Brenner. *Sad and Luminous Days: Cuba's Struggle with the Superpowers After the Missile Crisis* (2002).

Chang, Laurence, and Peter Kornbluh, eds. *The Cuban Missile Crisis, 1962: A National Security Archive Documents Reader* (1992).

Cold War International History Project. "The Cuban Missile Crisis," *CWIHP Bulletin* 5 (Spring 1995).

Dobrynin, Anatoli. *In Confidence* (1995).

Fursenko, Aleksandr, and Timothy Naftali. *"One Hell of a Gamble": Khrushchev, Castro, and Kennedy, 1958–1964* (1997).

Garthoff, Raymond L. *Reflections on the Cuban Missile Crisis* (1989).

George, Alice L. *Awaiting Armageddon: How Americans Faced the Cuban Missile Crisis* (2003).

Gleijeses, Piero. *Conflicting Missions: Havana, Washington, and Africa* (2002).

Gribkov, Anatoli I., and William Y. Smith. *Operation ANADYR: U.S. and Soviet Generals Recount the Cuban Missile Crisis* (1994).

Gross, Peter. *Gentleman Spy: The Life of Allen Dulles* (1994).

Higgins, Trumbull. *The Perfect Failure* (1987).

Hillsman, Roger. *To Move a Nation: The Politics of Foreign Policy in the Administration of John F. Kennedy* (1967).

Kennedy, Robert F. *Thirteen Days: A Memoir of the Cuban Missile Crisis* (1969).

Kern, Montague, Patricia W. Levering, and Ralph B. Levering. *The Kennedy Crises: The Press, the Presidency, and the Foreign Policy* (1983).

Khrushchev, Nikita. *Khrushchev Remembers: The Glasnost Tapes* (1990).

LaFeber, Walter. *Inevitable Revolutions: The United States in Central America* (1983).

Lechuga, Carlos. *In the Eye of the Storm: Castro, Khrushchev, Kennedy, and the Missile Crisis,* trans. Mary Todd (1995).

May, Ernest R., and Philip D. Zelikow, eds. *The Kennedy Tapes: Inside the White House During the Cuban Missile Crisis* (2002).

McCauliffe, Mary S., ed. *CIA Documents on the Cuban Missile Crisis* (1992).

McNamara, Robert. *Blundering into Disaster* (1986).

Nash, Philip. *The Other Missiles of October: Eisenhower, Kennedy and the Jupiters, 1957–1963* (1997).

Nathan, James A., ed. *The Cuban Missile Crisis Revisited* (1992).

Paterson, Thomas G. *Contesting Castro: The United States and the Triumph of the Cuban Revolution* (1994).

Pope, Ronald R., ed. *Soviet Views on the Cuban Missile Crisis: Myth and Reality in Foreign Policy Analysis* (1982).

Powers, Thomas. *The Man Who Kept the Secrets* (1981).

Quirk, Robert E. *Fidel Castro* (1993).

Smith, Gaddis. *The Last Years of the Monroe Doctrine, 1945–1993* (1994).

Stern, Sheldon M. *Averting "The Final Failure": John F. Kennedy and the Secret Cuban Missile Crisis Meetings* (2003).

————. *The Week the World Stood Still: Inside the Secret Cuban Missile Crisis* (2005).

Szulc, Tad. *Fidel* (1986).

Taylor, Maxwell, et al. *Operation ZAPATA: The "Ultrasensitive" Report and Testimony of the Board of Inquiry on the Bay of Pigs* (1981).

Welch, David A., ed. *Proceedings of the Hawk's Cay Conference on the Cuban Missile Crisis, March 5–8, 1987* (1987).

Welch, Richard E., Jr. *Response to Revolution: The United States and Cuba, 1959–1961* (1985).

White, Mark J. *The Cuban Missile Crisis* (1996).

CHAPTER
5

The African American Struggle for Equality

The African American struggle for freedom and equality is one of the most important and defining events in postwar America. The struggle played out not only in the courts and in the halls of Congress, but also in the workplace, in schools and churches, on college campuses, in the streets, and at lunchroom counters. No part of American life escaped its influence. Moreover, it was a struggle not just of individual leaders, however charismatic, but of ordinary men and women who found the courage and dignity to demand change. The changes they demanded, as the following documents and essays suggest, raise questions (many of them still unresolved) that go to the heart of the American experience. For example, what do Americans mean when they profess to believe in equality? Do we believe in equality of condition or in equality of opportunity? How has race (or gender or class) limited the application of such beliefs? What actions are appropriate for government and other institutions to take in the pursuit of equality, and which are inappropriate?

Between 1945 and the present, the many laws, court decisions, and public policies that had sustained racial segregation since the late nineteenth century were swept aside, transforming the nation's racial relations in a single genera-tion. Yet the history of those earlier days, their legacy, remains deeply embedded in the nation's social structure. While some middle-class African Americans have profited from the new economic and social opportunities created by the civil rights movement, the plight of many poor African Americans has actually worsened. Meanwhile, growing white opposition to affirmative action and other minority programs threatened to further slow the pace of change. At the beginning of the twenty-first century, the dream invoked by Martin Luther King Jr. remains only partially fulfilled.

DOCUMENTS

World War II marked a watershed in the struggle for equality. Many African Ameri-cans served in the armed forces, albeit in segregated units; others found work in defense plants. Wartime rhetoric about freedom and democracy raised expectations

of expanded rights and opportunities. Most importantly, African Americans themselves displayed a new confidence and determination. The return of African American soldiers was nevertheless greeted by violence in parts of the South, as suggested
by a *New York Times* report of July 27, 1946 (Document 1). In the war's wake,
African American parents renewed their efforts to secure more equal educational
opportunities for their children, as shown in the petition from parents in Clarendon,
South Carolina (Document 2). The Clarendon case, prepared by a team of NAACP
lawyers that included Thurgood Marshall, became one of the five cases decided by
the Supreme Court's historic decision in the matter of *Brown v. Board of Education,
Topeka, Kansas,* which held that racially segregated schools were "inherently unequal."
The *Brown* decision had an enormous symbolic impact, addressing as it did the deep-
seated conflict between the equalitarian rhetoric of America's founding and its long
history of slavery and segregation. However, the history of *Brown* itself was complicated. To be sure, the decision helped fuel an already growing civil rights movement.
But the Court temporized in enforcing the ruling, as did President Dwight D. Eisenhower, who privately voiced his disagreement with the decision. Not until 1968
would *Brown* be effectively enforced in the South. Meanwhile, as an excerpt from
novelist Alan Paton's 1954 article in *Collier's* suggests (Document 3), residential
segregation remained a powerful barrier to opportunity for African Americans.
Indeed, in both the North and South new patterns of suburban residential segregation
would increasingly assert themselves, while the Supreme Court's 1974 decision
in *Milliken v. Bradley* would effectively limit efforts to achieve school integration in
large metropolitan districts.

The history of the civil rights movement was shaped not only by national leaders
and court decisions, but also by the local actions of courageous men and women who
directly challenged the Jim Crow system of segregation and discrimination. While
some of these efforts predated *Brown,* the Court's decision spurred growing local
protests throughout the nation. In Document 4, Franklin McCain, then an eighteen-
year-old freshman at historically all-black North Carolina A&T University, recalls
the first sit-in of the 1960s. Only twenty-six years old when he helped lead the 1955
Montgomery Bus Boycott, Martin Luther King Jr. quickly became the movement's
most charismatic leader, drawing strength from and inspiring protests throughout the
nation. His "I Have a Dream" address before the Lincoln Memorial during the March
on Washington in August 1963, couched in the spiritual vernacular of the African
American church and the equal rights language of the Declaration of Independence,
is one of the most famous speeches in American history (Document 5). The years
that immediately followed King's historic speech were marked by continuing local
struggles throughout much of the South, many of them met by violent resistance. They
were also marked by a series of major new laws, court decisions, and administrative initiatives, including the Civil Rights Acts of 1964 and 1965, which prohibited
discrimination in voting, education, and the use of public facilities, and empowered
the federal government to act more decisively in ending segregation and other discriminatory practices. (See Document 2 in Chapter 6 for an excerpt from the 1964
Civil Rights Act.)

By the mid-1960s, however, King's leadership was increasingly challenged by
younger, more radical activists such as Stokely Carmichael, a leader of the Student
Nonviolent Coordinating Committee (SNCC), who in Document 6 defends the call
for "black power." Resistance to the civil rights movement occurred not just in the
South, where beatings and even murders were not infrequent, but throughout the
nation, including even federal law enforcement agencies such as the Federal Bureau

of Investigation, which carried out an elaborate secret campaign to discredit King and other civil rights leaders. Document 7 is excerpted from a 1976 investigation of the FBI by a U.S. Senate committee chaired by Democratic Senator Frank Church of Idaho. As the focus of the struggle for equality shifted from the South to the North, and from civil rights to economic justice, the level of anger and frustration on the part of African Americans steadily mounted, exploding in the mid-1960s in a series of riots that convulsed almost every major city in the United States. Document 8, reprinted from the *Milwaukee Journal,* logs the reports by police officers and firefighters in Milwaukee, Wisconsin, during a riot that erupted late at night on July 30, 1967.

1. The *New York Times* Reports a Murder in Georgia, 1946

Monroe, Ga., July 26—Two young Negroes, one a veteran just returned from the war, and their wives were lined up last night near a secluded road and shot dead by an unmasked band of twenty white men.

The ghastly details of the multiple lynching were told today by Loy Harrison, a well-to-do white farmer who had just hired the Negroes to work on his farm. Harrison was bringing the Negroes to his farm when his car was waylaid by the mob eight miles from Monroe. Questioning of one of the Negroes by the mob indicated, Harrison said, that he was suspected of having stabbed his former employer, a white man. The Negroes, Roger Malcolm and George Dorsey, both 27, were removed from the car and led down a side road.

The women, who were sisters and who had just recently married Malcolm and Dorsey, began to scream. Then a mob member said that one of the women had recognized him.

"Get those damned women, too," the mob leader shouted.

Several of the men then came back and dragged the shrieking women from the automobile. A few moments later Mr. Harrison heard the shots—many of them and the mob dispersed.

The grotesquely sprawled bodies were found in a clump of bushes beside a little-used side road, the upper parts of the bodies scarcely recognizable from the mass of bullet holes.

Dorsey's mother, Monia Williams, said that her son had just been discharged after five years in the Army and that she had received his discharge button in the mail just this week.

The lynching was the first in the nation in nearly a year and was the first multiple lynching since two 14-year-old Negro boys were hanged by a Mississippi mob in October 1942. For Georgia it was the first lynching of more than one person since 1918 when ten Negroes were lynched in Brooks County.

---

2. African American Parents Petition the Clarendon, S.C., School Board, 1949

STATE OF SOUTH CAROLINA)

)   PETITION

COUNTY OF CLARENDON   )

To: The Board of Trustees for School District Number 22, Clarendon County, South Carolina, R. W. Elliott, Chairman, J. D. Carson and George Kennedy, Members; The County Board of Education for Clarendon County, South Carolina, L. B. McCord, Chairman, Superintendent of Education for Clarendon County, A. J. Plowden, W. E. Baker, Members, and H. B. Betchman, Superintendent of School District #22.

Your petitioners, Harry, Eliza, Harry Jr., Thomas Lee, Katherine Briggs [ninety-eight additional names]. . . children of public school age, eligible for elementary and high school education in the public schools of School District #22, Clarendon County, South Carolina, their parents, guardians and next friends respectfully represent:

1. That they are citizens of the United States and of the State of South Carolina and reside in School District #22 in Clarendon County and State of South Carolina.
2. That the individual petitioners are Negro children of public school age who reside in said county and school district and now attend the public schools in School District #22, in Clarendon County, South Carolina, and their parents and guardians.
3. That the public school system in School District #22, Clarendon County, South Carolina, is maintained on a separate, segregated basis, with white children attending the Summerton High School and the Summerton Elementary School, and Negro children forced to attend the Scott Branch High School, the Liberty Hill Elementary School or Rambay Elementary School solely because of their race and color.
4. That the Scott's Branch High School is a combination of an elementary and high school, and the Liberty Hill and Rambay Elementary Schools are elementary schools solely.
5. That the facilities, physical condition, sanitation and protection from the elements in the Scott's Branch High School, the Liberty Hill Elementary School and Rambay Elementary School, the only three schools to which Negro pupils are permitted to attend, are inadequate and unhealthy, the buildings and schools are old and overcrowded and in a dilapidated condition; the facilities, physical condition, sanitation and protection from the elements in the Summerton High in the Summerton Elementary Schools in school district number twenty-two are modern, safe, sanitary, well equipped, lighted and healthy and the buildings and schools are new, modern, uncrowded and maintained in first class condition.

Petition, Harry Briggs et al., to the Board of Trustees for School District 22, Clarendon County, South Carolina, online at http://www.palmettohistory.org/exhibits/briggs/pages/Briggs1.htm.

6. That the said schools attended by Negro pupils have an insufficient number of teachers and insufficient class room space, whereas the white schools have an adequate complement of teachers and adequate class room space for the students.
7. That the said Scott's Branch High School is wholly deficient and totally lacking in adequate facilities for teaching courses in General Science, Physics and Chemistry, Industrial Arts and Trades, and has no adequate library and no adequate accommodations for the comfort and convenience of the students.
8. That there is in said elementary and high schools maintained for Negroes no appropriate and necessary central heating system, running water or adequate lights.
9. That the Summerton High School and Summerton Elementary School, maintained for the sole use, comfort and convenience of the white children of said district and county, are modern and accredited schools with central heating, running water, adequate electric lights, library and up to date equipment.
10. That Scott's Branch High School is without services of a janitor or janitors, while at the same time janitorial services are provided for the high school maintained for white children.
11. That Negro children of public school age are not provided any bus transportation to carry them to and from school while sufficient bus transportation is provided white children traveling to and from schools which are maintained for them.
12. That said schools for Negroes are in an extremely dilapidated condition, without heat of any kind other than old stoves in each room, that said children must provide their own fuel for said stoves in order to have heat in the rooms, and that they are deprived of equal educational advantages with respect to those available to white children of public school age of the same district and county.
13. That the Negro children of public school age in School District #22 and in Clarendon County are being discriminated against solely because of their race and color in violation of their rights to equal protection of the laws provided by the 14th amendment to the Constitution of the United States.
14. That without the immediate and active intervention of this Board of Trustees and County Board of Education, the Negro children of public school age of aforesaid district and county will continue to be deprived of their constitutional rights to equal protection of the laws and to freedom from discrimination because of race or color in the educational facilities and advantages which the said District #22 and Clarendon County are under a duty to afford and make available to children of school age within their jurisdiction.

Wherefore, Your petitioners request that: (1) the Board of Trustees of School District Number twenty-two, the County Board of Education of Clarendon County and the Superintendent of School District #22 immediately cease discriminating against Negro children of public school age in said district and county and immediately make available to your petitioners and all other Negro children of public school age similarly situated educational advantages and facilities equal in all respects to that which is being provided for whites; (2) That they be permitted to appear before the Board of Trustees of District #22 and before the County Board of Education of Clarendon, by their attorneys, to present their complaint; (3) Immediate action on this request.

Dated 11 November 1949

3. A South African Novelist Examines the Plight of "The Negro in the North," 1954

Housing and employment hold the key to the problem of integration of the Negro into the life of America. The cry of the Negro is no longer, "Let my people go"; it is, "Let my people in." There is hardly a community in America where the purchase of a house by a Negro in a hitherto "white" section does not cause resentment, leading at times to violence. In Louisville, shots are fired and bricks hurled through the windows of Andrew E. Wade, a veteran, and the cross is burned outside his house. In Philadelphia, mobs batter the house bought by Wiley Clark and force him and his wife and four children to sell out and look elsewhere for a home. In Levittown, Long Island, and in Levittown, Pennsylvania, Mr. Levitt builds 33,700 houses, but no Negro need apply. . . .

The great weapon of the segregator has always been the restrictive covenant, intended to guarantee forever that a white-owned house would pass only into white hands. . . . In 1926 such covenants were upheld by the courts. . . . [Restrictive covenants were ruled unconstitutional by the Supreme Court in 1948, yet continued to be used on a widespread basis.]

But I heard that there is yet another covenant, an unwritten one, that a white realtor must not sell white-owned property to any colored man. . . .

In 1934 the Federal Housing Administration regarded itself as a business organization, and regarded Negro occupancy as harmful from a business point of view. In 1937 it actually published a model race-restrictive covenant. In the words of Mr. Loren Miller, of Los Angeles, one of the most powerful Negro fighters against the covenant, "the FHA sowed race-restrictive covenants through the country far and wide." The FHA dropped the model covenant in 1949, and declared it would no longer insure loans in new developments where there were covenants. . . .

The American drama . . . the struggle between ideal and practice, . . . is being played today, in the theater of Trumbull Park.

Trumbull Park is a low-cost housing project of 462 apartments opened by the Chicago Housing Authority in the white section called South Deering. In 1950, the CHA declared that there would be no racial discrimination in its projects; "the laws of the state of Illinois make it a criminal offense." Thereafter, Negroes moved into a number of new developments, but no Negroes moved into older CHA projects in "white" neighborhoods.

As in so many cities in America, the congestion in housing occupied by Negroes and its generally squalid condition set up a pressure that endlessly seeks relief. That was how, on July 30, 1953, the Donald Howards came to Trumbull Park, hitherto an all-"white" project. It was Mrs. Howard, who does not look like many Negroes look, who got the apartment. Suddenly the CHA realized that its ideal had been fully translated into practice. There were Negroes at Trumbull Park.

Before that, the Howards had moved from room to room to room, always looking for something bigger and better and cleaner, a place where their children could play. And at last they got this place. Mrs. Howard could hardly believe it; Donald Howard said, "This is it."

Alan Paton, "The Negro in the North," *Collier's*, 29 October 1954, 70–72, 74–75, 77, 79–80. Reprinted by permission of the Alan Paton Will Trust via Ewing Trust Company Ltd., Hillcrest, South Africa.

That was it, sure enough; in the weeks that followed, the Howards lived as very few human families have had to live. There were people in South Deering who were determined to get them out. They milled about in front of the Howards' apartment; many times a day, and every day, they fired off giant fireworks, which are known as aerial bombs and are forbidden by Illinois law. They shouted insults and smashed windows; they were kept back by hundreds of policemen on duty day after day. The Howards lived behind boarded windows, their children in terror, all youngness gone, in a cacophony of bombs and curses and smashing glass. Christians did this, not knowing or not caring for the fierce words of their Lord. The Howards wanted their rights as Americans, and they wanted some place to live. In the end, tried beyond their strength, they moved away. . . .

I met Mr. Herman King, one of the colored tenants [of Trumbull Park], a veteran. He is a big man, and he talked to me quietly, but he talked to me like a man who has some deep internal pain, and wishes wistfully that it were not there, but that is how it is. Sometimes he stopped talking and looked out into space, which was not very far, because the blinds were down. . . .

"We nearly moved out once," he said. "Then we thought of all the work done to get Negroes in. I wasn't prepared to see it wasted. So I felt obligated to go on. I didn't come in as a crusader. I came to get a place to live. I'm a man of principle, but no man wants to die for it if he can live. But I'm going to stay. I had to become a crusader after all." . . .

"I was coming home from work one day last February," he said. "There was a tremendous crowd, shouting and yelling. I thought I would get out of the bus farther on, and get back through the south end. But in trying to avoid one crowd, I walked into another. They had sticks and stones and asked me where I lived. I told them I was lost, and lived in some other place.

"'Get out,' they said, 'and get out fast.'

"A woman shouted, 'Beat that nigger's brains out,' but there was an old man there who kept on saying, 'Don't hurt that nigger, he don't live around here.' I often think of that. I reckon that old man saved my life.

"I started walking. My heart was in my mouth, but I was acting calm. Someone yelled, 'Pick up some speed, nigger.'

"So I picked up some speed. A stone hit me. I am proud to this day that I had no weapon on me. Something told me to stop, and something told me to go on. They called out, 'Faster, nigger, faster' and something told me, 'No,' and something, 'Yes.' So I went faster.

"When I reached the big street, there was a bus right there, and I got in. But before I even sat down, every window on that side was broken. I moved over, out of the glass, and every window on the other side was broken too. The driver stopped the bus, which was the last thing I wanted. He sent for the police, and they took our names, but I didn't dare to give my right name, because of my wife and children. I got off the bus some long way off and sat down on the edge of the sidewalk for twenty-five minutes, trying to pull myself together. Then I got up, but there was hardly any strength in my legs."

He sat for a long time remembering it. His face was covered with sweat, and he wiped it off.

"That night took seven years off my life," he said. "I'll never get used to it."

We sat in silence for a long time. . . .

He saw me looking at a card that hangs on the wall. Smile, it said.
"Sometimes I can't," he said. . . .

4. Franklin McCain Remembers
the First Sit-in, 1960

[Howell Raines] It was one of those group friendships that spring up among college freshmen. In the first semester at all-black North Carolina A&T College
in Greensboro, he [Franklin McCain] and Ezell Blair Jr., David Richmond, and
Joseph McNeil became inseparable. They would study together, eat together, and "as
young freshmen often do in college dormitories late at night, when they finish
studying or when they want to cop out from studying . . . resort to the old-fashion
type bull session."

Through the fall, their talks continued. He remembers them as "elementary
philosophers," young idealists talking about justice and injustice, hypocrisy, how
imperfectly their society embodied its own ideals. Slowly their talks swung to a
debate as old as philosophy itself: at what point does the moral man act against
injustice? ". . . I think the thing that precipitated the sit-in, the idea of the sit-in,
more than anything else, was that little bit of incentive and that little bit of courage
that each of us instilled within each other."

[McCain] The planning process was on a Sunday night, I remember it quite well.
I think it was Joseph who said, "It's time that we take some action now. We've been
getting together, and we've been, up to this point, still like most people we've
talked about for the past few weeks or so—that is, people who talk a lot but, in fact,
make very little action." After selecting the technique, then we said, "Let's go down
and just ask for service." It certainly wasn't titled a "sit-in" or "sit-down" at that
time. "Let's just go down to Woolworth's tomorrow and ask for service, and the
tactic is going to be simply this: we'll just stay there." We never anticipated being
served, certainly, the first day anyway. "We'll stay until we get served." And I think
Ezell said, "Well, you know that might be weeks, that might be months, that might
be never." And I think it was the consensus of the group, we said, "Well, that's just
the chance we'll have to take."

What's likely to happen? Now, I think that that was a question that all of us
asked ourselves. . . . What's going to happen once we sit down? Of course, nobody
had the answers. Even your wildest imagination couldn't lead you to believe what
would, in fact, happen.

[Raines] Why Woolworth's?

[McCain] They advertise in public media, newspapers, radios, television, that
sort of thing. They tell you to come in: "Yes, buy the toothpaste; yes, come in and
buy the notebook paper. . . . No, we don't separate your money in this cash register;
but, no, please don't step down to the hot dog stand. . . ." The whole system, of

course, was unjust, but that just seemed like insult added to injury. That was just like pouring salt into an open wound. That's inviting you to do something. . . .

Once getting there . . . we did make purchases of schools supplies and took the patience and time to get receipts for our purchases, and Joseph and myself went over to the counter and asked to be served coffee and doughnuts. As anticipated, the reply was "I'm sorry, we don't serve you here." And of course we said, "We just beg to disagree with you. We've in fact already been served; you've served us already and that's just not quite true." The attendant or waitress was a little bit dumbfounded, just didn't know what to say under circumstances like that. And we said, "We wonder why you'd invite us in to serve us at one counter and deny service at another. If this is a private club or private concern, then we believe you ought to sell membership cards and sell only to persons who have a membership card. If we don't have a card, then we'd know pretty well that we shouldn't come in or even attempt to come in." That didn't go over too well, simply because I don't really think she understood what we were talking about, and for the second reason, she had no logical response to a statement like that. And the only thing that an individual in her case or position could do is, or course, call the manager. [Laughs] Well, at this time, I think we were joined by Dave Richmond and Ezell Blair at the counter with us, after that dialogue.

[Raines] Were you afraid at this point?

[McCain] Oh, hell yes, no question about that. [Laughs] At that point there was a policeman who had walked in off the street, who was pacing the aisle . . . behind us, where we were seated, with his club in his hand, just sort of knocking it in his hand, and just looking mean and red and a little bit upset and a little bit disgusted. And you had the feeling that he didn't know what the hell to do. You had the feeling that this is the first time that this big bad man with the gun and the club has been pushed in a corner, and he's got absolutely no defense, and the thing that's killing him more than anything else—he doesn't know what he can or what he cannot do. He's defenseless. Usually his defense is offense, and we've provoked him, yes, but we haven't provoked him outwardly enough for him to resort to violence. And I think this is just killing him; you can see it all over him.

People in the store were—we got mixed reactions from people in the store. A couple of old ladies . . . came up to pat us on the back sort of and say. "Ah, you should have done it ten years ago. It's a good thing I think you're doing."

[Raines] These were black ladies.

[McCain] No, these are white ladies.

[Raines] Really?

[McCain] Yes, and by the same token, we had some white ladies and white men come up and say to us, "Nasty, dirty niggers, you know you don't belong here at the lunch counter. There's a counter—" There was, in fact, a counter downstairs in the Woolworth store, a stand-up type counter where they sold hot dogs. . . .

[Raines] But at any rate, there were expressions of support from white people that day?

[McCain] Absolutely right. Absolutely. And I think probably that was certainly one incentive for additional courage on the part of us. And the other thing that helped us psychologically quite a lot was seeing the policeman pace the aisle and

not be able to do anything. I think that this probably gave us more strength, more encouragement, than anything else on that particular day, on day one.

[Raines] Unexpected as it was, the well-wishing from the elderly white women was hardly more surprising than the scorn of a middle-aged black dishwasher behind the counter. She said, "That's why we can't get anyplace today, because of people like you, rabble-rousers, troublemakers. . . . this counter is reserved for white people, it always has been, and you are all aware of that. So why don't you go on out and stop making trouble?"

He has since seen the woman at, of all places, a reunion commemorating the event in which she played so unsupportive a role.

[McCain] [She said] "Yes, I did say it and I said it because, first of all, I was afraid for what would happen to you as young black boys. Secondly, I was afraid of what would happen to me as an individual who had a job at the Woolworth store. I might have been fired and that's my livelihood. . . ."

It took me a long time to really understand that statement . . . but I know why she said it. She said it out of fear more than anything else. I've come to understand that, and my elders say to me that it's maturity that makes me understand why she said that some fifteen years ago.

[Raines] But, moved by neither praise nor scorn, he and the others waited for the waitress to return with the manager, a career Woolworth's employee named C. L. Harris.

[McCain] That was real amusin' as well [laughing] because by then we had the confidence, my goodness, of a Mack truck. And there was virtually nothing that could move us, there was virtually nothing probably at that point that could really frighten us off. . . . If it's possible to know what it means to have your soul cleansed—I felt pretty clean at that time. I probably felt better on that day than I've ever felt in my life. Seems like a lot of feelings of guilt or what-have-you suddenly left me, and I felt as though I had gained my manhood, so to speak, and not only gained it, but had developed quite a lot of respect for it. Not Franklin McCain only as an individual, but I felt as though the manhood of a number of other black persons had been restored and had gotten some respect from just that one day.

5. Martin Luther King Jr., "I Have a Dream," 1963

I am happy to join with you today in what will go down in history as the greatest demonstration for freedom in the history of our nation.

Fivescore years ago, a great American, in whose symbolic shadow we stand today, signed the Emancipation Proclamation. This momentous decree came as a great beacon light of hope to millions of Negro slaves who had been seared in the flames of withering injustice. It came as a joyous daybreak to end the long night of their captivity.

But one hundred years later, the Negro still is not free; one hundred years later, the life of the Negro is still sadly crippled by the manacles of segregation and the chains of discrimination; one hundred years later, the Negro lives on a lonely island of poverty in the midst of a vast ocean of material prosperity; one hundred years later, the Negro is still languished in the corners of American society and finds himself in exile in his own land.

So we've come here today to dramatize a shameful condition. In a sense we've come to our nation's capital to cash a check. When the architects of our republic wrote the magnificent words of the Constitution and the Declaration of Independence, they were signing a promissory note to which every American was to fall heir. This note was the promise that all men, yes, black men as well as white men, would be guaranteed the unalienable rights of life, liberty, and the pursuit of happiness.

It is obvious today that America has defaulted on this promissory note in so far as her citizens of color are concerned. Instead of honoring this sacred obligation, America has given the Negro people a bad check; a check which has come back marked "insufficient funds." We refuse to believe that there are insufficient funds in the great vaults of opportunity of this nation. And so we've come to cash this check, a check that will give us upon demand the riches of freedom and the security of justice.

We have also come to this hallowed spot to remind America of the fierce urgency of now. This is no time to engage in the luxury of cooling off or to take the tranquilizing drug of gradualism. Now is the time to make real the promises of democracy; now is the time to rise from the dark and desolate valley of segregation to the sunlit path of racial justice; now is the time to lift our nation from the quicksands of racial injustice to the solid rock of brotherhood; now is the time to make justice a reality for all God's children. It would be fatal for the nation to overlook the urgency of the moment. This sweltering summer of the Negro's legitimate discontent will not pass until there is an invigorating autumn of freedom and equality.

Nineteen sixty-three is not an end, but a beginning. And those who hope that the Negro needed to blow off steam and will now be content, will have a rude awakening if the nation returns to business as usual.

There will be neither rest nor tranquility in America until the Negro is granted his citizenship rights. The whirlwinds of revolt will continue to shake the foundations of our nation until the bright day of justice emerges.

But there is something that I must say to my people who stand on the warm threshold which leads into the palace of justice. In the process of gaining our rightful place we must not be guilty of wrongful deeds.

Let us not seek to satisfy our thirst for freedom by drinking from the cup of bitterness and hatred. We must forever conduct our struggle on the high plane of dignity and discipline. We must not allow our creative protest to degenerate into physical violence. Again and again we must rise to the majestic heights of meeting physical force with soul force.

The marvelous new militancy which has engulfed the Negro community must not lead us to a distrust of all white people, for many of our white brothers, as evidenced by their presence here today, have come to realize that their destiny is tied up with our destiny and they have come to realize that their freedom is inextricably bound to our freedom. This offense we share mounted to storm the battlements of injustice must be carried forth by a biracial army. We cannot walk alone.

And as we walk, we must make the pledge that we shall always march ahead. We cannot turn back. There are those who are asking the devotees of civil rights, "When will you be satisfied?" We can never be satisfied as long as the Negro is the victim of the unspeakable horrors of police brutality.

We can never be satisfied as long as our bodies, heavy with fatigue of travel, cannot gain lodging in the motels of the highways and the hotels of the cities. We cannot be satisfied as long as the Negro's basic mobility is from a smaller ghetto to a large one.

We can never be satisfied as long as our children are stripped of their selfhood and robbed of their dignity by signs stating "for whites only." We cannot be satisfied as long as a Negro in Mississippi cannot vote and a Negro in New York believes he has nothing for which to vote. No, we are not satisfied, and we will not be satisfied until justice rolls down like waters and righteousness like a mighty stream.

I am not unmindful that some of you have come here out of excessive trials and tribulation. Some of you have come fresh from narrow jail cells. Some of you have come from areas where your quest for freedom left you battered by the storms of persecution and staggered by the winds of police brutality. You have been the veterans of creative suffering. Continue to work with the faith that unearned suffering is redemptive.

Go back to Mississippi; go back to Alabama; go back to South Carolina; go back to Georgia; go back to Louisiana; go back to the slums and ghettos of the northern cities, knowing that somehow this situation can, and will be changed. Let us not wallow in the valley of despair.

So I say to you, my friends, that even though we must face the difficulties of today and tomorrow, I still have a dream. It is a dream deeply rooted in the American dream that one day this nation will rise up and live out the true meaning of its creed—we hold these truths to be self-evident, that all men are created equal.

I have a dream that one day on the red hills of Georgia, sons of former slaves and sons of former slave-owners will be able to sit down together at the table of brotherhood.

I have a dream that one day, even the state of Mississippi, a state sweltering with the heat of injustice, sweltering with the heat of oppression, will be transformed into an oasis of freedom and justice.

I have a dream my four little children will one day live in a nation where they will not be judged by the color of their skin but by [the] content of their character. I have a dream today!

I have a dream that one day, down in Alabama, with its vicious racists, with its governor having his lips dripping with the words of interposition and nullification, that one day, right there in Alabama, little black boys and black girls will be able to join hands with little white boys and white girls as sisters and brothers. I have a dream today!

I have a dream that one day every valley shall be exalted, every hill and mountain shall be made low, the rough places shall be made plain, and the crooked places shall be made straight and the glory of the Lord will be revealed and all flesh shall see it together.

This is our hope. This is the faith that I go back to the South with.

With this faith we will be able to hew out of the mountain of despair a stone of hope. With this faith we will be able to transform the jangling discords of our nation into a beautiful symphony of brotherhood.

With this faith we will be able to work together, to pray together, to struggle together, to go to jail together, to stand up for freedom together, knowing that we will be free one day. This will be the day when all of God's children will be able to sing with new meaning—"my country 'tis of thee; sweet land of liberty; of thee I sing; land where my fathers died, land of the pilgrim's pride; from every mountainside, let freedom ring"—and if America is to be a great nation, this must become true.

So let freedom ring from the prodigious hilltops of New Hampshire.

Let freedom ring from the mighty mountains of New York.

Let freedom ring from the heightening Alleghenies of Pennsylvania.

Let freedom ring from the snow-capped Rockies of Colorado.

Let freedom ring from the curvaceous slopes of California.

But not only that.

Let freedom ring from Stone Mountain of Georgia.

Let freedom ring from Lookout Mountain of Tennessee.

Let freedom ring from every hill and molehill of Mississippi, from every mountainside, let freedom ring.

And when we allow freedom to ring, when we let it ring from every village and hamlet, from every state and city, we will be able to speed up that day when all of God's children—black men and white men, Jews and Gentiles, Catholics and Protestants—will be able to join hands and to sing in the words of the old Negro spiritual, "Free at last, free at last; thank God Almighty, we are free at last."

6. Stokely Carmichael Explains "Black Power," 1967

One of the tragedies of the struggle against racism is that up to now there has been no national organization which could speak to the growing militancy of young black people in the urban ghetto. There has been only a civil rights movement, whose tone of voice was adapted to an audience of liberal whites. It served as a sort of buffer zone between them and angry young blacks. None of its so-called leaders could go into a rioting community and be listened to. In a sense, I blame ourselves— together with the mass media—for what has happened in Watts, Harlem, Chicago, Cleveland, Omaha. Each time the people in those cities saw Martin Luther King get slapped, they became angry; when they saw four little black girls bombed to death, they were angrier; and when nothing happened, they were steaming. We had nothing to offer that they could see, except to go out and be beaten again. We helped to build their frustration.

For too many years, black Americans marched and had their heads broken and got shot. They were saying to the country, "Look, you guys are supposed to be nice guys and we are only going to do what we are supposed to do—why do you beat us

"What We Want," by Stokely Carmichael explaining "Black Power" from *The New York Review of Books*. Vol. 7 (September 22, 1966), pp. 5–6, 8. Reprinted by permission of Kwame Ture (Stokely Carmichael).

up, why don't you give us what we ask, why don't you straighten yourselves out?" After years of this, we are at almost the same point—because we demonstrated from a position of weakness. We cannot be expected any longer to march and have our heads broken in order to say to whites: come on, you're nice guys. For you are not nice guys. We have found you out.

An organization which claims to speak for the needs of a community—as does the Student Nonviolent Coordinating Committee—must speak in the tone of that community, not as somebody else's buffer zone. This is the significance of black power as a slogan. For once, black people are going to use the words they want to use—not just the words whites want to hear. And they will do this no matter how often the press tries to stop the use of the slogan by equating it with racism or separatism.

An organization which claims to be working for the needs of a community— as SNCC does—must work to provide that community with a position of strength from which to make its voice heard. This is the significance of black power beyond the slogan.

Black power can be clearly defined for those who do not attach the fears of white America to their questions about it. We should begin with the basic fact that black Americans have two problems: they are poor and they are black. All other problems arise from this two-sided reality: lack of education, the so-called apathy of black men. Any program to end racism must address itself to that double reality. . . .

Ultimately, the economic foundations of this country must be shaken if black people are to control their lives. The colonies of the United States—and this includes the black ghettoes within its borders, north and south—must be liberated. For a century, this nation has been like an octopus of exploitation, its tentacles stretching from Mississippi and Harlem to South America, the Middle East, southern Africa, and Vietnam; the form of exploitation varies from area to area but the essential result has been the same—a powerful few have been maintained and enriched at the expense of the poor and voiceless colored masses. This pattern must be broken. As its grip loosens here and there around the world, the hopes of black Americans become more realistic. For racism to die, a totally different America must be born.

This is what the white society does not wish to face; this is why that society prefers to talk about integration. But integration speaks not at all to the problem of poverty, only the problem of blackness. Integration today means the man who "makes it," leaving his black brothers behind in the ghetto as fast as his sports car will take him. It has no relevance to the Harlem wino or to the cottonpicker making three dollars a day. As a lady I know in Alabama once said, "the food that Ralph Bunche eats doesn't fill my stomach."

Integration, moreover, speaks to the problem of blackness in a despicable way. As a goal, it has been based on complete acceptance of the fact that *in order to have* a decent house or education, blacks must move into a white neighborhood or send their children to a white school. This reinforces, among both black and white, the idea that "white" is automatically better and "black" is by definition inferior. This is why integration is a subterfuge for the maintenance of white supremacy. It allows the nation to focus on a handful of Southern children who get into white schools, at great price, and to ignore the 94 percent who are left behind in unimproved all-blacks schools. Such situations will not change until black people have power—to control their own school boards, in this case. Then Negroes become equal in a way that means something, and integration ceases to be a one-way street. . . .

7. A Senate Committee Reports on the FBI's Campaign Against Martin Luther King, 1963–1968 (1976)

From December 1963 until his death in 1968, Martin Luther King Jr. was the target of an intensive campaign by the Federal Bureau of Investigation to "neutralize" him as an effective civil rights leader. In the words of the man in charge of the FBI's "war" against Dr. King:

> No holds barred. We have used [similar] techniques against Soviet agents. [The same methods were] brought home against any organization against which we were targeted. We did not differentiate. This is a rough, tough business.

The FBI collected information about Dr. King's plans and activities through an extensive surveillance program, employing nearly every intelligence-gathering technique at the Bureau's disposal. Wiretaps, which were initially approved by Attorney General Robert F. Kennedy, were maintained on Dr. King's home telephone from October 1963 until mid-1965; the SCLC [Southern Christian Leadership Conference] headquarter's telephones were covered by wiretaps for an even longer period. Phones in the homes and offices of some of Dr. King's close advisers were also wiretapped. The FBI has acknowledged 16 occasions on which microphones were hidden in Dr. King's hotel and motel rooms in an "attempt" to obtain information about the "private activities of King and his advisers" for use to "completely discredit" them.

FBI informants in the civil rights movement and reports from field offices kept the Bureau's headquarters informed of developments in the civil rights field. The FBI's presence was so intrusive that one major figure in the civil rights movement testified that his colleagues referred to themselves as members of "the FBI's golden record club."

The FBI's formal program to discredit Dr. King with Government officials began with the distribution of a "monograph" which the FBI realized could "be regarded as a personal attack on Martin Luther King," and which was subsequently described by a Justice Department official as "a personal diatribe . . . a personal attack without evidentiary support."

Congressional leaders were warned "off the record" about alleged dangers posed by Reverend King. The FBI responded to Dr. King's receipt of the Nobel Peace Prize by attempting to undermine his reception by foreign heads of state and American ambassadors in the countries that he planned to visit. When Dr. King returned to the United States, steps were taken to reduce support for a huge banquet and a special "day" that were being planned in his honor.

The FBI's program to destroy Dr. King as the leader of the civil rights movement entailed attempts to discredit him with churches, universities, and the press. Steps were taken to attempt to convince the National Council of Churches, the Baptist World Alliance, and leading Protestant ministers to halt financial support of

Senate Select Committee to Study Governmental Operations with Respect to Intelligence Activities, *Supplemental Detailed Staff Reports . . .* , vol. 3 (Washington, D.C.: GPO, 1976), 81–83, 133–137, 158–160.

the Southern Christian Leadership Conference (SCLC), and to persuade them that "Negro leaders should completely isolate King and remove him from the role he is now occupying in civil rights activities." When the FBI learned that Dr. King intended to visit the Pope, an agent was dispatched to persuade Francis Cardinal Spellman to warn the Pope about "the likely embarrassment that may result to the Pope should he grant King an audience." The FBI sought to influence universities to withhold honorary degrees from Dr. King. Attempts were made to prevent the publication of articles favorable to Dr. King and to find "friendly" news sources that would print unfavorable articles. The FBI offered to play for reporters tape recordings allegedly made from microphone surveillance of Dr. King's hotel rooms.

The FBI mailed Dr. King a tape recording made from its microphone coverage. According to the Chief of the FBI's Domestic Intelligence Division, the tape was intended to precipitate a separation between Dr. King and his wife in the belief that the separation would reduce Dr. King's stature. The tape recording was accompanied by a note which Dr. King and his advisers interpreted as a threat to release the tape recording unless Dr. King committed suicide. The FBI also made preparations to promote someone "to assume the role of leadership of the Negro people when King has been completely discredited."

The campaign against Dr. King included attempts to destroy the Southern Christian Leadership Conference by cutting off its sources of funds. The FBI considered, and on some occasions executed, plans to cut off the support of some of the SCLC's major contributors, including religious organizations, a labor union, and donors of grants such as the Ford Foundation. One FBI field office recommended that the FBI send letters to the SCLC's donors over Dr. King's forged signature warning them that the SCLC was under investigation by the Internal Revenue Service. The IRS files on Dr. King and the SCLC were carefully scrutinized for financial irregularities. For over a year, the FBI unsuccessfully attempted to establish that Dr. King had a secret foreign bank account in which he was sequestering funds.

The FBI campaign to discredit and destroy Dr. King was marked by extreme personal vindictiveness. As early as 1962, Director Hoover penned on an FBI memorandum, "King is no good." At the August 1963 March on Washington, Dr. King told the country of his dream that "all the God's children, black men and white men, Jews and Gentiles, Protestants and Catholics, will be able to join hands and sing in the words of the old Negro spiritual, 'Free at last, free at last. Thank God, almighty, I'm free at last.'" The FBI's Domestic Intelligence Division described this "demagogic speech" as yet more evidence that Dr. King was "the most dangerous and effective Negro leader in the country." Shortly afterward, *Time* magazine chose Dr. King as the "Man of the Year," an honor which elicited Director Hoover's comment that "they had to dig deep in the garbage to come up with this one." Hoover wrote "astounding" across the memorandum informing him that Dr. King had been granted an audience with the Pope despite the FBI's efforts to prevent such a meeting. The depth of Director Hoover's bitterness toward Dr. King, a bitterness which he had effectively communicated to his subordinates in the FBI, was apparent from the FBI's attempts to sully Dr. King's reputation long after his death. Plans were made to "brief" congressional leaders in 1969 to prevent the passage of a "Martin Luther King Day." In 1970, Director Hoover told reporters that Dr. King was the "last one in the world who should ever have received" the Nobel Peace Prize.

8. Police and Fire Department Logs
Record an Urban Riot, 1967

Police and fire department radios blared out the urgent messages as the tempo of the riot built up Sunday night and Monday. The radios of the two departments were the only sure way to keep track of the riot's size and the direction it moved.

Not all of the calls could be heard because of different frequencies used to broadcast. Two that could be heard indicated the scope of the rioting.

The radio calls were monitored from 11:35 P.M. Sunday to 5:15 A.M. Monday, the time of the most intense activity. The messages recorded were reports by police and firemen on the street, the police command center at N. 4th st. and W. Garfield av., and dispatchers in city hall and the safety building. The log:

11:35 P.M.—Looters entering a Goodyear store at 1815 W. Fond du Lac.

11:42—Rubbish fire 2400 N. 3d st.

11:45—Get some help at 3rd and Lloyd; the fire's out of control.

11:45—Rubbish fire extinguished at 3rd and McKinley.

11:46—Garage fire at 21st and Concordia.

11:50—They're beginning to loot at 3rd and Brown.

11:51—We're pulling the beat man out at 3rd and Wright. We're getting nailed pretty hard. Watch out!

11:51—Unconfirmed report of squad car tipped over.

11:52—Have Chief Breier call the mayor or his administrator.

11:54—Kids throwing stones at passing cars on foot bridge over 6th st., just south of North av.

11:54—Notify owner show window broken at appliance store 3356 N. Green Bay.

11:56—Man shot at 3rd and Vine. Send ambulance. (Believed to be a looter.)

11:56—Battalion 2 reported from a fire scene that it needed protection.

11:57—Crowds out of control at Meinecke and Wright. Looting going on.

11:58—Businessman trapped in building at 2555 N. 3rd st. Being pummeled by rocks.

12:02 A.M.—All shotguns being brought down from headquarters and training school. Taken to command post at 4th and Garfield.

12:03—Fire 3rd and Meinecke, Martin service station.

12:05—Fires in alley 2300 block of N. 3rd.

12:08—See if you can raise some ministers.

12:09—Group breaking into convalescent home at 107 E. Garfield.

12:10—Box alarm of fire N. 5th and Vliet sts.

12:11—Sheriff's department advises 50 men standing by waiting for chief's order.

12:15—No. 5 captain advises that four reverends are on the way to the command post.

12:16—Burglary in progress at 13th and Burleigh.

12:16—Merchants police alarm at 2741 N. Teutonia.

12:17—Halyard and Lloyd, about 50 youths stoning automobiles.

12:20—Burglary in progress at 2401 N. 3rd st.

Diary of an Urban Riot, 1967, *Milwaukee Journal*, July 31, 1967.

12:24—Wagonload of patrolmen need helmets.

12:25—Call for fire department, rear of 2300 N. 3rd st. Also need additional officers.

12:26—Group going toward Wisconsin av.

12:28—1900 N. Buffum, another fire set.

12:28—Gang beating a white man at 4th and Wright.

12:28—Fire at National Food store, 2354 N. 3rd st.

12:28—2741 N. Teutonia. They've smashed windows wide open. Notify the owner.

12:30—Request Mount Sinai hospital remain open. Keep emergency personnel on.

12:31—3rd and Highland. Eight police confronting a crowd of 50 marching toward Wisconsin av.

12:32—Get hold of sheriff's department hard helmets and bring them to command post.

12:32—Cars being set on fire 16th and Vliet.

12:33—Fifth Dist. police station being attacked. (The message was garbled.)

12:35—They're breaking into Badger Plating. 1300 N. Water.

12:36—Telephone alarm of fire at N. 16th and W. Vliet.

12:37—Brink's called. They want to move their trucks from 431 W. Galena at 1 A.M.

12:40—Report from citizen that they've broken windows at Kaufman Motors at 3rd and Burleigh and they're stealing motorcycles.

12:40—Firemen report that they are being stoned at 3rd and Clark.

12:40—About 25 persons are attacking a service station at 3rd and Burleigh.

12:42—Request for more squads at 15th and Vliet. A crowd is gathering.

12:44—We need more squads at 3200 N. Green Bay.

12:44—3rd and Burleigh at the motorcycle shop. We've got motorcycles lying in the street.

12:46—We've got a large group of punks who need some attention at 1301 N. Center.

12:48—Squad is stuck in sand at 2nd and Meinecke.

12:49—Check bank at 27th and Vliet. Auto seen fleeing the scene.

12:50—We have a report of looters in a tavern. 3rd and Green Bay.

12:51—More looting at Woolworth's, 13th and Vliet.

12:52—Large group at 12th and Galena with guns and golf clubs.

12:53—Check injured man at 24th and Lisbon.

12:53—Large group breaking windows at 13th and Vliet.

12:58—Telephone alarm of fire, 3rd and Clark.

12:58—Breaking into Kellers, beer depot, 5th and Center.

12:59—Injured man, 12th and Lloyd.

12:59—Plankinton and Michigan; numerous lootings in area.

12:59—Box alarm, 2nd and Chambers.

1:00—Telephone alarm of fire, 2018 N. 5th st.

1:00—Looting reported at 21st and Walnut.

1:00—Group in white Cadillac throwing bricks and rocks at homes in the 2300 block of N. 20th.

1:00—Pedestrian struck, 24th and Lisbon.

1:03—Large group congregating at Teutonia and Center.

1:04—Auto accident, 12th and Lloyd. Passenger injured pretty badly.

1:04—Burglar alarm, Sangor Drugs, 800 W. North av.

1:05—Reports of shooting at 2nd and Clark.

1:05—Autos being tipped at 3rd and Meinecke.

1:05—Two white males with rifles in the 2900 block of N. 3rd.

1:06—Check 2nd and Wright. Report of woman being beaten.

1:07—Pedestrian struck 24th pl. and Lisbon.

1:08—Report of gas pump burning, 16th and Highland.

1:08—Report of looting, 12th and Cherry.

1:09—We have report of looting at 5th and North.

1:13—Large group in parking lot with weapons at 2nd and Michigan.

1:13—Looting at Super America station, 17th and Atkinson.

1:14—Groups throwing rocks at 6th and Cherry.

1:14—Ambulance sent. 2nd and Meinecke.

1:15—Box alarm of fire, 16th and Juneau.

1:16—They are entering grocery stores at 15th and Vliet and 16th and Cherry.

1:17—One reduced line (fire hose) working on buildings at 16th and Juneau.

1:22—Burglar alarm at Palay's Men's shop, 1200 W. Walnut st.

1:25—Looting at store at 11th and Center.

1:27—Group of 20 to 30 walking east on Meinecke armed with bottles, bricks and weapons.

1:28—Looting, Royal Cleaners, 5th and North.

1:30—Accident, 10th and Ring.

1:31—Sergeant reports that his group has no shotguns.

1:31—Large group approaching Teutonia and Center.

1:33—Fifteen cars loaded with Negroes going west on North av.

1:37—Group of 40 Negroes at 29th and Vliet.

1:38—Squad at 14th and Walnut has prisoners.

1:39—They're looting the Kohl's Beverage Center, 3700 N. Teutonia av.

1:40—They're beating a woman at 5th and Wright.

1:41—Large group of Negroes at jewelry store at 37th and North.

1:42—Large group of Negroes leaving 37th and North. We have just moved them.

1:43—Two burglar alarms, 925 W. North and 1400 W. North av.

1:44—People buying cans of gasoline at 35th and Meinecke.

1:45—Accident at 1st and Meinecke, large group gathering, send help.

1:46—We're closing down all service stations in the 3rd police district.

1:46—Box alarm fire, 12th and Garfield.

1:48—Broken window at 928 W. North, nobody around.

1:48—Box alarm fire at 2nd and Hadley.

1:49—We're standing by at Ken's Gun shop, 48th and North. Everything is OK here.

1:49—Check 15th and McKinley. People trapped in an auto.

1:50—Check a large group armed with bottles at 27th and Wells.

1:51—Bus driver reports rocks being thrown at busses at 14th and Fond du Lac.

1:51—Man being beaten at 1st and Meinecke.

1:56—Officer needs assistance, 15th and Center.

1:58—Send a couple of squads to 3rd and Hadley. They're looting up here.

1:59—We have shooting from an automobile in the vicinity of Buffum and Center.

2:00—Large fight at 12th and Reservoir.

2:01—Check for windows being broken, 2500 block of N. Downer.

2:02—We have 25 people following three patrolmen at 4th and Walnut.

2:02—We need a wagon at 6th and North. We've got a couple of stone throwers.

2:03—Send ambulance. One dead already. Send ambulance, 134 W. Center. Man shot in head by sniper.

2:05—Four cars of Negroes at 2nd and Vliet.

2:06—Truck on fire, 12th and Galena.

2:06—Another ambulance, 2nd and Center.

2:10—Window smashed at television store, 27th and Atkinson.

2:10—2nd and Center. [Bring] tear gas and ambulance. We're shooting at house.

2:12—Another ambulance, 2nd and Center.

2:12—Sound of gunshots, 12th and Walnut.

2:12—Get some tear gas here, 2nd and Center. We have at least one policeman shot.

2:12—We need shotguns here at 2nd and Center.

2:13—We're sending help.

2:13—2nd and Center. Two coppers shot. We're requesting help immediately. Two coppers shot.

2:15—Request for ambulances to stand by, 4th and Garfield. Ambulance, 2nd and Center, hurry, hurry.

2:16—Disregard the ambulance. We're taking the wounded officer ourselves.

2:17—1000 N. 3rd st. Camera shop broken into. We've got the guys.

2:18—Large fire at 3rd and Center.

2:19—Notify fire department, fire bomb at 3rd and Center.

2:20—Check for five carloads of Negroes at 3rd and Morgan.

2:20—Large crowd of juveniles gathering at 1st and Wright. Cars are burning.

2:22—Meet squad at 3rd and State. They are going in after looters.

2:22—Meet squad at 3rd and Cherry. We've got looters.

2:23—Negro juveniles with guns at 32nd and McKinley.

2:24—Negroes just broke into service station at 31st and Capitol.

2:24—Looting at beer depot at 23rd and Burleigh.

2:25—Looting at drugstore at 13th and Burleigh.

2:25—Looting at liquor store, 8th and North.

2:25—All squads—close up service stations for the night.

2:29—Supermarket on fire, 10th and Burleigh.

2:29—We're pinned down at 2nd and Center (by sniper).

2:38—Send fire department, 3rd and Center, big blaze.

2:40—Tell No. 3 squads to stop any roving cars with Negro males. Stop them and check the trunks for guns and contraband.

2:41—Large fire at 3rd and Center. Fire department unable to get into area.

2:42—We've got the prisoner. He has been shot. . . .

✦ E S S A Y S

The essays that follow challenge the classic textbook history of the civil rights movement, which focuses on the years 1954–1968, on the South, on the role of charismatic
leaders such as Martin Luther King Jr., on national organizations such as the NAACP,
and on the struggle in the courts and halls of Congress. But as the essays by Charles M.
Payne and Thomas J. Sugrue argue, the civil rights movement was both larger and more
complicated than this simple model might suggest. Payne's essay, based in part on his
award-winning book *I've Got the Light of Freedom: The Organizing Tradition and the
Mississippi Freedom Struggle* (1995), places the civil rights movement within a long
tradition of black resistance and protest, emphasizing the important roles played by local
communities and less widely heralded grassroots leaders. In the second essay, drawn
from his prize-winning study of race and inequality in postwar Detroit, *The Origins of
the Urban Crisis* (1996), Sugrue shifts the focus to deeply rooted struggles over jobs,
schools, and housing in the industrial North, a focus that helps explain the limits of
conventional civil rights politics and the growing anger and frustration of many African
Americans, as well as the white backlash on which George Wallace and Richard Nixon
would base their political strategies.

The View from the Trenches

CHARLES M. PAYNE

Brown was more than a legal battle. It was one element in a decades-long struggle
for equity in education, a struggle that required Blacks in local communities across
the South to expose themselves to physical violence and economic repression. In
1947 the Blacks of Clarendon County, South Carolina, for example, decided to ask
the school superintendent for a bus for their children. In a pattern that would be
repeated many times—Blacks ask for small adjustments in the system, the authorities refuse, Blacks then make more radical demands—the superintendent refused,
and the Black community decided to launch a fight for the complete equalization
of schools. The leaders of the Clarendon County movement expected trouble; you
could not attack white supremacy in South Carolina and not expect trouble. They
had not, however, fully considered the number of weapons the system could bring
to bear. The man they chose to lead them was a Methodist minister, J. A. Delaine,
and he caught nearly the full weight of the repression. In his history of *Brown*,
Richard Kluger says of Delaine:

> Before it was over, they fired him from the little schoolhouse at which he had taught
> devotedly for ten years. And they fired his wife and two of his sisters and a niece. And they
> threatened him with bodily harm. And they sued him on trumped up charges and con-
> victed him in a kangaroo court and left with a judgement that denied him credit from
> any bank. And they burned his house to the ground while the fire department stood
> around watching the flames consume the night. And they stoned the church at which he
> pastored. And fired shotguns at him out of the dark. But he was not Job, and so he fired

Charles M. Payne, "Debating the Civil Rights Movement: The View from the Trenches," from Steven F.
Lawson and Charles Payne, *Debating the Civil Rights Movement, 1945–1968* (Rowman & Littlefield,
2nd edition, 2006), pp. 116–124, 127–129, 147–149, 151–152. Reprinted by permission of Rowman &
Littlefield Publishers, Inc.

back and called the police, who did not come and kept not coming. Then he fled, driving north at eighty-five miles an hour over country roads, until he was across the state line. Soon after, they burned his church to the ground and charged him, for having shot back that night, with felonious assault with a deadly weapon, and so he became an official fugitive from justice.

Similar stories were being repeated across the South between the mid-1940s and the late 1950s. In the wake of World War II, Black activists were more aggressive, to which the white South responded with a wave of repression. Not all of those who got caught by it were men. Like Delaine, Septima Clark lost her career because of her social activism. Born around the turn of the century, the daughter of a cook and a washerwoman, Clark became a schoolteacher in the area around Charleston, South Carolina. After World War I, she became involved in a fight to get Black teachers and principals hired in Charleston. Following years brought other battles—to equalize pay between white and Black teachers, to get more funding for Black schools and a longer school year. By the mid-1950s, she was deeply involved in the state branch of the National Association for the Advancement of Colored People (NAACP) when the state declared the organization subversive and forbade any state or city employee to be a member. Clark refused to deny her membership and was immediately fired.

Fortunately, the year before, she had begun attending classes at the Highlander Folk School in Tennessee. Started during the Depression, Highlander was among the most unique institutions in the South. One of its founders was Myles Horton, who had grown up in a family of poor white Tennessee sharecroppers. He saw Highlander as a school for the poor of Appalachia, a school where the curriculum was essentially about activism, a place where coal miners, steel workers, mill workers, and others could come to learn how to organize. From its inception, it was also a place concerned with attacking white supremacy, a place where civil rights workers could find training and support. Few significant southern civil rights activists in the 1940s and 1950s did not have some contact with Highlander. It was at Highlander that "We Shall Overcome" was introduced to the movement. No matter what people came there for, Highlander insisted—in contradiction to Tennessee law and southern custom—on interracial living, a philosophy that initially discomfited Black visitors just as much as white ones. Visitor after visitor testified that the experience of egalitarian living in an interracial situation had greater impact on them than the courses and workshops.

Already an experienced activist when she first came to Highlander, Clark found the school a supportive, stimulating environment. She started bringing friends to workshops there and then running workshops herself. When she was fired, Highlander made her its director of education, a position from which she was able to refine Highlander's distinctive style of work. Highlander was founded on a philosophy of struggle that was an alternative to the legal gradualism of the NAACP, on the one hand, or to Dr. Martin Luther King's charisma, on the other. Rather, Highlander espoused a form of participatory democracy. Its statement of purpose, drafted by Clark, speaks of "broadening the scope of democracy to include everyone and deepening the concept to include every relationship." In practical terms, that meant that Highlander wanted to identify and groom leadership at the local level, not just provide it from the outside.

Nothing better illustrates the Highlander style than the Citizenship Schools that Clark developed. She had only been on staff a few months when one of her old students came to her for help. He had just lost an election for school board on Johns Island, one of the Sea Islands opposite Charleston. Blacks made up a large majority of the population, but only a few were able to navigate through the various obstacles the state used to prevent Blacks from voting. This situation was all the more complicated because most Black adults could neither read nor write. Clark, whose first teaching job had been on Johns, developed a program for teaching adults to read and write and then to register, which entailed being able to interpret a section of the state constitution to the satisfaction of the local registrar.

The first class, the existence of which was carefully hidden from whites on the island, had fourteen students, eleven of whom were able to register. From those modest beginnings, the Citizenship Schools grew into one of the most important civil rights initiatives of the late 1950s and early 1960s. Nearly ten thousand people would be trained as teachers and as many as two hundred schools would be in operation at one time "in people's kitchens, in beauty parlors and under trees in the summertime." Across the South, Citizenship Schools and teachers provided much of the on-ground leadership for other civil rights organizations.

This was very much in keeping with how Septima Clark saw the schools. Voting was not, for her, so much an end in itself as it was an organizing device. "The basic purpose of the Citizenship Schools," she wrote, "is discovering local community leaders. . . . It is my belief that creative leadership is present in any community and only awaits discovery and development." For some in the movement, finding and grooming leadership, transforming individuals, was as important as winning legislative victories, perhaps more so in the long run. Political victories are transitory; the powers that be can grant them today and withdraw them tomorrow unless the movement has created people who are always capable of fighting for themselves. Ella Baker certainly thought so. For her, the movement could not be something in which a few big leaders were going to lead the singing masses to freedom. People, she thought, had to learn to lead themselves.

> My basic sense of it has always been to get people to understand that in the long run they themselves are the only protection they have against violence or injustice. . . . People have to be made to understand that they cannot look for salvation anywhere but to themselves.

If one thinks of the movement that way, powerful oratory and big demonstrations may not be important, may even be counterproductive, unless they contribute to the goal of developing a broad leadership base. She was no fan of centralized, charismatic leadership precisely because of its antidemocratic tendencies.

> I have always felt it was a handicap for oppressed people to depend so largely on a leader, because unfortunately in our culture, the charismatic leader usually becomes a leader because he has found a spot in the public limelight. It usually means that the media made him, and the media may undo him.

What we need, she argued, is people "who are interested not in being leaders as much as in developing leadership in others. " If you can give them the light, people can find their own way. That meant you could not just lead people to change. They had to be a part of the work themselves. She would have agreed emphatically with what James Farmer of the Congress of Racial Equality (CORE) said about the need

> to involve the people themselves, individually, personally, in the struggle for their own freedom. Not simply because it was clear that no one else was going to confer liberty upon them, but because in the very act of working for the impersonal cause of racial freedom, a man experiences, almost like grace, a large measure of private freedom. Or call it a new comprehension of his own identity, an intuition of the expanding boundaries of his self, which, if not the same thing as freedom, is its radical source.

Baker came into the 1960s with more than three decades of activist experience. A product of rural North Carolina, by the Depression she was in Harlem teaching Black history and organizing domestic workers, economic cooperatives, and adult education programs. In one job application she noted that she had maintained at least a speaking acquaintance with the leaders of "the articulate mass and semi-mass movements" in the area. The application was for a position with the NAACP, the most important civil rights organization of the period. From 1941, she was an assistant field secretary, which meant spending half the year traveling through the South, organizing new branches and advising established ones. That eventually led to a position as national director of branches, a position she held during the organization's most dynamic period of growth.

She brought her distinctive philosophy to the position, which meant she had her misgivings about the organization for which she was working. The NAACP, she thought, was overly committed to a legal strategy that left most of its membership—four hundred thousand by 1944—little meaningful role in the development of policy and program. Like many of the leaders with whom she had worked in the Deep South, she was increasingly impatient with the organization's conservatism. The leadership was putting too much energy into worrying about how much recognition they were getting from important white people, a concern that helped prevent the organization from taking a confrontational stance even when that would have made tactical sense. The program was overly middle-class, not strong enough on the kinds of economic issues that meant most to working-class Black people. Perhaps above all, she found the organization too centralized; too many decisions were being made in New York. The annual conventions were carefully staged exercises in pseudodemocracy. The national staff was really calling the shots.

She wanted to use her position as director of branches to open the organization up somewhat. She tried to have more decisions made in the branches rather than in New York, and she was able to establish a training program for local leaders. By 1946, she decided that democratizing the NAACP was beyond even her considerable talents, and she resigned, working for a variety of causes over the next decade.

When the Southern Christian Leadership Conference (SCLC) was founded in 1957, it actually represented an alliance across generations of activists. The face that the public saw was that of the Reverend King, but in fact he was twenty-eight years old and politically inexperienced. A cadre of older activists formed around him to give him support, including Bayard Rustin, a longtime labor, peace, and civil rights activist, and Stanley Levison, a Jewish lawyer with much experience in left and radical causes. They were able to talk Ella Baker into going south once more where she eventually became the SCLC's first full-time executive director. She was the ideal choice for a fledgling organization in that she had such extensive net-works among southern activists. On the other hand, she was an outspoken woman in an organization that did not expect or appreciate that attitude from women; she was suspicious of charismatic leadership in an organization that was built on it, was impatient with ministerial conservatism, and did not personally believe in the non-violence the organization was espousing. Her years at SCLC were tense, but when the sit-ins erupted in 1960, she was in a position to help channel that energy into an organization that became a model for American activists of all types.

During the 1940s, when Baker was bemoaning the conservatism of the NAACP, one of the most significant alternatives to it was provided by A. Philip Randolph. Formerly the editor of an important African-American socialist magazine, in 1925 he organized the Brotherhood of Sleeping Car Porters, the most important Black union of its day. The presidency of the union gave him a pulpit from which he gave elo-quent voice to the concerns of Black workers for four decades. As befits a man with union roots, he was not much given to the moral suasion and legal gradualism in which the NAACP specialized. His style was to threaten, to embarrass, to put the masses into the street. When it became clear that World War II defense industries were excluding Blacks, Randolph, to the dismay of more timid Black leadership, threatened to march a hundred thousand protesting Negroes on Washington unless President Franklin D. Roosevelt did something. He was criticized for keeping the March on Washington Movement all-Black, but he was adamant about that. "You take ten thousand dollars from a white man," he said, "you've got his ten thousand dollars but he's got your movement." His thinking also echoed Ella Baker's in how it balanced concern for immediate tactical objectives with concern for larger questions about how the race was developing. In order for a people to develop, they had to fight for their own causes, not have friends do their fighting for them. Sympathetic whites could best help through their own organizations (a position the Black Panthers would revive a quarter-century later).

After the war, Randolph played a role in President Harry Truman's decision to desegregate the armed forces. In 1948, amid cries of treason, Randolph promised that if the services were not desegregated, he would lead a campaign of massive civil disobedience modeled after Gandhi's approach, and he pledged to "openly counsel, aid and abet youth, both white and Negro, to quarantine any jimcrow con-scription system." Randolph pushed Truman so that in one meeting the president virtually threw him out of his office. Much established Black leadership, including the NAACP, thought Randolph had gone too far, but 70 percent of young Black men polled in Harlem agreed with Randolph.

In terms of brass, at least, Birmingham's Fred Shuttlesworth was a worthy match for Randolph. In its attempt to harass the NAACP, Alabama went South Carolina one better. South Carolina merely decided that public employees could not be mem-bers of the NAACP; in 1956, Alabama declared the organization illegal. NAACP members immediately reconstituted themselves as the Alabama Christian Movement for Human Rights (ACMHR), which proceeded to give white Alabama even more trouble than had the NAACP. While the NAACP restricted itself mostly to filing lawsuits, the ACMHR, with Shuttlesworth as president, was willing to engage in boycotts, pickets, and demonstrations. When the Supreme Court decided, in Decem-ber 1956, that bus segregation in Montgomery was unconstitutional, the ACMHR decided to protest Birmingham's segregated buses. Black people had nicknamed Birmingham "Bombingham" and for very good reason. The night before the protest was to begin, The Shuttlesworth home was bombed, injuring a visiting deacon and two of the Shuttlesworth children, though Shuttlesworth himself was untouched. "I wasn't saved to run," he announced.

That kind of hard-headed determination frightened more traditional Black leaders, but it also inspired some people. Shuttlesworth got death threats constantly, the police harassed him in every way they could, including wiretaps, and both the police and the Ku Klux Klan (in Birmingham, it was hard to tell the two apart) harassed his followers. In 1957, in the wake of the Little Rock Crisis, Shuttlesworth was leading four Black youngsters, including two of his own children, to register at the white high school when he was attacked by a mob and beaten with brass knuckles and bicycle chains. His wife was stabbed. The following spring, there was another attempt to bomb his church. Nonetheless, for the rest of the decade, Shuttlesworth and his followers attacked white supremacy in Birmingham—pushing the city to hire Black police officers, open parks and libraries to Negroes, desegregate its schools, and allow Blacks to vote.

That Shuttlesworth survived the 1950s is a small miracle. Others were less fortunate. Harry T. Moore of Mims, Florida, was a schoolteacher, often described as a shy man. Nonetheless, he was staunch enough in his politics. The work that he was known for and that had propelled him to the presidency of the state NAACP was his persistent agitation for the equalization of the educational resources given to Black and white youngsters. In 1951, he campaigned for the prosecution of a sheriff who had shot two Negro youths, killing one. Shortly after he and his wife had retired on Christmas Eve that year, a bomb destroyed their bedroom. He died immediately and his wife a few days later.

In the prewar years, southern Blacks typically laid low after a racial killing. It was a sign of changing times that Blacks from across the state packed his funeral, paying homage to a man who was for them the kind of symbol of persistence and integrity that Medgar Evers would become for Blacks in Mississippi. The Black press saw another sign of change in the fact that the murder was one of a wave of bombings across the South in the early 1950s. The fact that the most dangerous defenders of racism were hiding behind bombs in the night rather then rallying lynch mobs in the open suggested that killers saw a need to be more cautious. It was a measure of progress, however grim.

When Americans speak of the "civil rights movement," they are unlikely to be thinking of Harry T. Moore or A. Philip Randolph, Septima Clark, Ella Baker, J. A. Delaine, . . . or Fred Shuttlesworth. They and the struggles they represent are not a part of American history as it is normally taught, with its streamlined, homogenized version of the movement. Saying that most Americans have been raised on a whitewashed version of movement history is more than a bad pun.

What difference does it make if we leave people like this out? At the very least, it means that we lose touch with the complexity of the historical process. All kinds of people are important to this history—Appalachian whites, Black professionals from quite privileged backgrounds, quasi socialists, radical democrats, church-based activists, advocates of self-defense for Black people, advocates of racial separatism, people as concerned with human development as with legislative victories, people who saw education, the need for self-affirmation, access to jobs, and access to the political system as intertwined. It is not a history that can be comprehended in terms of a couple of dominant figures or any one form of politics, and it is not at all clear that it can be well understood in terms of "civil rights." . . .

By way of example of illustrating a less sophisticated top-down approach, we can look at how the Montgomery bus boycott, perhaps our most familiar origin myth about the movement, is normally presented. What we are usually told is that a tired woman refused to give up her seat on the bus and an eloquent, nonviolent prophet rose up to lead the grateful masses, and the Supreme Court eventually saw the justness of their cause. That rendering hides more than it reveals.

For one thing, the traditional story obscures the fact that the people who made the boycott happen had long activist backgrounds, including the venerable E. D. Nixon, a pullman porter with a sixth-grade education, in his mid-fifties at the time of the boycott and probably the most influential Black man in town, at least in the eyes of the Black masses. Nixon had organized the state branch of the Brotherhood of Sleeping Car Porters in 1928. He attributed much of what he had learned about organizing to A. Philip Randolph, the founder of the Brotherhood. In the 1930s Nixon, along with Myles Horton at Highlander, tried to organize Alabama farm laborers, and he organized a committee to make sure that Alabama Blacks got their fair share of benefits from federal programs. In 1940, he helped organize the Montgomery Voters League; in 1944, he led a march of 750 people on the registrar's office; from 1939 to 1951, he headed the Montgomery NAACP; and from 1951 to 1953, the state conference.

The portrait of Rosa Parks as some simple woman who accidentally got caught up in great historical events is a complete distortion. She had spent her adult life looking for a way to make a difference. In 1943, she joined the NAACP under Nixon, became its secretary, and worked in voter registration campaigns; she first registered herself in 1945. She also ran the local NAACP Youth Council and served as secretary to the state NAACP Conference of Branches. She had attended one of Ella Baker's Leadership Training Conferences in the 1940s and had spent a week at the Highlander Folk School in 1955. From the 1940s on, she had refused on several occasions to comply with bus segregation laws, frequently enough that some bus drivers recognized her on sight and simply refused to stop for her. King's comment about her—"She was tracked down by the Zeitgeist—the spirit of the times"—is precisely wrong. She, like Nixon, had spent much of her adult life actively seeking levers of change, not waiting until the times were right.

Jo Ann Robinson was an English professor at nearby Alabama State College and president of the Women's Political Caucus, a group of three hundred educated Black women who had been concerned with voter registration and segregated public facilities since 1946. They had been agitating the city commission about segregated buses since the early 1950s and in May 1954 had sent a letter to the mayor threatening a boycott if improvements were not made. Between the spring of 1955 and the time of the Parks arrest in December, Nixon and the caucus had considered three bus incidents as potential test cases but decided against them on various tactical grounds. The Parks incident gave them the case they wanted.

Nixon and Robinson's group were largely responsible for the initial mobilization of Black Montgomery. Parks was arrested on a Thursday; Nixon started organizing the first meeting of Negro leadership on Friday; by Monday they had organized a boycott that was nearly completely effective among a community of over forty thousand people. That they could mobilize the Black community so thoroughly, so quickly, is a reflection of how well people such as Nixon and Robinson knew their community, knowledge acquired through long years of working in it. When Nixon called the first nineteen ministers, he had to have been making some calculations about which individuals had to be involved to carry the whole of Black Montgomery with them. That knowledge was the product of three decades of meetings, demonstrations, barbershop arguments, and beauty parlor conversations.

What does the background information, even in this sketchy form, add to our understanding of the movement? Potentially, it broadens our conception of leadership, ranging from a woman with a college education to a man whose real education came from union organizing. It leaves an impression of women as thinking, determined activists. It restores a sense of human agency, suggesting, as one scholar put it, "that reflective and purposeful people matter." Montgomery happened because many people worked to make it happen. When we take the high drama of moments such as the boycott out of the longer historical context, we implicitly undervalue the more mundane activities, the sheer persistence that helped make the dramatic breakthroughs possible.

Knowing even a little of the larger story also suggests something about how we might think about King's leadership. In some top-down treatments, of course, King comes to be almost equated with the movement. . . . In fact, what we see in Montgomery was that King was the inheritor of momentum that other people established, a pattern that was to be repeated often over the next several years. Other people constructed the stage, but once he stepped into the role of movement spokesperson, his charisma, broad appeal, and personal growth allowed him to project the message of the movement in ways that virtually no one could have predicted in 1956. . . .

. . . [A] case can be made that the way in which Martin Luther King is remembered—or disremembered, if you will—contributes to a dumbing down of the discussion. The King of popular memory is the King of August 1963, calling the peaceful throng to the ideal of brotherhood. That memory hardly does justice to the mature King. In the final years of his life, he articulated a more challenging vision of the American future and a more pessimistic assessment of America's capacity for achieving it. Thus, in those years, he was constantly at odds with the press, the White House, and much of the liberal establishment.

There was no way he could have avoided getting caught up in the Black power turmoil. The term derived much of its impact from the fact that it made white people uneasy, to understate the matter. King went to great lengths to explain it in less threatening ways, but he also refused to disavow the young people, many of whom he had worked with for years, who kept shoving the term in the nation's face. Other leaders of older civil rights organizations felt they had to distance themselves from the new radicalism, at least in part because they were worried about the loss of white support. King refused to join the general condemnation. He came to feel that some whites were exploiting the Black power controversy, using it as an excuse not to think about correcting social injustice. This was a part of King's growing disenchantment with liberal America. Too many who styled themselves liberal were only concerned with the problem when they could think of it as a southern problem, not as something in their own backyards. Too many could react supportively when racist violence was being directed against Negroes but were not much concerned with racial inequality as an evil in and of itself, could not see that poverty itself was violence, that the ghetto represented institutionalized violence against its inhabitants.

In his last years, King showed considerable capacity for sticking with what he saw as the principled position even when it was clearly costing him support. He was publically opposed to the Vietnam War when most of the country still supported it. With few exceptions, his advisers encouraged him to downplay his opposition. King did just the opposite; his criticism grew more caustic. On April 4, 1967, a year before his death, he gave a speech at Riverside Church in New York that did not equivocate.

> We must stop now. I speak as a child of God and brother to the suffering poor of Vietnam. I speak for those whose land is being laid waste, whose homes are being destroyed, whose culture is being subverted. I speak for the poor of America who are paying the double price of smashed hopes at home and death and corruption in Vietnam. I speak as a citizen of the world. . . . The great initiative in this war has been ours. The initiative to stop it must be ours.

The national press spent the next week castigating him. The *New York Times* warned that "to divert the energies of the civil rights movement to the Vietnam issue is both wasteful and self-defeating." The *Washington Post* concluded that he "has diminished his usefulness to his cause, to his country and to his people." The *Chicago Tribune* warned Negroes that if they wanted to continue to make progress, "they had better get responsible leadership and repudiate the Kings and the Carmichaels." These remarks pretty well reflect the tone of national press coverage of King in his last year.

His criticism of the Vietnam adventure caused a further deterioration of his relationship with the White House. His relationship with the FBI was already about as bad as it could get. The bureau—which had labeled the "I Have a Dream" speech "demagogic"—had long been engaged in a campaign to destroy King, taking every opportunity to feed rumors and negative information about him to opinion leaders here and abroad, even trying at one point to trick him into committing suicide. J. Edgar Hoover publically called King "the most notorious liar in America" and privately called him "the burrhead."

King's growing radicalism meant increasing skepticism about whether the nation's conscience could be reached on economic matters, that he put increasing emphasis on racism as a national problem, not a regional one, and as a problem closely tied to economic exploitation. It meant that he increasingly described problems of inequality in structural terms, not in terms of individual prejudice.

> If we look honestly at the realities of our national life, it is clear that we are not marching forward: we are groping and stumbling; we are divided and confused. Our moral values and our spiritual confidence sink, even as our material wealth ascends. In these trying circumstances, the black revolution is much more than a struggle for the rights of Negroes. It is forcing America to face all its interrelated flaws of racism, poverty, militarism and materialism. It is exposing evils that are deeply rooted in the whole structure of our society. It reveals systemic rather than superficial flaws and suggests that radical reconstruction of society itself is the real issue to be faced.

. . . The way we "remember" King . . . is, of course, only illustrative of the way we remember the larger movement. We tend to construct our memories in ways that make us feel good but that also obscure much of what the movement was trying to say. In 1998, for example, David Halberstram, who covered the movement as a journalist, wrote an admiring essay about the courage and the impact of the early sit-in participants:

> Consider what they did. When they had started out, they were virtually alone. Only the Supreme Court . . . seemed sympathetic. . . . Yet only five years later both parties in the Congress were competing to pass legislation trying to outlaw voting injustices; the Justice Department had become their activist partner; the FBI, however reluctantly, had come aboard; and the President of the United States, Lyndon Johnson, was their principal convert. . . . What they had accomplished in that brief time span still strikes me as a shining example of democracy at work.

There are arguable interpretations here, to be mild about it, but that's not the most important issue. The problem is that the thinking here is a perspective, just one possible perspective on the movement but one that few Americans are likely to recognize as such. From another perspective, we could emphasize another set of "facts" in summation of the movement—the many innocent lives, lives of some of the least privileged of Americans, that had to be sacrificed to make the Justice Department "activist"; the way federal agencies "came aboard" partly to control the movement; the way in which Black radicalism made civil rights legislation seem like a cheap way out; the fact that many of the young people who gave the movement so much of its dynamism think that what they experienced was not some shining example of democracy but the betrayal of it. The more one appreciates the price of a small number of people paid to liberate us from our past, the less miraculous the whole thing seems. Depending on how it is framed, even stressing the courage and idealism of the young people can be a dangerous game. The youngsters developed a series of powerful questions about how this society generates and sustains inequality. We praise their courage while ignoring their questions. In that context, "Our civil rights activists sure were brave" may serve the same ideological function for this generation that "Our nigras are happy" served for another, a way of denying the need for discussion of underlying problems.

Both the movement's achievements and its shortcomings can be taken out of context. If some seem prone to romanticizing the accomplishments of the movement, others, including some Black youth, seem to think the movement accomplished little or nothing, that racism is unchanged from what it used to be. In part, this thinking may reflect how little contemporary youngsters understand just what racism used to be. In part, it may be that some of them are proceeding from a Hollywoodesque version of historical change, where all problems have to be resolved by the last scene. Thinking about history in that way stands in sharp contrast to the way many movement veterans thought about it. They understood their lives as chapters in an ongoing struggle. Ella Baker, who had organized Black history programs in the 1920s and was organizing against South African apartheid in the 1970s, was asked once how she had kept at it so long. She answered in terms that reflected one enduring vision of the movement:

> But if people begin to place their values in terms of how high they get in the political world, or how much worldly goods they accumulate, or what kind of cars they have, or how much they have in the bank, that's where I begin to lose respect. To me, I'm part of the human family. What the human family will accomplish, I can't control. But it isn't

impossible that what those who came along with me went through might stimulate others to continue to fight for a society that does not have those kinds of problems. Somewhere down the line the numbers increase, the tribe increases. So how do you keep on? I can't help it. I don't claim to have any corner on an answer, but I believe the struggle is eternal. Somebody else carries on.

The Continuing Racial Crisis

THOMAS J. SUGRUE

In late July 1967, one of the most brutal riots in American history swept through Detroit. On July 23, 1967, in the middle of a summer heat wave, the police decided to bust a "blind pig," an illegal after-hours saloon on Twelfth Street in the center of one of Detroit's largest black neighborhoods. Arrests for illegal drinking were common in Detroit, but usually the police dispersed the crowd and arrested a handful of owners and patrons, taking the names of the remainder. On the steamy July night, they decided to arrest all eighty-five people present and detained them—hot, drunk, and angry—outside the saloon until reinforcements could arrive.

By four in the morning, an hour after the bust, nearly two hundred people, attracted by the commotion behind the blind pig, had gathered to watch the proceedings. As the arrestees shouted allegations of police brutality, tempers rose. The crowd began to jeer and to throw bottles, beer cans, and rocks at the police. William Scott II, a son of one of the bar's owners, threw a bottle at a police officer and shouted "Get your god damn sticks and bottles and start hurtin' baby." By 8:00 A.M., a crowd of over three thousand had gathered on Twelfth Street. The riot raged out of control until it was suppressed by a combined force of nearly seventeen thousand law enforcement officers, National Guardsmen, and federal troops. After five days of violence, forty-three people were dead, thirty of them killed by law enforcement personnel. Altogether 7,231 men and women were arrested on riot-related charges. The property damage, still visible in vacant lots and abandoned buildings in Detroit, was extensive. Rioters looted and burned 2,509 buildings. $36 million in insured property was lost and undoubtedly millions more were lost by those without insurance, not to mention wages, income, and government costs.

Detroit was twice torn by cataclysmic violence in a period of less than twenty-five years. The extent of social and economic changes in the postwar period, however, made the context of Detroit's long hot summer of 1967 profoundly different from the violent summer of 1943. The vast majority of participants in the 1967 Detroit uprising were black (with the exception of armed officials who were overwhelmingly white); 1943 had involved black and white participants in roughly equal proportions. The changed racial demography of 1967 was hardly surprising, for over a third of Detroit residents were black in 1967, and few whites lived anywhere near the riot's epicenters on Linwood and Twelfth Street on the West Side and on Mack and Kercheval on the East Side. The riot of 1943 came at a time of increasing black and white competition for jobs and housing; by 1967, discrimination and deindustrialization had ensured that blacks had lost the competition. White resistance and white flight left a bitter legacy that galvanized black protest in the 1960s. Detroit's attempts to take advantage of the largesse of the Great Society offered too little, too late for Detroit's poor, but raised expectations nonetheless. Growing resentment, fueled by increasing militancy in the black community, especially among youth, who had suffered the brunt of economic displacement, fueled the fires of 1967.

For those who cared to listen, there were rumblings of discontent in the late 1950s and early 1960s. The problems of limited housing, racial animosity, and reduced economic opportunity for a segment of the black population in Detroit had led to embitterment. When sociologist John Leggett and his colleagues interviewed black Detroiters in 1957 and 1958, they found that many were seething with anger about their living and working conditions. When Leggett asked unemployed blacks to predict what would happen if there were another Great Depression, their answers were grimly prophetic. "There'd be widespread riots," answered one. "The young people won't take it," stated another. "They will steal. A lot of them steal now because they aren't working." A third also raised the issue of a youthful rebellion. "The younger generation won't take it; a lot of bad things would happen." "Oh Hot!" remarked another. "Everybody would get a ball bat and start swinging." Black youths, as Leggett's respondents knew, were increasingly alienated. They were most severely affected by the city's shrinking job market. Young people coming of age in Detroit in the mid- and late 1950s and 1960s faced a very different economic world from that of the previous generation. A black male in Detroit in 1945 or 1950 could realistically expect factory employment, even if his opportunities were seriously limited by discrimination. Blacks continued to suffer levels of unemployment disproportionate to those of Detroit residents in general, although labor force participation rates fluctuated with economic cycles. Still, even in the most flush of times, somewhere close to 10 percent of Detroit's black population was unemployed. Over the next three decades, with the exception of a cyclical boom in automobile employment in the mid- and late 1960s, few could rely on steady employment.

A survey of over three hundred young people in one of Detroit's most depressed inner-city neighborhoods in the early 1960s revealed the extent to which limited opportunities in Detroit's job market had narrowed the horizon of Detroit's young African Americans. Not a single respondent mentioned a career in "the broad middle range of occupations such as skilled trades, office, clerical, or technical occupations." The report noted that "replacing the whole middle range of occupations" in the "perceptual worlds" of the youth were a "whole range of deviant occupations— prostitution, numbers, malicing, corn whiskey, theft, etc." A growing number of young people turned to criminal activity, for "Under conditions where a gap in legitimate opportunity exists in the world, such deviant occupations grow up to fill the void. The motif is one of survival; it is not based on thrill seeking. What we call deviant occupations are in fact perceived to be common and in fact legitimate within the context of the culture in which these youths live." The situation changed little in the mid-1960s, even though the overall economy of Detroit improved. At the time of the 1967 riot, somewhere between 25 and 30 percent of young blacks (between ages eighteen and twenty-four) were out of work.

The combination of persistent discrimination in hiring, technological change, decentralized manufacturing, and urban economic decline had dramatic effects on the employment prospects of blacks in metropolitan Detroit. What was even more striking was the steady increase of adults who were wholly unattached to the urban labor market. Nearly one in five of all Detroit adults did not work at all or worked in the informal economy in 1950. The number grew steadily in the 1960s. The economic transformation of the city launched a process of deproletarianization, as growing numbers of African Americans, especially young men, joined the ranks of those who gave up on work. By 1980, nearly half of the adult male population had only tenuous connections to the city's formal labor market. The deproletarianization of the city's black population had far-reaching consequences: it shaped a pattern of poverty in the postwar city that was disturbingly new. Whereas in the past, most poor people had had some connection to the mainstream labor market, in the latter part of the twentieth century, the urban poor found themselves on the economic margins.

The deproletarianization of a growing number of Detroit's black workers was exacerbated by the persistent racial divide between blacks and whites in the metropolitan area. Detroit's blacks lacked the geographic mobility—common to other groups in other periods of American history—to adapt to the changing labor market. A visitor to Detroit in the 1960s would have found that despite the tremendous growth of Detroit's black population, the pattern of segregation in the metropolitan area remained intact. Throughout the postwar period whole neighborhoods lost their white populations as hundreds of thousands of white Detroiters fled to the burgeoning ring of suburbs that surrounded the city. Detroit's black population was mobile, but its movement was contained within sharply defined racial barriers.

Plant relocations, especially to rural areas and the South, severely limited the economic opportunities of Detroit's blacks. Detroit's waning industrial economy had less and less to offer them. But few black Detroiters in the 1960s had the option of following the exodus of employment; residential segregation and lack of resources kept most trapped in the city. In addition, the alternatives were hardly more appealing. Few considered moving to other major Rust Belt cities, whose economies, like Detroit's, were rapidly declining. And fewer had any desire to move to the small, overwhelmingly white Midwestern towns that attracted much of the nonmetropolitan industrialization of the postwar era. Small numbers headed west, and beginning in the 1970s, some began to return to the South. But opportunities in Detroit were, for many, still better than in Alabama's Black Belt, the Mississippi Delta, or the coal mines of West Virginia. Many remembered the promise of the 1940s and early 1950s and clung to the reasonable expectations that Detroit's economy would pick up again. Hope about the city's future was one option available to the unemployed and jobless. But more and more black Detroiters responded with anger to the city's economic and racial crisis.

Beginning in the late 1950s, African American civil rights activists in the city, after a period of retrenchment, engaged in a renewed militancy. As part of the nationwide civil rights movement, black Detroiters founded new, insurgent organizations like the Trade Union Leadership Council and began to refashion the agenda of established groups like the National Association for the Advancement of Colored People. In the early and mid-1960s, organized African American resistance to discrimination in work and housing accelerated. In 1963, nearly 250,000 blacks and whites, led by the Reverend Martin Luther King Jr., marched through Detroit. Inspired by the successes of the civil rights movement in the South, African American activists in Detroit led boycotts against local stores and businesses that discriminated against blacks. And interracial liberals took the struggle for open housing in a new direction, turning their sights on Detroit's middle- and upper-class suburbs, including

Birmingham and Livonia, and lobbying hard for state and federal legislation that would prohibit discriminatory real estate practices. In all these ways, 1960s-era Detroit witnessed the emergence of a revitalized civil rights movement.

But many civil rights activists grew impatient with the glacial pace of change in Detroit. Black power organizations burgeoned in Detroit in the 1960s, offering an alternative to the mainstream civil rights activism of the postwar years. Detroit was home to the Reverend Albert Cleage, founder of the nationalist Shrine of the Black Madonna and an early and outspoken advocate of black power. At the same time, a younger generation of African Americans, who watched entry-level jobs vanish and who chafed at ongoing discrimination in Detroit's factories, grew more militant on the shop floor, eschewing the consensus politics and integrationism of the UAW [United Auto Workers] for a new "revolutionary unionism." The black-led Revolutionary Union Movement (RUM) established footholds in Dodge and Chrysler plants, where whole departments remained devoid of African Americans, and where blacks remained underrepresented in local union offices.

The 1960s was a paradoxical time in Detroit. From the perspective of national politics, it seemed hopeful. The federal government enacted the most sweeping civil rights legislation since Reconstruction. At the same time, Detroit benefited tremendously from the expansion of federal urban spending during the Kennedy and Johnson administrations. In local politics, the balance of power also began to shift to the left, as Detroit's rapidly growing black populations gained electoral power. City politics remained stiffly polarized by the issues of race and housing, but as more blacks voted and were elected to office, they (and a small but vocal segment of white liberals) broke the stranglehold of the white neighborhood associations on local politics. Mayor Albert Cobo's successor, Louis Miriani, . . . recognized the power of blacks as a swing vote and tried, unsuccessfully, to accommodate both white neighborhood groups and blacks. His successor, Jerome Cavanagh, a little-known insurgent, won an upset victory in 1961 over Miriani. Cavanagh's election was almost accidental: he was supported by an unlikely alliance of African Americans and white neighborhood groups, both alienated (for different reasons) by Miriani's equivocal, middle-of-the-road position on race and housing.

Under Cavanagh, who astutely lobbied government officials for assistance, War on Poverty dollars flooded into Detroit. Detroit was second only to New York in the amount of federal dollars that it received in the 1960s. But officials channeled government assistance down familiar routes and established programs that did not fundamentally deviate from the limited agenda that social welfare, labor, and civil rights groups had set in the 1950s. By and large, War on Poverty programs embodied the conventional wisdom of mainstream economists and social welfare advocates, and focused on behavioral modification as the solution to poverty. The most far-reaching antipoverty programs targeted jobless youth. In 1962, Cavanagh established the Mayor's Committee on Community Action for Detroit Youth, and in 1963, the Michigan Employment Security Commissions established a special Detroit Metropolitan Youth Center. Both directed their energies largely toward black youth "deprived because of social, economic, cultural, or . . . personal conditions." Government, it was argued, should play a role in the transformation of youth culture. The problem with such initiatives, as Thomas F. Jackson has argued in his seminal article on antipoverty policy in the 1960s, was that they "failed to eliminate income poverty or reduce income inequality [or] to increase the aggregate supply of jobs in urban and other labor markets." The education, job training, and youth programs that were at the heart of the War on Poverty in Detroit were built on the same premises and suffered many of the same limitations as the previous generation of ad hoc programs. None responded adequately to deindustrialization and discrimination.

Simultaneous with the organized protest of civil rights groups were spontaneous outbursts of violent resistance on the streets of Detroit. A growing segment of the black population, especially young people who had little attachment to civil rights and reform organizations, began to vent their discontent at shopkeepers and police officers, the only two groups of whites who regularly appeared in largely black neighborhoods. Protests surrounding the shooting of a black youth by an East Side shopkeeper in 1964, a "mini-riot" on the Lower East Side in 1966, and the massive 1967 riot were the symptoms of growing discontent among Detroit's black poor in the 1960s. Detroit's rioters were disproportionately young black men, the group most affected by racial and economic dislocations, and the most impatient with the slow pace of civil rights reforms.

Further complicating the situation in the postwar era were hardening white racial prejudices. Whites grew increasingly bitter at the failure of their efforts to contain the city's expanding black population. The city was racked with housing protests throughout the mid-1960s, as mobile blacks continued to transgress the city's precarious racial boundaries. White neighborhood groups grew even more militant in their opposition to civil rights and open housing. In 1965, fresh off the Homeowners' Rights Ordinance campaign, white civic association advocate Thomas Poindexter revived the effort to abolish the Detroit Commission on Community Relations. The same year, twenty-five crosses burned throughout Detroit, including some in the Courville area, Lower West Side, and Wyoming Corridor, whose residents were involved in a last-ditch effort to stem racial transition. White Detroit groups pressured local politicians to oppose civil rights legislation. Their votes played a crucial role in the defeat of Michigan's Democratic governor, G. Mennen Williams, in 1966, and in the defeat of local referenda to raise taxes to pay for Detroit's increasingly African American public schools.

Most importantly, working- and lower middle-class whites continued to rally around racially conservative candidates. In 1968 and 1972, Detroit whites provided an impressive base of support for Alabama segregationist George C. Wallace as he forayed northward. The politician whose most famous declaration was "segregation now, segregation forever" found a receptive audience in one of the supposed bastions of liberal northern urban voters. Wallace's outspoken opposition to open housing, school integration, and the expansion of civil rights in the workplace resonated deeply with alienated white Detroiters. Wallace voters, to a far greater extent than supporters of other candidates, denounced racial integration and believed that the civil rights movement was moving too fast. Cheering crowds of thousands greeted Wallace when he appeared at Cobo Hall, the riverfront convention center. Like Wallace supporters elsewhere in the North, stalwart Democratic voters roared in applause when their candidate derided civil rights, "forced housing," welfare spending, urban crime, and big government. Wallace also tapped into the economic vulnerability of his blue-collar supporters. Pollsters found that Wallace voters were more pessimistic about the economy than the electorate at large. A UAW local in Flint, Michigan, endorsed Wallace, and Ford workers at the company's shrinking River Rouge plant supported him in a straw poll. Wallace's troubled campaign faltered in Detroit in 1968. But emboldened by the depth of grassroots support that he found in the Rust

Belt, Wallace returned stronger than ever in 1972. He won the 1972 Michigan Democratic primary, sweeping every predominantly white ward in Detroit. Wallace found some of his most fervent support on Detroit's Northwest and Northeast sides, the final remaining bastions of homeowners' association activity in a city that was now over 45 percent African American. Following the lead of Wallace, Richard Nixon and Spiro Agnew repudiated their party's moderate position on civil rights, wooed disaffected urban and southern white Democrats, and swept predominantly white precincts in Detroit in 1968 and 1972.

Racial cleavages also persisted in local politics. Whites provided the crucial margin of support to conservative Polish American mayoral candidate Roman Gribbs in 1969, who edged out his African American opponent Richard Austin. They rallied in support of Detroit's overwhelmingly white police force, including its paramilitary STRESS (Stop Robberies, Enjoy Safe Streets) squad that was regularly accused of brutality toward black suspects. Anti-integration sentiment came to a head when white Detroiters rebelled against the *Milliken v. Bradley* court decision that called for interdistrict busing to eliminate metropolitan-wide educational segregation. The combination of the riot and growing black political power gave urgency to white resistance, but opposition to school integration and support of white conservative candidates for public office was the logical extension of the white racial politics that had divided Detroit in the 1940s and 1950s.

As the invisible boundaries within Detroit frayed, whites continued to flee from the city. . . . Fleeing whites brought the politics of local defensiveness with them to the suburbs, and found protection behind the visible and governmentally defended municipal boundaries of suburbia. By 1980, metropolitan Detroit had eighty-six municipalities, forty-five townships, and eighty-nine school districts. It was far more difficult for African Americans to cross suburban lines than it was for them to move into white urban neighborhoods. But when a few intrepid blacks tried to move into communities like Redford, Wayne, and Warren, they faced attacks and hostility like those that had plagued them in the city. Window breakings, arson, and threats largely prevented blacks from joining the ranks of working-class suburbanites. Whites also fiercely battled the Department of Housing and Urban Development's attempt to mandate the construction of integrated low-income housing in all-white suburbs.

More importantly, the grassroots racial politics that had dominated Detroit since the 1940s took deep root in suburbia. As the auto industry continued to reduce its Detroit labor force and shut down Detroit-area plants in the 1970s and 1980s, blue-collar suburbanites turned their anger against government-sponsored programs for African Americans, particularly affirmative action. Macomb County, the refuge for so many white East Side residents who fled black movement into their neighborhoods, became a bellwether for the troubled Democratic party in the 1970s and 1980s. Like whites still living in the city of Detroit, Macomb residents overwhelmingly supported Wallace in 1972. And in the 1980s, Macomb County became a bastion of "Reagan Democrats," angry antiliberal white voters who repudiated the party of Franklin D. Roosevelt for the Republican Party. Macomb was combed by pollsters and pundits alike who sought to explain why its Catholic, blue-collar workers had abandoned the New Deal for the New Rights.

The virulence of the white backlash of the 1970s and 1980s seems to lend support to the thesis of many recent commentators that the Democratic party made a grievous political error in the 1960s by ignoring the needs of white, working-class and middle-class voters in favor of the demands of the civil rights movement, black militants, the counterculture, and the "undeserving" poor. "The close identification of the Democratic party with the cause of racial justice," argues Allen Matusow, "did it special injury." Jonathan Rieder contends that the 1960s rebellion of the "silent majority" was in part a response to "certain structural limitations of liberal reform," especially "black demands" that "ran up against the limits of liberalism." Wallace's meteoric rise seems to sustain Thomas and Mary Edsall's argument that the Alabama independent "captured the central political dilemma of racial liberalism and the Democratic party: the inability of Democrats to provide a political home for those whites who felt they were paying—unwillingly—the largest 'costs' in the struggle to achieve an integrated society."

The Edsalls, Rieder, and Matusow, although they correctly emphasize the importance of white discontent as a national political force, err in their overemphasis on the role of the Great Society and the sixties rebellions in the rise of the "silent majority." To view the defection of whites from Democratic ranks simply as a reaction to the War on Poverty, civil rights, and black power movements ignores racial cleavages that shaped local politics in the north well before the tumult of the 1960s. Urban antiliberalism had deep roots in a simmering politics of race and neighborhood defensiveness that divided northern cities well before George Wallace began his first speaking tours in the Snowbelt, well before Lyndon Johnson signed the Civil Rights Act, well before the long, hot summers of Watts, Harlem, Chicago, Newark, and Detroit, and well before affirmative action and busing began to dominate the civil rights agenda. From the 1940s through the 1960s, Detroit whites fashioned a language of discontent directed against public officials, blacks, and liberal reformers who supported public housing and open housing. The rhetoric of George Wallace, Richard Nixon, Spiro Agnew, and Ronald Reagan was familiar to the whites who supported candidates such as Edward Jeffries, Albert Cobo, and Thomas Poindexter. The "silent majority" did not emerge de novo from the alleged failures of liberalism in the 1960s; it was not the unique product of the white rejection of the Great Society. Instead it was the culmination of more than two decades of simmering white discontent and extensive antiliberal political organization.

The most enduring legacy of the postwar racial struggles in Detroit has been the growing marginalization of the city in local, state, and national politics. Elected officials in Lansing and Washington, beholden to a vocal, well-organized, and defensive white suburban constituency, have reduced funding for urban education, antipoverty, and development programs. At the same time, Detroit—like its counterparts around the country—grapples with a declining tax base and increasingly expensive social, economic, and infrastructural problems.

⬥ *F U R T H E R   R E A D I N G*

Adams, Julianne Lewis, and Thomas A. DeBlack. *Civil Obedience: An Oral History of School Desegregation in Fayetteville, Arkansas, 1954–1965* (1994).
Balkin, J. M., and Bruce A. Ackerman. *What* Brown v. Board of Education *Should Have Said* (2001).

Bartley, Numan V. *The Rise of Massive Resistance: Race and Politics in the South During the 1950s* (1969; with a new preface, 1999).

Belknap, Michal R. *Federal Law and Southern Order: Racial Violence and Constitutional Conflict in the Post-Brown South* (1987).

Bell, Derrick. *Silent Covenants:* Brown v. Board of Education *and the Unfulfilled Hopes for Racial Reform* (2004).

Berman, Daniel M. *It Is So Ordered: The Supreme Court Rules on School Segregation* (1966).

Borstelmann, Thomas. *The Cold War and the Color Line: American Race Relations in the Global Arena* (2001).

Branch, Taylor. *At Canaan's Edge: America in the King Years, 1965–68* (2006).

———. *Parting the Waters: Martin Luther King and the Civil Rights Movement, 1954–1963* (1988).

———. *Pillar of Fire: America in the King Years, 1963–1965* (1998).

Brauer, Carl M. *John F. Kennedy and the Second Reconstruction* (1977).

Burner, Eric. *And Gently Shall He Lead Them: Robert Moses and Civil Rights in Mississippi* (1994).

Burns, Stewart, ed. *Daybreak of Freedom: The Montgomery Bus Boycott* (1997).

Cashin, Sheryll. *The Failures of Integration: How Race and Class Are Undermining the American Dream* (2004).

Cecelski, David S. *Along Freedom Road: Hyde County, North Carolina, and the Fate of Black Schools in the South* (1994).

Chafe, William H. *Civilities and Civil Rights: Greensboro, North Carolina, and the Black Struggle for Freedom* (1980).

Chappell, David. *Inside Agitators: White Southerners in the Civil Rights Movement* (1994).

Clotfelter, Charles T. *After* Brown: *The Rise and Retreat of School Desegregation* (2004).

Colburn, David R. *Racial Change and Community Crisis: St. Augustine, Florida, 1877–1980* (1985).

Crawford, Vickie L., et al., eds. *Women in the Civil Rights Movement: Trailblazers and Torchbearers* (1990).

Dittmer, John. *Local People: The Struggle for Civil Rights in Mississippi* (1994).

Donato, Ruben. *The Other Struggle for Equal Schools: Mexican Americans During the Civil Rights Era* (1997).

Dudziak, Mary L. *Cold War Civil Rights: Race and the Image of American Democracy* (2002).

Eskew, Glen T. *But for Birmingham: The Local and National Movements in the Civil Rights Struggle* (1997).

Fairclough, Adam. *Race and Democracy: The Civil Rights Movement in Louisiana, 1915–1972* (1995).

———. *To Redeem the Soul of America: The Southern Christian Leadership Conference and Martin Luther King, Jr.* (1987).

Findlay, James F., Jr. *Church People in the Struggle: The National Council of Churches and the Black Freedom Movement, 1950–1970* (1993).

Formisano, Ronald P. *Boston Against Busing: Race, Class and Ethnicity in the 1960s and 1970s* (1991).

Garrow, David J. *Bearing the Cross: Martin Luther King, Jr. and the Southern Christian Leadership Conference* (1986).

———. *The Montgomery Bus Boycott and the Women Who Started It* (1987).

———. *Protest at Selma: Martin Luther King, Jr. and the Voting Rights Act of 1965* (1978).

Glen, John M. *Highlander: No Ordinary School, 1932–1962* (1988).

Graham, Hugh Davis. *The Civil Rights Era: Origins and Development of National Policy* (1990).

Grant, Joanne. *Ella Baker: Freedom Bound* (1998).

Horne, Gerald. *The Fire This Time: The Watts Uprising and the 1960s* (1995).

Kellar, William Henry. *Make Haste Slowly: Moderates, Conservatives, and School Desegregation in Houston* (1999).

Klarman, Michael J. *From Jim Crow to Civil Rights: The Supreme Court and the Struggle for Racial Equality* (2004).

Kluger, Richard. *Simple Justice: The History of* Brown v. Board of Education *and Black America's Struggle for Equality* (1976).

Lawson, Steven F. *Running for Freedom: Civil Rights and Black Politics Since 1941* (1991).

Marsh, Charles. *God's Long Summer: Stories of Faith and Civil Rights* (1997).

Masey, Douglas S., and Nancy A. Denton. *American Apartheid: Segregation and the Making of the Underclass* (1993).

McMillin, Neil. *The Citizens Council: Organized Resistance to the Second Reconstruction* (1971).

McNeil, Genna Rae. *Groundwork: Charles Hamilton Houston and the Struggle for Civil Rights* (1983).

Morris, Aldon. *The Origins of the Civil Rights Movement: Black Communities Organizing for Change* (1984).

Morris, Vivian Gunn, and Curtis L. Morris. *The Price They Paid: Desegregation in an African American Community* (2002).

Norrell, Robert. *Reaping the Whirlwind: The Civil Rights Movement in Tuskegee* (1985).

O'Reilly, Kenneth. *Nixon's Piano: Presidents and Racial Politics from Washington to Clinton* (1995).

———. *"Racial Matters": The FBI's Secret File on Black America, 1960–1972* (1989).

Ogletree, Charles J. *All Deliberate Speed: Reflections on the First Half-Century of* Brown v. Board of Education (2004).

Orfield, Gary. *Public School Desegregation in the United States, 1968–1980* (1986).

———, Susan E. Eaton, and the Harvard Project on School Desegregation. *Dismantling Desegregation* (1996).

Patterson, James T. Brown v. Board of Education: *A Civil Rights Milestone and Its Troubled Legacy* (2001).

Payne, Charles M. *I've Got the Light of Freedom: The Organizing Tradition and the Mississippi Freedom Struggle* (1995).

Pratt, Robert A. *The Color of Their Skin: Education and Race in Richmond, Virginia, 1954–1989* (1994).

Prendergast, Catherine. *Literacy and Racial Justice: The Politics of Learning After* Brown v. Board of Education (2003).

Ransby, Barbara. *Ella Baker and the Black Freedom Movement: A Radical Democratic Vision* (2003).

Robnett, Belinda. *How Long? How Long? African-American Women in the Struggle for Civil Rights* (1997).

Self, Robert O. *American Babylon: Race and the Struggle for Postwar Oakland* (2003).

Steinberg, Stephen. *Turning Back: The Retreat from Racial Justice in American Thought and Policy* (1995).

Sugrue, Thomas J. *The Origins of the Urban Crisis: Race and Inequality in Postwar Detroit* (1996).

Theoharis, Jeanne F., and Komozi Woodward, eds. *Freedom North: Black Freedom Struggles Outside the South, 1940–1980* (2003).

Tushnet, Mark V. *Making Civil Rights Law: Thurgood Marshall and the Supreme Court, 1936–1961* (1994).

Tyson, Michael Eric. *The Making of Malcolm: The Myth and Meaning of Malcolm X* (1995).

Tyson, Timothy B. *Radio Free Dixie: Robert F. Williams and the Roots of Black Power* (1999).

Van Deburg, William L. *New Day in Babylon: The Black Power Movement and American Culture, 1965–1975* (1992).

Whitfield, Stephen J. *A Death in the Delta: The Story of Emmett Till* (1991).

Wilson, William Julius. *The Truly Disadvantaged: The Inner City, the Underclass, and Public Policy* (1987).

Woodard, K. Komozi. *A Nation Within a Nation: Amiri Baraka (LeRoi Jones) and Black Power Politics* (1999).

CHAPTER
6

The Great Society and the
Politics of Liberal Reform

*The Great Society, as President Lyndon B. Johnson and others called the flood
of domestic reform legislation enacted between 1964 and 1968, was the high
watermark of modern American liberalism. Greatly expanding the social welfare
safety net created by the New Deal of the 1930s, it also moved into new areas
relatively untouched by the New Deal, most notably, African American civil rights.
During the Great Depression of the 1930s, the federal government had assumed
new responsibilities toward the unemployed, the elderly, and the poor. The Social
Security Act of 1935, with its provisions for unemployment insurance, old-age
pensions, and support for dependent children, laid the foundation for the modern
welfare state. Many Americans came to expect that in times of economic trouble, the
federal government would step in to help. As early as 1936, President Franklin D.
Roosevelt claimed that "[p]rotection of the family and home," "[e]stablishment of a
democracy of opportunity for all people," and "[a]id to those overtaken by disaster"
were birthrights of all Americans; in 1944, Roosevelt elaborated an "economic
bill of rights" that promised food, housing, jobs, and education. However, conservative opposition to what critics called the "welfare state" blocked fulfillment
of most of these promises during the Fair Deal or New Frontier of later Democratic administrations.*

*All of this changed in the mid-1960s, when Johnson, with the aid of an
expanding economy and large Democratic majorities in Congress, won passage
of a host of new laws on health, housing, education, workplace safety, civil rights,
consumer protection, poverty, and the environment. Moreover, the momentum of
the Great Society continued, even after the Democrats lost the White House in 1968.
Indeed, under President Richard Nixon, federal spending on social welfare programs actually increased. New environmental legislation was enacted, including
the establishment of the Environmental Protection Agency (EPA); and new workplace safety initiatives were put in place under the new Occupational Safety and
Health Administration (OSHA). Affirmative action plans for African Americans,
women, and other groups were also begun during the Nixon years. Indeed, Nixon
even proposed a guaranteed annual income plan as a replacement for the welfare*

system, although a combination of liberal and conservative members of Congress defeated the plan.

Liberal public policies drew criticism even in the heyday of the Great Society. According to some, welfare's intrusive bureaucracy stripped recipients of dignity; to others, it sapped their willingness to work. Public housing projects often concentrated the poor in what rapidly became crime-ridden, high-rise buildings, destroyed urban neighborhoods, and enriched politically connected contractors. Regulation, depending on one's viewpoint, did not go far enough in protecting consumers and the environment or wrapped businesses and homeowners in crippling red tape. During the 1980s, President Ronald Reagan and other conservatives tapped into discontent with Great Society liberalism. While many specific programs remained, liberal dominance of the public policy agenda was clearly over.

✦ D O C U M E N T S

Although President John F. Kennedy had called in his Inaugural Address for Americans to seek a "New Frontier" at home and abroad, he was unable to win congressional passage of much of his domestic legislative program. When Lyndon B. Johnson took office after Kennedy's assassination, he greatly expanded his predecessor's commitments to a broad range of programs designed to reduce poverty, extend equal rights to African Americans, provide health care for the elderly, protect consumers, and expand educational opportunities. In his first annual message to Congress on January 8, 1964 (Document 1), President Johnson called for "an unconditional war on poverty." By the summer of 1964, Johnson had won passage of the Civil Rights Act, the first meaningful civil rights legislation since Reconstruction (Document 2); a tax cut designed to expand the economy; and the Economic Opportunity Act, which signaled the beginning of his administration's campaign against poverty. Although the rate of poverty declined during the late 1960s and early 1970s, the accompanying expansion of the nation's welfare system sparked sharp debate among both liberals and conservatives. Conservatives, led by 1964 Republican presidential candidate Barry M. Goldwater, attacked Johnson's "Great Society" as an unwarranted expansion of federal power. In a 1964 campaign speech on behalf of Goldwater, former actor and General Electric spokesman Ronald Reagan warned of the dangers of the "welfare state" (Document 3). An expanding economy, together with the 1964 landslide victory over Goldwater and the Republicans, enabled Johnson to translate many more of his promises into law. By the end of the Eighty-Ninth Congress (1965–1967), new Great Society programs had expanded to include almost every aspect of American life, as summarized in a report to President Johnson by presidential aides Lawrence O'Brien and Joseph Califano (Document 4). By 1968, however, faced with growing conservative opposition to his policies at home and mounting liberal protest over the war in Vietnam, Johnson abandoned his quest for reelection. In the fall election, Democratic Vice President Hubert Humphrey won only 42.6% of the popular vote, against the combined totals of 43.2% for Republican Richard Nixon and 12.9% for third-party candidate George Wallace. The following year, young Nixon aid Kevin Phillips presciently hailed the election as signaling an "emerging Republican majority" (Document 5). Although Richard Nixon was elected on a backlash against the war in Vietnam, civil rights, and the Great Society, the energies unleashed during the 1960s continued to roil the waters of American politics. In Document 6, Dennis Hayes, given the task of organizing the first Earth Day by Senator Gaylord Nelson, expresses how the new environmentalism grew beyond a widespread concern with clean air and clean water.

1. President Lyndon B. Johnson Declares War on Poverty, 1964

Let this session of Congress be known as the session which did more for civil rights than the last hundred sessions combined; as the session which enacted the most far-reaching tax cut of our time; as the session which declared all-out war on human poverty and unemployment in these United States; as the session which finally recognized the health needs of all our older citizens; as the session which reformed our tangled transportation and transit policies; as the session which achieved the most effective, efficient foreign aid program ever; and as the session which helped to build more homes, more schools, more libraries, and more hospitals than any single session of Congress in the history of our Republic. . . .

This budget, and this year's legislative program, are designed to help each and every American citizen fulfill his basic hopes—his hopes for a fair chance to make good; his hopes for fair play from the law; his hopes for a full-time job on full-time pay, his hopes for a decent home for his family in a decent community; his hopes for a good school for his children with good teachers; and his hopes for security when faced with sickness or unemployment or old age.

Unfortunately, many Americans live on the outskirts of hope—some because of their poverty, and some because of their color, and all too many because of both. Our task is to help replace their despair with opportunity.

This administration today, here and now, declares unconditional war on poverty in America. I urge this Congress and all Americans to join with me in that effort.

It will not be a short or easy struggle, no single weapon or strategy will suffice, but we shall not rest until that war is won. The richest Nation on earth can afford to win it. We cannot afford to lose it. One thousand dollars invested in salvaging an unemployable youth today can return $40,000 or more in his lifetime.

Poverty is a national problem, requiring improved national organization and support. But this attack, to be effective, must also be organized at the State and the local level and must be supported and directed by State and local efforts.

For the war against poverty will not be won here in Washington. It must be won in the field, in every private home, in every public office, from the courthouse to the White House.

The program I shall propose will emphasize this cooperative approach to help that one-fifth of all American families with incomes too small to even meet their basic needs.

Public Papers of the Presidents of the United States: Lyndon B. Johnson, 1963–69, (Washington, D.C.: GPO, 1965), 704–707.

Our chief weapons in a more pinpointed attack will be better schools, and better health, and better homes, and better training, and better job opportunities to help more Americans, especially young Americans, escape from squalor and misery and unemployment rolls where other citizens help to carry them.

Very often a lack of jobs and money is not the cause of poverty, but the symptom. The cause may lie deeper—in our failure to give our fellow citizens a fair chance to develop their own capacities, in a lack of education and training, in a lack of medical care and housing, in a lack of decent communities in which to live and bring up their children.

But whatever the cause, our joint Federal-local effort must pursue poverty, pursue it wherever it exists—in city slums and small towns, in sharecropper shacks or in migrant worker camps, on Indian Reservations, among whites as well as Negroes, among the young as well as the aged, in the boom towns and in the depressed areas.

Our aim is not only to relieve the symptom of poverty, but to cure it and, above all, to prevent it. No single piece of legislation, however, is going to suffice.

We will launch a special effort in the chronically distressed areas of Appalachia.

We must expand our small but our successful area redevelopment program.

We must enact youth employment legislation to put jobless, aimless, hopeless youngsters to work on useful projects.

We must distribute more food to the needy through a broader food stamp program.

We must create a National Service Corps to help the economically handicapped of our own country as the Peace Corps now helps those abroad.

We must modernize our unemployment insurance and establish a high-level commission on automation. If we have the brain power to invent these machines, we have the brain power to make certain that they are a boon and not a bane to humanity.

We must extend the coverage of our minimum wage laws to more than 2 million workers now lacking this basic protection of purchasing power.

We must, by including special school aid funds as part of our education program, improve the quality of teaching, training, and counseling in our hardest hit areas.

We must build more libraries in every area and more hospitals and nursing homes under the Hill-Burton Act, and train more nurses to staff them.

We must provide hospital insurance for our older citizens financed by every worker and his employer under Social Security, contributing no more than $1 a month during the employee's working career to protect him in his old age in a dignified manner without cost to the Treasury, against the devastating hardship of prolonged or repeated illness.

We must, as a part of a revised housing and urban renewal program, give more help to those displaced by slum clearance, provide more housing for our poor and our elderly, and seek as our ultimate goal in our free enterprise system a decent home for every American family.

We must help obtain more modern mass transit within our communities as well as low-cost transportation between them.

Above all, we must release $11 billion of tax reduction into the private spending stream to create new jobs and new markets in every area of this land.

2. Congress Strikes Down Segregation in Public Accommodations: The Civil Rights Act of 1964, Title II (1964)

Sec. 201. **(a)** All persons shall be entitled to the full and equal enjoyment of the goods, services, facilities, and privileges, advantages, and accommodations of any place of public accommodation, as defined in this section, without discrimination or segregation on the ground of race, color, religion, or national origin.

(b) Each of the following establishments which serves the public is a place of public accommodation within the meaning of this title if its operations affect commerce, or if discrimination or segregation by it is supported by State action:

(1) any inn, hotel, motel, or other establishment which provides lodging to transient guests, other than an establishment located within a building which contains not more than five rooms for rent or hire and which is actually occupied by the proprietor of such establishment as his residence;

(2) any restaurant cafeteria, lunchroom, lunch counter, soda fountain, or other facility principally engaged in selling food for consumption on the premises, including, but not limited to, any such facility located on the premises of any retail establishment; or any gasoline station;

(3) any motion picture house, theater, concert hall, sports arena, stadium or other place of exhibition or entertainment; and

(4) any establishment (A)(i) which is physically located within the premises of any establishment otherwise covered by this subsection, or (ii) within the premises of which is physically located any such covered establishment, and (B) which holds itself out as serving patrons of such covered establishment.

(c) The operations of an establishment affect commerce within the meaning of this title if (1) it is one of the establishments described in paragraph (1) of subsection (b); (2) in the case of an establishment described in paragraph (2) of subsection (b), it serves or offers to serve interstate travelers or a substantial portion of the food which it serves, or gasoline or other products which it sells, has moved in commerce; (3) in the case of an establishment described in paragraph (3) of subsection (b), it customarily presents films, performances, athletic teams, exhibitions, or other sources of entertainment which move in commerce; and (4) in the case of an establishment described in paragraph (4) of subsection (b), it is physically located within the premises of, or there is physically located within its premises, an establishment the operations of which affect commerce within the meaning of this subsection. For purposes of this section, "commerce" means travel, trade, traffic, commerce, transportation, or communication among the several States, or between the District of Columbia and any State, or between any foreign country or any territory or possession and any State or the District of Columbia, or between points in the same State but through any other State or the District of Columbia or a foreign country.

(d) Discrimination or segregation by an establishment is supported by State action within the message of this title if such discrimination or segregation (1) is

Excerpt from the Civil Rights Act of 1964, Public Law 88-352, 88th Cong., 2d sess. (July 2, 1964). Title II, Injunctive Relief Against Discrimination in Places of Public Accommodation, http://usinfo.state.gov/usa/infousa/laws/majorlaw/civilr19.htm.

carried on under color of any law, statute, ordinance, or regulation; or (2) is carried on under color of any custom or usage required or enforced by officials of the State or political subdivision thereof; or (3) is required by action of the State or political subdivision thereof.

(e) The provisions of this title shall not apply to a private club or other establishment not in fact open to the public, except to the extent that the facilities of such establishment are made available to the customers or patrons of an establishment within the scope of subsection (b).

3. Ronald Reagan Warns of the Dangers of the Welfare State, 1964

It's time we asked ourselves if we still know the freedoms intended for us by the Founding Fathers. James Madison said, "We base all our experiments on the capacity of mankind for self-government." This idea that government was beholden to the people, that it had no other source of power except the sovereign people, is still the newest, most unique idea in all the long history of man's relation to man. For almost two centuries we have proved man's capacity for self-government, but today we are told we must choose between a left and right or, as others suggest, a third alternative, a kind of safe middle ground. I suggest to you there is no left or right, only an up or down. Up to the maximum of individual freedom consistent with law and order, or down to the ant heap of totalitarianism; and regardless of their humanitarian purpose those who would sacrifice freedom for security have, whether they know it or not, chosen this downward path. Plutarch warned, "The real destroyer of the liberties of the people is he who spreads among them bounties, donations, and benefits."

Today there is an increasing number who can't see a fat man standing beside a thin one without automatically coming to the conclusion the fat man got that way by taking advantage of the thin one. So they would seek the answer to all the problems of human need through government. Howard K. Smith of television fame has written, "The profit motive is outmoded. It may be replaced by the incentives of the welfare state." He says, "The distribution of goods must be effected by a planned economy."

Another articulate spokesman for the welfare state defines liberalism as meeting the material needs of the masses through the full power of centralized government. I for one find it disturbing when a representative refers to the free men and women of this country as the masses, but beyond this the full power of centralized government was the very thing the Founding Fathers sought to minimize. They knew you don't control things; you can't control the economy without controlling *people*. So we have come to a time for choosing. Either we accept the responsibility for our own destiny, or we abandon the American Revolution and confess that an intellectual belief in a far-distant capitol can plan our lives for us better than we can plan them ourselves.

Already the hour is late. Government has laid its hand on health, housing, farming, industry, commerce, education, and, to an ever-increasing degree, interferes with the people's right to know. Government tends to grow; government programs take on weight and momentum, as public servants say, always with the best of intentions, "What greater service we could render if only we had a little more money and a little more power." But the truth is that outside of its legitimate function, government does nothing as well or as economically as the private sector of the economy. . . .

Federal welfare spending is today ten times greater than it was in the dark depths of the Depression. Federal, state, and local welfare combined spend 45 billion dollars a year. Now the government has announced that 20 percent, some 9.3 million families, are poverty-stricken on the basis that they have less than a $3,000 a year income.

If this present welfare spending was prorated equally among these poverty-stricken families, we could give each family more than $4,500 a year. Actually, direct aid to the poor averages less than $600 per family. There must be some administrative overhead somewhere. Now, are we to believe that another billion dollar program added to the half a hundred programs and the 45 billion dollars, will, through some magic, end poverty? For three decades we have tried to solve unemployment by government planning, without success. The more the plans fail, the more the planners plan.

The latest is the Area Redevelopment Agency, and in two years less than one-half of one percent of the unemployed could attribute new jobs to this agency, and the cost to the taxpayer for each job found was $5,000. But beyond the great bureaucratic waste, what are we doing to the people we seek to help?

Recently a judge told me of an incident in his court. A fairly young woman with six children, pregnant with her seventh, came to him for a divorce. Under his questioning it became apparent her husband did not share this desire. Then the whole story came out. Her husband was a laborer earning $250 a month. By divorcing him she could get an $80 raise. She was eligible for $350 a month from the Aid to Dependent Children Program. She had been talked into the divorce by two friends who had already done this very thing. But any time we question the schemes of the do-gooders, we are denounced as being opposed to their humanitarian goal. It seems impossible to legitimately debate their solutions with the assumption that all of us share the desire to help those less fortunate. They tell us we are always against, never for anything. Well, it isn't so much that liberals are ignorant. It's just that they know so much that isn't so.

4. Two White House Aides Report the Achievements of the Great Society, 1966

Final Report to President Lyndon B. Johnson on the 89th Congress by Lawrence F. O'Brien and Joseph A. Califano Jr.

Here is our final summary of the 89th Congress.

A. Our Overall Assessment.   In a word, this was a fabulous and remarkable Congress. We say this not because of its unprecedented productivity—but because what was passed has deep meaning and significance for every man, woman, and

Public Papers of the Presidents of the United States: Lyndon B. Johnson, 1963–69, vol. 2 (Washington, D.C.: GPO, 1967), 1193–1194.

child in this country—and for future generations. A particularly striking feature about the 89th was that its second session was as equally productive as the first.

Attached is a detailed appendix. It tells an impressive story of achievement.

In brief summary this is the record of the major legislation this Administration initiated and sponsored:

First session:	*87 measures*
	84 passed
Second session:	*113 measures*
	97 passed
Grand total:	*200 measures*
	181 passed
	19 did not
Batting average:	*.905*

B. The Major Accomplishments.   Of this list of 181 measures passed, we regard the following 60 as of landmark and historic significance:

The First Session

1. Medicare
2. Elementary and Secondary Education
3. Higher Education
4. Farm Bill
5. Department of Housing and Urban Development
6. Omnibus Housing Act (including rent supplements, and low and moderate income housing)
7. Social Security Increases
8. Voting Rights
9. Immigration Bill
10. Older Americans Act
11. Heart Disease, Cancer, and Stroke Research and Facilities
12. Law Enforcement Assistance Act
13. National Crime Commission
14. Drug Controls
15. Mental Health Research and Facilities
16. Health Professions Education
17. Medical Library Facilities
18. Vocational Rehabilitation
19. Inter-American Bank Fund Increases
20. Stepping Up the War Against Poverty
21. Arts and Humanities Foundation
22. Appalachia
23. Highway Beautification
24. Air Pollution (auto exhausts and research)
25. Water Pollution Control (water quality standards)
26. High Speed Ground Transportation
27. Extension and Strengthening of MDTA [Manpower Development and Training Act of 1962]

28. Presidential Disability and Succession
29. Child Health Medical Assistance
30. Regional Development

The Second Session

1. The Department of Transportation
2. Truth in Packaging
3. Demonstration Cities
4. Funds for Rent Supplements
5. Funds for Teacher Corps
6. Asian Development Bank
7. Water Pollution (Clean Rivers)
8. Food for Peace
9. March Anti-inflation Package
10. Narcotics Rehabilitation
11. Child Safety
12. Viet-Nam Supplemental
13. Foreign Aid Extension
14. Traffic Safety
15. Highway Safety
16. Public Health Service Reorganization
17. Community Relations Service Reorganization
18. Water Pollution Control Administration Reorganization
19. Mine Safety
20. Allied Health Professions Training
21. International Education
22. Child Nutrition
23. Bail Reform
24. Civil Procedure Reforms
25. Tire Safety
26. Protection for Savers (increase in Federal Insurance for savings accounts)
27. The GI Bill
28. Minimum Wage Increase
29. Urban Mass Transit
30. Elementary and Higher Education Funds

5. A Conservative Strategist Hails an "Emerging Republican Majority," 1969

The long-range meaning of the political upheaval of 1968 rests on the Republican opportunity to fashion a majority among the 57 per cent of the American electorate which voted to eject the Democratic Party from national power. To begin with, more than half of this protesting 57 per cent were firm Republicans from areas—Southern

Excerpts from Kevin P. Phillips, *The Emerging Republican Majority* (New Rochelle, N.Y.: Arlington House, 1969), pp. 461–474. Reprinted by permission of the Leigh Bureau.

California to Long Island's Suffolk County—or sociocultural backgrounds with a growing GOP bias. Some voted for George Wallace, but most backed Richard Nixon, providing the bulk of his Election Day support. Only a small minority of 1968 Nixon backers—perhaps several million liberal Republicans and independents from Maine and Oregon to Fifth Avenue—cast what may be their last Republican presidential ballots because of the partisan re-alignment taking place. The third major anti-Democratic voting stream of 1968—and the most decisive—was that of the fifteen million or so conservative Democrats who shunned Hubert Humphrey to divide about evenly between Richard Nixon and George Wallace. Such elements stretched from the "Okie" Great Central Valley of California to the mountain towns of Idaho, Florida's space centers, rural South Carolina, Bavarian Minnesota, the Irish sidewalks of New York and the Levittowns of Megalopolis. . . .

Although most of George Wallace's votes came from Democrats rather than Republicans, they were conservatives—Southerners, Borderers, German and Irish Catholics—who had been trending Republican prior to 1968. . . . [T]he Wallace vote followed the cultural geography of obsolescent conservative (often Southern) Democratic tradition. There was no reliable Wallace backing among blue-collar workers and poor whites as a class; industrial centers in the Yankee sphere of influence from Duluth to Scranton, Fall River and Biddeford shunned the Alabama ex-governor with a mere 2 per cent to 3 per cent of the vote. Areas of eroding Democratic tradition were the great breeding grounds of Wallace voters.

In the South, Wallace drew principally on conservative Democrats quitting the party they had long succored and controlled. Generally speaking, Wallace's Southern strength was greatest in the Democratic Party's historic (pre-1964) lowland strongholds, while the Alabaman's worst Southern percentages came in the Republican highlands. White voters throughout most sections of the Deep South went two-to-one for Wallace, In the more Republican Outer South, only one white voter out of three supported the third-party candidate. In the South as a whole, 85 to 90 per cent of the white electorate cast Nixon or Wallace votes against the re-aligning national Democratic Party in 1968, an unprecedented magnitude of disaffection which indicates the availability of the Wallace vote to the future GOP.

Four of the five Wallace states had gone Republican in 1964, and although the Alabaman greatly enlarged the scope of Southern revolt by attracting most of the (poor white or Outer South Black Belt) Southerners who had hitherto resisted Republican or States Rights candidacies, much of his tide had already been flowing for Goldwater [in 1964]. Nor does the Nixon Administration have to bid much ideologically for this electorate. Despite his success in enlarging the scope of white Southern revolt, George Wallace failed to reach far enough or strongly enough beyond the Deep South to give his American Independent Party the national base required for a viable future. Republican Nixon won most of the Outer South, establishing the GOP as the ascending party of the local white majority. Having achieved statewide success only in the Deep South, and facing competition from a Southern Republicanism mindful of its opportunity, the Wallace movement cannot maintain an adequate political base and is bound to serve, like past American third parties, as a way station for groups abandoning one party for another. Some Wallace voters were longtime Republicans, but the great majority were conservative Democrats who have been moving—and should continue to do so—towards the GOP. . . .

In addition to Western or Southern Democrats of conservative or populist bent, Wallace also scored well among Catholics, but only in certain areas. From Maine to Michigan, across most of the belt of Yankee-settled territory where local cleavage, though changing, still pits Protestant Republicans against urban Catholic Democrats, the Catholic trend away from the Democrats was slight. However, in the greater New York area, as well as Gary and Cleveland, where minority group (Negro and/or Jewish) power has taken control of local Democratic machinery, Catholic backing of Wallace was considerable. Here, . . . Catholics are leaving the Democratic Party. . . .

Although the appeal of a successful Nixon Administration and the lack of a Wallace candidacy would greatly swell the 1972 Republican vote in the South, West, Border and the Catholic North, the 1972 GOP may well simultaneously lose a lesser number of 1968 supporters among groups reacting against the party's emerging Southern, Western and New York Irish majority. . . . Yankees, Megalopolitan silk-stocking voters and Scandinavians from Maine across the Great Lakes to the Pacific all showed a distinct Democratic trend in the years between 1960 and 1968. Such disaffection will doubtlessly continue, but its principal impact has already been felt. Richard Nixon won only 38 per cent of the total 1968 presidential vote on Manhattan's rich East Side; he took only 44 per cent of the ballots in Scarsdale, the city's richest suburb; New England's Yankee counties and towns produced Nixon majorities down 10 per cent to 15 per cent from 1960 levels; fashionable San Francisco shifted toward the Democrats; and Scandinavian Minnesota and Washington state backed Humphrey, as did the Scandinavian northwest of Wisconsin. . . .

The upcoming cycle of American politics is likely to match a dominant Republican Party based in the Heartland, South and California against a minority Democratic Party based in the Northeast and the Pacific Northwest (and encompassing Southern as well as Northern Negroes). With such support behind it, the GOP can easily afford to lose the states of Massachusetts, New York and Michigan—and is likely to do so except in landslide years. Together with the District of Columbia, the top ten Humphrey states—Hawaii, Washington, Minnesota, Michigan, West Virginia, New York, Connecticut, Rhode Island, Massachusetts and Maine—should prove to be the core of national Democratic strength. . . . [T]he new battlegrounds of quadrennial presidential politics are likely to be California, Ohio and Pennsylvania.

Unluckily for the Democrats, their major impetus is centered in stagnant Northern industrial states—and within those states, in old decaying cities, in a Yankee countryside that has fewer people than in 1900, and in the most expensive suburbs. Beyond this, in the South and West, the Democrats dominate only two expanding voting blocs—Latins and Negroes. From space-center Florida across the booming Texas plains to the Los Angeles–San Diego suburban corridor, the nation's fastest-growing areas are strongly Republican and conservative. Even in the Northeast, the few rapidly growing suburbs are conservative-trending areas. . . . Because of this demographic pattern, the South and West are gaining electoral votes and national political power at the expense of the Northeast. . . .

The emerging Republican majority spoke clearly in 1968 for a shift away from the sociological jurisprudence, moral permissiveness, experimental residential, welfare and educational programing and massive federal spending by which the Liberal (mostly Democratic) Establishment sought to propagate liberal institutions and ideology—and all the while reap growing economic benefits. The dominion of this impetus is inherent in the list of Republican-trending groups and potentially Republican Wallace electorates of 1968: Southerners, Borderers, Germans, Scotch-Irish, Pennsylvania Dutch, Irish, Italians, Eastern Europeans and other urban Catholics, middle-class suburbanites, Sun Belt residents, Rocky Mountain and Pacific Interior populists. Democrats among these groups were principally alienated from their party by its social programs and increasing identification with the Northeastern Establishment and ghetto alike. . . .

Because the Republicans are little dependent on the Liberal Establishment or urban Negroes—the two groups most intimately, though dissimilarly, concerned with present urban and welfare policies—they have the political freedom to disregard the multitude of vested interests which have throttled national urban policy. The GOP is particularly lucky not to be weighted down with commitment to the political blocs, power brokers and poverty concessionaires of the decaying central cities of the North, now that national growth is shifting to suburbia, the South and the West. The American future lies in a revitalized countryside, a demographically ascendant Sun Belt and suburbia, and new towns—perhaps mountainside linear cities astride monorails 200 miles from Phoenix, Memphis or Atlanta. National policy will have to direct itself towards this future and its constituencies; and perhaps an administration so oriented can also deal realistically with the central cities where Great Society political largesse has so demonstrably failed. . . .

One of the greatest political myths of the decade—a product of liberal self-interest—is that the Republican Party cannot attain national dominance without mobilizing liberal support in the big cities, appealing to "liberal" youth, empathizing with "liberal" urbanization, gaining substantial Negro support and courting the affluent young professional classes of "suburbia." The actual demographic and political facts convey a very different message. . . .

[T]he big city political era is over in the United States. . . . With Negroes moving into the cities, whites have moved out. Moreover, white urban populations are getting increasingly conservative. . . .

While urbanization *is* changing the face of America, and the GOP must take political note of this fact, it presents the opposite of a problem. A generation ago, the coming of age of the working-class central cities condemned the Republican Party to minority status, but the new "urbanization"—suburbanization is often a better description—is a middle-class impetus shaping the same ignominy for the Democrats. All across the nation, the fastest-growing urban areas are steadily increasing their *Republican* pluralities, while the old central cities—seat of the New Deal era—are casting steadily fewer votes for Democratic liberalism. No major American city is losing population so rapidly as arch-Democratic and establishmentarian Boston, while the fastest-growing urban area in the nation is Southern California's staunchly conservative Orange County, and the fastest-growing cities are conservative strongholds like Phoenix, Dallas, Houston, Anaheim, San Diego and Fort Lauderdale.

Substantial Negro support is not necessary to national Republican victory in light of the 1968 election returns. Obviously, the GOP can build a winning coalition without Negro votes. Indeed, Negro-Democratic mutual identification was a major source of Democratic loss—and Republican or American Independent Party profit—in many sections of the nation.

6. Earth Day, 1970

I suspect that the politicians and businessmen who are jumping on the environmental bandwagon don't have the slightest idea what they are getting into. They are talking about filters on smokestacks while we are challenging corporate irresponsibility. They are bursting with pride about plans for totally inadequate municipal sewage treatment plants; we are challenging the ethics of a society that, with only 6 percent of the world's population, accounts for more than half of the world's annual consumption of raw materials.

Our country is stealing from poorer nations and from generations yet unborn. We seem to have a reverse King Midas touch. Everything we touch turns to garbage—142 tons of smoke, 7 million junked cars, 30 million tons of paper, 28 billion bottles, 48 billion cans each year. We waste riches in planned obsolescence and invest the overwhelming bulk of our national budget in ABMs [anti-ballistic-missiles] and MIRVs [multiple independently targeted re-entry vehicles; ballistic missiles with multiple warheads each capable of guiding itself to its target] and other means of death. Russia can destroy every American twelve times; America can destroy every Russian forty times. I guess that is supposed to mean that we are ahead.

We're spending insanely large sums on military hardware instead of eliminating hunger and poverty. We squander our resources on moon dust while people live in wretched housing. We still waste lives and money on a war that we should never have entered and should get out of immediately.

We have made Vietnam an ecological catastrophe. Vietnam was once capable of producing a marketable surplus of grain. Now America must feed her. American bombs have pockmarked Vietnam with more than 2.6 million craters a year, some of them thirty feet deep. We spent $73 million on defoliation in Vietnam last year alone, much of it on 2,4,5–T, a herbicide [*Dixon* or *Agent Orange*] we've now found causes birth defects. We dumped defoliants on Vietnam at the rate of 10,000 pounds a month, and in the last fiscal year alone we blackened 6,600 square miles. We cannot pretend to be concerned with the environment of this or any other country as long as we continue the war in Vietnam or wage war in Cambodia. Laos, or anywhere else.

But even if that war were over tomorrow, we would still be killing this planet. We are systematically destroying our land, our streams, and our seas. We foul our air, deaden our senses, and pollute our bodies. And it's getting worse.

America's political and business institutions don't seem yet to have realized that some of us want to live in this country thirty years from now. They had better come to recognize it soon. We don't have very much time. We cannot afford to give them very much time.

When it comes to salvaging the environment, the individual is almost powerless. You can pick up litter, and if you're diligent, you may be able to find some returnable bottles. But you are forced to breathe the lung-corroding poison which companies spew into the air. You cannot buy electricity from a power company which does not pollute. You cannot find products in biodegradable packages. You cannot even look to the manufacturer for reliable information on the ecological effects of a product.

"The Beginning" by Dennis Hayes from *Earth Day—The Beginning, 1970*, pp. xiii–xv. Reprinted by permission of Dennis Hayes, Green Seal Inc.

You simply can't live an ecologically sound life in America. That is not one of the options open to you. Go shopping and you find dozens of laundry products; it seems like a tremendous array unless you know that most are made by three companies, and the differences in cleaning power are almost negligible. If you really want to be ecologically sound, you won't buy any detergents—just some old-fashioned laundry soap and a bit of soda. But there's nothing on those packages to tell you the phosphate content, and there's nothing in the supermarket to tell you, only meaningless advertising that keeps dunning you.

We are learning. In response, industry has turned the environmental problem over to its public relations men. We've been deluged with full-page ads about pollution problems and what's being done about them. It would appear from most of them that things are fine and will soon be perfect. But the people of America are still coughing. And our eyes are running, and our lungs are blackening, and our property is corroding, and we're getting angry. We're getting angry at half-truths, angry at semitruths, and angry at outright lies.

We are tired of being told that we are to blame for corporate depredations. Political and business leaders once hoped that they could turn the environmental movement into a massive antilitter campaign. They have failed. We have learned not to place our faith in regulatory agencies that are supposed to act in the public interest. We have learned not to believe that advertising that sells us presidents the way it sells us useless products.

We will not appeal any more to the conscience of institutions because institutions have no conscience. If we want them to do what is right, we must make them do what is right. We will use proxy fights, lawsuits, demonstrations, research, boycotts, ballots—whatever it takes. This may be our last chance. If environment is a fad, it's going to be our last fad.

Things as we know them are falling apart. There is an unease across this country today. People know that something is wrong. The war is part of it, but most critics of that war have, from the beginning, known that the war is only a symptom of something much deeper. Poor people have long known what is wrong. Now the alley garbage, the crowding and the unhappiness and the crime have spread beyond the ghetto and a whole society is coming to realize that it must drastically change course.

We are building a movement, a movement with a broad base, a movement which transcends traditional political boundaries. It is a movement that values people more than technology, people more than political boundaries and political ideologies, people more than profit. It will be a difficult fight. Earth Day is the beginning.

◆ *E S S A Y S*

Early analyses of the Great Society tend to focus on whether reform thwarted more radical possibilities and on the nature of the new expectations for government that developed in the late 1960s and the 1970s. The current debate, which takes its measure of the Great Society from the vantage point of a time when the liberal approach to domestic policy no longer commands the field as it once did, has moved in several new directions. One such direction, illustrated here in the selection by historian James T. Patterson, emphasizes some of the enduring contributions of Great Society liberalism. Another line of analysis questions whether the public commitment to Great Society liberalism was ever that broad and deep. Matthew D. Lassiter finds the suburban middle class only weakly tied to the claims of the Great Society, even when voting for Democrats. This "volatile center" is viewed as part of a rightward shift in American politics.

The Rise of "Rights Consciousness"

JAMES T. PATTERSON

Searching for a title to an essay on American politics between the 1930s and 1980, many writers might choose something like "From Roosevelt to Reagan: The Rise and Fall of American Liberalism in Mid-Twentieth-Century America." My title, however, has no presidents in it, and my essay tells a different story. It focuses less on presidents or political rhetoric than on long-term structural developments, notably the rise of interest groups—old as well as new—and of an ever-growing state and its bureaucracies and courts.

Reflecting a great increase in popular rights consciousness, these expanding institutions managed to protect a broad range of civil rights, civil liberties, and entitlements. As a result, many policies crafted by liberals, far from falling, were standing tall as bulwarks of a wide-ranging administrative state in 1980, though not always in the shape that their creators had anticipated. To tell this story, I begin by sketching some of the major political changes and continuities during these fifty years and then backtrack to focus on the most important plot line of the narrative: the rise of rights and rights consciousness. . . .

The changes are difficult to miss. They took place gradually, of course, but most dramatically in three bursts: during the mid-1930s, during World War II, and again during the mid to late 1960s. In all three periods, large structural developments—mainly economic or war-related—drove notable transformations, among them a considerable expansion of authority at all levels of American government. Most importantly, economic growth and unimaginable affluence after 1940 greatly widened popular rights consciousness, thereby encouraging the rise of numerous and clamorous interest groups and bureaucracies and bringing the courts into unprecedented activism in many areas of policy. My account of key changes, therefore, emphasizes the role of economic and international forces and stresses the increasingly pluralistic, bureaucratic, and litigious politics that emerged over time.

Yet important continuities are also a major part of this tale. Generally, these can be called ideological and necessarily take us beyond primarily structural models of political change. Some of these ideological forces were—and are—conservative. Deeply rooted in the American historical experience prior to the 1930s, they are

From James T. Patterson, "The Rise of Rights and Rights Consciousness in American Politics, 1930s–1970s," in Byron E. Shafer and Anthony J. Badger, eds., *Contesting Democracy: Substance and Structure in American Political History, 1775–2000* (Lawrence, KS: University Press of Kansas, 2001), 201–205, 210–219. Copyright © 2001 by the University Press of Kansas. Reprinted by permission of the University Press of Kansas.

familiar to any student of American history: popular resistance to substantial growth of the state, especially when it seeks to expand welfare for the "undeserving"; distrust of authority, governmental and otherwise; and faith in localism, federalism, and the separation of powers as outlined in the Constitution. Amid all the change that transformed American politics in these years—and it was in many ways dramatic—these ideas remained strong, thereby ensuring that the United States continued to feature an unusually decentralized polity compared with most industrialized nations in the world.

As Samuel Huntington argues, Americans have also been prone to display what he calls "moral passion" in a quest for a more egalitarian society. Rooted in the ideals of the Declaration of Independence, this passion (Huntington, like Gunnar Myrdal, labels it the "American Creed") exploded with special intensity during the 1960s, thereby exposing the limitations of consensus models of American politics that had captivated many scholars during the 1950s. Indeed, social and political conflict seemed for a time in the late 1960s to threaten basic institutions. But it was conflict within limits. Most of the protesters who agitated for change in the 1960s were neither anti-American nor advocates of social leveling. What they expressed was mainly a moral passion aimed at forcing the nation to live up to its democratic ideals. . . .

Perhaps the strongest ideological continuity during much of this era, however, was the staying power of liberal—not social democratic—ideas and policies. These liberal ideas rested on that firmest of modern American faiths: although the federal government should be limited in size and scope, it should also help individuals to enjoy equal opportunity. Franklin D. Roosevelt's New Deal in the 1930s determined that government must engage in this process. This idea took firmer root over time and flowered in the Great Society programs of Lyndon Johnson.

Some of this blossoming was too fast for people, prompting a backlash that seemed threatening to many liberal observers in the late 1970s and the early 1980s. The journalist Theodore White, writing in the immediate aftermath of what he called Reagan's "landslide" presidential victory in 1980, concluded in 1982 that American politics—by which he meant liberal politics—had come to "the end of an era." In retrospect, it seems that White exaggerated. But he expressed a generally accurate and widely held view concerning the strength of liberalism during the nearly fifty years before that.

Indeed, the long-range thrust of American political preferences between 1932 and the late 1960s—and of most public policies—was in a liberal direction. And liberal policies established in those years did not die in the 1970s. Conservative efforts notwithstanding, the years from 1932 into the late 1970s were not an era in which liberal programs rose and then fell. Rather, these were years of considerable continuity, in which a growing number of federal efforts became bureaucratically well established and judicially well protected.

We may also consign political ideas on both the Right and the Left during these years to the somewhat dim edges of the political spectrum. Although political conservatives were frequently able to block new liberal legislation—notably, between 1937 and 1963, and again between 1966 and 1980—they never came close to dismantling the New Deal or its subsequent expansion. In 1964–1965, they were powerless before the legislative juggernaut that Johnson engineered. Thereafter, they could not stem the near-inexorable growth of public authority and of bureaucratic and judicial interventions on behalf of a lengthening list of rights and entitlements.

The Left between 1930 and 1980 was weaker still. . . . Notwithstanding gusts of anti-corporate rhetoric that ruffled political life from time to time, most reformers from the 1930s into the 1970s did not call for social democratic programs that would have significantly expanded progressive taxation or redistributed income or resources. Instead, they expressed liberal ideas and called for the expansion of economic opportunity, so that the American dream of socioeconomic mobility might become a reality.

Liberals—and others—lamented a number of discouraging political trends during these years. Voting by eligible Americans plummeted after 1940, especially among the young. Despite the great spread of educational attainment after 1945, even those who seemed as ignorant as earlier voters about many aspects of government, which was becoming more complex and harder to fathom. Political parties fell apart in an age of electoral "dealignment," thereby (some thought) undermining orderly, productive policy formation. Organized interest groups developed greater power. Alonzo Hamby bewails the power during these years of a "conglomerate of special interests . . . [that had] little support in the larger body politic and no compelling vision of a general public interest." Reforms of these flaws in the 1970s had little practical effect.

Perhaps the most common scholarly lament about American politics and policies during these fifty years—a lament mainly from the Left—is that the United States only slowly and fitfully constructed a social safety net. There is no doubt that this was the case: although the New Deal ushered in the beginnings of an American welfare state, public spending for social welfare from all levels of government, education excepted, continued to be consistently lower as a percentage of gross domestic product than it was in most other industrial countries. By 1980, it was one-sixth below the average in such nations. It also seems clear that income inequality remained more pronounced in the United States during this era than in most other industrialized areas of the world.

But without succumbing to romantic nostalgia—who can forget McCarthyism or Jim Crow?—liberals can find much to celebrate in the years between 1930 and 1970. For many marginal groups, notably African Americans, this was a time of extraordinary political as well as economic progress. By the early 1970s, many Americans— blacks, the elderly, the welfare poor, political radicals, alleged criminals—enjoyed benefits, entitlements, legal protections, civil rights, and civil liberties that would scarcely have been imaginable in 1930, or even in 1960. In the early 1970s, other groups—environmentalists, women, the handicapped, and advocates of consumer protection—also secured greater protection and support from legislation, federal bureaucracies, and the courts.

This was also a time—notably, between World War II and the early 1970s—that huge numbers of people, especially in the rapidly expanding middle classes, developed grand and growing popular expectations about the future, both of the nation's salutary role in world affairs and of the socioeconomic possibilities of coming generations. For the millions of Americans who moved up the social ladder and came to enjoy the good life, these became realistic, achieved expectations. Economic growth drove many of these developments. As the pie enlarged, there was much more to share.

But, to repeat, less deterministic forces also mattered. For example, the surge of egalitarian ideas—many of them unleashed by the civil rights movement—was a key to the advance in the early 1960s of both liberal policies and a broader rights consciousness that gripped a host of claimant groups. So it was that a fortuitous combination of forces—of economic progress and moral fervor—worked together to promote significant, often beneficial changes for many previously marginalized people. The nation's political institutions, often maligned, ultimately proved capable of accommodating many of these changes. . . .

As late as 1960, shortly before the third great burst of political change, two key, related political forces of the near future were still to achieve prominence. The first was the explosion of moral passion, driven strongly by the civil rights movement, which increased rights consciousness in the culture, helped to multiply the number of interest groups, and thereby transformed political activism. By 1970, for instance, not only African Americans but also women, gay people, environmentalists, consumer advocates, and various ethnic minorities had become well organized and were clamoring for governmental attention. For a brief time in the late 1960s and early 1970s, there was even a vocal, visible National Welfare Rights Organization.

Prior to 1960, however, these groups were scarcely to be heard in politics. As a sign of those earlier times, politicians, knowing that they need not fear retribution from the electorate or the media, casually referred to the homeless as "bums," "drunks," and "psychos." Voters who had come of age in the 1930s, moreover, tended to retain durable loyalties to either the Democratic or the Republican Party. The percentage of voters who called themselves independents—mostly young people—rose slowly, from around 15 percent in the 1940s to 24 percent by the early 1960s. As far as most politicians could tell in 1960, the great electoral realignment of the 1930s was holding fairly firm outside of a few western states. It seemed a serene, largely unchanging time.

The second force that as of 1960 still lay largely in the future was structural: the fantastic performance of the economy. Following a recession that ended in 1961, the decade witnessed uninterrupted economic expansion. Economic growth between 1962 and 1965 was nothing short of sensational, at 5 percent or more per year. The poverty rate, at around 22 percent of the population in 1962, fell sharply to an all-time low of 11 percent by 1973. Liberal rhetoric to the contrary, these changes probably owed little to purposeful government policies. But liberal Democrats were naturally quick to claim credit for their expertise—it was an age of highly confident social science—and for the spread of affluence, which in turn prompted rising popular expectations about the government's capacity to ensure an even rosier future.

The combination of economic growth, moral passion, rising rights consciousness, and higher expectations from government played beautifully into the large and eager hands of Lyndon Johnson in the mid-1960s. Johnson, an extraordinarily skillful manager of Congress, proved that individuals can make a considerable difference in history. Driving hard for his so-called Great Society domestic programs, he secured from Capitol Hill a burst of liberal legislation that rivaled the output of FDR's first term: the War on Poverty, Medicare and Medicaid, immigration reform, and passage at last of general federal aid to public schools. Above all, Congress enacted two historic civil rights acts that did away with Jim Crow and guaranteed the voting rights of minorities. The Republican Party, damaged by the bizarre presidential candidacy of Barry Goldwater in 1964, seemed helpless before this onslaught of liberal policy making.

Johnson's programs, like FDR's, were generally liberal rather than redistributive in a social democratic sense. The War on Poverty, for instance, was a classic example of American liberal policy making; it aimed to enhance equality of opportunity, not establish equality of condition—to set up *doors* such as Head Start through which the poor might pass and move ahead, not *floors* of guaranteed income on which they could stand. The War on Poverty provided services, not cash, in the quintessentially American hope that services—and growth in employment—could, in the long run, render welfare almost unnecessary. The civil rights acts had immediate and lasting effects on American race relations. With Social Security, they rank as the most important domestic laws in the twentieth-century history of the United States. And most of the other Great Society programs remained on the books and expanded in the years ahead; it is highly misleading to label the years 1965 to 1980 as representing a sharp turn to the right or as a decisive repudiation of liberal programs.

Many of Johnson's laws, however, quickly aroused debate. Critics said correctly that Medicare and Medicaid would cost far more than had been anticipated, that public schools needed much more than money, and that the War on Poverty—never really more than a skirmish—was wildly oversold. All these laws, especially immigration reform (which resulted in great increases in the numbers of foreigners who came to America), thus had large and unforeseen consequences in later years. Drawing on criticisms like these, the GOP scored major gains in congressional elections as early as 1966, and in 1968, Richard Nixon won the presidency.

By the 1970s, the faith in government that people had demonstrated in 1964–1965 had dissipated. In 1964, only 43 percent of Americans had thought that the federal government was "too big." By 1976, following the loss in Vietnam and Watergate, more than 58 percent thought so. Even more skeptical responses concerning governmental competence greeted pollsters in later years. This decline of popular faith in the capacity of the state to do good things was one of the most lasting legacies of the 1960s and early 1970s.

President Johnson's mode of leadership contributed to a second lasting legacy: the remarkably rapid decomposition of the political parties. Eager to enhance his personal presidential power, he largely ignored the Democratic Party, which fell into disarray by 1968. It grew so weak that in 1976, Jimmy Carter, a no-name, set up his own organization and grabbed the presidential nomination. The Republican Party too became less hierarchical. In the same year, former governor Ronald Reagan of California nearly took the GOP nomination away from incumbent president Gerald Ford.

Larger structural forces abetted this dramatic trend: the already decaying state of Democratic urban machines, whose access to patronage had fallen dramatically after dissolution of the WPA [Works Progress Administration]; intraparty polarizations caused by conflict over the Vietnam War; the escalating spread of highly rights-conscious, issue-oriented interest groups; and the growing tendency of voters, dismayed by both parties after 1965, to split tickets and to call themselves independents. By the early 1970s, some two-thirds of voters split their tickets, compared with the one-fourth who had done so in the 1940s.

The ubiquitous and powerful impact of television especially facilitated these changes. First of all, television promoted the rise of telegenic candidates such as

John F. Kennedy, who could appeal beyond party. More significantly—neither Johnson nor Nixon could be said to be telegenic—television encouraged statewide and national candidates to ignore their party organizations and run their own campaigns, largely through ads and sound bites on the screen. Whether this was a good thing for American political life will forever generate debate; surely it was good for candidates with money. But there is no doubt that television further weakened grassroots party organizing and accelerated the emergence of candidate-centered politics in the United States.

Changes in party procedures further advanced these tendencies. As the parties grew weaker, activists managed to substitute primaries for conventions; the latter had previously enabled party leaders to maintain some control over their tickets. By 1980, thirty states had true Democratic presidential primaries, and thirty-one had Republican primaries. These selected 76 percent of Democratic delegates and 65 percent of Republican delegates to the party conventions. By contrast, only seventeen states in 1968 had had Democratic presidential primaries, choosing 40 percent of the delegates, and fifteen had had Republican primaries, accounting for 43 percent of delegates.

When the Democrats staggered forth from their fratricide in 1968, they also established new quotas for convention delegates that radically transformed their nominating base. Thereafter, the presidential Democratic Party became a shaky coalition of well-educated, upper-middle-class liberals—a "new class," they were called—and of blacks, Hispanics, feminists, environmentalists, and others on the left of the political spectrum. The more working-class-based Democratic electoral coalition of the 1930s and 1940s no longer held up well in presidential elections.

The decomposition of parties did not, however, mean that the national party organizations atrophied. On the contrary, they professionalized and grew in size, hiring a wide range of consultants, pollsters, and media experts. Using modernized money-raising techniques such as direct mailings, these professionals took advantage of the absence of meaningful controls on campaign expenditures and pulled in vast sums of money. In these ways, too, grassroots political activism lost importance.

Nor did the decomposition amount to a partisan realignment on the scale of those of the 1890s or the 1930s. Rather, it led to a *de*alignment, in which some groups—especially middle-class white southerners, religious conservatives and fundamentalists, and many working-class northerners—sheared off from the Democratic Party to vote Republican, principally in presidential elections. What realignment there was occurred mainly at this level, where Republican candidates for the White House scored well until 1992. Democratic congressional candidates, in contrast, continued to highlight their support of social programs from the New Deal and Great Society, such as Social Security and Medicare; to employ the advantages of incumbency; and, in most cases, to outpoll Republican conservatives. They controlled Capitol Hill throughout much of the late 1960s, 1970s, and 1980s, thereby creating many years of divided, highly partisan government. . . .

Arresting as these changes were, they were less significant than other dramatic developments during the late 1960s—a pivotal time of political transformation in recent American history. One key change involved the political agenda. As late as the 1960 election, the most contested national issues were familiar: the state of the economy and the cold war. In 1964, thanks to the civil rights movement, racial issues also rose to the top of the agenda. And by the early 1970s, a host of sociocultural issues—women's rights, environmentalism, prayer in the schools, rising crime, out-of-wedlock pregnancy, declining SAT scores, welfare dependency, concerns over rising immigration—greatly expanded the number of controversial items on the agenda of American politics. The salience of such sociocultural concerns was in some ways reminiscent of the Progressive Era, a time of high immigration when some of these same issues—mainly on the state level—had also preoccupied the public.

Perhaps the most stunning changes during the late 1960s and early 1970s arose from the rights consciousness that had been growing rapidly since the early 1960s. This rise sparked three big changes in American government. First, it led to what Hugh Davis Graham accurately called an "explosion in public law litigation," greatly broadening the role of the federal courts in American life. Cases involving civil rights alone—affirmative action, employment set-asides, and the like—increased from 300 in 1960 to 40,000 by 1985. Many of these cases reached the Supreme Court, which, following the landmark *Brown v. Board of Education* decision of 1954, issued a series of momentous rulings calling for the expansion and protection of rights. Blacks, political radicals, alleged criminals, welfare recipients, and many other out-groups hailed the liberalism of the Court under Chief Justice Earl Warren. Even under the more conservative Warren Burger, who succeeded Warren in 1969, the Court continued for a while along this liberal trail.

Between 1969 and 1973, it delivered a number of important decisions—favoring court-ordered busing to achieve racial balance in the schools, approving affirmative action in employment, and legalizing abortion rights, for instance—that the majority of democratically elected legislators would not have dared to support. Federal judges, indeed, sparked a due process revolution, interpreting vague legislative language in ways that led to the bureaucratic expansion of governmental activity on behalf of many well-organized groups. In so doing, these judges became eager partners in the growth of the administrative state. Then and for many years thereafter, judges also oversaw the decisions of hundreds of school districts in order to prevent or curb racially discriminatory practices. As conservatives were quick to point out, it was ironic at best that liberals, in the world's largest democratic system, had come to rely so heavily on nonelected, life-tenured, old men.

The rise in rights consciousness led secondly to a huge increase in federal regulation, as scores of well-organized groups—among them, governmental and public lobbies such as the National Governors Association, the United States Conference of Mayors, and the National Education Association—demanded federal protection and assistance. A raft of new social regulatory agencies came into being, such as the Equal Employment Opportunity Commission (EEOC), the Environmental Protection Agency (EPA), the Occupational Safety and Health Administration (OSHA), and the Department of Education. They joined ever-larger existing agencies and swelled the size of the federal bureaucracy. Although some deregulation—of transportation, banking, and communications—took place in the late 1970s, the spread of governmental activism was nonetheless relentless, continuing strongly into the 1980s as well.

Indeed, federal spending for nondefense purposes increased, in constant 1972 dollars, from $130 billion in 1970 to $222 billion in 1980—from 14 percent of the GNP to 17 percent. In the 1970s, the budgets of social regulatory agencies jumped from $1.4 billion to $7.5 billion. The number of pages in the *Code of Federal Regulations* leaped during the 1970s from 54,000 to 100,000. The regulators, far from protecting corporate groups, as many federal bureaucracies had done in the past, were normally proactive on behalf of the rights-conscious organizations that had helped bring them into being. The EEOC adopted stances (in favor of affirmative action, for instance) that astounded congressmen who had voted for the supposedly color-blind Civil Rights Act of 1964. Even President Nixon, ostensibly a foe of such stances, made no serious effort prior to 1973 to prevent the spread of bureaucratic activism. Many of the new agencies, such as the EPA and OSHA, were created on his watch; others, such as the EEOC, greatly windened their ken during his first term.

The third consequence of the rights revolution was a large increase in categorical federal aid programs and unfunded mandates to states as well as to private employers. In 1960, these numbered 160; by 1970, there were 530. In part for this reason, state-local activism expanded considerably in the 1960s and thereafter; in fact, spending on these levels grew more rapidly between 1960 and 1980 than it did in Washington. Legislation passed by a Democratic Congress in 1972 and signed by Nixon vastly expanded Social Security benefits and set up a generously funded federal program, Supplemental Security Income, for the needy aged and disabled. Congress also established programs—and regulatory bureaucracies—to promote bilingual education (1971) and to aid handicapped children (1974). It approved considerable growth in a food stamps program that had begun to increase during the late 1960s.

This expansion of federal programs, together with the growth in litigation and regulation, generally worked to the advantage of previously marginal groups and causes. Workers received better protection against accidents. Consumers hailed environmental laws concerned with water and air pollution. The welfare poor and the handicapped received more legal protection. Some blacks and women gained from affirmative action procedures. Bureaucratic and judicial administration such as this, often in the absence of legislation clearly authorizing such activity, broadened the reach and power of many federal programs in the United States. It transformed the American state, often confounding presidents, congressmen, employers, and state and local officials alike.

Suburban Politics and the Limits of the Great Society

MATTHEW D. LASSITER

During the late 1960s and early 1970s, a populist revolt of the Silent Majority rippled upward into national politics and established powerful constraints on Great Society liberalism and civil rights reform. In an opening phase, suburban parents in the Sunbelt South launched grassroots uprisings to defend their children's neighborhood schools against the legal challenge of court-ordered busing. White-collar home owners who claimed membership in the Silent Majority invented a potent

From Matthew D. Lassiter, "Suburban Strategies: The Volatile Center in Postwar American Politics," in Meg Jacobs, William J. Novak, and Julian E. Zelizer, eds., *The Democratic Experiment: New Directions in American Political History* (Princeton, N.J.: Princeton University Press, 2003), 327–341. © 2003 by Princeton University Press. Reprinted by permission of Princeton University Press.

"color-blind" discourse that portrayed residential segregation as the product of economic stratification rather than historical racism. This political formula eventually gained national traction as a bipartisan defense of middle-class consumer privileges and suburban residential boundaries. The rise of the Silent Majority reflected broader trends spreading throughout metropolitan America, a politics of middle-class consciousness based in subdivision associations, shopping malls, church congregations, PTA branches, and voting booths. The political culture of suburban populism—from taxpayer revolts and antibusing crusades to home owner movements and antisprawl campaigns—galvanized a top-down response marked by the persistent refusal of all three branches of the federal government to address the historical legacies of residential segregation through collective remedies for metropolitan inequality. From the "conservative" subdivisions of southern California to the "liberal" townships of New England, the suburbanization of American society and politics has empowered a bipartisan ethos of private-property values, individual taxpayer rights, children's educational privileges, family residential security, consumer freedom of choice, and middle-class racial innocence.

The growth policies of New Deal liberalism and the rise of the Cold War military-industrial complex shaped the patterns of postwar residential expansion and transformed the South and West into the booming Sunbelt. The Federal Housing Administration and the GI Bill subsidized the "American Dream" of middle-class home ownership for millions of white families who moved from rural regions and urban centers to the sprawling suburbs. By excluding racial minorities from new suburban developments and "redlining" racially mixed urban neighborhoods, federal mortgage policies during the initial postwar decades systematically enforced residential segregation and reinforced marketplace discrimination. The 1956 Interstate Highway Act facilitated automobile-based commuting and corporate mobility in the outlying suburbs and simultaneously enabled municipal governments to concentrate racial minorities within inner-city ghettos. Cold War spending priorities propelled a population shift to the South and West, where middle-class migrants settled in residentially segregated suburbs clustered around military bases, defense industries, and regional branch offices. The white-collar character of Sunbelt expansion also depended on the explosive growth of the technology-driven and service-oriented sectors of corporate capitalism. After the Rust Belt recession of the 1970s, industrial centers in the Midwest and Northeast increasingly emulated the Sunbelt model of high-tech innovation, capital mobility, corporate deregulation, flexible labor markets, and residential sprawl.

Suburban decentralization and Sunbelt development ultimately produced a volatile political climate in which neither the Democrats nor the Republicans could maintain a stable electoral majority. The upward mobility subsidized by the middle-class entitlement programs of the federal government undermined the working-class base of New Deal liberalism and turned suburban voters into a vital demographic that came to drive the electoral strategies of both parties. When the civil rights movement launched a direct assault on residential and educational segregation in suburban jurisdictions, the Silent Majority responded with a localist politics of home owner rights and middle-class warfare. In the affluent white-collar suburbs that have commanded the attention of national politicians, the celebratory ideology of the free market and the "color-blind" ethos of meritocratic individualism effectively

concealed the role of the state in forging metropolitan patterns of residential segregation and structural inequality. Although the Republican party initially benefited
from the grassroots surge of middle-class consciousness, the populist revolt of the
center transcended the conservative mobilization of the New Right. The reinvention
of the "New Democrats" as the champions of quality-of-life issues in suburban swing
districts and the fiscally responsible managers of the "new economy" has revitalized
the competitiveness of the center in a postliberal political order.

Historians have only begun to examine the local political culture of white-collar
voters and the grassroots movements of upper-middle-class home owners in the
suburban neighborhoods of postwar America. In recent years, the new urban history
has explored the racial contradiction at the heart of postwar liberalism as the promise
of equal opportunity for black citizens clashed with a grassroots white backlash that
defined segregated housing and secure neighborhoods as an essential feature of the
New Deal society contract. . . . The populist revolt of the Silent Majority fused
racial and class politics into a centrist ideology that created an underlying suburban
consensus in the electoral arena. Understanding the political culture of middle-class
entitlement requires analysis of the suburban strategies that simultaneously reshaped
the metropolitan landscape and the electoral map. . . .

The suburban strategies developed in the Sunbelt South, not a top-down "southern
strategy" inspired by the Deep South, provided the blueprint for the reconfiguration
of the political center in American politics. Many pundits and scholars have embraced a reductionist narrative of political realignment in the modern South, building
on GOP strategist Kevin Phillips's book *The Emerging Republican Majority* (1969).
In this account of the New Right, presidential candidates Barry Goldwater and
George Wallace emerge as the two most influential losers in American political history, the progenitors of a racialized conservatism that subsequently shaped the coded
appeals of the Republican party and united working-class and middle-class white
voters in an alliance of reactionary populism. To explain the national collapse of the
New Deal order, the "southern strategy" school offers a corollary called the "southernization of American politics"—a schematic portrait that highlights Nixon's "law
and order" platform, Reagan's "states' rights" rhetoric, [George H. W.] Bush's
"Willie Horton" television advertisements, and Gingrich's invective against "welfare
mothers." At the grassroots level, however, the "southern strategy" conspicuously
backfired in each of its four genuine incarnations: the Dixiecrat revolt of 1948,
the Goldwater debacle in 1964, the third-party Wallace movement in 1968, and the
Republican disaster in the 1970 midterm elections. Each of these campaigns failed
to carry the high-growth states of the peripheral South and instead achieved Pyrrhic
victories in the Deep South strongholds that supported the losing candidate in all but
one presidential election between 1948 and 1968. During the same era, the suburban
residents of the metropolitan regions and the white-collar migrants to the New South
increasingly diverged from the racial politics of the Black Belt and converged with
the class-based voting patterns in the rest of the nation. As a top-down and race-
driven account of regional transformation, the "southern strategy" framework
obscures a more compelling narrative that revolves around the class-stratified politics produced by the postwar suburbanization of southern society and the population
shift to the metropolitan Sunbelt.

The southern base of the Republican party always depended more on the middle-class corporate economy than on the top-down politics of racial backlash, and the region's pioneering contribution to national political realignment came primarily from the suburban ethos of New South metropolises such as Atlanta and Charlotte, North Carolina, not the exportation of the working-class racial politics of the Black Belt. In 1968, Richard Nixon triumphed through a de facto "suburban strategy" that, by calculation and by default, positioned the Republican party as the moderate alternative to the reactionary racial platform of George Wallace and the discredited Great Society liberalism of Hubert Humphrey. Recognizing that an overt appeal for the segregationist vote would alienate white moderates everywhere else, the Nixon campaign essentially conceded the Goldwater base in the Deep South to the Wallace insurgency and instead aimed directly at the middle-class voters who lived in the suburban South and had voted for Eisenhower during the 1950s. Through populist appeals to the political center and a consciously "color-blind" stance on controversial racial issues, Nixon forged an electoral coalition between the dynamic states of the Sunbelt South and West and the upwardly mobile voters of the Midwest and Northeast. The Republican candidate expressly adopted racially inclusive imagery in his convention speech, subsequently repackaged in a series of evocative television advertisements that contrasted burning cities and campus upheaval with happy nuclear families engaged in activities such as raking their leaves and making homemade ice cream. "Let us listen now to . . . the voice of the great majority of Americans, the forgotten Americans, the non-shouters, the non-demonstrators," implored Nixon. "They are black and they are white. . . . They work in America's factories. . . . They run America's businesses. . . . They give lift to the American dream. . . . They work, they save, they pay their taxes, they care." At a shopping mall in Charlotte, the future president launched his southeastern campaign swing with similar "color-blind" praise for the "people who pay their taxes and go to work and support their churches, white people and black people, people [who] are not rioters." The New South represented a progressive place to live, Nixon told the enthusiastic audience of middle-class suburbanites and grassroots Republican activists, a region that had become "a lot like the rest of the country."

Rather than illustrating the "southernization of American politics," the Republican victory in 1968 signaled the increasing suburbanization of both southern and national politics. Although Nixon quietly ratified backroom deals to appease the Goldwater-Reagan wing of the party, including a pledge to minimize federal enforcement of school desegregation and open-housing legislation, the candidate's public comments reflected the emerging suburban blueprint on civil rights issues, a nominally "color-blind" and frankly class-conscious ideology that revolved around the twin pillars of neighborhood schools and residential exclusivity. In his well-publicized Charlotte appearance, Nixon expressed support for the moral principle of racial integration, but he also charged that "busing for racial balance" would backfire because of the wide socioeconomic gap in academic aptitude between wealthy schools in the suburbs and poor students in the ghettos. In the three-way campaign of 1968, the first national election in which suburban residents constituted a plurality of the electorate, opinion surveys clearly identified Nixon as the status quo candidate regarding race relations, the overwhelming choice of white voters who endorsed equal opportunity in the abstract but opposed most of the specific remedial policies necessary to tackle historical structures of racial discrimination. Nixon's temperate rhetoric on civil rights became a crucial element in securing a narrow plurality of what political scientists called the "tripartite southern electorate," divided almost evenly among the GOP base in the middle-class suburbs, the Wallace supporters in the rural and working-class precincts, and the Humphrey coalition of white liberals and almost all black voters. Nixon carried the critical states of the Upper South with a much more substantial 45 percent plurality, powered by wide margins of victory in the new white-collar subdivisions of metropolitan regions such as Charlotte and Richmond. . . .

During the 1970s, a grassroots suburban strategy that revolved around a "color-blind" defense of the middle-class rights and residential privileges of the Silent Majority succeeded where the overtly racialized tactics of the top-down "southern strategy" had failed. In the 1968 campaign, Richard Nixon appealed to the white suburban electorate through a combination of racially inclusive imagery and residentially exclusive policies, framed by a populist outreach to the "forgotten Americans" who worked hard and played by the rules. Over the course of the next decade, in response to the civil rights movement's concerted attack on metropolitan patterns of residential segregation and educational inequality, a series of grassroots uprisings in the white-collar suburbs appropriated the populist discourse of the Silent Majority and forced a new class-driven version of "color-blind" politics into the national arena. The collective debut of the Silent Majority came during the summer of 1970, when representatives from antibusing movements throughout the New South suburbs gathered in Atlanta to forge a political alliance called the National Coalition of Concerned Citizens. The leaders of the grassroots revolt included physicians, dentists, attorneys, and other upper-middle-class professionals—the most affluent tier of the white parents and home owners mobilizing under the national banner of the Silent Majority. Claiming a membership of one million supporters of "neighborhood schools" in twenty-seven states, the confederation adopted a "color-blind" stance that demanded political protection for the socioeconomic and residential privileges of the middle-class suburbs. Two weeks later, more than one hundred local activists reconvened in Norfolk to launch a national membership drive, revolving around the constitutional claim that federal courts could not address the "de facto" segregation that allegedly prevailed throughout metropolitan America. The alliance warned that "government tyranny" threatened the tradition of neighborhood schools, denounced President Nixon for failing to keep his campaign promise to prevent "forced busing," and urged supporters to flood the White House and the United States Congress with letters of protest. "We are going on the offensive," promised a Miami Beach attorney named Ellis Rubin. "We are going to organize the largest, most effective lobby this country has ever seen. . . .

The New South metropolis of Charlotte, North Carolina, a white-collar banking center with a reputation for racial moderation, became the national test case for large-scale busing between the sprawling suburbs and the crowded ghettos. In the spring of 1969, the National Association for the Advancement of Colored People (NAACP) reopened desegregation litigation based on the pathbreaking contention that the prevailing distinction between "de jure" and "de facto" segregation was artificial, and therefore the Constitution required the school system to take affirmative action to overcome residential patterns shaped by government policies and reinforced by private discrimination. During the Cold War boom, municipal leaders and corporate executives in Charlotte had implemented the national model of residential segregation with the systematic efficiency of the Sunbelt economic blueprint, leveraging federal funds to construct a landscape of spatial apartheid achieved through the twin processes of suburban expansion and urban redevelopment. Between 1950 and 1970, when the metropolitan population doubled to include more than 350,000 residents, almost all white-collar families drawn into the corporate economy moved into newly developed subdivisions located to the south and east of the downtown business district. During the same period, the municipal government displaced more than 10,000 black residents through federal urban renewal and highway construction programs and relocated almost all of these families in public housing projects invariably located in the opposite quadrant of the city. Official planning policies meticulously separated the middle-class white suburbs of southeast Charlotte from the overwhelmingly black neighborhoods of northwest Charlotte through industrial zoning buffers and interstate highway placement. By the time of the busing litigation, about 96 percent of the African-American population lived in the highly segregated northwest sector, and more than 14,000 black students attended completely isolated public schools. In April 1969, in *Swann v. Charlotte-Mecklenburg,* district judge James McMillan issued an unprecedented and explosive remedy: the two-way exchange of students from the black neighborhoods of the central city and the white subdivisions on the metropolitan fringe, a comprehensive busing formula designed to integrate every facility throughout the consolidated metropolitan school system.

Tens of thousands of middle-class white families immediately joined forces in the Concerned Parents Association (CPA), a powerful grassroots organization based in the outer-ring suburbs of southeast Charlotte. From the beginning, the CPA rallied around a "color-blind" platform of middle-class respectability and insisted that opposition to busing had nothing to do with racial prejudice or segregationist preference. The accidental activists in this suburban social movement consisted of young professional couples and white-collar home owners who had moved to Charlotte from across the nation, settled in recently developed subdivisions marked by racial exclusivity and upward mobility, and cast more than 70 percent of their ballots for Richard Nixon in the 1968 presidential election. Tom Harris, an insurance executive who headed the CPA, explained that the membership did not represent either right-wing ideologues or the "upper crust" of the city but rather "essentially the middle class, and we have every intention of maintaining the proper dignity and respect." The petitions circulated by the group defended the rights of hardworking families who had purchased homes based on "proximity to schools and churches of their choice" and condemned busing as a violation of the equal protection clause of the Fourteenth Amendment and the original spirit of the *Brown* decision. "I am not opposed to integration in any way," claimed one suburban father during a CPA demonstration. "But I was 'affluent' enough to buy a home near the school where I wanted my children to go. And I pay taxes to pay for it. They can bring in anybody they like to that school, but I don't want my children taken away." Another member of the group warned that the "moderate majority . . . has civil rights too . . . and has tried to be very understanding, but we don't like having our feet stepped on repeatedly and we can't be expected to keep turning the other cheek forever." Identifying themselves as parents and taxpayers from the middle-class mainstream, the suburban populists in the CPA co-opted the rhetoric of the civil rights movement in their promises to take the political offensive in order to secure the defense of their homes and families. "The people of Charlotte have had it with Judge McMillan and liberal federal courts," warned Dr. Don Roberson, a physician who served as vice chairman of the organization. "The unorganized silent majority is about ready to take to the streets with tactics that have seemed to work so effectively for the vocal minority groups."

The antibusing movement in Charlotte represented a populist revolt of the center, as white-collar parents from secure suburban neighborhoods responded to the racial crisis of metropolitan desegregation through a "color-blind" politics of middle-class consciousness. "I couldn't believe such a thing could happen in America," Don Roberson explained. "So many of us made the biggest investment of our lives—our homes—primarily on the basis of their location with regard to schools. It seemed like an absurdity that anyone could tell us where to send our children." In a way, *Swann* plaintiff James Polk agreed with this class analysis of Charlotte's racial showdown: "We were smacking against the whole American dream. To whites, that meant pull yourself up by your bootstraps, buy a nice home and two cars, live in a nice neighborhood and go to a nice church, send your kids to the appropriate school. . . . We understood that a lot of white people would raise holy hell." During Charlotte's protracted busing crisis, the CPA platform never acknowledged the judicial finding that federal and municipal policies had shaped the methodical patterns of residential segregation that produced school segregation. The white parents who joined the antibusing movement thought of the location of their homes and the proximity of quality schools as nothing more and nothing less than the individual rewards for their willingness to work hard and make sacrifices for their children's future. This philosophy of middle-class accomplishment obscured the centrality of the state in the process of suburbanization and finessed the internal contradictions in the meritocratic ethos through an unapologetic defense of the rights of children to enjoy the fruits of their parents' success. The futuristic ethos of the white suburbs simply did not address the question of whether the black families systematically relocated by city planners to the northwest quadrant enjoyed "freedom of choice" to live in the upscale neighborhoods and attend the excellent schools of southeast Charlotte. The CPA's "anti-bus hysteria [seems] more mistaken than racist," observed one civil rights activist, in the context of fifteen years of municipal development and federal policy based on the "hypocrisy of blinding itself to the 'de jure' nature of most 'de facto' segregation." The federal government had permitted "leaders in a place like Charlotte to convince themselves or kid themselves into thinking that, even as they continued the process of building a ghetto and a system of segregated schools, they were in compliance with the law against segregation."

During the winter and spring of 1970, as antibusing movements spread from the suburban South to metropolitan centers such as Denver and Los Angeles, the Concerned Parents Association pioneered the emergence of the Silent Majority on the national political landscape. After taking control of the local board of education, the antibusing movement in Charlotte embraced a compromise position that reluctantly accepted one-way busing of black students to suburban facilities but fiercely rejected the transportation of white students away from their neighborhood schools. When the district court set a firm deadline for two-way busing, the CPA immediately demanded White House intervention in the judicial process. CPA leaders promptly secured private audiences with senior members of the executive branch, and the foot soldiers of the movement sent thousands of letters and telegrams to President Nixon. One suburban physician, identifying himself as a "concerned member of the silent majority which has possibly remained silent too long," asked the president why prosperous communities should be punished simply because their residents worked hard and bought respectable homes in safe neighborhoods near quality public schools. After clarifying that his views had "nothing to do with race or integration," this father insisted that the "thought that this course is un-American is simply untenable." A married couple from an upper-middle-class subdivision informed the president that they supported racial integration and believed that high-achieving black students deserved to attend the best white schools, but warned that two-way busing would drive away affluent families and destroy public education. Another resident of southeast Charlotte, explaining that he was neither a crack-pot nor a segregationist, denounced busing as reverse discrimination and asked Nixon "to come to the rescue of the silent majority who . . . has been pushed about as far as it will tolerate." "As a member of the silent majority," yet another Charlotte parent declared, "I have never asked what anyone in government or this country could do for me; but rather have kept my mouth shut, paid my taxes and basically asked to be left alone. . . . I think it is time the law abiding, tax paying white middle class started looking to the federal government for something besides oppression.

The suburban uprising of the Silent Majority established the busing controversy as an urgent and unavoidable crisis in national politics. The White House quickly responded to the pleas and demands of upper-middle-class voters with a major policy statement on school desegregation, released under President Nixon's signature in March 1970. The address attempted to stake out the middle ground by implicitly rejecting the recent Supreme Court mandate to eliminate racial segregation "root and branch," but offering no escape hatch for the segregationist movements based in the rural South. Instead, in a direct appeal to suburban voters throughout the nation, the president adopted the "color-blind" framework of the grassroots antibusing movement and defended an inviolable right to attend neighborhood schools even if they reflected residential segregation. In accord with his vocal constituents, Nixon argued that most school segregation in both the metropolitan South and the urban North resulted from "de facto" market forces beyond the jurisdiction of the federal courts. While civil rights groups expressed outrage, the White House promised to intervene against the comprehensive busing precedent in the Charlotte litigation, which clearly represented the primary target of the president's address. The administration position effectively endorsed a national antibusing standard that revolved around a laissez-faire approach to residential segregation and an overt defense of the spatial and socioeconomic privileges of middle-class suburbs throughout the country. A political agenda presented in constitutional wrapping, this policy represented a calculated effort to shift the heat for desegregation enforcement from the executive branch to the federal judiciary, and a prescient recognition that suburban hostility toward racial busing transcended partisan, class, and regional boundaries.

Court-ordered busing in Charlotte became a conspicuous exception to the national rule, because the prior existence of a metropolitan school system provided the leverage for a suburban remedy that achieved stable racial desegregation through a social-class-based integration resolution. In the case of *Swann v. Charlotte-Mecklenburg* (1971), the United States Supreme Court rejected the "color-blind" defense and approved busing as a legitimate remedy for state-sponsored racial discrimination. While the CPA soon faded as a grassroots force, the antibusing leaders on the school board adopted an unstable formula that exempted the affluent suburbs of southeast Charlotte from two-way integration and assigned working-class white students from residentially transitional neighborhoods to the historically black schools. After several years of "white flight" caused by the foreseeable flaws in this plan, Judge McMillan ordered the school district to prevent racial resegregation through an affirmative action commitment to "socioeconomic integration." In the most significant feature of the new approach, the board reluctantly agreed to reassign white students from the upper-middle-class suburbs to stabilize school enrollment in the black residential areas of northwest Charlotte. By including every section of the school district in the comprehensive integration formula, the emphasis on class and geographic fairness defused the controversy over the preferential treatment of southeast Charlotte and removed the incentive for white families to relocate to the suburban neighborhoods that had previously escaped two-way busing. The favorable conditions created by the class-based busing compromise eventually turned Charlotte-Mecklenburg into a national success story, a New South showcase that boasted a greater degree of racial integration and a lower percentage of "white flight" than most other large cities in the nation. Although the Charlotte example illustrates that an expansive metropolitan remedy could overcome the organized resistance of suburban home owners, by the end of the 1970s a powerful mythology had emerged that court-ordered busing caused the decline of urban school systems. This political consensus ignores the necessity of metropolitan strategies to stabilize racial integration and misapplies the lessons of cities such as Boston, where secure suburban spectators watched struggling white communities fight reassignment to poor black neighborhoods. "To understand reactionary populism," Ronald Formisano has concluded, "we must recognize the role of class and its consequences in the formation of public policy, particularly policies designed to alleviate racial injustice. If class is ignored, as it was in Boston and consistently tends to be in dealing with desegregation, then those policies have little chance of success."

The antibusing movement in Charlotte lost the local battle but won the national war. In the wake of *Swann,* the NAACP launched a campaign to overcome urban school segregation through city-suburban integration formulas and metropolitan consolidation remedies. During the same period, President Nixon appointed four justices to the Supreme Court, and the grassroots resistance of the Silent Majority converged with the top-down defense of suburban autonomy. In 1972, as an organized antibusing movement roiled the Virginia capital of Richmond, the Fourth Circuit Court of Appeals overturned a metropolitan integration plan that combined the black-majority city schools with two overwhelmingly white suburban districts. A deadlocked Supreme Court affirmed the appellate ruling that the "last vestiges of state-imposed segregation have been wiped out," and the striking conclusion that the "root causes of the concentration of blacks in the inner cities of America are simply not known." In 1974, in the landmark case of *Milliken v. Bradley,* a narrow majority on the Burger Court invalidated a three-county busing formula designed to stem "white flight" from the city schools of Detroit by including the entire metropolitan region in the quest for stable integration and equal opportunity. The majority opinion in *Milliken* immunized most suburbs throughout the nation from the burdens and opportunities of meaningful integration and foreshadowed the hypersegregation by race and income in large urban school districts across the United States. In a scathing dissent, Thurgood Marshall highlighted the uncomfortable truth that the judicial accommodation of political resistance had transformed residential segregation into a historical wrong without a constitutional remedy. Alluding to the broad antibusing movement in metropolitan Detroit, which ranged from the blue-collar subdivisions of Macomb County to the wealthy island suburbs of Grosse Pointe, Marshall portrayed the majority decision as "a reflection of a perceived public mood that we have gone far enough in enforcing the Constitution's guarantee of equal justice. . . . In the short run, it may seem to be the easier course to allow our great metropolitan areas to be divided up each into two cities—one white, the other black—but it is a course, I predict, our people will ultimately reject."

✦ F U R T H E R   R E A D I N G

Andrew, John A., III. *Lyndon Johnson and the Great Society* (1998).
Berkowitz, Edward D. *Something Happened: A Political and Cultural Overview of the Seventies* (2006).
Bernstein, Irving. *Guns or Butter: The Presidency of Lyndon Johnson* (1996).
Block, Fred, et al. *The Mean Season: The Attack on the Welfare State* (1987).
Bornet, Vaughan. *The Presidency of Lyndon B. Johnson* (1983).
Burke, Vincent J., and Lee Burke. *Nixon's Good Deed: Welfare Reform* (1974).
Califano, Joseph A. *The Triumph and Tragedy of Lyndon Johnson* (1991).
Caro, Robert A. *The Years of Lyndon Johnson: Means of Ascent* (1990).
———. *The Years of Lyndon Johnson: The Path to Power* (1982).
Conkin, Paul. *Big Daddy from the Pedernales: Lyndon Baines Johnson* (1986).
Dallek, Robert. *Flawed Giant: Lyndon B. Johnson, 1961–1973* (1999).
———. *Lone Star Rising: Lyndon Johnson and His Times, 1908–1960* (1991).
———. *Lyndon B. Johnson: Portrait of a President* (2004).
Davies, Gareth. *From Opportunity to Entitlement: The Transformation and Decline of Great Society Liberalism* (1996).
Divine, Robert A., ed. *The Johnson Years,* 3 vols. (1981, 1987, 1994).
Flippen, Brooks, J. *Nixon and the Environment* (2000).
Graham, Hugh Davis. *The Uncertain Triumph: Federal Education Policy in the Kennedy and Johnson Years* (1984).
Jordan, Barbara C., and Elspeth D. Rostow, eds. *The Great Society: A Twenty Year Critique* (1986).
Kaplan, Marshall, and Peggy L. Cuciti, eds. *The Great Society and Its Legacy: Twenty Years of U.S. Social Policy* (1986).
Kotz, Nick. *Judgment Days: Lyndon Baines Johnson, Martin Luther King, Jr., and the Laws That Changed America* (2005).
Lassiter, Matthew D. *The Silent Majority: Suburban Politics in the Sunbelt South* (2005).
Levitan, Sar, and Robert Taggert. *The Promise of Greatness* (1976).
Lieberman, Robert C. *Shifting the Color Line: Race and the American Welfare State* (1998).
MacLean, Nancy. *Freedom Is Not Enough: The Opening of the American Workplace* (2006).
McGirr, Lisa. *Suburban Warriors: The Origins of the New American Right* (2001).

Milkis, Sidney M., and Jerome M. Mileur, eds. *The Great Society and the High Tide of Liberalism* (2005).

Mittelstadt, Jennifer. *From Welfare to Workfare: The Unintended Consequences of Liberal Reform, 1945–1965* (2005).

Reeves, Richard. *President Nixon: Alone in the White House* (2002).

Rothman, Rozann. *The Great Society at the Grass Roots* (1984).

Schulman, Bruce J. *Lyndon B. Johnson and American Liberalism: A Brief Biography with Documents* (1994).

Sundquist, James L. *Politics and Policy: The Eisenhower, Kennedy, and Johnson Years* (1968).

Unger, Irwin. *The Best of Intentions: The Triumphs and Failures of the Great Society Under Kennedy, Johnson, and Nixon* (1996).

Warner, David C., ed. *Toward New Human Rights: The Social Policies of the Kennedy and Johnson Administrations* (1977).

Zarefsky, David. *President Johnson's War on Poverty: Rhetoric and History* (1986).

C H A P T E R
7

The New Radicalism:
Politics and Culture
in the 1960s

As the 1950s drew to a close and the chill of the McCarthy years faded and even Eisenhower's towering popularity waned, a new critical spirit quickened throughout much of America. It sprang from diverse sources: from the burgeoning struggle for civil rights; from the growing disquietude among women that would soon lead to a revival of feminism; from the growing awareness that despite wide prosperity, millions of Americans remained trapped in poverty; from the fear of nuclear war, the Cold War, and, especially, the growing "hot" war in Vietnam; from the dawning realization of the social and environmental costs of the postwar economy; and from the rising self-consciousness of the new postwar baby-boom generation. It was this spirit of disquietude to which John F. Kennedy appealed in his promise to "get America moving again" along a "new frontier." Of course, rhetoric aside, what Kennedy envisioned was a moderate liberalism not all that dissimilar from the moderate conservatism that had marked the Eisenhower years. But the new radicalism of the 1960s challenged the assumptions of conventional liberalism—the adequacy of economic growth and the necessity of the cold war in particular—and continues to shape American politics.

D O C U M E N T S

The Port Huron Statement, excerpts from which are reprinted as Document 1, was written in 1962 by student activist Tom Hayden and others and adopted at the annual Students for a Democratic Society (SDS) convention. SDS represented a self-consciously new radicalism that, shunning the Marxist clichés of the 1930s, called for "participatory democracy" and a reconstruction of American society that would replace "power rooted in possession, privilege, or circumstance [with] power and uniqueness rooted in love, reflectiveness, reason, and creativity." Reflecting the early history of the New Left in its lack of doctrinaire ideology as well as in its spirit of hope and optimism, SDS was initially dedicated to the more or less traditional politics of organization and struggle. Many among the founders of SDS leaders were veterans of the civil rights movement, and their early campaigns focused on urban poverty and, increasingly, opposition to the war in Vietnam. Rebels such as Abbie Hoffman and Jerry Rubin, on the other hand, owed more to the new *cultural* radicalism, which swept up many young Americans in a tide of generational self-expression that featured bold new styles of music, hairstyle, dress, and behavior. Document 2, an excerpt from Rubin's book *Do It! Scenarios of the Revolution* (1970), captures the emphasis of the new counterculture on theatricality and self-expression. By the late 1960s, SDS had become bitterly divided. Among its radical splinter factions were the Weathermen, who took their name from Bob Dylan's "Subterranean Homesick Blues." The Weathermen's 1969 call for revolution is reprinted from *New Left Notes* (June 18, 1969) as Document 3.

Most Americans, of course, were not students, were not young, and were not radical; and although some sympathized with the goals of student protesters, many others angrily opposed their methods and goals. The same decade in which SDS figured so prominently also witnessed the organization of Young Americans for Freedom (YAF). Conservative politicians such as Richard Nixon and Ronald Reagan regularly denounced student radicals, appealing to what Nixon called America's great "silent majority." The FBI even launched an illegal, secret campaign to disrupt and destroy the New Left (Document 4). Many ordinary college students were caught up in the turmoil of the 1960s and early 1970s, though few so dramatically as at Kent State University, where in 1970 four students were killed when Ohio National Guardsmen fired into a crowd protesting the Nixon administration's expansion of the Vietnam War into neighboring Cambodia. By this time, disillusionment had begun to set in. Some of the generation's new radicals sought to restore their own lives—and perhaps in their own small way to work for the reform of the larger society—by fleeing to communes in the rural countryside. Among them was Raymond Mungo; Document 5, an excerpt from his book *Total Loss Farm* (1970), captures something of the communal spirit of the era. By the early 1970s, the political radicalism that had characterized the sixties had all but subsided, much of the decade's cultural radicalism had been absorbed and converted into cultural commodities, and a faltering economy had dampened the heady optimism of the previous decade. In Document 6, pollster Daniel Yankelovich captures the chastened new spirit in a survey that mapped the changing attitudes and values of the 1970s.

1. Students for a Democratic Society Issue the Port Huron Statement, 1962

We are people of this generation, bred in at least modest comfort, housed now in universities, looking uncomfortably to the world we inherit.

When we were kids the United States was the wealthiest and strongest country in the world: the only one with the atom bomb, the least scarred by modern war, an initiator of the United Nations that we thought would distribute Western influence throughout the world. Freedom and equality for each individual, government of,

Excerpts from the Port Huron Statement, 1962, State Historical Society of Wisconsin.

by, and for the people—these American values we found good, principles by which we could live as men. Many of us began maturing in complacency.

As we grew, however, our comfort was penetrated by events too troubling to dismiss. First, the permeating and victimizing fact of human degradation, symbolized by the Southern struggle against racial bigotry, compelled most of us from silence to activism. Second, the enclosing fact of the Cold War, symbolized by the presence of the Bomb, brought awareness that we ourselves, and our friends, and millions of abstract "others" we knew more directly because of our common peril, might die at any time. We might deliberately ignore, or avoid, or fail to feel all other human problems, but not these two, for these were too immediate and crushing in their impact, too challenging in the demand that we as individuals take the responsibility for encounter and resolution.

While these and other problems either directly oppressed us or rankled our consciences and became our own subjective concerns, we began to see complicated and disturbing paradoxes in our surrounding America. The declaration "all men are created equal . . ." rang hollow before the facts of Negro life in the South and the big cities of the North. The proclaimed peaceful intentions of the United States contradicted its economic and military investments in the Cold War status quo.

We witnessed, and continue to witness, other paradoxes. With nuclear energy whole cities can easily be powered, yet the dominant nation-states seem more likely to unleash destruction greater than that incurred in all wars of human history. Although our own technology is destroying old and creating new forms of social organization, men still tolerate meaningless work and idleness. While two-thirds of mankind suffers undernourishment, our own upper classes revel amidst superfluous abundance. Although world population is expected to double in forty years, the nations still tolerate anarchy as a major principle of international conduct and uncontrolled exploitation governs the sapping of the earth's physical resources. Although mankind desperately needs revolutionary leadership, America rests in national stalemate, its goals ambiguous and tradition-bound instead of informed and clear, its democratic system apathetic and manipulated rather than "of, by, and for the people."

Not only did tarnish appear on our image of American virtue, not only did disillusion occur when the hypocrisy of American ideals was discovered, but we began to sense that what we had originally seen as the American Golden Age was actually the decline of an era. The worldwide outbreak of revolution against colonialism and imperialism, the entrenchment of totalitarian states, the menace of war, overpopulation, international disorder, supertechnology—these trends were testing the tenacity of our own commitment to democracy and freedom and our abilities to visualize their application to a world in upheaval.

Our work is guided by the sense that we may be the last generation in the experiment with living. But we are a minority—the vast majority of our people regard the temporary equilibriums of our society and world as eternally functional parts. In this is perhaps the outstanding paradox: we ourselves are imbued with urgency, yet the message of our society is that there is no viable alternative to the present. Beneath the reassuring tones of the politicians, beneath the common opinion that America will "muddle through," beneath the stagnation of those who have closed their minds to the future, is the pervading feeling that there simply are no alternatives, that our times have witnessed the exhaustion not only of Utopias, but of any new departures as well. Feeling the press of complexity upon the emptiness of life, people are fearful of the thought that at any moment things might thrust out of control. They fear change itself, since change might smash whatever invisible framework seems to hold back chaos for them now. For most Americans, all crusades are suspect, threatening. The fact that each individual sees apathy in his fellows perpetuates the common reluctance to organize for change. The dominant institutions are complex enough to blunt the minds of their potential critics, and entrenched enough to swiftly dissipate or entirely repel the energies of protest and reform, thus limiting human expectancies. Then, too, we are a materially improved society, and by our improvements we seem to have weakened the case for further change.

Some would have us believe that Americans feel contentment amidst prosperity—but might it not better be called a glaze above deeply felt anxieties about their role in the new world? And if these anxieties produce a developed indifference to human affairs, do they not as well produce a yearning to believe there *is* an alternative to the present, that something *can* be done to change circumstances in the school, the work-places, the bureaucracies, the government? It is to this latter yearning, at once the spark and engine of change, that we direct our present appeal. The search for truly democratic alternatives to the present, and a commitment to social experimentation with them, is a worthy and fulfilling human enterprise, one which moves us and, we hope, others today. On such a basis do we offer this document of our convictions and analysis: as an effort in understanding and changing the conditions of humanity in the late twentieth century, an effort rooted in the ancient, still unfulfilled conception of man attaining determining influence over his circumstances of life. . . .

Making values explicit—an initial task in establishing alternatives—is an activity that has been devalued and corrupted. The conventional moral terms of the age, the politician moralities—"free world," "people's democracies"—reflect realities poorly, if at all, and seem to function more as ruling myths than as descriptive principles. But neither has our experience in the universities brought us moral enlightenment. Our professors and administrators sacrifice controversy to public relations; their curriculums change more slowly than the living events of the world; their skills and silence are purchased by investors in the arms race; passion is called unscholastic. The questions we might want raised—what is really important? can we live in a different and better way? if we wanted to change society, how would we do it?—are not thought to be questions of a "fruitful, empirical nature," and thus are brushed aside. . . .

Theoretic chaos has replaced the idealistic thinking of old—and, unable to reconstitute theoretic order, men have condemned idealism itself. Doubt has replaced hopefulness—and men act out a defeatism that is labelled realistic. The decline of utopia and hope is in fact one of the defining features of social life today. The reasons are various: the dreams of the older left were perverted by Stalinism and never recreated; the congressional stalemate makes men narrow their view of the possible; the specialization of human activity leaves little room for sweeping thought; the horrors of the twentieth century, symbolized in the gas-ovens and concentration camps and atom bombs, have blasted hopefulness. To be idealistic is to be considered apocalyptic, deluded. To have no serious aspirations, on the contrary, is to be "tough-minded."

In suggesting social goals and values, therefore, we are aware of entering a sphere of some disrepute. Perhaps matured by the past, we have no sure formulas, no closed theories—but that does not mean values are beyond discussion and tentative determination. A first task of any social movement is to convince people that the search for orienting theories and the creation of human values is complex but worthwhile. We are aware that to avoid platitudes we must analyze the concrete conditions of social order. But to direct such an analysis we must use the guideposts of basic principles. Our own social values involve conceptions of human beings, human relationships, and social systems.

We regard *men* as infinitely precious and possessed of unfulfilled capacities for reason, freedom, and love. In affirming these principles we are aware of countering perhaps the dominant conceptions of man in the twentieth century: that he is a thing to be manipulated, and that he is inherently incapable of directing his own affairs. We oppose the depersonalization that reduces human beings to the status of things—if anything, the brutalities of the twentieth century teach that means and ends are intimately related, the vague appeals to "posterity" cannot justify the mutilations of the present. We oppose, too, the doctrine of human incompetence because it rests essentially on the modern fact that men have been "competently" manipulated into competence—we see little reason why men cannot meet with increasing skill the complexities and responsibilities of their situation, if society is organized not for minority, but for majority, participation in decision-making.

Men have unrealized potential for self-cultivation, self-direction, self-understanding, and creativity. It is this potential that we regard as crucial and to which we appeal, not to the human potentiality for violence, unreason, and submission to authority. The goal of man and society should be human independence: a concern not with image or popularity but with finding a meaning in life that is personally authentic; a quality of mind not compulsively driven by a sense of powerlessness, nor one which unthinkingly adopts status values, nor one which represses all threats to its habits, but one which has full, spontaneous access to present and past experiences, one which easily unites the fragmented parts of personal history, one which openly faces problems which are troubling and unresolved; one with an intuitive awareness of possibilities, an active sense of curiosity, an ability and willingness to learn.

This kind of independence does not mean egoistic individualism—the object is not to have one's way so much as it is to have a way that is one's own. Nor do we deify man—we merely have faith in his potential.

Human relationships should involve fraternity and honesty. Human interdependence is contemporary fact; human brotherhood must be willed however, as a condition of future survival and as the most appropriate form of social relations. Personal links between man and man are needed, especially to go beyond the partial and fragmentary bonds of function that bind men only as worker to worker, employer to employee, teacher to student, American to Russian.

Loneliness, estrangement, isolation describe the vast distance between man and man today. These dominant tendencies cannot be overcome by better personnel management, nor by improved gadgets, but only when a love of man overcomes the idolatrous worship of things by man.

As the individualism we affirm is not egoism, the selflessness we affirm is not self-elimination. On the contrary, we believe in generosity of a kind that imprints one's unique individual qualities in the relation to other men, and to all human activity. Further, to dislike isolation is not to favor the abolition of privacy; the latter differs from isolation in that it occurs or is abolished according to individual will. Finally, we would replace power and personal uniqueness rooted in possession, privilege, or circumstance by power and uniqueness rooted in love, reflectiveness, reason, and creativity.

As a *social system* we seek the establishment of a democracy of individual participation, governed by two central aims: that the individual share in those social decisions determining the quality and direction of his life; that society be organized to encourage independence in men and provide the media for their common participation.

In a participatory democracy, the political life would be based in several root principles:
- that decision-making of basic social consequence be carried on by public groupings;
- that politics be seen positively, as the art of collectively creating an acceptable pattern of social relations;
- that politics has the function of bringing people out of isolation and into community, thus being a necessary, though not sufficient, means of finding meaning in personal life;
- that the political order should serve to clarify problems in a way instrumental to their solution; it should provide outlets for the expression of personal grievance and aspiration; opposing views should be organized so as to illuminate choices and facilitate the attainment of goals; channels should be commonly available to relate men to knowledge and to power so that private problems—from bad recreation facilities to personal alienation—are formulated as general issues.

The economic sphere would have as its basis the principles:
- that work should involve incentives worthier than money or survival. It should be educative, not stultifying; creative, not mechanical; self-directed, not manipulated, encouraging independence, a respect for others, a sense of dignity, and a willingness to accept social responsibility, since it is this experience that has crucial influence on habits, perceptions, and individual ethics;
- that the economic experience is so personally decisive that the individual must share in its full determination;
- that the economy itself is of such social importance that its major resources and means of production should be open to democratic participation and subject to democratic social regulation.

Like the political and economic ones, major social institutions—cultural, education, rehabilitative, and others—should be generally organized with the well-being and dignity of man as the essential measure of success.

In social change or interchange, we find violence to be abhorrent because it requires generally the transformation of the target, be it a human being or a community of people, into a depersonalized object of hate. It is imperative that the means of violence be abolished and the institutions—local, national, international—that encourage nonviolence as a condition of conflict be developed.

These are our central values, in skeletal form. It remains vital to understand their denial or attainment in the context of the modern world.

2. Jerry Rubin Declares Himself a "Child of Amerika," 1970

I am a child of Amerika.

If I'm ever sent to Death Row for my revolutionary "crimes," I'll order as my last meal: a hamburger, french fries and a Coke.

I dig big cities.

I love to read the sports pages and gossip columns, listen to the radio and watch color TV.

I dig department stores, huge supermarkets and airports. I feel secure (though not necessarily hungry) when I see Howard Johnson's on the expressway.

I groove on Hollywood movies—even bad ones.

I speak only one language—English.

I love rock 'n' roll.

I collected baseball players' cards when I was a kid and wanted to play second base for the Cincinnati Reds, my home team.

I got a car when I was sixteen after flunking my first driver's test and crying for a week waiting to take it a second time.

I went to the kind of high school where you had to pass a test to get *in*.

I graduated in the bottom half of the class.

My classmates voted me the "busiest" senior in the school.

I had short, short, short hair.

I dug *Catcher in the Rye*.

I didn't have pimples.

I became an ace young reporter for the Cincinnati *Post and Times-Star*. "Son," the managing editor said to me, "*someday you're going to be a helluva reporter, maybe the greatest reporter this city's ever seen.*"

I loved Adlai Stevenson.

My father drove a truck delivering bread and later became an organizer in the Bakery Drivers' Union. He dug Jimmy Hoffa (so do I). He died of heart failure at fifty-two.

My mother had a college degree and played the piano. She died of cancer at the age of fifty-one.

I took care of my brother, Gil, from the time he was thirteen.

I dodged the draft.

I went to Oberlin College for a year, graduated from the University of Cincinnati, spent 1½ years in Israel and started graduate school at Berkeley.

I dropped out.

I dropped out of the White Race and the Amerikan nation.

I dig being free.

I like getting high.

I don't own a suit or tie.

I live for the revolution.

I'm a yippie!

I am an orphan of Amerika.

3. Radicals Proclaim: "You Don't Need a Weatherman to Know Which Way the Wind Blows," 1969

People ask, what is the nature of the revolution that we talk about? Who will it be made by, and for, and what are its goals and strategy?

The overriding consideration in answering these questions is that the main struggle going on in the world today is between U.S. imperialism and the national liberation struggles against it. This is essential in defining political matters in the whole world: because it is by far the most powerful, every other empire and petty dictator is in the long run dependent on U.S. imperialism, which has unified, allied with, and defended all of the reactionary forces of the whole world. Thus, in considering every other force or phenomenon, from Soviet imperialism or Israeli imperialism to "workers struggle" in France or Czechoslovakia, we determine who are our friends and who are our enemies according to whether they help U.S. imperialism or fight to defeat it.

So the very first question people in this country must ask in considering the question of revolution is where they stand in relation to the United States as an oppressor nation, and where they stand in relation to the masses of people throughout the world whom U.S. imperialism is oppressing.

The primary task of revolutionary struggle is to solve this principal contradiction on the side of the people of the world. It is the oppressed peoples of the world who have created the wealth of this empire and it is to them that it belongs; the goal of the revolutionary struggle must be the control and use of this wealth in the interests of the oppressed peoples of the world.

It is in this context that we must examine the revolutionary struggles in the United States. We are within the heartland of a world-wide monster, a country so rich from its world-wide plunder that even the crumbs doled out to the enslaved masses within its borders provide for material existence very much above the conditions of the masses of people of the world. The U.S. empire, as a world-wide system, channels wealth, based upon the labor and resources of the rest of the world, into the United States. The relative affluence existing in the United States is directly dependent upon the labor and natural resources of the Vietnamese, the Angolans, the Bolivians, and the rest of the peoples of the Third World. All of the United Airlines Astrojets, all of the Holiday Inns, all of Hertz's automobiles, your television set, car, and wardrobe already belong, to a large degree to the people of the rest of the world.

Therefore, any conception of "socialist revolution" simply in terms of the working people of the United States, failing to recognize the full scope of interests of the most oppressed peoples of the world, is a conception of a fight for a particular privileged interest, and is a very dangerous ideology. While the control and use of the wealth of the Empire for the people of the whole world is also in the interests of the vast majority of the people in this country, if the goal is not clear from the start we will further the preservation of class society, oppression, war, genocide, and the complete emiseration of everyone, including the people of the U.S.

The goal is the destruction of U.S. imperialism and the achievement of a classless world: world communism. Winning state power in the U.S. will occur as a result

---

From *New Left Notes*, June 18, 1969. Reprinted with permission from *Weatherman* by Harold Jacobs. © Ramparts Press, 1970, pp. 51–53.

of the military forces of the U.S. overextending themselves around the world and being defeated piecemeal; struggle within the U.S. will be a vital part of this process, but when the revolution triumphs in the U.S. it will have been made by the people of the whole world. For socialism to be defined in national terms within so extreme and historical an oppressor nation as this is only imperialist national chauvinism on the part of the "movement."

4. The FBI's Secret Campaign Against the New Left, 1968–1971 (1976)

COINTELPRO is the FBI acronym for a series of covert action programs directed against domestic groups. In these programs, the Bureau went beyond the collection of intelligence to secret action designed to "disrupt" and "neutralize" target groups and individuals. The techniques were adopted wholesale from wartime counter-intelligence, and ranged from the trivial (mailing reprints of *Reader's Digest* articles to college administrators) to the degrading (sending anonymous poison-pen letters intended to break up marriages) and the dangerous (encouraging gang warfare and falsely labeling members of a violent group as police informers).

This report is based on a staff study of more than 20,000 pages of Bureau documents, depositions of many of the Bureau agents involved in the programs, and interviews of several COINTELPRO targets. The examples selected for dis-cussion necessarily represent a small percentage of the more than 2,000 approved COINTELPRO actions. Nevertheless, the cases demonstrate the consequences of a Government agency's decision to take the law into its own hands for the "greater good" of the country.

COINTELPRO began in 1956, in part because of frustration with Supreme Court rulings limiting the Government's power to proceed overtly against dissident groups; it ended in 1971 with the threat of public exposure. In the intervening 15 years, the Bureau conducted a sophisticated vigilante operation aimed squarely at preventing the exercise of First Amendment rights of speech and association, on the theory that preventing the growth of dangerous groups and the propagation of dangerous ideas would protect the national security and deter violence.

Many of the techniques used would be intolerable in a democratic society even if all of the targets had been involved in violent activity, but COINTELPRO went far beyond that. The unexpressed major premise of the programs was that a law enforce-ment agency has the duty to do whatever is necessary to combat perceived threats to the existing social and political order. . . .

7. New Left.   The Internal Security Section had undergone a slow transition from concentrating on the "Old Left"—the CPUSA [Communist party, USA] and SWP [Socialist Workers party]—to focusing primarily on the activities of the "New Left"—a term which had no precise definition within the Bureau. Some agents defined "New Left" functionally, by connection with protests. Others defined it by philosophy, particularly antiwar philosophy.

Excerpt from Select Committee to Study Governmental Operations with Respect to Intelligence Activi-ties (the Church Committee), *Final Report* (Washington, D.C.: GPO, 1976), 3, 23–27.

On October 28, 1968, the fifth and final COINTELPRO was started against this undefined group. The program was triggered in part by the Columbia campus disturbance. Once again, law enforcement methods had broken down, largely (in the Bureau's opinion) because college administrators refused to call the police on campus to deal with student demonstrations. The atmosphere at the time was described by the Headquarters agent who supervised the New Left COINTELPRO:

> During that particular time, there was considerable public, Administration—I mean governmental Administration—[and] news media interest in the protest movement to the extent that some groups, I don't recall any specifics, but some groups were calling for something to be done to blunt or reduce the protest movements that were disrupting campuses. I can't classify it as exactly an hysteria, but there was considerable interest [and concern]. That was the framework that we were working with. . . . It would be my impression that as a result of this hysteria, some governmental leaders were looking to the Bureau.

And, once again, the combination of perceived threat, public outcry, and law enforcement frustration produced a COINTELPRO.

According to the initiating letter, the counterintelligence program's purpose was to "expose, disrupt, and otherwise neutralize" the activities of the various New Left organizations, their leadership, and adherents, with particular attention to Key Activists, "the moving forces behind the New Left." The final paragraph contains an exhortation to a "forward look, enthusiasm, and interest" because of the Bureau's concern that "the anarchist activities of a few can paralyze institutions of learning, induction centers, cripple traffic, and tie the arms of law enforcement officials all to the detriment of our society." The internal memorandum recommending the program further sets forth the Bureau's concerns:

> Our Nation is undergoing an era of disruption and violence caused to a large extent by various individuals generally connected with the New Left. Some of these activists urge revolution in America and call for the defeat of the United States in Vietnam. They continually and falsely allege police brutality and do not hesitate to utilize unlawful acts to further their so-called causes.

The document continues:

> The New Left has on many occasions viciously and scurrilously attacked the Director and the Bureau in an attempt to hamper our investigation of it and to drive us off the college campuses.

Based on those factors, the Bureau decided to institute a new COINTELPRO.

8. New Left Directives.   The Bureau's concern with "tying the hands of law enforcement officers," and with the perceived weakness of college administrators in refusing to call police onto the campus, led to a May 23, 1968, directive to all participating field offices to gather information on three categories of New Left activities:

> (1) false allegations of police brutality, to "counter the wide-spread charges of police brutality that invariably arise following student-police encounters";
> (2) immorality, depicting the "scurrilous and depraved nature of many of the characters, activities, habits, and living conditions representative of New Left adherents"; and
> (3) action by college administrators, "to show the value of college administrators and school officials taking a firm stand," and pointing out "whether and to what extent faculty members rendered aid and encouragement."

The letter continues, "Every avenue of possible embarrassment must be vigorously and enthusiastically explored. It cannot be expected that information of this type will be easily obtained, and an imaginative approach by your personnel is imperative to its success."

The order to furnish information on "immorality" was not carried out with sufficient enthusiasm. On October 9, 1968, headquarters sent another letter to all offices, taking them to task for their failure to "remain alert for and to seek specific data depicting the depraved nature and moral looseness of the New Left" and to "use this material in a vigorous and enthusiastic approach to neutralizing them." Recipient offices were again instructed to be "particularly alert for this type of data" and told:

> As the current school year commences, it can be expected that the New Left with its anti-war and anti-draft entourage will make every effort to confront college authorities, stifle military recruiting, and frustrate the Selective Service System. Each office will be expected, therefore, to afford this program continuous effective attention in order that no opportunity will be missed to destroy this insidious movement.

As to the police brutality and "college administrator" categories, the Bureau's belief that getting tough with students and demonstrators would solve the problem, and that any injuries which resulted were deserved, is reflected in the Bureau's reaction to allegations of police brutality following the Chicago Democratic Convention.

On August 28, 1968, a letter was sent to the Chicago field office instructing it to "obtain all possible evidence that would disprove these charges" [that the Chicago police used undue force] and to "consider measures by which cooperative news media may be used to counteract these allegations." The administrative "note" (for the file) states:

> Once again, the liberal press and the bleeding hearts and the forces on the left are taking advantage of the situation in Chicago surrounding the Democratic National Convention to attack the police and organized law enforcement agencies. . . . We should be mindful of this situation and develop all possible evidence to expose this activity and to refute these false allegations.

In the same vein, on September 9, 1968, an instruction was sent to all offices which had sent informants to the Chicago convention demonstrations, ordering them to debrief the informants for information "indicating incidents were staged to show police reacted with undue force and any information that authorities were baited by militants into using force." The offices were also to obtain evidence of possible violations of anti-riot laws.

The originating New Left letter had asked all recipient offices to respond with suggestions for counterintelligence action. Those responses were analyzed and a letter sent to all offices on July 6, 1968, setting forth twelve suggestions for counterintelligence action which could be utilized by all offices. Briefly the techniques are:

(1) preparing leaflets designed to discredit student demonstrators, using photographs of New Left leadership at the respective universities. "Naturally, the most obnoxious pictures should be used";

(2) instigating "personal conflicts or animosities" between New Left leaders;

(3) creating the impression that leaders are "informants for the Bureau or other law enforcement agencies";

(4) sending articles from student newspapers or the "underground press" which show the depravity of the New Left to university officials, donors, legislators, and parents. "Articles showing advocation of the use of narcotics and free sex are ideal";

(5) having members arrested on marijuana charges;

(6) sending anonymous letters about a student's activities to parents, neighbors, and the parents' employers. "This could have the effect of forcing the parents to take action";

(7) sending anonymous letters or leaflets describing the "activities and associations" of New Left faculty members and graduate assistants to university officials, legislators, Boards of Regents, and the press. "These letters should be signed 'A Concerned Alumni,' or 'A Concerned Taxpayer' ";

(8) using "cooperative press contacts" to emphasize that the "disruptive elements" constitute a "minority" of the students. "The press should demand an immediate referendum on the issue in question";

(9) exploiting the "hostility" among the SDS [Students for a Democratic Society] and other New Left groups toward the SWP, YSA [Young Socialist Alliance], and Progressive Labor Party;

(10) using "friendly news media" and law enforcement officials to disrupt New Left coffeehouses near military bases which are attempting to "influence members of the Armed Forces";

(11) using cartoons, photographs, and anonymous letters to "ridicule" the New Left; and

(12) using "misinformation" to "confuse and disrupt" New Left activities, such as by notifying members that events have been cancelled.

As noted earlier, the lack of any Bureau definition of "New Left" resulted in targeting almost every anti-war group, and spread to students demonstrating against anything. One notable example is a proposal targeting a student who carried an "obscene" sign in a demonstration protesting administration censorship of the school newspaper, and another student who sent a letter to that paper defending the demonstration. In another [example, an] article regarding "free love" on a university campus was anonymously mailed to college administrators and state officials since free love allows "an atmosphere to build up on campus that will be a fertile field for the New Left."

None of the Bureau witnesses deposed believes the New Left COINTELPRO was generally effective, in part because of the imprecise targeting.

5. Raymond Mungo Searches for a New Age at Total Loss Farm, 1970

Friday: Portsmouth, N.H.

The farm in Vermont had fooled us, just as we hoped it would when we moved there in early '68; it had tricked even battle-scarred former youth militants into seeing the world as bright clusters of Day-Glo orange and red forest, rolling open meadows, sparkling brooks and streams. I had lived in industrial, eastern New

Excerpts from Raymond Mungo, *Total Loss Farm: A Year in the Life* (New York: Bantam Books, 1970), 9–12, 158–160. Copyright © 1970 by Raymond Mungo. Reprinted with permission of the author.

England all my life, though, as well as worse places like New York and Washington, D.C., so I might have known better. But Vermont had blurred my memory, and when we finally left the farm for Portsmouth, I was all Thoreau and Frost, October up North, ain't life grand, all fresh and eager to begin rowing up the Concord and Merrimack rivers in the vanished footsteps of old Henry D. himself. Verandah Porche, queen of the Bay State Poets for Peace, packed the failing '59 VW and we went tearing down the mountain, kicking up good earth from the dirt road and barely slowing down for the 18th-century graveyard and all manner of wild animals now madly racing for shelter against the sharp winds of autumn in these hills. The frost was on the pumpkin, it was our second autumn together, and warm vibrations made the yellow farmhouse fairly glow in the dying daylight as we pointed east, over the Connecticut River, heading for our rendezvous with what *he* called "the placid current of our dreams." Knockout October day in 1969 in Vermont. All the trees had dropped acid.

The idea had come to me in a dream. It was one of those nights after Steve brought the Sunshine (wotta drug) when I'd wake up and sit bolt upright, alarmed at a sudden capacity, or *power,* I had acquired, to *see far.* I could see eternity in the vast darkness outside my window and inside my head, and I remembered feeling that way when but an infant. In my dream I was floating silently downstream in a birchbark canoe, speechless me watching vistas of bright New England autumn open up with each bend, slipping unnoticed between crimson mountains, blessing the warm sun by day and sleeping on beds of fresh leaves under a canary harvest moon by night. I was on the road to no special place, but no interstate highway with Savarinettes and Sunoco for this kid; in my dream, I was on a natural highway through the planet, the everlovin' me-sustainin' planet that never lets you down. Said Henry: "I have not yet put my foot through it."

It was the farm that had allowed me the luxury of this vision, for the farm had given me the insulation from America which the peace movement promised but cruelly denied. When we lived in Boston, Chicago, San Francisco, Washington (you name it, we lived there; some of us still live there), we dreamed of a New Age born of violent insurrection. We danced on the graves of war dead in Vietnam, every corpse was ammunition for Our Side; we set up a countergovernment down there in Washington, had marches, rallies, and meetings; tried to fight fire with fire. Then Johnson resigned, yes, and the universities began to fall, the best and oldest ones first, and by God every 13-year-old in the suburbs was smoking dope and our numbers multiplying into the millions. But I woke up in the spring of 1968 and said, "This is not what I had in mind," because the movement had become my enemy; the movement was not flowers and doves and spontaneity, but another vicious system, the seed of a heartless bureaucracy, a minority Party vying for power rather than peace. It was then that we put away the schedule for the revolution, gathered together our dear ones and all our resources, and set off to Vermont in search of the New Age.

The New Age we were looking for proved to be very old indeed, and I've often wondered aloud at my luck for being 23 years old in a time and place in which only the past offers hope and inspiration; the future offers only artifice and blight. I travel now in a society of friends who heat their houses with hand-cut wood and eliminate in outhouses, who cut pine shingles with draw-knives and haul maple sugar sap on sleds, who weed potatoes with their university-trained hands, pushing long hair out of their way and thus marking their foreheads with beautiful penitent dust. We till the soil to atone for our fathers' destruction of it. We smell. We live far from the marketplaces in America by our own volition, and the powerful men left behind are happy to have us out of their way. They do not yet realize that their heirs will refuse to inhabit their hollow cities, will find them poisonous and lethal, will run back to the Stone Age if necessary for survival and peace.

Yet this canoe trip had to be made because there was adventure out there. We expected to find the Concord and Merrimack rivers polluted but still beautiful, and to witness firsthand the startling juxtaposition of old New England, land and water and mountains, and new America, factories and highways and dams; and to thus educate ourselves further in the works of God and man. We pushed on relentlessly, top speed 50 mph, in our eggshell Volkswagen (Hitler's manifestly correct conception of the common man's car), 100 miles to the sea. The week following, the week we'd spend in our canoe, was the very week when our countrymen would celebrate Columbus Day (anniversary of the European discovery of Americans), the New York Mets in the World (American) Series, and the National Moratorium to demand an "early end to the war." Since we mourn the ruthless extinction of the natives, have outgrown baseball, and long ago commenced our own total Moratorium on constructive participation in this society, our presence and support was irrelevant to all of these national pastimes. . . .

We *are* saving the world, of course, as the world for us extends to the boundaries of Total Loss Farm and the limits of our own experience; and Total Loss Farm is everywhere now, perhaps under your own rhubarb patch if you looked at it a little closer, and our experience all that anyone could hope to know of life. We were born and raised by parents who loved us at least until they lost us to a certain high-pitched whistle in the wind which they had gotten too old to hear; we work at maintaining ourselves, though our shared labor is seldom very taxing, for it takes little enough work to make plants grow, most of it is out of our hands, and our relationship to the work one of direct gratification and reward, as children insist on; we have children of our own, though they are fully peers by the time they've learned to eat and eliminate without physical help, and soon become more our masters than our students; and we die, sometimes in sulphurous flames, dramatic and shocking, other times silent and mysterious like the gone children wandering Europe with scenes of the parents engulfed in atrocity scrawled across their minds, but never to be spoken: " I come from Auschwitz, or Hué, or Boston, my father was shot for believing in God and hangs limp forever in front of our home as a reminder to the others; my mother was sold to the grim green soldiers for their sport, and my brother to be used as a woman; I escaped the country of the somnambulent and blind on the back of a wolf who prowled the ruins and took pity on me; I have come here to begin again."

Our parents must wonder where we are. . . . [T]his story is, as much as anything else, an attempt to fill them in . . . but it grows harder and harder to speak. Fortunately, it grows simultaneously less necessary. I have clothes on my back, though they are old, and a roof over my head and food for my belly. In this, I am luckier than many. I am surrounded by people who would give their own lives in defense of mine, for they know we will make it together or not at all. I wish to be reconciled with all of my enemies, and to live on the planet and glory in peaches to a ripe old age. I am willing to help you as much as I'm able, as a single person can help another, not as a movement or government can help a mass. I may ask for some help from you as well. If you come to my house with love in your heart and there's room for one more—for there isn't always—you may know I will feed you and house you for the night, if you need it. You may see me walking from town to town with my thumb outstretched to the highway, seeking a lift: don't pass me by.

You have seen me everywhere. I am not asking for the vote. I do not seek to be represented. I do not seek to tear down your buildings or march on your castle or sit at your desk. I am interested neither in destroying what you have put up nor in gaining control of your empire. I demand nothing, and nothing is my inheritance. I live in the world, in the woods, with my friends, where not many people come by and the planet is entire and friendly; we like to be left alone except by those who can help. You can help by giving the planet, and peace, a chance. I ask only that you treat yourself right, give yourself the best of everything; and in so doing, you will be acting for me as well. If you can't stop, at least wave as you go by. Slow down, perhaps stop working: you'll find the time for everything you really want to do.

Who am I? In the world of the farm, I am Grampaw, who still finds himself able to deliver of such bombastic lectures as this, thinks he has lived through such madness and chaos, such orgasm and ecstasy, that he has some lessons to give, sleeps with the dogs. I am a fool. I am also Pan, who does in Captain Hook with a sweep of his wooden sword: saying: I am youth! I am joy! I am freedom!

6. A Pollster Reports on "The Big Chill," 1974

LATE 1960s	EARLY 1970s
The campus rebellion is in full flower.	The campus rebellion is moribund.
New life styles and radical politics appear together: granny glasses, crunchy granola, commune-living, pot smoking, and long hair seem inseparable from radical politics, sit-ins, student strikes, protest marches, draft card burnings.	An almost total divorce takes place between radical politics and new life styles.
A central theme on campus: the search for self-fulfillment *in place of* a conventional career.	A central theme on campus: how to find self-fulfillment *within* a conventional career.
Growing criticism of America as a "sick society."	Lessening criticism of America as a "sick society."
The Women's Movement has virtually no impact on youth values and attitudes.	Wide and deep penetration of Women's Liberation precepts is underway.
Violence on campus is condoned and romanticized; there are many acts of violence.	Violence-free campuses; the use of violence, even to achieve worthwhile objectives, is rejected.
The value of education is severely questioned.	The value of education is strongly endorsed.
A widening "generation gap" appears in values, morals, and outlook, dividing young people (especially college youth) from their parents.	The younger generation and older mainstream America move closer together in values, morals, and outlook.

Daniel Yankelovich, *The New Morality: A Profile of American Youth in the 70s,* McGraw-Hill (1974), pp. 3–5. Reproduced with permission of The McGraw-Hill Companies.

LATE 1960s (*continued*)	EARLY 1970s (*continued*)
A sharp split in social and moral values is found within the youth generation, between college students and the noncollege majority. The gap *within* the generation proves to be larger and more severe than the gap *between* the generations.	The gap within the generation narrows. Noncollege youth has virtually caught up with college students in adopting the new social and moral norms.
A new code of sexual morality, centering on greater acceptance of casual premarital sex, abortions, homosexuality, and extramarital relations is confined to a minority of college students.	The new sexual morality spreads both to mainstream college youth and also to mainstream working-class youth.
The challenge to the traditional work ethic is confined to the campus.	The work ethic appears strengthened on campus but is growing weaker among noncollege youth.
Harsh criticisms of major institutions, such as political parties, big business, the military, etc., are almost wholly confined to college students.	Criticism of some major institutions are tempered on campus but are taken up by the working-class youth.
The universities and the military are major targets of criticism.	Criticism of the universities and the military decrease sharply.
The campus is the main locus of youthful discontent; noncollege youth is quiescent.	Campuses are quiescent, but many signs of latent discontent and dissatisfaction appear among working-class youth.
Much youthful energy and idealism is devoted to concern with minorities.	Concern for minorities lessens.
The political center of gravity of college youth: left/liberal.	No clear-cut political center of gravity: pressures in both directions, left and right.
The New Left is a force on campus: there are growing numbers of radical students.	The New Left is a negligible factor on campus: the number of radical students declines sharply.
Concepts of law and order are anathema to college students.	College students show greater acceptance of law and order requirements.
The student mood is angry, embittered, and bewildered by public hostility.	There are few signs of anger or bitterness and little overt concern with public attitudes toward students.

✦ E S S A Y S

Historians—many of whom were themselves deeply influenced by the new radicalism of the 1960s—have only begun to unpack the movement's meanings and significance. Not surprisingly, they have disagreed vigorously among themselves: some, echoing criticisms by the Old Left, fault the movement's lack of coherent ideology and disciplined organization; others, sympathetic to the movement's origins, decry its disintegration into sectarian radicalism; still others, disillusioned or unsympathetic to begin with, view it as at best shallow and ephemeral, at worst hypocritical and destructive. Indeed, the debate over the meaning of the 1960s became one of the most contested battlegrounds in the "culture wars" of the 1980s and 1990s. In the first essay, historians Maurice Isserman of Hamilton College and Michael Kazin of Georgetown University offer a sympathetic but balanced account of the movement's failures and successes. In the second essay, political scientist Hugh Heclo of George Mason University provocatively places the 1960s in the context of a late twentieth-century transition from modernity to postmodernity.

The Contradictory Legacy of the Sixties

MAURICE ISSERMAN AND MICHAEL KAZIN

As easy it was to tell black from white
It was all that easy to tell wrong from right
And our choices were few and the thought never hit
That the one road we travelled would ever shatter and split.

—"Bob Dylan's Dream,"

from *The Freewheelin' Bob Dylan*

. . . So wrote Bob Dylan, not yet twenty-two years old, in what was in 1963 a prophetic—or at least prematurely nostalgic—elegy for the illusions of youthful commitment. Shatter and split the new radicalism certainly did, in the space of only a decade and in a way that left many of its adherents embittered and its historical reputation in tatters. After Ronald Reagan's two victories at the polls, the sixties, viewed at the time as the beginning of a new era of reform, seem instead a short interregnum amid the larger rightward shift in American politics that began during Franklin Roosevelt's troubled second term and continued through the 1980s. What difference, if any, did the decade of cultural and political upheaval encapsulated by the rise and fall of the New Left make?

Though the origins of the New Left can be traced back at least to the mid-1950s, radicalism only began to reemerge as a significant undercurrent on American campuses in 1960 when a heretofore obscure group called the Student League for Industrial Democracy (SLID) renamed itself Students for a Democratic Society (SDS). Under the leadership of two recent University of Michigan graduates, Al Haber and Tom Hayden, SDS became a small but increasingly influential network of campus activists. At its official founding convention, held in Port Huron, Michigan, in 1962, SDS adopted a manifesto declaring that the ideas and organizational forms familiar to earlier generations of Marxian radicals were outmoded. The "Port Huron Statement" dedicated SDS to the achievement of "participatory democracy" inside its own movement and within the larger society. Initially engaged on a wide variety of fronts, from civil rights to nuclear disarmament to university reform, by the mid-1960s, many SDS founders had left the campuses to concentrate on community organizing in the slums of northern cities. Ironically, just as SDS leaders began to forsake the campus, the Berkeley Free Speech Movement in the fall of 1964 and the Vietnam teach-in movement in the spring of 1965 signaled the growing responsiveness of college students to radical ideas.

The steady escalation of the war in Vietnam from the spring of 1965 up to the Spring of 1968 spurred the growth of both a broadly based antiwar movement and of the campus New Left, and led the latter to adopt increasingly militant rhetoric and tactics. By the fall of 1967 the New Left had moved "from dissent to resistance." Teach-ins and silent vigils gave way to the seizure of campus buildings and disruptive street demonstrations. Under new and younger leadership SDS continued to grow, and eventually some of its original leaders, like Tom Hayden and Rennie Davis, were attracted back to antiwar organizing from the slums of Newark and Chicago.

In the aftermath of the bloody confrontations at the Chicago Democratic convention in the summer of 1968, and the indictment of Hayden, Davis, and six others for "conspiracy," most New Leftists abandoned whatever hopes they still cherished of reforming the existing political system. Declaring themselves allies and disciples of third-world Communist revolutionaries like Mao Zedong and Che Guevara, SDS leaders now conceived their principal role as one of "bringing the war home" to the "imperialist mother country." In 1969, SDS collapsed as small, self-proclaimed revolutionary vanguards squabbled over control of the organization, but the ranks of student radicals continued to increase through the 1969–70 school year. Polls showed that as many as three quarters of a million students identified themselves as adherents of the New Left. The national student strike that SDSers had long dreamed of but had never been able to pull off became a reality in the spring of 1970. Spontaneously organized in response to the invasion of Cambodia and the killing of four students at Kent State University, it effectively paralyzed the nation's university system.

The American writer John Dos Passos, describing the revolutionary exaltation and illusion of 1919 in his novel, *Three Soldiers,* declared: "Any spring is a time of overturn, but then Lenin was alive, the Seattle general strike had seemed the beginning of the flood instead of the beginning of the ebb." It soon became apparent to despairing New Leftists that the spring of 1970 marked a similar "beginning of the ebb." Former SDS president Carl Oglesby was one among many who took to the hills (literally, in his case) at the start of the new decade. As Oglesby would say in a bittersweet reflection years later: "There were a lot of good, righteous people showing up in places like Vermont and New Hampshire in those days. Lots of parties, great reefer, good acid. Lovely friends . . . I remember it with great fondness. It was almost the best part of the struggle. The best part of the struggle was the surrender."

When the sixties were over, it seemed to many former activists that they had accomplished nothing. The "participatory democracy" the New Left sought in its early years remained a utopian dream; the "revolutionary youth movement" it built in its waning years had collapsed; the tiny "new communist parties" that one-time New Leftists tried to organize in the 1970s only illustrated once again the wisdom of Marx's comments in *The Eighteenth Brumaire* on the way history repeatedly turns tragedy into farce.

Yet in surveying the ruins of these successive political failures, it is striking that while "nothing" was accomplished by the New Left in its short life, everything was different afterward. If the years that followed the 1960s did not live up to the hopeful vision of the future sketched out in the Port Huron Statement, still they did not mark a return to the previous status quo. America certainly became a more politically and culturally contentious society because of what happened in the 1960s— and in some respects it also became a more just, open, and egalitarian one. On the coldest, darkest, and most reactionary days of the Reagan ascendancy, there was more radical belief and activity to be seen in the United States than was present anytime in the 1950s. As an organizational presence the New Left had vanished, but as a force in American political culture its impact continued to be felt.

The New Left was shaped by and came to embody a profound dislocation in American culture, and, in the end, it had more impact on the ideas that Americans had about themselves and their society than on structures of power that governed their lives. Young radicals articulated a critique of "everyday life" in the United States, which was, in time, taken up by millions of people who had little notion of where those ideas originated. In the course of the sixties and seventies, many Americans came to recognize and reject the prevalence of racial and sexual discrimination, to ask new questions about the legitimacy of established institutions and authority, and to oppose military adventures abroad. To understand the New Left's role in this transition, historians need both to explore the organizational dynamics of radical groups like SDS and to analyze the ways in which American culture shaped the young radicals who emerged to challenge the received wisdom of their society. . . .

. . . "Politics," as conventionally defined, was only of secondary importance in the rise of the new radicalism of the 1960s. The emergence and celebration of generationally defined life-styles preceded the appearance of the New Left and, for most Americans throughout the 1960s, continued to overshadow the fate of organizations, candidates, and causes. As contemporary observers and historians have since agreed, the phenomenon of the "baby boom" determined the contours of the sixties' dizzying pace of change. Between 1945 and 1946, the birth rate in the United States leaped 20 percent. Thereafter, it continued to climb, peaking in 1957 when over four million babies were born in a single year. The impact of this unexpected development, which reversed a century-long decline in the birth rate, had effects everywhere—from the spread of suburbia to the transformation of the university system. At each stage of its life, the baby-boom generation has proven to be a voracious consumer of material goods, from diapers and cribs to microwave ovens and video cassette recorders. It has also shown an enormous capacity to absorb new forms of entertainment, new images, and new ideas about politics and society.

Starting with the Davy Crockett fad of the early 1950s, cultural entrepreneurs seeking to tap the disposable income controlled by the nation's young perfected their pitch and inadvertently helped shape a distinctive generational consciousness. Hollywood soon learned to gear its offerings to the tastes of the new generation. While ostensibly condemning juvenile delinquency, such movies as *The Wild One* and *Rebel without a Cause* in effect established actors like Marlon Brando and James Dean as icons of youthful rebellion. Elvis Presley's fusion of country music and rhythm and blues combined with the frank sensuality of his stage presence signaled the arrival of a new musical era; major record producers were quick to take note and seek imitators. To a far greater extent than their parents, baby boomers grew up surrounded by and at home in a world of mass culture and mass consumption. And it was precisely because they were so deeply imbued with the promise and assumptions of that world—believing the advertisers who told them that a time of unending affluence and total freedom of choice was at hand—that they were willing, at least for a few years, to forego the quest for economic security and its material tokens that obsessed the older generation. The purveyors of mass culture were thus unintentionally acting as the gravediggers of a depression-inspired and cold war-reinforced conservative cultural consensus.

As a college education became the norm rather than a privilege, millions of young people found themselves in a new socially determined developmental stage that extended adolescence into the middle twenties or even later. By the early 1960s, "youth communities" had sprung up on the outskirts of college campuses, often in the cheap housing available on the edge of black ghettos. There, surrounded by their peers, largely freed from adult supervision and spared for the time being the responsibilities of career, family, and mortgage, young people began to experiment with new manners, mores, stimulants, sexual behavior, and, in due time, forms of political expression. . . .

At precisely the moment when the first wave of the baby boom reached the college campuses, the southern civil rights movement exploded into newspaper headlines and the nation's consciousness through the use of an innovative strategy of mass, nonviolent civil disobedience. The 1960 southern sit-in movement, which attracted fifty thousand participants in the space of a few months, was sparked by four black college freshmen in Greensboro, North Carolina, who decided on their own to challenge the segregation of a Woolworth's lunch counter. Rennie Davis, a founder of SDS who was a sophomore at Oberlin College in 1960, recalled: "Here were four students from Greensboro who were suddenly all over *Life* magazine. There was a feeling that they were us and we were them, and a recognition that they were expressing something we were feeling as well and they'd won the attention of the country."

For sympathetic college students, the civil rights movement blended the appeal of "making history" with the potential for testing one's own sense of personal "authenticity" through an existential (and for those who joined the freedom rides or the voter registration campaigns in the South, quite genuine) brush with danger. In her book *Personal Politics,* historian Sara Evans described the compelling example set by the young black volunteers of the Student Non-Violent Coordinating Committee: "Eating, sleeping, working side by side day after day, SNCC activists created a way of life more than a set of ideas." . . .

The superheated ideological atmosphere of 1950s cold war America played an important role in shaping the political outlook of college students at the start of the new decade. They had grown up in a political culture that stressed the division of the world into absolute good and absolute evil, freedom versus totalitarianism. The cold war was justified in much the same terms that had been used in the recent victorious struggle against the Axis powers. Yet, beneath the surface agreement among conservatives and liberals on the need to contain the Soviet threat, certain ambiguities still lurked. For many Americans, the cold war summoned up an uncritical identification with the emerging national security state. But some others, loyal to the liberatory and antiracist beliefs that had fueled the war against fascism, tendered their support for the "free world" on a more conditional basis. . . .

In 1961, John F. Kennedy had sounded the call for a selfless dedication to the (vaguely defined) national cause, significantly posed in terms of individual choice: "Ask not what your country can do for you, ask what you can do for your country." The same spirit of self-sacrificing idealism that led many students to volunteer for the Peace Corps led others to the civil rights movement. Many young white volunteers felt that their civil rights activism was sanctioned from on high (although SNCC's black field workers never shared that particular illusion, knowing how unresponsive the Justice Department was to their requests for protection against racist attacks). A succession of emotional and political blows followed, with the cumulative effect of redirecting the spirit of idealism away from the official agenda being set in Washington: there was fear of nuclear annihilation during the Cuban missile crisis in October 1962, indignation over the brutal treatment of civil rights demonstrators in Birmingham in the spring of 1963, shock at Kennedy's assassination that fall, distrust the following summer as a result of the Democratic convention's "compromise" that prevented the seating of Fannie Lou Hamer and other black delegates from the Mississippi Freedom Democratic Party, and dismay over the escalation of the war in Vietnam in the spring of 1965.

In the early-to-mid 1960s, an essential prop of the old order gave way in the minds of tens of thousands of young people. In more jaded times, like those which followed the Vietnam War and the Watergate scandal, disbelief in the official pronouncements of American foreign-policy makers would lead primarily to cynicism and apathy; but, in the 1960s, when the fervor of cold war liberalism was still a potent force, such disillusionment was often the prelude to an intensely moralistic conversion to political activism.

Bob Dylan's rapid rise to fame was emblematic of the newly emerging cultural and political sensibility. Dylan's first album, a combination of folk and blues interpretations and his own ironic ballads, was released in February 1962. It sold an unremarkable five thousand copies in its first year. But Dylan's second album, released in May of 1963, found a broad new audience. *The Freewheelin' Bob Dylan,* which featured protest songs like "Blowin' in the Wind," "Masters of War," and "A Hard Rain's A Gonna Fall," sold 200,000 copies by July 1963. The following month, Peter, Paul, and Mary released a single of Dylan's "Blowin' in the Wind" that sold over 300,000 copies in less than two weeks, making it the first protest song ever to grace the hit parade.

Where were Dylan's new fans coming from, and what message did they seek in his music? "Blowin' in the Wind" was simultaneously a song about coming-of-age ("How many roads must a man walk down / Before you call him a man?") and about moral choice ("Yes, 'n' how many times can a man turn his head / Pretending he just doesn't see?"), as well as a promise that those who understood its message would soon help redeem the nation ("The answer, my friend, is blowin' in the wind / The answer is blowin' in the wind"). Young Americans in the 1960s were not the first generation to feel that they were more sensitive to hypocrisy and injustice than their elders. But due to the structural and ideological framework that had emerged in postwar America, they were primed for an opening to the Left in the early 1960s. The demographic bulge, the delayed entry into the adult world, the encouragement of generational consciousness by advertisers, the cultural identification with outsiders and marginal groups, the inspirational example of the civil rights movement, and the paradoxical influence of cold war liberalism were the raw materials from which a mass New Left would be fashioned over the next few years. . . .

The chief organizational beneficiary of these trends would be SDS. As the [Vietnam] war and the protests it inspired escalated in the mid-1960s, SDS grew rapidly. This occurred despite the fact that, after organizing the first antiwar march on Washington in April 1965, its leaders disdained sponsorship of any more such events because they did not address the root issue of an imperialist foreign policy—"stopping the seventh Vietnam from now," as one slogan put it. But the policies SDS leaders chose to embrace or reject had little to do with the organization's growth. As Steve Max, an early leader of the group, recalled in a recent interview: "The progression in SDS was to be more and more movement and less and less organization. It was a situation of a movement looking for a place to happen."

There were national headlines in the spring of 1965 when SDS's antiwar march attracted some twenty thousand participants. By the end of that school year, the SDS National Office (NO) was receiving a flood of letters from individuals and groups eager to affiliate, from places like Dodge City Community College in Kansas not previously known as loci of radical activity. It was no longer necessary for SDS to organize chapters: they organized themselves. Many recruits were members of preexisting local groups who sought access to the resources and prestige that only a national organization could provide. . . .

The NO set up a system of campus "travelers" and regional offices, but these did little more than service existing chapters, distribute literature, and make an occasional statement to the media. New members were seldom "converted" to SDS ideology. If the SDS "old guard" had had its way, the organization would have functioned chiefly as a recruiting pool for future community organizers. Instead, reflecting the loosely formulated set of ideas, concerns, and political priorities that new members brought with them into the national organization, SDS chapters increasingly focused their efforts on resisting the war in Vietnam. Students did not become activists because they joined SDS; they joined SDS because they were already activists.

The SDS annual national conventions were important mainly as places where SDSers from around the country could make contacts and share experiences. Labored efforts to chart a coordinated national strategy (like an abortive "Ten Days to Shake the Empire" plan in 1968) were almost universally ignored by local chapters. To the extent that people in SDS chapters learned to speak a common language and pursue a common political agenda, they did so through a process of osmosis rather than central direction.

Just at the moment when it began to develop a significant national presence, SDS lost the ability to set its own agenda. Starting in 1965, SDS's concerns and the pace of its development were largely reactions to decisions being made in the White House and the Pentagon. The escalation of the Vietnam War thus simultaneously strengthened and weakened SDS. In the matter of a few months, it transformed the group from a small network of activists, most of whom knew one another, into a national movement with hundreds of chapters—and an organizational infrastructure that never managed to make the transition. And while the war galvanized protesters, it also bred frustration and extremism in their ranks. Vietnam was a particularly volatile issue around which to build a mass movement. No partial victories or breathing spaces could be won: the movement would either force the government to end the war, or it would fail. As a result the peace movement, with the New Left at its core, constantly swung back and forth between near-millennial expectations and dark and angry despair.

As the political climate changed after 1965, so did the New Left's cultural style. The new members who flooded into SDS (dubbed the "prairie power" contingent because so many of them came from places other than the usual urban centers of radical strength) were less likely to share a theoretical sophistication or intellectual ambitions of the group's founding generation. The new breed tended to be unschooled in and impatient with radical doctrine, intensely moralistic, suspicious of "elitism" and "bureaucracy," and immersed in the new cultural currents running through college towns.

In January 1966, three members of the newly organized SDS chapter at the University of Oklahoma were among those arrested in a marijuana raid on a private party in Norman. Newspapers throughout the country picked up the story, linking SDS with pot-smoking. The Norman police chief unabashedly revealed to local reporters that his suspicions of the students had been aroused by their politics as much as their alleged drug use: "Several of these people have been active in the Society [SDS]. . . . One of them had a receipt showing he had just joined the SDS." High bail was set for all the defendants, and two of them were locked up incommunicado in a state mental hospital for observation because of their long hair.

Jeff Shero, an SDS campus traveler and leading exponent of "prairie power" within the organization, visited Norman soon after the bust. He reported back to the NO that the police had assembled prescription drugs and antiwar literature for sensationalized photographs. Local newspapers reported that a book on "homosexuality" was found in the raided apartment. They neglected to mention the name of the book's author—Sigmund Freud. Shero was both indignant and amused at the crudity of the official antics, but he concluded that the affair had not done SDS any real political harm. "The chapter probably isn't irreparably damaged," he wrote to the NO. "Chapter people were mixed as to the effect of the raid, some actually thought it would be beneficial."

Steve Max and a few other "old guard" leaders of SDS had a different reaction. Speaking in a tone that reflected the assumptions of his earlier involvement with the Communist youth movement, Max regarded it a matter of "Socialist discipline" that "unless the organization votes to carry on a Legalize marijuana through a civil disobedience campaign, then our members ought not place themselves and the organization in a position where they can be put out of commission so easily." He wanted the Norman chapter suspended until it had, through some unspecified procedure, reformed itself. In a subsequent letter, he reiterated, "If we don't start to draw the line someplace we are going to wind up with a federation of dope rings instead of a national political organization."

But sentiment in the hinterland seemed to run in a completely opposite direction. One member from Ohio reported to the NO that news of the Norman arrests "strikes home in the Ohio area since a number of people including three friends have been arrested on charges involving pot." Although he realized that SDS might have good reasons to avoid involvement in a campaign to legalize pot-smoking, "nevertheless, I think this area is another expression of the lack of individual freedom in the society for an individual desiring to control his own life without interference."

The Norman SDS chapter was not suspended. Moreover, within a few years, SDS would not simply regard the use of drugs as a question of individual choice but would endorse it as yet another emblem of the revolutionary disaffection of the young. "Our whole life is a defiance of Amerika," the newspaper of the Weatherman SDS faction exulted in 1969. "It's moving in the streets, digging sounds, smoking dope . . . fighting pigs." By the late sixties, marijuana and LSD were circulating freely at national SDS conventions.

Underlying the ability and willingness of so many young radicals, along with others of their generation, to experiment with new "life-styles" (including drugs) was the economic prosperity of the postwar era. New Leftists took affluence for granted and despised its corrupting influence, unlike the Socialists and Communists of the 1930s who denounced capitalism for its inability to provide the minimum decencies of life to the poor. . . .

Earlier generations of radicals had derided capitalism as an anarchic, irrational system; the new radicals scorned the system because it was *too* rational, based on a soul-destroying set of technological and bureaucratic imperatives that stifled individual expression. From university reform, where the slogan was "I am a human being, do not fold, spindle, or mutilate," to draft resistance, where the buttons read "Not with my life, you don't," the New Left championed a form of radical individualism that was authentically American in derivation and flavor—ironically, all too "American" for the organizational well-being of the movement. For this deeply rooted individualism prepared the way for the development of a movement culture of "confrontation."

In the Communist, Socialist, and Trotskyist movements of the 1930s, young radicals had prided themselves on their analytic abilities, their skill in debate, their command of the intricacies of Marxist theory. In contrast, a kind of emotional and moral plain-speaking was the preferred rhetorical style among SDS leaders. Authenticity, usually described as "commitment," was the political and personal value New Leftists were most eager to display, a quality that could best be established by the willingness to "put your body on the line." Overcoming any lingering squeamishness about breaking the law (and plate-glass windows) was the ultimate "gut-check" that alone could establish whether you were "part of the problem or part of the solution."

The political deficiencies of this personal stance were not lost on some SDSers, though they found themselves powerless to correct the situation. As early as 1965, Lee Webb, former SDS national secretary, complained in an international document that "SDS influences its membership to become more militant rather than more radical. . . . Calls to fight the draft, stop a troop train, burn a draft card, avoid all forms of liberalism, have become . . . the substitute for intellectual analysis and understanding." Late sixties SDS rhetoric, composed of equal parts Maoist jargon and black street rap, communicated little but the angry alienation of its practitioners. Nevertheless, it had a very potent appeal to the already-converted or would-be recruits in defining the cultural terrain of the movement—if you spoke the language, you were already a revolutionary. "Brothers," a high school student wrote to the NO in the late 1960s, "I sympathize with the movement and its goals. But information on what's going on is hard to come by in rural, conservative western Pennsylvania. Dig?"

By the late 1960s, SDS had grown to as many as a hundred thousand loosely affiliated members, while tens of thousands more could be counted as supporters of the movement. But off-campus, the New Left's activities, and the increasingly outrageous and opaque language in which they were justified, found few supporters.

[Then governor of California] Ronald Reagan spoke for many Americans when he declared in the midst of the People's Park disorders in Berkeley in 1969 (which left one spectator dead from police buckshot), "If it's a blood bath they want, let it be now." The ferocity with which authorities sought to crack down on campus protest only exacerbated the appeal of extreme rhetoric and doctrines within SDS. In the summer of 1969 the organization splintered, with one small faction led by the Progressive Labor Party (PLP) heading for the factories, and another small faction led by Weatherman heading for the "underground." Neither the PLP nor Weatherman enlisted more than a tiny fraction of SDS members under their banners, but Weatherman's cultural style—which included a fervent if erratic promotion of drugs, sex, and rock and roll—gave it a measure of influence on campuses that the dour dogmatists in the PLP were never able to match. In the early 1970s underground newspapers gave extensive coverage to Weatherman's bombings and "communiqués"; posters in college dorms invited Bernardine Dohrn and other Weatherman fugitives to seek shelter. . . .

The demise of SDS did not retard the flowering of cultural radicalism. From campus towns to the "youth ghettos" of big cities and even to American military bases in Vietnam, a diffuse set of "countercultural" ideas, symbols, and behaviors circulated. "Liberation" was easy to achieve, since it was defined as the practice of a communal, playful, and sensual life-style. While they often ignored or explicitly rejected the politics advocated by "power-tripping" radicals, those immersed in the counterculture embraced beliefs the earlier New Left had first popularized. Alternative, participatory communities based on decentralized, small-scale technology and an ethic of loving mutuality had all been prefigured by the Port Huron Statement, the civil rights movement, and SDS's community-organizing projects. Garbed in apolitical dress, this vision continued to attract believers (many of them from working-class backgrounds) who never would have considered attending an SDS meeting. In the mid-1970s, pollster Daniel Yankelovich called attention to the ways in which new attitudes toward authority, sexual morality, and self-fulfillment had spread from elite college campuses to much of the younger population: "Indeed," he wrote, "we are amazed by the rapidity with which this process is now taking place."

As the sixties ended, some radical leaders withdrew from the increasingly fractious realm of left-wing politics to join rural communes or mystical cults, or to embrace various "new age" therapies. The well-publicized voyage of Jerry Rubin from yippie revolutionary to yuppie networker is the best known, if not most representative, example of this process. Paul Potter, a former SDS president, was less self-serving and more reflective when he recorded his own painful withdrawal from the movement in his 1971 book *A Name for Ourselves*. Potter reaffirmed his belief in the values and concerns that had initially led him to the New Left, but rejected organized politics as a means of achieving a better world:

> I am less involved in changing America. . . . This does not mean that I am less angry or upset or horrified by this country than before. If anything, I am more profoundly and intuitively aware, day to day, of what an ugly society this is and how desperately it needs change. But my information comes less and less from the papers—more and more from my own experience with it. . . .

The emergence of a new feminist movement had the paradoxical effect of draw-ing many New Left women into more active political participation while hastening the political withdrawal of many men. In the late 1960s and early 1970s few male leaders of the New Left escaped being taken to task for sexism by women in the movement. What more decisive step could men take to indicate repentance for past misdeeds than to abdicate any further claim to leadership? With the movement foundering, the "politically correct" decision often served to rationalize personal inclinations. Coinciding with the decline of the antiwar movement, a widespread and decentralized network of women's "consciousness raising" groups, health clinics, bookstores, newspapers, publishing houses, and similar enterprises emerged, giving new meaning to the original New Left call for a "beloved community." . . .

"The sixties are over," literary critic Morris Dickstein wrote in 1977, "but they remain the watershed of our recent cultural history; they continue to affect the ambiance of our lives in innumerable ways." The passage of more than a decade and Ronald Reagan's two terms in office have not lessened the truth of that observation. In the late 1980s, the conservative victors found it politically convenient to lump together the vestiges of New Deal–Great Society liberalism with the memory of the New Left to justify reversing both the social legislation and the "moral permis-siveness" associated with the sixties. They were quite successful in cutting back or abolishing domestic programs that had no wealthy or powerful constituency. But as the New Right's plaintive refrain "Let Reagan be Reagan" indicated, conservatives did not have everything their own way in the 1980s. The right was forced to govern within a cultural environment that, in significant ways, limited what it could accom-plish. Conservatives had to repackage many of their ideas and policies to appeal to a public that had caught a "democratic distemper" and was unwilling to defer automati-cally to its new governors. . . .

Right-wing movements also sought to exploit the mood of morally committed idealism that sixties radicals had done so much to create; in some instances, they proved more successful than their left-wing counterparts. The impulse to expose and attack illegitimate authority was turned against legislators who tried to "solve problems by throwing money at them," against a Democratic president who could neither free American hostages nor punish their captors, and against liberal judges perceived as protecting muggers, drug-pushers, or pornographers. At the same time, a vigorous libertarian spirit, itself a legacy of the sixties, acted as a countervailing force, preventing the New Right from imposing its version of morality on law and society. America's political culture in the 1980s thus contained enough contradictory impulses to baffle the pundits who assumed that Reagan's electoral victories repre-sented a fundamental rightward shift. . . .

In ways both trivial and serious, the example, language, and actions of sixties radicals offered millions of Americans a way to express the discontent generated by the triple debacle of Vietnam, Watergate, and seventies stagflation. Often it was the New Left's style rather than its politics that wound up being recycled in the 1970s and 1980s. Some otherwise law abiding "right-to-life" demonstrators risked arrest blockading abortion clinics while singing, in paraphrase of John Lennon, "All we are saying / is give life a chance." Campus conservatives distributed leaflets accusing Gulf Oil of "corporate murder" because the firm does business with the pro-Soviet government of Angola. New Leftists succeeded in exposing the bankrupt policies of the liberal state in the 1960s. But that very success activated right-wing critics of liberalism who championed a "counterculture" of their own, based on biblical injunctions, the patriarchal family, and the economic homilies of nineteenth-century capitalism.

The contradictory legacy of the sixties thus provides evidence of both the failures and successes of the new radicalism—"failures" that were sometimes unavoidable, and sometimes self-inflicted, and "successes" that usually were recognized and were often the opposite of what was intended. Richard Hofstadter wrote in *The Age of Reform* that while it may be "feasible and desirable to formulate ideal programs of reform, it is asking too much to expect that history will move . . . in a straight line to realize them." Despite the best efforts of the Reagan administration and the New Right, the 1980s did not represent a return to the "normalcy" of the 1950s. Young radicals never became serious contenders for state power, but the issues they raised and the language in which those issues were dramatized became the normal fare of American politics.

Whether scorned as pro-Communistic and nihilistic or smothered in bland nostalgia, the New Left's reputation in the late 1980s was not all that its founders might have hoped for. But the message of the young radicals had certainly been received.

The Sixties and the Origins of "Postmodern" America

HUGH HECLO

Mid-twentieth-century America [was in the grip of modernity]. Modernity refers here to those characteristic ways of living and thinking associated with a technologically advanced, commercially-oriented society, a society that has gone through the now familiar processes of industrialization and urbanization. Everyday life becomes "structurally differentiated" into specialized spheres of work and home, production and consumption, education and entertainment, and so on. Densely layered social bonds in self-contained communities with well-fixed traditions are gradually supplanted. They are replaced by transient, functionally separated relationships of isolated individuals in fluid groupings whose antitraditionalist tolerance tends toward relativism. New impersonal "systems" of rational organization and contract are self-consciously designed to coordinate economic, social, and political activities. And most important for present purposes, modernity brings with it a secularization of public life and thought. This does not mean that people become personally less religious. The secularization in view here refers to the relegation of religion to the distinctly private sphere of personal beliefs and choice, a refuge of psychological peace and communitarian warmth with no widely accepted authority over the utility-oriented public spheres of polity and economy. With the coming of modernity, science and rational calculation gradually expel any transcendent divinity

Hugh Heclo, "The Sixties' False Dawn: Awakenings, Movements, and Postmodern Policy-Making," *The Journal of Policy History,* 8:1 (1996), pp. 34–63. Copyright © 1996 by The Pennsylvania State University. Reproduced by permission of the publisher.

from the natural and social world, what Max Weber famously described as "the disenchantment of the world."

By the 1960s America exhibited all these signs of modernity to an extent that would have seemed incomprehensible to people only sixty or seventy years earlier. Automobile transportation and suburban/urban housing patterns, vast corporate organizations and the full flowering of a mass consumer market, the development of massive educational systems as a separate sphere for youth—these were merely some of the outward signs of the deeper forces of modernity. Sixty years earlier, education (or if one prefers, indoctrination) in the godly order of nature, history, the economy, and society had infused everything from first readers to university curricula. By the Sixties it was secular science that held center stage, not least of all a triumphant behavioralism in the social sciences that had much to say about the relation of processes to outcomes and little at all to say about the moral worth of any particular outcome. By self-report to pollsters and church attendance rates, Americans were still a remarkably religious people in the 1950s. But it was what many theologians themselves called a "secular Christianity" of private belief outside the public arena. Religiosity was a personal matter, one of many self-attributes in a socially fragmented and historically conditioned world that was deconsecrated of sacred or ultimate significance. "Multiculturalism" had not yet been affirmed. But the once robust socio-cultural-political reality of the Protestant establishment was becoming little more than a vaguely surviving mood of morally neutral civility.

By mid-century, the American public arena carried all the modern hallmarks of a rationalized sociopolitical order. It displayed the maturing form of what later leftist critics would call "corporate liberalism" and others would call "Cold War liberalism" or interest-group liberalism. . . . The once threatening Social Question had been resolved into something like an implicit social contract: a middle-class welfare state of social insurance for (mainly) male breadwinners, government-business cooperation to stabilize employment, and rationalized management of an ever-expanding consumer market. Chastened by their earlier experiences with the Left and the threat of McCarthyism, liberals were Cold War and social-reform "realists." Public affairs was an arena for tough-minded, analytic problem-solving, appropriately dominated by those with the necessary expertise and presumably tough minds. Policy problems were discrete issues where fact-finding, technical competence, and rational analysis had everything to offer, and ideology was an unproductive distraction. Descendants of a now thoroughly secularized Progressive impulse, mid-century liberals were the elite vanguard of modernity.

This Cold War liberalism was never as consistent and monolithic as its critics would later contend, but it did offer the central organizing principles for a stable political society in the 1940s, 1950s, and early 1960s. It embraced the modern system of large-scale, hierarchical organizations in business, labor, education, marketing, mainstream religious denominationalism, and government. It celebrated both the Realpolitik of pragmatic group politics and the use of dispassionate reason for problem-solving. Through public policy-making—a term increasingly in vogue—society could be rationally understood and steered. Ideological debates about the role of government or the meaning of social justice were considered a distracting echo from an early industrializing era misguided by class conflict and emotional bombast. The dominant view assumed a national government that would be actively devoted to (1) assuring a favorable business climate for the commercial culture of mass consumption, (2) projecting overwhelming anticommunist force abroad, and (3) marshaling the expertise to confront particular problems of domestic policy as these arose at home. From time to time the mid-century consensus could be heard mouthing the old sounds of transcendent idealism and providential exceptionalism. But the real voice was that of modernity speaking in the soothing, moderate tones of a consumer democracy.

As the 1950s turned into the 1960s, Cold War liberalism marched onward in its policy-making work. Fiscal policy gradually evolved from what had been generally perceived to be a "moral" issue of balancing the budget to a political-technocratic management tool of economic science. To deal with what were perceived to be pressing national problems, liberal reformers, policy experts, and mainstream interest groups struggled over what was coming to be known as the "national agenda." . . .

Slowly, moderately, "nonideologically," a liberal agenda emerged for new national commitments to regional economic development, aid to education, health, insurance for the elderly, environmental protection, and "moderate" civil rights legislation. To help implement this agenda, a stream of tough-minded, Cold War "action intellectuals" followed John Kennedy to Washington in 1960. With Lyndon Johnson the stream became a river of policy experts, task forces, and new ventures in federal domestic policy. While the overweening optimism about the capacity of experts for social engineering would soon fade, the forces of modernity pressed onward in American politics and society. Meanwhile, like a second great tectonic plate surfacing and grating alongside, there came a surge of personal discontent and social self-questioning that would constitute the Great Awakening of the 1960s. . . .

In particular, youths coming of age in the 1960s were well primed for such distress, quite apart from the remarkable events of assassination, war, and official deceit that would afflict their coming of age in the Sixties. If only because of its sheer size, this generation commanded special attention as it moved from birth toward adulthood. As youths raised in a culture of intense parenting and self-satisfied affluence, their age cohort was possibly the first group of children in history to be treated as a separate, specially privileged part of the population. Many, but by no means all, were conditioned to expect much—and to demand much—when the world did not live up to their expectations. As always, active engagement would be a minority taste. The numbers who became directly and indirectly involved "in the Sixties" were significant, but so too were the numbers of young Americans opposed or indifferent. Something less than a fifth of those under twenty in 1959 appear to have participated in organized protests associated with the social causes of the Sixties, but no doubt many others were affected by a faith-shaking cultural confusion. In the years 1965–68 two to three percent of U.S. students considered themselves "activists," although 20 percent said they had participated in at least one protest demonstration. Likewise we should recall that in 1968 Richard Nixon beat Hubert Humphrey by a 49 percent to 39 percent margin among those under twenty-five, and in 1972, among eighteen- to twenty-nine-year-old voters, George McGovern won by a 53 percent to 47 percent margin.

As youths and other people searched for a transformative understanding of themselves and their society, their searches often congealed to manifest . . . as social movements—"organized, non-governmental efforts of large numbers of people to attain significant social and personal change." More than anything else, it was this movement-referenced yearning for personal and social rebirth, expressed through political action and policy demands, that turned the mere decade of the 1960s into the larger historic moment that would become known as the Sixties. . . .

The archetypal movements of the 1960s defined themselves against, attacked, and rejected not conservatives but the liberal consensus and its institutional structures. First among blacks and white liberals awakening to the civil rights cause, and then in widening circles, [reformers] . . . perceived intolerable gaps between the espoused norms and the lived realities of the liberal system. Looking back from the 1990s, former activists who defend and those who regret their actions both agree that it was basically the working arrangements of the entrenched liberal administrative state and society that they were attacking.

For the early civil rights activists, it was the liberal order of "moderate," go-slow accommodation to state-sanctioned racial segregation in the Democratically controlled South. For the student New Left it was the interlocking liberal hegemony of corporate capitalism, state militarism, and antidemocratic bureaucratic structures of a consumerist society. For the emerging feminist movement the object of resistance was the dominant institutional-cultural paradigm of male privilege and female oppression, including, it turned out, within the New Left movement itself. For environmentalists or consumer advocates, the offending system was an unholy partnership of corporate power-holders pursuing profits with reckless abandon and captured bureaucracies failing to protect the public interest. The list could be extended for pages. In all manner of awakening activism, new struggles were deemed necessary to free people from isolated, oppressed lives lived under the spell of coercive elites in a bureaucratized, mass society. . . .

Although each of the Sixties movements had its own history, they were also interconnected, sometimes by overlapping memberships, but most especially by activists' mutual inspiration and critical motifs. Therefore as reinforcing forces, the Sixties movements and their activists had a cumulative impact well beyond any particular issue of the moment. The liberal system's gradualist, anti-idealistic acceptance of "things as they are" was rejected in favor of a visionary and fundamental restructuring of society. Essentially there were three interrelated motifs.

1. *Liberation.* The Sixties movements saw themselves as freedom struggles. Rights to personal autonomy had to be reasserted against the oppressions of the inherited order. To be truly fee was to be able to find self-fulfillment in one's own way, to grow, find meaning, and express one's true self. The movement, with its resources and arena for direct action, was the instrument for organizing against one's own oppression to achieve personal liberation. The liberation in question ranged from freedom defined against the oppression of racial segregation to freedom from limits on self-realization imposed by gender roles, consumerism, conventional morality— anything restricting the "range of alternatives for identity." From the stately Rosa Parks to counterculture dropouts at Woodstock, New Lights of all sorts awakened to their own power to overcome their oppression.

2. *Egalitarian inclusiveness.* The Sixties movements shared the basal presupposition that all people are to be equally included in society, since all are equal in their right to liberation. Thus despite their avant-garde pretensions, movement activists unknowingly restated the iron bond between liberation and equality captured by

John Milton's question three centuries earlier: ". . . for inferior who is free?" The inherited, hierarchical pecking orders of race, gender, wealth, and political power generally had to be supplanted by a community of equals where none would be marginalized.

Again, different branches of movement culture had their own particular versions of this common theme. For civil rights activists the issue was as plain as the equal inclusion promised but never delivered by the Constitution's Civil War amendments. The National Organization for Women's founding statement held out the promise of "a fully equal partnership of the sexes," and the SDS's well-known Port Huron statement ordained that "human brotherhood must be willed as the more appropriate form of social relations." Likewise, environmentalists and consumer advocates insisted they spoke for all those excluded and left voiceless in the liberal regime of interest-group politics and corporate-bureaucratic deal-making. Not least of all, each movement within itself was seen as embodying the ideal of a fraternal commonwealth (an expectation that led to much discord about those movement leaders becoming "media stars").

3. *Participatory openness.* If conditions of unfreedom are to be overcome for a community of equals, it follows that the closed structures of establishment power must be opened up so that all can share in the decisions affecting their lives. Activists saw themselves as part of what would be termed later in another context as pro-democracy movements. The liberated are not simply set free as individuals; they are empowered by virtue of being thoroughly embedded in participatory political and economic decision-making processes. In one sense this part of movement culture simply reflected a democratic vision rooted in American experience, a restatement of the Tocquevillian vision of large-spirited individualists who become such by being actively engaged in deliberating and managing their collective affairs.

Something more, however, was at work than good citizenship and participatory democracy. Institutional structures had to be opened and subjected to participatory scrutiny because they could not be trusted. Their spurious and elitist claims to disinterested knowledge and benevolent intentions created the conditions that made liberation necessary in the first place. Whatever the movement in question, activists saw elites of the "organized system" as self-serving establishments that had to be disestablished, something that could happen only through open access to decision-making processes. From university governance to the congressional committee process, from administrative implementation of the law to local zoning for trash dumps—all was to be opened to participatory democracy. And since the authority of even reformed institutions could not be trusted (given the ever-present tendency for oppression by the modern managerial technocracy/racist culture/sexist paradigm and so on), it would have to be activists themselves who used democratized procedures to pursue the just cause in question. Thus for many movement activists the real aim was not participation, which could simply mean cooptation by the process. The real aim was for your side, seen as the people's side, to win.

These, or at least something like them, seem to have been the common motifs of the awakened movement culture of the Sixties. For many of the participants, the movements represented "free spaces" between purely private lives and large-scale institutions. They were public environments of civil society where people voluntarily came together around visions of a new self and a new society. They were identity-breeding spaces in which people could create solidarity and break down the conventional oppositions of public and private, individual and community. Unlike conservatives' view of voluntary "mediating structures" as protectors of the social status quo, activists presented their movements as open, evolving forces for generating fundamental democratic change to "get back our country." . . .

The . . . movements of the Sixties helped to produce important changes in the policies, processes, and very tone of American politics. . . . However, it would be difficult to argue that the result of the changes ushered in by the Sixties was any sense of self-confident renewal or regained centeredness in American public life. . . . There were reforms in abundance, but a generation later, unlike the payoff of earlier upheavals, these seemed to add up to greater public distress and cultural confusion rather than to catharsis and revitalization.

At base the problem was that allegiances to cultural and political traditions were being dissolved with no replacement in sight. While aggressively and often successfully attacking the inherited moral authority of "the system," [reformers] . . . had no coherent alternative to put in its place. . . . This is not to say, obviously, that the . . . reformers were lacking in idealism. Movement culture was awash with moral indignation against the injustices and hypocrisy of the established system. . . . But with consciences awakened and disturbed, the question remained: What in the modern era could provide authoritative standards for constructive revitalization? What was the source of authority for the Truth claims made by the reformers?

As the 1960s progressed it became clear that any justifying warrant to legitimate reform demands was entirely self-referential. . . . Activists did not see themselves awakening penitently to a revived version of the nation's religious tradition or the established truths of its culture. They awakened to values and commitments they found personally fulfilling. To be free was to be able to live out one's subjectivity as a growing, self-realizing creator of meaning in one's life. The relevant guiding authority was the self-willed commitment to personal liberation and fulfillment in the world. Correspondingly, the rupture with the past was simply a healthy break with traditions of oppression. The long-standing national narrative of America's providential and benevolent moral mission in the world—a grounding component of earlier awakenings—became widely regarded by activists as little more than a conceit masking the country's failures and hypocrisy.

Herein lay a crucial though generally unacknowledged passage out of premodern and modern perspectives into what would increasingly become a postmodern sensibility. The concept of "pretending" in a *premodern* worldview could be invested with positive connotations of making believe—of claiming and behaving "as if" in order that the pretence might serve as an aspiration leading to the real, as yet unseen, thing. To the rationalistic *modern* perspective, pretending was an irrational, misleading escape inherently inferior to objective observation of the concrete, empirical facts. In contrast to both these views, the evolving *postmodern* sensibility attracted its audiences by showing the invariable falseness that underlay pretending. Pretence is only the disguise for the real thing, the system's way of concealing what the movement's critical powers had to continually unmask if liberation were to occur. Unmasking, the revealing of hidden agendas and unworthy motives of the powers that be, became a leitmotiv of movement culture. Perceptive observers sympathetic to the Sixties movements would later recognize that this rejection rather than engagement with normative tradition opened a dangerous gap between activists and the bulk of ordinary Americans' cultural understandings of patriotism and religion.

Many activists of the various movements of the Sixties displayed deep earnestness in the search for personal and social rebirth. . . . [They] proclaimed fulfillment to be the promise of self-fulfillment, the good to be what one freely chooses for one's own without the hegemonic pressure of institutions. . . . It was a secular version of what Dietrich Bonhoeffer called "cheap grace," the forgiving grace we bestow on ourselves. With "sin" passé, self-blame was out and system-blame was in. Postmodern sensibility would develop as a fervent search for answers based on the conviction that there are no "real" answers outside the self. . . .

For some in the movements, the personalized, self-referential basis of awakened faith soon made it fairly easy to give up on sociopolitical action and to concentrate on "doing one's own thing" to get on in life. As one of the founders of the student movement later described some in the New Left:

> A generation giddy about easy victories was too easily crushed by defeats, too easily placated by private satisfactions. . . . The premium the movement placed on the glories and agonies of pure existential will ill-equipped many of us to slog away.

This stands in striking contrast with the early civil rights movement's traditionalist faith in the transcendent strength available for eventual victory. As the Reverend Martin Luther King Jr. put it in his letter from the Birmingham jail: ". . . The opposition we face will surely fail. We will win our freedom because the sacred heritage of our nation and the eternal will of God are embodied in our echoing demands."

As the Sixties wore on, some activists counted on the revolutionary intensity and militancy of their convictions to intimidate opponents. Radical breakaway groups formed and re-formed on the student Left, in feminist and environmental circles, and in the black community. Generally these groups soon faded away, either into the mists of counterculture spontaneity and mind-trips or into the bomb smoke of vulgar Marxist anarchism.

In their central thrust, however, the Sixties movements eventually sought to advance their claims by nonrevolutionary confrontations of power with power, organization with counter organization. . . .

For those who chose to stay engaged in their causes, and for others who joined, to be a movement activist increasingly meant to have expert (if uncredentialed) knowledge about particular public issues, to be organizationally sophisticated (not least in foundation fund-raising and horizontal "networking" skills), and to understand the folkways of orchestrating media attention for your policy agenda. But notice too, participation in public deliberation was not simply a question of interest-group inclusion—getting one's voice heard. It was a strategic matter of constructing, defending, and advancing the "issues" that infused one's group identity against the designs of adversaries contesting for control of a social field. . . .

In general, the movements were not responses to economic crises or material breakdowns in society. On the contrary, everything about Cold War liberalism was proceeding *too* smoothly to suit thousands of movement activists. The deep-running issue was, to put it rather grandly, one of "meaning"—what people thought they were to make of themselves, individually and as a society. In an era of secular modernity, the raw materials of social life—identities, solidarities, and meanings—could not be considered as givens; they were constructions to be labored over and achieved by people increasingly aware of themselves as the creators and contenders for power involved in these constructive processes. Domains of social life once shielded by tradition and transcendent fixities—from procreation to death and all the production of culture in between—were unmasked and exposed to technocratic agendas of control as well as alternative "democratic" projects to control the newly opened domains. Thus the Sixties social movements would take on the modern organizational logic of rational resource mobilization, but they would also point toward a postmodern quest for the human design of meaning and identity, which is to say, toward the contests of a reflexive society self-consciously making itself. . . .

. . . [The Sixties were] transformative, for better or worse. [The decade] created an unprecedented openness of institutions to critical public view and correction. It established a presumption for an inclusive social union of equals beyond anything ever attempted by a nation-state. It nationalized policy-making on issues touching virtually every aspect of one's daily life. It drove a fundamental pluralism into the very heart of America's narrative understanding of itself. And it soon energized political forces that claimed to speak for the "true America's" religious and cultural traditions.

At the same time, a dangerous dissociation among government, policy politics, and the public was set in motion. Despite the forms of greater democratic openness in the system (in fact often because of them), policy-making in the postmodern era revolves around contending bodies of activists who are largely detached from the bulk of ordinary citizens. This is one thread that runs through our entire policy process broadly understood, from the focus-group consultants' framing of issues and the professional management of election campaigns to the details of the latest court hearing on agency regulations. The gap between policy activists and what have been called those with a commitment to everyday life is an equal-opportunity destroyer of public confidence, applying to the right and left of the political spectrum. It reflects something more than the familiar fact that serious political activity is a minority taste. The dissociation is structured in a post-Sixties policy culture that has institutionalized the distrust of institutions and their normative authority, whether in the public or private sector. The faithful activists of both right and left carry the antinomian banner.

For example, even on such a highly charged matter as the so-called culture wars over the public schools, the vast bulk of Americans are not preoccupied by concerns about multiculturalism and sex education. And traditional Christian parents (i.e., regular churchgoers who consider themselves born-again or biblical literalists) share most of the same concerns and support the same solutions for the public schools as do other Americans. On this and the host of other issues crowding the policy agenda, activists confront each other and do battle over competing claims to rights-victimhood, all sides claiming the moral right (and fund-raising necessity) to demonize their policy opponents. Huge expectations are invested in public-policy solutions to dire domestic problems, both by those who would have government do more and by those who would have it do much less, or nothing. But none of this adds up to a process or public philosophy that could provide ordinary citizens with a sense of coherent meaning to what is happening in their collective affairs. Everyday Americans find their lives entangled in a regime of activist government and activist antigovernment politics that they can little understand, much less sense they are controlling.

By the mid-1990s the Sixties were regnant. The now-adult, divided, radically pluralistic Sixties generation was taking over the reins of power. More than that, they were leading an inchoate debate on what political vision of the world could have authority over the nation. In effect, the search was on for a higher public moral order in a policy culture denying there could be any such thing. Here was a situation ripe with possibilities for demagoguery and for citizens' mounting disgust with the politics to which they were onlookers. Such are the perils of a basically religious people awakening in modernity.

✦ *F U R T H E R   R E A D I N G*

Anderson, Terry H. *The Movement and the Sixties* (1996).

Andrew, John A., III. *The Other Side of the Sixties: Young Americans for Freedom and the Rise of Conservative Politics* (1997).

Balogh, Brian, ed. *Integrating the Sixties* (1996).

Bloom, Alexander, ed. *Long Time Gone: Sixties America Then and Now* (2001).

———, and Wini Breines, eds. *"Takin' It to the Streets:" A Sixties Reader,* 2nd ed. (2003).

Braunstein, Peter. *Imagine Nation: The American Counterculture of the 1960s and '70s* (2001).

Breines, Wini. *Community and Organization in the New Left, 1962–1968: The Great Refusal,* 2nd ed. (1989).

Brennan, Mary C. *Turning Right in the Sixties* (1995).

Brick, Howard. *Age of Contradiction: American Thought and Culture in the 1960s* (1998).

Burner, David. *Making Peace with the 60s* (1996).

Caute, David. *The Year of the Barricades: A Journey Through 1968* (1988).

Chalmers, David Mark. *And the Crooked Places Made Straight: The Struggle for Social Change in the 1960s,* 2nd ed. (1996).

Chepesiuk, Ron. *Sixties Radicals, Then and Now* (1995).

Collier, Peter, and David Horowitz. *Destructive Generation: Second Thoughts About the Sixties* (1996).

Crow, Thomas. *The Rise of the Sixties: American and European Art in the Era of Dissent, 1955–69* (2005).

Cunningham, David. *There's Something Happening Here: The New Left, the Klan, and FBI Counterintelligence* (2004).

Davis, James Kirkpatrick. *Assault on the Left: The FBI and the Sixties Antiwar Movement* (1997).

Echols, Alice. *Scars of Sweet Paradise: The Life and Times of Janis Joplin* (1999).

———. *Shaky Ground: The '60s and Its Aftershocks* (2002).

Ellis, Richard J. *The Dark Side of the Left* (1998).

Ellwood, Robert S. *The Sixties Spiritual Awakening: American Religion Moving from Modern to Postmodern* (1995).

Evans, Sara. *Personal Politics: The Origins of Women's Liberation in the Civil Rights Movement and the New Left* (1979).

Farber, David R. *The Age of Great Dreams: America in the 1960s* (1994).

———. *Chicago '68* (1988).

———, ed. *The Sixties: From Memory to History* (1994).

———, and Beth Bailey, eds. *The Columbia Guide to America in the 1960s* (2001).

Farrell, James J. *The Spirit of the Sixties: Making Postwar Radicalism* (1997).

Fink, Carole, Philip Gassert, and Detlef Junker, eds. *1968: The World Transformed* (1998).

Flacks, Richard. *Making History: The American Left and the American Mind* (1988).

Frank, Thomas. *The Conquest of the Cool: Business Culture, Counterculture, and the Rise of Hip Consumerism* (1997).

Fraser, Ronald, et al. *1968: A Student Generation in Revolt* (1988).

Gitlin, Todd. *The Sixties: Years of Hope, Days of Rage* (1987).

Goldstein, Richard. *Reporting the Counterculture* (1989).

Gosse, Van. *Where the Boys Are: Cuba, Cold War America and the Making of a New Left* (1993).

Hall, James C. *Mercy, Mercy Me: African-American Culture and the American Sixties* (2001).

Hayden, Tom. *Reunion: A Memoir* (1988).

Heineman, Kenneth J. *Campus Wars: The Peace Movement at American State Universities in the Vietnam Era* (1994).

————. *Put Your Bodies upon the Wheels: Student Revolt in the 1960s* (2001).

Isserman, Maurice. *If I Had a Hammer: The Death of the Old Left and the Birth of the New Left* (1993).

————, and Michael Kazin. *America Divided: The Civil War of the 1960s*, 2nd ed. (2004).

Jacobs, Ron. *The Way the Wind Blew: A History of the Weather Underground* (1997).

Kaiser, Charles. *1968 in America: Music, Politics, Chaos, Counterculture, and the Shaping of a Generation* (1997).

Katsiaficas, George. *The Imagination of the New Left: A Global Analysis of 1968* (1987).

Klatch, Rebecca E. *A Generation Divided: The New Left, the New Right, and the 1960s* (1999).

Lyons, Paul. *New Left, New Right, and the Legacy of the Sixties* (1996).

Macedo, Stephen, ed. *Reassessing the Sixties: Debating the Political and Cultural Legacy* (1997).

Matusow, Allen J. *The Unraveling of America: A History of Liberalism in the 1960s* (1984).

McGirr, Lisa. *Suburban Warriors: The Origins of the New American Right* (2001).

Mendel-Reyes, Meta. *Reclaiming Democracy: The Sixties in Politics and Memory* (1995).

Miller, James. *Democracy Is in the Streets* (1987).

O'Neill, William. *The New Left: A History* (2001).

Oppenheimer, Mark. *Knocking on Heaven's Door: American Religion in the Age of Counterculture* (2003).

Pearlstein, Rick. *Before the Storm: Barry Goldwater and the Unmaking of the American Consensus* (2001).

Rorabaugh, W. J. *Berkeley at War: The 1960s* (1990).

Rossinow, Douglas C. *Politics of Authenticity: Liberalism, Christianity, and the New Left in America* (1998).

Roszak, Theodore. *The Making of a Counter-Culture* (1969).

Rubin, Jerry. *Do It! Scenarios of the Revolution* (1970).

Sale, Kirkpatrick. *SDS* (1973).

Steigerwald, David. *The Sixties and the End of Modern America* (1995).

Stevens, Jay. *Storming Heaven: LSD and the American Dream* (1998).

Suri, Jeremi. *Power and Protest: Global Revolution and the Rise of Detente* (2003).

Tischler, Barbara L., ed. *Sights on the Sixties* (1992).

Varon, Jeremy. *Bringing the War Home: The Weather Underground, the Red Army Faction, and Revolutionary Violence in the Sixties and Seventies* (2004).

Whalen, Jack, and Richard Flacks. *Beyond the Barricades: The Sixties Generation Grows Up* (1989).

Whitmer, Peter O. *Aquarius Revisited: Seven Who Created the Sixties Counterculture That Changed America* (1991).

Wynkoop, Mary Ann. *Dissent in the Heartland: The Sixties at Indiana University* (2002).

CHAPTER
8

From the Feminine Mystique
to "Second Wave" Feminism

The publication in 1963 of Betty Friedan's The Feminine Mystique *opened a new chapter in American women's fight for equality, a struggle that in ensuing decades would transform American social relations. Like most revolutions, it was the product of a long historical gestation. Its roots lay in the broad social changes wrought by industrialization, urbanization, and the rise of a new economy based on mass consumption; the emergence of a more democratic and companionate family life; and the self-conscious strivings of nineteenth- and early-twentieth-century women for suffrage and sexual equality. The movement's immediate antecedents included the massive entry of women into the workforce during World War II, a change only temporarily reversed during the late 1940s. But the postwar years also were marked by the insistence of virtually all of the country's cultural authorities that women ought to seek fulfillment exclusively as wives and mothers. It was the tension between this powerful "feminine mystique" and the as yet largely unarticulated aspirations of women for freedom and equality that Betty Friedan would record in her influential book.*

Through The Feminine Mystique, *women began to discover a common sense of frustration and even despair. Friedan, however, spoke for and to a largely middle-class audience of liberal women, some of whom would join her in 1966 in creating the National Organization for Women (NOW). Other, more radical voices were nurtured by the decade's civil rights movement and New Left. Out of the crucible of these movements, women (mostly young women) would forge the social agenda of the new feminism, an agenda that included not only the political and economic opportunities stressed by NOW but also a more radical challenge to definitions of gender roles in American society.*

The transformation sought by the new feminists would encounter strong opposition: the resistance of men and of male-dominated institutions, the sharp limits to change imposed by class and race, and the mobilization of social conservatives by the New Right during the 1980s. Feminists themselves remained divided over the means and ends of their movement. Women's fight for equality nevertheless continues to shape the landscape of American society. Like the civil rights movement, to which it has often been compared, it is an unfinished revolution whose final chapters will be written by Americans in the new millennium.

✦ D O C U M E N T S

Document 1 includes excerpts from the opening chapter of Betty Friedan's *The Feminine Mystique* (1963). An interpretive analysis of the lives of college-educated, middle-class women in the 1950s, the book became a classic of the new feminism. The next year, Friedan was among the founders of the National Organization for Women (NOW), whose statement of purpose is reproduced as Document 2. Younger radical feminists, often with roots in the civil rights and antiwar movements, argued that feminism was an analytic tool that opened new insights into a wide range of injustices. Document 3, the Redstockings Manifesto, illustrates the radical turn among some feminists. While both radical and mainstream feminists seemed to focus on the cause of women who were white and middle class, women who were neither applied its insights to their lives, as illustrated by Document 4, a 1972 critique of the welfare system by a recipient. An article from *Redbook,* a women's magazine, shows how feminist ideas had begun to penetrate the popular media by 1973 (Document 5). The power of the new, "second wave" of feminism was reflected both in the courts and in Congress. The Supreme Court, in its landmark 1973 decision in *Roe v. Wade* (Document 6), overturned a Texas law restricting women's right to abortion, a decision that polarized many Americans and that continues to arouse passions more than three decades later. Congress passed the Equal Rights Amendment (ERA) in 1972, a constitutional amendment that had been repeatedly introduced in Congress since 1923 (Document 7). The women's movement also sparked a powerful conservative backlash. The ERA failed ratification in the states, due in part to an anti-ERA campaign in state legislatures led by Phyllis Schlafly, a prominent conservative activist. An excerpt from her best-selling book *The Power of the Positive Woman,* in Document 8, argues against feminism as a threat to both women and the traditional family.

1. Betty Friedan on "The Problem That Has No Name," 1963

The problem lay buried, unspoken, for many years in the minds of American women. It was a strange stirring, a sense of dissatisfaction, a yearning that women suffered in the middle of the twentieth century in the United States. Each suburban wife struggled with it alone. As she made the beds, shopped for groceries, matched slipcover material, ate peanut butter sandwiches with her children, chauffeured Cub Scouts and Brownies, lay beside her husband at night—she was afraid to ask even of herself the silent question—"Is this all?"

For over fifteen years there was no word of this yearning in the millions of words written about women, for women, in all the columns, books, and articles by experts telling women their role was to seek fulfillment as wives and mothers. Over and over women heard in voices of tradition and of Freudian sophistication that they could desire no greater destiny than to glory in their own femininity. Experts told them how to catch a man and keep him, how to breastfeed children and handle their toilet training, how to cope with sibling rivalry and adolescent rebellion; how to buy a dishwasher, bake bread, cook gourmet snails, and build a swimming pool with their own hands; how to dress, look, and act more feminine and make marriage

---

more exciting; how to keep their husbands from dying young and their sons from growing into delinquents. They were taught to pity the neurotic, unfeminine, unhappy women who wanted to be poets or physicists or presidents. They learned that truly feminine women do not want careers, higher education, political rights—the independence and the opportunities that the old-fashioned feminists fought for. Some women, in their forties and fifties, still remembered painfully giving up those dreams, but most of the younger women no longer even thought about them. A thousand expert voices applauded their femininity, their adjustment, their new maturity. All they had to do was devote their lives from earliest girlhood to finding a husband and bearing children.

By the end of the nineteen-fifties, the average marriage age of women in America dropped to 20, and was still dropping, into the teens. Fourteen million girls were engaged by 17. The proportion of women attending college in comparison with men dropped from 47 per cent in 1920 to 35 per cent in 1958. A century earlier, women had fought for higher education; now girls went to college to get a husband. By the mid-fifties, 60 per cent dropped out of college to marry, or because they were afraid too much education would be a marriage bar. Colleges built dormitories for "married students," but the students were almost always the husbands. A new degree was instituted for the wives—"Ph.T." (Putting Husband Through).

Then American girls began getting married in high school. And the women's magazines, deploring the unhappy statistics about these young marriages, urged that courses on marriage, and marriage counselors, be installed in the high schools. Girls started going steady at twelve and thirteen, in junior high. Manufacturers put out brassieres with false bosoms of foam rubber for little girls of ten. And an advertisement for a child's dress, sizes 3–6x, in the *New York Times* in the fall of 1960, said: "She Too Can Join the Man-Trap Set."

By the end of the fifties, the United States birthrate was overtaking India's. The birth-control movement, renamed Planned Parenthood, was asked to find a method whereby women who had been advised that a third or fourth baby would be born dead or defective might have it anyhow. Statisticians were especially astounded at the fantastic increase in the number of babies among college women. Where once they had two children, now they had four, five, six. Women who had once wanted careers were now making careers out of having babies. So rejoiced *Life* magazine in a 1956 paean to the movement of American women back to the home. . . .

Interior decorators were designing kitchens with mosaic murals and original paintings, for kitchens were once again the center of women's lives. Home sewing became a million-dollar industry. Many women no longer left their homes, except to shop, chauffeur their children, or attend a social engagement with their husbands. Girls were growing up in America without ever having jobs outside the home. In the late fifties, a sociological phenomenon was suddenly remarked: a third of American women now worked, but most were no longer young and very few were pursuing careers. They were married women who held part-time jobs, selling or secretarial, to put their husbands through school, their sons through college, or to help pay the mortgage. Or they were widows supporting families. Fewer and fewer women were entering professional work. The shortages in the nursing, social work, and teaching professions caused crises in almost every American city. Concerned over the Soviet Union's lead in the space race, scientists noted that America's greatest source of unused brainpower was women. But girls would not study physics: it was "unfeminine." A girl refused a science fellowship at Johns Hopkins to take a job in a real-estate office. All she wanted, she said, was what every other American girl wanted, to get married, have four children, and live in a nice house in a nice suburb.

The suburban housewife—she was the dream image of the young American women and the envy, it was said, of women all over the world. The American housewife—freed by science and labor-saving appliances from the drudgery, the dangers of childbirth, and the illnesses of her grandmother. She was healthy, beautiful, educated, concerned only about her husband, her children, her home. She had found true feminine fulfillment. As a housewife and mother, she was respected as a full and equal partner to man in his world. She was free to choose automobiles, clothes, appliances, supermarkets; she had everything that women ever dreamed of.

In the fifteen years after World War II, this mystique of feminine fulfillment became the cherished and self-perpetuating core of contemporary American culture. Millions of women lived their lives in the image of those pretty pictures of the American suburban housewife, kissing their husbands goodbye in front of the picture window, depositing their stationwagonsful of children at school, and smiling as they ran the new electric waxer over the spotless kitchen floor. They baked their own bread, sewed their own and their children's clothes, kept their new washing machines and dryers running all day. They changed the sheets on the beds twice a week instead of once, took the rug-hooking class in adult education, and pitied their poor frustrated mothers, who had dreamed of having a career. Their only dream was to be perfect wives and mothers; their highest ambition to have five children and a beautiful house, their only fight to get and keep their husbands. They had no thought for the unfeminine problems of the world outside the home; they wanted the men to make the major decisions. They gloried in their role as women, and wrote proudly on the census blank: "Occupation: housewife." . . .

If a woman had a problem in the 1950s and 1960s, she knew that something must be wrong with her marriage, or with herself. Other women were satisfied with their lives, she thought. What kind of a woman was she if she did not feel this mysterious fulfillment waxing the kitchen floor? She was so ashamed to admit her dissatisfaction that she never knew how many other women shared it. If she tried to tell her husband, he didn't understand what she was talking about. She did not really understand it herself. For over fifteen years women in America found it harder to talk about this problem than about sex. Even the psychoanalysts had no name for it. When a woman went to a psychiatrist for help, as many women did, she would say, "I'm so ashamed," or "I must be hopelessly neurotic." "I don't know what's wrong with women today," a suburban psychiatrist said uneasily. "I only know something is wrong because most of my patients happen to be women. And their problem isn't sexual." Most women with this problem did not go to see a psychoanalyst, however. "There's nothing wrong really," they kept telling themselves. "There isn't any problem."

But on an April morning in 1959, I heard a mother of four, having coffee with four other mothers in a suburban development fifteen miles from New York, say in a tone of quiet desperation, "the problem." And the others knew, without words, that she was not talking about a problem with her husband, or her children, or her home. Suddenly they realized they all shared the same problem, the problem that has no name. They began, hesitantly, to talk about it. Later, after they had picked up their children at nursery school and taken them home to nap, two of the women cried, in sheer relief, just to know they were not alone.

2. NOW Statement of Purpose, 1966

We, men and women who hereby constitute ourselves as the National Organization for Women, believe that the time has come for a new movement toward true equality for all women in America, and toward a fully equal partnership of the sexes, as part of the world-wide revolution of human rights now taking place within and beyond our national borders.

The purpose of NOW is to take action to bring women into full participation in the mainstream of American society now, exercising all the privileges and responsibilities thereof in truly equal partnership with men.

We believe the time has come to move beyond the abstract argument, discussion, and symposia over the status and special nature of women which has raged in America in recent years; the time has come to confront, with concrete action, the conditions that now prevent women from enjoying the equality of opportunity and freedom of choice which is their right as individual Americans, and as human beings.

NOW is dedicated to the proposition that women first and foremost are human beings, who, like all other people in our society, must have the chance to develop their fullest human potential. We believe that women can achieve such equality only by accepting to the full the challenges and responsibilities they share with all other people in our society, as part of the decision-making mainstream of American political, economic, and social life.

We organize to initiate or support action, nationally or in any part of this nation, by individuals or organizations, to break through the silken curtain of prejudice and discrimination against women in government, industry, the professions, the churches, the political parties, the judiciary, the labor unions, in education, science, medicine, law, religion, and every other field of importance in American society. . . .

There is no civil rights movement to speak for women, as there has been for Negroes and other victims of discrimination. The National Organization for Women must therefore begin to speak.

WE BELIEVE that the power of American law, and the protection guaranteed by the U.S. Constitution to the civil rights of all individuals, must be effectively applied and enforced to isolate and remove patterns of sex discrimination, to ensure equality of opportunity in employment and education, and equality of civil and political rights and responsibilities on behalf of women, as well as for Negroes and other deprived groups.

We realize that women's problems are linked to many broader questions of social justice; their solution will require concerted action by many groups. Therefore, convinced that human rights for all are indivisible, we expect to give active support to the common cause of equal rights for all those who suffer discrimination

---

"NOW Statement of Purpose, 1966." Reprinted by permission of the National Organization for Women. This is a historical document (1966) and does not reflect the current language or priorities of the organization.

and deprivation, and we call upon other organizations committed to such goals to support our efforts toward equality for women.

WE DO NOT ACCEPT the token appointment of a few women to high-level positions in government and industry as a substitute for a serious continuing effort to recruit and advance women according to their individual abilities. To this end, we urge American government and industry to mobilize the same resources of ingenuity and command with which they have solved problems of far greater difficulty than those now impeding the progress of women.

WE BELIEVE that this nation has a capacity at least as great as other nations, to innovate new social institutions which will enable women to enjoy true equality of opportunity and responsibility in society, without conflict with their responsibilities as mothers and homemakers. In such innovations, America does not lead the Western world, but lags by decades behind many European countries. We do not accept the traditional assumption that a woman has to choose between marriage and motherhood, on the one hand, and serious participation in industry or the professions on the other. We question the present expectation that all normal women will retire from job or profession for ten or fifteen years, to devote their full time to raising children, only to reenter the job market at a relatively minor level. This in itself is a deterrent to the aspirations of women, to their acceptance into management or professional training courses, and to the very possibility of equality of opportunity or real choice, for all but a few women. Above all, we reject the assumption that these problems are the unique responsibility of each individual woman, rather than a base social dilemma which society must solve. True equality of opportunity and freedom of choice for women requires such practical and possible innovations as a nationwide network of child-care centers, which will make it unnecessary for women to retire completely from society until their children are grown, and national programs to provide retraining for women who have chosen to care for their own children full time.

WE BELIEVE that it is as essential for every girl to be educated to her full potential of human ability as it is for every boy—with the knowledge that such education is the key to effective participation in today's economy and that, for a girl as for a boy, education can only be serious where there is expectation that it will be used in society. We believe that American educators are capable of devising means of imparting such expectations to girl students. Moreover, we consider the decline in the proportion of women receiving higher and professional education to be evidence of discrimination. This discrimination may take the form of quotas against the admission of women to colleges and professional schools; lack of encouragement by parents, counselors, and educators; denial of loans or fellowships; or the traditional or arbitrary procedures in graduate and professional training geared in terms of men, which inadvertently discriminate against women. We believe that the same serious attention must be given to high school dropouts who are girls as to boys.

WE REJECT the current assumptions that a man must carry the sole burden of supporting himself, his wife, and family, and that a woman is automatically entitled to lifelong support by a man upon her marriage, or that marriage, home, and family are primarily woman's world and responsibility—hers, to dominate, his to support. We believe that a true partnership between the sexes demands a different concept of marriage, an equitable sharing of the responsibilities of home and children and of the economic burdens of their support. We believe that proper recognition should be given to the economic and social value of homemaking and child care. To these ends, we will seek to open a reexamination of laws and mores governing marriage and divorce, for we believe that the current state of "half-equality" between the sexes discriminates against both men and women, and is the cause of much unnecessary hostility between the sexes.

WE BELIEVE that women must now exercise their political rights and responsibilities as American citizens. They must refuse to be segregated on the basis of sex into separate-and-not-equal ladies' auxiliaries in the political parties, and they must demand representation according to their numbers in the regularly constituted party committees—at local, state, and national levels—and in the informal power structure, participating fully in the selection of candidates and political decision-making, and running for office themselves.

IN THE INTERESTS OF THE HUMAN DIGNITY OF WOMEN, we will protest and endeavor to change the false image of women now prevalent in the mass media, and in the texts, ceremonies, laws, and practices of our major social institutions. Such images perpetuate contempt for women by society and by women for themselves. We are similarly opposed to all policies and practices—in church, state, college, factory, or office—which, in the guise of protectiveness, not only deny opportunities but also foster in women self-denigration, dependence, and evasion of responsibility, undermine their confidence in their own abilities, and foster contempt for women.

NOW WILL HOLD ITSELF INDEPENDENT OF ANY POLITICAL PARTY in order to mobilize the political power of all women and men intent on our goals. We will strive to ensure that no party, candidate, President, senator, governor, congressman, or any public official who betrays or ignores the principle of full equality between the sexes is elected or appointed to office. If it is necessary to mobilize the votes of men and women who believe in our cause, in order to win for women the final right to be fully free and equal human beings, we so commit ourselves.

WE BELIEVE THAT women will do most to create a new image of women by *acting* now, and by speaking out in behalf of their own equality, freedom, and human dignity—not in pleas for special privilege, nor in enmity toward men, who are also victims of the current half-equality between the sexes—but in an active, self-respecting partnership with men. By so doing, women will develop confidence in their own ability to determine actively, in partnership with men, the conditions of their life, their choices, their future, and their society.

3. Redstockings Manifesto, 1970

I   After centuries of individual and preliminary political struggle, women are uniting to achieve their final liberation from male supremacy. Redstockings is dedicated to building this unity and winning our freedom.

II   Women are an oppressed class. Our oppression is total, affecting every facet of our lives. We are exploited as sex objects, breeders, domestic servants, and cheap labor. We are considered inferior beings, whose only purpose is to enhance men's lives. Our humanity is denied. Our prescribed behavior is enforced by the threat of physical violence.

Because we have lived so intimately with our oppressors in isolation from each other, we have been kept from seeing our personal suffering as a political condition. This creates the illusion that a woman's relationship with her man is a matter of interplay between two unique personalities, and can be worked out individually. In reality, every such relationship is a *class* relationship, and the conflicts between individual men and women are *political* conflicts that can only be solved collectively.

III   We identify the agents of our oppression as men. Male supremacy is the oldest, most basic form of domination. All other forms of exploitation and oppression (racism, capitalism, imperialism, etc.) are extensions of male supremacy: men dominate women, a few men dominate the rest. All power structures throughout history have been male-dominated and male-oriented. Men have controlled all political, economic, and cultural institutions and backed up this control with physical force. They have used their power to keep women in an inferior position. *All men* received economic, sexual, and psychological benefits from male supremacy. *All men* have oppressed women.

IV   Attempts have been made to shift the burden of responsibility from men to institutions or to women themselves. We condemn these arguments as evasions. Institutions alone do not oppress; they are merely tools of the oppressor. To blame institutions implies that men and women are equally victimized, obscures the fact that men benefit from the subordination of women, and gives men the excuse that they are forced to be oppressors. On the contrary, any man is free to renounce his superior position provided that he is willing to be treated like a woman by other men.

We also reject the idea that women consent to or are to blame for their own oppression. Women's submission is not the result of brainwashing, stupidity, or mental illness but of continual, daily pressure from men. We do not need to change ourselves, but to change men.

The most slanderous evasion of all is that women can oppress men. The basis for this illusion is the isolation of individual relationships from their political context and the tendency of men to see any legitimate challenge to their privileges as persecution.

V   We regard our personal experience, and our feelings about that experience, as the basis for any analysis of our common situation. We cannot rely on existing ideologies as they are all products of male supremacist culture. We question every generalization and accept none that are not confirmed by our experience.

Our chief task at present is to develop female class consciousness through sharing experience and publicly exposing the sexist foundation of all our institutions. Consciousness-raising is not "therapy," which implies the existence of individual solutions and falsely assumes that the male-female relationship is purely personal, but the only method by which we can ensure that our program for liberation is based on the concrete realities of our lives.

The first requirement for raising class consciousness is honesty, in private and in public, with ourselves and other women.

VI   We identify with all women. We define our best interest as that of the poorest, most brutally exploited woman.

We repudiate all economic, racial, educational, or status privileges that divide us from other women. We are determined to recognize and eliminate any prejudices we may hold against other women.

We are committed to achieving internal democracy. We will do whatever is necessary to ensure that every woman in our movement has an equal chance to participate, assume responsibility, and develop her political potential.

VII   We call on all our sisters to unite with us in struggle.

We call on all men to give up their male privileges and support women's liberation in the interest of our humanity and their own.

In fighting for our liberation we will always take the side of women against their oppressors. We will not ask what is "revolutionary" or "reformist," only what is good for women.

The time for individual skirmishes has passed. This time we are going all the way.

4. Welfare Is a Women's Issue, 1972

I'm a woman. I'm a black woman. I'm a poor woman. I'm a fat woman. I'm a middle-aged woman. And I'm on welfare.

In this country, if you're any one of those things you count less as a human being. If you're all those things, you don't count at all. Except as a statistic.

I am 45 years old. I have raised six children. There are millions of statistics like me. Some on welfare. Some not. And some, really poor, who don't even know they're entitled to welfare. Not all of them are black. Not at all. In fact, the majority—about two-thirds—of all the poor families in the country are white.

Welfare's like a traffic accident. It can happen to anybody, but especially it happens to women.

And that's why welfare is a women's issue. For a lot of middle-class women in this country, Women's Liberation is a matter of concern. For women on welfare it's a matter of survival.

Survival. That's why we had to go on welfare. And that's why we can't get off welfare now. Not us women. Not until we do something about liberating poor women in this country.

Because up until now we've been raised to expect to work, all our lives, for nothing. Because we are the worst educated, the least-skilled, and the lowest-paid people there are. Because we have to be almost totally responsible for our children. Because we are regarded by everybody as dependents. That's why we are on welfare. And that's why we stay on it.

Johnnie Tilmon, "Welfare Is a Women's Issue," *Ms.* (Spring 1972): 111–116.

Welfare is the most prejudiced institution in this country, even more than marriage, which it tries to imitate. Let me explain that a little.

Ninety-nine percent of welfare families are headed by women. There is no man around. In half the states there can't be men around because A.F.D.C. (Aid to Families with Dependent Children) says if there is an "able-bodied" man around, then you can't be on welfare. If the kids are going to eat, and the man can't get a job, then he's got to go.

Welfare is like a super-sexist marriage. You trade in a man for the man. But you can't divorce him if he treats you bad. He can divorce you, of course, cut you off anytime he wants. But in that case, he keeps the kids, not you. The man runs everything. In ordinary marriage, sex is supposed to be for your husband. On A.F.D.C., you're not supposed to have any sex at all. You give up control of your own body. It's a condition of aid. You may even have to agree to get your tubes tied so you can never have more children just to avoid being cut off welfare.

The man, the welfare system, controls your money. He tells you what to buy, what not to buy, where to buy it, and how much things cost. If things—rent, for instance—really cost more than he says they do, it's just too bad for you. He's always right.

That's why Governor [Ronald] Reagan can get away with slandering welfare recipients, calling them "lazy parasites," "pigs at the trough," and such. We've been trained to believe that the only reason people are on welfare is because there's something wrong with their character. If people have "motivation," if people only want to work, they can, and they will be able to support themselves and their kids in decency.

The truth is a job doesn't necessarily mean an adequate income. There are some ten million jobs that now pay less than the minimum wage, and if you're a woman, you've got the best chance of getting one. Why would a 45-year-old woman work all day in a laundry ironing shirts at 90-some cents an hour? Because she knows there's some place lower she could be. She could be on welfare. Society needs women on welfare as "examples" to let every woman, factory workers and housewife workers alike, know what will happen if she lets up, if she's laid off, if she tries to go it alone without a man. So these ladies stay on their feet or on their knees all their lives instead of asking why they're only getting 90-some cents an hour, instead of daring to fight and complain.

Maybe we poor welfare women will really liberate women in this country. We've already started on our own welfare plan. Along with other welfare recipients, we have organized so we can have some voice. Our group is called the National Welfare Rights Organization (N.W.R.O.). We put together our own welfare plan, called Guaranteed Adequate Income (G.A.I.), which would eliminate sexism from welfare. There would be no "categories"—men, women, children, single, married, kids, no kids—just poor people who need aid. You'd get paid according to need and family size only and that would be upped as the cost of living goes up.

As far as I'm concerned, the ladies of N.W.R.O. are the front-line troops of women's freedom. Both because we have so few illusions and because our issues are so important to all women—the right to a living wage for women's work, the right to life itself.

5. A *Redbook* Magazine Reader Discovers Consciousness-Raising, 1973

I have participated in a consciousness-raising group for some time now, exploring what it means to me to be a woman, discovering how I can transform the traditional female role into one that fits my own feelings and capabilities.

Consciousness-raising is basically a sensitizing process. Its purpose is to make a woman aware that as a woman she has been denied many opportunities for choice in her life. Through discussing her life on a personal level with others in her group, the reasoning goes, she will come to realize the extent to which the realities of her situation—including what has been expected of her and denied her, how she has been conditioned by parents, teachers, and other people to fit the "feminine" mold, and how she feels about herself—are shared by other women. Such new perspectives help prepare women to recognize and cope with discrimination and to take advantage of new opportunities arising for women today.

One of the first things consciousness-raising helped my group see is how unfair the institution of marriage is to women. Traditionally dependent upon her husband for financial support, a wife generally has been expected to fit in the community her husband chooses, be supportive of his career, wait on him and accommodate to his desires, fulfill housekeeping and childcare functions capably and do her best to "love, honor, and obey"—cheerfully.

Many women have accepted this secondary role and taken for granted the fact that their husbands have had more mobility and freedom of choice. In fact, few married women realize that marriage can restrict their legal rights—that in many states, for instance, a wife is not free to conduct such activities as taking out a loan, filing a suit, starting a business or disposing of personal property independently of her husband, legally marriage is not a partnership of equals.

Many women, including myself, believe that this inequality will not be overcome merely by the passage of fairer marriage and divorce legislation. We feel that married women must work for shared responsibility and privilege that may involve a difficult reassessment of marriage. In my case this has meant sharing child care, housework, and financial support of our family with my husband, a flexible arrangement that has taken into account our individual goals and interests and allowed us both to grow.

One function of the consciousness-raising group is to provide the support a woman needs to insist upon equality in her personal relationships and to work for more control over her own life, to give her the insight and strength to change aspects of her life—or of her marriage—that make her unhappy. Sometimes just knowing that other women share her feelings or face similar problems is enough. Or a group can suggest solutions to specific problems.

For example, when a 26-year old woman in my group was offered a job by a former boss, she was torn between her feelings of responsibility for her two-year old daughter and her desire to continue the work she'd enjoyed before her child was born—a conflict others of us also had faced. She realized that full-time work would make her feel she was missing the joys of watching her daughter grow; yet full-time motherhood left her lethargic and bored, she sometimes found it hard to summon the energy to do her housework. And she had been surprised, she told us, at her eagerness to take the job when it was offered.

Our group helped by listening as she voiced her qualms, by suggesting possibilities for child care and a part-time trial period on the job, and by supporting her right to choose what she wanted to do. Eventually she decided to take the job—working only three days a week—and before long she found that her daughter enjoyed her play group, her husband no longer came home to her complaints of boredom, and even the housework seemed easier. "Without the support of the group, taking a job again might have been an empty dream, a fantasy to turn over in my mind while I watched the soap operas," she said later.

If you are interested in joining a consciousness-raising group, there are many ways to go about it. You can check first with neighbors, friends, and acquaintances to find out if they know of any such group in your community. You can contact women's organizations in the area to see if they are helping to set up such groups—in many cities consciousness-raising groups are co-ordinated through women's centers and the YWCA. And you can watch the newspapers for items about or announcements of local group meetings. Also there are Women's Liberation groups at many colleges.

Some women I know who haven't found a group functioning in their community have started their own by encouraging interest on the part of friends, neighbors and acquaintances. If you are employed or do volunteer work in parents' or community projects you can talk with co-workers, and you can post a sign on a bulletin board where other women will see it, asking for those interested to contact you.

My group and most of the groups I know about follow certain basic guidelines. The best size for a group, for example, seems to be from seven to ten women—large enough for a variety of viewpoints, yet small enough for intimacy to develop—but anywhere from five to 15 members seems manageable. Usually meetings are held weekly at members' houses. The atmosphere of the meetings should be casual, with no interruptions from husband or children, so that each woman feels comfortable and able to speak frankly.

In general, groups follow similar patterns in their meetings. The first session is usually devoted to getting acquainted and overcoming the initial nervousness of those who don't know what to expect or who have misconceptions about the Women's Movement. Sometimes the women give their reasons for being drawn to the Movement and discuss what they hope it can accomplish.

The personalities and backgrounds of some women may make them better able to express themselves; a group should try to be aware of this and to insist that the more silent women participate. And it is important to stick to a weekly topic and not let the meeting deteriorate into chitchat or gossip.

Weekly topics are designed to trigger feelings the group can explore together and are best chosen the week before so that they can be mulled over during the week. Although it's natural for a group to stick at first to such subjects as how housekeeping can be less of a burden, most groups eventually get around to covering topics and answering questions like the following: Your parents and their relationship to each other and to you. Your feelings about marriage, having children, pregnancy and motherhood. Your relationship with other women, your relationships with men—are there recurring patterns? Do you ever feel invisible? How do you feel about growing old? Have you ever felt that men have pressured you into sexual relationships? Have you ever lied about orgasm? What would you like most to do in life and what has stopped you? Do you have difficulty expressing anger or asserting yourself? As a child were you encouraged in certain activities and discouraged from others? How were you educated? Do you see housework as a duty only you should perform or do you see it as a favor to your family?

Discussion proceeds in a circle with each woman speaking on the topic as it relates to her own life. While one woman is speaking others may question her, but she should finish before another woman begins.

In my group there were strained silences and halting testimony during the first few meetings, before members learned to trust one another and were able to overcome their nervousness. It takes a while to find the courage to expose problems that have been considered private; yet once women open up to one another, they often find that others share, or at least sympathize with, these problems. A friend of mine told me that members of her group found it easier to reveal themselves after they made a protective decision not to repeat to people outside the group personal information given at meetings. Several of my friends found that when they shared ideas from our group discussions with their husbands, they were better able to help them understand women's objections to some male attitudes and how these attitudes needed to be changed.

My experience in a consciousness-raising group has been tremendously exciting, and so have the experiences of my friends. Most of us went through periods of elation, anger, and frustration before achieving a new-found sense of power over our lives. We also felt a sense of closeness as we discovered how much we as women have in common and learned to work together. Once we realized how the stereotyped woman's role can limit individual growth, many of us reacted with anger, or with what one woman called "justifiable rage." But these feelings of anger are not the goal of consciousness-raising; they're part of the process. They motivate women to change, to develop their abilities, and to use these abilities with confidence in themselves.

Attempting to replace a traditional role with a new, self-determined one is a constant challenge to women like us who are working to liberate ourselves. But it is likely that the co-operation, sisterhood, individual initiative, and internal democracy that we develop through consciousness-raising will strongly influence the people and the institutions around us.

6. The Supreme Court Rules on Abortion: *Roe v. Wade,* 1973

Mr. Justice [Harry A.] Blackmun delivered the opinion of the Court. . . .

We forthwith acknowledge our awareness of the sensitive and emotional nature of the abortion controversy, of the vigorous opposing views, even among physicians, and of the deep and seemingly absolute convictions that the subject inspires. One's philosophy, one's experiences, one's exposure to the raw edges of human existence,

---

Roe v. Wade, 410 U.S. 113 (1973). Argued December 13, 1971; reargued October 11, 1972; decided January 22, 1973.

one's religious training, one's attitudes toward life and family and their values, and the moral standards one establishes and seeks to observe, are all likely to influence and to color one's thinking and conclusions about abortion. . . .

The Texas statutes that concern us here are Arts. 1191–1194 and 1196 of the State's Penal Code. These make it a crime to "procure an abortion," as therein defined, or to attempt one, except with respect to "an abortion procured or attempted by medical advice for the purpose of saving the life of the mother." Similar statutes are in existence in a majority of the States. . . .

Jane Roe, a single woman who was residing in Dallas County, Texas, instituted this federal action in March 1970 against the District Attorney of the country. She sought a declaratory judgment that the Texas criminal abortion statutes were unconstitutional on their face, and an injunction restraining the defendant from enforcing the statutes.

Roe alleged that she was unmarried and pregnant; that she wished to terminate her pregnancy by an abortion "performed by a competent, licensed physician, under safe, clinical conditions"; that she was unable to get a "legal" abortion in Texas because her life did not appear to be threatened by the continuation of her pregnancy; and that she could not afford to travel to another jurisdiction in order to secure a legal abortion under safe conditions. She claimed that the Texas statutes were unconstitutionally vague and that they abridged her right of personal privacy, protected by the First, Fourth, Fifth, Ninth, and Fourteenth Amendments. By an amendment to her complaint Roe purported to sue "on behalf of herself and all other women" similarly situated. . . .

The principal thrust of appellant's attack on the Texas statutes is that they improperly invade a right, said to be possessed by the pregnant woman, to choose to terminate her pregnancy. Appellant would discover this right in the concept of personal "liberty" embodied in the Fourteenth Amendment's Due Process Clause; or in personal, marital, familial, and sexual privacy said to be protected by the Bill of Rights . . . or among those rights reserved to the people by the Ninth Amendment. . . .

It perhaps is not generally appreciated that the restrictive criminal abortion laws in effect in a majority of States today are of relatively recent vintage. Those laws, generally proscribing abortion or its attempt at any time during pregnancy except when necessary to preserve the pregnant woman's life, are not of ancient or even of common-law origin. Instead, they derive from statutory changes effected, for the most part, in the latter half of the 19th century. . . . It is undisputed that at common law, abortion performed *before* "quickening"—the first recognizable movement of the fetus *in utero,* appearing usually from the 16th to the 18th week of pregnancy— was not an indictable offense. . . . In this country, the law in effect in all but a few States until mid-19th century was the pre-existing English common law. . . .

Gradually, in the middle and late 19th century the quickening distinction disappeared from the statutory law of most States and the degree of the offense and the penalties were increased. By the end of the 1950's, a large majority of the jurisdictions banned abortion, however and whenever performed, unless done to save or preserve the life of the mother. . . .

It is thus apparent that at common law, at the time of the adoption of our Constitution, and throughout the major portion of the 19th century, abortion was viewed with less disfavor than under most American statutes currently in effect. Phrasing it another way, a woman enjoyed a substantially broader right to terminate a pregnancy than she does in most States today. At least with respect to the early stage of pregnancy, and very possibly without such a limitation, the opportunity to make this choice was present in this country well into the 19th century. Even later, the law continued for some time to treat less punitively an abortion procured in early pregnancy. . . . When most criminal abortion laws were first enacted, the procedure was a hazardous one for the woman. . . . Modern medical techniques have altered this situation. . . . Mortality rates for women undergoing early abortions, where the procedure is legal, appear to be as low as or lower than the rates for normal childbirth. Consequently, any interest of the State in protecting the woman from an inherently hazardous procedure, except when it would be equally dangerous for her to forgo it, has largely disappeared. Of course, important state interests in the areas of health and medical standards do remain. The State has a legitimate interest in seeing to it that abortion, like any other medical procedure, is performed under circumstances that insure maximum safety for the patient. . . .

The Constitution does not explicitly mention any right of privacy. In a line of decisions, however, . . . the Court has recognized that a right of personal privacy, or a guarantee of certain areas or zones of privacy, does exist under the Constitution. . . . This right of privacy, whether it be founded in the Fourteenth Amendment's concept of personal liberty and restrictions upon state action, as we feel it is, or, as the District Court determined, in the Ninth Amendment's reservation of rights to the people, is broad enough to encompass a woman's decision whether or not to terminate her pregnancy. . . .

We . . . conclude that the right of personal privacy includes the abortion decision, but that this right is not unqualified and must be considered against important state interests in regulation. . . .

In view of all this, we do not agree that, by adopting one theory of life, Texas may override the rights of the pregnant woman that are at stake. We repeat, however, that the State does have an important and legitimate interest in preserving and protecting the health of the pregnant woman, whether she be a resident of the State or a nonresident who seeks medical consultation and treatment there, and that it has still *another* important and legitimate interest in protecting the potentiality of human life. These interests are separate and distinct. Each grows in substantiality as the woman approaches term and, at a point during pregnancy, each becomes "compelling."

With respect to the State's important and legitimate interest in the health of the mother, the "compelling" point, in the light of present medical knowledge, is at approximately the end of the first trimester. This is so because of the now-established medical fact . . . that until the end of the first trimester mortality in abortion may be less than mortality in normal childbirth. It follows that, from and after this point, a State may regulate the abortion procedure to the extent that the regulation reasonably relates to the preservation and protection of maternal health. . . .

This means, on the other hand, that, for the period of pregnancy prior to this "compelling" point, the attending physician, in consultation with his patient, is free to determine, without regulation by the State, that, in his medical judgment, the patient's pregnancy should be terminated. If that decision is reached, the judgment may be effectuated by an abortion free of interference by the State.

With respect to the State's important and legitimate interest in potential life, the "compelling" point is at viability. This is so because the fetus then presumably has the capability of meaningful life outside the mother's womb. State regulation protective of fetal life after viability thus has both logical and biological justifications. If the State is interested in protecting fetal life after viability, it may go so far as to proscribe abortion during that period, except when it is necessary to preserve the life or health of the mother.

Measured against these standards, Art. 1196 of the Texas Penal Code, in restricting legal abortions to those "procured or attempted by medical advice for the purpose of saving the life of the mother," sweeps too broadly. The statute makes no distinction between abortions performed early in pregnancy and those performed later, and it limits to a single reason, "saving" the mother's life, the legal justification for the procedure. The statute, therefore, cannot survive the constitutional attack made upon it here.

7. Equal Rights Amendment, 1972

House Joint Resolution 208

Proposing an amendment to the Constitution of the United States relative to equal rights for men and women.

Resolved by the Senate and House of Representatives of the United States of America in Congress assembled (two-thirds of each House concurring therein), That

The following article is proposed as an amendment to the Constitution of the United States, which shall be valid to all intents and purposes as part of the Constitution when ratified by the legislatures of three-fourths of the several States within seven years from the date of its submission by the Congress:

"Section 1. Equality of rights under the law shall not be denied or abridged by the United States or by any State on account of sex.

"Section 2. The Congress shall have the power to enforce, by appropriate legislation, the provisions of this article.

"Section 3. This amendment shall take effect two years after the date of ratification."

8. Phyllis Schlafly Proclaims the Power of the Positive Woman, 1977

The first requirement for the acquisition of power by the Positive Woman is to understand the differences between men and women. Your outlook on life, your faith, your behavior, your potential for fulfillment, all are determined by the parameters of your original premise. The Positive Woman starts with the assumption that the world is her oyster. She rejoices in the creative capability within her body and the power potential of her mind and spirit. She understands that men and women are different, and that those very differences provide the key to her success as a person and fulfillment as a woman.

Ninety-Second Congress, *U.S. Statutes At Large* 86 (1972): 152–1524. Online at: http://www.gpoaccess. gov/constitution/pdf/con002.pdf.

Excerpt from *The Power of the Positive Woman* by Phyllis Schlafly (1977). Reprinted by permission of the author.

The women's liberationist, on the other hand, is imprisoned by her own negative view of herself and of her place in the world around her. This view of women was most succinctly expressed in an advertisement designed by the principal woman's liberationist organization, the National Organization for Women (NOW), and run in many magazines and newspapers and as spot announcements on many television stations. The advertisement showed a darling curlyheaded girl with the caption: "This healthy, normal baby has a handicap. She was born female."

This is the self-articulated dog-in-the-manger, chip-on-the-shoulder, fundamental dogma of the women's liberation movement. Someone—it is not clear who, perhaps God, perhaps the "Establishment," perhaps a conspiracy of male chauvinist pigs— dealt women a full blow by making them female. It becomes necessary, therefore, for women to agitate and demonstrate and hurl demands on society in order to wrest from an oppressive male-dominated social structure the status that has been wrongfully denied to women through the centuries.

By its very nature, therefore, the women's liberation movement precipitates a series of conflict situations—in the legislatures, in the courts, in the schools, in industry—with man targeted as the enemy. Confrontation replaces cooperation as the watchword of all relationships. Women and men become adversaries instead of partners.

The second dogma of the women's liberationists is that, of all the injustices perpetrated upon women through the centuries, the most oppressive is the cruel fact that women have babies and men do not. Within the confines of the women's liberationist ideology, therefore, the abolition of this overriding inequality of women becomes the primary goal. This goal must be achieved at any and all costs—to the woman herself, to the baby, to the family, and to society. Women must be made equal to men in their ability *not* to become pregnant and *not* to be expected to care for babies they may bring into the world.

This is why women's liberationists are compulsively involved in the drive to make abortion and child-care centers for all women, regardless of religion or income, both socially acceptable and government-financed. Former Congresswoman Bella Abzug has defined the goal: "to enforce the constitutional right of females to terminate pregnancies that they do not wish to continue."

If man is targeted as the enemy, and the ultimate goal of women's liberation is independence from men and the avoidance of pregnancy and its consequences, then lesbianism is logically the highest form in the ritual of women's liberation. Many, such as Kate Millett, come to this conclusion, although many others do not.

The Positive Woman will never travel that dead-end road. It is self-evident to the Positive Woman that the female body with its baby-producing organs was not designed by a conspiracy of men but by the Divine Architect of the human race. Those who think it is unfair that women have babies, whereas men cannot, will have to take up their complaint with God because no other power is capable of changing that fundamental fact. On some college campuses, I have been assured that other methods of reproduction will be developed. But most of us must deal with the real world rather than with the imagination of dreamers. . . .

The third basic dogma of the women's liberation movement is that there is no difference between male and female except the sex organs, and that all those physi- cal, cognitive, and emotional differences you *think* are there, are merely the result of centuries of restraints imposed by a male-dominated society and sex-stereotyped schooling. The role imposed on women is, by definition, inferior, according to the women's liberationists.

The Positive Woman knows that, while there are some physical competitions in which women are better (and can command more money) than men, including those that put a premium on grace and beauty, such as figure skating, the superior physical strength of males over females in competitions of strength, speed, and short-term endurance is beyond rational dispute. . . .

The new generation can brag all it wants about the new liberation of the new morality, but it is still the woman who is hurt the most. The new morality isn't just a "fad"—it is a cheat and a thief. It robs the woman of her virtue, her youth, her beauty, and her love—for nothing, just nothing. It has produced a generation of young women searching for their identity, bored with sexual freedom, and despondent from the loneliness of living a life without commitment. They have abandoned the old commandments, but they can't find any new rules that work. . . .

The differences between men and women are also emotional and psychological. Without woman's innate maternal instinct, the human race would have died out centuries ago. There is nothing so helpless in all earthly life as the newborn infant. It will die within hours if not cared for. Even in the most primitive, uneducated societies, women have always cared for their newborn babies. They didn't need any schooling to teach them how. They didn't need any welfare workers to tell them it is their social obligation. Even in societies to whom such concepts as "ought," "social responsibility," and "compassion for the helpless" were unknown, mothers cared for their new babies.

Why? Because caring for a baby serves the natural maternal need of a woman. Although not nearly so total as the baby's need, the woman's need is nonetheless real.

The overriding psychological need of a woman is to love something alive. A baby fulfills this need in the lives of most women. If a baby is not available to fill that need, women search for a baby-substitute. This is the reason why women have traditionally gone into teaching and nursing careers. They are doing what comes naturally to the female psyche. The schoolchild or the patient of any age provides an outlet for a woman to express her natural maternal need. . . .

Finally, women are different from men in dealing with the fundamentals of life itself. Men are philosophers, women are practical, and 'twas ever thus. Men may philosophize about how life began and where we are heading; women are concerned about feeding the kids today. No woman would ever, as Karl Marx did, spend years reading political philosophy in the British Museum while her child starved to death. Women don't take naturally to a search for the intangible and the abstract. The Positive Woman knows who she is and where she is going, and she will reach her goal because the longest journey starts with a very practical first step. . . .

✥ *E S S A Y S*

Feminism encompassed both a reform movement, which aimed to erase inequalities between men and women, and a radical movement, inspired by the civil rights and anti-war movements, which aimed to level all hierarchies in society, including that housed in the traditional family. In the first essay, historian Alice Echols discusses radical feminism and its critique of the mainstream women's movement represented by organizations such as NOW. In the second, historian Beth Bailey traces the origins of the 1970s sexual revolution to three sorts of challenges in the 1960s, all of which challenged the nineteenth-century norms that had guided behavior of men and women in the past.

Women's Liberation and Sixties Radicalism

ALICE ECHOLS

On 7 September 1968 the sixties came to the Miss America Pageant when one hundred women's liberationists descended upon Atlantic City to protest the pageant's promotion of physical attractiveness and charm as the primary measures of women's worth. Carrying signs that declared, "Miss America Is a Big Falsie," "Miss America Sells It," and "Up Against the Wall, Miss America," they formed a picket line on the boardwalk, sang anti–Miss America songs in three-part harmony, and performed guerrilla theater. The activists crowned a live sheep Miss America and paraded it on the boardwalk to parody the way the contestants, and by extension, all women, "are appraised and judged like animals at a county fair." They tried to convince women in the crowd that the tyranny of beauty was but one of the many ways that women's bodies were colonized. By announcing beforehand that they would not speak to male reporters (or to any man for that matter), they challenged the sexual division of labor that consigned women reporters to the "soft" stories and male reporters to the "hard" news stories. Newspaper editors who wanted to cover the protest were thus forced to pull their female reporters from the society pages to do so.

The protesters set up a "Freedom Trash Can" and filled it with various "instruments of torture"—high-heeled shoes, bras, girdles, hair curlers, false eyelashes, typing books, and representative copies of *Cosmopolitan, Playboy,* and *Ladies' Home Journal.* They had wanted to burn the contents of the Freedom Trash Can but were prevented from doing so by a city ordinance that prohibited bonfires on the boardwalk. However, word had been leaked to the press that the protest would include a symbolic bra-burning, and, as a consequence, reporters were everywhere. Although they burned no bras that day on the boardwalk, the image of the bra-burning, militant feminist remains part of our popular mythology about the women's liberation movement.

The activists also managed to make their presence felt inside the auditorium during that night's live broadcast of the pageant. Pageant officials must have known that they were in for a long night when early in the evening one protester sprayed Toni Home Permanent Spray (one of the pageant's sponsors) at the mayor's booth. She was charged with disorderly conduct and "emanating a noxious odor," an irony that women's liberationists understandably savored. The more spectacular action occurred later that night. As the outgoing Miss America read her farewell speech, four women unfurled a banner that read, "Women's Liberation," and all sixteen protesters shouted "Freedom for Women," and "No More Miss America" before

"Nothing Distant About It" by Alice Echols, from *The Sixties: From Memory to History,* edited by Dave Farber. Copyright © 1994 by the University of North Carolina Press. Used by permission of the publisher.

security guards could eject them. The television audience heard the commotion and could see it register on Miss America's face as she stumbled through the remainder of her speech. But the program's producer prevented the cameramen from covering the cause of Miss America's consternation. The TV audience did not remain in the dark for long, because Monday's newspapers described the protest in some detail. As the first major demonstration of the fledgling women's liberation movement, it had been designed to make a big splash, and after Monday morning no one could doubt that it had.

In its wit, passion, and irreverence, not to mention its expansive formulation of politics (to include the politics of beauty, no less!), the Miss America protest resembled other sixties demonstrations. Just as women's liberationists used a sheep to make a statement about conventional femininity, so had the Yippies a week earlier lampooned the political process by nominating a pig, Pegasus, for the presidency at the Democratic National Convention. Although Atlantic City witnessed none of the violence that had occurred in Chicago, the protest generated plenty of hostility among the six hundred or so onlookers who gathered on the boardwalk. Judging from their response, this new thing, "women's liberation," was about as popular as the antiwar movement. The protesters were jeered, harassed, and called "commies" and "man-haters." One man suggested that it "would be a lot more useful" if the protesters threw themselves, and not their bras, girdles, and makeup, into the trash can.

Nothing—not even the verbal abuse they encountered on the boardwalk—could diminish the euphoria women's liberationists felt as they started to mobilize around their own, rather than other people's, oppression. Ann Snitow speaks for many when she recalls that in contrast to her involvement in the larger, male-dominated protest Movement, where she had felt sort of "blank and peripheral," women's liberation was like "an ecstasy of discussion." Precisely because it was about one's own life, "there was," she claims, "nothing distant about it." Robin Morgan has contended that the Miss America protest "announced our existence to the world." That is only a slight exaggeration, for as a consequence of the protest, women's liberation achieved the status of a movement both to its participants and to the media; as such, the Miss America demonstration represents an important moment in the history of the sixties.

Although the women's liberation movement only began to take shape toward the end of the decade, it was a paradigmatically sixties movement. It is not just that many early women's liberation activists had prior involvements in other sixties movements, although that was certainly true, as has been ably documented by Sara Evans. And it is not just that, of all the sixties movements, the women's liberation movement alone carried on and extended into the 1970s that decade's political radicalism and rethinking of fundamental social organization. Although that is true as well. Rather, it is also that the larger, male-dominated protest Movement, despite its considerable sexism, provided much of the intellectual foundation and cultural orientation for the women's liberation movement. Indeed, many of the broad themes of the women's liberation movement—especially its concern with revitalizing the democratic process and reformulating "politics" to include the personal— were refined and recast versions of ideas and approaches already present in the New Left and the black freedom movement.

Moreover, like other sixties radicals, women's liberationists were responding at least in part to particular features of the postwar landscape. For instance, both the New Left and the women's liberation movement can be understood as part of a gendered generational revolt against the ultradomesticity of that aberrant decade, the 1950s. The white radicals who participated in these movements were in flight from the nuclear family and the domesticated versions of masculinity and femininity that prevailed in postwar America. Sixties radicals, white and black, were also responding to the hegemonic position of liberalism and its promotion of government expansion both at home and abroad—the welfare/warfare state. Although sixties radicals came to define themselves in opposition to liberalism, their relation to liberalism was nonetheless complicated and ambivalent. They saw in big government not only a way of achieving greater economic and social justice, but also the possibility of an increasingly well-managed society and an ever more remote government.

In this essay I will attempt to evaluate some of the more important features of sixties radicalism by focusing on the specific example of the women's liberation movement. I am motivated by the problematic ways in which "the sixties" has come to be scripted in our culture. If conservative "slash and burn" accounts of the period indict sixties radicals for everything from crime and drug use to single motherhood, they at least heap guilt fairly equally upon antiwar, black civil rights, and feminist activists alike. By contrast, progressive reconstructions, while considerably more positive in their assessments of the period, tend to present the sixties as if women were almost completely outside the world of radical politics. Although my accounting of the sixties is in some respects critical, I nonetheless believe that there was much in sixties radicalism that was original and hopeful, including its challenge to established authority and expertise, its commitment to refashioning democracy and "politics," and its interrogation of such naturalized categories as gender and race.

Women's discontent with their place in America in the sixties was, of course, produced by a broad range of causes. Crucial in reigniting feminist consciousness in the sixties was the unprecedented number of women (especially married white women) being drawn into the paid labor force, as the service sector of the economy expanded and rising consumer aspirations fueled the desire of many families for a second income. As Alice Kessler-Harris has pointed out, "homes and cars, refrigerators and washing machines, telephones and multiple televisions required higher incomes." So did providing a college education for one's children. These new patterns of consumption were made possible in large part through the emergence of the two-income family as wives increasingly "sought to aid their husbands in the quest for the good life." By 1960, 30.5 percent of all wives worked for wages. Women's growing participation in the labor force also reflected larger structural shifts in the U.S. economy. Sara Evans has argued that the "reestablishment of labor force segregation following World War II ironically reserved for women a large proportion of the new jobs created in the fifties due to the fact that the fastest growing sector of the economy was no longer industry but services." Women's increasing labor force participation was facilitated as well by the growing number of women graduating from college and by the introduction of the birth control pill in 1960.

Despite the fact that women's "place" was increasingly in the paid work force (or perhaps because of it), ideas about women's proper role in American society were quite conventional throughout the 1950s and the early 1960s, held there by a resurgent ideology of domesticity—what Betty Friedan coined the "feminine mystique."

But, as Jane De Hart-Mathews has observed, "the bad fit was there: the unfairness of unequal pay for the same work, the low value placed on jobs women performed, the double burden of housework and wage work." By the mid-1960s at least some American women felt that the contradiction between the realities of paid work and higher education on the one hand and the still pervasive ideology of domesticity on the other had become irreconcilable.

Without the presence of other oppositional movements, however, the women's liberation movement may not have developed at all as an organized force for social change. It certainly would have developed along vastly different lines. The climate of protest encouraged women, even those not directly involved in the black movement and the New Left, to question conventional gender arrangements. Moreover, many of the women who helped form the women's liberation movement had been involved as well in the male-dominated Movement. If the larger Movement was typically indifferent, or worse, hostile, to women's liberation, it was nonetheless through their experiences in that Movement that the young and predominantly white and middle-class women who initially formed the women's liberation movement became politicized. The relationship between women's liberation and the larger Movement was at its core paradoxical. If the Movement was a site of sexism it also provided white women a space in which they could develop political skills and self-confidence, a space in which they could violate the injunction against female self-assertion. Most important, it gave them no small part of the intellectual ammunition—the language and the ideas—with which to fight their own oppression.

Sixties radicals struggled to reformulate politics and power. Their struggle confounded many who lived through the sixties as well as those trying to make sense of the period some thirty years later. One of the most striking characteristics of sixties radicals was their ever-expanding opposition to liberalism. Radicals' theoretical disavowal of liberalism developed gradually and in large part in response to liberals' specific defaults—their failure to repudiate the segregationists at the 1964 Democratic National Convention, their lack of vigor in pressing for greater federal intervention in support of civil rights workers, and their readiness (with few exceptions) to support President Lyndon B. Johnson's escalation of the Vietnam War. But initially some radicals had argued that the Movement should acknowledge that liberalism was not monolithic but contained two discernible strands—"corporate" and "humanist" liberalism. For instance, in 1965 Carl Oglesby, an early leader of the Students for a Democratic Society (SDS), contrasted *corporate liberals,* whose identification with the system made them "illiberal liberals," with *humanist liberals,* who he hoped might yet see that "it is this movement with which their own best hopes are most in tune."

By 1967 radicals were no longer making the distinction between humanist and corporate liberals that they once had. This represented an important political shift for early new leftists in particular who once had felt an affinity of sorts with liberalism. Black radicals were the first to decisively reject liberalism, and their move had an enormous impact on white radicals. With the ascendancy of black power many black militants maintained that liberalism was intrinsically paternalistic, and that black liberation required that the struggle be free of white involvement. This was elaborated by white radicals, who soon developed the argument that authentic radicalism involved organizing around one's own oppression rather than becoming involved, as a "liberal" would, in someone else's struggle for freedom. For instance, 1967 Gregory Calvert, another SDS leader, argued that the "student movement has to develop an image of its own revolution . . . instead of believing that you're a revolutionary because you're related to Fidel's struggle, Stokely's struggle, always someone else's struggle." Black radicals were also the first to conclude that nothing short of revolution—certainly not Johnson's Great Society programs and a few pieces of civil rights legislation—could undo racism. As leftist journalist Andrew Kopkind remembered it, the rhetoric of revolution proved impossible for white new leftists to resist. "With black revolution raging in America and world revolution directed against America, it was hardly possible for white radicals to think themselves anything less than revolutionaries." . . .

. . . [S]ixties radicals did (especially over time) appropriate, expand, and recast Marxist categories in an effort to understand the experiences of oppressed and marginalized groups. Thus exponents of what was termed "new working-class theory" claimed that people with technical, clerical, and professional jobs should be seen as constituting a new sector of the working class, better educated than the traditional working class, but working class nonetheless. According to this view, students were not members of the privileged middle class, but rather "trainees" for the new working class. And many women's liberationists (even radical feminists who rejected Marxist theorizing about women's condition) often tried to use Marxist methodology to understand women's oppression. For example, Shulamith Firestone argued that just as the elimination of "economic classes" would require the revolt of the proletariat and their seizure of the means of production, so would the elimination of "sexual classes" require women's revolt and their "seizure of control of reproduction."

If young radicals often assumed an arrogant stance toward those remnants of the Old Left that survived the 1950s, they were by the late 1960s unambiguously contemptuous of liberals. Women's liberationists shared new leftists' and black radicals' rejection of liberalism, and, as a consequence, they often went to great lengths to distinguish themselves from the liberal feminists of the National Organization for Women (NOW). (In fact, their disillusionment with liberalism was more thorough during the early stages of their movement building than had been the case for either new leftists or civil rights activists because they had lived through the earlier betrayals around the Vietnam War and civil rights. Moreover, male radicals' frequent denunciations of women's liberation as "bourgeois" encouraged women's liberationists to distance themselves from NOW.) NOW had been formed in 1966 to push the federal government to enforce the provisions of the 1964 Civil Rights Act outlawing sex discrimination—a paradigmatic liberal agenda focused on public access and the prohibition of employment discrimination. To women's liberation activists, NOW's integrationist, access-oriented approach ignored the racial and class inequities that were the very foundation of the "mainstream" that NOW was dedicated to integrating. In the introduction to the 1970 bestseller, *Sisterhood Is Powerful,* Robin Morgan declared that "NOW is essentially an organization that wants reform [in the] second-class citizenship of women—and this is where it differs drastically from the rest of the Women's Liberation Movement." In *The Dialectic of Sex,* Shulamith Firestone described NOW's political stance as "untenable even in terms of immediate political gains" and deemed it "more a leftover of the old feminism rather than a model of the new." Radical feminist Ti-Grace Atkinson went even further, characterizing many in NOW as only wanting "women to have the same opportunity to be oppressors, too."

Women's liberationists also took issue with liberal feminists' formulation of women's problem as their exclusion from the public sphere. Younger activists argued instead that women's exclusion from public life was inextricable from their subordination in the family and would persist until this larger issue was addressed. For instance, Firestone claimed that the solution to women's oppression was not inclusion in the mainstream, but rather the eradication of the biological family, which was the "tape worm of exploitation."

Of course, younger activists' alienation from NOW was often more than matched by NOW members' disaffection from them. Many liberal feminists were appalled (at least initially) by women's liberationists' politicization of personal life. NOW founder Betty Friedan frequently railed against women's liberationists for waging a "bedroom war" that diverted women from the real struggle of integrating the public sphere.

Women's liberationists believed that they had embarked upon a much more ambitious project—the virtual remaking of the world—and that theirs was the real struggle. Nothing short of radically transforming society was sufficient to deal with what they were discovering; that gender inequality was embedded in everyday life. In 1970 Shulamith Firestone observed that "sex-class is so deep as to be invisible." The pervasiveness of gender inequality and gender's status as a naturalized category demonstrated to women's liberationists the inadequacy of NOW's legislative and judicial remedies and the necessity of thoroughgoing social transformation. Thus, whereas liberal feminists talked of ending sex discrimination, women's liberationists called for nothing less than the destruction of capitalism and patriarchy. As defined by feminists, patriarchy, in contrast to sex discrimination, defied reform. For example, Adrienne Rich contended: "Patriarchy is the power of the fathers: a familial-social, ideological, political system in which men—by force, direct pressure, or through ritual, tradition, law and language, customs etiquette, education, and the division of labor, determine what part women shall or shall not play, and in which the female is subsumed under the male."

Women's liberationists typically indicted capitalism as well. Ellen Willis, for instance, maintained that "the American system consists of two interdependent but distinct parts—the capitalist state, and the patriarchal family." Willis argued that capitalism succeeded in exploiting women as cheap labor and consumers "primarily by taking advantage of women's subordinate position in the family and our historical domination by man."

Central to the revisionary project of the women's liberation movement was the desire to render gender meaningless, to explode it as a significant category. In the movement's view, both masculinity and femininity represented not timeless essences, but rather "patriarchal" constructs. (Of course, even as the movement sought to deconstruct gender, it was, paradoxically, as many have noted, trying to mobilize women precisely on the basis of their gender.) This explains in part the significance abortion rights held for women's liberationists, who believed that until abortion was decriminalized, biology would remain women's destiny, thus foreclosing the possibility of women's self-determination.

Indeed, the women's liberation movement made women's bodies the site of political contestation. The "colonized" status of women's bodies became the focus of much movement activism. (The discourse of colonization originated in Third World national liberation movements but, in an act of First World appropriation, was taken up by black radicals who claimed that African Americans constituted an "internal colony" in the United States.) Radical women trying to persuade the larger Movement of the legitimacy of their cause soon followed suit by deploying the discourse to expose women's subordinate position in relation to men. This appropriation represented an important move and one characteristic of radicalism in the *late* 1960s, that is, the borrowing of conceptual frameworks and discourse from other movements to comprehend the situation of oppressed groups in the United States— with mixed results at best. In fact, women's liberationists challenged not only tyrannical beauty standards, but also violence against women's sexual alienation, the compulsory character of heterosexuality and its organization around male pleasure (inscribed in the privileging of the vaginal over clitoral orgasm), the health hazards associated with the birth control pill, the definition of contraception as women's responsibility, and, of course, women's lack of reproductive control. They also challenged the sexual division of labor in the home, employment discrimination, and the absence of quality child-care facilities. Finally, women's liberationists recognized the power of language to shape culture.

The totalism of their vision would have been difficult to translate into a concrete reform package, even had they been interested in doing so. But electoral politics and the legislative and judicial reforms that engaged the energies of liberal feminists did little to animate most women's liberationists. Like other sixties radicals, they were instead taken with the idea of developing forms that would prefigure the utopian community of the imagined future. Anxious to avoid the "manipulated consent" that they believed characterized American politics, sixties radicals struggled to develop alternatives to hierarchy and centralized decision making. They spoke often of creating "participatory democracy" in an effort to maximize individual participation and equalize power. Their attempts to build a "democracy of individual participation" often confounded outsiders, who found Movement meetings exhausting and tedious affairs. But to those radicals who craved political engagement, "freedom" was, as one radical group enthused, "an endless meeting." According to Gregory Calvert, participatory democracy appealed to the "deep anti-authoritarianism of the new generation in addition to offering them the immediate concretization of the values of openness, honesty, and community in human relationships." Women's liberationists, still smarting from their first-hand discovery that the larger Movement's much-stated commitment to egalitarianism did not apply equally to all, often took extraordinary measures to try to ensure egalitarianism. They employed a variety of measures in an effort to equalize power, including consensus decision making, rotating chairs, and the sharing of both creative and routine movement work.

Fundamental to this "prefigurative politics," as sociologist Wini Breines terms it, was the commitment to develop counterinstitutions that would anticipate the desired society of the future. Staughton Lynd, director of the Mississippi Freedom Schools and a prominent new leftist, likened sixties radicals to the Wobblies (labor radicals of the early twentieth century) in their commitment to building "the new society within the shell of the old." According to two early SDSers, "What we are working for is far more than changes in the structure of society and its institutions or the people who are now making the decisions. . . . The stress should rather be on wrenching people out of the system both physically and spiritually."

Radicals believed that alternative institutions would not only satisfy needs unmet by the present system, but also, perhaps, by dramatizing the failures of the system, radicalize those not served by it but currently outside the Movement. Tom Hayden proposed that radicals "build our own free institutions—community organizations, newspapers, coffeehouses—at points of strain within the system where human needs are denied. These institutions become centers of identity, points of contact, building blocks of a new society from which we confront the system more intensely."

Among the earliest and best known of such efforts were the Mississippi Freedom Democratic party and the accompanying Freedom Schools formed during Freedom Summer of 1964. In the aftermath of that summer's Democratic National Convention, Bob Moses [Parris] of the Student Nonviolent Coordinating Committee (SNCC) even suggested that the Movement abandon its efforts to integrate the Democratic party and try instead to establish its own state government in Mississippi. And as early as 1966 SNCC's Atlanta Project called on blacks to "form our own institutions, credit unions, co-ops, political parties." This came to be the preferred strategy as the sixties progressed and disillusionment with traditional politics grew. Rather than working from within the system, new leftists and black radicals instead formed alternative political parties, media, schools, universities, and assemblies of oppressed and unrepresented people.

Women's liberationists elaborated on this idea, creating an amazing panoply of counterinstitutions. In the years before the 1973 Supreme Court decision decriminalizing abortion, feminists established abortion referral services in most cities of any size. Women's liberationists in Chicago even operated an underground abortion clinic, "Jane," where they performed about one hundred abortions each week. By the mid-1970s most big cities had a low-cost feminist health clinic, a rape crisis center, and a feminist bookstore. In Detroit, after "a long struggle to translate feminism into federalese," two women succeeded in convincing the National Credit Union Administration that feminism was a legitimate "field" from which to draw credit union members. Within three years of its founding in 1973, the Detroit credit union could claim assets of almost one million dollars. Feminists in other cities soon followed suit. Women's liberation activists in Washington, D.C., formed Olivia Records, the first women's record company, which by 1978 was supporting a paid staff of fourteen and producing four records a year. By the mid-1970s there existed in most cities of any size a politicized feminist counterculture, or a "women's community."

The popularity of alternative institutions was that at least in part they seemed to hold out the promise of political effectiveness without co-optation. Writing in 1969, Amiri Baraka (formerly LeRoi Jones), a black nationalist and accomplished poet, maintained, "But you must have the cultural revolution. . . . We cannot fight a war, an actual physical war with the forces of evil just because we are angry. We can begin to build. We must build black institutions . . . all based on a value system that is beneficial to black people." . . .

The move toward building counterinstitutions was part of a larger strategy to develop new societies "within the shell of the old," but this shift sometimes had unintended consequences. While feminist counterinstitutions were originally conceived as part of a culture of resistance, over time they often became more absorbed in sustaining themselves than in confronting male supremacy, especially as their services were duplicated by mainstream businesses. In the early years of the women's liberation movement this alternative feminist culture did provide the sort of "free space" women needed to confront sexism. But as it was further elaborated in the mid-1970s, it ironically often came to promote insularity instead—becoming, as Adrienne Rich has observed, "a place of emigration, an end in itself," where patriarchy was evaded rather than confronted. In practice, feminist communities were small, self-contained subcultures that proved hard to penetrate, especially to newcomers unaccustomed to their norm and conventions. The shift in favor of alternative communities may have sometimes impeded efforts at outreach for the women's liberationists, new leftists, and black radicals who attempted it.

On a related issue, the larger protest Movement's great pessimism about reform—the tendency to interpret every success a defeat resulting in the Movement's further recuperation (what Robin Morgan called "futilitarianism")—may have encouraged a too-global rejection of reform among sixties radicals. For instance, some women's liberation groups actually opposed the Equal Rights Amendment (ERA) when NOW revived it. In September 1970 a New York–based group, The Feminists, denounced the ERA and advised feminists against "squandering invaluable time and energy on it." A delegation of Washington, D.C., women's liberationists invited to appear before the senate subcommittee considering the ERA, testified: "We are aware that the system will try to appease us with their [*sic*] paper offerings. We will not be appeased. Our demands can only be met by a total transformation of society which you cannot legislate, you cannot co-opt, you cannot *control.*" In *The Dialectic of Sex,* Firestone went so far as to dismiss child-care centers as attempts to "buy women off" because they "ease the immediate pressure without asking why the pressure is on *women.*"

Similarly, many SDS leaders opposed the National Conference for New Politics (NCNP), an abortive attempt to form a national progressive organization oriented around electoral politics and to launch an antiwar presidential ticket headed by Martin Luther King Jr. and Benjamin Spock. Immediately following NCNP's first and only convention, in 1967, the SDS paper *New Left Notes* published two front-page articles criticizing NCNP organizers. One writer contended that "people who recognize the political process as perverted will not seek change through the institutions that process has created." The failure of sixties radicals to distinguish between reform and reformism meant that while they defined the issues, they often did little to develop policy initiatives around those issues. Moreover, the preoccupation of women's liberationists with questions of internal democracy (fueled in part by their desire to succeed where the men had failed) sometimes had the effect of focusing attention away from the larger struggle in an effort to create the perfect movement. As feminist activist Frances Chapman points out, women's liberation was "like a generator that got things going, cut out and left it to the larger reform engine which made a lot of mistakes." In eschewing traditional politics rather than entering them skeptically, women's liberationists, like other sixties radicals, may have lost an opportunity to foster critical debate in the larger arena.

If young radicals eschewed the world of conventional politics they nonetheless had a profound impact upon it, especially by redefining what is understood as "political." Although the women's liberation movement popularized the slogan "the personal is political," the idea that there is a political dimension to personal life was first embraced by early SDSers who had encountered it in the writings of C. Wright Mills. Rebelling against a social order whose public and private spheres were highly differentiated, new leftists called for a reintegration of the personal with the political. They reconceptualized apparently personal problems—specifically their alienation from a campus cultural milieu characterized by sororities and fraternities, husband and wife hunting, sports, and careerism, and the powerlessness they felt as college students without a voice in campus governance or curriculum—as political problems. Thus SDS's founding Port Huron Statement of 1962 suggested that for an American New Left to succeed, it would have to "give form to . . . feelings of helplessness and indifference, so that people may see the political, social, and economic sources of their private troubles and organize to change society." Theirs was a far more expansive formulation of politics than what prevailed in the Old Left, even among the more renegade remnants that had survived into the early sixties. Power was conceptualized as relational and by no means reducible to electoral politics.

By expanding political discourse to include personal relations, new leftists unintentionally paved the way for women's liberationists to develop critiques of the family, marriage, and the construction of sexuality. (Of course, nonfeminist critiques of the family and sexual repressiveness were hardly in short supply in the 1950s and 1960s, as evidenced by *Rebel without a Cause, Catcher in the Rye,* and Paul Goodman's *Growing Up Absurd,* to mention but a few.) Women's liberationists developed an understanding of power's capillarylike nature, which in some respects anticipated those being formulated by Michel Foucault and other poststructralists. Power was conceptualized as occupying multiple sites and as lodging everywhere, even in those private places assumed to be the most removed from or impervious to politics—the home and, more particularly, the bedroom.

The belief of sixties radicals that the personal is political also suggested to them its converse—that the political is personal. Young radicals typically felt it was not enough to sign leaflets or participate in a march if one returned to the safety and comfort of a middle-class existence. Politics was supposed to unsettle life and its routines, even more, to transform life. For radicals the challenge was to discover, underneath all the layers of social conditioning, the "real" self unburdened by social expectations and conventions. Thus, SNCC leader Stokely Carmichael advanced the slogan, "Every Negro is a potential black man." Shulamith Firestone and Anne Koedt argued that among the "most exciting things to come out of the women's movement so far is a new daring . . . to tear down old structures and assumptions and let real thought and feeling flow." Life would not be comfortable, but who wanted comfort in the midst of so much deadening complacency? For a great many radicals, the individual became a site of political activism in the sixties. In the black freedom movement the task was very much to discover the black inside the Negro, and in the women's liberation movement it was to unlearn niceness, to challenge the taboo against female self-assertion.

Sixties radicalism proved compelling to many precisely because it promised to transform life. Politics was not about the subordination of self to some larger political cause; instead, it was the path to self-fulfillment. This ultimately was the power of sixties radicalism. As Stanley Aronowitz notes, sixties radicalism was in large measure about "infus[ing] life with a secular spiritual and moral content" and "fill[ing] the quotidian with personal meaning and purpose." But "the personal is political" was one of those ideas whose rhetorical power seemed to sometimes work against or undermine its explication. It could encourage a solipsistic preoccupation with self-transformation. As new leftist Richard Flacks presciently observed in 1965, this kind of politics could lead to "a search for personally satisfying modes of life while abandoning the possibility of helping others to change theirs." Thus the idea that "politics is how you live your life, not who you vote for," as Yippie leader Jerry Rubin put it, could and did lead to a subordination of politics to life-style. If the idea led some to confuse personal liberation with political struggle, it led others to embrace an asceticism that sacrificed personal needs and desires to political imperatives. Some women's liberation activists followed this course, inter-preting the idea that the personal is political to mean that one's personal life should conform to some abstract standard of political correctness. At first this tendency was mitigated by the founders' insistence that there were no personal solutions, only collective solutions, to women's oppression. Over time, however, one's self-presentation, marital status, and sexual preference frequently came to determine one's standing or ranking in the movement. The most notorious example of this involved the New York radical group, The Feminists, who established a quota to limit the number of married women in the group. Policies such as these prompted Barbara Ehrenreich to question "a feminism which talks about universal sisterhood, but is horrified by women who wear spiked heels or call their friends 'girls.' At the same time, what was personally satisfying was sometimes upheld as politically correct. In the end, both the women's liberation movement and the larger protest Movement suffered, as the idea that the personal is political was often interpreted in such a way as to make questions of life-style absolutely central.

The social movements of the sixties signaled the beginning of what was come to be known as "identity politics," the idea that politics is rooted in identity. Although some New Left groups by the late 1960s did come to endorse an orthodox Marxism whereby class was privileged, class was not the pivotal category for these new social movements. (Even those New Left groups that reverted to the "labor metaphysic" lacked meaningful working-class participation.) Rather, race, ethnicity, gender, sexual preference, and youth were the salient categories for most sixties activists. In the women's liberation movement, what was termed "consciousness-raising" was the tool used to develop women's group identity.

As women's liberationists started to organize a movement, they confronted American women who identified unambiguously as women, but who typically had little of what Nancy Cott would call "we-ness," or "some level of identification with 'the group called women.'" Moreover, both the pervasiveness of gender inequality and the cultural understanding of gender as a natural rather than a social construct made it difficult to cultivate a critical consciousness about gender even among women. To engender this sense of sisterhood or "we-ness," women's liberationists developed consciousness-raising, a practice involving "the political reinterpretation of personal life." According to its principal architects, its purpose was to "awaken the latent consciousness that . . . all women have about our oppression." In talking about their personal experiences, it was argued, women would come to understand that what they had believed were personal problems were, in fact, "social problems that must become social issues and fought together rather than with personal solutions."

Reportedly, New York women's liberationist Kathie Sarachild was the person who coined the term *consciousness-raising*. However, the technique originated in other social movements. As Sarachild wrote in 1973, those who promoted consciousness-raising "were applying to women and to ourselves as women's liberation organizers the practice a number of us had learned in the civil rights movement in the South in the early 1960s." There they had seen that the sharing of personal problems, grievances, and aspirations—"telling it like it is"—could be a radicalizing experience. Moreover, for some women's liberationists consciousness-raising was a way to avoid the tendency of some members of the movement to try to fit women within existing (and often Marxist) theoretical paradigms. By circumventing the "experts" on women and going to women themselves, they would be able to not only construct a theory of women's oppression but formulate strategy as well. Thus women's liberationists struggled to find the commonalities in women's experiences in order to generate generalizations about women's oppression.

Consciousness-raising was enormously successful in exposing the insidiousness of sexism and in engendering a sense of identity and solidarity among the largely white, middle-class women who participated in "c-r" groups. By the early 1970s even NOW, whose founder Betty Friedan had initially derided consciousness-raising as so much "navel-gazing," began sponsoring c-r groups. But the effort to transcend the particular was both the strength and the weakness of consciousness-raising. If it encouraged women to locate the common denominators in their lives, it inhibited discussion of women's considerable differences. Despite the particularities of white, middle-class women's experiences, theirs became the basis for feminist theorizing about women's oppression. In a more general sense the identity politics informing consciousness-raising tended to privilege experience in certain problematic ways. It was too often assumed that there existed a kind of core experience, initially articulated as "woman's experience." Black and white radicals (the latter in relation to youth) made a similar move as well. When Stokely Carmichael called on blacks to develop an "ideology which speaks to our blackness," he, like other black nationalists, suggested that there was somehow an essential and authentic "blackness."

With the assertion of difference within the women's movement in the 1980s, the notion that women constitute a unitary category has been problematized. As a consequence, women's experiences have become ever more discretely defined, as in "the black female experience," "the Jewish female experience," or "the Chicana lesbian experience." But, as Audre Lorde has argued, there remains a way in which, even with greater and greater specificity, the particular is never fully captured. Instead, despite the pluralization of the subject within feminism, identities are often still imagined as monolithic. Finally, the very premise of identity politics—that identity is the basis of politics—has sometimes shut down possibilities for communication, as identities are seen as necessarily either conferring or foreclosing critical consciousness. Kobena Mercer, a British film critic, has criticized the rhetorical strategies of "authenticity and authentication" that tend to characterize identity politics. He has observed: "if I preface a point by saying something like, 'as a black gay man, I feel marginalized by your discourse,' it makes a valid point but in such a way that preempts critical dialogue because such a response could be inferred as a criticism not of what I say but of what or who I am. The problem is replicated in the familiar cop-out clause, 'as a middle-class, white, heterosexual male, what can I say?'"

The problem is that the mere assertion of identity becomes in a very real sense irrefutable. Identity is presented as not only stable and fixed, but as also insurmountable. While identity politics gives the oppressed the moral authority to speak (perhaps a dubious ground from which to speak), it can, ironically, absolve those belonging to dominant groups from having to engage in a critical dialogue. In some sense, then, identity politics can unintentionally reinforce Other-ness. Finally, as the antifeminist backlash and the emergence of the New Right should demonstrate, there is nothing inherently progressive about identity. It can be, and has been, mobilized for reactionary as well as for radical purposes. For example, the participation of so many women in the antiabortion movement reveals just how problematic the reduction of politics to identity can be.

Accounts of sixties radicalism usually cite its role in bringing about the dismantling of Jim Crow and disfranchisement, the withdrawal of U.S. troops from Vietnam, and greater gender equality. However, equally important, if less frequently noted, was its challenge to politics as usual. Sixties radicals succeeded both in reformulating politics, even mainstream politics, to include personal life, and in challenging the notion that elites alone have the wisdom and expertise to control the political process. For a moment, people who by virtue of their color, age, and gender were far from the sites of formal power became politically engaged, became agents of change.

Given the internal contradictions and shortcomings of sixties radicalism, the repressiveness of the federal government in the late 1960s and early 1970s, and changing economic conditions in the United States, it is not surprising that the movements built by radicals in the sixties either no longer exist or do so only in attenuated form. Activists in the women's liberation movement, however, helped to bring about a fundamental realignment of gender roles in this country through outrageous protests, tough-minded polemics, and an "ecstasy of discussion." Indeed, those of us who came of age in the days before the resurgence of feminism know that the world today, while hardly a feminist utopia, is nonetheless a far different, and in many respects a far fairer, world than what we confronted in 1967.

Women at Work

BETH BAILEY

In 1975, Arizona senator and 1964 Republican nominee for president Barry Goldwater was asked in a public forum whether he supported the equal rights amendment (ERA) to the Constitution. The ERA, which had been passed by both houses of Congress in 1972, was at the center of an enormous and controversial battle for ratification by the required two-thirds of America's fifty states. According to the newspaper account, Goldwater answered: "I don't think it is needed." It was a politically savvy answer for a conservative politician speaking in the South. Such an amendment could only stir up trouble, many argued, by mandating that men and women be treated identically—and the notion that women, like men, might be subject

---

Excerpts from Beth Bailey, "She 'Can Bring Home the Bacon,'" in Beth Bailey and David Farber, eds., *America in the Seventies* (Lawrence, KS: University Press of Kansas, 2004), 107–126. Copyright © 2004 by the University Press of Kansas. Reprinted by permission of the University Press of Kansas.

to the draft had been a powerful argument during the Vietnam War. Women, according to the position Goldwater was claiming, were already guaranteed equal rights and protections, along with all Americans, under the Constitution. Goldwater, however, did not stop there. "I was for it at one time," he told the audience, "but then I saw the women in Washington who were pushing it, and I said, 'Hell, I don't want to be equal to them.'" The audience laughed and applauded.

The campaign for the ERA failed, expiring in 1982 (after an extension) and falling three states short of ratification. But even as the ERA stalled in the face of organized opposition and grassroots resistance, opportunities for women in American society were growing almost exponentially. The calls for revolution had begun in the 1960s, and much of the legal and political groundwork for change had been laid during that era. But it was during the 1970s that Americans confronted what was arguably a revolution in gender roles. For as women's lives changed—whether by choice or simply as a result of the larger social forces that were transforming the nation—men's lives changed, too. And it was not easy. Looking back to the 1970s, it is striking how very hard the struggles over change were, how angry and ugly and confused the public culture was, as Americans debated the transformation of American life and of American lives "from bedroom to boardroom," as the saying went, and just about every place else. . . .

In many ways, the transformations of the 1970s appear to be the triumph of the liberal wing of the women's movement, which had worked hard since the early 1960s to secure political and legislative equality for women. In 1973, *Roe v. Wade* guaranteed women's right to choose abortion, and as of 1972, the unmarried could no longer be denied access to birth control. In 1975, new legislation ended practices that made it impossible for a married woman to obtain a credit card or a loan without her husband's written permission. Title IX of the 1972 Education Act amendments prohibited discrimination by sex in any program receiving federal aid, thus guaranteeing funding for women's athletics in high schools and colleges. Girls' participation in high school athletics increased almost fivefold by the end of the decade. And during the 1970s, women flooded the workplace. Some were drawn by new opportunities: the *U.S. News and World Report* article "The American Woman: On the Move—But Where?" noted that the percentage of female law students had risen from 4 percent in 1960 to 19 percent in 1974, gains similar to those made in medicine.

However, larger structural forces also were critically important in changing the landscape of gender in America. Seventies-era deindustrialization meant the loss of well-paid blue-collar jobs, most of them held by men. The vast majority of new jobs created in the service sector paid less than the jobs they replaced, and by 1976, according to one estimate, only 40 percent of the nation's jobs paid enough to support a family. The energy crisis that began in 1973 sent oil prices skyrocketing 350 percent, and as inflation topped 11 percent in 1974, many families were struggling to make ends meet. Women's earnings became critical. The influx of women into the job market was not a new trend, for the percentage of wives and mothers working outside the home had been growing throughout the past two decades. However, the economic crisis of the 1970s—along with better job opportunities for women—was a powerful catalyst for change. In 1970, 30 percent of women with children under six years of age held paid jobs. That total jumped to 43 percent by 1976 and then to 50 percent by

1985. Many women also found themselves in the paid labor force because of changes in family circumstances, as the divorce rate doubled between 1966 and 1976.

The importance of the economy, as opposed to ideology, in changing gender roles complicated matters. If women's liberation demanded equality in the workplace, did that mean that women who held jobs were "women's libbers"? If a great many women who held relatively conservative views about gender roles nonetheless worked outside the home, where did they fit in the angry debates about women's proper roles? In a special report on women in 1975, *U.S. News and World Report* heralded the "millions of unreconstructed housewives" who rejected "women's lib" and instead signed up for "full-time duty as chauffeurs, cooks, cleaning ladies, repair specialists, nurses, laundresses, baby-sitters and counselors—all for their own families" while at the same time noting that several million of these "career homemakers" were employed full or part time outside the home and that many found their jobs a "welcome change" from household duties. In such a complicated landscape, Americans sought ways to make sense of the changes taking place in men's and women's lives.

The women's movement provided one arena for discussion. But during the 1970s, feminists had no easy or clear answers. The movement was confronting its own divisions, and its most radical statements and occasionally rancorous exchanges were eagerly reported in the media, sometimes to discredit the movement, and sometimes simply because they were sensational. Thus, the women's movement influenced the ways Americans understood gender in this period, but its positions were not coherent enough to offer a firm foundation to sympathizers and were various enough to provide a multiplicity of targets for opponents. . . .

Throughout most of the decade, a variety of competing frameworks for understanding gender circulated in the public sphere, sometimes claimed by one group or another, sometimes highly politicized and strategic, sometimes vaguely coloring the oceans of ink spilled on the topic. Although discussions ranged widely, struggles over gender during this era were most commonly framed around the notion of liberation or around the critical question of difference: are men and women essentially different or essentially the same? And, significantly and somewhat surprisingly, changes in gender roles were negotiated and reconciled in the American consumer marketplace as much as in the realm of politics or of ideas. . . .

In the grand tradition of Sixties protest, the women's liberation movement had its symbolic beginning in a media-savvy and slightly wacky protest organized by very serious activists. On September 7, 1968, members of New York Radical Women gathered on the boardwalk in Atlantic City to protest the Miss America Pageant, which, they argued, perpetuated "an image that has oppressed women." Carrying banners proclaiming women's liberation, they crowned a sheep Miss America (remember, Yippies had nominated a pig for president in protests at the Democratic National Convention in Chicago the previous month). They distributed a pamphlet protesting the fact that "women in our society find themselves forced daily to compete for male approval, enslaved by ludicrous 'beauty' standards we ourselves are conditioned to take seriously." And they threw "instruments of torture"—hair curlers, high heels, girdles, bras, copies of magazines such as *Playboy* and *Cosmopolitan*— into a "Freedom Trashcan." The protesters had hoped to burn the contents but decided not to run the risk of setting fire to the wooden boardwalk. Robin Morgan, one of the organizers, told a reporter that the mayor of Atlantic City had expressed concern about fire safety: "We told him we wouldn't do anything dangerous—just a symbolic bra burning." (For context, think draft-card burning.) No bras were burned that day—or girdles, or magazines, or false eyelashes. But Morgan's statement would plague the women's movement for more than a decade.

On August 26, 1970, *ABC Evening News* concluded its coverage of Women's Strike for Equality, which was at that point the largest demonstration in American history for women's rights, with a comment from West Virginia senator Jennings Randolph. Senator Randolph dismissed the women's movement as "a small band of bra-less bubbleheads," and ABC News closed the segment with that phrase projected on the screen beside anchorman Howard K. Smith. In 1972, Amitai Etzioni, professor of sociology and director of the Center for Policy Research at Columbia University, published a "Test for Female Liberationists" in the *New York Times Magazine*." Are you inclined to believe that bra-burners are the most effective flag-carriers of a major social political revolutionary movement but that those who keep theirs on, while marching, despoil the image of American womanhood?" read question 5. Question 6 read, "Is believing that there are more important issues—Vietnam, pollution, crime, and the oppression of blacks—than who leaves what hankies where, a true sign of male pigheadedness?" As feminists Kate Swift and Casey Miller noted in a *New York Times Magazine* article later that year, "The word 'liberation' itself, when applied to women, means something less than when used of other groups of people."

How was women's liberation defined in American public culture during the 1970s? The original meanings of the term survived, as is evident in Etzioni's question 6 above. Women's liberation sought to free women from oppression. Many of the young women who helped initiate the women's liberation movement had begun their journey in the civil rights movement or the New Left, seeking social justice for African Americans or for the poor and dispossessed, and had gradually come to recognize that women, too, were an oppressed class within American society. But "oppression" was complicated territory; it invited comparisons. How could the sorts of oppressions claimed by women (symbolized in Etzioni's question by the issue of housework, reduced to the slightly ridiculous, "who leaves what hankies where") compare with the oppression of black people in America?

Opponents of women's liberation tended to see oppression as all-or-nothing: if women, as a group, were not so oppressed as black Americans, as a group, then claims of oppression were misplaced at best and ludicrous at worst. This position did not rule out the oppression of women altogether. Women of color might be oppressed because of their race; poor women might be oppressed because of their class. But women per se were not oppressed. This tendency to marginalize race and class (shared by parts of the women's movement) was further complicated by a tendency to treat "women" interchangeably with "married middle-class women with children." How could American women, supported comfortably by their husbands and able to stay home and care for their children and to gather with friends to drink coffee in the morning, claim to be oppressed? Compared with whom? Even allowing for the millions of women who did not fit this description, it was a significant sleight of hand. If oppression was measured primarily in terms of material comfort, then issues of choice, autonomy, and human dignity became largely irrelevant. With such self-defined parameters, skeptics found it east to reduce many of the less tangible claims of the women's liberation movement to what they saw as parody. . . .

[A] would-be parodist, writing in *Harper's* magazine in 1976, complained that the women's movement was putting satirists and parodists out of business by introducing ludicrous claims, such as the feminists' new issue of sexual harassment "or, as some of us would call it, flirting." Most women, she claimed, given a petition on "sex in the office," would "put a check next to 'not enough.'" But the author's larger target was the twinned notion of liberation and oppression. Unable to resist the satirical tone, she scoffed, "The feminists are to be congratulated for having rooted out still another area of injustice." Sexual harassment was a false issue, she concluded, not likely ever to make the evening news, but it was still a "graphic illustration of what's wrong with much of feminism":

> "Women's liberation," ironically, exists on its ability to persuade its adherents that, despite appearances, they are miserable and weak. With jesuitical ingenuity, they go about convincing white, middle-class, college-educated women that society has done them wrong, like the snake-oil salesmen whose suggestible listeners began to feel all the symptoms of sciatica, dropsy, and the botts.This way of thinking, of course, is not without appeal. Persons whose affluence and civility ensure they will never be beaten as punishment may find flagellation an interesting vice.

The author obviously was not prescient—sexual harassment has claimed a great deal of time on the evening news, in the nation's courts, and in congressional hearings over the past few decades. However, she was laying one more brick in the wall of arguments about comparative oppression and the meaning of liberation. The truly oppressed risked beatings. Women risked . . . flirting?

The network news programs, with tens of millions of viewers, also found ample opportunity to compare women's claims of oppression with "real" oppression. On ABC, anchor Howard K. Smith contrasted American women with "Indians and Negroes," who had been "genuinely mistreated." NBC's coverage of the 1970 Women's Strike for Equality cut from a black woman singing, "And before I'll be a slave, I'll be buried in my grave . . . Yes, goodbye slavery, hello freedom," to footage of well-dressed white women, lounging in the park, eating ice cream as they listened. And CBS concluded its three-part series on women's liberation that year: "So far, the women's rights movement has had one fundamental problem; not so much to persuade men, but to convince the majority of American women that there is something basically wrong with their position in life."

In the early 1970s, surprisingly, women's liberation tended to receive its most generous hearing (in the mainstream media) in traditional women's magazines such as *Redbook, Good Housekeeping,* and *Ladies' Home Journal.* (In July 1976, the month of America's bicentennial, thirty-five women's magazines produced special issues on the ERA.) Earlier in the decade, the editors of *Redbook* launched a series of articles on women's liberation, describing it as an issue that "matters very much to all of us." In the heading to each of the substantial articles, the editors stated straightforwardly that *Redbook* believed "every human being should have the right and the opportunity to make her own or his own choices in every area of life." They continued, "This seems to be a very simple and obvious point of view. But, of course, it is not, and it may not ever be a popular one. Yet we do not see how, in a free nation, freedom can be defined otherwise."

In several of the articles, *Redbook* confronted the tricky question of oppression and liberation for an audience made up largely of homemakers. The first article was an eight-page interview with feminist Gloria Steinem, who made an eloquent case for the women's movement. When asked whether she really believed women were exploited, she responded with statistics about how many hours per week the American housewife worked (ninety-nine and six-tenths, she said). When asked "what does the Movement have to say to those women who insist—as so many do—that they like being wives and mothers and are perfectly happy in these roles?" Steinem replied that the point of the movement was choice: all individuals, men and women, should be able to choose how to live their lives. With inset photographs and quotes from women such as Susan B. Anthony and Eleanor Roosevelt, the article gave the women's movement a full, respectful, and supportive hearing.

For the second installment, published in February 1972, *Redbook* sent writer Vivian Cadden to travel the nation and ask women what they thought about women's liberation and their own lives. The reporter's conclusions were grim, given *Redbook*'s own position: "Except in the larger cities and on the campuses, liberation does not yet seem to be an aspiration of young women."

Nonetheless, the complex picture of women's fears and desires offered in this article sheds light on the difficulty of framing a movement for women's rights around a framework of oppression and "liberation." A thirty-something-year-old farm wife in Indiana was bemused:

> Women's Liberation? I just laugh when I hear them talk about it. Today's women have all the freedom they please to come and go. Husbands have been brainwashed into letting women do anything. I suppose it's the economic thing—women having to go to work to help make ends meet. But it's not good for the family. I think the trouble with these women who complain about their lives is that they're disorganized. With a washer and a dryer, I don't see how any woman can get behind.

"I *like* what I'm doing," said one young housewife. "If I really wanted to go back to work, my husband would let me," said another. And another: "I don't want to go out and do what my husband is doing."

For many of the women Cadden interviewed, "women's lib" really meant going out to work. That "liberation," she noted, was not so appealing "to the wives of truck drivers and farmers and salesmen and auto workers and struggling small businessmen and beginning lawyers." Such women told her that "[n]o woman in her right mind who didn't have to" would trade her life of homemaking, mothering, gardening, the PTA, community politics, and bridge for a routine office job or worse. "For these women," Cadden explained, "cooking and marketing and child rearing are pleasant jobs"—much more pleasant than what they saw as their alternatives in paid employment. Cadden acknowledged that low-level, routine jobs might not seem like "liberation," but she suggested that women were perhaps steered from an early age toward a narrow range of possibilities, that the weight of sexism and discrimination in American society narrowed their own sense of possibility as well as their practical options. At the same time, she conceded, most of these women did not see the problem as sex discrimination or oppression. "By comparison to their husbands' work," she wrote, these women saw their work as "not a bit menial and not very hard."

If housewives in the heartland thought the term "liberation" was shorthand for working outside the home, it might seem that women already in the paid workforce would be more enthusiastic about its possibilities. Here, though, the slippery set of meanings attached to liberation complicated matters. Most of the employed women Cadden interviewed believed in equal pay for women, and many believed in equal job opportunities. But for them, women's liberation carried other connotations and threatened other sorts of loss. "I don't think men and women ought to be the same," explained a nineteen-year-old woman who worked in an insurance company office. A twenty-four-year-old factory worker at a General Electric plant in Warren, Ohio, scoffed: "This whole Women's Liberation thing is a crock of you-know-what. . . . I suppose you're going to start opening car doors for them. Next thing you know it'll be my turn to . . . pick him up on Saturday night. Before you know it, it'll be my turn to pay." Liberation, it seemed, meant different things to different people.

Liberation's most complicated association, and one scarcely touched in the *Redbook* series, was with sex, and it was in the realm of sex that notions of liberation were most confused and contradictory. During the 1970s, some women sought liberation from the oppressions of sex. "A large part of our oppressions stem from the sexual exploitation of our bodies," asserted a women's liberation article in a midwestern underground paper in 1970. "Women are viewed as objects. It is difficult for a woman to walk down the street without being weighed, measured, and judged.". . .

But some women also found another form of oppression in the American sexual landscape. If, as most believed, a woman's future status and material well-being depended on marriage to a successful man, she was in a difficult position. She must be sexually alluring enough to attract a man (hence the Miss America protest rejected "ludicrous beauty standards") while maintaining her marriage-ability through a "good reputation." Consider the terms "ruined" and "spoiled." Some women—most of them young—sought liberation from a system that equated a woman's value with her sexual virtue. And, finally, some sought liberation in sex itself, whether with men or with other women: sex on their own terms, sex for pleasure, sex as a way to explore previously forbidden experiences. Liberation was not always just an escape from oppression; sometimes it was an affirmative embrace of new freedoms.

Some of the most difficult struggles within the women's movement came over issues of sex and sexuality, and it was in the vexed relation of sex to liberation that many skeptics found their best targets. Throughout the 1970s, in American public life, women's liberation was frequently conflated with the sexual revolution. "Are you liberated?" did not mean "Do you believe that an individual should have the freedom to choose his or her own path?" It did not mean "Do you work outside the home?" It meant "Do you have sex?"

Sex sells, of course, and titillating images of bra-less women and sexual freedom made for livelier stories than statistics about women's wages and the lack of affordable childcare. The mainstream media—and often for reasons no more Machiavellian than a desire to attract viewers or readers—often treated women's liberation and sexual freedom interchangeably. But opponents of women's liberation also purposely conflated women's liberation with the sexual revolution to brand the women's movement as radical, immoral, and antifamily. A woman attending an anti-ERA rally at a Palm Beach, Florida, movie theater in 1977 asked Phyllis Schlafly, the wife and mother (and attorney and prominent conservative activist) who spearheaded the campaign against the amendment, "Wouldn't you say that the majority of these so-called females who are for ERA are AC-DC or lesbians who are naturally very loud, very vociferous, very wealthy? I mean, they are backed by the media." Her voice trailed off, "And unisex." As the *New York Times Magazine* correspondent who covered the rally noted, Schlafly found the question embarrassing, but only because it was too bald and incoherent a statement of themes her movement had been using in its quest to stop ratification of the ERA.

The conflation of the women's liberation movement with the sexual revolution, however, reached beyond the ranks of avowed antifeminists. Many who were somewhat sympathetic to the claims of the women's movement found the sexual revolution troubling, and the conflation of movements made it easier for them to draw a line between "reasonable" demands for decent wages and (as they saw it) the sex-obliterating role reversals and illegitimate intrusions into the "private" spheres of home, marriage, and the family demanded by "radical" women's libbers. . . .

For many Americans, the crux of the problem was that liberation freed women to compete with men and, in so doing, upset what they believed was the proper relationship between the sexes. Discussions about liberation, pro and con, were usually focused on women and their changing roles. But as the decade wore on, people were increasingly concerned not only about women but about women, men, and the relationship between the sexes. In these debates, competition was a key issue and not only in the bedroom. In 1973, Americans witnessed a tennis match between the aging star Bobby Riggs (then fifty-five years old and with a Wimbledon victory in 1939) and women's champion Billie Jean King (twenty-nine years old). The event drew more than fifty million television viewers to what was billed as the "Battle of the Sexes." King won. Feeding the flames, *Science Digest* explored the "facts" in "Biological Superiority: Female or Male." (The proponent of male superiority mused, "If a woman claims superiority on a genetic basis, must she exclude genetic females with characteristics of male behavior?")

When *Ladies' Home Journal* asked a male and a female author to respond to the question "Do Strong Women Frighten Men?" both answered with a qualified "yes." "As more and more women enter the workforce," the female author noted, "men are finding a frightening new challenge to their jobs and futures: a whole new crop of ambitious and serious people—women. Added to this new competition, men now have to wrestle with their conditioned feelings that the people they're forced to compete with are, well, inferior." . . . Thus, *Readers Digest* offered advice for the working woman on "How to Support Your Husband's Ego" (she should avoid making him feel "inadequate by flaunting her own contribution to the family income"), and a host of articles explored the phenomenon of the woman boss, giving advice on how to handle the situation when a woman "wears-the-pants-in-your-office" or "when the 'man at the top' is a woman." *Time*'s contribution to the genre was a portrait of "business bitches." Top female executives, *Time* explained, had "shelved their femininity" in "blind striving" for success; the most successful of them managed to reclaim femininity in midcareer and become more "open and effective," while those who continued "to act as much like men as possible" became "closed, bitter, defensive, and unhappy."

Emotionally charged debates over the changing relationships between men and women usually hinged on the vexed question of difference. Were men and women fundamentally and essentially different from one another? Or were they fundamentally the same? Difference was not just the fallback of traditionalist opponents of women's lib; many feminists embraced an essentialist vision during the 1970s, rejecting what they called patriarchal values for a more body-centered, noncompetitive, nurturing "women's culture." But in much of mainstream American thought, "difference" was the final answer to the challenge of feminists, the line drawn against the rapidly changing gender roles symbolized by the ERA. House Judiciary Committee chairman Emmanuel Celler, who had buried the ERA in committee for twenty-three years until Representative Martha Griffiths engineered a discharge petition supported by some of the most influential members of the House, fumed when confronted with the Congressionally passed ERA: "There is no equality except in a cemetery. There are differences in physical structure and biological function. . . . There is more difference between a male and a female than between a horse chestnut and a chestnut horse."

It was not a new concept. One major strand of the women's movement historically had strongly supported various forms of protective legislation for women—all based on women's biological and physical differences from men and the responsibilities of motherhood that were closely associated with those differences. Many opponents of the ERA feared that the amendment would overturn protective legislation that limited the physically strenuous tasks women could be required to do in the workplace and that defined support of the family as the man's responsibility and guaranteed (at least legally) alimony and child support in the case of divorce. Senator Sam Ervin, a wily opponent of the ERA, crafted a different version of the amendment that centered on the notion of the difference of the sexes. "Equality of rights under the law shall not be denied or abridged by the United States or by any state on account of sex," the amendment began, as did the original, but continued, "This article shall not impair, however, the validity of any law of the United States or any state which exempts women from compulsory military service or which is reasonably designed to promote the health, safety, privacy, education or economic welfare of women, or to enable them to perform their duties as homemakers or mothers." The second half of the amendment, in effect, nullified the first.

Difference was a complicated concept, especially for a society that had, until recently, allowed racial segregation predicated on the notion of difference embodied in "separate but equal." Opponents of the women's movement, therefore, had to square the assertion of difference with some understanding of equality. Reverend Billy Graham, the nation's most influential clergyman, offered one of the most eloquent arguments to that end in a *Ladies' Home Journal* article, "Jesus and the Liberated Woman." He portrayed mid-twentieth-century American gender roles as God-given and timeless, but his logic held outside the theological framework. Resuscitating an old argument, Graham and others like him attempted to reorient the debate. Men and women have different roles in society and in the family, but those roles are complementary. Abstract notions of equality are not the issue, for each role is dependent on the other, the survival of the family and of society itself dependent on both. To the skeptic, it seemed that men were allotted all the real power in society and beyond (Graham did not pull his punches, advising women to subordinate themselves to their husbands). But for many, the notion of complementary roles was an excellent answer.

It was an answer, however, that left an opening. In 1970s America, men and women did not occupy separate spheres. In the scheme of complementary roles, where did a woman fit if she were not a wife or mother? Where did the woman fit who worked outside the home? What about the woman who was her own sole support or the sole support of her family? Once again, the economic transformations of the 1970s made such issues more pressing. The framework of oppression had allowed a loophole for economic issues: most who scoffed at calls for liberation were willing to accept calls for equal pay for equal work. But the notion of complementary roles had no such loophole. What about those who, by choice or necessity, did not fit easily into such a predefined notion of women's sphere?

In the women's movement and its opposition alike, during the 1970s, notions of women as a class (whether an oppressed class or as males' complementary sex) confronted the old notions of American individualism. As *Redbook* asserted from the beginning of its pro-ERA campaign, "every human being should have the right and the opportunity to make her own or his own choices in every area of life." *Redbook*'s big push for the ERA, in the bicentennial month of July 1976, focused squarely on the issue of individual choice. "It is the individual," argued *Redbook,* "under Federal law, who will determine whether to play football, work a graveyard shift or join the Marines."

Although the debate over gender roles was largely waged in the language of liberation and oppression or of difference and competition, another framework would become dominant by the end of the decade. Magazines that had previously trotted out scores of experts to demonstrate the fundamental differences between men and women began offering expert condemnations of "sex roles." It was a short step from individual choice to individual difference and from there to a suspicion of gender roles entirely. "Androgyny vs. the Tight Little Lives of FLUFFY WOMEN AND CHESTY MEN," offered the widely read magazine *Psychology Today.* "Learning to Be a Boy, a Girl, or a Person," contributed *PTA Magazine.* Over and over, throughout America's public culture, the deadening effects of sex roles were condemned. "We need a new standard of psychological health for the sexes," wrote a Stanford professor in *Psychology Today,* "one that removes the burden of stereotype and allows people to feel free to express the best traits of men and women." What of the stereotypes that have created "agony for the countless 'sissy' boys and 'tomboy' girls[?]" asked a *Mademoiselle* columnist, advocating a society that "tolerated, even prized, individual variety over the dubious intellectual and social convenience of categories." And even Dr. Spock ventured the opinion that all people have a mixture of male and female identities.

In 1974, *New York Times Magazine* published, without editorial comment, the new guidelines distributed to all eight thousand authors and to editorial staff at the McGraw-Hill Book Company. Going well beyond suggestions for gender-neutral language, the lengthy guidelines began, "Men and women should be treated primarily as people, and not primarily as members of opposite sexes. Their shared humanity and common attributes should be stressed, not their gender difference." The memo reiterated, a few hundred words later, that both men and women should be "represented as whole human beings with *human* strengths and weaknesses, not masculine or feminine ones."

The new focus on common humanity finessed some of the tensions associated with gender oppression and liberation, for in this framework it was not women who needed liberation from men but men and women who needed liberation from the stifling stereotypes and confining sex roles that thwarted their true human potentials. Difference here was individual, falling along a continuum of masculine and feminine traits. And choice remained central. As the McGraw-Hill memo emphasized,

> Though many women will continue to choose traditional occupations such as homemaker or secretary, women should not be typecast in these roles. . . . Teaching materials should not assume or imply that most women are wives who are also full-time mothers, but should instead emphasize the fact that women have choices about their marital status, just as men do: that some women choose to stay permanently single and some are in no hurry to marry; that some women marry but do not have children, while others marry, have children, and continue to work outside the home.

(The memo also pointed out that statements such as "Jim Weiss allows his wife to work part-time" should be avoided, replaced with "Judy Weiss works part-time.") The issue of language—"firefighter" versus "fireman," for example—was one of the issues most parodied by those who found women's claims of oppression ridiculous and their proposed solutions more so. However, in the context of common humanity, these claims had weight. McGraw-Hill was a major educational publisher, and this memo signaled a transformation. The language of common humanity, the emphasis on avoiding gender-role stereotypes, was becoming a central part of America's public culture. And this new framework, encompassing and surpassing the frameworks of liberation and of difference, offered a fairly revolutionary path to the future.

The turmoil over gender was not put to rest in the 1970s, though women's role and power in American society continued to expand throughout the decade and beyond. What that meant, however, remained uncertain, and people relied on complicated and often incoherent combinations of these various frameworks—liberation and oppression, competition and difference, and common humanity—to make sense of changes that came rapidly and often without being sought.

While tensions remained high in the political realm and in the private lives of American men and women, those who managed the American consumer marketplace tried to avoid or, at the very least, negotiate the troubled ground. Struggles over changing gender roles threatened to divide and disrupt the mass market for consumer goods. In a 1970 article on advertising and women, *Time* described "liberationists" as embracing "oddball causes—from ban-the-bras to communal child rearing" but noted nonetheless that many (implicitly non-oddball) women were also unhappy with advertising. "Though nearly one-half of American women hold jobs," noted *Time,* "they are still depicted in many ads as scatterbrained homebodies, barely able to cope with piles of soiled laundry, dirty sinks and other mundane minutiae." Surveys by *Redbook* and *Good Housekeeping* also found high levels of dissatisfaction. But in such a contested atmosphere, how could companies appeal to the working woman? How could they avoid alienating the traditionalists who still saw themselves as homemakers despite having full-time jobs, while appealing to the liberationists who were perhaps more likely to hold well-paid, higher-status positions, and still manage the anxieties about gender roles that seemed to pervade American society?

Advertisers purposely set out to negotiate the complexities of the new gender relations and the new sex roles. Marketing research focused on women, making discoveries such as "Working Women No Monolith" (*Advertising Age,* 1975), and "New Era Women Need Fragrance to Define Their Roles" (*Product Marketing,* 1977). Advertisers and their clients were no more progressive than any other sector of American society, but they had a major stake in figuring out how to manage changing gender roles. Their task, as they were increasingly aware, was to avoid sexism and the portrayal of women as idiots while assuaging or at least not increasing the fears about changing gender roles that remained widespread even among many women in the workplace. Advertisers had to figure out how, for the sake of profit, to negotiate the fact that stagflation and desire for liberation had led women by different paths to a similar consumer position: the working woman. As Franchellie Cadwell, president of the Cadwell David advertising agency, explained in 1970, as she was building her agency's reputation on the notion that "the lady of the house is dead," replaced by a "new woman" (who had neither "the mentality of a six-year-old" nor "acute brain damage") to whom advertisers must learn to appeal: "This campaign we've got going is strictly a business thing. We've got the best interests of business at heart."

In their attempts to have it all, to belay anxieties about competition between men and women, and to portray women as both competent and liberated working women and competent and traditionalist homemakers, the advertising industry invented the superwoman. Her apotheosis came in the long-running Enjoli commercial, created for Charles of the Ritz in the late 1970s by the agency Advertising to Women. "I can bring home the bacon, fry it up in a pan, and never, ever, let him forget he's a man," sang the Enjoli woman (remember, "New Era Women Need Fragrance to Define Their Roles").

The Enjoli woman has survived, in American public culture, as a symbol of the 1980s superwoman. But the Enjoli woman was not a product of the 1980s; she was, instead, the best attempt of American advertising to manage the gender anxieties of the 1970s. As Americans struggled to make sense of the rapidly changing roles brought about by the complex combination of feminist activism and economic necessity, American advertising agencies and their clients in the business world had begun to portray a new image of the American woman—the superwoman. She was created from no particular ideological commitment; her all-encompassing role was simply a ploy to manage and neutralize the divisive debates over gender—in order to sell freeze-dried coffee, dishwasher detergent, and perfume. American advertisers, of course, did not create the phenomenon. However, as an industry with little ideological investment in women's equality or social change, American advertising nevertheless played a huge role in *normalizing* for the American public a world in which women can—and do—do it all.

◆ *F U R T H E R   R E A D I N G*

Banner, Lois. *Women in Modern America* (1984).
Bradley, Patricia. *Mass Media and the Shaping of American Feminism, 1963–1975* (2003).
Breines, Wini. *The Trouble Between Us: An Uneasy History of White and Black Women in the Feminist Movement* (2006).
———. *Young, White, and Miserable: Growing Up Female in the Fifties* (1992).
Chafe, William. *Women and Equality* (1977).
Coontz, Stephanie. *The Way We Never Were: American Families and the Nostalgia Trap* (1993).
Costain, Anne N. *Inviting Women's Rebellion* (1992).
Critchlow, Donald T. *Intended Consequences: Birth Control, Abortion, and the Federal Government in Modern America* (1999).
———. *Phyllis Schlafly and Grassroots Conservatism: A Woman's Crusade* (2005).
Cruikshank, Margaret. *The Gay and Lesbian Liberation Movement* (1992).
De Hart-Mathews, Jane, and Donald Mathews. *The Equal Rights Amendment and the Politics of Cultural Conflict* (1988).
Emilio, John. *Sexual Politics, Sexual Communities: The Making of a Homosexual Minority in the United States, 1940–1970* (1983).
———, and Estelle B. Freedman. *Intimate Matters: A History of Sexuality in America* (1988).
Evans, Sarah M. *Tidal Wave: How Women Changed America at Century's End* (2003).
Douglas, Susan J. *Where the Girls Are: Growing Up Female with the Mass Media* (1994).
Duggan, Lisa, and Nan D. Hunter. *Sex Wars: Sexual Dissent and Political Culture* (1995).
Echols, Alice. *Daring to Be Bad: Radical Feminism in America, 1967–1975* (1989).
Ehrenreich, Barbara. *The Hearts of Men* (1983).
Evans, Sara. *Personal Politics: The Roots of Women's Liberation in the Civil Rights Movement and the New Left* (1979).
Farrell, Amy Erdman. *Yours in Sisterhood:* Ms. *Magazine and the Promise of Popular Feminism* (1998).
Ferree, Myra, and Beth Hess. *Controversy and Coalition: The New Feminist Movement,* 2nd ed. (1994).
Fox-Genovese, Elizabeth. *Feminism Is Not the Story of My Life* (1996).
Freeman, Jo. *The Politics of Women's Liberation* (1975).
———, ed. *Social Movements of the Sixties and Seventies* (1983).
Friedan, Betty. *The Feminine Mystique* (1963).
———. *It Changed My Life: Writings on the Women's Movement* (1976).
Ginsberg, Faye. *Contested Lives: The Abortion Debate in an American Community* (1989).
Harrison, Cynthia. *On Account of Sex: The Politics of Women's Issues, 1945–1968* (1988).
Hoff-Wilson, Joan. *Rites of Passage: The Past and Future of the ERA* (1986).
Hooks, Bell. *Ain't I a Woman? Black Women and Feminism* (1981).
Horowitz, Daniel. *Betty Friedan and the Making of "The Feminine Mystique"* (1998).
Jacoby, Kerry N. *Souls, Bodies, Spirits: The Drive to Abolish Abortion Since 1973* (1998).
Jeansonne, Glen. *Women of the Far Right: The Mothers' Movement and World War II* (1996).
Joseph, Gloria, and Jill Lewis. *Common Differences: Conflicts in Black and White Feminist Perspectives* (1981).
Kessler-Harris, Alice. *In Pursuit of Equity: Women, Men, and the Quest for Economic Citizenship in 20th-Century America* (2001).
Klatch, Rebecca. *Women of the New Right* (1987).
Koedt, Anne, Ellen Levine, and Anita Rapone, eds. *Radical Feminism* (1973).
Luker, Kristin. *Abortion and the Politics of Motherhood* (1984).
May, Elaine Tyler. *Homeward Bound: American Families in the Cold War Era* (1988).
Meyerowitz, Joanne, ed. *Not June Cleaver: Women and Gender in Postwar America* (1994).

Mintz, Steven, and Susan Kellogg. *Domestic Revolutions: A Social History of American Family Life* (1988).

Mohr, James. *Abortion in America* (1980).

Morgan, Robin, ed. *Sisterhood Is Powerful* (1970).

Nicholson, Linda, ed. *The Second Wave: A Reader in Feminist Theory* (1997).

Rupp, Leila J., and Verta Taylor. *Survival in the Doldrums: The American Women's Rights Movement, 1945 to the 1960s* (1987).

Snitow, Ann, Christine Stansell, and Sharon Thompson, eds. *Powers of Desire: The Politics of Sexuality* (1983).

Sommers, Christina Hoff. *Who Stole Feminism? How Women Have Betrayed Women* (1994).

Umansky, Lauri. *Motherhood Reconceived: Feminism and the Legacies of the Sixties* (1996).

Vance, Carol, ed. *Pleasure and Danger: Exploring Female Sexuality* (1984).

Wandersee, Winifred. *On the Move: American Women in the 1970s* (1988).

CHAPTER
9

Vietnam and the Crisis

of American Empire

The Vietnam War was one of the most traumatic events in postwar American history; even more so for the Vietnamese. It cost the lives of more than fifty thousand Americans and of hundreds of thousands of Vietnamese and other Southeast Asians. It shattered the presidency of Lyndon Johnson, dealt the Democratic party a defeat from which it still has not recovered, and divided the American people more deeply than at any other time since the Civil War.

On one level, the war in Vietnam was the product of the Cold War and the projection of the ideas, interests, and strategies associated with that struggle onto a postcolonial world of nationalism and social revolution. The United States and the Soviet Union (and its sometimes ally, sometimes rival, China) sought to shape what sorts of states would emerge from the disintegration of the old colonial system. For the United States, the war in Vietnam was also the logical outcome of America's postwar effort to maintain what Truman adviser Clark M. Clifford had once described as "our conception of a decent world order" or what Henry Luce had earlier called "an American century." The U.S. defeat in Vietnam, combined with the economic uncertainties of the 1970s and early 1980s, led many Americans to wonder if the postwar "American era" had ended.

Among the many questions that continue to preoccupy historians and other students of the Vietnam War, three in particular stand out: How (and why) did the United States come to invest so much in the creation and maintenance of an American-dominated, anticommunist regime in Vietnam? Given that commitment, how (and with what consequences) did the United States conduct the war? And finally, what are the lessons of Vietnam, especially in a world no longer dominated by the Cold War but in which the forces of nationalism remain strong?

DOCUMENTS

As World War II drew to a close and Japanese control over Vietnam waned, the Vietminh, whose forces represented a powerful fusion of communism and nationalism, seized power throughout much of the country. With an eye toward gaining U.S. support (or at least sufferance), the Vietminh issued a Declaration of Independence (Document 1), which began with a familiar passage. The French effort to regain control of Vietnam and the resulting First Indochina War (1946–1954) posed a dilemma for U.S. policymakers: should the United States accept the victory of a movement that, like that in China, was both communist and nationalist, or should it support the French colonial regime led by Boa Dai? While there was debate within the Eisenhower administration, its decision was to support the French—with funds but not troops. President Dwight D. Eisenhower expressed grave concerns about the consequences of a Vietminh victory at an April 27, 1954, press conference (Document 2), in which he suggested that if the Vietminh took control, other nations in the region would fall like a "row of dominoes."

The French defeat was sealed on July 21, 1954, by the Geneva Accords (Document 3), which temporarily divided Vietnam along the seventeenth parallel, established procedures for the nation's reunification, and sought to insulate it from further outside intervention. Despite the Geneva Accords, the United States soon replaced France as the dominant Western power in Vietnam. Its efforts to create and sustain a new anti-communist government that could gain popular support, however, drew the United States deeper into conflict with the National Liberation Front (NLF, or "Vietcong"), which was supported by the armies of the Democratic Republic of Vietnam (North Vietnam). At the center of the struggle were the many Vietnamese peasants whose poverty and alienation from the U.S.-backed southern government made them easy recruits for the NLF. In Document 4, excerpted from David Chanoff and Doan Van Toai's *Portrait of the Enemy* (1985), Nguyen Tan Thanh explains why he joined the Vietcong. In 1964, when American warships were fired upon in the Gulf of Tonkin off the North Vietnamese coast (where U.S. ships had been conducting electronic surveillance and providing cover for South Vietnamese operations), President Lyndon Johnson seized the opportunity to push through Congress the Gulf of Tonkin Resolution (Document 5), which he would later use to justify the continuing U.S. war in Vietnam.

Although U.S. military advisers had been present in Vietnam since the 1950s, American combat troops did not arrive in large numbers until early 1965, and it was not until the summer of 1965 that the Johnson administration acknowledged the full extent of its military commitments. Document 6 is composed of excerpts from two memoranda, one by Secretary of Defense Robert S. McNamara urging escalation and one by Undersecretary of State George W. Ball arguing that the United States should seek a negotiated solution. Johnson, of course, followed the advice of McNamara and other "hawkish" advisers. Soon both American and Vietnamese casualties mounted; so did disturbing reports of a war in which it was often difficult to tell friends from enemies and in which civilian casualties were very high. In Document 7, an American soldier describes the events that unfolded in the Vietnamese hamlet of My Lai on the morning of March 16, 1968. As casualties mounted and no end to the war was in sight, both Johnson and the war grew increasingly unpopular. Johnson declined to run for president in 1968, and Republican Richard Nixon, who promised a plan to achieve "peace with honor," won in a close election. The war dragged on; however, as did the death and destruction it brought in its wake. Not until 1973 did the Paris Accords (Document 8) bring an end to the U.S. military presence in Vietnam.

1. The Vietnamese Declare Their Independence, 1945

"We hold truths that all men are created equal, that they are endowed by their Creator with certain unalienable Rights, among these are Life, Liberty and the pursuit of Happiness."

Ho Chi Minh, *Selected Writings, 1920–1969* (Hanoi: Foreign Language Publishing House, 1973), 53-56.

This immortal statement is extracted from the Declaration of Independence of the United States of America in 1776. Understood in the broader sense, this means: "All peoples on the earth are born equal; every person has the right to live to be happy and free."

The Declaration of Human and Civic Rights proclaimed by the French Revolution in 1791 likewise propounds: "Every man is born equal and enjoys free and equal rights."

These are undeniable truths.

Yet, during and throughout the last eighty years, the French imperialists, abusing the principles of "Freedom, equality and fraternity," have violated the integrity of our ancestral land and oppressed our countrymen. Their deeds run counter to the ideals of humanity and justice.

In the political field, they have denied us every freedom. They have enforced upon us inhuman laws. They have set up three different political regimes in Northern, Central, and Southern Viet Nam (Tonkin, Annam, and Cochinchina) in an attempt to disrupt our national, historical, and ethical unity.

They have built more prisons than schools. They have callously ill-treated our fellow-compatriots. They have drowned our revolutions in blood.

They have sought to stifle public opinion and pursued a policy of obscurantism on the largest scale; they have forced upon us alcohol and opium in order to weaken our race.

In the economic field, they have shamelessly exploited our people, driven them into the worst misery, and mercilessly plundered our country.

They have ruthlessly appropriated our rice fields, mines, forests, and raw materials. They have arrogated to themselves the privilege of issuing banknotes, and monopolized all our external commerce. They have imposed hundreds of unjustifiable taxes, and reduced our countrymen, especially the peasants and petty tradesmen, to extreme poverty.

They have prevented the development of native capital enterprises; they have exploited our workers in the most barbarous manner.

In the autumn of 1940, when the Japanese fascists, in order to fight the Allies, invaded Indochina and set up new bases of war, the French imperialists surrendered on bended knees and handed over our country to the invaders.

Subsequently, under the joint French and Japanese yoke, our people were literally bled white. The consequences were dire in the extreme. From Quang Tri up to the North, two millions of our countrymen died from starvation during the first months of this year.

On March 9th, 1945, the Japanese disarmed the French troops. Again the French either fled or surrendered unconditionally. Thus, in no way have they proved capable of "protecting" us; on the contrary, within five years they have twice sold our country to the Japanese.

Before March 9th, many a time did the Viet Minh League invite the French to join in the fight against the Japanese. Instead of accepting this offer, the French, on the contrary, let loose a wild reign of terror with rigour worse than ever before against Viet Minh's partisans. They even slaughtered a great number of our "*condamnés politiques*" imprisoned at Yen Bay and Cao Bang.

Despite all that, our countrymen went on maintaining, vis-à-vis the French, a humane and even indulgent attitude. After the events of March 9th, the Viet Minh League helped many French to cross the borders, rescued others from Japanese prisons, and, in general, protected the lives and properties of all the French in their territory.

In fact, since the autumn of 1940, our country ceased to be a French colony and became a Japanese possession.

After the Japanese surrender, our people, as a whole, rose up and proclaimed their sovereignty and founded the Democratic Republic of Viet Nam.

The truth is that we have wrung back our independence from Japanese hands and not from the French.

The French fled, the Japanese surrendered. Emperor Bao Dai abdicated, our people smashed the yoke which pressed hard upon us for nearly one hundred years, and finally made our Viet Nam an independent country. Our people at the same time overthrew the monarchical regime established tens of centuries ago, and founded the Republic.

For these reasons, we the members of the Provisional Government representing the entire people of Viet Nam, declare that we shall from now on have no more connections with imperialist France; we consider null and void all the treaties France has signed concerning Viet Nam, and we hereby cancel all the privileges that the French arrogated to themselves on our territory.

The Vietnamese people, animated by the same common resolve, are determined to fight to the death against all attempts at aggression by the French imperialists.

We are convinced that the Allies who have recognized the principles of equality of peoples at the Conferences of Teheran and San Francisco cannot but recognize the independence of Viet Nam.

A people which has so stubbornly opposed the French domination for more than 80 years, a people who, during these last years, so doggedly ranged itself and fought on the Allied side against Fascism, such a people has the right to be free, such a people must be independent.

For these reasons, we, the members of the Provisional Government of the Democratic Republic of Viet Nam, solemnly declare to the world:

"Viet Nam has the right to be free and independent and, in fact, has become free and independent. The people of Viet Nam decide to mobilise all their spiritual and material forces and to sacrifice their lives and property in order to safeguard their right of Liberty and Independence."

2. President Dwight D. Eisenhower Explains the Domino Theory, 1954

Q. Robert Richards, Copley Press Mr. President, would you mind commenting on the strategic importance of Indochina to the free world? I think there has been, across the country, some lack of understanding on just what it means to us.

The President You have, of course, both the specific and the general when you talk about such things.

First of all, you have the specific value of a locality in its production of materials that the world needs.

Public Papers of the Presidents of the United States: Dwight D. Eisenhower, 1954 (Washington, D.C.: GPO, 1960), 382–383.

Then you have the possibility that many human beings pass under a dictatorship that is inimical to the free world.

Finally, you have broader considerations that might follow what you would call the "falling domino" principle. You have a row of dominoes set up, you knock over the first one, and what will happen to the last one is the certainty that it will go over very quickly. So you could have a beginning of a disintegration that would have the most profound influences.

Now, with respect to the first one, two of the items from this particular area that the world uses are tin and tungsten. They are very important. There are others, of course, the rubber plantations and so on.

Then with respect to more people passing under this domination, Asia, after all, has already lost some 450 million of its peoples to the Communist dictatorship, and we simply can't afford greater losses.

But when we come to the possible sequence of events, the loss of Indochina, of Burma, of Thailand, of the Peninsula, and Indonesia following, now you begin to talk about areas that not only multiply the disadvantages that you would suffer through loss of materials, sources of materials, but now you are talking about millions and millions and millions of people.

Finally, the geographical position achieved thereby does many things. It turns the so-called island defensive chain of Japan, Formosa, of the Philippines and to the southward; it moves in to threaten Australia and New Zealand.

It takes away, in its economic aspects, that region that Japan must have as a trading area or Japan, in turn, will have only one place in the world to go—that is, toward the Communist areas in order to live.

So, the possible consequences of the loss are just incalculable to the free world.

3. Final Declaration of the Geneva Conference on Indochina, 1954

Final declaration, dated the 21st July, 1954, of the Geneva Conference on the problem of restoring peace in Indo-China, in which the representatives of Cambodia, the Democratic Republic of Viet-nam, France, Laos, the People's Republic of China, the State of Viet-nam, the Union of Soviet Socialist Republics, the United Kingdom, and the United States of America took part.

1. The Conference takes note of the Agreements ending hostilities in Cambodia, Laos, and Viet-nam and organizing international control and the supervision of the execution of the provisions of these agreements.

2. The Conference expresses satisfaction at the ending of hostilities in Cambodia, Laos, and Viet-nam; the Conference expresses its conviction that the execution of the provisions set out in the present Declaration and in the Agreements on the cessation of hostilities will permit Cambodia, Laos, [and] Viet-nam henceforth to play their part, in full independence and sovereignty, in the peaceful community of nations.

Democratic Republic of Viet-Nam, *Documents Related to the Implementation of the Geneva Agreements Concerning Viet-Nam* (Hanoi, 1956), 181–183.

3. The Conference takes note of the declarations made by the Governments of Cambodia and of Laos of their intention to adopt measures permitting all citizens to take their place in the national community, in particular by participating in the next general elections, which, in conformity with the constitution of each of these countries, shall take place in the course of the year 1955, by secret ballot and in conditions of respect for fundamental freedoms.

4. The Conference takes note of the clauses in the Agreement on the cessation of hostilities in Viet-nam prohibiting the introduction into Viet-nam of foreign troops and military personnel as well as of all kinds of arms and munitions. The Conference also takes note of the declarations made by the Governments of Cambodia and Laos of their resolution not to request foreign aid, whether in war material, in personnel, or in instructors except for the purpose of the effective defence of their territory and, in the case of Laos, to the extent defined by the Agreements on the cessation of hostilities in Laos.

5. The Conference takes note of the clauses in the Agreement on the cessation of hostilities in Viet-nam to the effect that no military base under the control of a foreign State may be established in the regrouping zones of the two parties, the latter having the obligation to see that the zones allotted to them shall not constitute part of any military alliance and shall not be utilized for the resumption of hostilities or in the service of an aggressive policy. The Conference also takes note of the declarations of the Governments of Cambodia and Laos to the effect that they will not join in any agreement with other States if this agreement includes the obligation to participate in a military alliance not in conformity with the principles of the Charter of the United Nations or, in the case of Laos, with the principles of the Agreement on the cessation of hostilities in Laos or, so long as their security is not threatened, the obligation to establish bases on Cambodian or Laotian territory for the military forces of foreign Powers.

6. The Conference recognizes that the essential purpose of the Agreement relating to Viet-nam is to settle military questions with a view to ending hostilities and that the military demarcation line is provisional and should not in any way be interpreted as constituting a political or territorial boundary. The Conference expresses its conviction that the execution of the provisions set out in the present Declaration and in the Agreement on the cessation of hostilities creates the necessary basis for the achievement in the near future of a political settlement in Viet-nam.

7. The Conference declares that, so far as Viet-nam is concerned, the settlement of political problems, effected on the basis of respect for the principles of independence, unity, and territorial integrity, shall permit the Vietnamese people to enjoy the fundamental freedoms, guaranteed by democratic institutions established as a result of free general elections by secret ballot. In order to ensure that sufficient progress in the restoration of peace has been made and that all the necessary conditions obtain for free expression of the national will, general elections shall be held in July 1956, under the supervision of an international commission composed of representatives of the Member States of the International Supervisory Commission, referred to in the Agreement on the cessation of hostilities. Consultations will be held on this subject between the competent representative authorities of the two zones from 20 July 1955 onwards.

8. The provisions of the Agreements on the cessation of hostilities intended to ensure the protection of individuals and of property must be most strictly applied

and must, in particular, allow everyone in Viet-nam to decide freely in which zone he wishes to live.

9. The competent representative authorities of the Northern and Southern zones of Viet-nam, as well as the authorities of Laos and Cambodia, must not permit any individual or collective reprisals against persons who have collaborated in any way with one of the parties during the war, or against members of such persons' families.

10. The Conference takes note of the declaration of the Government of the French Republic to the effect that it is ready to withdraw its troops from the territory of Cambodia, Laos, and Viet-nam, at the request of the governments concerned and within periods which shall be fixed by agreement between the parties except in the cases where, by agreement between the two parties, a certain number of French troops shall remain at specified points and for a specified time.

11. The Conference takes note of the declaration of the French Government to the effect that for the settlement of all the problems connected with the re-establishment and consolidation of peace in Cambodia, Laos, and Viet-nam, the French Government will proceed from the principle of respect for the independence and sovereignty, unity, and territorial integrity of Cambodia, Laos, and Viet-nam.

12. In their relations with Cambodia, Laos, and Viet-nam, each member of the Geneva Conference undertakes to respect the sovereignty, the independence, the unity, and the territorial integrity of the above-mentioned States, and to refrain from any interference in their internal affairs.

13. The members of the Conference agree to consult one another on any question which may be referred to them by the International Supervisory Commission, in order to study such measures as may prove necessary to ensure that the Agreements on the cessation of hostilities in Cambodia, Laos, and Viet-nam are respected.

4. A South Vietnamese Peasant Explains Why He Joined the Vietcong, 1961 (1986)

I joined the VC [Vietcong—formally, the National Liberation Front] when I was thirty-five years old. I was married and had four children. I was leasing farmland— one hectare [about 2.5 acres]—that was very poor in quality, almost sterile. That was why the owner rented it out to us. Despite working hard all year round, we got only about 100 *gia* of rice out of it. Of this amount, 40 *gia* went to the landlord. We borrowed money to buy ducks and geese. We lived a very hard life. But I cultivated the land carefully, and in time it became fertile. When it did, the owner took it back; my livelihood was gone. I had to go back to my parents, to raise ducks for my father.

I was poor. I had lost my land and I didn't have enough money to take care of my children. In 1961 propaganda cadres of the [National Liberation] Front contacted me. These guys had joined the resistance against the French, and after Geneva they had stayed underground in the South. They came to all the poor farmers and made an analysis of the poor and rich classes. They said that the rich people had always served the French and had used the authority of the French to oppress the poor. The majority of the people were poor, not because they wasted their money but because they had been exploited by the landlords who had worked with the French. In the past, the ancestors of the poor had broken ground for tillage. Then powerful people had seized their land. Without any other means to live, the poor had become slaves of the landlords. The cadres told us that if the poor people don't stand up [to] the rich people, we would be dominated by them forever. The only way to ensure freedom and a sufficient life was to overthrow them.

When I heard the cadres, I thought that what they said was correct. In my village there were about forty-three hundred people. Of these, maybe ten were landlords. The richest owned five hundred hectares [1,236 acres], and the others had at least twenty hectares [49 acres] apiece. The rest of the people were tenants or honest poor farmers. I knew that the rich oppressed the poor. The poor had nothing to eat, and they also had no freedom. We had to get rid of the regime that allowed a few people to use their money and authority to oppress the others.

So I joined the Liberation Front. I followed the VC to fight for freedom and prosperity for the country. I felt that this was right.

5. The Gulf of Tonkin Resolution, 1964

Whereas naval units of the Communist regime in [North] Vietnam, in violation of the principles of the Charter of the United Nations and of international law, have deliberately and repeatedly attacked United States naval vessels lawfully present in international waters, and have thereby created a serious threat to international peace; and

Whereas these attacks are part of a deliberate and systematic campaign of aggression that the Communist regime in North Vietnam has been waging against its neighbors and the nations joined with them in the collective defense of their freedom; and

Whereas the United States is assisting the peoples of southeast Asia to protect their freedom and has no territorial, military, or political ambitions in that area, but desires only that these peoples should be left in peace to work out their own destinies in their own way: Now, therefore, be it

Resolved by the Senate and House of Representatives of the United States of America in Congress assembled, That the Congress approves and supports the determination of the President, as Commander in Chief, to take all necessary measures to repel any armed attack against the forces of the United States and to prevent further aggression.

Sec. 2. The United States regards as vital to its national interest and to world peace the maintenance of international peace and security in southeast Asia. Consonant with the Constitution of the United States and the Charter of the United Nations and in accordance with its obligations under the Southeast Asia Collective Defense Treaty, the United States is, therefore, prepared, as the President determines, to take all necessary steps, including the use of armed force, to assist any member or protocol state of the Southeast Asia Collective Defense Treaty requesting assistance in defense of its freedom.

Department of State Bulletin 51, no. 1313 (August 24, 1964): 268.

Sec. 3. This resolution shall expire when the President shall determine that the peace and security of the area is reasonably assured by international conditions created by action of the United Nations or otherwise, except that it may be terminated earlier by concurrent resolution of the Congress.

6. President Lyndon Johnson's Advisers Debate Expanding the War, 1965

Robert S. McNamara

[26 June 1965; revised 1 July 1965]

Introduction

Our objective is to create conditions for a favorable settlement by demonstrating to the VC [Viet Cong]/DRV [Democratic Republic of Vietnam—North Vietnam] that the odds are against their winning. Under present conditions, however, the chances of achieving this objective are small—and the VC are winning now—largely because the ratio of guerrilla to antiguerrilla forces is unfavorable to the government. With this in mind, we must choose among three courses of action with respect to South Vietnam: (1) Cut our losses and withdraw under the best conditions that can be arranged; (2) continue at about the present level, with U.S. forces limited to say, 75,000, holding on and playing for the breaks while recognizing that our position will probably grow weaker; or (3) expand substantially the U.S. military pressure against the Viet Cong in the South and the North Vietnamese in the North and at the same time launch a vigorous effort on the political side to get negotiations started. An outline of the third of these approaches follows.

I. Expanded Military Moves

The following military moves should be taken together with the political initiatives in Part II below.

A. Inside South Vietnam.   Increase U.S./SVN [South Vietnam] military strength in SVN enough to prove to the VC that they cannot win and thus to turn the tide of the war. . . .

B. Against North Vietnam.   While avoiding striking population and industrial targets not closely related to the DRV's supply of war material to the VC, we should announce to Hanoi and carry out actions to destroy such supplies and to interdict their flow into and out of North Vietnam. . . .

Robert S. McNamara, Memorandum for the President, June 26, 1965; revised July 1, 1965; George W. Ball to the President, memorandum, July 1, 1965; both in National Security File, National Security Council History, "Deployment of Major U.S. Forces to Vietnam, July 1965," Lyndon B. Johnson Library, Austin, Tex.

II. Expanded Political Moves

Together with the above military moves, we should take the following political initiatives in order (a) to open a dialogue with Hanoi, Peking, and the VC looking toward a settlement in Vietnam, (b) to keep the Soviet Union from deepening its military involvement and support of North Vietnam until the time when settlement can be achieved, and (c) to cement the support for U.S. policy by the U.S. public, allies, and friends, and to keep international opposition at a manageable level. While our approaches may be rebuffed until the tide begins to turn, they nevertheless should be made. . . .

George W. Ball

[1 July 1965]

1. A Losing War: The South Vietnamese are losing the war to the Viet Cong [formally, the National Liberation Front]. No one can assure you that we can beat the Viet Cong or even force them to the conference table on our terms no matter how many hundred thousand *white foreign* (U.S.) troops we deploy.

No one has demonstrated that a white ground force of whatever size can win a guerrilla war—which is at the same time a civil war between Asians—in jungle terrain in the midst of a population that refuses cooperation to the white forces (and the SVN [South Vietnam]) and thus provides a great intelligence advantage to the other side. Three recent incidents vividly illustrate this point:

(a) The sneak attack on the Danang Air Base which involved penetration of a defense perimeter guarded by 9,000 Marines. *This raid was possible only because of the cooperation of the local inhabitants.*

(b) The B-52 raid that failed to hit the Viet Cong *who had obviously been tipped off.*

(c) The search-and-destroy mission of the 173rd Airborne Brigade which spent three days looking for the Viet Cong, suffered 23 casualties, and never made contact with the enemy *who had obviously gotten advance word of their assignment.*

2. The Question to Decide: Should we limit our liabilities in South Viet-Nam and try to find a way out with minimal long-term cost?

The alternative—no matter what we may wish it to be—is almost certainly a protracted war involving an open-ended commitment of U.S. forces, mounting U.S. casualties, no assurance of a satisfactory solution, and a serious danger of escalation at the end of the road.

3. Need for a Decision Now: So long as our forces are restricted to advising and assisting the South Vietnamese, the struggle will remain a civil war between Asian peoples. Once we deploy substantial numbers of troops in combat it will become a war between the United States and a large part of the population of South Viet-Nam, organized and directed from North Viet-Nam and backed by the resources of both Moscow and Peiping [sic].

The decision you face now, therefore, is crucial. Once large numbers of U.S. troops are committed to direct combat they will begin to take heavy casualties in a war they are ill-equipped to fight in a non-cooperative if not downright hostile countryside.

Once we suffer large casualties we will have started a well-nigh irreversible process. Our involvement will be so great that we cannot—without national humiliation—stop short of achieving our complete objectives. *Of the two possibilities I think humiliation would be more likely than the achievement of our objectives— even after we had paid terrible costs.*

4. A Compromise Solution: Should we commit U.S. manpower and prestige to a terrain so unfavorable as to give a very large advantage to the enemy—or should we seek a compromise settlement which achieves less than our stated objectives and thus cut our losses while we still have the freedom of maneuver to do so?

5. Costs of Compromise Solution: The answer involves a judgment as to the costs to the United States of such a compromise settlement in terms of our relations with the countries in the area of South Viet-Nam, the credibility of our commitments, and our prestige around the world. In my judgment, if we act before we commit substantial U.S. forces to combat in South Viet-Nam we can, by accepting some short-term costs, avoid what may well be a long-term catastrophe. I believe we have tended greatly to exaggerate the costs involved in a compromise settlement. . . .

7. A "Tunnel Rat" Testifies About the My Lai Massacre, 1969

We were picked up by helicopters at LZ Dottie early in the morning and we were flown to My Lai. We landed outside the village in a dry rice paddy. There was no resistance from the village. There was no armed enemy in the village. We formed a line outside the village.

The first killing was an old man in a field outside the village who said some kind of greeting in Vietnamese and waved his arms at us. Someone—either Medina or Calley—said to kill him and a big heavy-set white fellow killed the man. I do not know the name of the man who shot this Vietnamese. This was the first murder.

Just after the man killed the Vietnamese, a woman came out of the village and someone knocked her down and Medina shot her with his M16 rifle. I was 50 or 60 feet from him and saw this. There was no reason to shoot this girl. Mitchell, Conti, Meadlo, Stanley, and the rest of the squad and the command group must have seen this. It was a pure out and out murder.

Then our squad started into the village. We were making sure no one escaped from the village. Seventy-five or a hundred yards inside the village we came to where the soldiers had collected 15 or more Vietnamese men, women, and children in a group. Medina said, "Kill everybody, leave no one standing." Wood was there with an M-60 machine gun and, at Medina's orders, he fired into the people. Sgt Mitchell was there at this time and fired into the people with his M16 rifle, also. Widmer was there and fired into the group, and after they were down on the ground, Widmer passed among them and finished them off with his M16 rifle. Medina, himself, did not fire into this group.

CID Deposition Files, My Lai Investigation, CID Statement, file no. 69-CID0011-00074, U.S. Army Crimes Records Center, Fort Belvoir, Virginia.

Just after this shooting, Medina stopped a 17 or 18 year old man with a water buffalo. Medina said for the boy to make a run for it—he tried to get him to run—but the boy wouldn't run, so Medina shot him with his M16 rifle and killed him. The command group was there. I was 75 or 80 feet away at the time and saw it plainly. There were some demolition men there, too, and they would be able to testify about this. I don't know any other witnesses to this murder. Medina killed the buffalo, too.

Q: I want to warn you that these are very serious charges you are making. I want you to be very sure that you tell only the truth and that everything you say is the truth?

A: What I have said is the truth and I will face Medina in court and swear to it. This is the truth: this is what happened.

Q: What happened then?

A: We went on through the village. Meadlo shot a Vietnamese and asked me to help him throw the man in the well. I refused and Meadlo had Carney help him throw the man in the well. I saw this murder with my own eyes and know that there was no reason to shoot the man. I also know from the wounds that the man was dead.

Also in the village the soldiers had rounded up a group of people. Meadlo was guarding them. There were some other soldiers with Meadlo. Calley came up and said that he wanted them all killed. I was right there within a few feet when he said this. There were about 25 people in this group. Calley said when I walk[ed] away, I want them all killed. Meadlo and Widmer fired into this group with his M16 on automatic fire. Cowan was there and fired into the people too, but I don't think he wanted to do it. There were others firing into this group, but I don't remember who. Calley had two Vietnamese with him at this time and he killed them, too, by shooting them with his M16 rifle on automatic fire. I didn't want to get involved and I walked away. There was no reason for this killing. These were mainly women and children and a few old men. They weren't trying to escape or attack or anything. It was murder.

A woman came out of a hut with a baby in her arms and she was crying. She was crying because her little boy had been in front of her hut and between the well and the hut and someone had killed the child by shooting it. She came out of the hut with her baby and Widmer shot her with an M16 and she fell. When she fell, she dropped the baby and then Widmer opened up on the baby with his M16 and killed the baby, too.

I also saw another woman come out of a hut and Calley grabbed her by the hair and shot her with a caliber .45 pistol. He held her by the hair for a minute and then let go and she fell to the ground. Some enlisted man standing there said, "Well, she'll be in the big rice paddy in the sky."

Q: Do you know any witnesses to these incidents?

A: Stanley might have [seen] the one Calley killed. There were a lot of people around when Widmer shot the woman with the baby. I can't definitely state any one person was there, but there were a lot of people around.

I also saw a Vietnamese boy about 8 years old who had been wounded, I think in the leg. One of the photographers attached to the company patted the kid on the head and then Mitchell shot the kid right in front of the photographer and me. I am sure the boy died from the fire of Mitchell.

About that time I sat down by a stack of dying people and Widmer asked me if he could borrow my caliber .45 pistol and finish off the people. I gave him my pistol and he walked in among the people and would stand there and when one would move, he would shoot that person in the head with the pistol. He used three magazines of caliber .45 ammunition on these people. These were men, children, women, and babies. They had been shot by machinegunners and riflemen from Company C, 1/20th Infantry. This was at a T-junction of two trails on the outskirts of the village. I got my pistol back from Widmer and holstered it again.

Q: How many people do you figure Widmer finished off when he used your pistol?

A: I know he shot some twice, so I figure he shot fifteen or so with my pistol. I know he shot one guy in the head and I imagine that was where he was shooting them all.

Q: What happened then?

A: We went on through the village and there was killing and more killing. I was with Stanley, mainly. I sat down with Stanley and Widmer came up again and asked to borrow my pistol again. I gave it to him. I saw a little boy there—wounded, I believe in the arm—and Widmer walked up close to the kid and shot him with my pistol. Widmer said something like, "Did you see me shoot that son of a bitch," and Stanley said something about how it was wrong. My gun had jammed when Widmer shot the kid. As far as I could tell, the kid died as a result of this gunshot. Then Widmer gave me my pistol back and walked off. I was trying to clean it when it accident[al]ly went off and I was shot in the left foot. Stanley gave me medical aid and then the medics came. Medina and some of the command group came up and then I was flown out in a helicopter. The next day the medics brought Meadlo into the hospital. He had stepped on a booby-trap and had lost his foot. He said he thought God might be punishing him for what he had done in My Lai. . . .

Q: Did you murder anyone in Vietnam?

A: The only people I killed in Vietnam I killed in combat. I didn't kill any women or kids or unarmed persons at all, ever.

Q: How many people do you think were killed in My Lai?

A: There were more than 100, but I couldn't tell you accurately how many people were killed. I don't believe there were any people left alive.

8. The Paris Accords, 1973

Article 1

. . . The United States and all other countries respect the independence, sovereignty, unity, and territorial integrity of Viet-Nam as recognized by the 1954 Geneva Agreements on Viet-Nam. . . .

Article 2

A cease-fire shall be observed throughout South Viet-Nam as of 2400 hours G.M.T., on January 27, 1973. At the same hour, the United States will stop all its military activities against the territory of the Democratic Republic of Viet-Nam by ground,

U.S. Secretary of State (ed.), *United States Treaties and Other International Agreements* (Washington, D.C.: GPO, 1974).

air and naval forces, wherever they may be based, and end the mining of the territorial waters, ports, harbors, and waterways of the Democratic Republic of Viet-Nam. The United States will remove, permanently deactivate or destroy all the mines in the territorial waters, ports, harbors, and waterways of North Viet-Nam as soon as this Agreement goes into effect. The complete cessation of hostilities mentioned in this Article shall be durable and without limit of time. . . .

Article 4

The United States will not continue its military involvement or intervene in the internal affairs of South Viet-Nam.

Article 5

Within sixty days of the signing of this Agreement, there will be a total withdrawal from South Viet-Nam of troops, military advisers, and military personnel including technical military personnel and military personnel associated with the pacification program, armaments, munitions, and war material of the United States and those of the other foreign countries mentioned in Article 3(a). Advisers from the above-mentioned countries to all paramilitary organizations and the police force will also be withdrawn within the same period of time.

Article 6

The dismantlement of all military bases in South Viet-Nam of the United States and of the other foreign countries mentioned in Article 3(a) shall be completed within sixty days of the signing of this Agreement.

Article 7

From the enforcement of the cease-fire to the formation of the government provided for in Article 9(b) and 14 of this Agreement, the two South Vietnamese parties shall not accept the introduction of troops, military advisers, and military personnel including technical military personnel, armaments, munitions, and war material into South Viet-Nam. . . .

Article 11

Immediately after the cease-fire, the two South Vietnamese parties will:

—achieve national reconciliation and concord, end hatred and enmity, prohibit all acts of reprisal and discrimination against individuals or organizations that have collaborated with one side or the other;

—ensure the democratic liberties of the people: personal freedom, freedom of speech, freedom of the press, freedom of meeting, freedom of organization, freedom of political activities, freedom of belief, freedom of movement, freedom of residence, freedom of work, right to property ownership, and right to free enterprise. . . .

Article 15

The reunification of Viet-Nam shall be carried out step by step through peaceful means on the basis of discussions and agreements between North and South Viet-Nam, without coercion or annexation by either party, and without foreign interference. The time for reunification will be agreed upon by North and South Viet-Nam. . . .

✦ *E S S A Y S*

The war in Vietnam remains one of the most controversial experiences in modern American history, its lessons learned, unlearned, and still debated long after the signing of the Paris Peace Accords in 1973. In the first essay that follows, University of North Carolina historian Michael H. Hunt traces the aftermath of the war in both the United States and Southeast Asia. In the second essay, Arnold R. Isaacs, who covered the war's final years for the *Baltimore Sun,* reflects on the ways in which the war is remembered by his generation—the Vietnam generation—and by that of his father, who came of age during World War II.

The Wages of War

MICHAEL H. HUNT

William Shakespeare's *Henry V* has an English soldier about to face a superior French force remark grimly on the mayhem to come and the responsibility borne by leaders whose embrace of war produces that mayhem:

> [I]f the cause be not good, the King himself hath a heavy reckoning to make, when all those legs and arms and heads, chopped off in a battle, shall join together at the latter day and cry all, "We died at such a place"; some swearing, some crying for a surgeon, some upon their wives left poor behind them, some upon the debts they owe, some upon their children rawly left. I am afeard there are few die well that die in a battle.

This eloquent call from the ranks directs our attention to the "heavy reckoning" to which leaders, foremost Lyndon Johnson in this case, must submit.

In Vietnam an estimated 1.4 million—civilians as well as combatants on one side or the other—died during the U.S. combat phase of the war (1965 through 1972), and another 300,000 fell in the subsequent period down to April 1975. (Of these deaths perhaps only about 50,000 were the result of the controversial bombing of the North.) Saigon's forces alone suffered a total of 220,000 killed. By 1972 South Vietnam, with a population short of eighteen million, may have had a total of over ten million refugees. By the war's end a united Vietnam had 300,000 combatants lost without trace, some 1.4 million disabled and half a million orphans to care for, and schools, hospitals, and other public facilities to rebuild. The environment, especially in the South, had suffered long-term damage from the concentrated, even stupefying, application of U.S. ordnance (some fifteen million tons down to 1972) and from extensive spraying of herbicides (nineteen million gallons, well over half deadly dioxins). Unexploded bombs and shells seeded the soil both north and south.

While postwar Vietnam escaped the bloodbath that some had predicted, unification still proved a rocky road for a leadership good at struggle but less skillful at managing the politics of peace and development. Hanoi moved quickly to clap some 100,000 of those prominent in the old regime into "reeducation camps." It followed in the late 1970s by imposing roughshod a program of integrating the south (with its distinct style and strong French and American imprint) into the existing northern system of centralized political control and economic planning. Joblessness, already high because of the large numbers of demobilized soldiers, climbed still higher. A newly collectivized agricultural sector suffered an immediate fall in rice output. The resulting economic crisis together with persecution of ethnic Chinese produced a second round of refugees, the "boat people."

These domestic difficulties were intensified by conflict within the region. Relations with Cambodia deteriorated following border skirmishes provoked by the new Pol Pot regime and climaxing in 1979 with the Vietnamese invasion and occupation of a country gripped by a frenzy of self-destruction. An already suspicious Beijing at once responded by sending a punitive expedition against the upstart Vietnamese. With few friends and with influential Chinese and American enemies, Vietnam became heavily dependent on the Soviet Union both strategically and economically. An annual Soviet subsidy of $1–$2 billion kept a struggling Vietnam afloat through the 1980s.

Hanoi fundamentally revised its course in December 1986 following the death of the dominant figure in the Workers' Party, Le Duan. His replacement, Nguyen Van Linh, was a northerner who had served in the south between 1945 and 1975 and thereafter established a reputation as a maverick reformer. Linh implemented a new economic policy that returned land to peasants, stimulated free markets, encouraged foreign investment, promoted production for export, and tapped the agricultural and commercial expertise of the south. His foreign policy, geared to resolving outstanding conflicts, helped open foreign markets and attract foreign capital, both critical to developing one of the poorest countries in the world. Détente with China followed in 1991 and with the United States in 1995. Returning Americans were astonished by the lack of animosity and bitterness they encountered. Vietnamese had seemingly submerged the trauma of the war in the old and deep tradition of resistance and patriotism. They had played by a familiar national script, and, despite the high price, the promise of victory had been realized.

Cambodia, though it sought to remain a bystander to the conflict in Vietnam, may have suffered even more death and destruction. Incursions by NLF [National Liberation Front], DRV [Democratic Republic of Vietnam—North Vietnam], Saigon, and American forces, together with devastating and repeated U.S. bombing raids, intensified the havoc already created by civil war and radicalized Cambodia's own revolutionary forces, the Khmer Rouge. Following [Prime Minister Norodom] Sihanouk's overthrow in 1970, this multifaceted conflict cost the lives of approximately a half million (mostly noncombatants), and roughly half the rural population (more than two million) became refugees, straining the cities and reducing agricultural production. Just as the war in Vietnam died out in April 1975, the Khmer Rouge came to power in what would turn into a reign of terror, starvation, and death. Pol Pot emptied the cities in his quest to purify his country of class enemies, those urbanites tainted by privilege and foreign influence. While some 300,000 of the elite fled into exile, perhaps 20 percent (roughly 1.5 million) of the remaining population died between 1975 and 1979 from revolutionary violence or deprivation. Vietnam's intervention in 1979 toppled the genocidal Khmer Rouge but also set off another cycle of civil conflict. Only in the early 1990s did the turmoil begin to ease.

In comparative terms, it is fair to say that the United States suffered only a flesh wound, although this estimate of the price Americans paid may be particularly difficult to accept for those whose lives were disrupted or whose loved ones were lost in the war. American soldiers killed in action, numbering slightly over 58,000, were but a quarter of the losses suffered by the despised Saigon forces and less than a twentieth of all the Vietnamese lives lost during the U.S. phase of the war. The treasure spent in waging the distant war came to but a small proportion of total national wealth, although a look at the actual numbers can be disconcerting. Military outlays between 1961 and 1975 totaled $141 billion. Long-term obligations such as care for veterans push the figure (by one rough estimate) into the range of $350 billion.

The American wound has been slow to heal, perhaps because the damage was more deeply psychic than physical. Involvement in Vietnam created bitter, deep, and lasting divisions within the country and left painful memories for many who served there (in all, some 2.7 million). So central has Vietnam become as a point of political and cultural reference that it invites comparison to the commanding place of Munich in the mind of an earlier generation. But while Munich and the broader experience of World War II gave rise to the crystalline certainties of the Cold War, Vietnam has assumed a far more ambiguous status that has made it a source of confusion and contention.

The willed amnesia that set in as the war drew to a close was broken by veterans. They began writing and talking as a form of therapy for what seemed to many troubling, wasted sacrifice. Their personal need to remember and understand forced the Vietnam experience back into the national consciousness. The rediscovery of Vietnam gave rise to acts of homage to those who served, nowhere more dramatically than at the Vietnam Veterans Memorial, built in 1982 in the heart of the capital, hardly a stone's throw from the White House, where the decisions for war had been made. Americans flocked to visit the low, stark black stone slab covered with the names of those who did not return.

The rediscovery of Vietnam also gave rise to disputes over what went wrong and what lessons to draw. Politicians, pundits, and the entertainment industry were soon in full cry. They generally agreed that Vietnam represented a national fall from grace, but differed fundamentally over whether the war was the best and the protest the worst or whether the war itself reflected the worst in the country and the protest the best.

Descendants of the wartime hawks took as their task expunging the blot on U.S. history and character. They placed blame for the first decisive American military defeat and the humiliation of a superpower at the apogee of its strength on Lyndon Johnson's poor leadership, irresponsible guidance by his team of advisers, and a national decline that had eroded patriotism and given rise to a radical antiwar movement. Ronald Reagan's estimate that the Vietnam War was a justified effort to stop the fall of dominoes and "counter the master plan of the communists for world conquest" and that, once America was committed, victory was the only acceptable goal expressed this influential "revisionist" point of view. The triumphant Grenada and Panama interventions and the Gulf War reflected the determination of Reagan as well as his successor, George Bush, to disprove what many feared Vietnam had shown—that the United States had become a pitiful, helpless giant.

The descendants of the doves traced the origins of Vietnam back to a lamentable Cold War arrogance. The United States had taken upon itself the role of world policeman without knowing the neighborhoods it presumed to patrol and without the informed consent of the American people. The practical conclusion drawn by latter-day doves and shared by much of the public was to approach intervention warily, a viewpoint that put a brake on the foreign-policy activism which was so marked a feature of the Cold War. As a result, Reagan had to reverse course following his intervention in Lebanon, and his involvement in Nicaragua and El Salvador encountered public and congressional opposition so strong that he had to pursue his goals covertly (resulting in the Iran-Contra affair).

The U.S. military drew its own lessons from Vietnam. Commentators took due note of the public impatience with an inconclusive war, the dangers of civilian interference in the conduct of war, and the risks inherent in free media access to the combat zone. The conclusion—applied in Grenada, Panama, and the Persian Gulf—was to fight only where U.S. goals were clear, public support assured, power overwhelming, and thus victory certain. How cautious Vietnam had left the U.S. military became dramatically evident in the Gulf War. The war did yield the quick military victory at a low cost in American lives, as it was designed to do. But it also ended inconclusively, with the agent of aggression, Saddam Hussein, still in power. This outcome did not so much kick as confirm the Vietnam syndrome. Americans nonetheless celebrated the triumph over Iraq as the surrogate for the victory that had eluded them in Vietnam.

Like any dramatic and controversial event, the Vietnam War was soon appropriated by Hollywood and conveyed to a fascinated public as a fantasy world where Americans tested their character, underwent youthful rites of passage, embarked on perilous rescues, suffered personal or national corruption, or replayed frontier dramas with the Vietnamese as the "wild Indians." Seldom in these re-creations did Vietnamese figure as anything more than two-dimensional stock figures. The war remained, as much as during the Cold War, an American drama in which the people of Vietnam played only minor parts.

The crosscurrents at work within the American mind were nowhere more evident than in the issue of normalizing relations with the former tormentor, the Communist leadership still in charge in Hanoi. Standing in the way of normalization were not only families of the missing-in-action but also the gnawing sense of humiliation over the war's outcome and the natural instinct to seek revenge rather than reconciliation. (Hanoi also threw up obstacles, none more troublesome than a 1977 demand for $3 billion in reparations.) But the 1986 changing of the guard in Hanoi led to greater cooperation in accounting for U.S. missing-in-action, thus removing one major obstacle. It also led to the opening of a new market attractive to U.S. corporations. By the early 1990s a majority of Americans supported normalization, and veterans groups were becoming vocal in support of reconciliation. President Bill Clinton, though embarrassed by his own avoidance of service in Vietnam, began the intricate process of rebuilding ties. Accounting for the missing-in-action (down to 1,621 by mid-1995) was the first serious step; removing the travel and trade embargoes was the next; establishing diplomatic relations in 1995 became the last.

The American wound is healing, but a scar remains. The small and distant country of Vietnam is intrinsically hardly more important today than it was when Franklin Roosevelt casually contemplated its future in 1943 or when [Harry] Truman fatefully placed it within the containment framework in 1950. Vietnam figured, above all else, at each of these and other critical turning points as a test—a test of American character and ideals. How Americans responded was a kind of referendum on their world leadership and the viability of their institutions and values.

But confident Americans with their globe-girdling organization and awesome technology did not prevail. Caught up in their Cold War crusade, U.S. leaders had plunged reluctantly and blindly into Vietnam. What they encountered was a people with a will and solidarity that far exceeded their own, with allies ready to take real risks, and, in the final analysis, with a capacity to absorb the blows of an uneven war undeterred until the enemy—demoralized in the field, divided at home—abandoned Vietnam to its stubborn people, just as the Chinese and the French had done. Americans are likely to continue to examine the war with its unsettling outcome as they might look into a mirror, the better to reflect on not just their recent tumultuous Cold War past but also their long-held claim as a special people.

Competing Memories

ARNOLD R. ISAACS

"Dear Michael: Your name is here but you are not. I made a rubbing of it, thinking that if I rubbed hard enough I would rub your name off the wall and you would come back to me. I miss you so."

No one leaves notes or offerings at the rest of Washington's many monuments. But the Vietnam Veterans Memorial is different. From the moment of its dedication, the wall, with its 58,209 names inscribed on slabs of polished black granite, has seemed to give physical form to a whole nation's feelings of pain and loss. The names unify, while other words about the war continue to divide. "It doesn't say whether the war was right or wrong," a man whose son was wounded in Vietnam, but survived, said about the wall. "It just says, 'Here is the price we paid.'"

The memorial's emotional power is easier to describe than to explain. In part it comes from the names, which make the war's loss personal and concrete and immediate instead of distant and abstract. In part it comes from the reflecting surface, where those looking at the wall can also see the sky and trees and their own faces mirrored in the black stone behind the names of the dead.

There is a kind of mystery in those reflected images. It is as if the stone surface really became what its creator, Maya Ying Lin, imagined: a meeting place "between

---

the sunny world and the quiet dark world beyond, that we can't enter." That sense of closeness between the dead and the living may explain why visitors so often do not just look, but touch, as if they can send their messages of sorrow and love through their fingertips. At the memorial, communication with the dark world seems possible. Thus, along with tears and touching, the wall of names became a place for tokens of remembrance: not only letters but also photographs, old dog tags and decorations, flags, religious medals, birthday and Christmas cards, faded scraps of uniforms and military equipment, souvenirs of war and high school and childhood.

These offerings expressed love and grief for the dead and often something more: a laying down of burdens, a release from the past. People came there to make peace with their memories—like a former marine sergeant named Frederick Garten, who left a ring and a note: "This wedding ring belonged to a young Viet Cong fighter. He was killed by a Marine unit in the Phu Loc province of South Vietnam in May of 1968. I wish I knew more about this young man. I have carried this ring for eighteen years and it's time for me to lay it down. This boy is not my enemy any longer."

Lin's design, selected when she was only twenty-one years old and studying architecture at Yale University, was at first bitterly denounced by those favoring a more conventionally patriotic monument. Opponents didn't like her design and some of them didn't like her, either: a young Chinese American woman who had only been in her early teens when the war ended, had no connection with it, hadn't even known anyone who had served in it.

When the U.S. Fine Arts Commission met to give final approval to the plan, Tom Carhart, a twice-wounded West Point graduate who had been one of the original fund-raisers for the memorial, arrived wearing his two Purple Hearts pinned on his suit jacket to tell the commissioners his reaction:" "A black gash of shame and sorrow. . . . Black walls, the universal color of sorrow and dishonor. Hidden in a hole, as if in shame." (Later, Carhart told a television interviewer: "We want something that will make us feel a part of America.") If Carhart and many like him were outraged because the memorial wasn't heroic enough, a few others were bitter for exactly the opposite reason. "I didn't want a monument," wrote the poet Bill Ehrhart, who also came home from Vietnam with a Purple Heart, "not even one as sober as that / Vast black wall of broken lives. . . . / What I wanted / Was an end to monuments."

Eventually, in an attempt to make the memorial less "antiheroic," as Tom Carhart called it, Lin's austere plan was modified by adding a U.S. flag and a statue, sculpted by Frederic Hart, naturalistically representing three GIs and carrying the inscription: "Our nation honors the courage, sacrifice and devotion to duty and country of its Vietnam veterans."* Not all critics were reconciled, even then. But by the time Hart's statue was completed, two years after the wall was dedicated, the initial criticisms of the memorial had long since been overwhelmed by the public's reaction. The controversy over the design, which had attracted a good deal of coverage before the memorial's dedication, quickly faded from view, to be replaced by images of veterans, children, parents, and other visitors shedding healing tears and finding solace in the sight and touch of the names. The wall quickly became one of the most-visited of all Washington's attractions, and certainly the most emotionally compelling. Some

---

*In 1993, a second sculpture was erected, honoring women veterans.

veterans still wouldn't go, but others found themselves returning again and again. "It is exactly the right memorial," said a retired three-star general, "for that war."

Powerful as it was, though, the wall did not close the book on America's confusion and pain about Vietnam. The war and its ghosts continued to hover over the national life and spirit. Rather than becoming a historical event that would automatically recede into the past, Vietnam lingered as a symbol, a metaphor for everything that troubled Americans in the closing years of what had once been called the American Century.

It was the war that "cleaves us still," as George [H. W.] Bush once said. Presumably, Bush was referring to the obvious divisions: between those who supported the policy and those who opposed it, between those who served and those who didn't, between those who denounced the United States and its symbols and those who put flag pins in their lapels and bumper stickers on their cars proclaiming "America— Love it or Leave it."

But the country's division over Vietnam could also be something more elusive and profound. I think, for example, of the only time I had a serious discussion about our respective wars with my father, who was a war correspondent in the China-Burma-India theater in World War II—and had, as a young man a decade earlier, also seen the early stages of Japan's brutal war in China. (He was also in Vietnam shortly after the Japanese surrender in 1945, at the very start of the Viet Minh uprising against French rule. It is a curious bit of family history that my father, who reported on some of the first skirmishes of that long conflict, lived to see his son cover the end, three decades later.)

From childhood, I knew that my father accepted none of the sentimental myths of war. He saw, as clearly as anyone I have known, the waste and degradation and cruelty. Probably that is why I assumed for years that he had come out of his war, in some fundamental way, with the same vision that I took from mine: that war, at its dark, bloody heart, is insanity. In Vietnam, from time to time during the nearly three years I spent reporting there, I would feel myself waking up, as if from a dream, thinking, *Who's the lunatic who invented this? Who figured out that this is how we decide what color bit of cloth will be fluttering in the morning over this village or that crossroads?* And whoever it was, I wondered, why wasn't he in an asylum, where he belonged?

That feeling came only intermittently, in what I came to think of as lucid moments. The truth is that the landscape of war was so completely familiar to my generation, the children of World War II, that most of the time it didn't seem crazy at all, but quite normal and sane. When I first arrived in Vietnam, in fact, one of the surprises was how much of the scenery and sensations felt familiar and well known: not everything, but a lot. But there was a kind of clarity in those moments of seeing the war as insane. I couldn't make the feeling last—it was like catching a fish with your bare hands and then having it slip away. Yet it was in those fleeting intervals that I thought I had grasped the truth of what I was experiencing. It had never occurred to me that my father didn't feel the same way. But that evening when we talked about it, the year before he died, ten years after my war ended and forty years after his, I learned—to my amazement—that I was wrong. His war was ugly and degrading, even tragic, but not absurd. It was necessary. The Japanese had to be beaten, and there wasn't any other way to do it. With all its cruelty and waste, it was still sane.

I was so surprised by that realization that I don't remember much of what we actually said to each other. I do remember thinking that I now understood in a new way just how profoundly, and in how many different ways, Vietnam had split this country apart. My father and I had no serious disagreements on Vietnam itself. But our generations' different experiences divided us on a much deeper level than that. Vietnam taught me (and, I think, most Americans who were there) that the world is, ultimately, absurd. World War II taught my father and his generation that the world may contain vast terror and evil—but also rationality and, even, a rough and approximate kind of justice. Between those two visions lay a gulf that was, and remains, almost impossible to cross.

The abyss between Americans whose lives were shaped by the great crusade of World War II and their children who grew up in the Vietnam era emerged clearly in a major survey of the baby boom generation conducted in 1986. Reporting on the survey, the writer William Greider wrote:

> The victory in World War II was not only a glorious triumph for the nation, but it taught deeper lessons about what one could expect in life. The United States could stand up for just causes, and if everyone pulled together, it could win. . . . The Sixties experience taught the opposite, . . . that the structure itself was corrupt, that individuals must follow their own moral compass and that they could not expect much moral leadership from above. The nation's framework, the sense of larger purpose and possibilities inherited from their parents' era, collapsed for this generation. It no longer seemed believable. And nothing has happened since to restore it.

It did not occur to me until many years after that conversation with my father that it didn't just have to do with America after Vietnam. It revealed something about our history during Vietnam, too. The men who made the choices that got the United States into the war, and who decided how to fight it, were also my father's age, sharing his experiences if not his particular knowledge or views about Vietnam. It was a generation whose vision of the world was shaped largely by the experience of World War II and the great triumph achieved by American resources and technological skill in that war. "A generation of men who believed that the world makes sense," one journalist wrote in an article about former Defense Secretary Robert S. McNamara. "That human events could be mastered. That if enough planes drop enough bombs on a backward Asian country, victory must follow."

The same article, whose subject was McNamara's long-delayed apologia for the war in his 1995 book *In Retrospect,* quoted one of its "lessons" from Vietnam: "We failed to recognize," McNamara acknowledged, "that in international affairs, as in other aspects of life, there may be problems for which there are no immediate solutions. For one whose life has been dedicated to the belief and practice of problem solving, this is particularly hard to admit. But at times, we may have to live with an imperfect, untidy world."

To which the reporter added a one-word comment: "May?"

The Vietnam War was not the only thing that changed America. It was probably not even the most important. A vast windstorm of changes in technology, in economic and family life, in racial and ethnic relations, and—possibly most profound of all—in matters of gender and sexual identity, gathered strength and speed during the last third of the twentieth century, swirling away old certainties, making everyone's world a more confusing, unstable, and uncertain place. Looking back, it's possible to trace the beginnings of the storm back far before Vietnam: taking shape in the huge turbulence of World War II, like a tropical storm forming in unseen air currents far out at sea; gently ruffling the seemingly placid air of the 1950s before reaching gale force in the following decades.

Even if the United States had never gone to war in Vietnam, the old system of racial segregation would still have been challenged, and fallen, and new racial tensions would have arisen. Women would still have assumed new roles, inside and outside the home, and men would still have felt troubled and threatened by challenges to old, deeply rooted concepts of masculinity. Suburbs would have provided unprecedented green comfort for millions while also dividing Americans ever more sharply by income and class. Tides of immigrants would still have arrived, making this a much more varied, multicolored society, with correspondingly more jostling and conflict as different groups vied for a place in their new country. Global business trends and technology would have wiped out traditional industrial jobs, transforming the occupational landscape and stranding millions of less-skilled, less-educated workers in poorly paid, unsatisfying, and impermanent jobs. Television would still have transformed the ways in which Americans saw themselves, and revolutionized the political process and the way we debate and decide national policies. And with all of these changes, old rules and traditions and standards of taste and conduct would have weakened; more people would have experimented with more freedoms, and, inevitably, more would also feel deeply threatened and anguished by the pace and wrenching nature of change.

Erase Vietnam from our history and one can reasonably speculate that America in the 1990s would still probably look much the same as it does: fragmented, self-doubting, cynical about its leaders, uncertain of its future, confused about its standards and beliefs. But, of course, Vietnam did happen, and became the era's most powerful symbol of damaged ideals and the loss of trust, unity, shared myths, and common values. Like a magnet, which draws steel shavings scattered on a sheet of paper into a particular form and pattern, Vietnam gave visible shape to the great cultural changes sweeping over American society, defining, more than any other event, the era and its pains.

Perhaps because it was such an exact reverse image of America's epic victory in World War II, Vietnam—the "bad war"—had an extraordinarily shattering effect on the national spirit. World War II ("the last good war," American officers in Vietnam often called it, in tones ranging from sour to sardonic to wistful) had become in many ways the culminating myth of the American experience and national character. It was "such a triumph of American resources, technology, and industrial and military genius," as the author Neil Sheehan put it, that during the next twenty years of unprecedented prosperity at home and military and economic dominance abroad, Americans came to think the success of their society was guaranteed.

Following World War II, the country's military and political leaders and "the greater part of the political, academic, and business leadership" as well, Sheehan wrote, took their supremacy for granted: "the elite of America had become stupefied by too much money, too many material resources, too much power, and too much success." The country that marched into Vietnam in the mid-1960s, two decades after the great crusade against Germany and Japan, had forgotten that it could fail. America's generals of the sixties "assumed that they would prevail in Vietnam simply because of who they were," Sheehan wrote. The same could have been said of American society as a whole.

There had been the ambiguous Korean War, of course. But as the nation gradually stepped up its effort in Vietnam, the towering triumph in World War II was still the dominant image in the imagination of most Americans—and their soldiers, as well. The great majority of men who fought in Vietnam were born between 1945 and 1953, growing up in the sunlit, high noon of postwar prosperity and national self-confidence. A large number were certainly the sons of World War II veterans. Virtually everything in their culture—novels, movies, family stories, childhood games, schoolbooks, the traditional patriotic rhetoric of Veterans Day speeches and graduations and political campaigns—conditioned young men entering military service in the mid-1960s to think of Vietnam as their generation's turn to be, as one veteran said, "the good guys against the bad guys."

If their war was on a smaller scale, they still imagined it—at least in the first few years—as essentially the same experience as World War II, the memory of which was now softened and sentimentalized by twenty years of heroic legends. And when Vietnam turned out to be such a different and disappointing war, the contrast with their fathers' experience made the disillusionment even sharper. One veteran, in a poem that may not have been great literature but achieved a kind of eloquence in its sadness, closed with these lines: "I want to say out loud, had we been in your war, dad, we would have made you proud."

Perhaps because it struck at such powerful myths, Vietnam acquired a mythical nature of its own. The word became a synonym for all kinds of national failure or frustration, as when the mayor of one crime-ridden city referred to the failed war on drugs as "a domestic Vietnam." The country seemed unable to shake its memories of the war or the cultural and political divisions associated with it.

The moral confusion of the war was mirrored in the postwar debate over how to remember it. "We want to give ourselves absolution," one journalist wrote, "although we remain deeply divided—as individuals and as a people—over what it is we need to absolve (whether it is what we did fighting the war in Indochina or what we did protesting it at home)." In fact, the more one examines it, the more one comes to feel the issue lingered so long because it wasn't really about how we fought or protested the war, after all, but something much more profound. America's continuing divisions about Vietnam reflected, more than anything else, an unfinished argument about who we are—about just who it is, when we look at our reflected selves in the black granite of the wall of names, that we really see.

◆ FURTHER READING

Anderson, David L. *Facing My Lai: Moving Beyond the Massacre* (1998).
———. *Trapped by Success: The Eisenhower Administration and Vietnam, 1953–1961* (1991).
Appy, Christian G. *Working-Class War: American Combat Soldiers and Vietnam* (1993).
Barrett, David M. *Uncertain Warriors: Lyndon Johnson and His Vietnam Advisers* (1993).
Beattie, Keith. *The Scar That Binds: American Culture and the Vietnam War* (1998).
Berman, Larry. *Lyndon Johnson's War: The Road to Stalemate in Vietnam* (1989).
Bradley, Mark Philip. *Imagining Vietnam and America: The Making of Postcolonial Vietnam, 1919–1950* (2000).

Braestrup, Peter. *Big Story: How the American Press and Television Reported and Interpreted the Crisis of Tet 1968 in Vietnam and Washington* (1983).

Brands, H. W. *The Wages of Globalism: Lyndon Johnson and the Limits of American Power* (1995).

Bundy, William P. *A Tangled Web: The Making of Foreign Policy in the Nixon Presidency* (1998).

Burkett, B. G., and Jay Wurts. *Stolen Valor: How the Vietnam Generation Was Robbed of Its Heroes and Its History* (1998).

Buzzanco, Robert. *Masters of War: Military Dissent and Politics in the Vietnam Era* (1996).

———. *Vietnam and the Transformation of American Life* (1999).

Clodfelter, Mark. *The Limits of Air Power: The American Bombing of North Vietnam* (1989).

Cohen, Warren I., and Nancy Bernkopf Tucker, eds. *Lyndon Johnson Confronts the World: American Foreign Policy, 1963–1968* (1994).

De Benedetti, Charles, and Charles Chatfield. *An American Ordeal: The Antiwar Movement of the Vietnam Era* (1990).

Duiker, William J. *Sacred War: Nationalism and Revolution in a Divided Vietnam* (1995).

Gardner, Lloyd C. *Pay Any Price: Lyndon Johnson and the Wars for Vietnam* (1995).

Gilbert, Marc Jason, ed. *Why the North Won the Vietnam War* (2002).

Hallin, David C. *The "Uncensored War"* (1986).

Hayslip, Le Ly, and Jay Wurts. *When Heaven and Earth Changed Places: A Vietnamese Woman's Journey from War to Peace* (1990).

Heineman, Kenneth. *Campus Wars: The Peace Movement at American State Universities in the Vietnam Era* (1993).

Hendrickson, Paul. *The Living and the Dead: Robert McNamara and Five Lives of a Lost War* (1996).

Herring, George C. *America's Longest War: The United States and Vietnam, 1950–1975*, 3rd ed. (1995).

———. *LBJ and Vietnam: A Different Kind of War* (1994).

Hess, Gary. *The United States Emergence as a Southeast Asian Power* (1987).

Hunt, Michael H. *Lyndon Johnson's War: America's Cold War Crusade in Vietnam* (1996).

Kaiser, David. *American Tragedy: Kennedy, Johnson, and the Origins of the Vietnam War* (2000).

Kaplan, Lawrence S., Denise Artaud, and Mark R. Rubin, eds. *Dien Bien Phu and the Crisis of Franco-American Relations, 1954–1955* (1990).

Khong, Yuen Foong. *Analogies at War: Korea, Munich, Dien Bien Phu, and the Vietnam Decisions of 1965* (1992).

Kimball, Jeffrey P. *Nixon's Vietnam War* (1998).

Lind, Michael. *Vietnam: The Necessary War* (1999).

Logevall, Fredrik. *Choosing War: The Lost Chance for Peace and the Escalation of War in Vietnam* (1999).

Maraniss, David. *They Marched into Sunlight: War and Peace in Vietnam and America, October 1967* (2003).

McNamara, Robert S., James G. Blight, and Robert K. Brigham. *Argument Without End: In Search of Answers to the Vietnam Tragedy* (1999).

Moïse, Edwin E. *Tonkin Gulf and the Escalation of the Vietnam War* (1996).

Morris, Stephen J. *Why Vietnam Invaded Cambodia: Political Culture and the Causes of War* (1999).

Moss, George Donelson. *Vietnam: An American Ordeal* (1989).

Neu, Charles E., ed. *After Vietnam: Legacies of a Lost War* (2000).

Newman, John M. *JFK and Vietnam: Deception, Intrigue, and the Struggle for Power* (1992).

Palmer, Bruce, Jr. *The 25-Year War: America's Military Role in Vietnam* (1984).

Pike, Douglas E. *PAVN: People's Army of Vietnam* (1986).

Pribbenow, Merle L., trans. *Victory in Vietnam: The Official History of the People's Army of Vietnam* (2002).

Rust, William J. *Kennedy in Vietnam* (1987).

Schandler, Herbert Y. *Lyndon Johnson and Vietnam: The Unmaking of a President* (1977).

Schulzinger, Robert. *A Time for War: The United States and Vietnam, 1941–1975* (1997).

Shawcross, William. *Sideshow: Kissinger, Nixon, and the Destruction of Cambodia* (1979).

Sheehan, Neil. *A Bright Shining Lie: John Paul Vann and America in Vietnam* (1988).

Small, Melvin. *Covering Dissent: The Media and the Anti-Vietnam War Movement* (1994).

Smith, R. B. *An International History of the Vietnam War,* 2 vols. (1983, 1985).

Sorley, Lewis. *A Better War: The Unexamined Victories and the Final Tragedy of America's Last Years in Vietnam* (1999).

Spector, Ronald H. *The United States Army in Vietnam: Advice and Support, the Early Years, 1941–1960* (1983).

Summers, Harry G., Jr. *On Strategy: A Critical Analysis of the Vietnam War* (1982).

Thompson, James C. *Rolling Thunder* (1980).

Truong, Nhu Tang, David Chanoff, and Doan Van Toai. *A Vietcong Memoir* (1986).

Van, Tien Dung. *Our Great Spring Victory: An Account of the Liberation of South Vietnam* (1977).

VanDeMark, Brian. *Into the Quagmire: Lyndon Johnson and the Escalation of the Vietnam War* (1991).

Vo, Nguyen Giap, and Van Tien Dung. *How We Won the War* (1976).

Young, Marilyn B. *The Vietnam Wars: 1945–1990* (1991).

Zhai, Qiang. *China and the Vietnam Wars, 1950–1975* (2000).

CHAPTER
10

Ronald Reagan and the

Transformation of America

The presidency of Ronald Reagan, many have argued, marked a critical turning point in the history of postwar America—a "revolution" in politics, economics, international affairs, and culture. Indeed, some have argued that the changes associated with the Reagan presidency were at the least comparable with those that occurred during the Democratic presidencies of John F. Kennedy and Lyndon B. Johnson, if not the transformation in politics and public life wrought during the New Deal and Cold War presidencies of Franklin D. Roosevelt and Harry S Truman. Yet if there is seemingly widespread consensus that the Reagan years somehow constituted a revolution of sorts, there has been far less agreement as to its extent and character, the degree of its success or failure, and whether or not it was truly Reagan's—that is to say, did he create it or was he merely its legatee?

As journalists and political scientists have noted, the Reagan years were marked by the continued decomposition of the old New Deal Democratic coalition forged by Roosevelt during the 1930s and by the growing ascendancy of the Republican party at the national level. Despite Democratic control of the House of Representatives (and the Senate, too, after 1986), Reagan secured passage of a series of major legislative initiatives. Through his power of appointment, moreover, he reshaped the nation's courts. He became the first president since Dwight D. Eisenhower to complete two terms in office successfully. Perhaps most important, he exercised a profound influence over the country's political agenda, molding the issues and terms of political debate throughout the decade.

The economic changes of the Reagan era were no less dramatic. By 1979, the Democratic administration of President Jimmy Carter was beset by a host of problems, chief among them an economy wracked by stalled growth, inflation, high unemployment, declining profits, and stagnant wages. Symptomatic of a more fundamental crisis in the postwar system of regulated capitalism forged during the 1930s and 1940s, these economic woes weakened Carter's Democratic base among working Americans, even as they prompted a massive mobilization by business leaders determined to refashion the nation's politics and political economy. Reagan entered the White House pledged to stem inflation, lower taxes, reduce government spending, and cut federal regulation of the economy. He succeeded in many of these *efforts, although not always in ways that he and his supporters had predicted and not necessarily in ways that produced all the benefits that they claimed would follow. He halted inflation through the classic Republican strategy of high interest rates and the cold bath of a major recession, a process begun during the late Carter years by Federal Reserve Board Chairman Paul Volcker. He lowered taxes, especially on the well-to-do, although it is unclear whether this reduction spurred increased investment or only fueled an orgy of conspicuous consumption by the rich. He presided over a wave of deregulation (begun during the 1970s) during which regulatory structures in place for decades were eliminated or radically revised. Finally, and perhaps ironically, Reagan conspicuously failed to reduce government spending. Indeed, steep increases in defense costs, coupled with lower taxes, contributed to what were then the largest annual deficits in American history. In the short run, these policies paid rich political dividends: a huge military buildup without cuts in middle-class entitlements such as Social Security and Medicare, combined with a tax cut that left many Americans with more money for private consumption, helped sustain the president's popularity.*

Reagan's success as president must also be understood in light of the powerful tensions coursing through American society and culture during the 1970s and 1980s: the polarizing impact of race and the reemergence of Christian conservatism in politics. Slowly, white southern Democratic conservatives and blue-collar ethnics continued to shift their allegiance from the Democratic to the Republican party. Reagan also appealed to conservative Christians, whose political mobilization around "traditional values" became one of the decade's defining characteristics. Indeed, much of Reagan's success as a national leader seemed to derive from a paradox: on the one hand, Reagan was himself the product of a technologically progressive, corporate, and media-driven modern culture that was changing America in so many fundamental ways; on the other hand, he continually evoked images of an America of individualism and traditional values. There can be no doubt that in doing so he deftly captured the ambivalence felt by many Americans.

In foreign affairs, too, Reagan offered the nation what seemed to be a sharp break with the policies of his predecessors. Richard Nixon, Gerald Ford, and Jimmy Carter had sought to engineer what some have called America's "retreat from empire"— a scaling back of the rampant globalism of the Kennedy and Johnson years and the beginnings of détente with the Soviet Union and China. By 1980, however, many conservatives were charging that the Soviet invasion of Afghanistan, the transfer of control of the Panama Canal, and especially the Iranian hostage crisis all signaled a dangerous decline in American power. Reagan campaigned for the White House on a platform that promised to restore American leadership in world affairs. During his presidency, the United States embarked on a massive military buildup, first in more or less conventional weapons and then through Star Wars, the highly controversial Strategic Defense Initiative (SDI), which proposed to defend the United States with a high-tech "umbrella" of costly and sophisticated electronic weapons. The United States also pursued a renewed interventionism, especially in the Caribbean, where the Reagan administration invaded the tiny island of Grenada and launched a covert campaign to overthrow the left-wing Sandinista government of Nicaragua. Reagan's revival of Cold War patriotism touched a popular nerve, perhaps best symbolized by the flag-waving and chanting of "We're Number One" by Americans at the 1984 Summer Olympic Games in Los Angeles.

By 1986, nevertheless, the administration was in deep trouble. Massive military spending, coupled with reduced taxes, sent the nation's indebtedness skyrocketing. The Iran-Contra scandals, meanwhile, revealed that the president and his top advisers were clearly implicated in an illegal attempt to trade arms for hostages and divert the proceeds to the U.S.-sponsored Contras in Nicaragua. The administration abruptly changed course during its final two years. The president abandoned Cold War confrontation for a new pragmatism that included the Intermediate-Range Nuclear Forces (INF) Treaty with the Russians and progress toward a more comprehensive reduction of all nuclear weapons. Much of this change owed to developments that neither Reagan nor most Americans anticipated—the growing economic and political paralysis of the Soviet Union, the rapid dismantling of its empire in Eastern Europe, and the rise of Mikhail Gorbachev and a new leadership dedicated to sweeping political and economic reforms. Some saw in these developments a vindication of Reagan's policies. The United States, they claimed, had won the Cold War. Others viewed the shift as a happy coincidence. Ronald Reagan, the "Teflon president," had lucked out again. Still others saw in these developments an end not only to the Cold War but to an entire era in international relations.

✦ D O C U M E N T S

By 1979, the Democratic administration of President Jimmy Carter was beset by a host of problems, many of which he had inherited but few of which he had successfully resolved. Chief among them was an economy wracked by inflation and high unemployment, and an energy crisis that was in part the product of the explosive politics of the Middle East and that signaled the end of an era of cheap energy. In Washington, D.C., political gridlock had set in, virtually paralyzing the efforts of either Congress or the administration to act decisively. In his July, 15, 1979, speech to the nation (Document 1), Carter addressed not only the problems of economics and energy but also the larger crisis of confidence that he believed pervaded the nation. Republican presidential candidate Ronald Reagan skillfully capitalized on the economic and political failures of the Carter administration, as is clear from his September 9, 1980, campaign speech before the International Business Council (Document 2). Carter, reflecting the chastened spirit of the 1970s, had emphasized sacrifice and restraint in his speeches and policies. Reagan, in what would become one of the dominant themes of the 1980s, stressed economic growth and freedom from governmental restraint, a message that appealed strongly to business leaders.

Equally important was Reagan's appeal to Americans worried about what they believed to be a decline in traditional values. And just as popular concerns over the economy were mobilized by the business community, concerns over "values" were organized by a cadre of new cultural entrepreneurs who skillfully used modern communication techniques—radio, television, and direct mail—to convey traditional messages. In Document 3, excerpted from his book *The New Right: We're Ready to Lead* (1980), New Right leader Richard A. Viguerie describes the innovative techniques used to build a powerful conservative movement. In the 1980 campaign, Reagan had promised strong leadership in foreign affairs. In a March 8, 1983, speech to the National Association of Evangelicals (Document 4), Reagan emphasized his support for conservative social values at home and denounced the Soviet Union as "the focus of evil in the modern world."

The policies of the Reagan administration also prompted sharp criticism. In Document 5, a congressional committee reports on a secret and illegal deal to sell arms to Iran (a country Reagan had once denounced as a sponsor of "international terrorism") in return for money that would be used to fund the Contra rebels in Nicaragua. In Document 6, Sierra Club leader Carl Pope condemns the administration's environmental policies; while in Document 7, former Surgeon General C. Everett Koop recalls his struggles to draw the administration's attention to the burgeoning AIDS crisis.

1. President Jimmy Carter and the Crisis of the American Spirit, 1979

. . . It's clear that the true problems of our Nation are much deeper—deeper than gasoline lines or energy shortages, deeper even than inflation or recession. And I realize more than ever that as President I need your help. So, I decided to reach out and listen to the voices of America.

I invited to Camp David people from almost every segment of our society—business and labor, teachers and preachers, Governors, mayors, and private citizens. And then I left Camp David to listen to other Americans, men and women like you. It has been an extraordinary 10 days, and I want to share with you what I've heard.

First of all, I got a lot of personal advice. Let me quote a few of the typical comments that I wrote down.

This from a southern Governor: "Mr. President, you are not leading this Nation—you're just managing the Government." . . .

I want to talk to you right now about a fundamental threat to American democracy.

I do not mean our political and civil liberties. They will endure. And I do not refer to the outward strength of America, a nation that is at peace tonight everywhere in the world, with unmatched economic power and military might.

The threat is nearly invisible in ordinary ways. It is a crisis of confidence. It is a crisis that strikes at the very heart and soul and spirit of our national will. We can see this crisis in the growing doubt about the meaning of our own lives and in the loss of a unity of purpose for our Nation.

The erosion of our confidence in the future is threatening to destroy the social and the political fabric of America.

The confidence that we have always had as a people is not simply some romantic dream or a proverb in a dusty book that we read just on the Fourth of July. It is the idea which founded our Nation and has guided our development as a people. Confidence in the future has supported everything else—public institutions and private enterprise, our own families, and the very Constitution of the United States. Confidence has defined our course and has served as a link between generations. We've always believed in something called progress. We've always had a faith that the days of our children would be better than our own.

Our people are losing that faith, not only in government itself but in the ability as citizens to serve as the ultimate rulers and shapers of our democracy. As a people we know our past and we are proud of it. Our progress has been part of the living history of America, even the world. We always believed that we were part of a great movement of humanity itself called democracy, involved in the search for freedom and that belief has always strengthened us in our purpose. But just as we are losing our confidence in the future, we are also beginning to close the door on our past.

In a nation that was proud of hard work, strong families, close-knit communities, and our faith in God, too many of us now tend to worship self-indulgence and

Excerpts from Jimmy Carter, "Energy and National Goals: Address to the Nation," July 15, 1979, in *Public Papers of the Presidents of the United States, 1977–1981* (Washington, D.C.: GPO). Online at http://www.presidency.ucsb.edu/ws/index.php?pid=32596

consumption. Human identity is no longer defined by what one does, but by what one owns. But we've discovered that owning things and consuming things does not satisfy our longing for meaning. We've learned that piling up material goods cannot fill the emptiness of lives which have no confidence or purpose.

The symptoms of this crisis of the American spirit are all around us. For the first time in the history of our country a majority of our people believe that the next 5 years will be worse than the past 5 years. Two-thirds of our people do not even vote. The productivity of American workers is actually dropping, and the willingness of Americans to save for the future has fallen below that of all other people in the Western world.

As you know, there is a growing disrespect for government and for churches and for schools, the news media, and other institutions. This is not a message of happiness or reassurance, but it is the truth and it is a warning.

These changes did not happen overnight. They've come upon us gradually over the last generation, years that were filled with shocks and tragedy.

We were sure that ours was a nation of the ballot, not the bullet, until the murders of John Kennedy and Robert Kennedy and Martin Luther King, Jr. We were taught that our armies were always invincible and our causes were always just, only to suffer the agony of Vietnam. We respected the Presidency as a place of honor until the shock of Watergate.

We remember when the phrase "sound as a dollar" was an expression of absolute dependability, until 10 years of inflation began to shrink our dollar and our savings. We believed that our Nation's resources were limitless until 1973 when we had to face a growing dependence on foreign oil.

These wounds are still very deep. They have never been healed.

Looking for a way out of this crisis, our people have turned to the Federal Government and found it isolated from the mainstream of our Nation's life. Washington, D.C., has become an island. The gap between our citizens and our Government has never been so wide. The people are looking for honest answers, not easy answers; clear leadership, not false claims and evasiveness and politics as usual.

What you see too often in Washington and elsewhere around the country is a system of government that seems incapable of action. You see a Congress twisted and pulled in every direction by hundreds of well-financed and powerful special interests. You see every extreme position defended to the last vote, almost to the last breath by one unyielding group or another. You often see a balanced and a fair approach that demands sacrifice, a little sacrifice from everyone, abandoned like an orphan without support and without friends.

Often you see paralysis and stagnation and drift. You don't like it, and neither do I. What can we do?

First of all, we must face the truth, and then we can change our course. We simply must have faith in each other, faith in our ability to govern ourselves, and faith in the future of this Nation. Restoring that faith and that confidence to America is now the most important task we face. It is a true challenge of this generation of Americans. . . .

All the traditions of our past, all the lessons of our heritage, all the promises of our future point to another path, the path of common purpose and the restoration of American values. That path leads to true freedom for our Nation and ourselves. . . .

2. Presidential Candidate Ronald Reagan Calls for New Economic Policies, 1980

Almost two months ago, in accepting the Presidential nomination of my party, I spoke of the historically unique crisis facing the United States. At that time I said:

> Never before in our history have Americans been called upon to face three grave threats to our very existence, any one of which could destroy us. We face a disintegrating economy, a weakened defense and an energy policy based on the sharing of scarcity. . . .

I'd like to speak to you today about a new concept of leadership, one that has both the words and the music. One based on faith in the American people, confidence in the American economy, and a firm commitment to see to it that the Federal Government is once more responsive to the people.

That concept is rooted in a strategy for growth, a program that sees the American economic system as it is—a huge, complex, dynamic system which demands not piecemeal Federal packages, or pious hopes wrapped in soothing words, but the hard work and concerted programs necessary for real growth.

We must first recognize that the problem with the U.S. economy is swollen, inefficient government, needless regulation, too much taxation, too much printing-press money. We don't need any more doses of Carter's eight- or 10-point programs to "fix" or fine tune the economy. . . .

Only a series of well-planned economic actions, taken so that they complement and reinforce one another, can move our economy forward again.

We must keep the rate of growth of government spending at reasonable and prudent levels.

We must reduce personal income tax rates and accelerate and simplify depreciation schedules in an orderly, systematic way to remove disincentives to work, savings, investment, and productivity.

We must review regulations that affect the economy and change them to encourage economic growth.

We must establish a stable, sound, and predictable monetary policy.

And we must restore confidence by following a consistent national economic policy that does not change from month to month. . . .

One of the most critical elements of my economic program is the control of government spending. Waste, extravagance, abuse, and outright fraud in Federal agencies and programs must be stopped. . . . [B]illions of the taxpayers' dollars . . . are wasted every year throughout hundreds of Federal programs, and it will take a major, sustained effort over time to effectively counter this. . . .

The second major element of my economic program is a tax rate reduction plan. This plan calls for an across-the-board, three-year reduction in personal income tax rates—10 percent in 1981, 10 percent in 1982, and 10 percent in 1983. . . .

Another vital part of this strategy concerns government regulation. . . .

Government regulation, like fire, makes a good servant but a bad master. No one can argue with the intent of this regulation—to improve health and safety and

Excerpts from Ronald Reagan, Speech delivered before the International Business Council (Chicago: September 9, 1980), *Vital Speeches of the Day* 46, no. 24 (October 1, 1980), 738–741.

to give us cleaner air and water—but too often regulations work against rather than for the interests of the people. When the real take-home pay of the average American worker is declining steadily, and 8 million Americans are out of work, we must carefully re-examine our regulatory structure to assess to what degree regulations have contributed to this situation. In my administration there should and will be a thorough and systematic review of the thousands of Federal regulations that affect the economy.

Along with spending control, tax reform, and deregulation, a sound, stable, and predictable monetary policy is essential to restoring economic health. The Federal Reserve Board is, and should remain, independent of the Executive Branch of government. But the President must nominate those who serve on the Federal Reserve Board. My appointees will share my commitment to restoring the value and stability of the American dollar.

A fundamental part of my strategy for economic growth is the restoration of confidence. If our business community is going to invest and build and create new, well-paying jobs, they must have a future free from arbitrary, government action. They must have confidence that the economic "rules-of-the-game" won't be changed suddenly or capriciously.

In my administration, a national economic policy will be established, and we will begin to implement it, within the first 90 days.

Thus, I envision a strategy encompassing many elements—none of which can do the job alone, but all of which together can get it done. This strategy depends for its success more than anything else on the will of the people to regain control of their government. . . .

The time has come for the American people to reclaim their dream. Things don't have to be this way. We can change them. We must change them. Mr. Carter's American tragedy must and can be transcended by the spirit of the American people, working together.

Let's get America working again.

The time is now.

3. A New Right Activist Explains
Conservative Success, 1980

Our success is built on four elements—single issue groups, multi-issue conservative groups, coalition politics and direct mail.

Conservative single issue groups have been accused of not only fragmenting American politics but threatening the very existence of our two-party system. Congressman David Obey of Wisconsin, a liberal Democrat, has even charged that government has nearly been brought to a standstill by single issue organizations.

Nonsense!

In the first place, all the New Right has done is copy the success of the old left.

Liberal single issue groups were around long before we were, and the liberals still have as many or more than we do.

Civil rights was a single issue that Hubert Humphrey used to rise to national office. The Vietnam War was a single issue that George McGovern used to rise to national prominence. The environment, consumerism, anti-nuclear power—these are all single issues around which liberals have organized and exercised power and influence.

In the area of public interest law, liberal groups such as the Environmental Defense Fund, the National Prison Project, the Mexican-American Legal Defense and Educational Fund, the Southern Poverty Law Center, the National Veterans Law Center, the Women's Legal Defense Fund have drastically changed the direction of the Federal government.

Ralph Nader is nothing if not a collection of single issues. The liberals who are upset now about conservative single issue groups were not upset about the groups pushing for legalization of marijuana . . . homosexual rights . . . or ERA. . . .

Single issue groups naturally emerge because the political parties run away from issues. Single issue groups are the result *of* not the reason *for* the decline of political parties.

If one of the two major political parties had concerned itself more with issues like right to life, high taxes, the growth of the federal government, the right to keep and bear arms, a strong national defense, prayer in the schools, strengthening the family, sex on TV and in the movies, there probably would not have been an explosion of conservative single issue groups. . . .

The second key to our success is the multi-issue group which is part of the conservative movement and makes no bones about it. Such a group is conservative first, last and always. It takes strong positions on every important conservative vs. liberal issue.

The multi-issue conservative movement group also takes a broad overview of where we are going and the best way to get there.

It usually does not have as many members or supporters as single issue groups because its ranks are made up of individuals who are solidly conservative across the board.

The National Right to Work Committee can find over a million people who strongly oppose compulsory unionism.

The National Rifle Association can find nearly two million people who oppose federal gun registration.

Right to Life groups can find over a million people who oppose abortion.

But a conservative group which is pro-Right to Work, pro-Right to Life and pro-gun simply can't find a million contributors who agree on 20 different conservative issues.

For example, a local union leader may dislike the National Right to Work Committee but also oppose additional gun controls.

A pro-life supporter may not care one way or the other about compulsory unionism. And so forth.

But it is a sign of conservative strength that several of our broad spectrum groups do have, if not a million members, several hundred thousand.

Multi-issue broad spectrum groups such as The Conservative Caucus, the American Conservative Union, the Committee for the Survival of a Free Congress, the Heritage Foundation and the National Conservative Political Action Committee, to name but a few, are trying and succeeding in covering all the bases and all the issues for the conservative movement. . . .

Which brings me to the third part of the New Right's success—coalition politics.

Coalition politics is as old as the United States of America. You could call the original Thirteen Colonies a collection of issue groups who banded together to fight and defeat a common enemy—Great Britain.

The Republican Party was originally a coalition of issue groups—Free-Soil party members, pro-business northern Whigs, and some Democrats opposed to slavery.

FDR's New Deal was basically a coalition of groups—Southern farmers, blacks, Jews, organized labor, big city Democrats and the unemployed.

In fact, a liberal coalition based on the New Deal, the Fair Deal and the Great Society has dominated the nation for almost five decades.

But in the last 12 years, since Hubert Humphrey lost the Presidency to Richard Nixon in 1968, that coalition has begun to unravel. Conservatives didn't have the institutions to fill the gap then, but we do now. . . .

Coalition politics includes working within the Republican and Democratic parties to nominate conservative candidates, promote conservative positions and create conservative majorities in both parties. . . .

I want to talk now about the fourth reason for the New Right's success—direct mail.

Like all successful political movements, we must have a method of communicating with each other, and for conservatives in the 1970's it was direct mail.

Frankly, the conservative movement is where it is today because of direct mail. Without direct mail, there would be no effective counterforce to liberalism, and certainly there would be no New Right. . . .

We sell our magazines, our books, and our candidates through the mail. We fight our legislative battles through the mail. We alert our supporters to upcoming battles through the mail. We find new recruits for the conservative movements through the mail.

Without the mail, most conservative activity would wither and die.

Most political observers agree that liberals have effective control of the mass media—a virtual monopoly on TV, radio, newspapers and magazines. . . .

However, there is one method of mass commercial communication that the liberals do not control—direct mail. In fact, conservatives excel at direct mail. . . .

Raising money is only one of several purposes of direct-mail advertising letters. A letter may ask you to vote for a candidate, volunteer for campaign work, circulate a petition among your neighbors, write letters and postcards to your Senators and Congressmen, urging them to pass or defeat legislation and also ask you for money to pay for the direct mail advertising campaign. . . .

Where would conservatives be without direct mail? We would be where we were 20 years ago, on the defensive, isolated, fighting losing battles. . . .

There is another key to New Right success—our positive attitude toward the news media.

From the time I started in politics in the mid 1950's until the early 1970's, most conservatives and the national media were like cats and dogs, or oil and water—they just didn't mix.

Then in the early 1970's some of the national media began to notice our political activities.

I have to be honest and say that I shared the traditional conservatives' position on the press. Which was avoid them, recognize that they are all liberals, and be convinced that their basic purpose is to attack conservatives.

I remember one day a fairly well known writer for a major newspaper called and wanted an appointment to come and talk to me.

I was a little short of terrified. I told my secretary that we'd get back to him.

I then called some of my conservative associates and asked what I should do. Almost all advised me to avoid the reporter.

The advice went something like this—that newspaper is no friend of the conservative movement, that reporter will try to do you in, etc., etc.

But then I got to thinking. I and my conservative friends are not playing in the big leagues—but we want to.

We're not having a major influence on national policies—but we want to.

We're not close to our goal of governing America—but we want to.

I called the reporter back and said, "Why don't you come over and, if you've got time, why don't we go to lunch?"

Well, I spent an enjoyable three hours with the reporter. He wrote a basically fair and accurate story (although it wasn't as fair and objective as my mother would have written).

And from that day forward, I felt that I and other conservatives had to change our view of the press.

I can think of no better example of the differences between the New Right and the old right.

We realize that reporters and editors are not monsters, or even hopeless ideologues.

The vast majority are good, decent men and women who are trying to do a professional job and are looking for the kind of news which will put their stories on the front page or the nightly TV newscasts.

During the next few years, the New Right's relationship with the press improved. We felt comfortable with the press and they began to cover our activities.

However, in the spring of 1977 I realized that my associates in the New Right and I needed a more professional approach to the media.

We were dealing with the media in a casual, almost accidental way. We needed someone to introduce us to the major media, to teach us how to call and conduct a press conference, how to have a press breakfast, how to get our thoughts across in a few seconds on TV, how to hold activities that the press would be interested in covering. . . .

Single issue groups—multi-issue groups—coalition politics—direct mail—these have been the four cornerstones of conservative growth and success in the 1970's. They will help us build a new majority in America in the 1980's.

As Congressman Newt Gingrich of Georgia has put it: "The way you build a majority in this country is you go out and put together everybody who's against the guy who's in. And instead of asking the question, What divides us?, you ask the question, What unites us?"

And what unites most conservatives, Republican, Democratic and Independent, is a desire for less government and more freedom for every American.

4. President Ronald Reagan Proclaims America's "Spiritual Reawakening," 1983

. . . I'm pleased to be here today with you who are keeping America great by keeping her good. Only through your work and prayers and those of millions of others can we hope to survive this perilous century and keep alive this experiment in liberty, this last, best hope of man.

I want you to know that this administration is motivated by a political philosophy that sees the greatness of America in you, her people, and in your families, churches, neighborhoods, communities—the institutions that foster and nourish values like concern for others and respect for the rule of law under God.

Now, I don't have to tell you that this puts us in opposition to, or at least out of step with, a prevailing attitude of many who have turned to a modern-day secularism, discarding the tried and time-tested values upon which our very civilization is based. No mater how well intentioned, their value system is radically different from that of most Americans. And while they proclaim that they're freeing us from superstitions of the past, they've taken upon themselves the job of superintending us by government rule and regulation. Sometimes their voices are louder than ours, but they are not yet a majority. . . .

But the fight against parental notification is really only one example of many attempts to water down traditional values and even abrogate the original terms of American democracy. Freedom prospers when religion is vibrant and the rule of law under God is acknowledged. When our Founding Fathers passed the first amendment, they sought to protect churches from government interference. They never intended to construct a wall of hostility between government and the concept of religious belief itself. . . .

Last year, I sent the Congress a constitutional amendment to restore prayer to public schools. Already this session, there's growing bipartisan support for the amendment, and I am calling on the Congress to act speedily to pass it and to let our children pray. . . .

More than a decade ago, a Supreme Court decision literally wiped off the books of 50 States statutes protecting the rights of unborn children. Abortion on demand now takes the lives of up to 1½ million unborn children a year. Human life legislation ending this tragedy will some day pass the Congress, and you and I must never rest until it does. Unless and until it can be proven that the unborn child is not a living entity, then its right to life, liberty, and the pursuit of happiness must be protected. . . .

There's a great spiritual awakening in America, a renewal of the traditional values that have been the bedrock of America's goodness and greatness. . . .

There is sin and evil in the world, and we're enjoined by Scripture and the Lord Jesus to oppose it with all our might. Our nation, too, has a legacy of evil with which it must deal. . . .

Excerpts from Ronald Reagan, "Remarks at the Annual Convention of the National Association of Evangelicals in Orlando, Florida, March 8, 1983," *The Public Papers of President Ronald Reagan* (Simi Valley, Calif.: Ronald Reagan Presidential Library). Online at http://www.reagan.utexas.edu/archives/speeches/1983/30883b.htm.

But whatever sad episodes exist in our past, any objective observer must hold a positive view of American history, a history that has been the story of hopes fulfilled and dreams made into reality. Especially in this century, America has kept alight the torch of freedom, but not just for ourselves but for millions of others around the world. . . .

[L]et us pray for the salvation of all of those who live in that totalitarian darkness—pray they will discover the job of knowing God. But until they do, let us be aware that while they preach the supremacy of the state, declare its omnipotence over individual man, and predict its eventual domination of all peoples on the Earth, they are the focus of evil in the modern world. . . .

5. A Congressional Committee Reports on "Irangate," 1987

The full story of the Iran-Contra Affair is complicated, and, for this Nation, profoundly sad. In the narrative portion of this Report, the Committees present a comprehensive account of the facts, based on 10 months of investigation, including 11 weeks of hearings.

But the facts alone do not explain how or why the events occurred. In this Executive Summary, the Committees focus on the key issues and offer their conclusions. Minority, supplemental, and additional views are printed in Section II and Section III.

Summary of the Facts

The Iran-Contra Affair had its origin in two unrelated revolutions in Iran and Nicaragua.

In Nicaragua, the long-time President, General Anastasio Somoza Debayle, was overthrown in 1979 and replaced by a Government controlled by Sandinista leftists.

In Iran, the pro-Western Government of the Shah Mohammed Riza Pahlavi was overthrown in 1979 by Islamic fundamentalists led by the Ayatollah Khomeini. The Khomeini Government, stridently anti-American, became a supporter of terrorism against American citizens.

United States policy following the revolution in Nicaragua was to encourage the Sandinista Government to keep its pledges of pluralism and democracy. However, the Sandinista regime became increasingly anti-American and autocratic; began to aid a leftist insurgency in El Salvador; and turned toward Cuba and the Soviet Union for political, military, and economic assistance. By December 1981, the United States had begun supporting the Nicaraguan Contras, armed opponents of the Sandinista regime.

The Central Intelligence Agency (CIA) was the U.S. Government agency that assisted the Contras. In accordance with Presidential decisions, known as Findings, and with funds appropriated by Congress, the CIA armed, clothed, fed, and supervised

U.S. Congress, *Report of the Congressional Committees Investigating the Iran-Contra Affair* (Washington, D.C.: GPO, 1987), 3–11.

the Contras. Despite this assistance, the Contras failed to win widespread popular support or military victories within Nicaragua.

Although the President continued to favor support of the Contras, opinion polls indicated that a majority of the public was not supportive. Opponents of the Administration's policy feared that U.S. involvement with the Contras would embroil the United States in another Vietnam. Supporters of the policy feared that, without U.S. support for the Contras, the Soviets would gain a dangerous toehold in Central America.

Congress prohibited Contra aid for the purpose of overthrowing the Sandinista Government in fiscal year 1983, and limited all aid to the Contras in fiscal year 1984 to $24 million. Following disclosure in March and April 1984 that the CIA had a role in connection with the mining of the Nicaraguan harbors without adequate notification to Congress, public criticism mounted and the Administration's Contra policy lost much of its support within Congress. After further vigorous debate, Congress exercised its Constitutional power over appropriations and cut off all funds for the Contras' military and paramilitary operations. The statutory provision cutting off funds, known as the Boland Amendment, was part of a fiscal year 1985 omnibus appropriations bill, and was signed into law by the President on October 12, 1984.

Still, the President felt strongly about the Contras, and he ordered his staff, in the words of his National Security Adviser, to find a way to keep the Contras' "body and soul together." Thus began the story of how the staff of a White House advisory body, the NSC [National Security Council], became an operational entity that secretly ran the Contra assistance effort, and later the Iran initiative. The action officer placed in charge of both operations was Lt. Col. Oliver L. North.

Denied funding by Congress, the President turned to third countries and private sources. Between June 1984 and the beginning of 1986, the President, his National Security Adviser, and the NSC staff secretly raised $34 million for the Contras from other countries. An additional $2.7 million was provided for the Contras during 1985 and 1986 from private contributors, who were addressed by North and occasionally granted photo opportunities with the President. In the middle of this period, Assistant Secretary of State A. Langhorne Motley—from whom these contributions were concealed—gave his assurance to Congress that the Administration was not "soliciting and/or encouraging third countries" to give funds to the Contras because, as he conceded, the Boland Amendment prohibited such solicitation.

The first contributions were sent by the donors to bank accounts controlled and used by the Contras. However, in July 1985, North took control of the funds and—with the support of two National Security Advisers (Robert McFarlane and John Poindexter) and, according to North, [CIA] Director [William] Casey—used those funds to run the covert operation to support the Contras.

At the suggestion of Director Casey, North recruited Richard V. Secord, a retired Air Force Major General with experience in special operations. Secord set up Swiss bank accounts, and North steered future donations into these accounts. Using these funds, and funds later generated by the Iran arms sales, Secord and his associate, Albert Hakim, created what they called "the Enterprise," a private organization designed to engage in covert activities on behalf of the United States.

The Enterprise, functioning largely at North's direction, had its own airplanes, pilots, airfield, operatives, ship, secure communications devices, and secret Swiss bank accounts. For 16 months, it served as the secret arm of the NSC staff, carrying out with private and non-appropriated money, and without the accountability or restrictions imposed by law on the CIA, a covert Contra aid program that Congress thought it had prohibited.

Although the CIA and other agencies involved in intelligence activities knew that the Boland Amendment barred their involvement in covert support for the Contras, North's Contra support operation received logistical and tactical support from various personnel in the CIA and other agencies. Certain CIA personnel in Central America gave their assistance. The U.S. Ambassador in Costa Rica, Lewis Tambs, provided his active assistance. North also enlisted the aid of Defense Department personnel in Central America, and obtained secure communications equipment from the National Security Agency. The Assistant Secretary of State with responsibility for the region, Elliot Abrams, professed ignorance of this support. He later stated that he had been "careful not to ask North lots of questions."

By Executive Order and National Security Decision Directive issued by President Reagan, all covert operations must be approved by the President personally and in writing. By statute, Congress must be notified about each covert action. The funds used for such actions, like all government funds, must be strictly accounted for.

The covert action directed by North, however, was not approved by the President in writing. Congress was not notified about it. And the funds to support it were never accounted for. In short, the operation functioned without any of the accountability required of Government activities. It was an evasion of the Constitution's most basic check on Executive action—the power of the Congress to grant or deny funding for Government programs.

Moreover, the covert action to support the Contras was concealed from Congress and the public. When the press reported in the summer of 1985 that the NSC staff was engaged in raising money and furnishing military support to the Contras, the President assured the public that the law was being followed. His National Security Adviser, Robert C. McFarlane, assured Committees of Congress, both in person and in writing, that the NSC staff was obeying both the spirit and the letter of the law, and was neither soliciting money nor coordinating military support for the Contras. . . .

The NSC staff was [thus] already engaged in covert operations through Secord when, in the summer of 1985, the Government of Israel proposed that missiles be sold to Iran in return for the release of seven American hostages held in Lebanon and the prospect of improved relations with Iran. The Secretaries of State and Defense repeatedly opposed such sales to a government designated by the United States as a supporter of international terrorism. They called it a straight arms-for-hostages deal that was contrary to U.S. public policy. They also argued that these sales would violate the Arms Export Control Act, as well as the U.S. arms embargo against Iran. The embargo had been imposed after the taking of hostages at the U.S. Embassy in Tehran on November 4, 1979, and was continued because of the Iran-Iraq war.

Nevertheless, in the summer of 1985 the President authorized Israel to proceed with the sales. The NSC staff conducting the Contra covert action also took operational control of implementing the President's decision on arms sales to Iran. The President did not sign a Finding for this covert operation, nor did he notify the Congress.

Israel shipped 504 TOW anti-task missiles to Iran in August and September 1985. Although the Iranians had promised to release most of the American hostages in return, only one, Reverend Benjamin Weir, was freed. The President persisted. In November, he authorized Israel to ship 80 HAWK anti-aircraft missiles in return for all the hostages, with a promise of prompt replenishment by the United States, and 40 more HAWKs to be sent directly by the United States to Iran. Eighteen HAWK missiles were actually shipped from Israel in November 1985, but no hostages were released.

In early December 1985, the President signed a retroactive Finding purporting to authorize the November HAWK transaction. That Finding contained no reference to improved relations with Iran. It was a straight arms-for-hostages Finding. National Security Adviser Poindexter destroyed this Finding a year later because, he testified, its disclosure would have been politically embarrassing to the President.

The November HAWK transaction had additional significance. The Enterprise received a $1 million advance from the Israelis. North and Secord testified this was for transportation expenses in connection with the 120 HAWK missiles. Since only 18 missiles were shipped, the Enterprise was left with more than $800,000 in spare cash. North directed the Enterprise to retain the money and spend it for the Contras. The "diversion" had begun.

North realized that the sale of missiles to Iran could be used to support the Contras. He told Israeli Defense Ministry officials on December 6, 1985, one day after the President signed the Finding, that he planned to generate profits on future arms sales for activities in Nicaragua. . . .

In February 1986, the United States, acting through the Enterprise, sold 1,000 TOW's to the Iranians. The U.S. also provided the Iranians with military intelligence about Iraq. All of the remaining American hostages were supposed to be released upon Iran's receipt of the first 500 TOW's. None was. But the transaction was productive in one respect. The difference between what the Enterprise paid the United States for the missiles and what it received from Iran was more than $6 million. North directed part of this profit for the Contras and for other covert operations. Poindexter testified that he authorized this "diversion."

The diversion, for the Contras and other covert activities, was not an isolated act by the NSC staff. Poindexter saw it as "implementing" the President's secret policy that had been in effect since 1984 of using nonappropriated funds following passage of the Boland Amendment.

According to North, CIA Director Casey saw the "diversion" as part of a more grandiose plan to use the Enterprise as a "stand-alone," "off-the-shelf," covert capacity that would act throughout the world while evading Congressional review. To Casey, Poindexter, and North, the diversion was an integral part of selling arms to Iran and just one of the intended uses of the proceeds.

In May 1986, the President again tried to sell weapons to get the hostages back. This time, the President agreed to ship parts for HAWK missiles but only on condition that all the American hostages in Lebanon be released first. A mission headed by Robert McFarlane, the former National Security Adviser, traveled to Tehran with the first installment of the HAWK parts. When the mission arrived, McFarlane learned that the Iranians claimed they had never promised to do anything more than try to obtain the hostages' release. The trip ended amid misunderstanding and failure, although the first installment of HAWK parts was delivered.

The Enterprise was paid, however, for all of the HAWK parts, and realized more than an $8 million profit, part of which was applied, at North's direction, to the Contras. Another portion of the profit was used by North for other covert operations, including the operation of a ship for a secret mission. The idea of an off-the-shelf, stand-alone covert capacity had become operational. . . .

The sale of arms to Iran was a "significant anticipated intelligence activity." By law, such an activity must be reported to Congress "in a timely fashion" pursuant to Section 501 of the National Security Act. If the proposal to sell arms to Iran had been reported, the Senate and House Intelligence Committees would likely have joined Secretaries Schultz and Weinberger in objecting to this initiative. But Poindexter recommended—and the President decided—not to report the Iran initiative to Congress.

Indeed, the Administration went to considerable lengths to avoid notifying Congress. The CIA General Counsel wrote on January 15, 1986, "the key issue in this entire matter revolves around whether or not there will be reports made to Congress." Shortly thereafter, the transaction was restructured to avoid the pre-shipment reporting requirements of the Arms Export Control Act, and place it within the more limited reporting requirements of the National Security Act. But even these reporting requirements were ignored. The President failed to notify the group of eight (the leaders of each party in the House and Senate, and the Chairmen and Ranking Minority Members of the Intelligence Committees) specified by law for unusually sensitive operations.

After the disclosure of the Iran arms sales on November 3, 1986, the American public was still not told the facts. The President sought to avoid any commitment on the ground that it might jeopardize the chance of securing the remaining hostages' release. But it was impossible to remain silent, and inaccurate statements followed. . . .

While the President was denying any illegality, his subordinates were engaging in a coverup. Several of his advisers had expressed concern that the 1985 sales violated the Arms Export Control Act, and a "cover story" had been agreed on if these arms sales were ever exposed. After North had three conversations on November 18, 1986, about the legal problems with the 1985 Israeli shipments, he, Poindexter, Casey, and McFarlane all told conforming false stories about the U.S. involvement in these shipments. . . .

In light of the destruction of material evidence by Poindexter and North and the death of Casey, all of the facts may never be known. The Committees cannot even be sure whether they heard the whole truth. . . . But enough is clear to demonstrate beyond doubt that fundamental processes of governance were disregarded and the rule of law was subverted.

The common ingredients of the Iran and Contra policies were secrecy, deception, and disdain for the law. A small group of senior officials believed that they alone knew what was right. They viewed knowledge of their actions by others in the Government as a threat to their objectives. They told neither the Secretary of State, the Congress, nor the American people of their actions. When exposure was threatened, they destroyed official documents and lied to Cabinet officials, to the public, and to elected representatives in Congress. They testified that they even withheld key facts from the President.

The United States Constitution specifies the process by which laws and policy are to be made and executed. Constitutional process is the essence of our democracy and our democratic form of Government is the basis of our strength. Time and again we have learned that a flawed process leads to bad results, and that a lawless process leads to worse.

6. An Environmentalist Attacks the Administration's Record, 1988

At half past four on election day, 1980, Sierra Club volunteers and staff gather around a borrowed television set at the Club's San Francisco headquarters to watch the returns.

For the first time the Club has conducted a major voter-education drive. It's been a discouraging effort. Republican presidential candidate Ronald Reagan has barnstormed the country, attacking the Carter administration and even its Republican predecessors for turning environmental agencies over to "extremists." He has made some outlandish statements, ranging from a promise to invite the steel and oil industries to rewrite the EPA's [Environmental Protection Agency] regulations to a charge that 80 percent of the nation's air pollution problems are caused by chemicals released by trees. Despite growing controversy over Reagan's reactionary environmental stands, polls indicate that he is likely to defeat the incumbent, Jimmy Carter.

Groans fill the room as soon as the television is turned on. Even though the polls will remain open for several hours in the far West, the networks are already proclaiming Reagan the winner.

Spirits slump further as the Senate and House results pour in. In state after state, senators who have fought for the environment are being upset by their opponents. . . . Frank Church of Idaho, one of the Senate's leading proponents of wilderness, is narrowly defeated by Steve Symms, a virulent advocate of public-land exploitation. By seven o'clock only a scattering of sorrowful Sierra Clubbers remain at the election-night party.

The next morning it is clear that very few pro-environment candidates have managed to claw their way to the top of the Reagan avalanche. Representative Morris Udall, chair of the House Interior Committee, is reelected, as are most of the other key environmental players in the House. Of the environmental leaders in the Senate facing strong 1980 challenges, only Alan Cranston of California wins a decisive victory. Senator Gary Hart of Colorado wins, but barely.

Reagan's coattails are so long that the Republicans finally wrest control of the Senate from the Democrats. The new chair of the Senate Energy Committee, with jurisdiction over the nation's public-land and energy resources, is Symms' ideological soulmate and fellow Idahoan, James McClure. The new head of the Senate Agriculture Committee is archconservative and wilderness foe Jesse Helms of North Carolina.

"The end of the environmental movement" is proclaimed by NBC News (along with the demise of feminism and civil rights). Mainstream Republicans who served on the staffs of environmental agencies under presidents Nixon and Ford, some of

Carl Pope, "The Politics of Plunder," is reprinted from pp. 48–55 of the November/December 1988 issue of *Sierra* magazine, the magazine of the Sierra Club.

whom worked for Reagan when he was governor of California in the late 1960s and early '70s, are passed over for jobs. By Inauguration Day environmental policy is firmly in the hands of the "sagebrush rebels"—abrasive, conservative ideologues from the West. The rebels' antigovernment bias is strongly supported by Office of Management and Budget (OMB) Director David Stockman, a former Republican congressman from Michigan who only months earlier told Congress that toxic waste dumps are not a proper federal concern.

The Reagan Era has begun.

Today environmentalists are breathing slightly easier, and counting the few days left in Reagan's reign. The Sierra Club has moved to larger headquarters, a necessary response to a membership that soared from 180,000 during the Carter years to 480,000 in September of 1988. Ironically, Ronald Reagan has motivated far more people to join the Club and other environmental organizations than all of his predecessors combined.

Reagan, in effect, has reinvented the national environmental movement. He has done so with appointments and policy initiatives that have offended and alarmed the American people—efforts consistent with the President's general hostility toward activist government and his unlimited faith in private economic institutions. But it is one thing to promise to get the government off the taxpayers' backs. It is an altogether different proposition—and an unacceptable one to most Americans—to relieve polluting industries of the burden of complying with environmental laws. It's one thing to extol the virtues of free markets; it's another to extend that principle *ad absurdum,* offering to sell national parks to geothermal companies or amusement-park operators.

For nearly eight years the American people have been confronted with a difficult choice. In the White House a charismatic political leader has made taxpayers an appealing promise of limited government. A majority of voters have felt that Reagan and his economic programs fit well with their values of personal freedom and achievement. At the same time, in the EPA, in the Department of the Interior, in the OMB, and elsewhere in the federal bureaucracy, Reagan's zealous and often hard-edged political appointees have openly displayed their contempt for the environmental values and programs that have long since become an accepted part of American life.

The public's reaction has been to support Reagan as a person, but to make sure that his anti-environmental ethic is not translated into concrete policy. Citizens demanded and got the ouster of Interior Secretary James Watt, EPA Administrator Anne Burford, and EPA Assistant Administrator Rita Lavelle—the first generation of Reagan's hard-line appointees. They joined environmental groups and told pollsters that their commitment to those issues was stronger than ever before. In 1984 they elected a Congress that stopped virtually all of Reagan's anti-environmental initiatives.

Faced with this formidable resistance, the Reagan administration gradually abandoned the environmental front. By the middle of Reagan's second term his administration's new initiatives were far closer to the mainstream than to the privatized, deregulated world the President's pre-inauguration team had laid out. The administration came in adamantly opposed to federal cleanup of abandoned hazardous waste dumps, for instance, yet eventually agreed to a strong Superfund bill that would provide for just that.

Now, at the end of Reagan's second term, it's clear that the past eight years have not turned out to be as disastrous as the environmentalists who watched the 1980 election returns feared; nor have U.S. businesses reaped the rich harvest they anticipated in the early months of 1981. The most disappointed of all must be the ideologues, the Watts, Burfords, and Stockmans. They had their best shot ever at the American environmental ethos. Yet they strengthened, rather than weakened, the public's determination to protect the environment—and that is one of the more surprising legacies of Ronald Reagan. . . .

There can be no question that Reagan's appointees tried on numerous fronts to weaken America's commitment to the environment.

—They talked loosely of selling some units of the National Park System, and for eight years regularly proposed eliminating federal funding for park acquisition.

—A dentist from South Carolina, James Edwards, began dismantling conservation and renewable-energy programs soon after he was named Secretary of Energy.

—Through Reagan's Task Force on Regulatory Reform, headed by Vice President George Bush, the OMB's Stockman targeted scores of environmental regulations that were later weakened, delayed, or eliminated.

—Administration officials offered mineral leases at bargain-basement prices on millions of acres of public land. They recommended putting the entire outer continental shelf (OCS) on the auction block, under lease procedures that ranged from honest giveaways to outright corruption. In its first ten OCS lease sales, the administration managed to transfer titles to prime oil tracts for $7 billion less than would have been realized using the leasing methods of previous administrations.

—Reagan appointees rebuffed repeated pleas from Canada for a reduction of the acid rain that is destroying its forests, its economy, and life in its lakes. Instead of solutions, some Reaganites talked of "more studies" while Stockman made scornful references to "billion-dollar fish."

—Appointees at the EPA crippled the Superfund toxic-waste-cleanup program, and the program's key administrator, Rita Lavelle, went to jail.

—Morale at the EPA, the National Park Service, the Fish and Wildlife Service, and the Bureau of Land Management collapsed in the face of inadequate budgets, the administration's repeated refusals to enforce the laws, and its political interference in regulatory decisions. . . .

[But] hundreds of thousands of Americans stood up to Reagan, Bush, Watt, and Burford and preserved and strengthened the country's environmental ethic. Good laws were passed and harmful ones blocked; lawsuits argued and won on their merits; scoundrels evicted from office. More people signed the Sierra Club's petition to remove Watt from Interior than had ever simultaneously petitioned Congress on any other issue. Thousands of dedicated civil servants in public agencies resisted the efforts of political appointees to disrupt the execution and enforcement of the nation's environmental statutes. The media covered environmental issues with more intensity than ever before. State and local governments assumed much of the burden that the Reaganites refused to shoulder.

Thanks in large part to environmentalist campaigns, more acreage was added to the National Wilderness Preservation System in the lower 48 states under Reagan than under any other president. Twenty-nine new wildlife refuges were established, encompassing a total of 500,000 acres; 200 new plants and animals were added to the nation's list of endangered species. The Clean Water Act, the Resources Conservation and Recovery Act, and the Comprehensive Environmental Response, Compensation, and Liability Act (the Superfund) have all been reauthorized and greatly strengthened. Lead is finally being phased out of gasoline after two generations of use. An international agreement to reduce the production of chlorofluorocarbons (CFCs), chemicals that destroy the protective stratospheric ozone layer, has been ratified. Oil leasing along the California coast has been stalled, and the Arctic National Wildlife Refuge is still closed to oil drilling.

Just this summer, the Senate renewed the Endangered Species Act by the largest margin ever—92 to 2. A majority of the House of Representatives, including 64 Republicans, went on record as favoring a massive strengthening and renewal of the Clean Air Act. The Senate declined to confirm Robert Bork and Bernard Siegan, viewed by environmentalists as Reagan's two worst judicial nominees.

In the end, even the delegates to the Republican National Convention in August demonstrated surprising disagreement with Reagan's environmental policies. In a survey conducted for the Sierra Club and other conservation groups, the delegates showed strong support for federal leadership in protecting the country's natural resources.

But . . . we should not forget that on mountaintops and beaches, in small woodlands and majestic rainforests, in cities and playgrounds, in the oceans and the atmosphere itself, reminders of the Reagan Era will linger for decades. . . .

Eight precious years have been lost. The patterns set by Reagan's policies could have irreversible consequences in ten, or twenty, or thirty years—very brief times to change the direction of cumbersome national and international economies and polities. . .

We now need a global environmental Reconstruction. We need to ask of ourselves and our leaders more self-discipline than ever before, in part to compensate for the callousness of the last eight years. We need greater fidelity to facts, in part because our most recent leaders tried to wish them away. We need above all to remember that time matters, that events have consequences, and that the world is a wondrous and intermingled web that, when torn in one place, may unravel a thousand miles or a hundred years away.

7. Surgeon General C. Everett Koop Recalls the Administration's Response to the AIDS Crisis, 1981–1988 (2001)

. . . AIDS entered the consciousness of the public health service very quietly, very gradually, and with no fanfare at all. And it was 20 years ago today [on June 5, 1981] that the Center for Disease Control [CDC] published its report on five previously healthy homosexuals who had a rare type of . . . pneumonia. It wasn't until the next day . . . that the public health service staff discussed this issue. And it wasn't long

Transcript of remarks by C. Everett Koop, from the Kaiser Family Foundation National Symposium, *U.S. AIDS Policy—Entering the Third Decade,* Washington, D.C. (June 5, 2001), Reprinted by permission of C. Everett Koop, MD, ScD.

after that, just about a month, when in July of '81, we heard another report at a staff meeting from CDC, that 26 previously healthy young homosexual men had turned up with . . . Kaposi sarcoma, which they described as an uncommonly reported cancerous condition found usually in elderly men, if at all. Now the public health service had never come upon anything like this in its history and it was given a somewhat awkward title of Acquired Immune Deficiency Syndrome. For a short while before that, we were calling it GRID, which stood for Gay Related Immune Deficiency. But then when more cases came in that were not homosexual, we called it A.I.D.S. and eventually just AIDS and it has remained that ever since.

By August of that same year, we learned from CDC that there had been 108 cases reported of HIV and 43 of those had already died. . . . But for some reason, due to intradepartmental politics that I still cannot truly understand or explain to you, I was cut off from AIDS discussions and statements over the next five years. But I did have a very definite impression about what was going on on Pennsylvania Avenue. Domestic policy folks in the White House isolated Ronald Reagan from the whole subject of AIDS. And because transmission of AIDS was understood [to be] primarily in the homosexual population and in those who abused intravenous drugs, the advisors to the President took the stand [that] they are only getting what they justly deserve. And the domestic policy people, as well as the majority of the President's cabinet, did not see any need to come to grips with AIDS, or indeed to have a governmental policy towards this disease. And these combined attitudes did nothing to dampen . . . indeed, they . . . very well may have aided and [abetted] the hatred of homosexuals in this country, the discrimination against innocent school children like Ryan White, and the acts of arson on the homes of hapless children with hemophilia, such as the Ray Children. . . .

[T]he first public health priority . . . to stop further transmission of the virus, became needlessly mired in homosexual politics of the early 1980s. In 1985, there was the death of Rock Hudson, a movie star, the first national figure to die of AIDS. And this at least got the attention of the White House. Also in 1985, we had a test for the first time to identify the presence of antibodies to the HIV and we couldn't see the virus, but we first at last saw its footprint.

Now, in spite of many charges that have been leveled against the public health service for foot dragging, I would like to remind you that we learned as much about the virus of AIDS in six years as we had learned about the polio virus in the previous 40 years. And although we acknowledge that there was much we didn't know about AIDS, we really made extraordinary progress in understanding the syndrome. We identified the virus. We named it. We renamed it. We understood the epidemiology among homosexual men and drug abusers. We identified antibodies to the AIDS virus, developed a screening test that made it possible to have a safer blood supply for transfusion. And we learned how to kill the virus in blood products and to make clotting factors for hemophiliacs safer. Above all, we were concerned how the disease was transmitted. And we learned that, although the virus had been identified in multiple body fluids, it seemed to be transmitted only by blood and semen. . . .

It was clear that, in spite of all kinds of unsubstantiated claims about mosquitoes and toilet seats, AIDS could be transmitted in only four ways, through sexual contact, blood contact associated with IV drug abuse, through pregnancy or delivery, and through transfused blood. . . . President Reagan asked me to write a report to the American people about AIDS. And then for the next two years, AIDS took over my life. . . .

Among all the experiences I had and that the public health service absorbed, I think the hemophilia experience nailed down the evidence that AIDS was not spread by non-sexual casual contact. 600 families of hemophiliacs were studied and their members, with a two year exposure to the virus, touched each other, used the same utensils, kissed each other, shared razors without passing the virus. Even the 7 percent who shared toothbrushes saw no transmission of the virus from patient to patient. And that was very good news for us because, along with other studies, it showed that most Americans were not at risk if they did not engage in high-risk behavior with sex and drugs. It also meant, very fortunately, that persons with AIDS should not suffer discrimination and that the stride and calls we constantly heard from the unknowing, that we should quarantine patients with AIDS, deny them housing, insurance, employment or public schooling were dead wrong.

I began to write that report in August of 1986. . . . [I]n my report I called for sex education at the earliest possible moment. And that seemed to be the most important thing that the press heard. And that simple statement was responsible for more threats on my life then everything else I said put together over eight years. So be careful when you get into sex education.

The official response to AIDS, as far as our government was concerned, hinged on two meetings of the Cabinet. The first was just before the AIDS report was released by me to the public. And the second was in May of 1987, a meeting of the entire Cabinet with the President. In each of these meetings, I had to skate on rather thin ice and do it fast because I had to get by political appointees who placed conservative ideology above saving lives. . . .

In the meantime, having failed to come to grips with the AIDS report when they first read it, the political meddlers in the White House tried to bottle up the report and then, in an unusual move, two White House members of the Domestic Policy Council came across town to see me and wondered if it wasn't time to update the report. It was only three weeks old. And I said it didn't need updating then and I can tell you it doesn't really, except for medications[,] need updating now. But it was very clear that they wanted four words removed from a government publication: penis, vagina, rectum and condom [—] and, of course, I refused.

And at last with that report, the people of the country knew what was myth and what was reality about the AIDS epidemic and they knew it in plain English. But the American people because of that, I think, finally became mobilized against AIDS. . . . [T]here was no mandatory premarital sex testing. There was no tax on visitors to the United States to put that in escrow in case they got sick with AIDS while they were here. And there was no quarantine of either the [c]ity of New York or of San Francisco. . . .

I think that we really began to drop the silliness from the national dialogue on AIDS. And I think it was because the AIDS report had done its job. It made accurate information available to the American people. . . .

Looking back on it, I divide my experience with AIDS into two phases. The first was from 1981 and the first cases until the AIDS report in 1986. And it was a period that was marked by mystery and fear and suspicion, judgment and the concern about the unknown.

The second phase saw health officials overcome considerable opposition, some of it misguided, some of it just mean spirited, and to at last bring the facts of AIDS before the American people in the AIDS report. . . .

✥ *E S S A Y S*

The 1990s witnessed a flood of memoirs on the Reagan presidency as well as the first scholarly assessments by historians and political scientists. In the first essay, an excerpt from the widely read *Politics by Other Means* (2002), political scientists Benjamin Ginsberg and Martin Shefter trace the "Republican offensive" that accompanied Reagan's election. While much of the recent literature stresses Reagan's skill as a great communicator, Ginsberg and Shefter focus on the hard politics of public policy, political economy, and institutional competition. In the second essay, historian Jules Tygiel offers a broad, critical overview of the Reagan presidency.

The Republicans Take Control

BENJAMIN GINSBERG AND MARTIN SHEFTER

After winning control of the presidency in 1980, the Republicans launched the first phase of an effort to undermine Democratic strongholds and to create a constellation of institutions, policies, and political forces to solidify their power. The principal weapons the GOP deployed against its opponents were domestic spending cuts, tax reductions, and deregulation. These weapons have weakened important institutional bastions of the Democratic party and disrupted the social groups and forces upon which it depended for support. At the same time, through national security, monetary, and fiscal policy, the Republicans undertook to reorganize social forces and establish mechanisms of governance to maintain their own rule. These Republican efforts were partially successful. The GOP was able to control the White House for twelve successive years. During these years the Republicans disrupted a number of key Democratic constituencies and at least temporarily weakened a number of important institutions linked to the Democrats.

Republican efforts suffered a serious setback when Democrat Bill Clinton won the 1992 presidential election. The GOP, however, regrouped its forces and, in 1994, took control of both houses of Congress for the first time in decades. From this new position of power Republicans launched what might be called Phase 2 of their attack upon Democratic political bastions.

Of course these disparate strategies were not components of some master plan that the Republicans devised prior to gaining power. Rather, they emerged in the course of conflicts both within the GOP and between the White House and institutions

---

controlled by the Democrats. The Republicans' political weapons have been shaped not only by the victories they have achieved but also by the compromises the GOP has been compelled to make and the defeats it has suffered in these struggles.

The GOP's Phase 1: Disrupting Democratic Institutions

Beginning in 1981, the Republicans worked to weaken social service and regulatory agencies in which the Democrats were entrenched. The Reagan and Bush administrations promoted tax reductions, domestic spending cuts, and efforts at deregulation to limit these agencies' powers. These Republican policies reduced the extractive, distributive, and regulatory capabilities of institutions over which the Democrats exercised influence. This diminished the Democrats' ability to achieve their policy objectives, overcome divisions in their coalition, and provide benefits to groups allied with the party.

In 1981 the Reagan administration sponsored legislation that substantially cut individual and corporate income tax rates and indexed these rates to inflation. Congressional Democrats responded to the administration's bill by introducing a proposal of their own. A bidding war ensued, and the tax bill that was enacted reduced revenues more sharply than the White House had planned. Coupled with the administration's military buildup and inability to secure reductions in domestic spending as drastic as it had proposed, these tax cuts produced the enormous budget deficits of the 1980s. The federal government's annual deficit increased from approximately sixty billion dollars at the end of the Carter administration to a peak of more than two hundred billion dollars during the Reagan presidency. Annual deficits began to decline from that peak in the late 1980s, although the decline was largely a result of surpluses in the Social Security trust fund.

Five years later, in the 1986 Tax Reform Act, tax rates were further reduced, and numerous loopholes—deductions, exemptions, and tax preferences—were eliminated from the federal tax code. By closing the loopholes for influential groups that had made nominally high income tax rates politically feasible, the 1986 Tax Reform Act made it more difficult for Congress to restore any of the lost revenues. Thus, when seeking to reduce the budget deficit at the beginning of the Bush administration, Congress was only able to consider increasing those taxes that produced little in the way of revenue, such as those on alcohol, gasoline, and tobacco.

These restrictions on the extractive capacities of Congress impaired that institution's distributive capabilities. Because the federal government was strapped for revenues, funding levels for domestic programs came under pressure, and it was all but impossible for congressional Democrats to enact new social programs, despite demands that more be done to cope with such problems as the AIDS epidemic and homelessness.

Republican tax policies also exacerbated cleavages within the Democratic party. During the New Deal and postwar decades, many groups made claims on the federal treasury; their claims were accommodated through logrolling arrangements that characteristically were negotiated by the Democratic leadership of Congress. These arrangements entailed a steady growth of the public sector through a process of budgetary incrementalism, as Aaron Wildavsky then called it. This pattern of policy making depended on a steady expansion of public revenues, which was achieved—without the political conflict that would have resulted from repeated increases in nominal tax rates—by allowing inflation to increase real rates of federal income taxation steadily through what came to be called bracket creep.

By slashing federal tax rates and introducing indexation to prevent bracket creep, the Republicans at least temporarily undermined the fiscal foundations of the New Deal pattern of accommodations among the beneficiaries of federal expenditure programs. The enormous deficit created by Republican fiscal policies exerted constant pressure on the funding levels of domestic programs. To protect their favorite programs in this fiscal environment, lobbyists representing such groups as farmers, organized labor, senior citizens, advocates of welfare spending, and local government officials were compelled to engage in zero-sum conflict, in contrast with the positive-sum politics of the New Deal and postwar systems. One group's gain now became another group's loss. This state of affairs placed strains on the Democratic coalition.

The 1989 outcry over catastrophic health insurance for the elderly illustrates how Reaganite fiscal policies altered the political environment in which Congress operated. To avoid an increase in either tax rates or the deficit, Congress found it necessary to impose the costs of the new coverage on the program's beneficiaries. This generated a firestorm of protest among the elderly, compelling Congress to curtail the program. Thus, members of Congress discovered that under the Republican fiscal regime the enactment of new spending measures was no longer a sure means of winning political support.

After gaining control of the White House in the 1980s, the Republicans also undertook to restrict the regulatory capabilities of the federal government. They promoted deregulation in the transportation, energy, banking, and financial sectors of the economy, and they curtailed enforcement of environmental, health, safety, consumer, and antitrust laws. Regulatory agencies were consequently less able to intervene against business on behalf of groups disadvantaged by market processes. For example, financial deregulation and the relaxation of antitrust enforcement in the 1980s left labor and other Democratic constituencies with little protection against the threat to their interests posed by the largest wave of corporate reorganizations—hostile takeovers, leveraged buyouts, plant closings—since the days of J. P. Morgan.

Deregulation also eroded the accommodations between business and labor that had been fashioned by the Democrats. During the New Deal period the federal government established or extended a regime of regulation over numerous sectors of the American economy. Characteristically these regulations restricted price competition among firms within the regulated industry and, in some cases, erected barriers to the entry of new firms. To the extent that firms within such industries could pass added costs to their customers without fear of being undersold by competitors, they lost an incentive to control their labor costs. Union-management relations in most regulated industries were consequently more cooperative than adversarial in character. Rather than fight each other over wages and work rules, unions and employers entered the political arena as allies to defend and extend the regulatory regime and to secure direct or indirect public subsidies for their industries.

Asserting that these business-labor accommodations served "special interests" at the expense of the "public interest," an unlikely coalition of conservatives and liberal consumer advocates secured a substantial measure of deregulation during the late 1970s. Through deregulation, conservatives hoped to get business to break its alliance with organized labor. Consumer advocates, for their part, were happy to weaken the labor unions and business interests that had been their rivals for influence within the Democratic party.

In the face of the threats that Reaganism posed to them both, liberals and labor rekindled their coalition in the 1980s. Increasingly, organized labor supported liberal causes, such as the nuclear freeze and comparable worth, that it would formerly have disdained. Liberals, for their part, began to see merit in a number of causes supported by organized labor, such as protectionism, and lost their enthusiasm for deregulation.

The Republicans, though, continued to press for deregulation, and with good reason. Particularly in airlines, telecommunications, and trucking, deregulation allowed nonunion firms to undersell the established giants in their industry. Established firms were compelled to demand givebacks from their unions to lower their own labor costs, and alliances between business and labor were disrupted.

Reorganizing Political Forces

By undermining the governing capacities of institutions over which the Democrats exercised influence, the Republicans also weakened the Democrats' social base. They destabilized some of the major political forces upon which the Democrats depended and reorganized them under Republican auspices.

Most observers assume that politicians must deal with whatever groups they find in society, but it is important to note that political leaders are not limited to working with some predefined constellation of forces. At times politicians can destroy established centers of power, reorganize interests, and even call new groups into being. Leaders can attempt to reorganize the constellation of interests central to the political process in several ways. They may be able to transform the political identities of the established groups, create new political forces by dividing existing groups, or construct new interests by uniting previously disparate elements. In these ways the Republicans worked to reshape the political attachments of business executives, middle-class suburbanites, blue-collar ethnics, and white southerners.

Reunifying Business   In the 1980s the Republicans sought to unify the business community under their auspices. After World War II the Democrats had come to terms with many segments of big business: internationally competitive firms that benefited from free trade policies, firms in capital-intensive industries that found it relatively easy to make concessions to organized labor, and defense contractors who benefited from a foreign policy of internationalism. However, proprietors of smaller firms that were not involved in international markets often found Democratic labor and social programs onerous, and they characteristically aligned themselves with the Republican party. This breach between Wall Street and Main Street undermined the political potency of American business.

During the 1970s the accord between big business and the Democratic party was severely strained by two developments that the Republicans sought to exploit. The erosion of America's position in the world economy caused many business leaders to reject the high labor costs and taxes associated with the Democrats that they had previously accepted. Also, Democratic support for environmental, consumer, and other new regulatory programs further alienated many of the party's allies in the business community. In his 1980 presidential campaign Ronald Reagan appealed for the support of business by indicating that he would trim costly social programs, weaken the influence of organized labor, and relax the environmental rules and other forms of regulation that had been sponsored by Democratic politicians during the 1960s and 1970s. Moreover, Reagan offered the thousands of firms that stood to benefit from military contracts substantial increases in defense spending.

Enacted into law, these policies helped reunify American business and attach it to the Republican party, where it remained until Bill Clinton's probusiness policies lured some segments of the business community back into the Democratic fold. Even before Clinton, Reaganite budget and trade deficits produced a conflict between what may be termed the traditionalist and supply-side camps within the Republican party. The traditionalists asserted that the nation's first economic priority was to reduce the budget deficit—through budget cuts and, if necessary, tax increases. The supply-siders were prepared to accept continuing deficits in order to protect tax cuts and to avoid reductions in defense spending.

The conflict between traditionalists and supply-siders had two sources. The first was a difference in economic and political perspectives. Traditionalist Republicans feared that continuing huge deficits could wreck the economy and hence their party's electoral fortunes. Supply-siders asserted that the deficit posed no immediate threat to the economy, and they feared that steps taken to cut the deficit—such as raising taxes—could severely damage Republican electoral prospects.

The second source of disagreement between traditionalists and supply-siders was the conflict between two sets of economic interests in the Republican party. Large budget and trade deficits hurt sectors of the economy that produced goods in the United States for export (e.g., agriculture) and faced competition in the American market from goods produced abroad (such as steel). Larger budget deficits also exerted upward pressure on interest rates, hurting local banks and thrift institutions. Together, these interests were the mainstays of the traditionalist camp.

Other sectors of American business (notably, domestic importers of goods produced by foreign manufacturers), however, benefited from Reagan's economic policies. Firms in the service sector were not severely affected by interest rates or the trade deficit, but they prospered as a result of the macroeconomic stimulus provided by budget deficits.

In the battle for the 1988 Republican presidential nomination, George Bush was the leader of the supply-side forces and Senator Robert Dole spoke for the traditionalists. But once Bush wrapped up the nomination, all segments of the business community united behind his candidacy. However uneasy some business executives might have been over budget deficits, they were even more distrustful of a Democratic party whose leading representatives then called for the enactment of plant-closing legislation, higher levels of social service spending, and increased taxes on the wealthy.

From Beneficiaries to Taxpayers   Middle-income suburbanites were a second group to which the Republicans appealed. The GOP attempted to convince these voters to regard themselves less as beneficiaries of federal expenditure programs than as taxpayers. After World War II many suburbanites were integrated into the political process and linked to the Democratic party by federal programs that subsidized mortgages, built arterial highways, and expanded access to higher education.

By placating the poor and reducing working-class militancy, Democratic welfare and labor programs also promoted social peace. In exchange for the benefits they received, members of the middle class gave their support to the various expenditure programs through which the Democratic party channeled public funds to its other constituency groups: crop subsidies for farmers, maritime subsidies for the shipping industry, and so on. This system of interest group liberalism enabled the Democrats to accommodate the claims of a host of disparate groups in their electoral coalition.

During the 1960s and 1970s many benefits that middle-income Americans had come to expect from federal programs and policies were sharply curtailed. For example, rising mortgage interest rates increased housing costs, affirmative action programs seemed to threaten the middle class's privileged access to higher education, social peace was disrupted by urban violence and riots, and above all, double-digit inflation during the late 1970s eroded the middle class's real income and standard of living. The curtailment of these benefits undermined the political basis of the loyalty that many middle-income individuals had shown to the Democrats. This provided the GOP with an opportunity to win their support.

In wooing suburbanites, the GOP chose not to promise new federal benefits although, to be sure, it did not seek to repeal existing middle-class benefit programs. Instead it sought to link these individuals to the Republican camp in their capacity as taxpayers. In 1980 Reagan declared tax relief to be a central political issue. The Republicans argued that taxation was linked to inflation and blamed high rates of inflation on Democratic tax and spending policies. Indeed, Reagan called inflation the "cruelest tax of all."

After Reagan's 1980 election his administration cooperated with Federal Reserve Board Chairman Paul Volcker in a relentless attack on inflation. The Reagan-Volcker war on inflation was successful, albeit at the cost of a severe recession and high rates of unemployment for blue-collar workers. At the same time the Reagan administration provided middle- and upper-income groups with a sizable reduction in federal income tax rates. Reagan's warning to middle-income voters that the Democrats wanted to take their tax cuts away was a crucial element of his successful 1984 campaign against Democratic presidential candidate Walter Mondale. This theme was echoed by George Bush in 1988. Bush promised to oppose any efforts to raise federal income tax rates and heaped scorn on Michael Dukakis's proposal to step up collection of delinquent federal taxes. Bush derided what he characterized as a Democratic plan to put an Internal Revenue Service auditor into every taxpayer's home.

In the 1980s the Republican party was successful in convincing middle-income Americans to focus on taxes. In 1976 only 2 percent of middle-class voters identified taxes and spending as important national problems; by 1984, 23 percent of voters with above-average incomes did so. Of these voters, 67 percent cast their ballots for the Republican presidential candidate.

Republicans appealed to members of the middle class as taxpayers rather than as beneficiaries of spending programs chiefly because they hoped to erode middle-income support for domestic expenditures in general. Transforming middle-class Americans into taxpayers not only linked them to the Republican party but also helped undermine the entire apparatus of interest group liberalism through which the Democrats maintained their various constituencies' allegiances. This helped disorganize the Democrats' political base.

Republican tax policies also served to divide a politically important middle-class group—college-educated professionals—that had given substantial support to the Democrats during the 1960s and 1970s. Socially this group is heterogeneous, ranging from ill-paid social workers to lavishly compensated attorneys. The group is so heterogeneous that sociologists have debated whether it is meaningful to speak of this "new class" as a coherent social and political force. But groups are constituted in the political realm, and in the 1960s and 1970s political entrepreneurs were able to mobilize large numbers of professionals on behalf of such liberal causes as environmentalism and opposition to the Vietnam War.

The Republicans attempted to divide this new class by shifting the political debate to the issues of tax and budget cuts. The 1981 tax cut was promoted as a means of stimulating the private sector. The tax reform package that Reagan made the centerpiece of his second administration was especially beneficial to professionals with high salaries. Professionals in a position to take advantage of these new opportunities—namely, those who worked in the private sector—were attracted into the Republican party.

Republican reductions in federal domestic expenditures, however, restricted opportunities for professionals who worked in the public and nonprofit sectors. The Republicans were not altogether unhappy to see schoolteachers, social workers, and university professors try to defend their interests by becoming increasingly active in Democratic party politics. The more committed the Democrats became to the cause of boosting domestic expenditures, the more likely it was that taxpayers, business executives, and private sector professionals would flock to the Republican party.

This Republican strategy was quite successful. College graduates working in public sector occupations gave the Republicans only 40 percent of their votes in the 1984 presidential election. On the other hand, college graduates in the private sector supported the GOP by the overwhelming margin of 68 percent to 32 percent for the Democrats.

From Workers to Patriots   The GOP also sought to appeal to blue-collar voters. During the New Deal era, members of urban ethnic groups had been integrated into politics in their capacity as workers, through organizations informally affiliated with the national Democratic party: trade unions, political machines, and urban service bureaucracies. These institutions provided members of urban ethnic groups with public and private employment at relatively high wages, with social services, and with preferential access to locally administered federal programs. At the same time trade unions and urban machines and bureaucracies functioned as the local institutional foundations of the national Democratic party, mobilizing urban voters to support Democratic candidates.

The Republicans weakened the links between the Democrats and blue-collar workers by attacking these institutions. They undermined organized labor by encouraging employers to engage in antiunion practices; indeed, the Reagan administration set an example by destroying the Professional Air Traffic Controllers Organization when the group conducted a strike in 1981. The Republicans also appointed officials who were hostile to organized labor to the National Labor Relations Board (an agency formerly controlled by labor sympathizers). Moreover, as discussed above, the Reagan and Bush administrations supported policies of deregulation that provided business firms with a strong incentive to rid themselves of their unions. The Republican commitment to free trade also allowed foreign goods to flood American markets, increasing unemployment in heavily unionized industries and reducing labor's bargaining power. As a result of these policies, union membership dropped sharply during the 1980s.

The Republicans attacked urban political machines and national and municipal service bureaucracies mainly through domestic spending reductions. The programs whose budgets suffered most under Reagan and Bush were precisely those that once provided local governments with substantial funds, such as revenue sharing and the Comprehensive Employment and Training Act (CETA). The tax reform package whose enactment was secured by the Reagan administration in 1986 reduced the deductability of local sales taxes (thereby heightening taxpayers' resistance to rate increases) and restricted the ability of local governments to issue tax-free revenue bonds. These changes in the tax code further diminished the resources available to municipal governments. The Justice Department also attacked urban machines and bureaucracies by launching a series of investigations into municipal government corruption; these investigations primarily targeted large cities controlled by the Democrats.

The attack on labor unions, political machines, and social service agencies diminished the ability of these institutions to provide benefits to blue-collar voters; thus, this group's links to the Democratic party were undermined, and Republicans seized an opportunity to capture the support of a previously staunch Democratic constituency.

The Republicans' appeal to this constituency was hindered in one important way. In their capacity as workers, many urban ethnic voters were hurt by Republican economic and tax programs, which mainly served the interests of the upper middle class and segments of the business community. Instead of trying to appeal to members of urban ethnic groups on economic grounds, the Republicans therefore attempted to secure and institutionalize their support on three other bases. First, they sought to link urban ethnics to the GOP on the basis of their moral and religious convictions. The Republicans politicized these concerns by focusing on so-called family issues—above all, the issue of abortion. In this endeavor they sought to make use of Roman Catholic churches, which rally the faithful against proabortion candidates. The importance of this political focus became evident during the 1984 presidential election. White working-class voters who belonged to trade unions but did not regularly attend a church gave Reagan only 46 percent of their vote. By contrast, among white working-class voters who attended a church regularly but did not belong to a union, the Republicans received 67 percent of the vote.

The Republicans attempted to mobilize blue-collar voters with patriotic as well as moral appeals. In this effort they were at times able to harness the national media, an institution whose editorial pages and televised commentary frequently were hostile to Republican policies. Reagan and Bush created news events filled with patriotic symbols that the media could neither attack nor ignore. In addition, where the risks of failure were low, Republican administrations used military force abroad not only to demonstrate America's resolve to foreigners but also to reinforce national pride among Americans. The 1984 Grenada invasion and the 1986 bombing of Libya exemplify this strategy. During the 1988 presidential campaign, Bush sought to make political use of patriotic sentiments by charging that his Democratic rival, Massachusetts Governor Michael Dukakis, had demonstrated a lack of respect for the American flag when he vetoed a Massachusetts bill that mandated the daily recitation of the pledge of allegiance in public schools.

Finally, the Republicans made use of race-related issues to seek support from blue-collar whites. The Reagan and Bush administrations opposed affirmative action and school busing plans and promoted efforts to narrow the rights that the liberal Warren Court granted to persons accused of crimes. In his 1988 presidential campaign, Bush made a major issue of the Willie Horton case. Horton, a black man, had been convicted of murder and sentenced to life imprisonment without parole. Under a program supported by Governor Dukakis, Massachusetts prison authorities granted Horton a weekend furlough. While on furlough, Horton fled the state and raped a white woman in Maryland. Groups supporting the Bush campaign repeatedly broadcast television ads displaying a picture of Horton and asserting that Dukakis was soft on crime.

From Southerners to Evangelicals   Southern whites were the fourth constituency that the Republicans strove to add to their camp. For a century after the Civil War, white southerners had participated in politics through the Democratic party, which had defended the southern caste system. These voters were linked to the Democrats not simply by their racial attitudes but also by local political institutions that were connected with the party—county commissions, sheriffs, voting registrars—and that guaranteed white political power by excluding blacks from participation in government and politics.

The civil rights revolution—in particular the Voting Rights Act of 1965— destroyed the institutional foundations of the traditional southern Democratic regime. Local governmental institutions were prevented from maintaining white privilege at the expense of black political subordination. The disruption of this system gave Republicans an opportunity to win the support of southern whites. The GOP stance on affirmative action, busing, and the rights of defendants in criminal trials helped them win support among white southerners as well as northern blue-collar voters. The GOP also appealed to southerners on the basis of their religious orientations. By focusing on the issue of abortion, Republicans politicized the moral concerns of white southerners. They made use of fundamentalist Protestant churches, a prominent feature of the southern landscape, to forge institutional links between southern whites and the Republican party. Republicans in effect made these churches organizational components of their party. For example, funds and technical support were often provided to conservative Protestant churches for voter registration activities. As a result of these efforts, many southern whites were integrated into politics through their evangelical religious affiliations. This helped give the Republicans a firm social base in the white South for the first time in the party's history.

As in the case of urban ethnics, who are mainly Roman Catholic, the moral issue that Republicans used most effectively to appeal to white southerners was abortion. Indeed, Republicans used the question of abortion to promote an alliance between evangelical southern Protestants and conservative Catholics and to attach both to the Republican party. Political mobilization around the right-to-life issue was initiated by Richard Viguerie, Paul Weyrich, Howard Phillips, and other conservative Republican activists. Seeking to take advantage of the furor caused by the Supreme Court's prochoice decision in *Roe v. Wade,* these politicians convinced Catholic political activists and evangelical Protestant leaders that they had common interests and worked with these leaders to arouse public opposition to abortion. The right-to-life issue helped unite politically, under Republican auspices, two religious groups that had been bitter opponents through much of American history.

The Republicans also used foreign policy and military issues to mobilize support among southerners. Military bases and defense plants play a major role in the economy of many southern states. Republican support and Democratic opposition to a military buildup during the 1980s tied many southern workers, business executives, and local communities to the GOP. Defense spending was thus the material foundation for the GOP's patriotic appeals that so successfully wooed support in the white South. . . .

Monetary and Fiscal Policy   The complex [of] Republican policies . . . was sustained by a fiscal regime that was one of the most notable features of the contemporary American political economy. Central to this regime were the enormous budget and trade deficits of the Reagan-Bush years. The budget deficit resulted from the tax reductions and military spending increases of the first Reagan administration and from Congress's opposition to further domestic spending cuts. In conjunction with the restrictive monetary policies the Federal Reserve pursued in its fight against inflation, the budget deficit led to sharp increases in real interest rates and the value of the American dollar in the early 1980s. These increases greatly reduced American exports and encouraged a flood of foreign imports into the United States. During the second Reagan administration, coordinated central bank intervention led the dollar to fall, but by that time foreign manufacturers had established such a solid position in the American market that the nation's trade deficit continued to grow.

Despite the economic risks they posed, these deficits provided the Republicans with important political benefits and opportunities. The budget deficit made it difficult for politicians to appeal for votes with new public expenditure programs and impeded the Democrats' efforts to reconstruct their political base. More important, the twin deficits functioned as a novel revenue collection apparatus that, at least in the short run, enabled the Republicans to finance government expenditures without raising taxes and alienating their political constituency.

This apparatus worked as follows. The Reagan administration's fiscal policies encouraged Americans to purchase foreign—especially Japanese and German—goods. At the same time America's high interest rates and political stability encouraged foreign bankers—notably the Japanese—to purchase U.S. Treasury securities with the profits their nation's manufacturers made in the United States. Thus, during the 1980s what might be called autodollars came to be recycled by Japanese banks, much as petrodollars had been recycled by American banks in the 1970s. These autodollars, invested in U.S. government securities, were used to help finance the American budget deficit. In essence, Japanese industrialists and bankers served as revenue agents for the Republican administration. American voters demonstrated in 1980, in 1984, and again in 1988 that they opposed increased taxation, but as consumers they willingly—indeed, enthusiastically—handed over billions of dollars for this purpose whenever they purchased Japanese and other foreign-made goods.

The costs of this revenue system were borne by unemployed American workers in the industrial sector and by American manufacturers who failed to restructure their firms to meet foreign competition. The benefits of the system flowed to groups with which the Republicans were allied. Military spending benefited the defense industry and its thousands of subcontractors. The fiscal stimulus of the deficit boosted corporate profits. High-income professionals received substantial tax cuts, access to foreign goods at low prices, and high rates of return on their savings.

This fiscal regime came under attack during the 1980s, as Democrats and some Republicans argued that the growing budget and trade deficits were destroying the American economy and threatening America's place in the world. Concern about the deficit led to the 1990 budget crisis that wrecked George Bush's presidency. In 1992 the issue of the deficit was used very successfully by Ross Perot to launch a major third-party presidential bid. In a series of televised infomercials, Perot increased public concern about the deficit while further undermining Bush's chances for reelection.

After Bill Clinton's victory in 1992 the deficit continued to hamper Democratic efforts to increase levels of domestic social spending. Clinton's 1993 budget, for example, which called for substantial new domestic spending programs, was defeated by a coalition of Republicans and conservative Democrats who feared it would increase the deficit. Congressional "deficit hawks" continually pushed for spending cuts during the early and mid-1990s to erase what had come to be seen as America's major economic problem.

By 1998 expansion of the domestic economy had all but erased the current deficit, though leaving a substantial national debt. President Clinton moved to take advantage of this new opportunity to propose a substantial expansion of social spending in the realms of child care and health care. Republicans attacked the Clinton initiative as fiscally irresponsible.

Thus, by the end of the 1990s the political significance of the deficit seemed to be eroding. It is significant, however, that for nearly two decades this element of Republican fiscal policy substantially undermined efforts by Democrats to serve their party's constituencies and strengthen the institutions with which the party was associated. Thus, taken together, the fiscal, monetary, and national security policies of the Reagan and Bush administrations strengthened the institutional bastions and governing capacities of the Republicans and threatened those of the Democrats.

A Disputed Legacy

JULES TYGIEL

Ronald Reagan left office in 1989, an extraordinarily popular figure. He had become the first president to complete two terms since Dwight Eisenhower in the 1950s. Reagan, asserts Lou Cannon, had restored "the respect of Americans for themselves and their own government after the traumas of Vietnam and Watergate, the frustration of the Iran hostage crisis, and a succession of seemingly failed presidencies." He bequeathed to his successor, George H. W. Bush, a prosperous economy

---

and a world closer to peace and disarmament than he had inherited. Within two years of Reagan's departure not only the Soviet empire, but the Soviet Union itself collapsed. This momentous event, more than any other, cemented Reagan's reputation as not only a well-beloved, but highly effective president. A torrent of books written from a conservative perspective, with titles or subtitles proclaiming *Victory; How an Ordinary Man Became an Extraordinary Leader;* and *When Character Was King* celebrated the Reagan years as a triumphant era.

Yet Reagan's legacy remains highly disputed. A spate of tell-all books written by former members of the Reagan Administration portrayed his presidency, especially his management style, in less than flattering terms. Biographers and other historians wrestled with the gap between his phlegmatic personality and record of accomplishment. Liberal critics questioned the success of his economic policies, his role in the end of the Cold War, and the overall moral message of his leadership. Amid these disputes, however, there remained the undeniable extent to which Reagan had transformed America. In terms of prolonged political impact, the ability to define the national course for future generations, only Franklin D. Roosevelt, Reagan's early political hero, can rival the former actor's impact on twentieth-century American life. When Reagan entered formal electoral politics in 1966, conservatism had been a fringe ideology. When he left the presidency in 1989, it had become, although not a dominant viewpoint, the belief system around which American politics defined itself.

Reagan was once described as a "Teflon President." Mistakes and even serious misdeeds never seemed to adhere to him or seriously tarnish his image. He retained a reputation for personal morality and honesty even as the waters of corruption and abuse of power swirled around him. The number of exposés of the scandals that had tainted his administration swelled in the years after he left office. In the early 1990s congressional investigations revealed the depth of wrongdoing in Housing and Urban Development. A Justice Department probe depicted the widespread corruption in the Defense Department. The full extent of the savings and loan debacle, a textbook example of the dangers of the unregulated marketplace, grew undeniably apparent. A 1990 report by Reagan's own economists disparaged his administration's mishandling of the savings and loan industry. The General Accounting Office pegged the cost of the scandal to taxpayers at a minimum of one trillion dollars. The independent counsel investigation of the Iran-contra affair produced 14 indictments and 11 convictions of top Reagan aides, including John Poindexter and Oliver North. Defense Secretary Caspar Weinberger escaped prosecution due to a pre-trial pardon from President Bush. In his final report in 1994 Iran-contra Special Prosecutor Lawrence Walsh concluded that while Reagan's actions "fell well short of criminality which could be successfully prosecuted," he had "created the conditions which made possible the crimes committed by others." A disconnection clearly existed between the high moral principles that Reagan espoused, his law-and-order rhetoric, and an environment in which inconvenient laws were evaded and government officials sought to illegally cash in on the very programs they attacked as wasteful.

Reagan largely avoided blame for this state of affairs, seen by most Americans as separate from his performance as president and peripheral to his broader achievements in the more important arenas of foreign and economic policy. On these critical fronts the strategies of the Reagan Administration appear, at first glance, to have prevailed. In the United States at the start of 1989, the Reagan presidency had over-seen the longest period of peacetime economic growth in the nation's history, seem-ingly validating the precepts of "Reaganomics." Within a year of Reagan's departure from office, the "captive nations" of Eastern Europe had liberated themselves from communism and Soviet domination. By the end of 1991, the Soviet Union itself had imploded, with democracy transcending dictatorship and a rudimentary capitalism replacing a moribund communism. Reagan's secret strategy, argues conservative writer Peter Schweizer, had hastened the collapse of the Soviet Union. But surface impressions rarely satisfy the demands of history, and the judgment on Reagan on these and other matters remains highly contested.

In January 1989, when Reagan returned to California, the final outcomes of his foreign policy remained uncertain. The progress made on arms control and Gor-bachev's reforms notwithstanding, the Soviet Union remained a formidable foe, its eastern European empire shaken, but still intact. Within a year, however, the extent to which the longstanding Cold War reality had changed grew apparent. In March 1989, the Soviet Union held its first free elections. In June, elections in Poland propelled Solidarity to power. Soviet General Secretary Gorbachev made no effort to reverse the Polish results, confirming that, as he had promised, the Soviet Union would no longer use repressive military force to impose its rule on eastern Europe. On Octo-ber 18, the communist government of East Germany collapsed and on November 9 the new government ordered the opening of the Berlin Wall. At the site of Reagan's challenge to Gorbachev just two years earlier jubilant Germans destroyed the wall that had symbolized the Cold War. Before 1989 had ended, the brutal communist dictatorship of Nicolae Ceausescu fell in Romania, and the dissident leader Vaclev Havel assumed the reins of government in Czechoslovakia.

The next two years brought equally dramatic changes. In March 1990 Lithuania voted to declare its independence from the Soviet Union. In October, East and West Germany reunited after 45 years of division. The United States and the Soviet Union signed the START I arms control treaty in July 1991, cutting their nuclear arsenals by an additional 50 percent. Most dramatically, in December 1991, the Soviet Union itself dissolved, with its 11 republics forming independent states, the majority of which now pledged themselves to capitalism and democracy. In addition, the com-munist regimes in Afghanistan and Nicaragua both fell. As Reagan had prophe-sized, communism had been discredited and the Soviet Union's "evil empire" had fallen into "the ash heap of history."

The sudden and unexpected end of the Cold War and demise of communism in Europe appeared to bear out Reagan's foreign policy. "What was most brilliant about Reagan's view was that it rejected the assumption of Soviet immutability," writes Dinesh D'Sousa. "Reagan dared to imagine a world in which the communist regime in the Soviet Union did not exist." The logic of this argument seems unassailable. The Reagan Administration definitively changed the terms of the Cold War. From the start they predicted that the Soviets would be unable to counter an American arms buildup and expended tens of billions of dollars to prove that assumption. Reagan's Strategic Defense Initiative upped the ante even further, provoking considerable concern in the Soviet Union. Reagan had predicted that America's new position of military superiority would force the Soviets to the bargaining table, and at Geneva, Reykjavik, Washington, D.C., and Moscow, Gorbachev had capitulated to Reagan's demands. Furthermore, the Reagan Administration had reversed the defensive and reactive policies of previous Cold War presidencies, rejecting the Brezhnev Doctrine and supporting anti-communist insurgencies in Central America, Europe, and Africa. Reagan and his foreign policy team adopted a more aggressive stance against the Soviet Union itself, waging undeclared economic warfare designed to weaken, and ultimately topple, the Soviet regime. In the end, their wildest hopes and dreams had been fulfilled.

Yet, very often in history a wide gap exists between perception and reality, concurrent events and causation. The Reagan Administration enacted a policy to achieve a Cold War victory and victory was won. Whether or not Reagan's policies determined this outcome, however, remains problematical. Viewed from the Soviet rather than the American perspective, a far different analysis of the end of the Cold War emerges. Many scholars who study the Soviet Union downplay the significance of Reagan's role in the fall of the Soviet empire. The Reagan Administration, they argue, based its policies on misconceptions about Soviet military strength and an exaggeration of the Soviet role in Third World unrest and international terrorism. The Soviets never possessed the overweening military superiority projected by the Committee on the Present Danger, and Soviet leaders began to reduce both defense spending and foreign entanglements in the late 1970s before Reagan came to office.

Although Reagan invoked a new American supremacy in 1984 to justify renewed arms control talks, little changed in the existing balance between the two superpowers during the 1980s. Much of the vaunted United States defense buildup had been consumed by waste and inefficiency. The MX-missile program had expended $15 billion, but still lacked an acceptable plan for deployment. SDI had absorbed $26 billion in research funds, but was no closer to viability than it had been in 1983. The Soviets, moreover, did not respond to the Reagan-era defense buildup or the SDI threat with enhanced military spending that disrupted or bankrupted their economy as anticipated. The Soviet Union might well have muddled along indefinitely, its nuclear deterrent sufficient to ward off American advances, its conventional forces constraining eastern European dissent, if not for the ascension of Mikhail Gorbachev.

"The single most important factor underlying this important shift [in Soviet policy]," writes former CIA analyst and Soviet specialist Raymond L. Garthoff, "was the determination of Soviet leader Mikhail Gorbachev to overcome the military confrontation between East and West." Gorbachev believed that the Soviet political and economic system required a dramatic overhaul to rescue the nation from its inertial malaise. The key to this transformation lay in drastic reductions in defense spending that could only be achieved through arms control agreements with the United States and an end to the standoff in Europe. Gorbachev acted, according to Garthoff, "almost always because he saw the need for change and not because of Reagan's pressures."

Indeed, while Reagan had signaled his desire to engage in arms reductions talks as early as January 1984, more than a year before Gorbachev assumed power, the United States never initiated serious proposals at any of the summit meetings. Gorbachev, desperate for agreements that would advance and justify his domestic program, offered concession after concession. But Reagan refused to yield, especially on SDI, an experimental program with at best a distant chance of success. Garthoff suggests that Reagan's anti-Soviet rhetoric and intransigence strengthened hard-line opposition to Gorbachev in Moscow and may have delayed, rather than hastened, Soviet military reductions. "All that the Reagan Administration had ever done," writes Frances Fitzgerald, "was talk to the Soviets, pocket the concessions they made, and take credit for having forced Gorbachev to do what he was doing anyway for his own purposes."

Similarly, Garthoff and others argue that communist regimes in eastern Europe collapsed not as a result of the Reagan Doctrine, but rather from Gorbachev's commitment to *Glasnost* and his decision to withhold Soviet repression in the face of change. "What happened would not have happened without [Gorbachev]," argues Garthoff. "That cannot be said of anyone else." In addition, the Reagan Doctrine had broad moral and security consequences for the United States. Throughout the world, "authoritarian" forces embraced by the United States as anti-communist allies caused embarrassments or severe security threats. In 1989, President Bush sent 22,500 troops to Panama to arrest Dictator Manuel Noriega for his drug-running activities. In 1990 Iraq's Saddam Hussein, following his defeat in the Iran-Iraq war, invaded and occupied Kuwait. The United States responded with "Operation Desert Storm," a major American-led military action in 1991, to drive Iraqi troops out of Kuwait.

In Afghanistan, the withdrawal of Soviet support led to the collapse of the communist government and precipitated a civil war among rival warlords and fundamentalist groups. When the United States requested that former "freedom fighters" return their unused Stinger missiles, they met with resistance. "We will not return the Stingers. . . . We ourselves need them most," responded one mujahedin group. In 1991 the CIA initiated a new covert action in Afghanistan, seeking to buy back the Stingers. The agency expended $65 million to reacquire approximately 200 of the dangerous anti-aircraft missiles, but hundreds more remained either in Afghan hands or unaccounted for, available to shoot down both military and commercial aircraft. The Taliban, an extreme Muslim fundamentalist group, seized power in Afghanistan and welcomed the presence of Al Qaeda, a violent terrorist group. Al Qaeda, led by former mujahedin leader Osama Bin Laden, had its roots in the Soviet-Afghan conflict. Al Qaeda used Afghanistan to stage terrorist attacks on United States installations throughout the world, culminating in the September 11, 2001, assaults on the World Trade Center and the Pentagon. The United States responded by invading Afghanistan to drive out Al Qaeda and the Taliban. After more than two decades of invasions, civil war, and Taliban misrule, Afghanistan lay devastated.

The Soviet archives generally support the liberal revisionist view. Yet Reagan's contribution to the end of the Cold War remains significant. The Soviet empire might have ultimately faltered in the face of a less intransigent American policy. But Reagan's support for insurgent forces in Poland, Afghanistan, and elsewhere weakened the hold of communism on these countries. Although Gorbachev's decision to withdraw Soviet power ultimately created the conditions that allowed a change in regimes, American underwriting of resistance movements hastened the day of reckoning and helped to force the issue. On the nuclear disarmament front, Reagan defied hardliners in his own administration by engaging Gorbachev in the talks that led to the INF Treaty and the START I and START II accords completed by Presidents George H. W. Bush and Bill Clinton. His commitment to reducing the nuclear threat, sincere though erratically applied, made these gains possible.

The second pillar of Reagan's legacy is the nation's economic performance during his tenure. Basic statistics attest to a substantial record of growth. After the rocky "Reagan recession" of 1981–1982, the overall economy expanded steadily. When Reagan entered office, inflation hovered at 12 percent, interest rates had soared as high as 21 percent, and unemployment exceeded seven percent. The so-called "misery index" combining the unemployment and inflation rates stood at twenty points. In January 1989, inflation had dropped to 4.4 percent, the prime rate to 9.3 percent, and unemployment to 5.4 percent. The "misery index" had been halved. Over the course of the Reagan years the nation's gross national product had doubled and per capita income had jumped from $9,722 to $11,326. Nearly 18 million new jobs had been created.

The years from 1983 to 1989 marked the longest stretch of uninterrupted economic growth in United States history. Champions of the Reagan presidency hailed it as a triumph of Reaganomics and a validation of the often-maligned supply-side tax cuts. As with foreign affairs, the reality is far more complex. The primary components of the 1980s expansion were the taming of inflation and the stimulus provided by deficit spending. Cannon calls the victory over inflation "the most notable accomplishment of the Reagan years." Lower interest rates, accompanied by a dramatic drop in oil prices after 1985, freed money for investment and consumption, as did lower tax rates for the rich.

Nonetheless, public spending stimulated the economy far more than private investment. Federal budget deficits ranging from $128 billion to more than $200 billion annually pumped desperately needed capital into the system. These unprecedented shortfalls tripled the national debt. When added to the deficits accumulated by Reagan's successor, George H.W. Bush, the two Republican administrations created more debt than all of the nation's previous presidents combined. The deficits generated widespread concern at the time, as critics predicted that Reagan and Bush had purchased prosperity by creating an economic burden that would saddle Americans for generations. These jeremiads proved ill founded. The economy, as liberals had argued for decades, could sustain a substantial amount of deficit spending; the larger the gross national product, the greater the allowable deficit. An economic boom in the 1990s allowed the United States to project paying off its debts in less than two decades of Reagan's departure from office.

Reagan's vaunted tax cuts probably played a far lesser role than federal spending in generating economic growth. The Reagan tax reforms made fundamental changes in the nation's revenue system and lowered the highest tax rates, but barely affected the overall taxation of Americans. When Reagan came to office, 19.4 percent of the national income was diverted into federal taxes. Upon his departure this figure stood at 19.3 percent. The Reagan Administration passed far more bills raising taxes and fees than lowering them. Increases in payroll taxes to fund Social Security and Medicare offset other cuts, especially for working-class Americans. In addition, many states raised taxes to offset the decline in assistance flowing from the federal government.

The new tax regime proved far more regressive than the old. While most Americans saw modest tax reductions at best, the greatest benefits went to families earning more than $200,000 per year. According to the tenets of supply-side economics, this windfall for the wealthy should have generated greater savings and investment.

Economists, however, have uncovered little evidence of a strong correlation between the lower rates and the economic rise in the 1980s. The economy had grown spectacularly in the post-World War II era despite top rates often exceeding 70 percent. Reagan's tax reforms had dropped the top rate as low as 28 percent. According to economist Charles Kindleberger, much of the savings generated "seems to have been spent on consumption: second and third houses, travel, luxury apparel, cars, jewelry, yachts and the like, rather than being saved or invested." A substantial proportion of the available capital was pumped into the paper economy, speculative investments offered in the savings and loan and merger phenomena, rather than underwriting plants, equipment, or production. When these bubbles burst, the capital misallocated to these ventures evaporated. Shortly after Reagan left office, the economy entered a sharp recession. Recovery and a far more dramatic financial boom occurred in the 1990s after Presidents Bush and Clinton raised taxes.

Viewed in a broader historical perspective, the Reagan prosperity, its length notwithstanding, seems far weaker than indicated by an isolated glance. The economy grew at a slower rate in the 1980s than it had in the 1960s and 1970s and than it would in the 1990s. The real gross national product grew no faster during the Reagan era than it had during the much-maligned Carter years. From 1983 to 1989, at the peak of the Reagan prosperity, private wealth grew by eight percent; from 1975 to 1980, during the Carter downturn, private wealth had increased by 31 percent. While the traditional industrial segment of the economy continued the decline began in the 1970s, only relatively modest expansion took place in computers and technology. The less financially rewarding service sector generated most of the growth. Economists noted that of the millions of jobs created during the Reagan era, about half were minimum- and low-wage posts. Millions of people who lost jobs because of plant closings during the 1980s found new positions that paid less. The unemployment rate, while lower than at the trough of the recession, remained high by recent historical standards.

The supply-side tax cuts and the expansion of low-wage jobs represented parallel attributes of what political commentator Kevin Phillips has called the "Great Inversion." The nation that emerged from the Reagan-Bush era diverged greatly from the more egalitarian United States of the immediate post-World War II decades. In the 1940s and 1950s, notes Phillips, economic gains accrued largely to the broad middle class. From the 1970s onward, prosperity flowed disproportionately to the wealthiest Americans, as a culture that glorified intemperate accumulation materialized. The Reagan years accelerated this trend at mach speed. In 1979, the top one percent of the population held 22 percent of the nation's wealth; in 1989 that figure had almost doubled to 39 percent. Within the top one percent, the greatest gains went to the richest elite as billionaires increased their net worth from highs of $10 billion in 1982 to peaks of $100 billion and more. Compensation for corporate chief executive officers (CEOs) exemplified this phenomenon. In the 1960s CEOs had earned 25 times the income of hourly production workers. During the eighties, top CEO incomes leaped 500 to 700 percent. CEOs now made 93 times as much as their hourly employees, a figure that would skyrocket to 419 by the end of the 1990s. "The gap between the rich and everyone else was yawning to widths unseen since the 1920s and 1930s," writes Phillips.

Contrary to supply-side predictions, these gains did not trickle down to the average Americans. As historian Michael Schaller comments, "The rich got richer, and everyone else trod water." A wide variety of measures indicated that middle-class income stayed the same or actually declined in the 1980s and 1990s, prompting economist Lawrence Summers to lament a "quiet depression" in living standards. By the 1990s, typical Americans worked longer hours for fewer rewards than they had in the recent past. In the 1990s alone, the average American work year expanded by 184 hours, and the American workload surpassed that of all industrial nations. The percentage of Americans saying they always felt rushed jumped from 28 in 1975 to 38 in 1992. In a decade when labor union membership fell from 23 percent to less than 17 percent, fringe benefits, one of the perquisites of the "affluent society" lifestyle of the 1950s won by unions, also declined. In 1982, 49 percent of all workers in the bottom ten percent of the economy had health benefits provided by their employers. By 1996 this figure had plummeted to 26 percent. Slippage had also occurred for middle-ranked employees. Employers of those who received health coverage were also far less likely to pay the entire costs of the plan.

Individuals at the lower rungs of the economic ladder fared particularly poorly during the Reagan years. The average family income for the bottom fifth of Americans fell by seven percent during the 1980s. One out of five children dwelt below the poverty level. At the same time the proportion of government assistance expenditures, including food stamp and school lunch programs, shrank. The Reagan Administration tightened eligibility requirements for welfare and cut benefits for many of those on the rolls. Other indicators of social conditions also revealed the deterioration of life among the poor. In the nation's cities, homelessness increased, the use of hard drugs climbed, and the numbers of people in prison doubled.

Reagan's true legacy rests, however, neither in foreign policy nor in the economic sphere. Reagan's greatest accomplishments lay in the realm of ideology and politics. American conservatives came to embrace Reagan as a visionary, the triumphant personification of their beliefs and the foundation on which to consolidate their hold on the American electorate. There is some irony in this. Although his boosters had hailed a "Reagan Revolution," many conservatives in 1989 expressed disappointment with the timidity with which he advanced their cause. Some, on the far right, remained distrustful of his liaison with Mikhail Gorbachev and the Soviet Union. Economic conservatives expressed discontent with Reagan's failure to shrink the federal domain. The number of government workers actually expanded more under Reagan than under Jimmy Carter. In part this resulted from the defense buildup, but Social Security and Medicare had not only survived the "revolution," but expanded their expenditures. Total welfare spending in 1989 exceeded 1981 levels. Nor had the Reagan regime significantly enhanced states' rights. As Schaller observes, "In practice, the Reagan Administration shifted costs, not power, to local government. . . . Washington burdened state, county, and city governments with many new, expensive-to-administer regulations . . . but provided less federal money than before." The burgeoning deficits concerned many conservatives who had railed for generations against Democratic profligacy.

The religious right also had cause for complaint. Although Reagan had courted and legitimized political evangelists with appearances before their gatherings and his regular invocations of God and morality, he had done little to advance their social agenda. Reagan was unwilling to invest too much of his political capital in the "culture wars" so dear to the evangelical Christians, but so polarizing in the nation as a whole. During the Reagan years, the religious right made little headway in its calls for banning abortion, protecting school prayer, and warding off the growing acceptance of homosexuality in America.

Nor had Reagan established the type of durable political coalition that Franklin Roosevelt had. His vice-president, George H.W. Bush, won election in 1988, effectively decrying liberalism as the "L-word," but Democrats still controlled Congress, muting further conservative advances. The Republicans could not even hold the White House. In 1992 maverick billionaire Ross Perot, running as an independent candidate, sheared off the populist element of the Reagan vote, allowing Democrat Bill Clinton to unseat Bush as president.

But Reagan had advanced the conservative agenda in ways beyond the national ballot box. From the 1930s to the early 1980s, a large majority of Americans had identified themselves as Democrats. By the end of the Reagan era, the Republicans had drawn even. The nation's political discourse had shifted dramatically to the right. To win election, Clinton had had to portray himself as a "new Democrat," less wedded to public solutions to social problems, more committed to a rhetoric of individual responsibility and law and order. Despite the often spectacular failures of deregulation, Americans remained suspicious of bureaucratic agencies. They also maintained a heightened hostility to taxation, making it difficult for governments at the federal, state, or local level to generate additional revenues for basic purposes such as education and infrastructure.

Americans had also become determined to clean up the "welfare mess," long a target of Reagan's wrath. In 1987, the White House granted states the right to attain waivers from federal regulations to test experimental "workfare" programs, a goal advocated by Reagan when he was still governor of California. By the mid-1990s half the states had implemented workfare projects. President Clinton in 1996 would lead the fight to end "welfare as we know it," with a program that reflected Reagan's longtime demands, and declare with Reaganesque bluntness that "The age of big government is dead."

Conservatives also had made extraordinary gains in the federal judiciary. Robert Bork's bitter defeat in 1987 obscured the extent to which not only the Supreme Court, but the lower courts as well, had shifted to the right. Reagan appointed three new justices to the Supreme Court—Sandra Day O'Connor, Antonin Scalia, and Anthony M. Kennedy—and elevated Nixon appointee William Rehnquist to chief justice. The High Court thus moved closer to a conservative majority. Of greater long-term import, by the time he left office Reagan had appointed almost half of all federal judges. Carefully selected by the Judicial Selection Committee centered in the White House, the judges tended to be, according to legal historian David M. O'Brien, "predominantly young, upper middle-class white males, with . . . reputations for legal conservatism." Their relative youth would guarantee a longstanding rightward swing in the federal courts. The heated Bork dispute notwithstanding, Senate Democrats acknowledged the presidential prerogative in judicial selection, rejecting only three out of almost 400 Reagan appointments. Although for years conservatives had decried "judicial activism" on behalf of liberal causes, the new judges would often move aggressively to implement their own political, cultural, and social agendas.

The generation that came of age during the Reagan presidency also proved more conservative than its predecessors. Much as the New Deal had cemented their grandparents' allegiances to the Democratic Party, the "Reagan Revolution" led many young Americans, particularly white Americans, to identify as Republicans and conservatives. They viewed Reagan as a symbol of a renewed American spirit and shared his distrust of government. The rise of the religious right that began in the 1970s and lasted beyond the Reagan years brought many evangelical Christians not just to the ballot box, but into political office as well. In the 1994 midterm elections, the Republican leadership delineated a "Contract with America," which espoused a decidedly conservative agenda for the nation. Under its banner the Republicans gained control of both houses of Congress for the first time in 40 years. . . .

On June 5, 2004, Ronald Reagan, after a decade of decline, finally succumbed to the ravages of old age and Alzheimer's. His passing initiated a week of public mourning emblematic of his impact on the nation and characterized by the ceremonial trappings that Reagan had so loved. The occasion also offered a reminder of the carefully scripted nature of Reagan's public persona. Orchestrated much like a Hollywood spectacle, the ceremonies combined the military elements of traditional state funerals and the desires of the Reagans to shape his memory.

The mourning period reawakened Americans to the romance of Reagan's life. The Movie Channel presented a 24-hour marathon of Ronald Reagan movies. Millions of Americans watched seemingly nonstop footage of the ceremonies and retrospectives on network and cable broadcasts. Tens of thousands visited Reagan's closed casket at the Reagan Presidential Library in Simi, California, before his body was flown to Washington, D.C., where it lay in state in the Capitol Rotunda. Upwards of 100,000 people, some waiting in line for as long as seven hours, passed through the viewing area. Government leaders and former leaders from all over the world joined the four surviving former United States presidents among the dignitaries attending the memorial service at the National Cathedral. Reagan friends and family then flew with his body back to California to fulfill one last request. With the sun setting over the Pacific Ocean as a backdrop, Reagan was buried at a spectacular hilltop site that he had selected on the grounds of his presidential library.

His death revived the partisan debates over his legacy, albeit in a muted form. Conservatives uniformly hailed him as the savior of the nation and forefather of their modern ascendancy. Liberals reminded people of his failures and shortcomings, but grudgingly conceded his enormous impact on the nation's history. The glow remained one year later. In spring 2005 the Discovery Channel televised a series in which viewers could select the "Greatest American" in the nation's history. Participants selected Reagan as the top choice, immediately ahead of Abraham Lincoln, Martin Luther King, George Washington, and Benjamin Franklin.

Conservative theorist D'Souza argues that "Reagan's greatness derives from the fact that he was a visionary—a conceptualizer who was able to see the world differently from the way it was." Reagan had, as his political opposite Senator Edward Kennedy allowed, "stood for a set of ideas . . . he meant them, and he wrote them not only into public law, but into the national consciousness." At the time of Reagan's death, the United States and the world adhered more closely to his vision than at any time during his active adult life. The Soviet Union had disappeared, its communist ideology largely discredited. United States foreign policy operated in a unilateral universe, a dominant military power unchecked by powerful foes, treaty obligations, international law, or entangling alliances, a world where ideology shaped reality rather than the logical opposite. The extremes between not only rich and poor, but rich and middle class, had grown ever wider. Conservatism had replaced liberalism at the core of American political discourse. The social contract of mutual dependence and governmental oversight forged during the New Deal had been rewritten to reflect a less compassionate brand of unrestrained economic acquisition and individualism. Even immensely popular programs like Social Security and Medicare, long on Reagan's wish list for elimination, seemed endangered in the foreseeable future.

Ronald Reagan, like the hero of *That Printer of Udell's,* the book that had inspired him as a youth, had marched steadily into ever larger "fields of wider usefulness." His improbable life spanned, and at times encapsulated, the broad historical breadth of twentieth-century America. From his modest beginnings in the Midwest, he had advanced to radio broadcasting, then a respectable Hollywood career. As an actor he occupied only a second rank of stardom, but he eventually transcended all of his more celebrated film companions in his fame and influence. He became a union leader, television pioneer, business spokesperson, political advocate and governor of California. He ascended to the presidency of the United States and led the nation through one of the most momentous periods of its modern history. To Americans, living in a world that he had played an extraordinary role in creating, neither Ronald Reagan nor his contested legacy will ever be forgotten.

⊕ *F U R T H E R   R E A D I N G*

Ackerman, Frank. *Reaganomics: Rhetoric vs. Reality* (1982).

Anderson, Martin. *Revolution: The Reagan Legacy* (1990).

Berman, William. *America's Right Turn: From Nixon to Bush* (1994).

Beschloss, Michael R., and Strobe Talbot. *At the Highest Levels: The Inside Story of the End of the Cold War* (1993).

Bialer, Seweryn, and Michael Mandelbaum, eds. *Gorbachev's Russia and American Foreign Policy* (1988).

Blumenthal, Sidney. *The Rise of the Counter-Establishment: From Conservative Ideology to Political Power* (1986).

————, and Thomas Byrne Edsall, eds. *The Reagan Legacy* (1988).

Boyer, Paul, ed. *Reagan as President: Contemporary Views of the Man, His Politics, and His Policies* (1990).

Broder, David S. *Changing of the Guard: Power and Leadership in America* (1980).

Brownlee, W. Elliot, and Hugh Davis Graham, eds. *The Reagan Presidency: Pragmatic Conservatism and Its Legacies* (2003).

Cannon, Lou. *President Reagan: The Role of a Lifetime* (1991).

Crothers, Thomas. *In the Name of Democracy: U.S. Foreign Policy Toward Latin America in the Reagan Years* (1991).

Dallek, Matthew. *The Right Moment: Ronald Reagan's First Victory and the Decisive Turning Point in American Politics* (2004).

Dallek, Robert. *Ronald Reagan and the Politics of Symbolism* (1984).

D'Souza, Dinesh. *Ronald Reagan: How an Ordinary Man Became an Extraordinary Leader* (1997).

Duffy, Michael. *Marching in Place: The Status Quo Presidency of George Bush* (1992).

Edsall, Thomas Byrne, with Mary D. Edsall. *Chain Reaction: The Impact of Race, Rights, and Taxes on American Politics* (1991).

Erhman, John. *The Eighties: America in the Age of Reagan* (2005).

Evangelista, Matthew. *Unarmed Forces: The Transnational Movement to End the Cold War* (1999).

Gaddis, John Lewis. *The United States and the End of the Cold War* (1992).

Ginsberg, Benjamin, and Martin Shefter. *Politics by Other Means: Politicians, Prosecutors, and the Press from Watergate to Whitewater,* 3rd ed. (2002).

Glynn, Patrick. *Closing Pandora's Box: Arms Races, Arms Control, and the History of the Cold War* (1992).

Himmelstein, Jerome L. *To the Right: The Transformation of American Conservatism* (1990).

Hodgson, Godfrey. *More Equal Than Others: America from Nixon to the New Century* (2004).

———. *The World Turned Right Side Up: A History of the Conservative Ascendancy in America* (1996)

Hoeveler, J. David, Jr. *Watch on the Right: Conservative Intellectuals in the Reagan Era* (1991).

Johnson, Haynes. *Sleepwalking Through History: America in the Reagan Years* (1991).

Klare, Michael, and Peter Kornbluh, eds. *Low Intensity Warfare: Counterinsurgency, Proinsurgency, and Antiterrorism in the Eighties* (1988).

Lash, Jonathan. *A Season of Spoils: The Story of the Reagan Administration's Attack on the Environment* (1984).

Lawrence, David G. *The Collapse of the Democratic Presidential Majority* (1998).

LeoGrande, William M. *Our Own Backyard: The United States in Central America, 1977–1992* (1998).

Levy, Frank. *The New Dollars and Dreams: American Incomes and Economic Change* (1999).

McGirr, Lisa. *Suburban Warriors: The Origins of the New American Right* (2001).

Mills, Nicolaus. *The Triumph of Meanness: America's War Against Its Better Self* (1997).

Morris, Edmund. *Dutch: A Memoir of Ronald Reagan* (1999).

Noonan, Peggy. *What I Saw at the Revolution: A Political Life in the Reagan Era* (1990).

Parmet, Herbert S. *George Bush: The Life of a Lone Star Yankee* (1997).

Pemberton, William E. *Exit with Honor: The Life and Presidency of Ronald Reagan* (1998).

Phillips, Kevin. *The Politics of Rich and Poor: Wealth and the American Electorate in the Reagan Aftermath* (1990).

Piven, Frances Fox, and Richard A. Cloward. *The Breaking of the American Social Compact* (1997).

Reeves, Richard. *President Reagan: The Triumph of Imagination* (2005).

Ribuffo, Leo. *Right Center Left: Essays in American History* (1992).

Rosenstiet, Tom. *Strange Bedfellows: How Television and the Presidential Candidates Changed American Politics, 1992* (1993).

Schmertz, Eric J., Natalie Datlof, and Alexej Ugrinsky. *Ronald Reagan's America* (1997).

Sexton, Patricia Cayo. *The War on Labor and the Left: Understanding America's Unique Conservatism* (1991).

Shafer, Byron E., and Richard Johnston. *The End of Southern Exceptionalism: Class, Race, and Partisan Change in the Postwar South* (2006).

Stefancic, Jean, Richard Delgado, and Mark Tushnet. *No Mercy: How Conservative Think Tanks and Foundations Changed America's Social Agenda* (1997).

Stockman, David A. *The Triumph of Politics: How the Reagan Revolution Failed* (1986).

Strober, Deborah Hart, and Gerald S. Strober, eds. *The Reagan Presidency: An Oral History of the Era,* 2nd ed. (2003).

Troy, Gil. *Morning in America: How Ronald Reagan Invented the 1980s* (2004).

Vogel, David. *Fluctuating Fortunes: The Political Power of Business in America* (1989).

Weir, Margaret, ed. *The Social Divide: Political Parties and the Future of Activist Government* (1998).

Wills, Garry. *Reagan's America: Innocents at Home* (1987).

Woodward, Bob. *Veil: The Secret Wars of the CIA, 1981–1987* (1987).

CHAPTER
11

The Promises and Perils
of a New Economy

As the twentieth century gave way to the new millennium, it became increasingly clear that a new era in American history had begun. The Cold War was over; so was liberal dominance of the nation's political agenda. International trade, travel, and communication—in a word, globalization—all increased at a rapid rate. In the United States, this new global era was marked by the emergence of what some called a "new economy"—that is, an economy marked not only by the continuing shift from manufacturing to services but also by heightened competition, rapid innovation, increased organizational flexibility, and more fluid capital and labor markets. The introduction of new computer technologies radically changed patterns of work and consumption, while deregulation, accompanied by widespread corporate restructuring, transformed the face of American business. The U.S. economy, which in the 1970s had faltered and stagnated, entered the longest period of sustained growth since World War II. As the twentieth century ended, the country seemed awash in a rising tide of computers, cell phones, and sport utility vehicles.

There were downsides to the new economy as well. While the economy of the old postwar order had been characterized by stability and security, the new economy was marked by almost continuous change. In the 1950s, many blue-collar and white-collar workers could realistically anticipate lifetime employment by a single company. By the 1990s, students graduating from college were told to expect as many as six to seven careers, much less jobs, over the course of their working lives. Moreover, the benefits of the new economy were distributed with startling inequality, reversing the trend toward greater equality that had prevailed from World War II through the 1960s. The power of organized labor was greatly reduced, and with it labor's share of increased productivity. The rich became much richer—by the end of the twentieth century, the top 1 percent of U.S. households possessed more wealth than the bottom 95 percent—while almost thirty-five million people remained below the poverty line, earning about $13,000 per year for a three-person family. For many, remaining in the middle class required two incomes, mounting consumer debt, and long commutes that left less and less time for family and friends.

The rapid diffusion of new technologies, especially in communications and biotechnology, was accompanied by growing uneasiness over how these new technologies might reshape people's lives. While millions joined the rush to shop online, others worried about new breaches in the walls that had once separated families from the marketplace. The rapid spread of genetically engineered foods boosted America's much-vaunted agricultural productivity even higher, although consumers both in the United States and abroad worried about the impact of such foods on health and the environment. The successful mapping of the human genome promised breathtaking new advances in medical science but also prompted disturbing ethical questions that Americans had never before confronted. Uncontrolled economic growth, many feared, posed an irreparable threat to the global environment.

While some enthusiasts boasted that the U.S. economy had entered a "long boom" from which the business cycle itself had been banished, more sober-minded critics warned of an impending reckoning produced by a growing federal deficit, lower rates of savings, a worsening trade balance, and growing disparities of income and wealth.

✥ D O C U M E N T S

Document 1, a brief analysis by economists associated with the new centrist Democrats closely associated with the presidency of Bill Clinton, contrasts characteristics of the "old" and "new" economies. Document 2 explains the economics of "mass customization," one of the many new processes that characterized the changing economy. Documents 3 and 4 outline the extraordinary story of Wal-Mart—the company's innovative business model and application of new information technologies. Wal-Mart's amazing growth also elicited strong local opposition. Consumers wanted low prices and affordable variety, even as some of them bemoaned Wal-Mart's deleterious effects on local communities. The company discouraged efforts to unionize its workforce and used its market power to obtain volume discounts and undercut its competitors. The emergence of a new economy in the United States was paralleled by and closely interrelated with globalization—the growing integration of international markets in capital, labor, goods, and services. Both phenomena changed traditional patterns of work and consumption. Moreover, there were both winners and losers in the new global economy. In Document 5, a critic of globalization decries outsourcing, the movement of jobs out of the United States and into low-wage nations. In Document 6, the liberal group Americans for Democratic Action reports on the growing poverty and inequality in the new economy. Finally, Document 7, features a chart used by a market research firm to track the spending habits of sixty-two demographic lifestyle groups.

1. "New Democrats" Hail the New Economy, 1998

The U.S. economy is undergoing a fundamental transformation at the dawn of the new millennium. Some of the most obvious outward signs of change are in fact among the root causes of it: revolutionary technological advances, including powerful personal computers, high-speed telecommunications, and the Internet. The market environment facilitated by these and other developments in the last decade and a half has been variously labeled the "information economy," "network economy," "digital

"The 'New Economy' of the 1990s," by Robert D. Atkin and Randolph H. Court. Introduction to "The New Economy Index: Understanding America's Economic Transformation" (Policy Report, 1995). Reprinted by permission of the Progressive Policy Institute.

economy," "knowledge economy," and the "risk society." Together, the whole package is often simply referred to as the "New Economy."

The story of how businesses are changing in today's economy has been told and retold with such frequency in recent years that it has become something of a cliché: the new rules of the game require speed, flexibility, and innovation. New, rapidly growing companies are selling to global markets almost from their inception, and established companies are being forced to reinvent their operations to stay competitive in the new terrain. This is the part of the New Economy that was born in Steve Jobs' and Steve Wozniak's garage, at Bell Labs, Xerox PARC, and in the trunk of Michael Dell's car. It is Silicon Valley: Netscape, Yahoo!, and the next Big Thing. And of course it is Microsoft, with a market capitalization now second only to General Electric's.

But this New Economy is about more than high technology and the frenetic action at the cutting edge. Most firms, not just the ones actually producing technology, are organizing work around it. The New Economy is a metal casting firm in Pittsburgh that uses computer-aided manufacturing technology to cut costs, save energy, and reduce waste. It is a farmer in Nebraska who sows genetically altered seeds and drives a tractor with a global satellite positioning system. It is an insurance company in Iowa that uses software to flatten managerial hierarchies and give its workers broader responsibilities and autonomy. It is a textile firm in Georgia that uses the Internet to take orders from customers around the world.

It is also as much about new organizational models as it is about new technologies. The New Economy is the Miller brewery in Trenton, Ohio, which produces 50 percent more beer per worker than the company's next-most-productive facility, in part because a lean, 13-member crew has been trained to work in teams to handle the overnight shift with no oversight. . . .

Beyond the technological advances, what is actually new about the so-called New Economy? In one respect, nothing. We still work at jobs for a living, and we still buy, sell, and trade products and services, just like we always have. As Federal Reserve Chairman Alan Greenspan has noted, the heart of the economy is, as it always has been, grounded in human nature, not in any new technological reality. In Greenspan's analysis,

> The way we evaluate assets, and the way changes in those assets affect our economy, do not appear to be coming out of a set of rules that is different from the one that governed the actions of our forebears. . . . As in the past, our advanced economy is primarily driven by how human psychology molds the value system that drives a competitive market economy. And that process is inextricably linked to human nature, which appears essentially immutable and, thus anchors the future to the past.

Nonetheless, Greenspan and other economists agree that some of the key rules of the game are changing, from the way we organize production, to our patterns of trade, to the way organizations deliver value to consumers. . . .

The United States is ahead of the curve in a number of areas. Here, one of the most noticeable structural changes in the New Economy is the degree to which dynamism, constant innovation, and adaptation have become the norm. One of the keys to the recent strong U.S. economic performance has been the country's ability to embrace these changes. Nearly three quarters of all new jobs are being created by 350,000 new fast-growing "gazelle" firms (companies with sales growth of at least 20 percent per year for four straight years). Almost a third of all jobs are now in flux (either being born or dying, added or subtracted) every year. This churning of the economy is being spurred by new technology, but also by increasing competition, a trend that is in turn partly a product of increasing globalization. Between 1970 and 1997, U.S. imports and exports grew three and a half times faster than GDP [Gross Domestic Product] in 1992 dollars.

Another striking structural characteristic of the New Economy is occupational change. Between 1969 and 1995, virtually all the jobs lost in the production or distribution of goods have been replaced by jobs in offices. Today, almost 93 million American workers (which amounts to 80 percent of all jobs) do not spend their days making things—instead, they move things, process or generate information, or provide services to people. . . .

Today, though the foundations for the New Economy are in place, widespread benefits haven't yet been realized. Despite job growth, low unemployment, and other notable signs of economic progress—and despite gushing press accounts of fabulous new wealth and opportunities—a central paradox of the emerging New Economy is that the 1980s and 1990s have seen productivity and per capita GDP growth rates languish in the 1.25 percent range, while income inequality has grown. Our challenge is to create a progressive economic policy framework that will encourage a new era of higher growth, while promoting and enabling a broad-based prosperity that produces the widest possible winner's circle.

Old economic policy, shaped by the Great Depression, largely focused on creating jobs, controlling inflation, and managing the business cycle. The New Economy brings new concerns. Technology, as well as a highly competent Federal Reserve policy, may have lessened the importance and severity of the domestic business cycle. . . .

The New Economy puts a premium on what Nobel Laureate economist Douglas North calls "adaptive efficiency"—the ability of institutions to innovate, continuously learn, and productively change. In the old economy, fixed assets, financing, and labor were principal sources of competitive advantage for firms. But now, as markets fragment, technology accelerates, and competition comes from unexpected places, learning, creativity, and adaptation are becoming the principal sources of competitive advantage in many industries. Enabling constant innovation has become the goal of any organization committed to prospering, and should also become the goal of public policy in the New Economy. . . .

2. A Federal Reserve Report Extols "Mass Customization," 1998

Henry Ford's first great contribution to America was the Model T, which rolled off the assembly lines at his Highland Park, Michigan, plant at the rate of one every 24 seconds. At the time, it was an amazing display of industrial efficiency. By

---

Excerpts from W. Michael Cox and Richard Alm, "The Right Stuff: America's Move to Mass Customization," *1998 Annual Report* (Dallas: Federal Reserve Bank of Dallas, 1998). Online at http://www.dallasfed.org/fed/annual/1999p/ar98.html.

streamlining automation in his factories, Ford advanced an era of mass production that built his fortune and brought the automobile within reach of an emerging middle class. But while the miracle of mass production delivered the goods, it didn't adapt easily, so all Model T's looked alike. Ford's approach can be summed up in what he said about the car's exterior: "The consumer can have any color he wants so long as it's black."

Ford's take-it-or-leave-it attitude wouldn't cut it in today's economy. Americans are blessed—some might say overwhelmed—by an ever-expanding variety of goods and services. . . . Just since the early 1970s, there's been an explosion of choice in the marketplace—the assortment of new vehicle models has risen from 140 to 260, soft drinks from 20 to more than 87, TV channels from 5 to 185, over-the-counter pain relievers from 17 to 141. The U.S. market offers 7,563 prescription drugs, 3,000 beers, 1,174 amusement parks, 340 kinds of breakfast cereal, 50 brands of bottled water. Whole milk sits on the supermarket shelf beside skim milk, half-percent, 1 percent, 2 percent, lactose-reduced, hormone-free, chocolate, buttermilk and milk with a shelf life of six months. Today's consumers have access to more book titles, more movies and more magazines. Ford's company still makes black cars for buyers who want them, but it also offers a palette of 46 other colors—toreador red, jalapeño green, Atlantic blue, mocha frost, autumn orange, teal and more.

This proliferation of products, models and styles isn't capitalism run amok. Variety shouldn't be dismissed as a trivial extravagance. It's a wealthy, sophisticated society's way of improving the lot of consumers. The more choices, the better. A wide selection of goods and services increases the chance each of us will find, somewhere among all the shelves and showrooms, products that meet our requirements. . . .

From clothing to computers, businesses are working to become more consumer friendly. They do it to gain new sales and stay competitive. They do it because pleasing the customer isn't just about producing more stuff. It's about producing the right stuff.

Just what is the right stuff? It's more of what we do want and less of what we don't want. The economy provides more of what we do want by customizing products to our particular tastes. It eliminates what we don't want through preventive products. Vaccines, childproof caps, safety gear on cars and antipollution devices are valuable for the misfortunes they avert. Preventive goods and services are often taken for granted—until they're needed. They raise living standards by replacing treatment with immunity, repair with safer design, helping protect consumers from some of life's tragedies.

The rich have always enjoyed the luxury of custom-made products. Now, though, personalized goods and services are increasingly within the budgets of middle-class consumers. Computers, the Internet, DNA research and other technologies are forging a whole new paradigm that makes possible the delivery of custom-designed products to the masses—at ever lower prices. The descriptive phrase for the phenomenon is mass customization. "Once you know exactly what you want, you'll be able to get it just that way," says Bill Gates, founder of software giant Microsoft. "Computers will enable goods that today are mass produced to be both mass produced and custom-made for particular customers."

The economy's progression to customization isn't a fad. It arises from the free market's relentless drive to bring what we buy closer to what we want. What we buy yields a lot more utility when it exactly matches our needs, and Americans are reaping enormous benefits as new tools help business cater to markets of one. We're getting more for less, helping keep inflation in check.

There's just one glitch in this otherwise serendipitous story: traditional measures of the economy may not reflect how much our living standards are improving. Conceived in an era of mass production, the nation's GDP [Gross Domestic Product] and productivity statistics may ably count more stuff, but they give little credit for right stuff. Mass customization and prevention—just like variety—deliver their gains in important but subtle ways, so gross domestic product and productivity statistics fail to capture the extent of our progress. . . .

Whether companies are seeking to expand sales or just stay in business, mass customization enables producers to snare buyers by offering extra value. It's no surprise that consumer satisfaction lies at the core of this phenomenon; what consumers want always shapes market economies. Econ 101 professors have taught this straightforward notion since Adam Smith published *The Wealth of Nations* in 1776. Markets serve as complex information machines that collect and communicate buyers' needs, tastes, desires and whims. Producers that do the best job of catering to consumers gain market share and make greater profits. Burger King got it right in its advertising slogan: Have it your way!

Companies prosper by delivering what customers want. This conventional view of consumer sovereignty is correct—as far as it goes. What's missing is a description of how meeting buyers' needs and wants evolves over time. . . . Americans have always preferred customized products, but they couldn't always afford them. Now, companies are finding ways to deliver exactly what we want at prices competitive with those of mass production. . . .

What's increasingly shaping today's economy isn't the raw power of machines but the subtle power of knowledge. Information Age technology—primarily the computer—has erased yesterday's edict that customization must carry a high price. Mass customization offers consumers the best of both worlds. It embodies the good qualities from the era of hand production—custom design and individualized service. And it retains the most significant gain from the era of mass production—low cost.

Mass production was about producing more stuff. Mass customization is about producing the right stuff.

Customization for the mass market isn't just economists' jargon for variety. The difference lies in which side of the market calls the shots. Variety represents producers' best guess about what consumers will buy. Companies tweak their designs, hoping what they offer is close enough. Even when companies rely on market research, they're still aiming at broad groups of consumers. Variety has delivered great benefits in recent decades, but it is mass production's response to the fact that everybody's tastes differ. . . . Even at its best, variety is an imperfect substitute for true customization, which eliminates the need for guesswork. Companies that customize don't make anything until they know precisely what the customer wants.

One size fits all? Not anymore. What served as a good slogan for mass production doesn't cut it in today's world.

Technology's Role: Driving Down Costs

Why have Americans had to wait until the tail end of the 20th century for mass customization? The simplest answer: until now, the country didn't have the know-how to customize at low cost. Today's technology, though, makes it possible.

If there's a signature tool of mass customization, it's the microprocessor. This tiny device is indispensable to many of today's "smart" tools—most notably, powerful computers that process, store and send information. The Internet moves vast amounts of information at the click of a button—not just words and numbers but pictures and sound as well. Search engines—software that brings order to the Internet's chaos—are key to customizing because they find and organize information based on users' profiles and inquiries. Lasers are used in bar-code scanners, measurement devices and fiber-optic cables that can transmit whole libraries in seconds. Artificial intelligence programs simplify the design of new products. Computer-controlled manufacturing makes it faster and cheaper to modify designs and assemble one-of-a-kind items. Breakthroughs in biotechnology are unlocking the secrets of individual cells. The leap from analog to digital greatly expands the capacity of all kinds of communications technologies to process and deliver that most precious of commodities—information.

The tools of the Information Age are indeed powerful. These technologies spawn mass customization by revolutionizing the calculus of production costs. Nearly all business expenses fall into two broad categories—fixed and marginal. Fixed costs include conceiving, designing and organizing the operation, setting up plants, installing equipment, bringing in utilities, hiring workers and slogging through the usual morass of red tape. These costs are incurred before the first sale is made. Marginal costs, on the other hand, aren't incurred until an enterprise is up and running. They cover expenses for producing additional units of output, including wages, raw materials, electricity, marketing and distribution.

The interplay of fixed and marginal costs explains both mass production and mass customization. In the Industrial Age, electric motors, engines, winches, conveyor belts, machine tools and other advances reshaped the economy. They were the high technology of the times. These innovations allowed companies to turn out identical products cheaply. The order of the day was standardization—from nuts and bolts to accounting procedures and time zones. The world of mass production usually involved high fixed costs and low marginal costs. Producers made money by cranking out as many units as possible, driving down the average production cost by spreading the huge fixed cost over more and more units. That's precisely what Henry Ford and his successors did. Customers paid lower prices for automobiles, appliances, clothing and household goods, but companies could only bring a limited number of standardized models to the marketplace. With high fixed costs and low marginal costs, it's cheap to make the same product for everybody but expensive to produce a different product for each customer.

Industrial Age technology replaced muscle power with machine power, which ran the assembly lines. Information Age technology complements machine power

with brain power, enabling us to recognize each consumer's preferences and deliver what they want at a reasonable price. . . . Once again, the key is costs. Mass
customization becomes optimal when both fixed and marginal costs—particularly
fixed—are low. If producers can change designs quickly and inexpensively, they'll
win customers by targeting individual tastes and preferences. Average costs decline
even without long production runs, permitting low prices along with the bonus of
getting exactly what we want.

Mass production was the by-product of Industrial Age tools. Mass customization is the dividend of Information Age tools.

Modern technologies slash fixed costs in three areas: information, production
and distribution. By making it easy to supply information, the Internet gives consumers a cheap and easy way to find out what goods and services are on the market.
Companies can display immense amounts of product information on their web pages
and take orders from anywhere in the world. More important, the Internet frees producers from the expensive proposition of paying firms to gather information on what
buyers want. . . .

By making it cheaper to personalize during production, Information Age tools
remove the last barriers to providing goods and services for individual customers. . . .
Even assembly lines are no longer limited to endless iterations of the same product.
Computer-aided designs are replacing costly prototypes. . . . Computer-guided machinery allows production to shift from one style to another with a few lines of
computer code. At Motorola's pager factory in Boynton Beach, Florida, the speci-
fications for each order arrive in a direct transmission from sales representatives'
laptop computers. Within minutes, these specs are translated into bar-code instructions for the assembly process. In theory, the factory could produce 29 million different pagers on the same line, one right after another, without the time and expense
of retooling.

Improvements in distribution, made possible by such technologies as lasers and
computers, reduce the fixed costs of getting products to consumers. Bar-code scanners
allow Federal Express and other overnight shippers to improve speed and accuracy
while reducing outlays for a global system to pick up, sort, track and deliver packages. As the Internet spreads into more homes and businesses, it makes the delivery
of information products relatively inexpensive. . . .

Information Age technology thrusts our economy toward mass customization,
but other factors also contribute. The globalization of commerce, for example,
makes goods and services more widely available, especially as cutting-edge electronic media reduce the time and expense involved in gathering information. Access
to products from around the world also makes us more sophisticated consumers,
so that even in the home market we demand the nuances of Italian suits or German beer.

Just as mass customization couldn't take root in an isolated society, it couldn't
emerge in a poor one. Low-income countries are still dominated by mass production.
That's to be expected, because producing quantity is the quickest way out of poverty.
Once a nation becomes wealthy, most families' basic needs are satisfied. As they
move up the economic ladder, consumers typically move down a list of wants from
food, clothing and shelter to luxuries. All of us desire the luxury of goods and services that embody our own tastes and preferences. It's money in the pocket, though,

that makes it possible. We're becoming a society of mass customization because we can now afford it.

First we meet basic needs through mass production. Then we gratify individual wants through mass customization.

Right Stuff, Wrong Statistics

As mass customization becomes part of our everyday lives, most Americans will intuitively understand how it represents an improvement over mass production. Clothes will fit better. Entertainment will be more enjoyable. Doctors and hospitals will have individualized tools to make us healthier.

Yet it may be hard for many Americans to assess how much better off we are. The problem lies in how we measure our economic progress. We tend to rely on a handful of well-publicized statistics—mostly notably, gross domestic product, the Consumer Price Index and productivity figures. The benefits of mass customization, however, are hard to quantify, especially with the rudimentary economic yardsticks now available.

GDP is a statistic designed for mass production. It's a simple counting—the number of units made. It falls short in measuring intangible benefits. Economic research demonstrates that GDP often fails to capture consumers' gains from better quality and new products. Mass customization introduces a similar bias, one tied to the fact that we can measure production but not consumers' satisfaction. They aren't the same, even though many commentators casually link them. . . .

Inflation-adjusted GDP puts economic growth at an annual average of 2.7 percent over the past two decades. GDP may be entirely accurate as a tally of how much our farms, factories and offices produce, but it's increasingly inadequate as a measure of how well the economy provides what we want—the satisfaction produced. As we grow wealthier, Americans are taking more of our progress in ways that aren't readily quantified. We're refining what we produce—making the right stuff, not just stuff.

If GDP can't detect the benefits of mass customization, it will also miss the mark on productivity, a number that derives straight from the GDP calculations. Some economists are disappointed in America's productivity performance over the past quarter century, a time of rapid spread of new technologies—most notably the computer. They see measured productivity slowing to 1 percent a year and worry that Information Age advances aren't delivering the same economic punch as Industrial Age inventions. It just isn't so. Our statistics don't recognize how the economy is making us better off by producing for us individually rather than en masse. . . .

Our statistics are a rearview mirror, looking back at the past. We need to focus on the economy that's emerging rather than the one that has been. Tomorrow's progress can't be judged with yesterday's gauges. What's needed are analytical tools that can capture the benefits of mass customization and preventive products.

After all, output and productivity aren't the goals of the economy. Consumer satisfaction is. . . .

Two centuries of American economic progress have brought us a standard of living that's the envy of the world. We wouldn't have it so good without the immense variety provided as companies move from standardization to custom-made. Our economy offers a veritable feast for consumers. Mass customization will make it even better. An economy that's delivering more of what we want and less of what we don't is doing its job in raising living standards. As we enter the 21st century, the United States is moving into a new economic era, one where consumers will be better off than ever before—because we'll live in a world of our own design.

3. *Money* Magazine Asks of Wal-Mart, "How Big Can It Get?" 1999

When you think of the great blue-chip growth stocks of the past quarter-century, what names come to mind? Coke? General Electric? Merck? Well, guess what. Wal-Mart has crushed them all. Since 1977, the stock has returned 35% annually, turning a hypothetical $10,000 investment into an astounding $6.9 million. . . . Going forward, it figures to outstrip most of today's crop of silicon start-ups and dotcoms—maybe all of them—over the long term.

Wal-Mart isn't in a sexy industry, isn't run by a young, entrepreneurial million-aire and doesn't woo Generation X-ers with promises of stock options. It's simply a juggernaut, built on a combination of cutting-edge technology—yes, it's a tech company—smiley-face service and good old-fashioned business skill. Wal-Mart has figured out how to pile up billions of dollars in profit by selling staggering quantities of low-margin goods. Its $147 billion in sales for the latest 12 months are double the sales of competitors Sears and K Mart combined, while its $4.9 billion profit in that period is nearly triple their total.

Relentless execution of its basic business model had helped Wal-Mart stock soar even while other retailers have been battered by fears of rising interest rates and de-clining consumer spending. . . . [T]he shares[, which were recently $55, have been] up 61% for the past 12 months. That's a tough pace to maintain, particularly in the cutthroat retail arena, where profit margins are slim, competition is tough, Internet start-ups are encroaching on traditional retailers' turf and many of the country's legendary stores have hit the wall. Can the Wal-Mart juggernaut keep going?

To answer that question, we spoke with Wal-Mart execs, Wall Street analysts, major shareholders, retail consultants, rivals and customers. We started in the small town of Bentonville, Ark., where Wal-Mart runs its far-flung operations from a converted warehouse building on Walton Boulevard. In a series of exclusive inter-views, chairman Rob Walton (son of founder Sam), CEO David Glass and other top executives gave us a detailed picture of the company's strategy. They are plan-ning growth on a mind-boggling scale for a company this big; their projections call for boosting both revenues and profits at least 15% a year (excluding any potential acquisitions). To hit those numbers—which would push sales past $200 billion in two years—Wal-Mart is steamrolling ahead on three main fronts: the grocery busi-ness, foreign markets and the Internet. We'll look at each in detail below.

Has Wal-Mart reached the point where it's just too big to keep growing rapidly? Perhaps. But the company's history is one of proving the naysayers wrong. "Our prospects are better today than at any point in our history," contends Glass. "We can be anything that we want to be. Any limits are self-imposed, because we can do whatever we want."

If that sounds more like an inspirational spiel from Tony Robbins than a dispassionate assessment of business prospects, that's simply the Wal-Mart way. At the shareholder meeting last June, more than 20,000 investors and employees descended on the local university's Bud Walton stadium for a morning of chatting and cheering ("Give me a W! Give me an A! . . . Who's No. 1? The customer!"). "It's like a cult," says Jerry Rascona, who runs the lawn-and-garden department in Wal-Mart's Middle Island, N.Y. store and owns some 700 shares of WMT stock. "We believe; therefore, it will happen."

Wal-Mart remains imbued with the spirit of Sam Walton, who died in 1992. Photos of Mr. Sam line the walls of the corporate headquarters, and the hokey customs he initiated, like cookie-stacking contests and "people greeters" at the stores' entrances, endure. But don't let the folksiness fool you. Like its founder, Wal-Mart is one big, tough, shrewd operator. It uses its size to wring the best deals from suppliers, and it carefully calibrates the price and placement of every item it sells, using reams of computer-generated data on the buying patterns of the 100 million people who come to its stores each week.

Indeed, Wal-Mart has shown how technology can revolutionize even the most mundane business. The backbone of the company's success is not the products or the stores but its 101-terabyte computer system, which Wal-Mart says is the second largest in the world, surpassed only by the Pentagon's. By analyzing the constantly updated information, Wal-Mart executives and store managers can track customer behavior with startling precision—and to great effect.

At Wal-Mart No. 0001 in Rogers, Ark., store manager Mike Walker points a hand-held scanner at a package of Kraft American cheese singles on special for $1.98. With the click of a button, the machine shows how many have been sold in the store that day and how many are in transit, in the warehouse and on order. Click again, and the hand-held pulls up the price Wal-Mart paid for the cheese and tallies its profit margin. "We know everything about every item," Walker says. "We can get more sales and make more money based on what we know."

What are the bestsellers in each store by total dollars? By profits? By volume? Wal-Mart knows and can position its hottest items in the best locations for boosting sales. How well did a new product fare on its first day of introduction? Wal-Mart knows and can tweak the color or size or flavor of the product with the supplier immediately. Are golf balls flying out of one Florida store but languishing in another? Wal-Mart knows and can move the sluggish product to the place where it will sell, rather than having to mark it down.

What Wal-Mart is now learning to do with the data, however, goes beyond traditional inventory management. By looking into the shopping baskets of its customers, the chain is learning which items to stock near one another (bananas close to cereal, alarm clocks with suitcases). And by working closely with more than 7,000 vendors who have access over the Internet to the company's data on all of their products, Wal-Mart can hammer out deals for special flavors and sizes and instantly nix products that don't sell in early tests. By constantly learning what works and what doesn't, in real time, Wal-Mart can shift gears faster than many small merchants, let alone other giants. The payoff from all this number crunching: Wal-Mart has sliced its inventory costs (because goods sit on the shelves for less time) and increased its sales per square foot (to $374, vs. $222 K Mart). "They make a lot of mistakes, but they are smart and very quick to react," says PaineWebber analyst Jeff Edelman. "That is what has enabled Wal-Mart to maintain that kind of momentum."

If you don't think of Wal-Mart as a grocery store yet, you will soon. Across the country, Wal-Mart is creating enormous 200,000-square-foot "supercenters" that offer all the usual items but also devote about a fifth of their floor space to groceries. Wal-Mart's foray into food will turn it into the country's No. 1 supermarket within five years, analysts predict, catapulting it ahead of Kroger and Safeway and pummeling many of the smaller chains.

Why would Wal-Mart move into a field with even lower margins, fiercer competition and more vexing distribution difficulties than the discount business? For starters, filling America's shopping carts is a $450-billion-a-year business, dwarfing the discount sector. And Wal-Mart executives see it as a field where the company's unparalleled skill at pushing large volumes of cheap goods will give it an unbeatable edge. People shop for food twice as often as for hard goods, so food brings more shoppers to Wal-Mart's supercenters, creating more potential buyers for the chain's higher-margin items, like books, CDs and computers. And tracking food purchases gives Wal-Mart information on its customers' ethnicity and demographics that it can't get any other way—letting it fine-tune its merchandising efforts even further. "Everything we do is a driver of volume," says Lee Scott, a 20-year Wal-Mart veteran who was tapped as chief operating officer early this year and is expected to become the next CEO. "Additional customers let us lower the price, and lower prices draw additional customers."

Moreover, Wal-Mart sees the food sector as ripe for conquest. It is extremely fragmented—with the top two chains, Kroger and Safeway, accounting for just 12% of sales last year—and in the throes of consolidation, with many smaller players declaring bankruptcy. While many of the country's grocers are preoccupied with the problems of integrating acquisitions, says Barrett Ladd, a retailing consultant at Management Ventures, Wal-Mart is simply rolling out new stores. (Wal-Mart prefers not to buy existing chains, because it wants to sell food and its traditional merchandise under one roof.) There are already 650 supercenters, and next year alone, Wal-Mart figures on adding at least 160 new ones, mostly by knocking down the walls of existing discount stores to create space for food. . . .

4. A Critic Assails the Influence of Wal-Mart, 1999

The table inside the door of the old Baptist church was laden with refreshments: ginger and peach iced tea (regular and decaffeinated), mango Ceylon tea, freshly made lemonade. As seven o'clock approached, they tested the public address system and finished arranging the white plastic chairs on the lawn outside to accommodate the expected overflow. Bowls of home-made chocolate cookies arrived. Slowly they began to gather, the men in their polo shirts and chinos, khaki shorts and loafers, the women in their linen dresses and summer frocks. These were the good citizens

Maurice Walsh, "America Learns to Hate Wal-Mart," *New Statesman,* Vol. 128, Issue 4446 (July 26, 1999), 15–16. © New Statesman. All rights reserved. Reprinted by permission.

of Ashland, Virginia (pop 6,000) and they were passionate in a way they had not been in decades. They did not want another Wal-Mart store near their town.

Ashland is a pretty place, a mid-19th-century summer resort transformed by the railway into a comfortable town. The train tracks run right through it, between the little blocks of clapboard houses. But if you drive from Ashland's town centre towards Interstate 95, where the town sprawls toward Richmond, you encounter a more familiar version of America, a series of shopping malls and fast-food restaurants. There's the drive-in Burger King and, naturally, a McDonald's, and there are relative newcomers such as Office Depot, a store known in the business as a "category killer" because it sells every conceivable piece of office equipment or stationery and thus kills all other stores in that sector of retailing. But the most impressive site, in sheer scale, is the Wal-Mart supercentre and its enormous car park. Here is the biggest retailing chain in the world, recognisably a supermarket but one so vast, with so many aisles of goods—from garden chairs to nappies, from shoes to guns—that when you are inside it you feel you may never need to visit another shop ever again.

The problem for Ashland is that Wal-Mart—whose takeover bid for Asda, the British supermarket chain, will be resolved by a shareholders' vote on 26 July—is not satisfied with just one store. It wants to build another one on wooded land near the edge of the town, to generate another $53 million in sales and draw people in their cars from far and wide.

But Wal-Mart has its enemies, and they are spearheaded by the youngish middle classes whose migrations from the big cities have led them to rediscover the virtues of small-town America: neighbours, mom-and-pop stores, a sense of history and property values not threatened by the turmoil of constant urban development. Wal-Mart and the other big shopping stores regard these proponents of so-called "smart growth" as snooty troublemakers, imbued with a sense of superiority over the millions who, fixated by low prices, drive for miles down the highways to push overflowing shopping trolleys through the checkouts. But it says something for the potential of their stealthy activism that Al Gore, launching his presidential campaign last January [1999], identified urban sprawl as an issue that might bring in votes. "In two many places across America," the vice-president said, "the beauty of local vistas has been degraded by decades of ill-planned and ill co-ordinated development."

Wal-Mart's phenomenal success—it has nearly 3,000 stores across the U.S.— has made it the latest epitome of corporate rapacity. Star billing at the town meeting in Ashland went to Al Norman, a fortysomething part-time political activist who conducts virtual guerrilla warfare against Wal-Mart from his Sprawlbusters website on the Internet. He travels from state to state to visit groups preparing to resist a Wal-Mart store, explaining to them how to organise and campaign, connecting each local fight to the others and painting Wal-Mart as a giant monopoly sapping the life out of American towns. And it's easy to sense that, through Wal-Mart, he's re-fighting some of the battles of the sixties, trying to establish some control over unrestrained commerce, pitting humanism against consumerism in an age of triumphant capitalism.

Yet Sam Walton, when he opened the first Wal-Mart discount store in Arkansas in 1962, must have seen it all quite differently. Back then, Walton wanted to replicate the feel of a small country store in his big supermarkets. He combined his image as a plain-speaking folk hero with an ability to adapt and learn from others' ideas and a hugely efficient information system to keep track of what to buy and sell. As Wal-Mart expanded outside Arkansas, so did the myth of Walton. Notoriously frugal, he made his executives share their rooms on business trips. Walton himself was re-nowned for driving an old pick-up truck and thinking of nothing but how to improve Wal-Mart.

He would leave his wife and family for weeks on end to visit stores, walking the aisles to get a feel for how they were performing, talking graciously with his employees (described as "associates," to keep them from joining trade unions) and listening to their experience of where the best place to display garden chairs or children's clothes was. "Mr. Sam's way" became a retailing religion, in which shoppers were so many consuming souls to be saved from the damnation of high prices. Trainee managers at Wal-Mart ended their pledge to customer service with a distortion of the oath of allegiance: "So help me, Sam."

In Hearne, Texas, a small town between Dallas and Houston that once pros-pered as a railroad crossing surrounded by cotton plantations, the Wal-Mart founder is still known as "Mr. Sam" to the employees who worked at the store the company opened there nearly 20 years ago. But if you visit it now, on the edge of town you will find an ugly brown-brick box, empty for nearly a decade, with weeds covering the car park. Hearne, the locals say, is the town that Wal-Mart killed twice.

The Wal-Mart store forced local traders out of business and then disappeared itself, moving 20 miles up the road. "Loyalty, friendship, history and civic pride," wrote a local preacher, "could not keep us from spending our money at Wal-Mart. . . . The savings that we made shopping at Wal-Mart cut off the life-blood of the businesses that had served Hearne for years." A real estate broker likens Mr. Sam's creation to a vast glacier, crushing all in its path. But, likely as not, he and other citi-zens of Hearne will be driving down the highway in a day or two to fill their cars at the new supercentre.

Walton was the epitome of the American dream, according to the citation that accompanied the Presidential Medal of Freedom presented to him by George Bush just before he died.

But Wal-Mart is worried about its image, worried that the story of Hearne and other towns like it will make it seem to represent American capitalism and con-sumerism at its worst. The company seems to fear that the low prices adored by its customers may not be enough to keep them happy. And so there are the large dona-tions to local charities, the patriotic "Buy American" campaign in every store and the constant claims that Wal-Mart is a responsible corporate citizen.

And indeed there are signs, beyond the Al Normans and the good folk of Ash-land and Hearne, that America is turning against Wal-Mart. In April a judge in Texas imposed a fine of $18 million on Wal-Mart for withholding evidence in a court case in which a woman who had been kidnapped in a superstore car park and then raped sued the company for not providing adequate security.

In May another Texas court awarded $624 million to a Mexican company that sued Wal-Mart for breaking an agreement to set up a joint business through a sub-sidiary. Wal-Mart settled the case out of court before the jury could award punitive damages. But the jurors said they were so shocked by Wal-Mart's arrogance that they would have doubled the award if they had been given the chance.

It is Wal-Mart's aim to become the largest corporation in the United States. Already, the vast retailing machine built by Walton and inherited by his managers has assumed the emblematic status in the new, service-based economy that General Motors occupied in the old economy.

To both its competitors and its admirers, Wal-Mart has acquired an air of invincibility. But the dilemmas raised by its success—masterly efficiency in the service of consumer needs vs. the hidden social costs of satisfying them—should make some demands on the thinking-time of the Third Way apostles in Washington and London.

5. A Columnist Decries "Outsourcing" in the New Global Economy, 2004

The people who insist that outsourcing is a trivial problem are wrong—but so are those who tell you that there is an easy solution.

The basic dilemma has several parts. First, the productivity of workers in poor countries is running far ahead of the wages they receive. That means Mexican autoworkers, unlike their American counterparts, can't afford to buy the cars they build.

This reality is unprecedented. There has always been a lot of trade between rich countries and poor ones. But the ability of the world's lowest-paid workers to work with advanced production technology, the dropping of barriers to trade, and the integration of a global information economy are all relatively new.

The analogy to trade within large countries is entirely false. Imagine that Massachusetts was paying an average wage of $15 an hour and Connecticut was paying $1. An awful lot of jobs would eventually go to Connecticut. The United States has always had regional disparities in pay levels—that's why New England's textile industry went south. But these were never anything like today's global disparities. And the United States, at least since the 1930s, has had nationwide minimum wage laws, followed by national laws on labor rights, workplace health and safety, and pollution standards. Not so the global economy. So the low-road countries are magnets for outsourcing.

It's surprising that a lot of economists dispute this. One of the most fundamental laws of economics is the law of one price. If Exxon is selling gas for $1.60 a gallon and Gulf tries to sell it for $2.60, everyone will go to Exxon. The technical term for this is "factor-price equalization." Wages are a price, and in an economy with free commerce, they will tend to converge. So unless wages rise in the Third World, global wages will tend to converge downward and American wages will move in the direction of Mexican and Indian wages.

As it happens, the outsourcing problem is occurring while three other factors are compounding the problem—productivity, the trade deficit, and deregulation. Rising productivity means workers are being replaced by machines. In the long run, this is a good thing; it makes the society wealthier. But who gets the increased wealth, and what does everyone do for a living?

A century ago, when people came off the farms and into factories and then into service work, the problem took care of itself. But where will today's displaced workers go if so many jobs are being drained overseas? In principle, as long as foreign countries buy from us as much as we sell them, their purchases will create a lot of American jobs. But a third factor, America's huge structural trade imbalance, keeps this from occurring.

Finally, these events are playing out in an era of deregulation. That means that even domestic jobs that could well pay higher wages are being battered down by businesses' new power to play off workers against each other.

A generation ago, industries such as telephones, gas and electric utilities, broadcasting, airlines, and hospitals were highly regulated. Prices were pegged and returns assured, so there was no competition between companies based on who could batter down wages. These industries had good, secure, middle-class jobs, blue collar as well as white.

This was also the era when basic industry, such as autos and steel, were largely sheltered from foreign competitors. Thanks to strong unions, they were spared wage competition, too. Deregulation of financial markets has also fostered a climate in which insiders can award themselves astronomical salaries and stock benefits.

In the 1960s, the ratio of chief executive pay to average worker pay was about 70 to 1. Today it's around 700 to 1.

There is no reason why a company has to pay $50 million to get a talented chief executive. People would line up to take the job for a paltry million. The reason for this shift is simply a shift in political power. Insiders grab these astronomical salaries because they can. Workers fail to defend their wages because they can't.

Another myth is that "it's all about skills." Some of the most highly skilled people in the economy, from computer programmers to brain surgeons, are suffering income declines.

The good news is that we do have the means to restore a high-wage economy. The remedy has several dimensions. All have more to do with the political power to make the right choices than with laws of economics. . . .

6. Americans for Democratic Action Reports Growing Poverty and Inequality, 2004

The widening income gap between the wealthiest Americans and the rest of Americans continues to be one of the most challenging economic trends facing this nation. Extreme inequality of income and wealth gives economic and political power to big corporations and the richest families and weakens the sense of community and common purpose essential to a democracy.

This assessment was expressed eloquently by Nobel Laureate economist Kenneth Arrow in the early '80's: "The vast inequalities of income weakens a society of mutual concern. The sense that we are all members of the social order is vital to the meaning of civilization."

Income inequality is far greater in the United States than in other major countries. Australia, Canada and 10 European countries have much more equal distribution of income.

The latest Census Bureau statistics show that the rich are still getting much richer, middle income Americans are just barely raising their incomes, and the poor are still falling further behind on the income ladder. The table below shows average

Excerpts from Americans for Democratic Action, Executive Summary, in *Income and Inequality: Millions Left Behind,* 3rd. ed. (February 2004). Online at http://www.adaction.org/income2004.htm. Reprinted with permission of Americans for Democratic Action.

family income from 1950 through 2002, expressed in constant 2002 dollars to eliminate the impact of inflation.

It shows the disproportionately greater gains for the top 20% of families and top 5%, ranked by income, compared to lower-income Americans.

The gap between rich and poor is now bigger than it has been since the 1930s. An incredible 98% of the 1979–1992 gain in total household income went to the wealthiest twenty percent of households. The remaining 2% gain in total household income was shared by the remaining 80% of households.

Two examples of these wide disparities are especially dramatic—the increase in the number of millionaires and income for corporation chief executive officers. In 1979 there were 13,500 households declaring income over $1 million. By the mid 90's the number of millionaires had jumped to close to 100,000. The steep trend continued during the late 90's when the number of millionaires more than doubled, rising to 205,000. And big business salaries for top corporation CEOs have skyrocketed out of sight. In 1980, CEO compensation was 42 times the average American worker's pay. In 2001, CEO compensation was 411 times the average worker's pay, jumping spectacularly in the past twenty years. Also, the average CEO compensation of FORTUNE 500 companies was $37.5 million, while the average worker's salary of all companies was $38,000. or a ratio of 1000 to 1. Note the difference in other industrial countries: in Japan a typical executive makes eleven times what a typical worker brings home and in Britain, twenty-two times.

When we take wealth, in addition to income, into consideration, note that the top 20% of American households control 83 percent of the nation's wealth, while the bottom 80 percent of Americans control only about 17 percent of the nation's wealth.

Poverty is still a blot on America's conscience. A total of 34.6 million Americans, 12.1% of the population in 2002, live in poverty. One-third of America's poor are White, with a 10% poverty rate; at 20%, the rate for African Americans and Hispanics is twice that of Whites. Black and Hispanic median family income is 37% below the median income of White families. Nationally, one out of six children—11.7 million— lives in poverty. One out of every three Black and Hispanic children lives in poverty.

Many poor people are working people, and many of them work full-time, year-round but don't earn enough to lift themselves and their families out of poverty. Of

---

Table 1. Average Real Family Income 1950–2002 by Fifths (Twenty Percent) and Top 5% of Families

QUINTILE	1950	1970	1980	2002	PERCENT CHANGE 1950–1980	PERCENT CHANGE 1980–2002
Poorest 20%	$5,345	$12,096	$13,252	$14,071	+147.9%	+5.8%
Second 20%	$14,254	$26,747	$28,848	$32,521	102.4%	12.7%
Middle 20%	$20,668	$38,674	$43,580	$51,869	110.9%	19.0%
Fourth 20%	$27,795	$52,168	$60,462	$77,145	117.5%	27.6%
Top 20%	$50,719	$89,168	$101,800	$159,298	100.7%	56.5%
Top 5%	$82,196	$136,602	$144,717	$278,790	76.1%	92.6%

(Constant 2002 dollars)

8.5 million people in poverty who did work in 2002, there were 2.6 million on the job full-time, year-round. Another 6.0 million worked full time for part of the year, but remained in poverty. With the minimum wage of $5.15 an hour enacted in September 1997, the $10,700 annual earnings of a minimum wage worker employed full-time, year-round is still *$3,628* less than the three-person family poverty line, and *$7,604* below the four-person family poverty threshold.

Wages and salaries—the main source of income for most Americans—have been lagging and stagnating, while corporate business profits have been booming. This is a central cause of growing inequality. Bureau of Labor Statistics data show that average hourly wages for private non-farm production and non-supervisory workers (about 80% of all workers) were $14.95 in 2002. By comparison, in the last years of the 1970s, the average hourly wage in 2002 dollars was $14.50. These official government figures tell us that the buying power of workers' hourly wages in 2002 were virtually the same as twenty years earlier!

Inequality and poverty do not have simple causes. Huge campaign contributions from big-money corporations and wealthy individuals too often dominate politics, economics, and social policies. Conservative and reactionary government policies such as the unfair Reagan tax cuts of the 1980's, attacks on unions by anti-union employers, the extremely regressive Bush tax cuts of 2001 and 2002, continued delays in raising the minimum wage to an adequate level. Republican attacks against basic social welfare programs, including Social Security and Medicare, are among the many factors contributing to growing inequality and poverty in the United States. . . .

7. A Research Firm "Segments" the American Market, 2000

America's Clustered Lifestyles

According to Claritas's PRIZM cluster system, America consists of 62 classic lifestyle types, divided into 15 socioeconomic groupings. They are listed below with demographic descriptions.

CLUSTERS	DEMOGRAPHIC SNAPSHOTS	SOCIAL GROUPINGS
Blue Blood Estates	Elite super-rich families	Elite Suburbs
Winner's Circle	Executive suburban families	
Executive Suites	Upscale white-collar couples	
Pools & Patios	Established empty-nesters	
Kids & Cul-de-Sacs	Upscale suburban families	
Urban Gold Coast	Elite urban singles and couples	Urban Uptown
Money & Brains	Sophisticated town-house couples	
Young Literati	Upscale urban singles and couples	
American Dreams	Established urban immigrant families	
Bohemian Mix	Bohemian singles and couples	

(*continued*)

Sources: PRIZM, Claritas Inc. From Michael J. Weiss, *The Clustered World* (New York: Little, Brown, 2000), 12–13. Reprinted by permission of Elaine Markson Agency.

CLUSTERS	DEMOGRAPHIC SNAPSHOTS	SOCIAL GROUPINGS
Second City Elite	Upscale executive families	Second City Society
Upward Bound	Young upscale white-collar families	
Gray Power	Affluent retirees in Sunbelt cities	
Country Squires	Elite exurban families	Landed Gentry
God's Country	Executive exurban families	
Big Fish, Small Pond	Small-town executive families	
Greenbelt Families	Young middle-class town families	
Young Influentials	Upwardly mobile singles and couples	The Affluentials
New Empty Nests	Upscale suburban fringe couples	
Boomers & Babies	Young white-collar suburban families	
Suburban Sprawl	Young suburban town-house couples	
Blue-Chip Blues	Upscale blue-collar families	
Upstarts & Seniors	Middle-income empty-nesters	Inner Suburbs
New Beginnings	Young mobile city singles	
Mobility Blues	Young blue-collar / service families	
Gray Collars	Aging couples in inner suburbs	
Urban Achievers	Midlevel white-collar urban couples	Urban Midscale
Big City Blend	Middle-income immigrant families	
Old Yankee Rows	Empty-nest middle-class families	
Mid-City Mix	African American singles and families	
Latino America	Hispanic middle-class families	
Middleburg Managers	Midlevel white-collar couples	Second City Centers
Boomtown Singles	Middle-income young singles	
Starter Families	Young middle-class families	
Sunset City Blues	Empty-nesters in aging industrial cities	
Towns & Gowns	College town singles	
New Homesteaders	Young middle-class families	Exurban Blues
Middle America	Midscale families in midsize towns	
Red, White & Blues	Small-town blue-collar families	
Military Quarters	GIs & surrounding off-base families	
Big Sky Families	Midscale couples, kids, and farmland	Country Families
New Eco-topia	Rural white- or blue-collar and farm families	
River City, USA	Middle-class rural families	
Shotguns & Pickups	Rural blue-collar workers and families	
Single City Blues	Ethnically mixed urban singles	Urban Cores
Hispanic Mix	Urban Hispanic singles and families	
Inner Cities	Inner-city solo-parent families	
Smalltown Downtown	Older renters and young families	Second City Blues
Hometown Retired	Low-income, older singles & couples	
Family Scramble	Low-income Hispanic families	
Southside City	African American service workers	
Golden Ponds	Retirement town seniors	Working Towns
Rural Industria	Low-income blue-collar families	
Norma Rae-ville	Young families, biracial mill towns	
Mines & Mills	Older families, mines and mill towns	
Agri-Business	Rural farm town and ranch families	The Heartlanders
Grain Belt	Farm owners and tenants	
Blue Highways	Moderate blue-collar / farm families	Rustic Living
Rustic Elders	Low-income, older, rural couples	
Back Country Folks	Remote rural / town families	
Scrub Pine Flats	Older African American farm families	
Hard Scrabble	Old families in poor, isolated areas	

The new economy of the late postwar era was marked by an accelerated shift of work out of the old manufacturing sector and into the burgeoning service sector. The service sector itself, however, was extremely heterogeneous, encompassing as it did highly compensated doctors, lawyers, and accountants, as well as lowly paid clerks and sales-people. In the first essay, excerpted from her best-selling book *Nickel and Dimed* (2001), author and social commentator Barbara Ehrenreich gives a firsthand account of what it was like to work an entry-level job at Wal-Mart. In gathering research for her book, Ehrenreich posed as an unskilled worker and held a series of low-wage jobs to document the plight of the working poor. Wal-Mart's success typifies the contractions of the new economy. Also characterized by new patterns of consumption and lifestyle, the new economy included a high degree of what advertising executives called "market segmen-tation." While the notion of "consumption communities" was scarcely new, historian Daniel J. Boorstin coined the term more than thirty years ago; in the new economy of the late twentieth and early twenty-first centuries, retailers used increasingly sophisticated demographic algorithms to reach increasingly segmented markets. The second essay, excerpted from Michael J. Weiss's *The Clustered World* (2000), explores the fragmented world of ZIP-code demographics used by the market research firm Claritas. Here, too, the structures and cultural understandings of the modern era of the mid-twentieth cen-tury have given way to a new, seemingly more diverse postmodern era.

Working at Wal-Mart

BARBARA EHRENREICH

. . . Don't ask me why Minneapolis came to mind, maybe I just had a yearning for de-ciduous trees. It's a relatively liberal state, I knew that, and more merciful than many to its welfare poor. A half an hour or so of Web research revealed an agreeably tight labor market, with entry-level jobs advertised at $8 an hour or more and studio apart-ments for $400 or less. If some enterprising journalist wants to test the low-wage way of life in darkest Idaho or Louisiana, more power to her. Call me gutless, but what I was looking for this time around was a comfortable correspondence between income and rent, a few mild adventures, a soft landing.

I pick up my Rent-A-Wreck from a nice fellow—this must be the famous "Minnesota nice"—who volunteers the locations of NPR and classic rock on the radio. We agree that swing sucks and maybe would have discovered a few more points of convergence, only I'm on what a certain Key West rock jock likes to call "a mission from God." I've got my map of the Twin Cities area, purchased for $10 at the airport, and an apartment belonging to friends of a friend that I can use for a few days free of charge while they visit relatives back East. . . .

I'm off first thing in the morning to look for a job. No waitressing, nursing homes, or housecleaning this time; I'm psyched for a change—retail, maybe, or factory work. I drive to the two nearest Wal-Marts, fill out applications, then head for a third

Excerpt from "Selling in Minnesota" from *Nickel and Dimed: On (Not) Getting By in America* (New York: Henry Holt, 2001), 121–186. © 2001 by Barbara Ehrenreich. Reprinted by permission of Henry Holt and Company, LLC.

one a forty-five-minute drive away on the opposite edge of the city. I drop off my application and am about to start hitting the Targets and Kmarts when I get an idea: no one is going to hire me based on an application showing no job experience—I have written, as usual, that I am a divorced homemaker reentering the workforce. What I have to do is make a personal appearance and exhibit my sunny, self-confident self. So I go to the pay phone in the front of the store, call the store's number, and ask for personnel. I'm put through to Roberta, who is impressed by my initiative and tells me I can come on in to her office in the back of the store. Roberta, a bustling platinum-haired woman of sixty or so, tells me there's nothing wrong with my "app"; she herself raised six children before starting at Wal-Mart, where she rose to her present position in just a few years, due mainly to the fact that she's a "people person." She can offer me a job now, but first a little "survey," on which there are no right or wrong answers, she assures me, just whatever I think. . . . Roberta takes it off to another room, where, she says, a computer will "score" it. After about ten minutes, she's back with alarming news: I've gotten three answers wrong—well, not exactly *wrong* but in need of further discussion.

Now, my approach to preemployment personality tests has been zero tolerance vis-à-vis the obvious "crimes"—drug use and theft—but to leave a little wriggle room elsewhere, just so it doesn't look like I'm faking out the test. My approach was wrong. When presenting yourself as a potential employee, you can never be too much of a suck-up. Take the test proposition that "rules have to be followed to the letter at all times": I had agreed to this only "strongly" rather than "very strongly" or "totally" and now Roberta wants to know why. Well, rules have to be interpreted sometimes, I say, people have to use some discretion. Otherwise, why, you might as well have machines do all the work instead of actual human beings. She beams at this—"Discretion, very good!"—and jots something down. With my other wrong answers similarly accounted for, Roberta introduces me to "what Wal-Mart is all about." She personally read Sam Walton's book (his autobiography, *Made in America*) before starting to work here and found that the three pillars of Wal-Mart philosophy precisely fit her own, and these are service, excellence (or something like that), and she can't remember the third. Service, that's the key, helping people, solving their problems, helping them shop—and how do I feel about that? I testify to a powerful altruism in retail-related matters and even find myself getting a bit misty-eyed over this bond that I share with Roberta. All I have to do now is pass a drug test. . . .

For sheer grandeur, scale, and intimidation value, I doubt if any corporate orientation exceeds that of Wal-Mart. I have been told that the process will take eight hours, which will include two fifteen-minute breaks and one half-hour break for a meal, and will be paid for like a regular shift. When I arrive, dressed neatly in khakis and clean T-shirt, as befits a potential Wal-Mart "associate," I find there are ten new hires besides myself, mostly young and Caucasian, and a team of three, headed by Roberta, to do the "orientating." We sit around a long table in the same windowless room where I was interviewed, each with a thick folder of paperwork in front of us, and hear Roberta tell once again about raising six children, being a "people person," discovering that the three principles of Wal-Mart philosophy were the same as her own, and so on. We begin with a video, about fifteen minutes long, on the history and philosophy of Wal-Mart, or, as an anthropological observer might call it, the Cult of Sam. First young Sam Walton, in uniform, comes back from the war. He starts a store, a sort of five-and-dime; he marries and fathers four attractive children; he receives a Medal of Freedom from President Bush, after which he promptly dies, making way for the eulogies. But the company goes on, yes indeed. Here the arc of the story soars upward unstoppably, pausing only to mark some fresh milestone of corporate expansion. 1992: Wal-Mart becomes the largest retailer in the world. 1997: Sales top $100 billion. 1998: The number of Wal-Mart associates hits 825,000, making Wal-Mart the largest private employer in the nation. Each land-mark date is accompanied by a clip showing throngs of shoppers, swarms of asso-ciates, or scenes of handsome new stores and their adjoining parking lots. Over and over we hear in voiceover or see in graphic display the "three principles," which are maddeningly, even defiantly, nonparallel: "respect for the individual, exceeding customers' expectations, strive for excellence."

"Respect for the individual" is where we, the associates, come in, because vast as Wal-Mart is, and tiny as we may be as individuals, everything depends on us. Sam always said, and is shown saying, that "the best ideas come from the associates"— for example, the idea of having a "people greeter," an elderly employee (excuse me, associate) who welcomes each customer as he or she enters the store. Three times during the orientation, which began at three and stretches to nearly eleven, we are reminded that this brainstorm originated in a mere associate, and who knows what revolutions in retailing each one of us may propose? Because our ideas are wel-come, more than welcome, and we are to think of our managers not as bosses but as "servant leaders," serving us as well as the customers. Of course, all is not total harmony, in every instance, between associates and their servant-leaders. A video on "associate honesty" shows a cashier being caught on videotape as he pockets some bills from the cash register. Drums beat ominously as he is led away in handcuffs and sentenced to four years.

The theme of covert tensions, overcome by right thinking and positive attitude, continues in the twelve-minute video entitled *You've Picked a Great Place to Work.* Here various associates testify to the "essential feeling of family for which Wal-Mart is so well-known," leading up to the conclusion that we don't need a union. Once, long ago, unions had a place in American society, but they "no longer have much to offer workers," which is why people are leaving them "by the droves." Wal-Mart is booming; unions are declining: judge for yourself. But we are warned that "unions have been targeting Wal-Mart for years." Why? For the dues money of course. Think of what you would lose with a union: first, your dues money, which could be $20 a month "and sometimes much more." Second, you would lose "your voice" because the union would insist on doing your talking for you. Finally, you might lose even your wages and benefits because they would all be "at risk on the bargaining table." You have to wonder—and I imagine some of my teenage fellow orientees may be doing so—why such fiends as these union organizers, such outright extortionists, are allowed to roam free in the land.

There is more, much more than I could ever absorb, even if it were spread out over a semester-long course. On the reasonable assumption that none of us is plan-ning to go home and curl up with the "Wal-Mart Associate Handbook," our trainers start reading it out loud to us, pausing every few paragraphs to ask, "Any questions?" There never are. Barry, the seventeen-year-old to my left, mutters that his "butt hurts." Sonya, the tiny African American woman across from me, seems frozen in terror. I have given up on looking perky and am fighting to keep my eyes open. No nose or other facial jewelry, we learn; earrings must be small and discreet, not dangling, no blue jeans except on Friday, and then you have to pay $1 for the privilege of wearing them. No "grazing," that is, eating from food packages that somehow become open; no "time theft." . . . "What is time theft?" Answer: Doing anything other than working during company time, anything at all. . . .

[On Monday, a]fter the rigors of orientation, I am expecting a highly structured welcome, perhaps a ceremonial donning of my bright blue Wal-Mart vest and a forty-five-minute training on the operation of the vending machines in the break room. But when I arrive in the morning for the ten-to-six shift, no one seems to be expecting me. I'm in "softlines," which has a wonderful, sinuous sound to it, but I have no idea what it means. Someone in personnel tells me I'm in ladies' wear (a division of softlines, I learn) and sends me to the counter next to the fitting rooms, where I am passed around from one person to the next—finally ending up with Ellie, whose lack of a vest signals that she is management. She sets me to work "zoning" the Bobbie Brooks knit summer dresses, a task that could serve as an IQ test for the severely cognitively challenged. First the dresses must be grouped by color—olive, peach, or lavender, in this case—then by decorative pattern—the leafy design on the bodice, the single flower, or the grouped flowers—and within each pattern by size. When I am finished, though hardly exhausted by the effort, I meet Melissa, who is, with only a couple of weeks on the job, pretty much my equivalent. She asks me to help her consolidate the Kathie Lee knit dresses so the Kathie Lee silky ones can take their place at the "image," the high-traffic corner area. I learn, in a couple of hours of scattered exchanges, that Melissa was a waitress before this job, that her husband works in construction and her children are grown. There have been some disorganized patches in her life—an out-of-wedlock child, a problem with alcohol and drugs—but that's all over now that she has given her life to Christ.

Our job, it emerges in fragments throughout the day, is to keep ladies' wear "shoppable." Sure, we help customers (who are increasingly called "guests" here as well), if they want any help. At first I go around practicing the "aggressive hospitality" demanded by our training videos: as soon as anyone comes within ten feet of a sales associate, that associate is supposed to smile warmly and offer assistance. But I never see a more experienced associate do this—first, because the customers are often annoyed to have their shopping dazes interrupted and, second, because we have far more pressing things to do. In ladies' wear, the big task, which has no real equivalent in, say, housewares or lawn and garden, is to put away the "returns"— clothes that have been tried on and rejected or, more rarely, purchased and then returned to the store. There are also the many items that have been scattered by customers, dropped on the floor, removed from their hangers and strewn over the racks, or secreted in locations far from their natural homes. Each of these items, too, must be returned to its precise place, matched by color, pattern, price, and size. Any leftover time is to be devoted to zoning. When I relate this to Caroline on the phone, she commiserates, "Ugh, a no-brainer."

But no job is as easy as it looks to the uninitiated. I have to put clothes away— the question is, Where? Much of my first few days is devoted to trying to memorize the layout of ladies' wear, one thousand (two thousand?) square feet of space bordered by men's wear, children's wear, greeting cards, and underwear. Standing at the fitting rooms and facing toward the main store entrance, we are looking directly at the tentlike, utilitarian plus sizes, also known as "woman" sizes. These are flanked on the left by our dressiest and costliest line (going up to $29 and change), the all-polyester Kathie Lee collection, suitable for dates and subprofessional levels of office work. Moving clockwise, we encounter the determinedly sexless Russ and Bobbie Brooks lines, seemingly aimed at pudgy fourth-grade teachers with important barbecues to attend. Then, after the sturdy White Stag, come the breezy, revealing Faded Glory, No Boundaries, and Jordache collections, designed for the younger and thinner crowd. Tucked throughout are nests of the lesser brands, such as Athletic Works, Basic Equipment, and the whimsical Looney Tunes, Pooh, and Mickey lines, generally decorated with images of their eponymous characters. Within each brand-name area, there are of course dozens of items, even dozens of each *kind* of item. This summer, for example, pants may be capri, classic, carpenter, clam-digger, boot, or flood, depending on their length and cut, and I'm probably leaving a few categories out. So my characteristic stance is one of rotating slowly on one foot, eyes wide, garment in hand, asking myself, "Where have I seen the $9.96 Athletic Works knit overalls?" or similar query. Inevitably there are mystery items requiring extra time and inquiry: clothes that have wandered over from girls' or men's, clearanced items whose tags haven't been changed to reflect their new prices, the occasional one-of-a-kind.

Then, when I have the layout memorized, it suddenly changes. On my third morning I find, after a few futile searches, that the Russ shirt-and-short combinations have edged Kathie Lee out of her image. When I groaningly accuse Ellie of trying to trick me into thinking I'm getting Alzheimer's, she's genuinely apologetic, explaining that the average customer shops the store three times a week, so you need to have the element of surprise. Besides, the layout is about the only thing she *can* control, since the clothes and at least the starting prices are all determined by the home office in Arkansas. So as fast as I can memorize, she furiously rearranges.

My first response to the work is disappointment and a kind of sexist contempt. I could have been in plumbing, mastering the vocabulary of valves, dangling tools from my belt, joshing around with Steve and Walt, and instead the mission of the moment is to return a pink bikini top to its place on the Bermuda swimwear rack. Nothing is heavy or, as far as I can see, very urgent. No one will go hungry or die or be hurt if I screw up; in fact, how would anyone ever know if I screwed up, given the customers' constant depredations? I feel oppressed, too, by the mandatory gentility of Wal-Mart culture. This is ladies' and we are all "ladies" here, forbidden, by store-wide rule, to raise our voices or cuss. Give me a few weeks of this and I'll femme out entirely, my stride will be reduced to a mince, I'll start tucking my head down to one side.

My job is not, however, as genteel as it at first appears, thanks to the sheer volume of clothing in motion. At Wal-Mart, as opposed to say Lord & Taylor, customers shop with supermarket-style shopping carts, which they can fill to the brim before proceeding to the fitting room. There the rejected items, which are about 90 percent of try-ons, are folded and put on hangers by whoever is staffing the fitting room, then placed in fresh shopping carts for Melissa and me. So this is how we measure our workload—in carts. When I get in, Melissa, whose shift begins earlier than mine, will tell me how things have been going—"Can you believe, eight carts this morning!"—and how many carts are awaiting me. At first a cart takes me an average of forty-five minutes and there may still be three or four mystery items left at the bottom. I get this down to half an hour, and still the carts keep coming.

Most of the time, the work requires minimal human interaction, of either the collegial or the supervisory sort, largely because it's so self-defining. I arrive at the start of a shift or the end of a break, assess the damage wrought by the guests in my absence, count the full carts that await me, and plunge in. I could be a deaf-mute as far as most of this goes, and despite all the orientation directives to smile and exude personal warmth, autism might be a definite advantage. Sometimes, if things are slow, Melissa and I will invent a task we can do together—zoning swimsuits, for example, a nightmarish tangle of straps—and giggle, she in her Christian way, me from a more feminist perspective, about the useless little see-through wraps meant to accompany the more revealing among them. Or sometimes Ellie will give me something special to do, like putting all the Basic Equipment T-shirts on hangers, because things on hangers sell faster, and then arranging them neatly on racks. I like Ellie. Gray-faced and fiftyish, she must be the apotheosis of "servant leadership" or, in more secular terms, the vaunted "feminine" style of management. She says "please" and "thank you"; she doesn't order, she asks. Not so, though, with young Howard—*assistant manager* Howard, as he is uniformly called—who rules over all of softlines, including infants', children's, men's, accessories, and underwear. On my first day, I am called off the floor to an associates' meeting, where he spends ten minutes taking attendance, fixing each of us with his unnerving Tom Cruise–style smile, in which the brows come together as the corners of the mouth turn up, then reveals (where have I heard this before?) his "pet peeve": associates standing around talking to one another, which is, of course, a prime example of time theft. . . .

I arrive at work full of bounce, pausing at the fitting room to jolly up the lady on duty—usually the bossy, self-satisfied Rhoda—because the fitting room lady bears the same kind of relation to me as a cook to a server: she can screw me up if she wants, giving me carts contaminated with foreign, nonladies' items and items not properly folded or hangered. "Here I am," I announce grandiosely, spreading out my arms. "The day can begin!" For this I get a wrinkled nose from Rhoda and a one-sided grin from Lynne, the gaunt blonde who's working bras. I search out Ellie, whom I find shooting out new labels from the pricing gun, and ask if there's anything special I need to be doing. No, just whatever needs to be done. Next I find Melissa to get a report on the cartage so far. Today she seems embarrassed when she sees me: "I probably shouldn't have done this and you're going to think it's really silly . . ." but she's brought me a sandwich for lunch. This is because I'd told her I was living in a motel almost entirely on fast food, and she felt sorry for me. Now *I'm* embarrassed, and beyond that overwhelmed to discover a covert stream of generosity running counter to the dominant corporate miserliness. Melissa probably wouldn't think of herself as poor, but I know she calculates in very small units of currency, twice reminding me, for example, that you can get sixty-eight cents off the specials at the Radio Grill every Tuesday, so a sandwich is something to consider. I set off with my cart, muttering contentedly, "Bobbie Brooks turquoise elastic-waist shorts" and "Faded Glory V-neck red tank top."

Then, in my second week, two things change. My shift changes from 10:00–6:00 to 2:00–11:00, the so-called closing shift, although the store remains open 24/7. No one tells me this; I find it out by studying the schedules that are posted, under glass, on the wall outside the break room. Now I have nine hours instead of eight, and although one of them is an unpaid dinner hour, I have a net half an hour a day more on my feet. My two fifteen-minute breaks, which seemed almost superfluous on the 10:00–6:00 shift, now become a matter of urgent calculation. Do I take both before dinner, which is usually about 7:30, leaving an unbroken two-and-a-half-hour stretch when I'm weariest, between 8:30 and 11:00? Or do I try to go two and a half hours without a break in the afternoon, followed by a nearly three-hour marathon before I can get away for dinner? Then there's the question of how to make the best use of a fifteen-minute break when you have three or more urgent, simultaneous needs—to pee, to drink something, to get outside the neon and into the natural light, and most of all, to sit down. I save about a minute by engaging in a little time theft and stopping at the rest room before I punch out for the break (and, yes, we have to punch out even for breaks, so there's no padding them with a few stolen minutes). From the time clock it's a seventy-five-second walk to the store exit; if I stop at the Radio Grill, I could end up wasting a full four minutes waiting in line, not to mention the fifty-nine cents for a small-sized iced tea. So if I treat myself to an outing in the tiny fenced-off area beside the store, the only place where employees are allowed to smoke, I get about nine minutes off my feet.

The other thing that happens is that the post–Memorial Day weekend lull definitely comes to an end. Now there are always a dozen or more shoppers rooting around in ladies', reinforced in the evening by a wave of multigenerational gangs— Grandma, Mom, a baby in the shopping cart, and a gaggle of sullen children in tow. New tasks arise, such as bunching up the carts left behind by customers and steering them to their place in the front of the store every half hour or so. Now I am picking up not only dropped clothes but all the odd items customers carry off from foreign departments and decide to leave with us in ladies'—pillows, upholstery hooks, Pokémon cards, earrings, sunglasses, stuffed animals, even a package of cinnamon buns. And always there are the returns, augmented now by the huge volume of items that have been tossed on the floor or carried fecklessly to inappropriate sites. Sometimes I am lucky to achieve a steady state between replacing the returns and picking up items strewn on the racks and the floor. If I pick up misplaced items as quickly as I replace the returns, my cart never empties and things back up dangerously at the fitting rooms, where Rhoda or her nighttime replacement is likely to hiss: "You've got three carts waiting, Barb. What's the *problem?*" Think Sisyphus here or the sorcerer's apprentice.

Still, for the first half of my shift, I am the very picture of good-natured helpfulness, fascinated by the multiethnic array of our shoppers—Middle Eastern, Asian, African American, Russian, former Yugoslavian, old-fashioned Minnesota white— and calmly accepting of the second law of thermodynamics, the one that says entropy always wins. Amazingly, I get praised by Isabelle, the thin little seventyish lady who seems to be Ellie's adjutant: I am doing "wonderfully," she tells me, and—even better—am "great to work with." I prance from rack to rack, I preen. But then, somewhere around 6:00 or 7:00, when the desire to sit down becomes a serious craving, a Dr. Jekyll/Mr. Hyde transformation sets in. I cannot ignore the fact that it's the customers' sloppiness and idle whims that make me bend and crouch and run. They are the shoppers, I am the antishopper, whose goal is to make it look as if they'd never been in the store. At this point, "aggressive hospitality" gives way to aggressive hostility. Their carts bang into mine, their children run amok. Once I stand and watch helplessly while some rug rat pulls everything he can reach off the racks, and the thought that abortion is wasted on the unborn must show on my face, because his mother finally tells him to stop.

I even start hating the customers for extraneous reasons, such as, in the case of the native Caucasians, their size. I don't mean just bellies and butts, but huge bulges in completely exotic locations, like the backs of the neck and the knees. This summer, Wendy's, where I often buy lunch, has introduced the verb *biggiesize,* as in "Would you like to biggiesize that combo?" meaning double the fries and pop, and something like biggiesizing seems to have happened to the female guest population. All right, everyone knows that midwesterners, and especially those in the lower middle class, are tragically burdened by the residues of decades of potato chips and French toast sticks, and I probably shouldn't even bring this up. In my early-shift, Dr. Jekyll form, I feel sorry for the obese, who must choose from among our hideous woman-size offerings, our drawstring shorts, and huge horizontally striped tees, which are obviously designed to mock them. But compassion fades as the shift wears on. Those of us who work in ladies' are for obvious reasons a pretty lean lot—probably, by Minnesota standards, candidates for emergency IV nutritional supplementation—and we live with the fear of being crushed by some widebody as she hurtles through the narrow passage from Faded Glory to woman size, lost in fantasies involving svelte Kathie Lee sheaths.

It's the clothes I relate to, though, not the customers. And now a funny thing happens to me here on my new shift: I start thinking they're mine, not mine to take home and wear, because I have no such designs on them, just mine to organize and rule over. Same with ladies' wear as a whole. After 6:00, when Melissa and Ellie go home, and especially after 9:00, when Isabelle leaves, I start to *own* the place. Out of the way, Sam, this is Bar-Mart now. I patrol the perimeter with cart, darting in to pick up misplaced and fallen items, making everything look spiffy from the outside. I don't fondle the clothes, the way customers do; I slap them into place, commanding them to hang straight, at attention, or lie subdued on the shelves in perfect order. In this frame of mind, the last thing I want to see is a customer riffling around, disturbing the place. In fact, I hate the idea of things being sold—uprooted from their natural homes, whisked off to some closet that's in God-knows-what state of disorder. I want ladies' wear sealed off in a plastic bubble and trucked away to some place of safety, some museum of retail history. . . .

The breakthrough comes on a Saturday, one of our heavier shopping days. There are two carts waiting for me when I arrive at two, and tossed items inches deep on major patches of the floor. The place hasn't been shopped, it's been looted. In this situation, all I can do is everything at once—stoop, reach, bend, lift, run from rack to rack with my cart. And then it happens—a magical flow state in which the clothes start putting *themselves* away. Oh, I play a part in this, but not in any conscious way. Instead of thinking, "White Stag navy twill skort," and doggedly searching out similar skorts, all I have to do is form an image of the item in my mind, transpose this image onto the visual field, and move to wherever the image finds its match in the outer world. I don't know how this works. Maybe my mind just gets so busy processing the incoming visual data that it has to bypass the left brain's verbal centers, with their cumbersome instructions: "Proceed to White Stag area in the northwest corner of ladies', try bottom racks near khaki shorts . . ." Or maybe the trick lies in understanding that each item *wants* to be reunited with its sibs and its clan members and that, within each clan, the item *wants* to occupy its proper place in the color/size hierarchy. Once I let the clothes take charge, once I understand that I am only the means of their reunification, they just fly out of the cart to their natural homes.

On the same day, perhaps because the new speediness frees me to think more clearly, I make my peace with the customers and discover the purpose of life, or at least of my life at Wal-Mart. Management may think that the purpose is to sell things, but this is an overly reductionist, narrowly capitalist view. As a matter of fact, I never see anything sold, since sales take place out of my sight, at the cash registers at the front of the store. All I see is customers unfolding carefully folded T-shirts, taking dresses and pants off their hangers, holding them up for a moment's idle inspection, then dropping them somewhere for us associates to pick up. For me, the way out of resentment begins with a clue provided by a poster near the break room, in the back of the store where only associates go: "Your mother doesn't work here," it says. "Please pick up after yourself." I've passed it many times, thinking, "Ha, that's all I do—pick up after people." Then it hits me: most of the people I pick up after are mothers themselves, meaning that what I do at work is what *they* do at home—pick up the toys and the clothes and the spills. So the great thing about shopping, for most of these women, is that here *they* get to behave like brats, ignoring the bawling babies in their carts, tossing things around for someone else to pick up. And it wouldn't be any fun—would it?—unless the clothes were all reasonably orderly to begin with, which is where I come in, constantly re-creating orderliness for the customers to maliciously destroy. It's appalling, but it's in their nature: only pristine and virginal displays truly excite them. . . .

With competence comes a new impatience: *Why does anybody put up with the wages we're paid?* True, most of my fellow workers are better cushioned than I am; they live with spouses or grown children or they have other jobs in addition to this one. I sit with Lynne in the break room one night and find out this is only a part-time job for her—six hours a day—with the other eight hours spent at a factory for $9 an hour. Doesn't she get awfully tired? Nah, it's what she's always done. The cook at the Radio Grill has two other jobs. You might expect a bit of grumbling, some signs here and there of unrest—graffiti on the hortatory posters in the break room, muffled guffaws during our associate meetings—but I can detect none of that. Maybe this is what you get when you weed out all the rebels with drug tests and personality "surveys"— a uniformly servile and denatured workforce, content to dream of the distant day when they'll be vested in the company's profit-sharing plan. They even join in the "Wal-Mart cheer" when required to do so at meetings, I'm told by the evening fitting room lady, though I am fortunate enough never to witness this final abasement.

But if it's hard to think "out of the box," it may be almost impossible to think out of the Big Box. Wal-Mart, when you're in it, is total—a closed system, a world unto itself. I get a chill when I'm watching TV in the break room one afternoon and see . . . *a commercial for Wal-Mart.* When a Wal-Mart shows up within a television within a Wal-Mart, you have to question the existence of an outer world. Sure, you can drive for five minutes and get somewhere else—to Kmart, that is, or Home Depot, or Target, or Burger King, or Wendy's, or KFC. Wherever you look, there is no alternative to the megascale corporate order, from which every form of local creativity and initiative has been abolished by distant home offices. Even the woods and the meadows have been stripped of disorderly life forms and forced into a uniform made of concrete. What you see—highways, parking lots, stores—is all there is, or all that's left to us here in the reign of globalized, totalized, paved-over, corporatized everything. I like to read the labels to find out where the clothing we sell is made— Indonesia, Mexico, Turkey, the Philippines, South Korea, Sri Lanka, Brazil—but the labels serve only to remind me that none of these places is "exotic" anymore, that they've all been eaten by the great blind profit-making global machine.

The only thing to do is ask: Why do you—why do *we*—work here? Why do you stay? So when Isabelle praises my work a second time (!), I take the opportunity to say I really appreciate her encouragement, but I can't afford to live on $7 an hour, and how does she do it? The answer is that she lives with her grown daughter, who also works, plus the fact that she's worked here two years, during which her pay has shot up to $7.75 an hour. She counsels patience: it could happen to me. Melissa, who has the advantage of a working husband, says, "Well, it's a job." Yes, she made twice as much when she was a waitress but that place closed down and at her age she's never going to be hired at a high-tip place. I recognize the inertia, the unwillingness to start up with the apps and the interviews and the drug tests again. She thinks she should give it a year. *A year?* I tell her I'm wondering whether I should give it another week.

A few days later something happens to make kindly, sweet-natured Melissa mad. She gets banished to bras, which is terra incognita for us—huge banks of shelves bearing barely distinguishable bi-coned objects—for a three-hour stretch. I know how she feels, because I was once sent over to work for a couple of hours in men's wear, where I wandered uselessly through the strange thickets of racks, numbed by the sameness of colors and styles. It's the difference between working and pretending to work. You push your cart a few feet, pause significantly with item in hand, frown at the ambient racks, then push on and repeat the process. "I just don't like wasting their money," Melissa says when she's allowed back. "I mean they're *paying* me and I just wasn't accomplishing anything over there." To me, this anger seems badly mis-aimed. What does she think, that the Walton family is living in some hidden room in the back of the store, in the utmost frugality, and likely to be ruined by $21 worth of wasted labor? I'm starting in on that theme when she suddenly dives behind the rack that separates the place where we're standing, in the Jordache/No Boundaries section, from the Faded Glory region. Worried that I may have offended her somehow, I follow right behind. "*Howard,*" she whispers. "Didn't you see him come by? We're not allowed to talk to each other, you know."

"The point is our time is so cheap they don't care if we waste it," I continue, aware even as I speak that this isn't true, otherwise why would they be constantly monitoring us for "time theft"? But I sputter on: "That's what's so insulting." Of course, in this outburst of militance I am completely not noticing the context—two women of mature years, two very hard-working women, as it happens, dodging behind a clothing rack to avoid a twenty-six-year-old management twerp. That's not even worth commenting on.

Alyssa is another target for my crusade. When she returns to check yet again on that $7 polo, she finds a stain on it. What could she get off for that? I think 10 percent, and if you add in the 10 percent employee discount, we'd be down to $5.60. I'm trying to negotiate a 20 percent price reduction with the fitting room lady when—rotten luck!—Howard shows up and announces that there are no reductions and no employee discounts on clearanced items. Those are the rules. Alyssa looks crushed, and I tell her, when Howard's out of sight, that there's something wrong when you're not paid enough to buy a Wal-Mart shirt, a *clearanced* Wal-Mart shirt with a stain on it. "I hear you," she says, and admits Wal-Mart isn't working for her either, if the goal is to make a living.

The Fragmenting of America

MICHAEL J. WEISS

At first glance, Berwyn, Illinois, resembles many of the close-in suburbs of Chicago, a settled middle-class community of beige brick bungalows known as a gateway for immigrants. Since Berwyn's founding a century ago, waves of Czechs, Italians, Poles, and Irish have come to work in the area's foundries and patronize the ethnic bakeries and restaurants along Cermak Street. Proud of their toehold on the American Dream, homemakers in babushkas would sweep their back alleys clean enough to eat dinners of stuffed cabbage, sausage, and spaghetti off the asphalt.

But times changed, the factories closed, and Berwyn's old-world residents aged. More recently, Central and South American immigrants have discovered Berwyn, carving up the neat bungalows into overcrowded apartments and sending their children to schools where 80 percent of the students speak Spanish. Today, Berwyn is a simmering stew of foreign-born residents who work side by side at blue-collar jobs but go their separate ways after hours. Italians congregate at the Italian-American Club for dinners and boccie tournaments. Hispanics meet at new Mexican restaurants and super *mercados,* and throw noisy parties on Cinco de Mayo, Mexico's independence day. Regular proposals to unify the ethnic groups and merge a Hispanic festival with the Czechs' Houby Days parade (celebrating an old-world mushroom) inevitably fail. Relative newcomer Rana Khan, a Pakistani doctor who came to Berwyn in 1994 with her husband and three children, found an insular community. "I went to a PTA meeting, and for two hours not one person said a word to me," she recalled. "With Americans, it's always 'hi and bye.'"

Few places present a greater refutation of the American "melting pot" image than contemporary Berwyn. But cultural dissonance has developed, to some degree, in communities all around the country. On the eve of the twenty-first century, America has become a splintered society, with multi-ethnic towns like Berwyn reflecting a nation more diverse than ever. In the 1990 census, Americans identified themselves as belonging to 300 races, 600 Native American tribes, 70 Hispanic groups, and 75 ethnic combinations. Since 1970, the number of immigrants living in the U.S.

has nearly tripled, increasing to 26.3 million and creating school districts in New York, Los Angeles, and Chicago where students speak more than 100 languages and take bilingual classes in everything from Armenian to Tagalog. The explosion of niche cable TV programming, on-line chat rooms, and targeted businesses like Urban Outfitters and Zany Brainy all point to a population with a classic case of multiple personality disorder. The mind plugged into the next set of Walkman headphones may be attuned to Christian rap, New Age drumming, or Deepak Chopra–style self-improvement.

For a nation that's always valued community, this breakup of the mass market into balkanized population segments is as momentous as the collapse of Communism. Forget the melting pot. America today would be better characterized as a salad bar. From the high-rises of Manhattan's Upper East Side to the trailer parks of South Texas, from the techno-elite professionals with their frequent-flier cards to the blue-collar laborers who frequent corner bars, America has fractured into distinctive lifestyles, each with its own borders. The horrors of urban living have sparked a migration of city dwellers to the countryside, creating a nation polarized between cosmopolitan cities and homogeneous exurban communities—not to mention pockets of latte-and-Lexus culture appearing amid cows and country music. At the same time, the rise of gated communities in America bespeaks a population trying to get away from children, gangs, the poor, immigrants, anyone unlike themselves.

Today, the country's new motto should be "*E pluribus pluriba*": "Out of many, many."

Evidence of the nation's accelerated fragmentation is more than anecdotal. According to the geodemographers at Claritas, American society today is composed of sixty-two distinct lifestyle types—a 55 percent increase over the forty segments that defined the U.S. populace during the 1970s and '80s. These clusters are based on composites of age, ethnicity, wealth, urbanization, housing style, and family structure. But their boundaries have undergone dramatic shifts in recent years as economic, political, and social trends stratify Americans in new ways. Immigration, women in the workforce, delayed marriage, aging baby boomers, economic swings: All these trends have combined to increase the number of distinct lifestyles. And advances in database technology that link the clusters to marketing surveys and opinion polls are permitting more accurate portraits of how these disparate population groups behave—whether they prefer tofu or tamales, Mercedes or Mazda, legalizing pot or supporting animal rights.

In today's clustered world, America has become a nation of Executive Suites (upscale suburban couples), Big Fish, Small Pond (midscale exurban families), and Rustic Elders (downscale rural retirees). If you live in a new cluster called Young Literati, present in North Brooklyn, New York, and Hermosa Beach, California, your neighbors are likely coffee bar-addicted Generation Xers into hardback books and music videos. If you've fled the city for the country lifestyle of Graft, Vermont, or Sutter Creek, California, you more than likely inhabit New Eco-topia, where your baby-boom neighbors enjoy country music, camping, and protesting to their congresspeople over the encroachment of big business. In Mid-City Mix, a cluster of working-class African American neighborhoods, residents believe O. J. Simpson was properly acquitted of murdering his former wife and her friend. In Greenbelt Families, an upscale white enclave typically located near Mid-City Mix communities, residents almost universally believe he was guilty. When you say "oil" in Rural Industria, a blue-collar heartland cluster, residents think "Quaker State." In the family suburbs of Winner's Circle, the second most affluent lifestyle, they think "extra virgin olive."

These lifestyles represent America's modern tribes, sixty-two distinct population groups each with its own set of values, culture, and means of coping with today's problems. A generation ago, Americans thought of themselves as city dwellers, suburbanites, or country folk. But we are no longer that simple, and our neighborhoods reflect our growing complexity. Clusters, which were created to identify demographically similar zip codes around the U.S., are now used to demarcate a variety of small geographic areas, including census tracts (500–1,000 households) and zip plus 4 postal codes (about ten households). Once used interchangeably with *neighborhood type,* however, the term *cluster* now refers to population segments where, thanks to technological advancements, no physical contact is required for cluster membership. The residents of Pools & Patios, a cluster of upper-middle-class suburban couples, congregate in La Crescenta, California, and Rockville, Maryland, but they also can be found on one block in Spring Hill, Tennessee, and in a few households in Portland, Maine. These residents can meet their neighbors across a fence to borrow a cup of sugar or argue issues, or they can schmooze on-line in the nonphysical world, debating the merits of a vacation in Austria or Hungary. In the clustered world, geographic communities united by PTAs, political clubs, and Sunday schools have given way to consumption communities defined by demographics, intellect, taste, and outlook. Today's town square is the on-line chat room.

The cluster system serves as a barometer in this changing world, monitoring how the country is evolving in distinct geographical areas. No longer can sociologists lump "American" behavior into a single trend line. Despite what network newscasters might have you believe, Americans are not becoming smarter or fatter or more indebted—but particular clusters most assuredly are. When Georgia's Division of Public Health cluster-coded the state's entire population, it found higher rates of breast cancer among women who lived in the factory towns classified Mines & Mills; afterward, it targeted mammography programs to those cluster communities. Nationwide, the poorly educated, small-town residents of Back Country Folks are typically more overweight than the college graduates of Urban Gold Coast, who heed the fat and cholesterol information printed on packaged foods. Surveys find that one in three Americans smoke, but many city-based Money & Brains sophisticates would be hard-pressed to name a smoker in their circle of friends and family (not counting, of course, those men and women caught up in the recent yuppie-stoked cigar-sucking craze). Smokers thrive in other lifestyle types, like Grain Belt and Scrub Pine Flats, a long geographic and demographic distance from upscale, college-educated, health-conscious surroundings. As the "American Way" becomes more elusive, the insights offered by the cluster system help us to appreciate who we are and where we're headed.

Sometimes, the clusters simply underscore realities already apparent, such as the widening gap between the richest and poorest Americans. The nation's most affluent neighborhood type, Blue Blood Estates (where the heirs to "old money" fortunes reside), has been joined by other wealthy havens, such as Winner's Circle (new-money suburbs dotted with split-levels) and Country squires (ritzy small towns like Middleburg, Virginia, characterized by horse farms and sport-utility vehicles). At the other end of the spectrum, America's poorest citizens are no longer confined to the urban ghettos of Inner Cities or the isolated settlements of Hard Scrabble, where hunting and fishing help put food on the table. For the first time, the poorest neighborhoods in America are found outside the nation's largest metros, in Southside City, a cluster of midsized city districts where blue-collar African Americans have a median income of $15,800, barely above the poverty line of $15,570 for a family of four. Between the 1980 and 1990 census, the median income of the wealthiest cluster jumped 55 percent, to $113,000 annually, while that of the poorest cluster increased only 39 percent, to $15,000. Sociologists say global competition and the cyber-revolution have widened the gap that divides the haves from the have-nots. But long-term contracts for workers in blue-collar industries are also disappearing. No longer are Americans rising and falling together, as if in one large national boat," former labor secretary Robert Reich observed. "We are, increasingly, in different, smaller boats." And not all of us are assured of life rafts.

At the same time, the American family is evolving into many different kinds of households with wildly different needs. Marketers once pitched products nationally on network TV to just a few dominant prototypes, the favorite being the white middle-class housewife wearing a sweater and fake pearls who worried herself sick over ring around the collar. Today, there's no overwhelming type of household in the United States. The most common model, married couples without children, represents 30 percent of the nation's households. Married couples with children make up about 25 percent, and about the same percentage of Americans live alone, up from less than 8 percent in 1940. One result of the continuing singles boom is the emergence of a cluster called Upstarts & Seniors, which contains both young and older singles living in modest homes and apartments often located in inner-ring suburbs. Despite their differences in age, they share a fondness for movies, health clubs, and coffee bars. In Upstarts & Seniors communities like Lakeside, Virginia, outside of Richmond, a visitor can find a shopping center with a tanning salon next to a shop specializing in denture care.

If there is any successor to the traditional homemaker who dominated popular culture a generation ago, it's today's Soccer Mom, that working mother of school-aged children whom commentators celebrated as the key to the 1996 presidential election. Found in a dozen lifestyle types, Soccer Moms typically describe themselves as political moderates concerned about family values, reducing military spending, and increasing environmental programs. Although some political commentators doubted their impact on the election, the pervasiveness of their lifestyle cannot be overlooked. In Upward Bound, a midsized city cluster of new subdivisions filled with dual-income couples, Soccer Moms swarm the streets every afternoon and weekend in their GMC Suburbans and Mercury Villagers, carting kids to chess clubs, tae kwon do lessons, and, yes, soccer leagues. In the cluster community of Federal Way, Washington, south of Seattle, many women log three hundred miles a week in after-school schlepping. A local marketing survey found that more people eat meals in their cars than any other place—including the home.

Under the cluster system, the "average American"—that is, the typical citizen trumpeted by network commentators—proves to be a figment of statisticians' imaginations, since the "average" lifestyle cluster represents less than 2 percent of the population. The "middle class" now comes in variations ranging from suburban white-collar couples (New Empty Nests) to rural blue-collar families (Shotguns & Pickups). Even the most populous cluster lifestyles are too small to have much meaning. Ten years ago, the largest cluster in America was Blue-Chip Blues, a collection of blue-collar family suburbs like Ronkonkoma, New York, and Mesquite, Texas, where the lifestyle resembled an old episode of *Roseanne*. Residents liked to relax by drinking beer or going to the Elks Club, and meals included heavily processed food like Hamburger Helper, potato chips, and creamed corn. But as manufacturing jobs disappeared and the children of Blue-Chip Blues grew up and moved out, the cluster population dropped from 6 percent of U.S. households to 2 percent. And its working-class lifestyle faded. In recent years, membership in fraternal organizations has dropped, beer sales have nosedived, and *Roseanne* has disappeared, to be replaced by sitcoms like *Friends,* whose characters pursue typical Bohemian Mix lifestyles. *Roseanne* just couldn't compete, despite an abrupt story-line shift that found the blue-collar family suddenly rich beyond their imagination after hitting the lottery—one working-class version of the American Dream.

Although hip urban lifestyles may be in vogue on TV, the most populous cluster in the nation today is Kids & Cul-de-Sacs, a collection of white-collar family suburbs like Wheaton, Illinois, known for its noisy medley of bikes, boom boxes, carpooled kids, and dogs. Home to about 9 million people, this cluster is the nation's largest— eleven times larger than the smallest cluster, Urban Gold Coast. But by no means does it represent the "average American" type. Even with its sprawling families— this cluster ranks first for having families with four or more people—only 3.5 percent of all Americans live in Kids & Cul-de-Sacs. The median household income, $61,600, is 40 percent higher than the national average. And the cluster contains half as many blacks and twice as many Asians as the U.S. norm. Together, these demographics have a singular effect on consumer patterns. Kids & Cul-de-Sacs households are much more likely than the general population to eat Brie cheese, drive Infinitis, buy CD-ROM disks, and shop at Price Club. When it comes to television, *This Old House* outranks *NYPD Blue.* On the sidewalks of Wheaton, it's not unusual to see traffic jams involving strollers; the lives and crimes of the *NYPD Blue* squad just don't resonate here.

On the other hand, there's plenty of evidence that a thriving homogenized culture exists in America, with identically dressed counter people flipping identically dressed hamburgers in strip malls from coast to coast. In this slice of Anywhere, U.S.A., giants like Wal-Mart and Home Depot offer almost anything to anybody, smothering the local shops that in the past gave cities and small towns their character and charm. On local TV stations, the bland voices of anchorpeople have supplanted regional accents. Social scientists have dubbed this process "the McDonaldization of society." They could just have well have termed it the salsa-dipping, Cajun-seasoning, Carolina-barbecuing of America, as fast-food chains have watered down and dispersed these once-regional food trends throughout the nation.

A journey through the clustered world reveals that such mass-appeal businesses do not reach out and touch millions. Not all Americans have equal access to McDonald's and mall outlets; indeed, there are many clusters where consumers have never sampled the tart taste of an Arch Deluxe. And the creeping sameness of malls is one reason that over the last three years, some analysts estimate, as many as 600 of the nation's 2,000 malls have experienced financial trouble. In contemporary America, different products and brands mean different things to different people. The hip city dwellers of Young Literati and Urban Gold Coast may look down on McDonald's as a déclassé purveyor of fat-laden meat and fries, counter to their lifestyle, which celebrates lean, low-cholesterol health food. In Norma Rae-ville, a cluster of mill towns concentrated in the Southeastern states, having a McDonald's in town is a sign that your community is no longer a backwater. In Monroe, Georgia, a cluster community where the closest white-tablecloth restaurants are a twenty-minute-drive away in Athens, residents were tickled when a McDonald's outlet recently arrived. On a Saturday afternoon, it's often the center of community activity, the cars lined up fifteen deep at the drive-in window. Many wish more chains would move in. As one resident observes, "I'd really feel like we made it if a Red Lobster came to town."

Of course, regional loyalties that once thrived in geographic isolation still affect values and consumer patterns. In the kitchens of the Northwest, coffee bean grinders are mandatory. Salsa has outsold ketchup for years in the Southwest. "If it ain't fried, it ain't Southern" is how one resident of the Red, White & Blues town of Hiram, Georgia, describes her regional cuisine, which includes fried peach pie. Sales of grits still mimic the old boundaries of the Confederate States of America. Fashion designers have long known that logos confer different degrees of status depending on where shoppers live. When Rough Hewn clothiers slapped logos on shirts and sweaters, they became hot items in the Southeast; in the Northeast, sales plummeted.

And yet, as major corporations continually foist their uniform products and national brands on consumers across the land, regional differences are having less and less influence. Sharper distinctions of taste occur up and down the cluster ladder. Along the mean streets of Inner Cities neighborhoods in the South Bronx, some young adults will literally kill for a Starter jacket or pair of Timberland shoes, their logos prominently displayed. An hour away in the upscale Second City Elite town of Northport, some shoppers cut out the designer labels of new clothes so they won't be judged by anything so superficial. These consumers look to other products and brands—albeit with more subtle logos—to connect them to their cluster community.

More and more, Americans define their world view through a cluster lens. In Big Fish, Small Pond, an upper-middle-class lifestyle typified by Mount Juliet, Tennessee, a bedroom suburb of Nashville, an important measure of success is which college your child attends. Befitting their interest in education, residents are more likely than the general population to buy the latest books and computers. But in Lynchburg, Tennessee, a downscale rural town classified as Shotguns & Pickups, what matters is how your son or daughter performs on a basketball court or athletic field. Residents speak of the importance of athletics over academics in a community where the major employer is Jack Daniel's distillery. "The most popular kids in high school are the ones who play on the basketball team, not who get the good grades," says librarian Sara Hope, adding that patrons resist reading newsweeklies and out-of-town papers. "People here aren't looking for the latest product seen on a TV commercial," explains Clayton Knight, assistant manager of the Lynchburg Hardware and General Store. "They all know the good old products." Indeed, at the local pharmacy, shoppers can still buy liniment, lye soap, and Watkin's vanilla flavoring, as their grandparents did before them.

In an age of overwhelming consumer choices, cluster residents look to brand names and product myths as distinguishing lifestyle markers. Saturn car owners can now gather for company-sponsored "reunions"—though they've never previously met. The upscale, politically correct urban residents of Money & Brains support the Body Shop and the myth of its founder, Anita Roddick, who supposedly jets around the globe in search of ancient potions that can save the rainforests by making their plants and peoples—at last—economically viable. David Brooks, an editor at the *Weekly Standard* in Washington, D.C., noticed that many of his neighbors in the Money & Brains neighborhood of Cleveland Park liked things "rough." "Smoothness connotes slickness, glitz, the Reagan '80s," he wrote in the *Washington Post.* "Roughness connotes authenticity, naturalness, virtue. Whether it's bread, clothing, or furniture, you can never have too much texture. That's why unrefined sugar is now considered the height of refinement." While his neighbors may all agree that coffee bars like Starbucks are essential to their community, they can still realize individual self-actualization by ordering complex concoctions like a half-decaf, no-foam, double-shot skim latte with almond syrup and a dash of cinnamon.

Moving to other clusters causes people to adopt new buying patterns, but most Americans inhabit only a handful throughout the course of their lives. Mobility rates have been steadily declining even while fracturing trends have increased due to economic shifts and increasing divorce rates, among other trends. Twenty years ago, 20.1 percent of all Americans moved every year. Today that figure is 16.7 percent. "Most people move to where they've been before, either where they went to school or vacation," reports Kristin Hansen, a mobility expert at the Census Bureau. Now even laid-off workers are reluctant to move for a new job, though the cluster system may reflect a downshift in lifestyle at the same address. According to Challenger, Gray & Christmas, an international outplacement firm, only 18 percent of laid-off managers and executives were willing to relocate for a new position in 1995—the lowest figure in a decade. "We are becoming a nation of isolates in which we are apprehensive about venturing outside of the lives in which we have become so comfortable, even after we lose a job," observed John Challenger, executive vice president of the firm. Rather than risk moving to an unfamiliar setting, workers stay put, taking comfort in what real or imagined social and emotional support their communities provide.

This process has left too many Americans alienated from each other, divided by a cultural chasm. Just how wide and deep the differences are hit home when journalist Peter A. Brown examined whether the popular press is as out of touch with mainstream America as some critics claim. Brown cluster-coded the home addresses of 3,400 editors, reporters, and columnists for publications like *USA Today,* the *Washington Post,* and the *Milwaukee Journal.* He found that the vast majority of full-time journalists live in the ten wealthiest urban and suburban neighborhood types—clusters like Urban Gold Coast, Pools & Patios, and Blue Blood Estates. By contrast, they were markedly underrepresented in forty-eight of the clusters, including suburban middle-class lifestyle types that more closely aligned with their papers' readership—clusters such as Greenbelt Families and Middleburg Managers. As Brown observed, "Most journalists are different from real Americans. And their perspective on the world is different from how most Americans live." The American experience, most often seen from the viewpoint of educated and affluent white European descendants, must now be told in different ways.

In clusters like Hispanic Mix, home to downscale, predominantly Hispanic families, you can live most of your life without needing to speak or read English. In Atwater Village, a typical cluster neighborhood in Los Angeles, residents shop at *carnicería* meat markets, watch soap opera *novellas* on TV, and sing along in Spanish karaoke bars. It can be a dangerous place, with gang violence erupting over territory and drugs. But the local Chevy Chase Recreation Center serves as a sanctuary for children arriving after school to do homework, take art classes, or play basketball. When local gang members hang out at the center's parking lot or hand-ball court, director Sophia Pina-Cartez tries to cool hot tempers and maintain peace in the neighborhood. "I tell them, 'Don't tell me what you're up to, just don't make the children your victims,' " she says. "I just want to make this a safe haven."

Across the country in Glen Rock, New Jersey, an affluent suburb west of Man-hattan classified as Money & Brains, residents faced a different sort of problem. Several years ago, the unmistakable odor of a nearby landfill wafted down their stately streets lined with solid Tudors and shady trees. People of eminently good taste and environmental sensitivity, these residents devised a solution apropos of their appreciation for the finer things in life. The local government scented the garbage dump with lemon, as if it were a huge cup of espresso. When that plan failed to clear the air, they did the next best thing. They hired a trucking outfit to haul all their garbage to another town. End of problem.

Today, the notion of a star-spangled melting pot seems quaint, of another age. Increasingly, America is a fractured landscape, its people partitioned into dozens of cultural enclaves, its ideals reflected through differing prisms of experience. And this fracturing is likely to continue as the self-concept of America shifts from a majority white–minority black nation to a pluralistic society of many ethnic and racial groups. At the close of what's been called the American Century, during which the nation emerged as the dominant world power in commerce and politics, old myths are dying hard and new ones are just being forged. In this clustered world, the national identity is changing, and most of us don't even know it. . . .

The splintering society is no surprise to corporate marketers, who have been working with clusters for twenty-five years. An estimated fifteen thousand North American companies, nonprofit groups, and politicians have used clusters as part of their mar-keting strategies. . . .

[In] the U.S.A., marketers now spend an estimated $300 million annually on clustering techniques, which have become well-accepted tools in targeting direct-mail campaigns, selecting sites for new stores, and profiling the behavior of the nation's 100 million households. With the increased precision in data collection and greater power of desktop computing, the demand for information segmented by clusters is exploding. The new marketing buzzwords are *narrowcasting, particle mar-keting,* and *segments of one.* Claritas now calls itself a "precision marketing" com-pany, able to target the households on any given street. Even corporate giants are now trying to hone their messages to the diverse tastes of America's splintered consumers. Ethnic minorities control some $600 billion in annual buying power in the U.S. Today there are three TV networks and 350 newspapers catering to Latinos alone.

In the current business climate, marketing wars are being waged in micro-neighborhoods with surgical precision. No longer can businesses target-market a whole city or even a zip code. In 75081, the zip code of affluent Richardson, Texas, a camera store looking to sell Nikons would score big by targeting the households on Oakwood Drive, classified as Winner's Circle and filled with well-educated mobile executives and teenagers, who buy a lot of expensive photo equipment. Meanwhile, less than a mile west on Woodoak, merchants would do better selling cordless drills and circular saws to these Kids & Cul-de-Sacs households, with their large families and upscale incomes.

Such information can be translated into bottom-line results. Until fairly recently, beer was marketed as a mass-appeal product much like milk. Major brewers stuck to limited product lines, rarely launched new brands, and fought over market share during routine price wars. But today liquor stores sell dozens of microbrews, and big brewers masquerade as microbrewers—Anheuser-Busch makes Elk Mountain Amber Ale—in aggressive fights over market share. With baby boomers aging out of their wild beer-guzzling days (consumers over fifty-five drink only about half as much as twenty-something-year-old drinkers), brewers have introduced non-alcoholic beers, such as Coors Cutter, to hold on to older consumers.

And it's worked. In Urban Gold Coast, a cluster of densely populated urban neighborhoods filled with singles and young couples, residents drink imported beer at rates three times the national average but nonalcoholic beer 50 percent less often than the general population. In Gray Collars, a cluster of inner suburbs home to aging couples, consumers drink imported beer at a rate one-third below the national average and nonalcoholic beers at 50 percent above the average. To compete in this landscape of shrinking niches, Miller now targets its brews to customers one corner bar at a time.

In the past, national retail chains and catalog companies have been the most aggressive users of geodemographic marketing systems. But a new generation of small and midsized users are finding even more creative ways to employ the cluster system and retain core customers. On college campuses, admissions officers have been particularly innovative in employing the clusters to recruit and retain students. American University in Washington, D.C., matches the clusters of its applicants with alumni recruiters to make the interview process less of a culture clash. At Concordia College, a small liberal arts school in Seward, Nebraska, marketers dispatch targeted brochures to students requesting information. The mailer sent to students from upscale suburban clusters like Winner's Circle and Executive Suites focuses on careers previous graduates have entered in copy titled "A Stepping Stone to Your Future." Those from the middle-class Middle America cluster receive another, headlined "An Affordable Education" and focusing on scholarship opportunities at the school. At Hood College in Frederick, Maryland, officials assign roommates based on their home clusters in an effort to reduce conflicts. "It helps link people with similar backgrounds, so they're more comfortable in the residence hall," says Theodore Kelly, president of CERR, a cluster-based college consulting firm in Falls Church, Virginia. "And it sure beats making roommate assignments based on five general questions." No longer will parents hear about their child's "roommate from another planet."

Even government agencies have turned to clusters for social marketing projects. The Centers for Disease Control and Prevention use the clusters to ensure that their health and safety messages are understood in the communities needing assistance. When the CDC was called on to provide workers at an Alabama beryllium plant with safety information, a cluster analysis of the neighborhoods surrounding the factory gave CDC field-workers "cultural sensitivity training beyond the stereotypes to help them better reach their audience," says Susan Kirby, a CDC marketing communications scientist. In Kansas, adoption officials at the state's Social Rehabilitation Services Office had difficulty finding couples who would adopt special-needs children. Accordingly, they cluster-coded couples who'd adopted children with physical or learning disabilities in an attempt to find their "clones." Their work yielded some surprises: Among the most receptive couples were those in New Homesteaders, a midscale town cluster, and Southside City, a downscale African American neighborhood type. With several different target groups, Kansas officials developed a statewide direct-mail campaign with multiple messages, featuring a photo of a white or black youngster, depending on the cluster, with the same caption. "A kid like this deserves a home like yours." The response outstripped that of any previous campaign, notes Bob Nunley, director of the Kansas Geographic Bureau. "It also tickled the hell out of me because many of my white liberal friends didn't believe that black couples adopt black kids. And the clusters proved that they did."

The beauty of the cluster system is that it can reveal consumer niches in the unlikeliest of places. Executive Suites, the third-wealthiest lifestyle type, has lots of Beef Jerky fans; the blue-collar households of Rural Industria are a good market for pagers; and Golden Ponds seniors have a devilish desire to visit theme parks. Young Literati, a cluster of urban singles with a high concentration of writers and artists, displays an unusual fondness for Cheerios. When Time Inc. Ventures launched its urban culture magazine *VIBE,* its advertisers believed that the target audience was inner-city kids. But receptive readers were also found among white-collar suburbanites living in Young Influentials and Money & Brains communities—those who parrot the in-your-face street styles of the inner city. Accordingly, the magazine began selling advertising space for consumer electronics that would appeal to upscale suburban tastes. . . .

While its insights are undeniable, this clustered view of life is not universally accepted. Charges of oversimplification, stereotyping, and redlining are often leveled, and there are revolts against the "I am what I buy" mentality inherent in a consumer-based construct. There's something unnerving about being measured and pigeonholed on the basis of address or purchase patterns. Do you feel as if you belong to Money & Brains or Mobility Blues? Are you really a hunk of Brie or a country cottage by a lake? How much do you really have in common with others who watch *The X-Files* or join investment clubs?

Like many systems used to understand and predict consumer behavior, the clusters have raised privacy concerns along with the specter of an evil, all-knowing marketing monster. Many companies that operate data warehouses containing information on consumers use cluster systems, the better to divine the desired Boomtown Singles or Greenbelt Families consumers among lists of magazine readers or political contributors. And the information-gathering business is booming, projected to grow to a $10 billion industry this year. Companies like Metromail and The Polk Company gather and sort information on the lifestyles and spending habits of most of the 100 million individual households in the nation.

Of course, databases filled with personal information have existed since computers were invented, but the current explosion in data collecting—and abuses through inaccurate credit reports and zealous promotions—has understandably alarmed consumers. A 1996 survey by Louis Harris & Associates for Equifax Inc., a giant credit bureau, found that nearly nine out of ten Americans expressed concern about threats to their privacy. In 1997, more than 8,500 privacy bills were introduced in state legislatures. And there's every fear that without strong federal oversight of the data-collection industry, breaches of privacy in the information age will increase. Today, companies rake in information from loan applications, medical histories, driver's licenses, warranty cards, and credit card receipts. "In the not too distant future," warns Democratic congressman Bob Wise of West Virginia, "consumers face the prospect that a computer somewhere will compile records about every place they go and everything they purchase." . . .

Still other critics are less concerned by the cluster systems themselves than what they reflect: an increasingly fragmented society divided by income, race, ethnicity, sexual behavior, and the percentage of fat in our diets. A recent *Newsweek* poll found that nearly 60 percent of Americans believe the national identity is threatened by the increasing diversity of the populace. Economist Paul A. Jargowsky worries about "a pronounced trend toward increasing economic segregation." In the 1990s, the United States had the least equitable income distribution among all developed nations—including England, with its aristocratic traditions. If present trends toward more fragmented lifestyles continue, this gap between Americans will only widen.

Concerns over a thinning social fabric can't be easily dismissed. In America's past, various institutions crossed cultural divides: public schools, the military draft, and the English language. Today, rising minority populations are threatening all these institutions and, thus, the social fabric. Sometime within the next fifty years, whites will be outnumbered by minorities in the U.S. Already, a white backlash of sorts is taking shape as evidenced by rising enrollments in private schools and an estimated eight million Americans now living in gated communities. More and more, people are turning to the private sector to insulate themselves from the rest of society; the latest retail experiment is the notion of so-called membership malls. Some critics wonder if the nation will splinter like the Soviet Union. As historian Arthur Schlesinger Jr. worried in his 1992 book *The Disuniting of America,* "Will the center hold? Or will the melting pot give way to the Tower of Babel?"

There's no clear answer. The clusters merely show that although the nation is far from being one big leafy suburb, Americans today are managing to find happiness within their patches on the national quilt. And as society continues its fragmentation in the future, cluster systems will be essential tools for understanding the changes affecting the U.S. population. One day in the future, we may be sliced and diced 275 million ways, one for every American citizen: You'll have your own personal lifestyle type known by you, your family, and any businessperson or politician with access to a database. But even in that fractured state of affairs, America will manage to endure, united in the recognition of its historic role as a great experiment in diversity. In this clustered world, you are where you live, even if your country is splintered into countless, clamorous lifestyles.

⊕ *FURTHER   READING*

Abate, Janet. *Computers: Inventing the Internet* (2000).

Bagby, Meredith. *Rational Exuberance: The Influence of Generation X on the New American Economy* (1999).

Benner, Chris. *Work in the New Economy: Flexible Labor Markets in Silicon Valley* (2002).

Bhagwati, Jagdish. *In Defense of Globalization* (2004).

Brooks, David. *Bobos in Paradise: The New Upper Class and How They Got There* (2000).

Brown, John Seely, and Paul Duguid. *The Social Life of Information* (2002).

Carnoy, Martin. *Sustaining the New Economy: Work, Family, and Community in the Information Age* (2002).

Castells, Manuel. *The Internet Galaxy: Reflections on the Internet, Business, and Society* (2001).

Ehrenreich, Barbara. *Nickel and Dimed: On (Not) Getting By in America* (2001).

Frank, Thomas. *One Market Under God: Extreme Capitalism, Market Populism, and the End of Economic Democracy* (2000).

Friedman, Thomas L. *The Lexus and the Olive Tree: Understanding Globalization* (2000).

———. *The World Is Flat: A Brief History of the Twenty-first Century* (2005).

Gee, Henry. *Jacob's Ladder: The History of the Human Genome* (2004).

Graham, Otis L. *Losing Time: The Industrial Policy Debate* (1992).

Kass, Leon. *Life, Liberty, and the Defense of Dignity: The Challenge for Bioethics* (2002).

Levy, Frank. *The New Dollars and Dreams: American Incomes and Economic Change* (1998).

Lewis, Michael. *The New New Thing: A Silicon Valley Story* (2000).

Lowenstein, Roger. *Origins of the Crash: The Great Bubble and Its Undoing* (2004).

McCall, Leslie. *Complex Inequality: Gender, Race, and Class in the New Economy* (2001).

McCloskey, Donald. *Second Thoughts: Myths and Morals of U.S. Economic History* (1993).

Pellow, David N., and Lisa Sun-Hee Park. *The Silicon Valley of Dreams: Environmental Injustice, Immigrant Workers, and the High-Tech Global Economy* (2003).

Ritzer, George. *The McDonaldization of Society: An Investigation into the Changing Character of Contemporary Social Life* (1996).

Robbins-Roth, Cynthia. *From Alchemy to IPO: The Business of Biotechnology* (2001).

Schiller, Robert J. *Irrational Exuberance*, 2nd ed. (2005).

Schwartz, Peter. *The Long Boom: A Vision for the Coming Age of Prosperity* (2001).

Sennett, Richard. *The Corrosion of Character: The Personal Consequences of Work in the New Capitalism* (2001).

———. *The Culture of the New Capitalism* (2006).

Shipler, David K. *The Working Poor: Invisible in America* (2004).

Smith, Vicki. *Crossing the Great Divide: Worker Risk and Opportunity in the New Economy* (2001).

Stiglitz, Joseph E. *Globalization and Its Discontents* (2003).

Vogel, David. *Fluctuating Fortunes: The Political Power of Business in America* (1989).

Weiss, Michael J. *The Clustered World: How We Live, What We Buy, and What It All Means About Who We Are* (2000).

C H A P T E R
12

E Pluribus Unum:
Race and Ethnicity
in a Changing World

*The last decades of the twentieth century were marked by a series of noisy, com-
plicated, and increasingly contentious debates over difference, over what is and
is not acceptable behavior, over the rights and privileges of citizenship (including
who gets to be a citizen), and over what it means to be an American at the start
of the twenty-first century. Many of these debates were rooted in the history of the
civil rights movement, in the larger "rights revolution" it helped foster, and in
the changing rules that govern race, gender, and sexual orientation. Others were
products of the renewal of large-scale immigration during the 1980s and 1990s.
Both developments helped produce a growing consciousness of America's diversity
and a variety of claims to representation in the culture—over whose history was
told, whose heroes were honored, whose holidays were celebrated, whose language
was spoken. Both developments were in turn rooted in the real (and perceived)
impact of economic restructuring, globalization, new patterns of work and consumption, and the uneasy embrace of modern secular culture. As more and more
Americans have been drawn into the "fast" culture of the new information age,
many have also sought refuge in the invocation of traditional values, including
values associated with race, ethnicity, and national origin. This chapter explores
the arrival of America's newest immigrants and some of the resulting ferment in
contemporary American society.*

D O C U M E N T S

Between World War I and the end of the Cold War, the United States had seemed a
relatively homogenous nation. Immigration restrictions, two world wars, and the
Great Depression had closed America's borders to immigration, and fifty years of
assimilation had blurred many of the differences that had characterized the American

people at the beginning of the twentieth century. However, the arrival in the 1980s and 1990s of a new "fourth wave" of immigrants began a transformation of the nation's demographics rivaling that which had occurred during the late nineteenth and early twentieth centuries. The tale of this new immigration is told in part by Document 1, which features two charts and a table. The first chart places the volume of immigration in a broad historical perspective. The second chart and the table highlight the new immigration's changing composition. The renewal of large-scale immigration aroused fears on the part of some Americans, fears that typically flared up during recessions but died down during periods of growth and prosperity. The late 1980s and early 1990s were marked by campaigns to restrict immigration, eliminate bilingual education, and declare English the nation's "official" language. In California, fears aroused by large numbers of undocumented immigrants led to the 1994 passage of Proposition 187 (Document 2). Moreover, the new immigrants of the 1980s and 1990s arrived in an America still struggling to resolve its own long history of racial discrimination, especially in inner cities where deindustrialization and the decline of manufacturing had disrupted traditional avenues of upward mobility. In the major cities, where most new immigrants settled initially, their presence often added complications to an already troubled urban environment—as suggested by Document 3, a 1995 newspaper report on Los Angeles's complex ethnic mix. Concerns about America's growing immigrant presence prompted a 1997 study of immigration by a panel of social scientists supported by the National Council of Sciences. Document 4 summarizes the panel's findings.

While new immigrants competed in some labor and housing markets with African Americans, such competition was often exaggerated by what novelist Toni Morrison calls "race talk," which sought to portray conflicts through the lens of a deeply rooted white-black binary (Document 5). In fact, the new immigrants included many Asians and Africans, as well as Hispanics, whose skin color ranged from black to brown to white. Intermarriage further blurred racial boundaries. In the introduction to his autobiography *Brown: The Last Discovery of America* (2002), writer Richard Rodriguez ponders how his brown skin and Mexican American heritage unsettles traditional racial categories (Document 6). As for assimilation, Americans appear to hold somewhat contradictory views. As a survey conducted in 2003 suggests, while many believe that the country should be bound together by common moral and religious values, many also express support for cultural and religious diversity (Document 7).

1. Coming to America, 1900–2002

Chart A
Immigrants Admitted: Fiscal Years 1900–2002

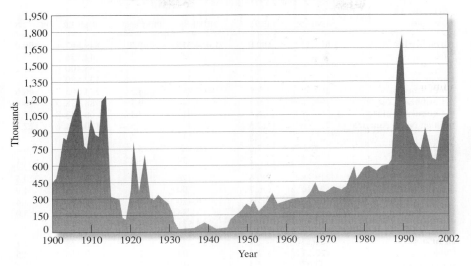

Chart B
Legal Immigrants by Region of Birth: Fiscal Years 1925–2002

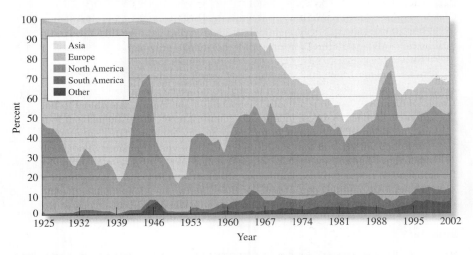

Note: North America includes Mexico, Central America, the Caribbean, and Canada.

From *Yearbook of Immigration Statistics, 2002* (Office of Immigration Statistics, Office of Management, Department of Homeland Security, 2002). Online at http://uscis.gov/graphics/shared/aboutus/statistics/IMM02yrbk/IMM2002.pdf.

Immigrants Admitted by Region and Top 20 Countries of Birth: Fiscal Years 2000–02

CATEGORY OF ADMISSION	2002		2001		2000	
	NUMBER	PERCENT	NUMBER	PERCENT	NUMBER	PERCENT
All countries	**1,063,732**	**100.0**	**1,064,318**	**100.0**	**849,807**	**100.0**
Africa	60,269	5.7	53,948	5.1	44,731	5.3
Asia	342,099	32.2	349,776	32.9	265,400	31.2
Europe	174,209	16.4	175,371	16.5	132,480	15.6
North America	404,437	38.0	407,888	38.3	344,805	40.6
Caribbean	96,489	9.1	103,546	9.7	88,198	10.4
Central America	68,979	6.5	75,914	7.1	66,443	7.8
Other North America	238,969	22.5	228,428	21.5	190,164	22.4
Oceania	5,557	.5	6,113	.6	5,136	.6
South America	74,506	7.0	68,888	6.5	56,074	6.6
Unknown	2,655	.2	2,334	.2	1,181	.1
Mexico	219,380	20.6	206,426	19.4	173,919	20.5
India	71,105	6.7	70,290	6.6	42,046	4.9
China	61,282	5.8	56,426	5.3	45,652	5.4
Philippines	51,308	4.8	53,154	5.0	42,474	5.0
Vietnam	33,627	3.2	35,531	3.3	26,747	3.1
El Salvador	31,168	2.9	31,272	2.9	22,578	2.7
Cuba	28,272	2.7	27,703	2.6	20,831	2.5
Bosnia-Herzegovina	25,373	2.4	23,640	2.2	11,828	1.4
Dominican Republic	22,604	2.1	21,313	2.0	17,536	2.1
Ukraine	21,217	2.0	20,975	2.0	15,810	1.9
Korea	21,021	2.0	20,742	1.9	15,830	1.9
Russia	20,833	2.0	20,413	1.9	17,110	2.0
Haiti	20,268	1.9	27,120	2.5	22,364	2.6
Canada	19,519	1.8	21,933	2.1	16,210	1.9
Colombia	18,845	1.8	16,730	1.6	14,498	1.7
Guatemala	16,229	1.5	13,567	1.3	9,970	1.2
United Kingdom	16,181	1.5	18,436	1.7	13,385	1.6
Jamaica	14,898	1.4	15,393	1.4	16,000	1.9
Pakistan	13,743	1.3	16,448	1.5	14,535	1.7
Iran	13,029	1.2	10,497	1.0	8,519	1.0
Subtotal	739,902	69.6	728,009	68.4	567,842	66.8
Other	323,830	30.4	336,309	31.6	281,965	33.2

2. Proposition 187: Californians Seek to Close the Door to Undocumented Immigrants, 1994

Summary

[By the California Secretary of State]. ILLEGAL ALIENS. INELIGIBILITY FOR PUBLIC SERVICES. VERIFICATION AND REPORTING. INITIATIVE STATUTE. Makes illegal aliens ineligible for public social services, public health care services

Excerpt from University of California Hastings College of Law database. Online at http://holmes.uchastings .edu/cgi-bin/starfinder/6377/calinits.txt.

(unless emergency under federal law), and attendance at public schools (elementary, secondary, and post-secondary). Requires various state and local agencies to report persons who are apparent illegal aliens to the California Attorney General and the U.S. Immigration and Naturalization Service (INS). Mandates California Attorney General to transmit reports to INS and maintain records of such reports. Makes it a felony to manufacture, distribute, sell or use false citizenship or residence documents. Summary of estimate by Legislative Analyst and Director of Finance of fiscal impact on state and local government: Annual savings at the state level potentially in excess of $100 million from withholding health and social services to undocumented persons. Annual savings at the local level potentially exceeding $200 million primarily from withholding medical care from undocumented persons. School districts would likely incur additional costs of tens of millions of dollars in the first two years of implementation and in excess of $10 million annually thereafter, to verify the legal status of students, parents and guardians. Savings to education, if any, are unknown.

Proponent

Ronald Prince Citizens for Legal Immigration Reform; P.O. Box 26288; Santa Ana, California 92799–6288; (714) 777–4653.

Initiative Text

SECTION 1. Findings and Declaration.

The People of California find and declare as follows:

That they have suffered and are suffering economic hardship caused by the presence of illegal aliens in this state.

That they have suffered and are suffering personal injury and damage caused by the criminal conduct of illegal aliens in this state.

That they have a right to the protection of their government from any person or persons entering this country unlawfully.

Therefore, the People of California declare their intention to provide for co-operation between their agencies of state and local government with the federal government, and to establish a system of required notification by and between such agencies to prevent illegal aliens in the United States from receiving benefits or public services in the State of California. . . .

3. Two Reporters Describe Los Angeles's Racial Tensions, 1995

The high-flown public image of Los Angeles sprang up as if by magic: a searchlight-swept Hollywood facade, obscuring the nastier blemishes—frustration, anger, urban strife—which periodically threatened to mar the veneer.

Then came Watts, and Rodney G. King, and now O. J. Simpson, and the city's racial rapport teeters, the factions staunchly divided. A place once viewed as idyllic

---

Excerpts from Lynell George and David Ferrell, "L.A.'s Veneer Stripped to Show Blemishes," *Los Angeles Times,* October 10, 1995. Reprinted by permission.

and tolerant, a palm-lined paradise, has come to be seen as quite the opposite—a worst-case example.

"In many ways, L.A. symbolizes the racism in this country like probably no other city," said Richard G. Majors, a senior researcher at the Urban Institute in Washington, D.C. "It's become the poster city for racism in America."

The truth is, Los Angeles has never been the perfect melting pot, with equal opportunity for all—nor is it the most racist of major urban hubs. It is, instead, a fast-changing metropolis where race relations are complicated by many of the same traits that lent the city its distinctive character: its newness, its wealth, its sprawling landscape, even its snaking system of freeways.

L.A.'s racial complexity is staggering. . . . [V]arious subgroups form an array of micro-cities divided by class, race, ethnicity and religion. As some neighborhoods merge, others secede from one another.

"You have neighborhoods changing ethnically literally overnight, displacing people—and displaced people never feel good," said Fernando Guerra, director of the Center for the Study of Los Angeles at Loyola Marymount University. "And it's not only a Latino, black, white thing: You can see it in Monterey Park, which went from being white to increasingly Latino, to now increasingly Asian, and you hear Latinos talking about Asians the way blacks talk about Latinos, and the way whites talk about blacks."

Situations arise that seldom, if ever, exist anywhere else in the world, demonstrating time and again the vexing nature of racial problems in Los Angeles.

On a single street in South-Central a few years ago, four cultures came together, clashing like mismatched gears. The home-owners were mostly black, living side by side with newly arrived Latino immigrants who occupied several large apartment houses. At each end of the block was a family-owned convenience store—one run by Koreans, the other by Vietnamese.

The blacks thought the Latinos were ruining the neighborhood: growing corn in their front yards, working on junker cars in the street. The Asian store owners refused to allow schoolchildren to place fund-raising signs in their shop windows. Language and cultural barriers prevented anyone from talking, so the anger smoldered until some blacks began moving out; others mounted a "Don't move, improve" campaign. . . .

It used to be . . . that most neighborhoods had individuals—typically older men and women—who would step in and mediate . . . problems. But cultural tensions in Los Angeles have ratcheted up so far, become so entwined with violence and crime, that would-be peacemakers have retreated to the safety of their homes. . . .

Newcomers are often startled by the intricacy of Los Angeles' racial dynamics, especially after arriving from less-fragmented cities where racial issues involve only two or three groups. . . .

One thing people learn is that Los Angeles' sprawling size makes it a highly contradictory place. There are communities—Culver City, Pasadena, Silver Lake—where racial mixing is rich, and usually amicable. And then there are communities entirely cut off from one another, either by freeways or hillsides or by sheer distance. In some segregated white enclaves, the appearance of minorities causes unease. They are watched with suspicion, followed through stores, discouraged in subtle ways from ever coming back.

"You're not treated very well," said social worker Mike Neely, who said huge segments of the black community thus never venture to beaches, art galleries or trendy hangouts. . . .

For many, the easiest answer to L.A.'s racial tensions is to avoid contact with other groups. . . .

The great labyrinth of freeways, one of the hallmarks of L.A. life, also complicates racial relations, setting Los Angeles apart from other cities because of the great distances that people travel in the insular confines of a car. Freeway driving prevents even the most superficial interaction with other racial groups. A subway commuter in Manhattan might encounter scores of blacks, Latinos and Asians in a single five-mile trip to the office; but a white commuter from Sherman Oaks might drive 40 minutes Downtown, day in, day out, for years, and never really see people of other races except at work, or possibly the gas station.

A *Times* poll in 1992 found that 35% of the city's white population has never been in South-Central or Watts. And thus many have no idea that those communities are filled with stucco homes, churches, furniture stores, palm trees and families working and raising their children.

Instead, many whites tend to see those areas as a featureless shadow land, a danger zone that symbolizes black rage, gangs, drive-by shootings and welfare mothers. In the resulting climate of distrust, racial biases harden; there is less interest in bridging differences, erasing stereotypes. . . .

More than any other single dynamic, the tension between the black community and the police represents the city's most enduring and defining racial problem. How it came to be that way involves not only the profound social problems of the city core but also the geographic and social forces that shaped Los Angeles.

Whites dominated the city's early growth, seeking out the beaches and claiming many communities just inland of those—or near Downtown—by placing restrictions on property: "*Said property shall not at any time be lived upon by any person whose blood is not entirely that of the Caucasian race,*" one typical deed read. Racial minorities were excluded from Inglewood, Glendale, Culver City and Mid-Wilshire.

Blacks found homes in inland communities, which merged during the heavy migrations of the 1940s and '50s into one of the nation's largest predominantly black centers, an area spanning close to 50 square miles. In it were doctors['] offices, corner grocers, clubs—everything. There was little reason for blacks to venture outside. . . .

There were also plenty of industrial jobs—until the big factories began to close. Bethlehem Steel, Firestone, Goodyear. In the four-year period ending in 1982, 75,000 manufacturing jobs disappeared in greater Los Angeles. . . .

Economic decline heightened racial tensions. To struggling blacks, whites represented the financial power-brokers who closed up those factories and who kept blacks from gaining work elsewhere. Eventually, the Latinos who immigrated by the thousands to South-Central came to be seen as competition for the jobs that were left. Koreans were resented for owning stores that blacks could not afford for lack of loans or personal assets.

Social problems also grew out of the economic despair—notably drug dealing and gang warfare. In cracking down, LAPD officers sometimes resorted to excessive force, using race as a means to identify "crimnals." . . .

L.A.'s fascination with wealth—mansions, Rolls-Royces—further complicates the picture. . . .

L.A. thrives as a center for sports, film and music—all fields in which minorities have excelled. That influence opens doors for blacks and other groups in Los Angeles. . . .

Yet the percentage of minorities who achieve entree into those elite circles is still small . . . [and] racial relations here suffer because of the yawning chasm between rich and poor. That gulf creates enormous frustration, . . . especially in a city where every facet of life is chronicled by the mass media. . . .

Ads and TV series tout the lifestyles of the rich and famous. . . . And all the while, TV and radio newscasts create the impression that gangsters, drugs and violence run rampant through all communities of color. . . .

Racial issues are allowed to fester; even the language of discussion—"riots," "minorities"—has become a minefield of potential conflict.

"We're so sensitive, so raw," said [Christopher] McCauley, the city human relations executive. "People are afraid that if they voice a concern, they'll cross a social border—and the consequences will be hellish."

Instead, they do nothing—usually. But there are exceptions, people who are sufficiently concerned by the complexity of the problem that they are breaking out of old habits, trying new things, being very L.A. in that respect. . . .

[They learn] that there are still vast racial differences, but that there is a healing power in being able to listen.

4. Social Scientists Report on the "New Americans," 1997

Throughout its history, the United States has been a nation of immigrants. The door may not always have been wide open, but it has never been completely shut. The current debate over the wisdom of high rates of immigration is not new; it stretches back even to colonial times. There are concerns about the effect of immigration on the economic prospects of native-born residents, on population growth, and on the ability of immigrants to interweave themselves into the social fabric of the nation.

Responding to these concerns, Congress in 1990 appointed a bipartisan Commission on Immigration Reform to review the nation's policies and laws and to recommend changes. In turn, the commission in 1995 asked the National Research Council to convene a panel of experts to assess the demographic, economic, and fiscal consequences of immigration. . . .

The panel's charge was to address three key questions:
•   What is the effect of immigration on the future size and composition of the U.S. population?
•   What is the influence of immigration on the overall economy?
•   What is the fiscal impact of immigration on federal, state, and local governments? . . .

Excerpts from James P. Smith and Barry Edmonston, eds., *The New Americans: Economic, Demographic and Fiscal Effects of Immigration* (Washington, D.C.: National Academy Press, 1997), pp. 1–13. Online at http://www.nap.edu/books/0309063566/html/index.html. Reprinted with permission, courtesy of the National Academy Press, Washington, D.C.

The modern era of immigration policy dates from the 1965 Immigration and Naturalization Act. This act removed the quotas for immigrants based on national origins and replaced them with a preference system based primarily on family unification and, to a lesser extent, on occupational skills. One consequence of the 1965 legislation has been a decline in the labor market skills of new immigrants relative to those of native-born workers. This decline has accompanied a decrease in immigration from more prosperous Western Europe and a rise in immigration from Asian and Latin and South American countries. Recent legislation, notably the Personal Responsibility and Work Opportunity Reconciliation Act of 1996, restricted access to public assistance programs for noncitizen legal immigrants, and set a lifetime limit on public assistance for all residents.

In 1994, there were nearly 800,000 legal immigrants. This number is considerably smaller than the number in the peak year of the early twentieth century wave of immigration—1.3 million immigrants in 1913. Moreover, since the resident population has more than tripled during the course of the twentieth century, the number of immigrants in the earlier decades represented a much higher proportion: 13 immigrants per 1,000 resident population in 1913, compared with 3 immigrants per 1,000 residents in 1994. However, immigration now plays a greater role in population growth than it did eight decades ago: it accounts for 37 percent of total growth, partly because of the decline in the fertility rates of residents.

Besides legal immigrants admitted for permanent residence, there were in 1994 some 22 million visits by aliens admitted for short stays—students, tourists, short-term employees of international companies. Most stay no more than a few weeks, but others live in the United States for several years; some overstay their allotted time and swell the number of illegal immigrants. . . .

What influence will immigration have on the size and composition of the U.S. population over the next half century? . . .

If net immigration continues indefinitely at its current levels, there will be 387 million people in the United States in 2050, 124 million more than at present. Immigration will play the dominant role in that growth, accounting for 80 million, or two-thirds, of the increase. Even if net immigration were halved, to 410,000 a year, the population would still rise to 349 million. And if it were increased by half, to 1,230,000 a year, the population would be 426 million by the middle of the 21st century. . . .

Under any immigration scenario, both the absolute and the relative sizes of the Asian-ancestry and Hispanic-ancestry populations will grow rapidly. Assuming continued net immigration at current levels, the size of the Asian population will increase from 9 to 34 million in 2050 (growing from 3 to 8 percent of the population). This growth stems mainly from the large fraction of Asians in the immigrant population. Similarly, fueled by higher fertility, high rates of immigration, and high affiliation rates, the Hispanic population will grow substantially over this period. Assuming continued net immigration at current levels, and current rates of intermarriage and ethnic affiliation, the Hispanic population will rise from 27 million in 1995 (about 1 in 11 of the population) to 95 million in 2050 (about 1 in 4 of the population).

These projections incorporate the assumption that current levels of intermarriage will continue, and thus that the proportion of people with multiple ancestry will increase. Multiple ancestry adds complexity and ambiguity to ethnic definitions, and it is possible that, by the middle of the next century, ethnic and racial lines will be even more blurred. . . .

The second charge to the panel concerned the impact of immigration on the U.S. economy. . . .

Using a basic economic model, with plausible assumptions, we show that immigration produces net economic gains for domestic residents, for several reasons. At the most basic level, immigrants increase the supply of labor and help produce new goods and services. But since they are paid less than the total value of these new goods and services, domestic workers as a group must gain.

The gains to the domestic economy come from a number of sources. On the production side, immigration allows domestic workers to be used more productively, specializing in producing goods at which they are relatively more efficient. Specialization in consumption also yields a gain.

Immigration thus breaks the rigid link between domestic consumption and domestic production. From this perspective, the effects of immigration are comparable to those of international trade. That the two processes are so similar suggests that, when trade is relatively free, any change in the number of immigrants will affect the incomes of domestic workers less than it would have without trade. . . .

Even when the economy as a whole gains, however, there may be losers as well as gainers among different groups of U.S. residents. Along with immigrants themselves, the gainers are the owners of production factors that are complementary with the labor of immigrants—that is, domestic, higher-skilled workers, and perhaps owners of capital—whose incomes will rise. Those who buy goods and services produced by immigrant labor also benefit. The losers may be the less-skilled domestic workers who compete with immigrants and whose wages will fall. . . .

. . . The one group that appears to suffer substantially from new waves of immigrants are immigrants from earlier waves, for whom the recent immigrants are close substitutes in the labor market.

While some have suspected that blacks suffer disproportionately from the inflow of low-skilled immigrants, none of the available evidence suggests that they have been particularly hard-hit on a national level. Some have lost their jobs, especially in places where immigrants are concentrated. But the majority of blacks live elsewhere, and their economic fortunes are tied largely to other factors. . . .

How do immigrants affect the revenues and expenditures of the various levels of government in the United States? Does additional immigration raise the amount that current residents must pay in taxes to receive a constant level of government services? Fiscal impacts are a much more important policy issue today than for earlier immigrant waves, because the relative size of all levels of government is so much larger. . . .

Taking the difference between taxes paid and benefits received at each age, immigrants (like others) are costly in childhood and in old age, but are net payers of taxes during their working ages. For this reason, the long-term net fiscal impact of an immigrant (measured as a present dollar value) varies greatly with age at arrival. Immigrants arriving at ages 10 to 25 produce fiscal benefits for natives under most scenarios, whereas immigrants arriving in their late sixties generally impose a long-term fiscal burden. In fact, most immigrants tend to arrive at young working ages, which partly explains why the net fiscal impact of immigration is positive under most scenarios. . . .

Although the average fiscal impacts of new immigration measured in present values are found to be positive under most scenarios, the impact of an increase in the annual flow of immigrants would initially be negative overall for a couple of decades before turning positive. The timing and extent of such a period depends crucially on federal fiscal policy. Given that near-term fiscal burdens will be offset by later fiscal gains, the present-value estimates of the long-term fiscal impact will be sensitive to the choice of a discount rate for comparing future expenditures and revenues with current ones.

Finally, under most scenarios, the long-run fiscal impact is strongly positive at the federal level, but substantially negative at the state and local levels. The federal impact is shared evenly across the nation, but the negative state and local impacts are concentrated in the few states and localities that receive most of the new immigrants. Consequently, native residents of some states, such as California, may incur net fiscal burdens from immigrants while residents of most states reap net fiscal benefits. . . .

How well are immigrants and their descendants integrated into American society, and how does immigration affect important American institutions? These are complex research issues, in which speculation and public discourse often run ahead of conclusive research findings. Despite fears in the past about the effects of immigration on the social fabric of the nation, few socioeconomic differences now separate the descendants of immigrants from Europe. Whether the same generational progress will characterize present-day immigrants and their children remains to be seen. Early readings suggest that some recent immigrants and their children—especially Asian Americans—match native-born whites in education and occupation, although not in incomes, fairly quickly.

Residential segregation is another visible measure of social distance. Recent immigrants tend to cluster in neighborhoods with others from their country of origin. But with convergence in socioeconomic status across generations, most immigrants disperse from the ethnic neighborhoods where they first tend to settle, and integrate with the overall population.

This residential movement has parallels in intermarriage among immigrant groups. Today, the children, grandchildren, and great-grandchildren of immigrants from various European countries and of various religions—once so distinct as to be referred to as "races"—have intermarried to such an extent as to virtually erase differences in education, income, occupation, and residence.

The picture is similar on the sensitive issue of the English language. Many immigrants arrive with at least a working knowledge of English. The 1990 decennial census found that three-fifths of the immigrants who came in the 1980s spoke English well or even very well; and of those who had been here 30 years or more, only 3 percent reported that they could not speak English well.

Attempts to draw empirical conclusions about the relation between immigration and crime rates founder on problems of measurement. Crime rates rose from the 1960s until about 1990, and since then have declined; there is no obvious link with trends in immigration in this period. Studies at the local level have found no association of immigrant concentrations with crime rates, with the exception of high rates of nonviolent crime near the borders.

Americans have always been ambivalent toward immigration, welcoming flows of foreigners in one era, blocking them in the next. In the past 50 years, polling data have charted a deepening opposition to immigration, linked in part, it appears, to economic concerns. Interethnic tensions have surfaced, especially in areas of high unemployment and poverty. Attitudes are by no means monolithic, however: Americans of African, Hispanic, and Asian descent are more accepting of immigration than non-Hispanic whites are. At present, about 68 percent of non-Hispanic whites favor decreasing immigration, compared with 57 percent of blacks. Asians and Hispanics are even more favorable toward immigration than blacks. Persons with more education tend to accept immigration more than those with less education. Finally, attitudes toward immigrants are no more negative in states with large immigrant populations than in the rest of the country.

5. An African American Novelist Decries "Race Talk," 1993

Fresh from Ellis Island, Stavros gets a job shining shoes at Grand Central Terminal. It is the last scene of Elia Kazan's film *America, America,* the story of a young Greek's fierce determination to immigrate to America. Quickly, but as casually as an afterthought, a young black man, also a shoe shiner, enters and tries to solicit a customer. He is run off the screen—"Get out of here! We're doing business here!"—and silently disappears.

This interloper into Stavros' workplace is crucial in the mix of signs that make up the movie's happy-ending immigrant story: a job, a straw hat, an infectious smile—and a scorned black. It is the act of racial contempt that transforms this charming Greek into an entitled white. Without it, Stavros' future as an American is not at all assured.

This is race talk, the explicit insertion into everyday life of racial signs and symbols that have no meaning other than pressing African Americans to the lowest level of the racial hierarchy. Popular culture, shaped by film, theater, advertising, the press, television and literature, is heavily engaged in race talk. It participates freely in this most enduring and efficient rite of passage into American culture: negative appraisals of the native-born black population. Only when the lesson of racial estrangement is learned is assimilation complete. Whatever the lived experience of immigrants with African Americans—pleasant, beneficial or bruising—the rhetorical experience renders blacks as noncitizens, already discredited outlaws.

All immigrants fight for jobs and space, and who is there to fight but those who have both? As in the fishing ground struggle between Texas and Vietnamese shrimpers, they displace what and whom they can. Although U.S. history is awash in labor battles, political fights and property wars among all religious and ethnic groups, their struggles are persistently framed as struggles between recent arrivals and blacks. In race talk the move into mainstream America always means buying into the notion of American blacks as the real aliens. Whatever the ethnicity or nationality of the immigrant, his nemesis is understood to be African American.

Toni Morrison, "On the Backs of Blacks," *Time,* December 2, 1993, 57. Online at http://www.time.com/time/community/morrisonessay.html. Reprinted by permission of International Creative Management, Inc. Copyright © 1993 by Toni Morrison.

Current attention to immigration has reached levels of panic not seen since the turn of the century. To whip up this panic, modern race talk must be revised downward into obscurity and nonsense if antiblack hostility is to remain the drug of choice, giving headlines their kick. PATTERNS OF IMMIGRATION FOLLOWED BY WHITE FLIGHT, screams the *Star-Ledger* in Newark. The message we are meant to get is that disorderly newcomers are dangerous to stable (white) residents. Stability is white. Disorder is black. Nowhere do we learn what stable middle-class blacks think or do to cope with the "breaking waves of immigration." The overwhelming majority of African Americans, hardworking and stable, are out of the loop, disappeared except in their less than covert function of defining whites as the "true" Americans.

So addictive is this ploy that the fact of blackness has been abandoned for the theory of blackness. It doesn't matter anymore what shade the newcomer's skin is. A hostile posture toward resident blacks must be struck at the Americanizing door before it will open. The public is asked to accept American blacks as the common denominator in each conflict between an immigrant and a job or between a wannabe and status. It hardly matters what complexities, contexts and misinformation accompany these conflicts. They can all be subsumed as the equation of brand X vs. blacks.

But more than a job is at stake in this surrender to whiteness, more even than what the black intellectual W.E.B. Du Bois called the "psychological wage"—the bonus of whiteness. Racist strategies unify. Savvy politicians always include in the opening salvos of their campaigns a quick clarification of their position on race. It is a mistake to think that Bush's Willie Horton or Clinton's Sister Souljah was anything but a candidate's obligatory response to the demands of a contentious electorate unable to understand itself in any terms other than race. Warring interests, nationalities and classes can be merged with the greatest economy under that racial banner.

Race talk as bonding mechanism is powerfully on display in American literature. When Nick in F. Scott Fitzgerald's *The Great Gatsby* leaves West Egg to dine in fashionable East Egg, his host conducts a kind of class audition into WASP-dom by soliciting Nick's support for the "science" of racism. "If we don't look out the white race will be . . . utterly submerged," he says. "It's all scientific stuff; it's been proved." It makes Nick uneasy, but he does not question or refute his host's convictions.

The best clue to what the country might be like without race as the nail upon which American identity is hung comes from Pap in Mark Twain's *Huckleberry Finn,* who upon learning a Negro could vote in Ohio, "drawed out. I says I'll never vote ag'in." Without his glowing white mask he is not American; he is Faulkner's character Wash, in *Absalom, Absalom!,* who, stripped of the mask and treated like a "nigger," drives a scythe into the heart of the rich white man he has loved and served so completely.

For Pap, for Wash, the possibility that race talk might signify nothing was frightening. Which may be why the harder it is to speak race talk convincingly, the more people seem to need it. As American blacks occupy more and more groups no longer formed along racial lines, the pressure accelerates to figure out what white interests really are. The enlisted military is almost one-quarter black; police forces are blackening in large urban areas. But welfare is nearly two-thirds white; affirmative-action beneficiaries are overwhelmingly white women; dysfunctional white families jam the talk shows and court TV.

The old stereotypes fail to connote, and race talk is forced to invent new, increasingly mindless ones. There is virtually no movement up—for blacks or whites, established classes or arrivistes—that is not accompanied by race talk. Refusing, negotiating or fulfilling this demand is the real stuff, the organizing principle of becoming an American. Star spangled. Race strangled.

6. Richard Rodriguez Ponders What It Means to Be "Brown," 2002

I write of a color that is not a singular color, not a strict recipe, not an expected result, but a color produced by careless desire, even by accident; by two or several. I write of blood that is blended. I write of brown as complete freedom of substance and narrative. I extol impurity.

I eulogize a literature that is suffused with brown, with allusion, irony, paradox—ha!—pleasure.

I write about race in America in hopes of undermining the notion of race in America.

Brown bleeds through the straight line, unstaunchable—the line separating black from white, for example. Brown confuses. Brown forms at the border of contradiction (the ability of language to express two or several things at once, the ability of bodies to experience two or several things at once).

It is that brown faculty I uphold by attempting to write brownly. And I defy anyone who tries to unblend me or to say what is appropriate to my voice. . . .

Brown is the color most people in the United States associate with Latin America.

Apart from stool sample, there is no browner smear in the American imagination than the Rio Grande. No adjective has attached itself more often to the Mexican in America than "dirty"—which I assume gropes toward the simile "dirt-like," indicating dense concentrations of melanin.

I am dirty, all right. In Latin America, what makes me brown is that I am made of the conquistador and the Indian. My brown is a reminder of conflict.

And of reconciliation.

In my own mind, what makes me brown in the United States is that I am Richard Rodriguez. My baptismal name and my surname marry England and Spain, Renaissance rivals.

North of the U.S.–Mexico border, brown appears as the color of the future. The adjective accelerates, becomes a verb: "America is browning." South of the border, brown sinks back into time. Brown is time.

. . . Hispanics brown an America that traditionally has chosen to describe itself as black-and-white. I salute Richard Nixon, the dark father of Hispanicity. But . . . I think of . . . more elementary considerations. I mean the meeting of the Indian, the African, and the European in colonial America. Red. Black. White. The founding palette.

Some months ago, a renowned American sociologist predicted to me that Hispanics will become "the new Italians" of the United States. (What the Sicilian had been for nineteenth-century America, the Colombian would become for the twenty-first century.)

His prediction seems to me insufficient because it does not account for the influence of Hispanics on the geography of the American imagination. Because of Hispanics, Americans are coming to see the United States in terms of a latitudinal vector, in terms of south-north, hot-cold; a new way of placing ourselves in the twenty-first century.

America has traditionally chosen to describe itself as an east-west country. I grew up on the east-west map of America, facing east. I no longer find myself so easily on that map. In middle age (also brown, its mixture of loss and capture), I end up on the shore where Sir Francis Drake first stepped onto California. I look toward Asia.

As much as I celebrate the browning of America (and I do), I do not propose an easy optimism. . . .

I think brown marks a reunion of peoples, an end to ancient wanderings. Rival cultures and creeds conspire with Spring to create children of a beauty, perhaps of a harmony, previously unknown. Or long forgotten. Even so, the terrorist and the skinhead dream in solitude of purity and of the straight line because they fear a future that does not isolate them. In a brown future, the most dangerous actor might likely be the cosmopolite, conversant in alternate currents, literatures, computer programs. The cosmopolite may come to hate his brownness, his facility, his indistinction, his mixture; the cosmopolite may yearn for a thorough religion, ideology, or tribe.

Many days, I wander[ed] the city, to discover the city . . . was comically browning. Walking down Fillmore Street one afternoon, I was enjoying the smell of salt, the brindled pigeons, brindled light, when a conversation overtook me, parted around me, just as I passed the bird-store window: Two girls. Perhaps sixteen. White, Anglo, whatever. Tottering on their silly shoes. Talking to boys. The one girl saying to the other: . . . *His complexion is so cool, this sort of light—well, not that light.* . . .

I realized my book will never be equal to the play of the young.

. . . *Sort of reddish brown, you know.* . . . The other girl nodded, readily indicated that she did know. But still Connoisseur Number One sought to bag her simile. . . . *Like a Sugar Daddy bar—you know that candy bar?*

. . . I believe it is possible to describe a single life thrice, if from three isolations: *Class. Ethnicity. Race.*

. . .[S]ome . . . would take "race" for a tragic noun, a synonym for conflict and isolation. Race is not such a terrible word for me. Maybe because I am skeptical by nature. Maybe because my nature is already mixed. The word race encourages me to remember the influence of eroticism on history. For that is what race memorializes. Within any discussion of race, there lurks the possibility of romance.

7. Americans Express Support for Both Unity and Diversity, 2003

Discussions of cultural diversity in the United States traditionally juxtapose two models or visions of the ideal future. One is the so-called "melting pot," where the emphasis is on all Americans assimilating social and cultural differences into a blended amalgam. Through most of American history this has been the dominant vision. The second is a more pluralist or "salad bowl" model in which the stress is laid on diverse groups preserving their cultural uniqueness. This is the model associated in recent years with multiculturalism. Initial findings from our "Difference and Democracy" survey reveal that neither of these images by itself expresses the deepest longings of Americans for our nation's future.

Respondents were asked a series of questions exploring which of the two opposing visions for the future came closest to their own. Americans overwhelmingly look to a future in which: Americans will stand strongly behind their personal convictions (87%); they will be more religious, rather than more secular (71%); the lines between good and bad will be firmer, rather than more flexible (76%); Americans will be more courteous and respectful, rather than more relaxed in their habits (76%); and they will have more unity of moral commitment, rather than more diversity (60%). In each of these areas, Americans have a centripetal urge; they hope to be bound together by common moral goals undergirded by a religious sensibility. The pluralist dream of cultural groups being left to their own designs, stitched together loosely in a secular, civil society would appear to have little popular resonance.

But then we encounter an alternate vision. Over half of those surveyed (53%) hope that America will be a land where many languages are spoken, rather than English alone. Six in ten Americans wish for the American family to take many forms, rather than to conform to a traditional model. And though Americans desire to live in a nation where people are religious, only one in four prefers the image of a "Christian nation" to one in which "America will be a mix of people of many faiths." Add to this the preference for a land in which there will be less government involvement in people's lives (72%), and we see a vision of a country in which people, and groups, are free to live their own lives, whatever their cultural heritage or religious "preference."

These two visions for the future—one that yearns for common commitments, and the other, cultural and religious diversity—are distributed unevenly between age groups, regions of the country, and metropolitan and rural areas, but the lines are not as predictable as one might guess. Almost as many senior citizens as young adults, for example, embrace the diversity vision, while two-thirds of Northeasterners share the longing for a more religious rather than a more secular nation. In fact, the picture is complicated and most Americans do not subscribe solely to one model or the other. Nearly four out of every ten (38%) who wished for more diversity

From Carl Bowman, "The Survey of American Political Culture: Difference and Democracy," *Insight* (Spring 2003): 4–5; published by the Institute for Advanced Studies in Culture, Center on Religion and Democracy, University of Virginia. Reprinted by permission.

Salad Bowl and Melting Pot

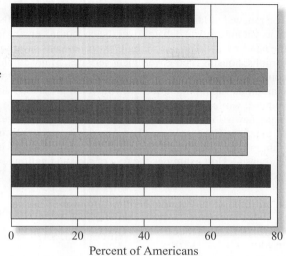

Americans will speak many languages

American families will take many different forms

America will be a mix of people of many faiths

Americans will be more unified in their moral commitments

America will be more religious

Americans will be more courteous in public

The lines between good and bad will be firmer

Percent of Americans

Lines of Opinion Regarding the American Family

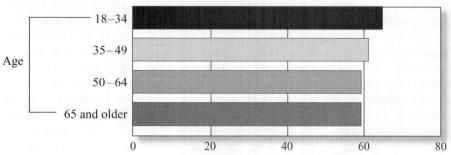

Age

18–34

35–49

50–64

65 and older

Percent who hope American families will take many forms rather than conforming to a traditional pattern

of moral commitment also wished for an English-only America. And nearly half (46%) of those who hoped for more unity of moral commitment hoped for a nation in which many languages would be spoken.

In short, most Americans seek some balance or tension between commonality and diversity. Neither of the standard models, the melting pot or the salad bowl, do a good job of distilling this tension. A satellite or solar system is perhaps a better model for the ideal: one in which cultural groups have their own trajectories and orbits, but in which there is enough moral "gravity" at the center to keep things orderly, both preventing Americans from flying completely off in their own direction and from bumping haphazardly into each other. . . .

◈ *E S S A Y S*

The renewal of large-scale immigration in the late 1980s and 1990s touched off a series of as yet unresolved debates over the economic, environmental, and cultural impact of the new arrivals. Some working-class Americans saw the new immigrants as competitors for jobs, housing, and government services. Many employers, on the other hand, welcomed the influx of newcomers willing to work for low wages. Some environmentalists feared that rapid population growth would press too hard on the nation's limited resources, while cultural conservatives worried about the "disuniting" influence of so many new strangers. In the first essay, historian George J. Sanchez of the University of Southern California uses Los Angeles in the 1990s to explore the intersections of immigration, race, and nativism. In the second essay, University of Chicago historian Thomas C. Holt examines the role of race and nationhood in the new, "post-Fordist" global economy of the late twentieth and early twenty-first centuries.

Race, Immigration and Nativism

GEORGE J. SANCHEZ

On April 30, 1992, Americans across the nation sat transfixed by a television event that grew to symbolize the sorry state of race relations in late twentieth century urban America. The image of Reginald Denny, a white truck driver, being pulled from his cab at the corner of Florence and Normandie Avenues in South Central Los Angeles, beaten and spat upon by a group of young African-American males, quickly became a counterimage of the inhumane beating of black motorist Rodney King a year earlier. These two events of racial conflict, both captured on videotape, dominated representations of the Los Angeles riots in a city haunted by poverty, racism and police brutality. So focused have all Americans become of a bipolar racial dynamic in this country, usually framed in white/black terms, that we lost an opportunity to dissect one of the most important and complex events of our time. As the perceptive playwright and artist Anna Deveare Smith has observed, "We tend to think of race as us and them—us or them being black or white depending on one's own color." Indeed, the Los Angeles riots provides stark, critical evidence of the rise of a racialized nativism directed at recent immigrants and the American born who racially represent those newcomers, one of the most important social movements of our era.

A closer look at the victims of violence at the corner of Florence and Normandie reveals the way in which the Los Angeles Riots were fundamentally an antiimmigrant spectacle at its very beginning. Most people outside of Los Angeles are surprised to hear that Reginald Denny was not the only person injured on that corner. Mesmerized by video images of a single beating of one white man, it is difficult to imagine that at least 30 other individuals were beaten at that same spot, most pulled from their cars, some requiring extensive hospitalization. Most importantly for my purposes, only one other victim of the violence at that corner besides Denny was white—and he was, like Denny, a truckdriver passing through the region.

Excerpts from George J. Sanchez, "Face the Nation: Race, Immigration, and the Rise of Nativism in Late Twentieth Century America," *International Migration Review* (Winter 1997): 1009–1030. Reprinted with permission of Blackwell Publishing.

All others were people of color, including a Mexican couple and their one-year-old child, hit with rocks and bottles; a Japanese-American man, stripped, beaten and kicked after being mistaken for Korean; a Vietnamese manicurist, left stunned and bloodied after being robbed; and a Latino family with five-year-old twin girls, who each suffered shattered glass wounds in the face and upper body. All of these acts of violence occurred before Reginald Denny appeared.

Indeed, the first victims at Florence and Normandie were Latino residents who lived in the neighborhood. Marisa Bejar was driving her car through the intersection at 5:45 pm when a metal-covered phone book sailed through her car window, opening up a wound that took thirteen stitches to close. Her husband, Francisco Aragon, was hit on the forehead with a piece of wood, while their seven-month-old infant suffered minor scratches when a large metal sign was hurled through the rear window. Minutes later, when Manuel Vaca drove his 1973 Buick into the intersection, Antonine Miller and Damian Williams threw rocks through the windshield, causing Vaca to stop the car. Six men pulled Vaca, his wife and his brother from their car, then beat and robbed them. As Anthony Brown remembered, he kicked at Vaca "because he was Mexican and everybody else was doin' it." Sylvia Castro, a fourth generation Mexican American and prominent activist in South Central, was shocked when bricks and bottles shattered her car window. Having worked closely with gang members in the area, she was able to escape with only a bloodied nose by speeding away.

Later, after Denny's assault was recorded and broadcast worldwide, several shocked black residents of the area risked their lives to save other victims. James Henry left his porch to pull Raul Aguilar, an immigrant from Belize, to safety after he had been beaten into a coma and a car had run over his legs. Donald Jones, an off-duty fireman, protected Sai-Choi Choi after several men beat and robbed him. Gregory Alan-Williams pulled a badly wounded Takao Hirata from the bloody intersection. Another savior at that corner was 59-year-old Reverend Bennie Newton, pastor of the Light of Love Church. He rescued the life of Fidel Lopez, a twenty-year resident of Los Angeles from Guatemala. Lopez, driving to his home one block from the intersection, was pulled from his car and later required 29 stitches in his forehead for a wound received by a blow with an auto stereo, 17 stitches to his ear, which someone had tried to slice off, and 12 stitches under his chin. Laying unconscious in the street from the beating, Lopez had motor oil poured down his throat and his face and genitals spraypainted blue. His life was saved when Newton began praying over his prostrate body with a bible in the air.

Over the four days of the Los Angeles riots, the dynamics of racial and class tensions, rage against the police, and antiforeign sentiment came together in violent, unpredictable fashion. From that corner of Florence and Normandie, the mayhem spread to engulf the city, creating the worst modern race riot in American history. Fifty-two lives were lost and 2,383 people were injured. About $1 billion of damage was done to residences and businesses, and over 14,000 arrests were made. In the first three days of rioting, over 4,000 fires were set and 1,800 people were treated for gunshot wounds. The destruction occurred throughout the Los Angeles basin, and the participants and victims were indeed multiethnic. But at its core, the Los Angeles riots provide stark evidence of the way in which immigrants provided the perfect scapegoat for American populations frustrated with developments in their society.

The decisions made by angry, young African Americans at that corner as they chose whom to hurt speak volumes to anyone interested in the intertwining of issues of race and immigration in late twentieth century America. For some, the decision was not about who was white, but about who was not black. For others it centered around how Latinos and Asians had "invaded the territory" of South Central, one which they claimed as their own turf, despite the fact that South Central Los Angeles had a majority Latino population in 1992. Others shouted (as heard on various video-tapes) to "let the Mexicans go," but "show the Koreans who rules." Although the violence began as a response to a verdict passed by an almost all-white jury against an almost all-white set of police officers, quickly other people of color—those deemed foreign or foreign looking—were engaged in the deadly exchange. The meaning of racial and national identities were consistently at issue at the corner of Florence and Normandie, with serious and sometimes bloody outcomes for all participants.

Since May 1992, more clearly visible evidence has appeared which allows most social commentators to identify our current historical moment as one experiencing a particularly sharp rise in American nativism. Two years after the Los Angeles riots, California voters would resurrect their longstanding history as leaders in anti-immigrant efforts since the days of Chinese Exclusion by passing Proposition 187, a state initiative intended to punish illegal immigrants by restricting their access to schools, medical care, and other social services. This would be accomplished by deputizing social service providers as immigration inspectors, including teachers, social workers and doctors, and forcing them to identify to local law enforcement officials students and clients who had entered the country illegally. Here was legislation that tied issues of crime and immigration into a tidy package and allowed voters to voice nativist fears in the anonymous sanctity of the voting booth, a populist solution long well-known in California. Polls showed that this piece of legislation won widespread approval across a range of ethnic groups, including 67 percent of whites (who formed 80% of the total electorate) and 50 percent of both Asian Americans and African Americans, with only 23 percent of Latinos voting in favor.

One feature of the campaign in favor of Proposition 187 was the prominent role played by California Governor Pete Wilson, a "moderate" Republican that had lost favor with the California electorate when his term coincided with the worst economic performance in the state since the Great Depression. His support of anti-immigrant positions was a centerpiece of his political comeback in California, where he won reelection from rival Kathleen Brown in November 1994 after coming from as much as 20 percentage points behind. . . .

During the past year, we also have witnessed the publication and media hype of a book which can easily be characterized as our era's equivalent to *The Passing of a Great Race,* the 1916 classic by Madison Grant, the man John Higham has called "intellectually the most important nativist in recent American history." Grant's contemporary counterpart is Peter Brimelow, senior editor at *Forbes* and *National Review.* His *Alien Nation: Common Sense About America's Immigration Disaster* (1995) unabashedly claims that recent immigration is likely "to transform—and ultimately, perhaps, even to destroy . . . the American nation." Within the first ten pages of the book, recent immigrants are blamed for rising crime rates, the health care crisis, lowering overall educational standards, and causing Americans to feel alienated from each other. Unlike other nativists, Brimelow wants to be clear to offer an overtly racial argument: "Race and ethnicity are destiny in American politics," declares Brimelow repeatedly, so all Americans should be concerned about restricting immigration of people who are colored differently than they.

Signs, therefore, point to a resurgence of a nativism unparalleled in this country since the 1920s. From attacks on immigrants in urban unrest to legislative action attacking immigration policies to academic and media discussions resonating the familiar intellectualized examinations of racialized dissonance of the past, today's nativism is as virulent as any that has gone before. Yet this era's nativism, like this era's immigration, has unique characteristics which differentiate it from that which appeared in the early twentieth century at the height of European immigration to the United States. Traditional hostility towards new immigrants has taken on a new meaning when those immigrants are racially identifiable and fit established racial categories in the American psyche. With the increase of immigration from Asia and Latin America, a new American racism has emerged which has no political boundaries or ethnic categorizations. From the left and right of the political spectrum, and from both white and black individuals, this new racism continually threatens to explode in contemporary American society.

One point worth making is that while nativist discourse is often decidedly linked to racial discourse, they are not one and the same, and they often lead in different directions. Part of the problem in separating racism from nativism is the fact that our collective understanding of what constitutes racism has become murkier since the 1960s. . . .

Although many philosophers and theorists have stressed that "race matters" in understanding American society, race in the national imagination has usually been reserved to describe boundaries between whites and blacks. . . . Indeed, the 1990s has produced many important works by noted social commentators that continue to utilize a strick white/black racial dichotomy. Andrew Hacker, author of *Two Nations: Black and White, Separate, Hostile, Unequal,* justifies his title and emphasis by claiming that Asians and Hispanics "find themselves sitting as spectators, while the two prominent players (Blacks and Whites) try to work out how or whether they can coexist with one another." While including voices of Asian Americans and Latinos in his collection of oral histories about "race," Studs Terkel subtitles his 1992 book, *How Blacks and Whites Think and Feel about the American Obsession.*

Asian Americans and Latinos, despite their active presence in American society in the mid-nineteenth century, are depicted as only the latest of immigrant groups to America, and they are described as engaging in patterns which more clearly represent early twentieth-century European immigrant groups than separate racial populations. Hacker, for example, rather than using the actual history of Asian groups or Latinos in the United States, argues that second and subsequent generations of Hispanics and Asians are merging into the "white" category, partly through intermarriage and also by personal achievement and adaptation. No more important figure than Nobel Prize winner Toni Morrison has made this claim recently in the newsmagazine, *Time.* In a special issue dedicated to immigration, Morrison writes:

> . . . All immigrants fight for jobs and space, and who is there to fight but those who have both? As in the fishing ground struggle between Texas and Vietnamese shrimpers, they displace what and whom they can. Although U.S. history is awash in labor battles, political fights and property wars among all religious and ethnic groups, their struggles are

persistently framed as struggles between recent arrivals and blacks. In race talk the move into mainstream America always means buying into the notion of American blacks as the real aliens. Whatever the ethnicity or nationality of the immigrant, his nemesis is understood to be African American.

This perspective, for all its insight into the crucial place of African Americans in American history, ignores the long history of racial discrimination aimed specifically at Asian Americans and Latinos in the United States. National scholars have a responsibility to study the whole nation and its history, but too often East Coast social commentators present a very thin knowledge of U.S. history more than a few miles away from the eastern seaboard. Both "Asians" and "Latinos" have been decidedly constructed as races in American history, long before the decade of the 1960s, and today both these subgroups have become lightning rods for discussions of race, equality, and the meaning of citizenship in contemporary America. . . .

It is time to consider what factors are at work during our current age which inform and promote our own brand of American nativism. Let me suggest three different antiforeign sentiments which mark the racialized nativism of the end of the twentieth century. The first is an extreme antipathy towards non-English languages and a fear that linguistic difference will undermine the American nation. Despite the fact that English has become the premier international language of commerce and communication, fueled by forces as widespread as multinational corporations, the Internet, popular culture and returning migrants, Americans themselves consistently worry that immigrants refuse to learn English and intend to undermine the preeminence of that language within American borders. Captured by statewide "English Only" proposals, which began in California but spread quickly across the nation, this fear seems to emanate from Americans' own linguistic shortcomings and their feeling of alienation from the discourse—be it personal, on the job, or on the radio—that monolingualism creates.

A second fear is one directly tied into issues of multiculturalism and affirmative action. Like papist conspiracy theories, this fear involves the uneasy belief that racialized immigrants take advantage of, in the words of Michael Lind, "a country in which racial preference entitlements and multicultural ideology encourage them to retain their distinct racial and ethnic identities." Going beyond the denial of white privilege in contemporary U.S. society, this sentiment directly believes that contrived, misguided, and sometimes secretive government policies have tilted against white people in the 1990s. Though tied to a general antipathy towards people of color, the place of immigrants and those perceived as racially connected to Latino and Asian immigrants heighten the nature of some of these fears. Even some pro-affirmative action activists bemoan the extension of programs to nonblacks, having equated the history of U.S. racism as that directed against only one racial group incorrectly defined as wholly nonimmigrant. These programs, then, are deemed to be un-American, not only because they contradict America's supposed commitment to equality of opportunity, but also because they are literally favoring "non-Americans" in their results. While invoking the name of the CORE national director in the early 1960s, Lind writes:

> One wonders what James Farmer, the patron saint of quotas, would have said, if he had been told, in 1960, that by boycotting Northern corporations until they hired fixed numbers of black Americans, he was inspiring a system whose major beneficiaries would

ultimately be, not only well-to-do white women, but immigrants and the descendants of immigrants who, at the time of his struggles, were living in Mexico, Cuba, Salvador, Honduras, and Guatemala.

A third antiforeign sentiment has emerged in the 1990s, embodied in California's Proposition 187, which is quite unique and has not been seen since the Great Depression. Current anti-immigrant rhetoric focuses on the drain of public resources by immigrants, both legal and illegal, particularly their utilization of welfare, education and health care services. Unlike nativist calls which center around immigrants taking jobs from citizens, this sentiment feeds into stereotypes of nonworking loafers, particularly targeting women who supposedly come to the United States to give birth and sustain their families from the "generous" welfare state. . . . Even when presented with evidence that immigrants are less likely to seek out government assistance than citizens, today's nativists scoff at the data and the researchers, like 187 proponent Harold Ezell who retorted to one study showing immigrant under-utilization of government-sponsored medical programs by saying, "He's obviously never been to any of the emergency rooms in Orange County to see who's using them—it's non-English speaking young people with babies." . . . The notion that immigrants are now coming to the United States to take advantage of welfare, health and education benefits has led directly to federal legislation which allows states to ban such assistance to even legal immigrants, and this has enabled Governor Wilson to mandate such cut-offs in California.

Although cultural antipathies are often at work in producing fear of newcomers, more often than not economic fears of competition have also played a critical role. Nativism has always cut across political lines, finding adherents on both the right and left. . . . Today's nativists similarly stretch across the political spectrum, from rightwingers like Pat Buchanan, to political "moderates" like Pete Wilson, to self-proclaimed liberals like Michael Lind.

What binds these individuals together is a profound sense of the decline of the American nation. With the rise of nativism since 1965, we are once again witnessing a defensive nationalism in the wake of profound economic restructuring. In place of a period of modernization which pushed the U.S. agricultural economy towards wide-spread industrial production, we are now witnessing rapid deindustrialization, the rise of a service and high tech economy, and the worldwide movement of capital which undercuts the ability of American unions to protect U.S. jobs. This economic trans-formation, coupled with antagonistic government policies, has certainly undermined central cities in the United States and made for fertile ground for nativist sentiments.

Indeed, underlying much of the frustration of the Los Angeles riot participants was the collapse of the inner-city economy, the negative flipside of the new "Pacific Rim" global economy. Los Angeles had lost 150,000 manufacturing jobs in the previous three years, and each of these jobs were estimated to take another three associated jobs with them. The new jobs which were created were disproportion-ately low-wage and dead-end forms of employment; in fact, 40 percent of all jobs created in Los Angeles from 1979 to 1989 paid less than $15,000 a year. Most of these jobs were taken by recent immigrants to the area, leaving African Americans few viable options for secure employment. The average earnings of employed black men fell 24 percent from 1973 to 1989, and unemployment swelled to record levels in the inner city. Middle-income Los Angeles was rapidly disappearing, leaving little opportunity for anyone to move up the economic ladder. This inequality was also highly racialized; the median household net worth for Anglos in the city in 1991 was $31,904, while only $1,353 for non-Anglos. . . .

It is clear that we are in a period of economic transformation which can and should be compared to the period of industrialization that occurred a century ago and that has provided the social context for the rise of nativism in the United States that occurred in both periods. Yet today's economic transformation is intimately tied to an economic globalization propelled by multinational corporations and an age where capital and information flows relatively freely across national borders. From 1890 to the 1920s, the industrial transformation which changed the American economy and fueled international migration led to a breaking down of local community control towards a national interdependency which propelled Americans to "search for order" in new and varied ways. Not only did bureaucracy and science rise to provide this national order, but so did immigration restriction and scientific racism emerge to provide ideological comfort to Americans in search of a glue to keep together a nation undergoing fundamental social and economic change.

Many Americans have been shielded since World War II from the convulsions of the international economic order by the enormous strength of the U.S. economy, and liberal policies of inclusion have been crafted which assume the continuation of this extraordinary growth. Most important in coming to terms with the complexities of race, immigration and nativism in the late twentieth century is a perspective which can deal with the multiple meanings of race and equality in American society in an age of liberal political retrenchment and widespread economic restructuring. During the Reagan/Bush administrations, and the . . . era of Republican ascendancy in Congress, hard-fought victories in racial and economic policy were and are continually threatened with extinction. In addition, supposedly "race-neutral" policies, such as tax reform and subsidies to the private sector, have disproportionally and adversely affected racial minorities.

Yet increasingly we must account for the fact that at least the Reagan/Bush era did not see a reversal of government spending despite all the rhetoric, but instead witnessed its redirection towards wealthy and corporate interests and away from long-term investment in education, infrastructure and safety nets for the poor. This "trickle-down" theory of social advancement has become the biggest failure of the 1980s, and it has left in its wake a sizable, disgruntled white electorate, one disaffected with politics that clamors for "change" at every turn. This group helped give the White House to the Democrats in 1992, handed large numbers of votes to Ross Perot, and offered the Republican Party a majority in both houses of Congress for the first time in thirty years in 1994. In this setting, one in which expectations of newfound prosperity grow with every change of political power, a scapegoat must be found amidst the citizenry that can be blamed for delaying the promised economic security. For many Americans in our era, the poor, especially the black poor, have served this role of scapegoat; increasingly, however, that role is being transferred to or combined with the blaming of the immigrant.

While the industrial economy was being sent through convulsions over the past thirty years, Americans produced largely cultural explanations for structural social problems. The demonization of black families, for example, served for white Americans as a plausible justification for the economic backwardness of African

Americans, despite affirmative action and civil rights. Instead of focusing on the ravages of deindustrialization in both black and white communities, white Americans increasingly revived traditional stereotypes of black laziness. While these racialized beliefs were no longer acceptable public discourse in the post-civil rights era, researchers who take anonymous polls can still ferret out extensive negative race stereotyping rampant in the white community.

Indeed, it seems to me that cultural beliefs in innate difference have worked together with structural forces of inequality to frame (and hide) discussions of white privilege. Literary scholar Eric Lott has argued that attitudes towards blackness are shaped by white self-examination and insecurity, rather than by the realities of African-American life. Indeed, contemporary white perceptions of blacks probably tell us more about the dangers of being "white" in this era than about strongly held beliefs regarding black inferiority. In fact, it is the language of liberal individualism that keeps many whites from seeking structural explanations for racial inequality. However, liberalism has always been a two-edged sword. When economic conditions become tenuous for whites, meritocratic rhetoric about the rewards of hard work and self-reliance also generates individual anxiety and a fear of personal victimization. Whites who are faced with economic failure or insecurity in spite of their racial privilege become a sure breeding ground for the scapegoating of racial others. This classic projection further obscures the need to acknowledge or understand the structural and economic sources of one's own oppression. . . .

Race, Nation, and the Global Economy

THOMAS C. HOLT

The racial regime of the pre-Fordist era was organized to transport racialized groups to places of labor and to keep them physically in place—whether on slave plantations, in sharecroppers' cabins, in convict labor gangs, or tied to indentured contracts. Resistance, individual and collective, most often took the form of escape from those places. Openings within those spaces for frontal attacks on the system of racial oppression occurred only for brief moments, and then usually in the context of life-and-death struggles among the white ruling classes, the American Civil War and Reconstruction being the most obvious such moment.

The racial regime that evolved in the Fordist era was of a very different sort, involving more-complex constraints but also more diverse possibilities for resistance. A high-powered consumer society could be vulnerable to more diversified and effective attack by a demographic minority. First, a mass-production economy called forth mass-production unions whose vulnerability to unskilled scab labor made them more receptive to black members than the traditional crafts-based unions. Second, the state became a powerful and interested player with business and labor in the management of the national economy, making it a potentially decisive arbitrator of private-sector conflicts in which state or political interests were

Excerpts from Thomas C. Holt, "Race, Nation, and the Global Economy," in *The Problem of Race in the Twenty-first Century* (Cambridge, Mass.: Harvard University Press, 2000), pp. 89–115. Reprinted by permission of the publisher. Copyright © 2000 by the President and Fellows of Harvard College.

perceived to be at stake. Third, mass-consumption outlets and products depended on national markets, making them vulnerable to locally focused but nationally publicized protest campaigns. . . .

Revisiting the Civil Rights Movement a generation later perhaps enables us to see the ways in which it grew out of, or at least found its material for fashioning, an effective resistance in the changes wrought by the Fordist era. Charles Payne and others have detailed many of the social transformations set in motion by the Second World War, tracing them to the grassroots level of specific families and communities. Others have pushed back to the 1930s and to various movements and personalities, like Ella Baker, who later challenged the dominant black male leadership and organizational structures, in the process laying the basis for the emergence of a youth movement of a special character. Baker's biography also reflects, however, the signal impact of the urban spaces and ideological ferment that shaped her own formative years as she literally trained on Harlem streets for the civil rights revolution to come. . . .

The political movement depended in the first instance on the demographic movement to cities, southern as well as northern. The civil rights revolution was born in northern cities and southern towns, not on plantations, which had imprisoned black folk for much of their history in America, first as slaves and then as sharecroppers or leased convicts. . . .

As we all know, the American Civil Rights Movement unfolded not on shop floors but within a social and cultural terrain. Not only did its confrontations emerge at sites of consumption rather than of production, its relation to the labor movement was by turns weak, ambivalent, and hostile. There were many reasons for this lack of convergence: the basic conservatism of American labor, the antileftist purges during the McCarthy era, and the crucial decisions taken to foster a higher standard of living rather than to push for more fundamental social change. For their part, postwar black leaders inherited a well-earned distrust of American labor and, with some notable exceptions, had little personal experience in that arena. . . .

Only in isolated localities did such labor-community alliances unfold, most notably in Memphis in 1967–68, and significantly enough at a time when most observers assumed the Civil Rights Movement was dead. Thus although the U.S. movement put an end to petty apartheid and unleashed the great potential of grassroots communities (some of which was realized or reflected in local and national political campaigns in the ensuing decades), in general its most radical potential was contained. Unable to challenge the political-economic status quo either substantively or conceptually, progressive forces could only fight rearguard actions to defend comparatively limited socioeconomic reforms. At the beginning of the twenty-first century, the social advances won by the 1960s movements are threatened by a broad front of conservative politicians and intellectuals.

Efforts to account for the stalling of progressive change have blamed the socially and financially costly Vietnam War, the backlash of disaffected white working and middle classes, and the shift of focus to the more intractable social problems of northern inner cities. It may be, however, that a broader set of changes framed all these developments, changes that move the discussion beyond the idiosyncrasies of

American political realignments. The downturn in progressive politics coincided with the advent of post-Fordist political-economic developments. . . .

What changed in the late twentieth century that could so profoundly affect movements for social justice and even the very meaning of race?

Obviously, some features of the Fordist era are still quite visible. We still have an economy dominated by multinationals and mass consumption—only even more so. Indeed, our collective economic fate depends on the ever-increasing purchases of automobiles, houses and their furnishings (those closely tracked durable goods). The black role in production via consumption is even more pronounced: Aunt Jemima—a caricature born on the eve of the Fordist era of the 1893 Chicago World's Fair, one in whose bosom the new commerce and the old racial culture were united— has been joined by a plethora of black images and symbols that sell us everything from cars, appliances, and sneakers to getaway vacations. So what's new?

First, since the 1970s, mechanisms for mobilizing capital and productive resources have become more geographically dispersed and yet more institutionally powerful than ever before. Second, the changed geography of economic relations has created new geographies of social and cultural relations as well, quite literally created new spaces of social interaction and imparted new meanings to those relations. . . . [T]he creation of global relations of labor and consumption is to some extent constitutive of the advent of modernity, and, as Du Bois suggested, the Atlantic slave trade formed its nexus. In some ways, the changes set in motion in the late twentieth century can be thought of as the further unfolding of that trend; the old is not entirely effaced, the new never entirely new. And yet, there are also radical changes in the time-space dimension of the contemporary world that taken altogether constitute an epistemic shift of historic proportions.

One of the formative moments for the post-Fordist economy was the late 1960s, when major industries seeking lower labor costs and less state regulation moved parts of their production to offshore sites in developing countries, especially to the Caribbean basin and southeast Asia. Within the developed economies this shift in the locus of part of their production paralleled a significant reduction in industrial labor, generally referred to as "deindustrialization." A short time later the partial breakdown of the Bretton Woods international financial system (with respect to currency exchanges) and a Third World debt crisis set in motion radical changes in how investment capital flows were managed and by whom. New financial service providers emerged and, with them, new technologies and technical expertise that fostered innovations in the mobilization and management of capital.

Central to this new economic nexus was a new sociospatial phenomenon that Saskia Sassen has dubbed "global cities." Preeminent among these were cities like New York, Tokyo, and London that emerged as the service centers for the global economy and enabled a concentration of professional expertise to manage transnational production sites and investment capital flows. These "strategic nodes in the organization of the world economy," as Sassen describes them, brought together new forms of telecommunications and a concentration of complementary professional services (law, accounting, computer programming, and so on) and, with these, created a new internationally linked elite.

Highly paid and highly urbanized, this new elite class of "service workers" required services of its own, leading to the growth of a poor, nonunionized, and largely immigrant working class in those same global cities. Some of these workers are employed in small, sweatshop enterprises making luxury goods for the newly emergent elites. Others are found in the informal economy of household help, gypsy cabdrivers, street vendors, and the like. The immigrants among this group were set in motion toward these global cities by the dislocations prompted by the 1960s and 1970s investments in offshore production in their countries of origin. Much like the industrialization of the early nineteenth century, this one drew women out of traditional economies, first into the wage-labor pools of their native land and then channeled them into immigrant streams and the low and casual wage labor sectors of developed countries. Thus the new service sector and sweatshops in the global cities are strikingly feminized. Like all immigrant groups historically, these newly displaced workers are prone to self-exploitation, often accepting lower wages and worse working conditions than natives or exploiting unpaid family labor in small shops and stores. All of which sets the stage for new racial tensions between the native-born and immigrant workers in those same global cities.

The scale and nature of this new immigration have recast the problem of race in the modern world. Practically every member of the industrialized economic elite of nations—the so-called G-7 countries—has witnessed politically dangerous and sometimes violent xenophobic outbursts against this new class of immigrants. In much of the developed world the boundaries of race and the boundaries of the nation are politically and conceptually intertwined. Racial issues are also issues of national integrity. Unlike in the early twentieth century, however, race no longer follows a color line. The racialized other may well be white and hail from the Caucasus. Nevertheless, as ostensibly indigenous citizens of the G-7 nations watch their birthrates decline, the need for immigrant labor grows and, with it, a collective anxiety about national *and racial* integrity.

Flowing from these material and socioeconomic changes is a palpable change of our contemporary *habitus*. Some years ago David Harvey suggested that there had been "a sea-change in cultural as well as in political-economic practices." He argued that we now literally experience time and space in new ways and that this experience is related to or expressed in a "time-space compression" in the very organization of contemporary capitalism as well as in our cultural forms and practices. Perhaps Harvey's insights can provide a point of departure for our analysis of the implication this new economic nexus held for racial issues.

I suggest . . . that there is a new indeterminacy in our measures of racial phenomena and an inscrutability that confounds our understandings of them—all of which is strikingly congruent with descriptions of the deindustrialized, globalized, service economy in which we now live. As Harvey suggests, it is an economy that gives new meaning to the Shakespearean (and later Marxian) line: "All that is solid melts into air." Not only is capital in some sense "fictive," but corporate ownership—and thus responsibility—can itself disappear at "warp speed" into an opaque cyberspace. The stock-market investment instruments called "derivatives," though much maligned recently, reflect the fragmented, recombinant quality of much modern stock ownership. One may own not actual shares of companies, but shares of the rights to buy or sell their stock or their debts at a given moment, under given conditions.

In the novel *Germinal,* Emile Zola satirized the nineteenth-century French stockholders of an oppressive mining company as self-satisfied bourgeois who clipped their coupons but took no responsibility for how the companies they profited from were managed. Today we might well find it practically impossible to trace the actual links between an individual investor and any specific, material corporate enterprise. Meanwhile corporations spend millions to cultivate an image of social responsibility ("goodwill") in general, while making decisions about downsizing and outsourcing that take no responsibility for any actual living communities.

What work does race do in this political economy? First of all, it is clear that although race may indeed do conceptual work in this economy, blacks-as-a-race have no economic role. Despite the dramatic rise in the number of middle-income blacks and, by historical measures, their visible integration into major institutions of the national life, one of the clearest consequences of the transformed economy has been the massive exclusion of blacks from the *formal* economy. And with that exclusion comes the loss of the standard of living and social securities envisaged for industrial workers under a Fordist regime. . . . [A]t the dawn of the twenty-first century, everybody does *not* have a job. Indeed, whereas under earlier regimes racialization was linked to the mobilization of blacks into productive relations, it is now marked by the exclusion of a significant plurality of black people from productive relations.

Of course, this story—of deindustrialization, the service economy, and the so-called underclass—is by now a familiar one. Less familiar, or at least both complicating and suggesting new approaches to this story, are the new relations between production and consumption, between both of these and the state and the nation, and how all of them figure in the delineation of new social spaces and a new transnational racial regime.

As modes of production and consumption undergo radical change, so too do the roles and responsibilities of the state. First, nation-states have become much less autonomous, and in some ways less powerful, in the face of new information technologies and global capital volatility. Eric Hobsbawm has suggested that the palpable growth of nationalism may well reflect the less visible decline of nation-states as structures around which collective identities can be effectively formed. Indeed, governments have surrendered more and more control to multinational bodies like those established by GATT, the World Bank, and the International Monetary Fund in an effort to gain some leverage over market forces. And rather than disciplining the markets, even "first-world" governments are increasingly disciplined *by* the markets. Thus was France rewarded or punished by the financial markets a few years ago according to how far its government succeeded in reducing social welfare spending. And even the all-powerful United States has from time to time found its credit rating and interest rates somewhat dependent on draconian reductions in its welfare state.

The powers that define our livelihoods are increasingly located in transnational processes and follow different social and moral logics. Thus as Zygmunt Bauman puts it:

> The way in which the world economy operates today (and there is today a genuine world economy) favours state organisms that cannot effectively impose conditions under which economy runs; economy is effectively transnational—and in relation to virtually

any state, big or small, most of the economic assets crucial for the daily life of its population are "foreign." The divorce between political autarchy (real or imaginary) and economic autarchy seems to be irrevocable.

At the dawn of the twenty-first century, not only does everybody not have a job, but the conventional economic wisdom is that it would be bad for the economy if everybody did. Some structural unemployment is necessary, we are told—to keep inflation down. Every interest-rate hike approved by the Federal Reserve gives renewed credence to the old Marxian charge that the welfare of capital depends on maintaining "a reserve army of unemployed."

Other parts of the state apparatus, traditionally more sympathetic to the needs of labor and the poor, are under increasing pressure to withdraw their support. The impact of such policies on the poor are obvious, but the recently emergent black middle class is especially at risk as state functions are retrenched. This historically novel class differentiation within the black population—an upper middle class, a working class, and the so-called underclass—was highly dependent on the expansion of state activity and expenditures under the Fordist regime. Thus the employment of that middle class is heavily concentrated in the public and/or public-contracted sector; and its wealth consists largely of salaries rather than financial assets. A great deal of attention has been given recently to the bifurcation of the American black class experience; that is, that there are historically high levels of both social-economic inclusion *and* exclusion. We might complicate that image by noting the very real vulnerability at both ends of the class structure.

The meanings, anomalies, and ambivalences produced by these transnational pressures are complicated further by the fundamental, continuing changes in our *habitus*—our everyday, lived, built, and perceptual environments. Housing, one of the new terrains of racial confrontation that emerged in the Fordist era, is no longer a simple matter of segregated neighborhoods but of gated communities, a phenomenon of privatized urban space that has emerged in locales as disparate as Los Angeles and São Paulo. Unlike the images from the *Sweet* case and Detroit in the 1950s, however, such communities may well have at least a token black or other minority presence. Are they, by virtue of that fact, any less racial?

Just as Fordism eventually changed the way people lived and how they thought about how they lived, so has/will the post-Fordist social order. Musing over whether the new inequality has produced new social forms, Saskia Sassen concludes that the new global-city elites have embraced an ideology of consumption strikingly different from those found in Fordist-era suburbs. "Style, high prices, and an ultraurban context characterize the new ideology and practice of consumption, rather than functionality, low prices, and suburban settings." Diplomatic historian Walter LaFeber finds a radically new mode of cultural transmission among nations. Cultural influences were once carried across national boundaries by migrants, elite travelers, or a literate readership. Now via television satellites culture moves "with the speed of sound," reaching billions of people in an instant.

In both time and space, local and global venues, the meanings, modalities, and consequences of consumption decisions have fundamentally changed. No longer simply a matter of Henry Ford's workers having the means to buy an automobile or a house to keep the economy purring, consumption now permeates—even regulates perhaps—practically all aspects of social life, including our politics. "Values" and "identities" have become consumables—they are packaged, advertised, and purchased. Our existence has never before been so commodified; our understanding, our knowing never before so dependent on representations of, symbols of putatively underlying realities that are not otherwise apparent; our perceptual universe never before so fragmented and fluid. Our social world is littered with the cultural equivalents of financial "derivatives."

Is it possible that the whole complex, post-Fordist system depends upon this *habitus,* much as the fragmenting, reductive qualities of the computer are necessary to construct a stock market derivative? Our fin-de-siècle political economy simultaneously promotes "homogenization" and "differentiation." It requires each of us individually to desire different goods that signify our distinction and individuality; but it also requires us to accept the same basis of evaluation, the same kind of commodity so that production can be viable.

In a global marketplace, therefore, all commodities are cultural, and they thrive on real and simulated differences—on containable signs of difference, on distinction. A pair of bluejeans, Nike running shoes, Suchard chocolates, a BMW are not just clothing, food, or a means of transportation. Among other things they variously connote American casualness, a virile leisure class, the French "smart" set, well-being and power.

All this suggests that in this post-Fordist world we are more dependent than ever on a veritable "economy of symbols." Of course, the unwritten codes embedded in signs and symbols have always been crucial to our ability to negotiate our way through our everyday worlds. But the material and psychic shocks of the time compression of this era have intensified the process of such symbolic negotiation.

Could it be that in such a marketplace, black bodies—no longer a means of production—have become a means of consumption? Could it be that Michael Jordan, the model for Suchard chocolates, Grace Jones modeling *as an automobile*—or for that matter, Colin Powell—notwithstanding their general attractiveness otherwise can now become meaningful as signs, not despite their blackness but because of it? Could it be that the issue now is less the utter ignorance of other cultures, as in times past, but too great a surface (sound-bite) familiarity; less stereotypes of the other than the voracious consumption of its metonymic parts? It is difficult, perhaps impossible, to answer such questions definitively. Difficult to know even how such propositions might be tested. A closer look at some of the icons of the new economy might help us tease out some of the work that race does.

. . . [I]t might be possible to trace an interesting trajectory from Jack Johnson at the opening of the Fordist era through Joe Louis at its maturation (incidentally Louis also worked in the auto plants of Detroit before turning to professional boxing) down to Michael Jordan today. Already evident in those earlier black sports figures was the tendency to turn them into texts on which the nation could work out its tensions and anxieties—much like the work minstrel shows did in the antebellum era. The articulation of race and consumption was merely emergent in the Johnson-Louis era, however. In the selling of Michael Jordan it has come full circle.

Not only is the Jordan phenomenon rife with the fragmentation and contradiction discussed earlier, it is thoroughly embedded in and reflective of the post-Fordist economy. Notwithstanding the incredible basketball skills, competitive character, and magnetic personality Jordan brings to the mix, his professional success is ultimately built on two powerful multinational capital enterprises—the National Basketball Association and Nike. (And in recent years they, of course, have been built largely on him.) Through the marriage of new communications technology, aggressive capitalist expansion, and image, both of these enterprises flourished in the late twentieth century. The NBA merged television and slick advertising to transform a sport in crisis in the 1980s into a domestic and international cultural and economic marvel in the 1990s. By the peak of Jordan's career in 1997, the number of TV sets per hundred of the world's people had doubled. Consequently, when Jordan announced his retirement from basketball on January 13, 1999, a Japanese newspaper banner headline read: "Jordan Retires! Shock Felt around the World." Although basketball was a minor sport in Japan, Air Jordan sneakers sold for as much as $1,000 a pair and "were collected like jewels."

Nike, meanwhile, though founded in little Beavertown, Oregon, secured its startup capital, made its shoes, and earned most of its profits overseas. Moving from one Asian country to another in search of lower wages, Nike was a veritable archetype of a post-Fordist multinational. In a well-worn pattern, noted earlier, its overseas labor force was heavily feminized; 90 percent of the workers in its Vietnamese plant, for example, were women.

But if Michael Jordan's career was made by Nike's multinational reach, Nike's success was just as surely built on Jordan's image. Indeed, that image, in silhouette, is copyrighted by Nike. Some of the troubling aspects of the enterprises built on Jordan's image are well known. The firm paid Jordan $20 million annually to promote its products, which was more than the total annual wages earned by Indonesian workers who made the shoe. Little girls in those same plants earn the equivalent of under $2 for an eleven-hour day, making shoes that sell for $70 to $150 in the West and that cost $5.60 to make. Michael Jordan is merely a cog—albeit a highly paid cog—in the complex machinery of the post-Fordist economy, however. Through that well-known logo based on the image of his black body soaring through the air is revealed the now intimate connection between a new international political economy, a transnational pattern of consumption, and black identity. Jordan, it has been observed, "was an image much like the Swoosh." Or, as Phil Knight, the entrepreneur behind Nike's success, explains it: "You can't explain much in 60 seconds, but when you show Michael Jordan, you don't have to. People already know a lot about him. It's that simple." What Jordan sold was not just a product but a life-style. "Just do it!" is now familiar to youth across the globe and needs no translation.

What can it mean that kids all over the world, in many different languages, can say, "I want to be like Mike"? Does this phenomenon still lie within the orbit of the racial? Just posing the question might be startling to some because Jordan is widely celebrated as a figure who transcends race. With some poignancy his friend and fellow basketball great, Julius Irving, observed that Jordan seemed "less a person than something of a 24-hour commodity." The conjunction of those two observations—a person who transcends race; a commodified personality—may well speak to a central issue in the social transformation that has engaged us. What can it mean that a commodified Jordan "transcends" race when just a few years earlier the premier black professional players were routinely denied endorsement contracts because it was assumed that their endorsements would not sell products to whites? Indeed what does it mean to transcend race in a sport from which blacks were first excluded and then had their eventual success attributed to racial biology?

Certainly, nineteenth- and early-twentieth-century meanings of race and racism are not sufficient to explain such phenomena. One of the standard definitions of racism assumes that it is always a response to an alleged inferiority of the racialized other, but contemporary racial images often refer merely to difference, exoticism, and sometimes even to an ostensible superiority.

And with that observation we can return to that other enigmatic icon of the new racial regime, Colin Powell. Powell's successful, if brief, courtship of American public opinion has also been attributed to his ability to transcend race—the "un-Negro." But again, what can it mean to claim that Powell transcends race in a political culture that is saturated with racially coded images and language? Just three years before Powell's phantom candidacy unfolded, a political observer began an analysis of American politics with the following characterization: "considerations of race are now deeply embedded in the strategy and tactics of politics, in competing concepts of the function and responsibility of government, and in each voter's conceptual structure of moral and partisan identity."

But leaving aside the poisonous racial climate in which Powell's potential candidacy unfolded, any claims to racial transcendence beg the question: Why Powell? If the answer is character or the appeal of his biography, then both his race and the overcoming of racism are part of the story. Or, alternatively, it is a life story—like Jordan's—ostensibly in which race "didn't matter." Either way, a crucial "truth" about the national character and identity appears to be affirmed—its justice, its fairness, its color-blindness. Though invisible, race does its work. It is conceivable that the need for that work to be done reflects the difficulty in defining and sustaining an integrated, psychologically satisfying identity under contemporary social conditions. As at other moments in American history, then, race is the medium through which other fundamental conflicts in the social system are "lived" and "fought through."

It remains to be seen whether some of this work that race does today, and will no doubt continue to do, is relatively innocuous or harmful. Which way it cuts may depend on whether and how the relatively benign images of the Michael Jordans and Colin Powells of the world articulate with—or perhaps are actually dependent on—those of ghetto youth and "welfare queens."

This issue may well be the key to unraveling the meaning of race in the twenty-first century. In sorting through all this we might again take note of the Geertzian observation that a game is often more than merely a game. Likewise it may be that symbols cannot always be confined to the safe terrain of the merely symbolic. So mundane an aspect of our everyday lives as the clothing we wear, whose labels are sewn onto the *outside* of the garment, suggests the pervasive link between symbol and the hard currency of the economic. When ghetto kids kill each other for a pair of brand-name sneakers, it brings home that this economy of symbols is not just serious; it's deadly serious.

. . . Even as I emphasize the novelty of the present moment in history—a new political economy and a new racial regime—I am also cognizant of shards of our racial past sedimented in this brave new world. Take the slogan of the Memphis movement that unfolded in the twilight days of the civil rights era, its possibility for catching and shaping the winds of change nationally perhaps snuffed out with the life of Martin Luther King Jr. on that fateful balcony. In 1968 the Memphis workers marched under the banner—"I am a man." The slogan strikingly echoes the one emblazoned on nineteenth-century abolitionist banners protesting the slave trade. For Memphis workers it invoked the issue of identity, indeed a claim—in the broadest terms—to citizenship, to membership in the polity as the covering rationale for what was essentially a labor action. For victims of the slave trade it was a claim to, a plea for, recognition of a common humanity.

In each of these senses it resonates yet again with the condition of the most recent victims of the racialization process in this global economy. I mentioned . . . that sweatshop workers in our era are to be found not just in East Asia but also in East Los Angeles. I was referring to a case brought to light a few years ago of Mexican and Thai women laboring under slavelike conditions in sweatshops in Los Angeles, making goods for the luxury consumer market. The word "slavelike" in this case is not hyperbole. Once discovered, these workers brought suit under laws based on the Thirteenth Amendment to the Constitution—the one outlawing slavery. They are not the last such workers to be discovered in such straits; and all such discoveries continue to raise the issue of how race, labor, and citizenship are to be articulated in the twenty-first century.

In some sense, perhaps, these poignant images take us full circle from the economy of symbols to a hard-edged political economy—or more accurately perhaps to where race and political economy join up with the superconsumption of our post-Fordist era. But we have also, in some more disturbing sense, returned to those ships plying their way across the Atlantic laden with human cargo—humans shorn of a place in a bewilderingly transformed world. Perhaps, more than ever, we can feel—and in more than simply a historical sense—our fate linked with theirs.

✦ *F U R T H E R   R E A D I N G*

Alba, Richard, and Victor Nee. *Remaking the American Mainstream: Assimilation and Contemporary Immigration* (2003).

Archdeacon, Thomas J. *Becoming American: An Ethnic History* (1983).

Barkan, Elliott R. *And Still They Come: Immigrants and American Society, 1920s to the 1990s* (1996).

———, ed. *A Nation of Peoples: A Sourcebook on America's Multicultural Heritage* (1999).

Barone, Michael. *The New Americans: How the Melting Pot Can Work Again* (2001).

Bean, Frank D., and Gillian Stevens. *Newcomers and the Dynamics of Diversity* (2003).

Borjas, George. *Friends or Strangers? The Impact of Immigrants on the U.S. Economy* (1990).

Briggs, Vernon, Jr., and Stephen Moore. *Still an Open Door? U.S. Immigration Policy and the American Economy* (1994).

Brimelow, Peter. *Alien Nation: Common Sense about America's Immigration Disaster* (1995).

Chavez, Linda. *Out of the Barrio: Toward a New Politics of Hispanic Assimilation* (1992).

Daniels, Roger. *Coming to America: A History of Immigration and Ethnicity in American Life* (1990).

Dinnerstein, Leonard, Roger L. Nichols, and David M. Reimers. *Natives and Strangers: Blacks, Indians and Immigrants in America* (1990).

Fitzgerald, Keith. *The Face of the Nation: Immigration, the State, and National Identity* (1996).

Fuchs, Lawrence. *The American Kaleidoscope: Race, Ethnicity, and the Civic Culture* (1990).

Gitlin, Todd. *The Twilight of Common Dreams: Why America Is Wracked by Culture Wars* (1995).

Glazer, Nathan. *We Are All Multiculturalists Now* (1997).

Hacker, Andrew. *Two Nations: Black and White, Separate, Hostile, Unequal* (1992).

Hollinger, David A. *Postethnic America: Beyond Multiculturalism* (1995).

Holt, Thomas C. *The Problem of Race in the Twenty-first Century* (2000).

Hughes, Robert. *The Culture of Complaint: The Fraying of America* (1993).

Huntington, Samuel P. *Who Are We: The Challenges to America's National Identity* (2004).

Ignatieff, Michael. *Blood and Belonging: Journeys into the New Nationalism* (1994).

Jacobson, Matthew Frye. *Whiteness of a Different Color: European Immigrants and the Alchemy of Race* (1998).

Jacoby, Tamar, ed. *Reinventing the Melting Pot: The New Immigrants and What It Means to Be American* (2004).

Johnston, William B., and Arnold Packer. *Workforce 2000: Work and Workers for the Twenty-First Century* (1987).

Kessner, Thomas, and Betty Boyd Caroli. *Today's Immigrants, Their Stories: A New Look at the Newest Immigrants* (1981).

Kinder, Donald R., and Lynn M. Sanders, eds. *Divided by Color: Racial Politics and Democratic Ideals* (1997).

Lamm, Richard, and Gary Imhof. *The Immigration Time Bomb: The Fragmenting of America* (1985).

Lind, Michael. *The Next American Nation: The New Nationalism and the Fourth American Revolution* (1995).

Lusane, Clarence. *Race in the Global Era: African Americans at the Millennium* (1997).

Massey, Douglas S., and Nancy A. Denton. *American Apartheid: Segregation and the Making of the Underclass* (1993).

Miller, John J. L., ed. *Strangers at Our Gate: Immigration in the 1990s* (1994).

Mills, Nicolaus, ed. *Arguing Immigration: The Debate over the Changing Face of America* (1994).

Minow, Martha. *Making All the Difference: Inclusion, Exclusion, and American Law* (1991).

———. *Not Only for Myself: Identity, Politics, and the Law* (1999).

Ono, Kent A., and John M. Sloop. *Shifting Borders: Rhetoric, Immigration, and California's Proposition 187* (2002).

Reed, Ishmael, ed. *Multiamerica: Essays on Cultural Wars and Cultural Peace* (1997).

Reimers, David M. *Unwelcome Strangers: American Identity and the Turn Against Immigration* (1998).

Roediger, David R. *The Wages of Whiteness: Race and the Making of the American Working Class* (1996).

Rose, Peter I. *Tempest-Tost: Race, Immigration, and the Dilemmas of Diversity* (1997).

Schlesinger, Arthur, Jr. *The Disuniting of America: Reflections on a Muticultural Society* (1992).

Simon, Julian L. *The Economic Consequences of Immigration* (1999).

Simon, Rita J., and Susan H. Alexander. *The Ambivalent Welcome: Print Media, Public Opinion, and Immigration* (1992).

Smith, James P., and Barry Edmonston, eds. *The New Americans: Economic, Demographic, and Fiscal Effects of Immigration* (1997).

Smith, Peter, and Joe R. Feagin, eds. *The Bubbling Cauldron: Race, Ethnicity and the Urban Crisis* (1995).

Sollors, Werner. *Beyond Ethnicity: Consent and Descent in American Culture* (1986).

Spencer, Jon Michael. *New Colored People: The Mixed-Race Movement in America* (1997).

Steinberg, Stephen, ed. *The Ethnic Myth: Race, Ethnicity, and Class in America* (1999).

Suro, Roberto. *Strangers Among Us: How Latino Immigration Is Transforming America* (1998).

Takaki, Ronald. *A Different Mirror: A History of Multicultural America* (1993).

Tichenor, Daniel J. *Dividing Lines: The Politics of Immigration Control in America* (2002).

Ungar, Sanford J. *Fresh Blood: The New American Immigrants* (1995).

Vecoli, Rudolph J., ed. *Gale Encyclopedia of Multicultural America* (1995).

Walzer, Michael. *What It Means to Be an American* (1992).

CHAPTER
13

Politics and Political Culture
in "Postmodern" America

The politics of the late twentieth and early twenty-first centuries were shaped by the continued disintegration of the Democratic New Deal coalition and the growing strength of a Republican-forged coalition of social and business conservatives. During the 1990s, so-called "new Democrats" led by President Bill Clinton sought to replace their party's older and shrinking industrial and agricultural bases with a new, if unwieldy, coalition of women, minorities, social liberals, and technological progressives. Both the Democratic and Republican parties paid obeisance to older voters, whose ranks were swollen by aging baby boomers; both parties sought to position themselves with younger voters from Generation X (as the children of the baby boomers were sometimes called); and both tried to come to terms with the ways in which globalization was reorganizing the contours of domestic politics. Although Bill Clinton won election in 1992 by stressing domestic issues—"It's the economy, stupid," proclaimed Democratic party strategist James Carville—the nation's political agenda was dominated by cultural issues—gun control, abortion, and gay rights—as well as by issues such as crime and welfare reform that were invariably discussed in terms heavily freighted with cultural resonances. In 1994, Republicans captured control of Congress by promising a new "Contract with America," and the ensuing struggle between Clinton and the Republicans became so acrimonious that it even led to a brief shutdown of the government in the winter of 1995–1996. Although Clinton would win reelection in 1996, Congress would remain in the hands of the GOP throughout the years that followed.

In 2000, George W. Bush, the governor of Texas and son of former President George H. W. Bush, won the presidency in the nation's first disputed election since 1876. The September 11, 2001, attacks on the World Trade Center and the Pentagon, followed by wars in Afghanistan and Iraq, once again pushed national security to the forefront, assuring Bush's reelection in 2004, as well as continued Republican control of Congress.

Meanwhile, deep beneath the surface clash of political parties, powerful currents continued to reshape the fundamental character of American politics and *civic life. Chief among these were the continued decline of political parties and other, older intermediary institutions; the rise of more narrowly segmented and professionally organized interest groups; the increasingly dominant role of the media in campaigning; and the associated rise of a professional class of campaign managers, fundraisers, media consultants, and pollsters. By the beginning of the new millennium, commentators would wonder if citizenship had been replaced by consumption in the "fast world" of the new century; if government (and political democracy itself) had become irrelevant in a world ruled by distant markets; if a corrosive individualism had irrevocably eroded the bonds of community on which politics had been traditionally erected; and if, in an increasingly media- and information-driven world, those who controlled the media and the technologies of information had become the new and dominant class in American politics and society.*

✦ D O C U M E N T S

In Document 1, from his speech accepting the Democratic nomination for the presidency, Bill Clinton attacks the record of Republican incumbent George H. W. Bush and sounds the "new Democratic" themes of economic growth and social inclusion. Within a year, however, his presidency was stalled. The issue of gay rights in the military (Document 2) sidetracked the administration initially and mobilized the president's opponents—particularly social conservatives and others in the military. New health care legislation, which Clinton had hoped to make a centerpiece of his first administration, was defeated by a welter of powerful interest groups, by the federal deficit he had inherited from the Republicans, and by the ineptness of his own administration. Capitalizing on Clinton's miscues, Republicans, led by Newt Gingrich (R-Ga.), captured control of Congress by promising a new "Contract with America" (Document 3). Clinton deftly turned the Republican victory to his own advantage, depicting the new congressional leadership as partisan extremists, while at the same time capturing conservative issues such as deficit reduction and welfare reform as his own. Although liberals were dismayed by Clinton's abandonment of traditional liberalism (Document 4), the president's strategy paid rich political dividends in the 1996 presidential campaign, when he easily defeated Republican candidate Robert Dole.

The scandal involving Clinton and White House intern Monica Lewinsky, which became public during the winter of 1997–1998, fused cultural issues with media frenzy and led to an effort to impeach the president. Although there was a long history of sexual scandals in American history—such as attacks on Thomas Jefferson in 1802 and Grover Cleveland in 1884—most twentieth-century journalists were noticeably reluctant to write about what they knew of presidential indiscretions. All of this changed in the wake of Watergate and the more permissive standards that accompanied the cultural changes of the 1960s and 1970s. Document 5, from the Report of Special Prosecutor Kenneth Starr, detailing President Clinton's relations with Lewinsky, is itself a telling example of the new notoriety given to sexual scandal. Cultural values loomed large in the nation's politics. Indeed, by the end of the twentieth century, political commentators frequently invoked the image of an America sharply divided between conservative "red" states and liberal "blue" states. Document 6 suggests that income, education, and other factors divided upscale cosmopolitan states from poorer, rural conservative states. Of course, other commentators and social scientists debunked such sweeping generalizations, insisting that most Americans shared moderate political views; and that "polarization," insofar as it existed, was largely the product of competing elites and the media. Certainly politicians and advocacy groups paid careful attention to cultural issues and how they were framed—for example, whether someone who supported a woman's right to abortion was characterized as "pro-abortion" or "pro-choice," or someone who opposed abortion was described as "anti-abortion" or "pro-life."

Both Clinton and his successor, George W. Bush, were extremely sensitive to the role played by the nation's media—and not just traditional institutions such as newspapers, magazines, and the major television networks, but also new phenomena such as talk radio, twenty-four-hour news channels such as CNN, and the Internet. Together with the parties, the media, interest groups, and lobbyists became increasingly important in shaping the nation's politics and political culture. In Document 7, newspaper columnist Jeffrey H. Birnbaum reports on the role played by such groups in determining the political agenda in the nation's capital.

1. Presidential Candidate Bill Clinton Promises a "New Covenant," 1992

We meet at a special moment in history, you and I. The Cold War is over. Soviet communism has collapsed and our values—freedom, democracy, individual rights, free enterprise—they have triumphed all around the world. And yet, just as we have won the Cold War abroad, we are losing the battles for economic opportunity and social justice here at home.

Now that we have changed the world, it's time to change America.

I have news for the forces of greed and the defenders of the status quo: Your time has come and gone. It's time for a change in America.

Tonight 10 million of our fellow Americans are out of work, tens of millions more work harder for lower pay. The incumbent President says that unemployment always goes up a little before a recovery begins, but unemployment only has to go up by one more person before a real recovery can begin. And Mr. President, you are that man.

This election is about putting power back in your hands and putting government back on your side. It's about putting people first. . . .

The thing that makes me angriest about what has gone wrong in the last 12 years is that our government has lost touch with our values, while our politicians continue to shout about them. I'm tired of it!

I was raised to believe the American Dream was built on rewarding hard work. But we have seen the folks in Washington turn the American ethic on its head.

For too long those who play by the rules and keep the faith have gotten the shaft, and those who cut corners and cut deals have been rewarded.

Excerpts from William J. Clinton, Acceptance Speech to the Democratic National Convention, New York, July 16, 1992. Online at http://www.presidency.ucsb.edu/shownomination.php?convid=7.

People are working harder than ever, spending less time with their children, working nights and weekends at their jobs instead of going to PTA and Little League or Scouts. And their incomes are still going down. Their taxes are still going up. And the costs of health care, housing and education are going through the roof.

Meanwhile, more and more of our best people are falling into poverty even though they work 40 hours a week.

Our people are pleading for change, but government is in the way. It has been hijacked by privileged private interests. It has forgotten who really pays the bills around here. It has taken more of your money and given you less in return. We have got to go beyond the brain-dead politics in Washington and give our people the kind of government they deserve, a government that works for them. . . .

Listen. Hear me now. I am not pro-abortion; I am pro-choice, strongly. I believe this difficult and painful decision should be left to the women of America.

I hope the right to privacy can be protected and we will never again have to discuss this issue on political platforms. But I am old enough to remember what it was like before *Roe v. Wade,* and I do not want to return to the time when we made criminals of women and their doctors.

Jobs, education, health care—these are not just commitments from my lips; they are the work of my life.

Our priorities must be clear; we will put our people first again. . . .

Now, I don't have all the answers, but I do know the old ways don't work. Trickledown economics has sure failed. And big bureaucracies, both private and public, they've failed too.

That's why we need a new approach to government, a government that offers more empowerment and less entitlement. More choices for young people in the schools they attend—in the public schools they attend. And more choices for the elderly and for people with disabilities and the long-term care they receive. A government that is leaner, not meaner; a government that expands opportunity, not bureaucracy; a government that understands that jobs must come from growth in a vibrant and vital system of free enterprise.

I call this approach the New Covenant, a solemn agreement between the people and their government based not simply on what each of us can take but what all of us must give to our Nation.

We offer our people a new choice based on old values. We offer opportunity. We demand responsibility. We will build an American community again. The choice we offer is not conservative or liberal. In many ways, it is not even Republican or Democratic. It is different. It is new. And it will work. It will work because it is rooted in the vision and the values of the American people. . . .

And so I say again: Where there is no vision, America will perish. What is the vision of our New Covenant?

An America with millions of new jobs and dozens of new industries, moving confidently toward the 21st century.

An America that says to entrepreneurs and businesspeople: We will give you more incentives and more opportunity than ever before to develop the skills of your workers and to create American jobs and American wealth in the new global economy. . . .

An America in which the doors of colleges are thrown open once again to the sons and daughters of stenographers and steelworkers. . . .

An America in which health care is a right, not a privilege. . . .

An America in which middle-class incomes, not middle-class taxes, are going up.

An America, yes, in which the wealthiest few, those making over $200,000 a year, are asked to pay their fair share. . . .

An America where we end welfare as we know it. . . .

An America with the world's strongest defense, ready and willing to use force when necessary.

An America at the forefront of the global effort to preserve and protect our common environment—and promoting global growth.

An America that will not coddle tyrants, from Baghdad to Beijing.

An America that champions the cause of freedom and democracy from Eastern Europe to Southern Africa—and in our own hemispheres, in Haiti and Cuba.

The end of the Cold War permits us to reduce defense spending while still maintaining the strongest defense in the world, but we must plow back every dollar of defense cuts into building American jobs right here at home. I know well that the world needs a strong America, but we have learned that strength begins at home.

But the New Covenant is about more than opportunities and responsibilities for you and your families. It's also about our common community.

Tonight every one of you knows deep in your heart that we are too divided. It is time to heal America.

And so we must say to every American: Look beyond the stereotypes that blind us. We need each other—all of us—we need each other. We don't have a person to waste, and yet for too long politicians have told the most of us that are doing all right that what's really wrong with America is the rest of us—them.

Them, the minorities. Them, the liberals. Them, the poor. Them, the homeless. Them, the people with disabilities. Them, the gays.

We've gotten to where we've nearly them'ed ourselves to death. Them, and them, and them.

But this is America. There is no them. There is only us.

One nation, under God, indivisible, with liberty and justice for all.

That is our Pledge of Allegiance, and that's what the New Covenant is all about. . . .

2. "Gays in the Military" Prompts Mobilization of Conservatives, 1993

Atlanta, Jan. 31—Emboldened by the furor over President Clinton's proposal to allow homosexuals in the military, conservative and evangelical Christian groups are furiously organizing, raising money and looking ahead to the battles to come against the first Democratic President in 12 years.

From Peter Applebome, "Gay Issue Mobilizes Conservatives Against Clinton," *New York Times,* February 1, 1993. Copyright © 1993 by The New York Times Co. Reprinted with permission.

"It's a bonanza for building organizations and raising money; the fund-raising letters are already in the mail," said John Green, a professor at the University of Akron who is an expert on the Christian right. "I've been talking to several of these people, and they all say that they could not have scripted Bill Clinton's first weeks any better."

Some of these groups have made homosexual issues their main focus for organizing and fund-raising over the past year. For moral traditionalists, many of them evangelical Christians, homosexuality is a more clear-cut issue even than abortion, Professor Green said, because it is explicitly forbidden in the Bible. And when the issue was fused to conservative views on the military and the objections of the nation's military leadership, it attained extraordinary emotional power, both for committed conservatives and for Americans in the political mainstream.

The issue is so potent that some conservatives, like Randall Terry, the anti-abortion crusader, are expanding their activities to become part of it.

"Clinton has done us a great favor," said Mr. Terry, who calls his efforts to mobilize opinion on the issue "the resistance." "This is going to help us mobilize people to take action for the next four years."

Because the question of homosexuals in the military is so volatile, some experts doubt that last week's furor is indicative of broader problems Mr. Clinton could face. Todd Gitlin, a sociologist at the University of California at Berkeley, said the current furor was a reminder of how split Americans were on social issues, but he added that he did not expect cultural issues to overwhelm economic ones.

"I wouldn't exaggerate the degree to which he's landed in a storm here," he said. "These may be just gusts."

Still, even liberal groups like People for the American Way concede the public opinion often flows toward the conservative side on issues like homosexual rights. No one doubts that Mr. Clinton won by focusing on the economy and by coming across as a moderate, bus-riding new-style Democrat rather than because voters endorsed liberal social policies.

And some experts say the intensity of the feelings last week reflects the depth of the cultural divide in America and the perils it raises for Democratic Presidents, in an era when no Democrat from north of the Mason-Dixon line has been elected President since 1960.

Professor Green, who is director of the Ray Bliss Institute of Applied Politics at the University of Akron, said: "This is a very conservative country, and cultural liberalism is a loser in American politics. There are more cultural conservatives than cultural liberals, and their ability to mobilize should not be underestimated. You've got 300,000 to 400,000 churches out there, and there's nothing like that on the left."

Strong Conservative Instincts

As the departing Republican national chairman, Richard N. Bond, made clear last week when he warned his party against zealotry, the kind of strident conservatism that many saw at the Republican Convention last year can be as unpopular as liberal excesses. But poll results indicate just how strong the conservative instincts of the American people remain.

When voters leaving polling booths in November were asked whether it was more important for government to encourage traditional family values or tolerance for nontraditional families, 70 percent said traditional families. Although most Americans oppose efforts to ban abortion, a *New York Times*/CBS News poll in October found that only 43 percent of respondents felt abortion should be generally available to all who want it. Thirty-seven percent favored stricter limits than are in effect now, and 16 percent favored an abortion ban.

Although polls show Americans feel homosexuals should not be discriminated against in hiring, they show a majority of Americans say homosexuality is not an acceptable life style and more Americans feel homosexual relations should be illegal than think they should be legal. Other polls have indicated that more than three-quarters of Americans favor prayer in school and the death penalty.

"Democrats make a mistake in thinking that because the social issues won't hurt the Democrats when there's a failed Republican economic manager in the White House, that those same issues can be ignored when you've got a Democrat in the White House," said Kevin Phillips, the maverick Republican political analyst. "What you've got working now calls up the ghosts of 1972 and of things that don't resonate in the subdivisions and malls."

A Promise of More to Come

Conservative groups are looking toward similar cultural issues they say could come up repeatedly during the Clinton Presidency, as the gay issue did last week. "This is a train wreck for Bill Clinton, and there will be more to come," said the Rev. Louis Sheldon, chairman of the conservative Traditional Values Coalition, based in Anaheim, Calif., which includes 25,000 churches.

Conservatives cite the coming debate over extending the 1964 Civil Rights Act, which is likely to include proposals to protect homosexuals; curriculum disputes around the country like the one in New York City over the Children of the Rainbow curriculum; National Endowment for the Arts financing for controversial artists; fetal tissue research and other issues as ones with the potential to polarize Americans on value-laden issues.

Not everyone, including some Republicans, is convinced that such issues need be losers for the Democrats. Vince Breglio, a Republican poll taker, said that despite the uproar over the military ban, the divide in American life had narrowed sharply since the 1960's. With their emphasis on meeting the social and economic needs of families, jobs, health care and education, the Democrats may be more in touch with the values people really care about than the Republicans, he said.

"If you limit it to a more restrictive set of social values, I would say the Republicans come out looking pretty good," he said. "But on the broader cross-section of cultural and economic values, I would have to say the Democrats strike a more resonating chord."

Even the most ardent conservatives say it's dangerous to read too much into a President's first two weeks. But many also say this week's uproar was neither manufactured nor a fluke.

"I think these cultural issues have an enormous opportunity to divide Clinton from this country, deeply and perhaps irretrievably," said Karl Rove, a Republican political consultant in Texas. "It's a marathon, and he can make a couple of mistakes. One would be to start too fast. He didn't do that. Another would be to start running in the wrong direction. I think he's making that mistake."

3. The Republican "Contract with America," 1994

The Contract's Core Principles

The Contract with America is rooted in 3 core principles:

Accountability—The government is too big and spends too much, and Congress and unelected bureaucrats have become so entrenched [as] to be unresponsive to the public they are supposed to serve. The GOP contract restores accountability to government.

Responsibility—Bigger government and more federal programs usurp personal responsibility from families and individuals. The GOP contract restores a proper balance between government and personal responsibility.

Opportunity—The American Dream is out of the reach of too many families because of burdensome government regulations and harsh tax laws. The GOP contract restores the American dream.

The Contract

As Republican Members of the House of Representatives and as citizens seeking to join that body we propose not just to change its policies, but even more important, to restore the bonds of trust between the people and their elected representatives.

That is why, in the era of official evasion and posturing, we offer instead a detailed agenda for national renewal, a written commitment with no fine print.

This year's election offers the chance, after four decades of one-party control, to bring to the House a new majority that will transform the way Congress works. That historic change would be the end of government that is too big, too intrusive, and too easy with the public's money. It can be the beginning of a Congress that respects the values and shares the faith of the American family.

Like Lincoln, our first Republican president, we intend to act "with firmness in the right, as God gives us to see the right." To restore accountability to Congress. To end its cycle of scandal and disgrace. To make us all proud again of the way free people govern themselves.

On the first day of the 104th Congress, the new Republican majority will immediately pass the following major reforms, aimed at restoring the faith and trust of the American people in their government:

FIRST, require all laws that apply to the rest of the country also apply equally to the Congress;

From www.newt.org/contract.htm.

SECOND, select a major, independent auditing firm to conduct a comprehensive audit of Congress for waste, fraud, or abuse;

THIRD, cut the number of House committees, and cut committee staff by one-third;

FOURTH, limit the terms of all committee chairs;

FIFTH, ban the casting of proxy votes in committee;

SIXTH, require committee meetings to be open to the public;

SEVENTH, require a three-fifths majority vote to pass a tax increase;

EIGHTH, guarantee an honest accounting of our Federal Budget by implementing zero base-line budgeting.

Thereafter, within the first 100 days of the 104th Congress, we shall bring to the House Floor the following bills, each to be given full and open debate, each to be given a clear and fair vote, and each to be immediately available this day for public inspection and scrutiny.

1. The Fiscal Responsibility Act.   A balanced budget/tax limitation amendment and a legislative line-item veto to restore fiscal responsibility to an out-of-control Congress, requiring them to live under the same budget constraints as families and businesses.

2. The Taking Back Our Streets Act.   An anti-crime package including stronger truth-in-sentencing, "good faith" exclusionary rule exemptions, effective death penalty provisions, and cuts in social spending from this summer's "crime" bill to fund prison construction and additional law enforcement to keep people secure in their neighborhoods and kids safe in their schools.

3. The Personal Responsibility Act.   Discourage illegitimacy and teen pregnancy by prohibiting welfare to minor mothers and denying increased AFDC [Aid to Families with Dependent Children] for additional children while on welfare, cut spending for welfare programs, and enact a tough two-years-and-out provision with work requirements to promote individual responsibility.

4. The Family Reinforcement Act.   Child support enforcement, tax incentives for adoption, strengthening rights of parents in their children's education, stronger child pornography laws, and an elderly dependent care tax credit to reinforce the central role of families in American society.

5. The American Dream Restoration Act.   A $500 per child tax credit, begin repeal of the marriage tax penalty, and creation of American Dream Savings Accounts to provide middle class tax relief.

6. The National Security Restoration Act.   No U.S. troops under UN command and restoration of the essential parts of our national security funding to strengthen our national defense and maintain our credibility around the world.

7. The Senior Citizens Fairness Act.   Raise the Social Security earnings limit which currently forces seniors out of the work force, repeal the 1993 tax hikes on Social Security benefits, and provide tax incentives for private long-term care insurance to let Older Americans keep more of what they have earned over the years.

8. The Job Creation and Wage Enhancement Act.   Small business incentives, capital gains cut and indexation, neutral cost recovery, risk assessment/cost-benefit analysis, strengthening the Regulatory Flexibility Act, and unfunded mandate reform to create jobs and raise worker wages.

9. The Common Sense Legal Reform Act.   "Loser pays" laws, reasonable limits on punitive damages, and reform of product liability laws to stem the endless tide of litigation.

10. The Citizen Legislature Act.   A first-ever vote on term limits to replace career politicians with citizen legislators.

Further, we will instruct the House Budget Committee to report to the floor and we will work to enact additional budget savings, beyond the budget cuts specifically included in the legislation described above, to ensure that the Federal budget deficit will be less than it would have been without the enactment of these bills.

Respecting the judgment of our fellow citizens as we seek their mandate for reform, we hereby pledge our names to this Contract with America.

4. President Bill Clinton Ends "Welfare as We Know It," 1996

I hate welfare. To be more precise, I hate the welfare system we had until last August, when Bill Clinton signed a historic bill ending "welfare as we know it." It was a system that contributed to chronic dependency among large numbers of people who would be the first to say they would rather have a job than collect a welfare check every month—and its benefits were never enough to lift people out of poverty. In April of 1967 I helped Robert Kennedy with a speech in which he called the welfare system bankrupt and said it was hated universally, by payers and recipients alike. Criticism of welfare for not helping people to become self-supporting is nothing new.

But the bill that President Clinton signed is not welfare reform. It does not promote work effectively, and it will hurt millions of poor children by the time it is fully implemented. . . .

Governor Clinton campaigned in 1992 on the promise to "end welfare as we know it" and the companion phrase "Two years and you're off." He knew very well that a major piece of welfare-reform legislation, the *Family Support Act,* had already been passed, in 1988. As governor of Arkansas he had been deeply involved in the

---

"The Worst Thing Bill Clinton Has Done" by Peter Edelman, from *Atlantic Monthly,* pp. 43–58 (March 1997). Copyright © 1997. Reprinted by permission of the author.

enactment of that law, which was based on extensive state experimentation with new welfare-to-work initiatives in the 1980s, especially *GAIN* in California. The 1988 law represented a major bipartisan compromise. The Democrats had given in on work requirements in return for Republican concessions on significant federal funding for job training, placement activities, and transitional child care and health coverage.

The Family Support Act had not been fully implemented, partly because not enough time had passed and partly because in the recession of the Bush years the states had been unable to provide the matching funds necessary to draw down their full share of job-related federal money. Candidate Clinton ought responsibly to have said that the Family Support Act was a major piece of legislation that needed more time to be fully implemented before anyone could say whether it was a success or a failure.

Instead Clinton promised to end welfare as we know it and to institute what sounded like a two-year time limit. This was bumper-sticker politics— oversimplification to win votes. Polls during the campaign showed that it was very popular, and a salient item in garnering votes. Clinton's slogans were also cleverly ambiguous. On the one hand, as President, Clinton could take a relatively liberal path that was nonetheless consistent with his campaign rhetoric. In 1994 he proposed legislation that required everyone to be working by the time he or she had been on the rolls for two years. But it also said, more or less in the fine print, that people who played by the rules and couldn't find work could continue to get benefits within the same federal-state framework that had existed since 1935. . . .

Candidate Clinton, however, had let a powerful genie out of the bottle. During his first two years it mattered only insofar as his rhetoric promised far more than his legislative proposal actually offered. When the Republicans gained control of Congress in 1994, the bumper-sticker rhetoric began to matter. So you want time limits? the Republicans said in 1995. Good idea. We'll give you some serious time limits. We now propose an absolute lifetime limit of five years, cumulatively, that a family can be on welfare. End welfare as we know it? You bet. From now on we will have block grants. And what does that mean? First, that there will be no federal definition of who is eligible and therefore no guarantee of assistance to anyone; each state can decide whom to exclude in any way it wants, as long as it doesn't violate the Constitution (not much of a limitation when one reads the Supreme Court decisions on this subject). And second, that each state will get a fixed sum of federal money each year, even if a recession or a local calamity causes a state to run out of federal funds before the end of the year.

This was a truly radical proposal. For sixty years Aid to Families with Dependent Children had been premised on the idea of entitlement. "Entitlement" has become a dirty word, but it is actually a term of art. It meant two things in the AFDC program: a federally defined guarantee of assistance to families with children who met the statutory definition of need and complied with the other conditions of the law; and a federal guarantee to the states of a matching share of the money needed to help everyone in the state who qualified for help. (AFDC was never a guarantor of income at any particular level. States chose their own benefit levels, and no state's AFDC benefits, even when coupled with food stamps, currently lift families out of poverty.) The block grants will end the entitlement in both respects, and in addition the time limits say that federally supported help will end even if a family has done everything that was asked of it and even if it is still needy. . . .

This was *the* major milestone in the political race to the bottom. The President had said he was willing to sign legislation that would end a sixty-year commitment to provide assistance to all needy families with children who met the federal eligibility requirements. In the floor debate Senator Edward Kennedy, who voted against the bill, described it as "legislative child abuse." . . .

The game was over. Now no one could ever say again with any credibility that this President is an old liberal.

5. Special Prosecutor Kenneth Starr's Indictment of President Bill Clinton, 1998

According to Ms. Lewinsky, she and the President had ten sexual encounters, eight while she worked at the White House and two thereafter. The sexual encounters generally occurred in or near the private study off the Oval Office—most often in the windowless hallway outside the study. During many of their sexual encounters, the President stood leaning against the doorway of the bathroom across from the study, which, he told Ms. Lewinsky, eased his sore back.

Ms. Lewinsky testified that her physical relationship with the President included oral sex but not sexual intercourse. According to Ms. Lewinsky, she performed oral sex on the President; he never performed oral sex on her. Initially, according to Ms. Lewinsky, the President would not let her perform oral sex to completion. In Ms. Lewinsky's understanding, his refusal was related to "trust and not knowing me well enough." During their last two sexual encounters, both in 1997, he did ejaculate.

According to Ms. Lewinsky, she performed oral sex on the President on nine occasions. On all nine of those occasions, the President fondled and kissed her bare breasts. He touched her genitals, both through her underwear and directly, bringing her to orgasm on two occasions. On one occasion, the President inserted a cigar into her vagina. On another occasion, she and the President had brief genital-to-genital contact.

Whereas the President testified that "what began as a friendship came to include [intimate contact]," Ms. Lewinsky explained that the relationship moved in the opposite direction: "[T]he emotional and friendship aspects . . . developed after the beginning of our sexual relationship." . . .

As the relationship developed over time, Ms. Lewinsky grew emotionally attached to President Clinton. She testified: "I never expected to fall in love with the President. I was surprised that I did." Ms. Lewinsky told him of her feelings. At times, she believed that he loved her too. They were physically affectionate: "A lot of

---

Excerpts from the Starr Report, Referral to the United States House of Representatives, pursuant to Title 28, United States Code, §595(c), Submitted by the Office of the Independent Counsel, September 9, 1998 (Washington, D.C.: GPO, 1998). Online at http://icreport.access.gpo.gov/report/2toc.htm.

hugging, holding hands sometimes. He always used to push the hair out of my face." She called him "Handsome"; on occasion, he called her "Sweetie," "Baby," or sometimes "Dear." He told her that he enjoyed talking to her—she recalled his saying that the two of them were "emotive and full of fire," and she made him feel young. He said he wished he could spend more time with her.

Ms. Lewinsky told confidants of the emotional underpinnings of the relationship as it evolved. According to her mother, Marcia Lewis, the President once told Ms. Lewinsky that she "had been hurt a lot or something by different men and that he would be her friend or he would help her, not hurt her." According to Ms. Lewinsky's friend Neysa Erbland, President Clinton once confided in Ms. Lewinsky that he was uncertain whether he would remain married after he left the White House. He said in essence, "[W]ho knows what will happen four years from now when I am out of office?" Ms. Lewinsky thought, according to Ms. Erbland, that "maybe she will be his wife." . . .

Ms. Lewinsky testified that she and the President "enjoyed talking to each other and being with each other." In her recollection, "We would tell jokes. We would talk about our childhoods. Talk about current events. I was always giving him my stupid ideas about what I thought should be done in the administration or different views on things." One of Ms. Lewinsky's friends testified that, in her understanding, "[The President] would talk about his childhood and growing up, and [Ms. Lewinsky] would relay stories about her childhood and growing up. I guess normal conversations that you would have with someone that you're getting to know."

The longer conversations often occurred after their sexual contact. Ms. Lewinsky testified: "[W]hen I was working there [at the White House] . . . we'd start in the back [in or near the private study] and we'd talk and that was where we were physically intimate, and we'd usually end up, kind of the pillow talk of it, I guess, . . . sitting in the Oval Office. . . ." During several meetings when they were not sexually intimate, they talked in the Oval Office or in the area of the study.

Along with face-to-face meetings, according to Ms. Lewinsky, she spoke on the telephone with the President approximately 50 times, often after 10 p.m. and sometimes well after midnight. The President placed the calls himself or, during working hours, had his secretary, Betty Currie, do so; Ms. Lewinsky could not telephone him directly, though she sometimes reached him through Ms. Currie. Ms. Lewinsky testified: "[W]e spent hours on the phone talking." Their telephone conversations were "[s]imilar to what we discussed in person, just how we were doing. A lot of discussions about my job, when I was trying to come back to the White House and then once I decided to move to New York. . . . We talked about everything under the sun." On 10 to 15 occasions, she and the President had phone sex. After phone sex late one night, the President fell asleep mid-conversation.

6. Who Voted for Whom in 2000: A Chart

Top Five and Bottom Five States by Income, Education, Non-English Speakers, Commuting Times, and Vote for President in 2000

MEDIAN INCOME	PRESIDENTIAL VOTE	COLLEGE EDUCATION	PRESIDENTIAL VOTE	NON-ENGLISH SPEAKERS	PRESIDENTIAL VOTE	COMMUTING TIMES (IN MINUTES)	PRESIDENTIAL VOTE
Top Five States							
1. New Jersey ($54,226)	Gore	1. District of Columbia (41.1%)	Gore	1. California (39.5%)	Gore	1. New York (31.2)	Gore
2. Connecticut ($53,108)	Gore	2. Massachusetts (34.9%)	Gore	2. New Mexico (35.5%)	Gore	2. Maryland (29.2)	Gore
3. Alaska ($52,876)	Bush	3. Colorado (33.4%)	Bush	3. Texas (32.0%)	Bush	3. New Jersey (28.7)	Gore
4. Maryland ($52,436)	Gore	4. Connecticut (33.3%)	Gore	4. New York (27.5%)	Gore	4. District of Columbia (28.5)	Gore
5. Hawaii ($51,046)	Gore	5. Maryland (31.5%)	Gore	5. Hawaii (26.1%)	Gore	5. Illinois (27.0)	Gore
U.S. Median $41,343		*U.S. Median 25.1%*		*U.S. Median 17.6%*		*U.S. Median 24.3*	
Bottom Five States							
1. Kentucky ($32,843)	Bush	1. Mississippi (18.6%)	Bush	1. Arkansas (3.8%)	Bush	1. Wyoming (17.1)	Bush
2. Arkansas ($32,714)	Bush	2. Nevada (18.3%)	Bush	2. Kentucky (3.5%)	Bush	2. Nebraska (16.1)	Bush
3. Mississippi ($32,955)	Bush	3. Kentucky (17.2%)	Bush	3. Alabama (3.3%)	Bush	3. Montana (16.0)	Bush
4. Louisiana ($31,034)	Bush	4. Arkansas (16.6%)	Bush	4. Mississippi (2.9%)	Bush	4. South Dakota (15.6)	Bush
5. West Virginia ($28,569)	Bush	5. West Virginia (14.1%)	Bush	5. West Virginia (2.2%)	Bush	5. North Dakota (15.4)	Bush

Source: Eric Schmitt, "Census Data Show a Sharp Increase in Living Standard," *New York Times*, August 6, 2001, A1. Copyright © 2001 by The New York Times Co. Reprinted with permission.

7. A Columnist Reports on How the Nation's Agenda Is Set, 2000

In the grand scheme of things, Social Security isn't the nation's biggest fiscal problem. That's not my view. That's the assessment of Douglas Holtz-Eakin, a [George W.] Bush political appointee before he became head of the nonpartisan Congressional Budget Office, who says that looming financial calamities in Medicare and Medicaid are larger and more immediate worries in a strictly budgetary sense.

As economic calamities go, more significant crises confront the states, which are responsible for our kids' education; the nation's hospitals, which bear the brunt of an overburdened health care system; and international institutions, which have to deal with famine, poverty and HIV/AIDS.

With all these pressing woes, how did Social Security, Terri Schiavo's end-of-life fight and judicial nominations make it to the top of the Washington agenda? It's not merely because the White House or the party in power wants them to be there. It's because deep-rooted, well-heeled organizations have been targeting those issues for years. What seems like serendipity to the public—why *is* Congress talking about trial lawyers again?—is more often the result of an interest group's advance work combining with the right circumstances to send an issue hurtling into the limelight.

Like it or not, we increasingly live in a stage-managed democracy where highly orchestrated interests filter our priorities. These groups don't have absolute power, of course. In the nation's capital, home to 30,000 registered lobbyists, hundreds of politicians, thousands of journalists and untold numbers of entrenched bureaucrats, no one's in charge. But long-established entities like the AARP [American Association of Retired Persons], the Family Research Council and the U.S. Chamber of Commerce mold our collective thinking and regularly dictate the language and tenor of our civic debates.

This notion runs counter to an abiding myth—that political leaders actually lead. That's true sometimes, of course, but more often than not, the ideas and movements that get on the government's to-do list come from the broad middle and not from the top.

A case in point: More than a decade ago, the National Federation of Independent Business, the country's premier small-business lobby, began to methodically contact its half-million members by phone and mail to categorize them by political leanings and their willingness to contact federal lawmakers. The lobby group trained its most eager members at local seminars and sent staffers door-to-door during elections in critical congressional districts. Regular "grass-roots" outpourings from this made-to-order machine vaulted NFIB-championed issues onto center stage—especially when the Republicans it favored took control of the White House and Congress. In particular, the inheritance tax (which NFIB loyalists redubbed the "death tax" for marketing purposes) was repealed (temporarily so far, but Congress is now considering whether to make the repeal permanent). This was the organization's No. 1 priority.

The process is a lot like surfing. Interest groups float along, waiting for the perfect wave of public sentiment or official fiat to carry their issues to victory. They

---

From Jeffrey H. Birnbaum, "The Forces That Set the Agenda," *Washington Post,* April 24, 2005,: B1+.
© 2005, The Washington Post, reprinted with permission.

can't create the wave, but they can be ready for the moment when it comes. The key is to be prepared for that moment: Not every issue has an organization with the wealth and staying power to be in that position. Those that do have a shot at winning.

"Lobbying is subtle and complicated," says John W. Kingdon, a professor emeritus of political science at the University of Michigan who studies interest groups. But the most important attribute of a successful lobbying campaign, he says, is persistence—something that only entrenched organizations possess.

"It takes a sustained organization, mobilized followers and an immense amount of power to get onto a legislative agenda," agrees Theodore J. Lowi, a professor of government at Cornell University.

In many ways, interest groups have replaced political parties as the real influence brokers. Candidates for office rely on these groups for campaign cash, for campaign workers and, increasingly, for campaign issues—all of which had once been the domain of the Republican and Democratic national committees.

Republican ground troops come from such diverse groups as the NFIB, the U.S. Chamber of Commerce, the Family Research Council and the National Rifle Association. Democratic soldiers are recruited from places like labor unions, the trial bar and Moveon.org. "The standard distinction between interest groups and parties used to be that parties were committed to winning elections and that pressure groups let elections happen and then tried to influence the people who got elected," Lowi said. "Now interest groups through their PACs and a variety of other methods are very much involved in the pre-policy arena."

Such involvement has become a prime factor in agenda-setting. Take Social Security. Few federal programs attract as much scrutiny. AARP, the nation's largest lobbying organization, is dedicated to keeping Social Security alive and well, as are groups such as the National Committee to Preserve Social Security and Medicare. The reason: Large portions of their membership depend on Social Security checks to survive in old age. AARP has taught a million and a half of its 35 million members how to hammer elected officials by mail, phone and in person, primarily about Social Security.

But AARP has learned that it needs to be careful what it wishes for. Its obsession with the issue has made Social Security a front-of-the-mind topic and, therefore, a perennial contender to shoot to Washington's upper tier. Ideological opponents of the current Social Security system have also been active, raising the issue's profile even higher. Free market think tanks such as the Cato Institute and anti-tax-increase lobbies have been churning out position papers for a quarter-century promoting partial privatization of Social Security as a way to undercut what they see as "big government." One appreciator of that work: George W. Bush.

So when the president went looking for a problem to solve that could guarantee him a lasting legacy—and, perhaps, realign party domination—he went for that old chestnut Social Security. He also embraced a proposal that AARP dislikes—the creation of private accounts. That notion has fallen flat largely because of more than $15 million worth of AARP advertising against it. When the process moves to another phase and compromises are explored, AARP is likely to become an important negotiator and perhaps the key indicator of whether the effort will succeed or fail.

The same high-stakes maneuvering couldn't have happened with, say, Medicaid, the health care program for the poor, even though it's in more dire financial straits. Medicaid doesn't have similarly situated citizens' groups beating the bushes on its behalf. So while Social Security is the watchword of the day, Medicaid's fate will be to languish and occasionally fend off budget cuts until its finances reach an emergency.

Terri Schiavo is another example of interest-group politics at work. The 41-year-old brain-damaged woman was in many ways not out of the ordinary. She was one of thousands of people whose families annually struggle with the question of when a relative's life has ended. But skilled marketers on the well-established, pro-life side of the abortion debate seized on her situation. The National Right to Life Committee, Operation Rescue, Priests for Life, the Family Research Council and others set up Web sites, held news conferences and raised lots of money for lawyers and for themselves.

Their pleas touched a chord with millions of Americans and made Schiavo's plight a cause celebre. The omnipresence of her situation in direct-mail communications from those groups and on talk radio made her synonymous with the battle over life and death issues of all kinds—from the womb to the grave. By the time Schiavo's parents had finally exhausted their legal options and her feeding tube was about to be removed permanently, the public policy pump had been thoroughly primed. Republican leaders sympathetic to the cause brought Congress back for an extraordinary weekend session. Only later did it appear, based on various polls, that the majority of Americans did not see Schiavo's case the way the Republican leadership did.

As a result, the starvation of a solitary middle-class woman in Florida riveted government for a couple of weeks while similar—and more severe—situations went almost unnoticed. Mass starvation in Sudan, for instance, was a legislative footnote by comparison. Why? It's not only that Sudan is far away and hard to solve. Help for the Sudan catastrophe lacks the backing of as many obsessively focused and widely dispersed interest groups.

The brewing battle in the Senate over a mere seven judicial nominees is another telling example. Groups on the political left and right are making the coming confrontation seem like World War III. (Witness the use of the word "nuclear" to describe the Republicans' effort to force a vote.) In fact, the debate is a warm-up for the more consequential conflict over filling the next Supreme Court vacancy as well as a stand-in for other divisive issues, such as gay rights, abortion rights and affirmative action.

Why such tumult and passion? Organizations with wide and longstanding interest have been on the prowl for supporters on these matters for years. On the anti-Bush side are the Alliance for Justice, the Leadership Conference on Civil Rights and People for the American Way, which was instrumental in derailing Robert Bork's nomination to the Supreme Court in 1987. The president's allies include groups such as the Committee for Justice, Focus on the Family, the Federalist Society, Americans for Tax Reform and FreedomWorks, which have not only raised millions for the purpose but coordinate their activities in conference calls among their leaders.

In an odd way, all this attention to Washington ways is heartening. The common view is that elites run the show and sheep-like citizens allow them to. In fact, organized interests able to motivate blocs of voters really can make a difference, as long as they can stick around for a while.

Unfortunately, not every vital issue has a group or groups that are clever or rich enough to generate unrelenting support from back home. That leaves out of the mix too many people with worthy woes: the unemployed, the uninsured, the unaligned.

There's probably an opportunity there for yet another powerful interest.

✦ E S S A Y S

Historians and social scientists are only beginning to decode the meaning of the political transformations that have occurred during the past several decades. In the first essay, political scientist Bruce Miroff, writing before the 2000 election and, especially, before the events of September 11, 2001, locates Bill Clinton within a "postmodern moment" in which the "organizing themes of modern American politics are superseded by fleeting images and issues that do not produce any consistent or coherent political understanding." In the second essay, by contrast, political scientists Matthew A. Crenson and Benjamin Ginsberg trace the continued growth of presidential power during the presidency of George W. Bush and what they view as the continued disintegration of grassroots politics. In the wake of September 11, they suggest, new "organizing themes" focused on terrorism and national security have replaced the vacuum created by the demise of the Cold War.

Bill Clinton and the Postmodern Presidency

BRUCE MIROFF

The paradoxes of Bill Clinton have bemused observers of his presidency ever since its oddly troubled beginning. Puzzling questions have piled up during Clinton's two terms: How can a president who is so bright make so many dumb moves? How can a president who is so beleaguered make so many bold comebacks? How can a president who is tainted by immorality succeed as the champion of middle-class values? Most important for the purposes of this chapter, how can a president who wins so little trust from the public gain such a strong standing in public evaluations of his presidential performance?

I do not aspire in this essay to resolve all of these paradoxes, but I do aim to provide a perspective on Clinton's ability to achieve popularity despite the low public regard for his character and morality. Bill Clinton has thrived as a public performer because he is a postmodern character attuned to a postmodern moment in American political history. By postmodern character, I mean a political actor who lacks a stable identity associated with ideological and partisan values and who is, thereby, free to move nimbly from one position to another as political fashion dictates. By postmodern moment, I mean an era where the organizing themes of modern American

From Bruce Miroff, "Courting the Public: Bill Clinton's Postmodern Education," in Steven E. Schier, ed., *The Postmodern Presidency: Bill Clinton's Legacy in U.S. Politics* (Pittsburgh: University of Pittsburgh Press, 2000), pp. 106–123. © 2000 by University of Pittsburgh Press. Reprinted by permission of the University of Pittsburgh Press.

politics—the heroic presidency, the Cold War, the conflict between Democratic liberalism and Republican conservatism—are superseded by fleeting images and issues that do not produce any consistent or coherent political understanding.

The strength and weaknesses of Clinton's postmodern character have both been on vivid display during his presidency. Narrowing the distance between president and public, Clinton has emphasized the democratic connection between the two through his rhetoric, gestures, and travels; even while doubting his honesty, the public has responded . . . by believing that the president cares about their problems. Highlighting the application of intelligence, free of ideology or dogma, to issues large and small, he has made substance rather than symbolics the core of his presidential politics. But Clinton's repeated postmodern reinventions of himself have cast a shadow over these appealing qualities. Substance, it often seems in the Clinton presidency, is less the alternative to symbolism than it is a cleverer form of symbolic appeal. And the democratic bond between president and people often seems manipulative and hollow, a product of polling rather than democratic purpose.

Clinton's biography provides several clues to his affinity with the postmodern political moment. His transformation from a McGovern organizer in the 1972 presidential campaign to a New Democrat in his own 1992 presidential campaign parallels the decline of liberal idealism that is one cause of the postmodern turn in American politics. The contemporary Republican Party employs postmodern media and campaign techniques, but its core leadership is still imbued with traditional conservative values. On the Democratic side, however, ideological enthusiasm faded after McGovern's catastrophic defeat, and subsequent crusades to revive it, such as the run for the presidential nomination by Senator Edward Kennedy in 1980, never recaptured the party. Although Democratic liberalism still contains adherents in the party's congressional contingent, its presidential standard bearers from 1976 through 1988 deemphasized the old liberal faith, setting the stage for Clinton to redefine his party as a postmodern collage no longer held together by its modern reconstruction in Franklin D. Roosevelt's New Deal.

Clinton's close ties with business interests during his five terms as governor of Arkansas point to a second source of his affinity with postmodern politics. The ascendancy of market values and a market vocabulary has led to the eclipse of distinctly political and social discourses. Emphasis on profitability and attention to the bottom line are supplanting alternative modes of thinking in many areas of American life—medicine is a notorious example—and politics is hardly immune from the same kind of postmodern mindset. Commitment to core values is burdensome to a politician who seeks to adapt to the fluctuating demands of the political marketplace; the postmodern politician, as Clinton has demonstrated, can escape the encumbrance of ideology to repackage himself in line with the most profitable political fashions.

Despite his preparation for postmodern politics in his Arkansas years, the national political terrain of the 1990s did not immediately yield its hidden postmodern contours even to such a flexible and adroit political character as Bill Clinton, who only found his way after two years of feckless wandering. But from his 1995 comeback in the battle with the Gingrich Republicans to his survival strategy in the Year of Lewinsky, he demonstrated that he had learned how to master the media politics of the postmodern moment. His two terms can thus be understood as the story of a postmodern political education.

Clinton's legacy for the public presidency depends on whether the postmodern moment proves to be our permanent condition or whether it is merely transitional to some new organizing framework for political conflict. It also depends on how Clinton's successors regard him. Whether Republican or Democratic, they are almost certain publicly to set themselves off from him when it comes to moral character in the White House. But will they, nonetheless, covertly copy Clinton's methods—for example, the constant opinion polling and media spinning—because they recognize that the shifting stances these methods generated, while failing to give the public a solid presidential character it respected, offered it the multiple presidential identities it desired? . . .

It is possible to compile separate lists for the strengths and weaknesses of Bill Clinton's relationship with the American people. The problem is that the two lists turn out to look much alike, for Clinton's strengths and weaknesses are closely intertwined. Describing "the paradox of Bill Clinton," *New York Times* journalist Todd Purdum has written, "One of the biggest, most talented, articulate, intelligent, open, colorful characters ever to inhabit the Oval Office can also be an undisciplined, fumbling, obtuse, defensive, self-justifying rogue. His strengths and weaknesses not only spring from the same source but could also not exist without one another. In a real sense, his strengths are his weaknesses, his enthusiasms are his undoing, and most of the traits that make him appealing can make him appalling in the flash of an eye." Purdum is certainly on to something. Both the political insiders who have direct dealings with Clinton and the public that watches him from afar see the different sides of the president in frequent alternation. The "appealing" Clinton is exceptionally bright, energetic, optimistic, charming, and caring. The "appalling" Clinton is exceptionally cunning, manipulative, evasive, petulant, and self-indulgent.

Much of the time, Clinton comes across to the public as applying his outsized political talents to the nation's business with enthusiasm and skill. In these moments, he has the grace at presidential politics that marked his Democratic heroes, FDR and JFK. And the closer citizens come to him (in a town meeting or White House conference on some social issue), the more they are bathed in the glow of his concern for them; he is, Garry Wills observes, "a virtuoso empathizer. Clinton has never made the political mistake that cost George [H. W.] Bush so heavily in 1992: appearing distant from the anxieties and aspirations of ordinary American citizens. Running the opposite risk—seeming to lack the gravity and dignity appropriate to the nation's "First Citizen"—repeatedly Clinton has sought democratic connection to his mass public.

But some of the time, Clinton's charms are exposed to the public as the wiles of a political seducer. As another *Times* reporter, Jacob Weisberg, has commented, Clinton cannot "escape his reputation for being slippery. He is not the first president to lie, or lie under oath. But he will surely be remembered as someone who habitually played games with the truth. . . . It will also be recalled that he was disloyal to friends and took advantage of people who worked for him." Clinton's supporters generally like where he stands on the issues, and they find him an engaging public character (especially in comparison to his political enemies), but few can be said to believe in him. Many Americans have agreed in essence with what Clinton's adversaries say about his character even as they have reelected him and rallied to his defense against impeachment and removal from office.

These paradoxes that bewilder everyone else seem to nurture Clinton's public virtuosity: Take away the appalling traits and there might be little left of Clinton's appealing ones. Thus, a simpler and more honorable political figure would likely have been crushed by the defeats Clinton has suffered and constrained from pursuing the opportunistic and shape-shifting strategies that Clinton has followed to recover from them. Character, in the traditional sense of the word, would likely have made Bill Clinton into another Jimmy Carter. But Clinton lacks Carter's sense of shame. His former political lieutenant, George Stephanopoulos, observes: "I came to see how Clinton's shamelessness is a key to his political success, how his capacity for denial is tied to the optimism that is his greatest political strength."

If presidents were still judged by the heroic imagery of the Cold War presidency or evaluated by the Founders' standard of republican dignity, Clinton's flaws would have spelled political doom for him. But he has surmounted revelations of weak character that would have destroyed previous presidents because his public is prepared to accept a president as a larger-than-life version of Everyman. His is the archetypal story of the 1990s, with all the vital ingredients: self-absorption, ambition, sex, celebrity—and the promise of transcendence. As Weisberg has remarked: "To a public that consumes quantities of confessional entertainment and self-help advice, Clinton's turmoil seems not bizarre, but familiar. His cyclical progress through stages of sin, denial, contrition, and forgiveness has humanized him like no previous president."

Acceptance by the majority of Americans of a protean president whose "good" and "bad" sides oscillate is not simply the mark of growing tolerance for moral imperfection or concern for the protection of privacy. It also reflects the ways in which the public has been saturated with postmodern media that emphasizes discontinuity and irony over consistency and conviction. In the era of the modern presidency, from Franklin Roosevelt through Ronald Reagan (George [H. W.] Bush may have been a transitional figure), presidents were expected to have stable identities and consistent political projects. In the postmodern presidency of Bill Clinton, both identity and political projects can be fluid and even reversible. The new political culture, like the new popular culture, is skeptical of certainties and fixities and welcoming of novelties so long as they provide the audience with the satisfactions it seeks at that moment. To posit just one analogy between the two cultures, if we associate *Father Knows Best* with the Eisenhower years, we should associate *Seinfeld* with the Clinton ones.

Comparing Clinton with Ronald Reagan, a predecessor who also excelled at the arts of the public presidency, should serve to clarify Clinton's postmodern public character. The Reagan White House was just as focused on courting the public as the Clinton White House was; its techniques for manufacturing attractive images and "spinning" the press indeed provided useful templates for a Clinton administration that initially came to power pledged to undo core elements of its policy legacy. But there are fundamental differences between the two administrations in the presentation of presidential character, the understanding of how to win public support, and the relationship between the press and the presidency.

Although he had undergone a profound political transformation of his own, from New Deal Democrat to Goldwater Republican, by the time Ronald Reagan entered the presidency he had the most clear-cut identity of any major American political figure. Reagan was the very definition of a conservative Republican (although his amiable persona softened his ideology's harsh edges). He appeared in political ads and tableaux as the living embodiment of traditional American verities. Rugged individualist, independent thinker, strong father—these roles may have been more characteristic of Reagan's movie parts than his real life, but the "Gipper" was presented by his media strategists as an icon of American virtues. In a 1984 campaign memo, Reagan aide Richard Darman proposed that the president's reelection strategy pivot on his mythic appeal: "Paint RR as the personification of all that is right with or heroized by America. Leave Mondale in a position where an attack on Reagan is tantamount to an attack on America's idealized image of itself."

No one would take Bill Clinton seriously as an exemplar of American virtues. Indeed, most observers would have difficulty getting a clear fix on Clinton's political convictions. Where Reagan was identified as a man of firm principles (and admired for pragmatic adaptations of them), Clinton has been a shape-shifter on many of the major public issues during his presidency. His political identity, associated with the lower arts of political maneuver ("Slick Willie") and not the higher purposes of public philosophy, lacks symbolic resonance. But it also frees Clinton of ideological baggage, allowing him to case the landscape of political issues and seize the more popular positions as measured by the polls. His Republican adversaries, assuming that he would pay a price for his inconsistency and opportunism in the 1996 elections, created a campaign ad in which Clinton's changing positions on the subject of a balanced budget followed in rapid succession. But they did not understand that in a postmodern environment consistency is largely irrelevant: what mattered was that Clinton wound up precisely attuned to the most popular stance on the budget.

Deriving their approach to public opinion with television as the defining medium, Reagan's public-relations strategists perceived that in a television age the eye counts for more than the ear. Reagan's positions on issues were generally firm and frequently unpopular; a focus on the issues might alienate more citizens than it would attract. But appealing visual images on television could trump harsh words on the issues from journalistic or partisan critics. Writing about Michael Deaver, Reagan's top media adviser, John Anthony Maltese points out, "Deaver helped to create a counter-reality through his visuals. The idea was to divert people's attention away from substantive issues by creating a world of myths and symbols that made people feel good about themselves and their country."

Clinton's public-relations strategists scarcely eschewed good pictures; they knew the Reagan method well. Instead of diverting the public from the issues so as to define the president through visuals, however, Clinton's advisers used issues to redefine the president in a more flattering light. Dick Morris, the strategist with the greatest influence over Clinton, writes, "for years Clinton and I had believed that issues are the paddle you use to power yourself through the political swamp. Others prefer images, photos, adjectives, and negatives. We believed it was through issues that the public learned who you really were." Who Clinton "really was," to be sure, did not rest on a stable character structure or set of convictions that undergirded his stance on the issues; instead, his political identity would be established, and could be changed, by the issues he and his advisers decided to highlight or to slight. Rather than replacing substance with symbolism, Morris and Clinton used substance *as* symbolism. Many of President Reagan's public-relations specialists were veterans of Richard Nixon's protracted war with the press. From the Nixon experience they drew the precedent of an administration speaking to the media in unison through a common "line of the day," thereby keeping control of the press's agenda. But while undertaking extensive efforts to manage the news, they avoided the Nixon administration's tendency to attack reporters every time the president and his aides disliked the tone of press coverage. A cordial president and a solicitous staff kept White House relations with the press on a friendly basis and generated coverage so favorable that Reagan media advisers were pleasantly surprised by how well their boss was treated.

Bill Clinton has as much charm as Ronald Reagan, and he frequently bestows it on members of the public. But the press almost never receives the warm and fuzzy treatment from Clinton that it received from Reagan. From the opening day of his first term, when reporters were banned from areas of the White House where they had previously been able to seek information, Clinton and the press have approached each other with suspicion and sometimes hostility. Some talented media handlers, particularly David Gergen and Michael McCurry, have made periodic attempts to alleviate the mutual animosity between Clinton and the press. But nothing has eliminated the underlying causes of the friction; and in press coverage of the campaign finance and Monica Lewinsky scandals during Clinton's second term, Howard Kurtz relates, reporters could not conceal their belief that "Clinton simply could not be trusted to provide an unvarnished version of the truth." Nonetheless, while press coverage was kinder to President Reagan than to President Clinton, both achieved high levels of popularity. The appealing stances on issues that Clinton took impressed the public more than the critical judgments that journalists made about his character. Clinton's audience cared more about how his policies would affect their lives than about press charges of his duplicitous dealings.

Perhaps the best indicator of the difference between Clinton's politics and Reagan's politics is that there is no issue that can pin Clinton down, no issue that he cannot escape. In his first term, Reagan earned the nickname of "the Teflon president." Nonetheless, a president who had sought a reputation for "standing tall" against America's global foes saw his public approval ratings tumble during his second term, when he was revealed to have cut a deal with a terrorist regime he had denounced. (Similarly, President Bush suffered politically when he was forced to reverse himself on *his* signature issue: "No new taxes!") But Clinton can dance away from defeats on issues that would have damaged previous presidents because no issue is allowed to define him for very long. Thus, the champion of a massive new social program to provide universal health-care coverage in 1993–1994 can become the prophet of the end of big government by 1996. For the postmodern president, the only real trap is to stick to a policy that has become unfashionable. . . .

The political style that has characterized Bill Clinton's presidency was evident early in his life. Both the charm and the slickness in courting followers were on display in Clinton's races for office in high school, Boys Nation, and college. Many of the specific media techniques employed in the Clinton presidency were honed in his five terms as governor of Arkansas. Clinton entered the presidency already marked by the chief sign of the postmodern character: a readiness to reinvent the self to match the moment. But he still had much to learn about his moment in political time. National politics in the post-Cold War, post-heroic period posed snares Clinton had not encountered before, along with opportunities he had not yet learned to exploit.

Clinton entered the presidency with a strategy for capturing public support that had been designed to build on the precedents of his predecessors while going them one better. Seeking to reach his public audience by circumventing a hostile press, he traveled extensively and favored alternatives to press conferences with the White House press corps, such as town meetings and appearances on *Larry King Live* and MTV. The White House employed (while the Democratic National Committee picked up the tab) most of the political consultants who had managed Clinton's 1992 campaign for advice on matters ranging from policy to appointments. Polling was conducted on a scale that dwarfed previous administrations in scale and cost. Clinton thus approached the presidency as a "permanent campaign" (a term coined by Sidney Blumenthal, who served as a communications aide in Clinton's second term). But what was surprising about Clinton's initial forays into courting public opinion was not how elaborate they were but how poorly they worked. His popularity slumped as an alienated press played up embarrassing revelations of Travel Office firings and $200 haircuts. One small example can stand for the initial ineptitude of the Clinton White House at staging a spectacle of presidential leadership: at a reception for dignitaries attending the dedication of the Holocaust Museum in Washington, the Clinton White House served ham.

It was in the most dramatic political campaign of Clinton's first two years in office—the health-care-reform crusade—that the Clinton White House's weaknesses with the public were exposed. Yet the most disastrous defeat of the Clinton presidency proved its most important education in how to master postmodern politics. So many things went wrong with the Clinton health-care plan that its defeat seemed overdetermined. One crucial contributor to failure was the administration's clumsy approach in seeking public support for its plan. Clinton's political consultants came up with simple principles to sell the proposal—Quality, Responsibility, Choice, Savings, Simplicity, Security—but never crafted a message that explained the new government mechanisms at the core of the plan. As Theda Skocpol argues: "Vague and evasive explanations of how the reformed health-care system would work left Americans open to alternative descriptions purveyed by Health Security's fiercest opponents."

Dominating the debate over health-care reform, these opponents taught Bill Clinton a lesson about the manipulative possibilities in postmodern politics. Interest groups steadfastly opposed to the Clinton plan—especially the Health Insurance Association of America (HIAA) and the National Federation of Independent Business (NFIB)—got the jump on the Clinton administration in the battle for public opinion and took away the definition of the issue from its initiators. Coordinating their efforts with Republican leaders in Congress, these interest groups turned Clinton's bid for grand accomplishment into a political boomerang.

Money was crucial in the battle for public opinion about health care, and the interest groups opposed to the Clinton plan raised far more of it than the Clinton White House did. HIAA, for example, raised about $50 million for the health-care war and spent about $15 million on television ads attacking the Clinton proposal.

Its now classic attack ads, featuring the middle-class couple "Harry" and "Louise," trumped the Clinton promise of health-care security for the middle class with clever slogans that evoked the threat of rising costs and bureaucratic restrictions. The Clintons and their supporters protested the distortions in these and other advertisements assailing the administration's health plan, but the doubts they planted were more potent than the hopes that the Clintons had initially inspired. Interest-group money paid not only for television advertising but also for a vast effort at grassroots mobilization. For example, NFIB directed a constant flow of faxes to its small-business constituents to send them into action, staged public forums in states where swing members of Congress had been targeted, and contacted scores of talk-radio shows across the nation to pillory the Clinton plan.

Through television advertising and grassroots mobilization, interest-group and Republican foes of the Clintons turned each of their health-care reform positives into negatives. Bill Clinton had made "change" the mantra of his race for the presidency, and his health-care reform delivered on the promise that he would propose fundamental change. The reform's foes bested him by instilling the fear of change. Clinton targeted middle-class insecurities with his health-care plan, making its symbol a health security card guaranteeing "health care that's always there, health care that can never be taken away." Opponents successfully redefined the Clinton plan as a welfare-state scheme designed to benefit the uninsured in the working and lower classes at the expense of the already-insured middle class. Clinton presented his plan as a "managed care" system that was an innovative compromise between market-based and government-centered approaches. His adversaries overwhelmed this fuzzy presentation by depicting his plan as the latest and one of the largest incarnations of big government run amok.

In the course of the battle over health-care reform, the opposition's negatives also became sharply personal. Since Bill Clinton had tied himself closely to the issue of putting his wife in charge of the task force creating the administration's plan, hoping to draw thereby on the respect Hillary had earned as a new kind of First Lady, his opponents set out to tarnish the president and his plan by trashing his wife's role. As Skocpol writes: "By using Hillary Rodham Clinton as a target, cartoonists and talk radio hosts could ridicule the Clinton plan for its alleged governmental overweeningness—and in the process subliminally remind people how much they resent strong women."

Considering everything that was thrown against the Clinton health-care plan, it never really had a chance to maintain its initial public support and gain the momentum needed to pass Congress. After the administration proposal collapsed, one of the architects of its defeat commented to Haynes Johnson and David Broder that the Clintons had never realized what powerful forces and methods their opponents had mustered against them. But if Bill Clinton, for all of his supposed slickness, came across during the health-care campaign as something of the political innocent at postmodern politics on the national level, he lost that innocence with his defeat. In the next big battle with his foes, he would absorb the lessons they had taught him, and with perhaps the justification that the other side had victimized him first, he would outdo them in the techniques of political manipulation.

The health-care reform fiasco was a prime contributor to the drubbing that President Clinton and his party took in the historic off-year elections of 1994. As the architect of the Democrats' defeat, House Speaker Newt Gingrich, drove his Republican "revolution" through Congress in 1995, Clinton was thrown on the defensive. But Clinton not only played better on defense than Gingrich anticipated, he also took advantage of the power of negation that Gingrich himself had exploited in the past.

The vehicle for the Republican revolution was a balanced budget over seven years. Since Gingrich's Contract with America election platform had promised a major tax cut (eventually set at $245 billion), the Republicans had to find huge cuts in spending in order to balance the budget, and the biggest single source of savings appeared to be the Medicare program. Aware that the GOP had picked a risky target, party pollsters advised congressional leaders not to talk about the projected $270 billion in Medicare savings as a cut, but rather as a slowing down of anticipated increases in order to preserve a Medicare trust fund in jeopardy of insolvency.

Despite the care the Republicans took with their public-relations strategy, they had created a fat target for Bill Clinton and the political strategist he had summoned to mastermind his comeback, Dick Morris. Clinton and Morris seized on Medicare as a handy issue to deflate the Republican revolution. One of the few journalists to detect what they were up to was the *New York Times*'s Alison Mitchell: "When the Clinton health-care proposal died in Congress last year, the administration belatedly realized that it had allowed opponents to define the terms of the debate, using television, lobbying, and grass-roots politicking to capitalize on the public's fear of change. Now, taking a lesson from that defeat, the White House is using the same tactics against the Republicans who control Congress."

Badly outspent in the public-relations battle over health-care reform, the Clinton team would not let money beat it again. To pay for the flurry of polls and political commercials that turned the tables on the Republicans, the White House engaged in frenzied fund-raising among fat cats that, among other things, provided Clinton with an insurmountable lead for 1996 and a campaign finance scandal in 1997. Some of the Clinton ads this fund-raising financed borrowed brazenly from "Harry and Louise"; this time, the middle-class couple worried not about government bureaucracy but rather: "What would your parents be reduced to if their health care collapsed?" While Republicans decried the scare tactics being used against them, the commercials, personally approved by the president, effectively pounded home the message that Gingrich and his followers were decimating Medicare for the elderly in order to pay for tax cuts for the rich.

In the struggle over Medicare, a critical episode in the budget showdown of 1995–1996 that revitalized the president's political fortunes, the Clinton-Morris partnership was as adroit in its negative strategy as Clinton's opponents had been in 1993–1994. Clinton and Morris defined the issue: Republicans hurting seniors and jeopardizing the Medicare system in order to reward the party's rich supporters. They exploited the fear of change: instead of the party of big government threatening to expand the bureaucratic leviathan for the benefit of the disadvantaged, this time the danger was the party of the free market threatening to slash the social safety net for the parents of the middle class. They recast the characters: in place of Hillary Rodham Clinton as the emblem of feminist aggressiveness and government meddling, the demon figure in this drama would be Newt Gingrich, the emblem of white-male insensitivity and right-wing extremism.

The campaign to reposition the president in a more favorable light with the public was not restricted to the Medicare battle or the larger budget showdown. One of Dick Morris's postmodern insights was that with the right combination of issue stands (V-chips to screen out TV violence, curfews to keep adolescents home and studying, school uniforms to reduce gang battles and class resentments), Bill Clinton could become, improbably, the vessel of middle-class values. In fact, Morris had in mind an even more striking makeover for Clinton's political identity. If Clinton had campaigned as America's "buddy" in 1992, now he needed the air of maturity that would come from being "the nation's father." Morris even altered the president's wardrobe: the light-colored suits Clinton favored were replaced with the states-man's navy suit. Clinton the baby boomer took a lesson too from the oldest president ever to occupy the White House, studying videotapes of Ronald Reagan in order to emulate "the Gipper's bearing, his aura of command." In postmodern politics, Clinton and Morris concurred, who the president "really" was had become largely insignificant; by a shrewd calibration of issues and images, identified by polls and propagated through the media, the president could be whatever the public wanted him to be at that moment.

The same methods that propelled Clinton's remarkable political comeback in 1995–1996 stood him in good stead when he faced the ultimate test of his political survival in the Monica Lewinsky affair of 1998–1999. For Clinton's opponents, frustrated heretofore that they could not convince the public that he was too untrust-worthy and immoral to be president, the Lewinsky scandal seemed a golden oppor-tunity to affix on the president labels that would have been ruinous for any previous chief executive: philanderer, liar, abuser of the highest public trust. But once again Clinton evaded Republican definition; he appeared in the Year of Lewinsky as a moral delinquent but not a malefactor guilty of "high crimes and misdemeanors."

When the first details of the Lewinsky affair exploded in the media in January 1998, many political observers and pundits thought that Clinton's presidency was doomed. How could Clinton survive the charges that he had had an affair with a twenty-one-year-old intern in the White House and then conspired to cover it up? After a few days of hesitation, when Clinton unconvincingly voiced denials of the charges, he and his advisers hit on the strategy that quelled the initial furor. First, the finger-wagging president indignantly repudiated reality: "I did not have sex with that woman." Second, he shifted the focus from his character to his stand on the issues: he was too busy doing the work for which the people had reelected him to be diverted by a sex scandal. Third, he refused to answer further questions while the investigation proceeded. Fourth, his supporters assailed the motives and methods of his pursuer, independent counsel Kenneth Starr.

Ignoring advice to come clean and tell the public the whole story, Clinton, alerted of the risks in a poll taken by Dick Morris, put on the armor of his most suc-cessful past identities. Brushing off suggestions that he dare not appear before Con-gress for the scheduled State of the Union address, he turned this event, of which he was an acknowledged master, into a bravura reminder to the public of why they had reelected him. With a long string of popular, poll-tested proposals, presented with Clinton's trademark charm and good humor, he regained his political footing, soaring to over 70 percent in some opinion polls.

Clinton's original strategy set him up for later humiliation when he had to con-fess to the truth of his liaison with Lewinsky. More important, however, it bought him time by allowing the public to get used to the idea that a president might be a reprobate in his private behavior yet talented and effective in his public performance.

The drama that unfolded over the following months, endlessly fascinating to its afi-
cionados but increasingly tedious to the majority of Americans, was characteristic of
the postmodern moment. There were no heroes: the public had to choose between an
untrustworthy president, a zealous and relentless prosecutor, polarized partisans, and
a sensation-addicted press. There was little illumination: as the Starr Report vividly
demonstrated, high-minded constitutional disputation seemed repeatedly to sink into
sex talk. And there were Clinton's amazing poll ratings, which remained on an even
keel despite repeated blows to his original defenses.

Characteristic of Clinton's survival strategy was his response to the release of
the 445-page Starr Report in September 1998, which aimed to make an overwhelming factual and legal case for his impeachment and removal from office. In tested
fashion, the Clinton team supplied the press and public with a rapid rebuttal. Starr's
story, the White House said, was old news (in postmodern terms, what could be more
boring?). The report, it charged, was replete with salacious details and was all about
sex, not constitutional offenses (who was guilty of pandering to postmodern tastes?).
Besides, the president had already confessed his moral (though not his legal) turpi-
tude. A month earlier, forced to admit his liaison with Lewinsky in grand-jury testimony, Clinton had been insufficiently contrite in a televised address to the nation.
But hours before the Starr Report was released to Congress, the president told a
breakfast meeting of religious leaders: "I have sinned. I have repented." Although
Clinton's new identity as repentant sinner was not his most convincing one, it did
recast him in softer tones just as his hunter fired his sharpest barbs at the president.

By the scandal's endgame, Clinton's impeachment by the House and his trial
by the Senate, it had become fecund in postmodern ironies. Clinton had supposedly
been stigmatized in the history books by impeachment, yet at the moment he was
barely affected in his political identity, agenda, or popularity. Longtime critics in
his party and among the liberal intelligentsia had been driven to become his passionate defenders. Two leaders of the opposition—a Speaker and a Speaker-elect of
the House—had been driven into retirement. And the public was unhappier with his
attackers than with Clinton.

The factors that contributed to Clinton's political salvation were many: a vibrant
economy, a complacent public mood, scandal fatigue, conservative zealotry, and perhaps above all, the ideal foil for Clinton in Kenneth Starr. But Clinton's postmodern
character and political moment should not be neglected in any list of explanations.
Had Clinton had a stable character that the public had come to trust, revelations of
his secret life in the White House would have come as more of a shock. But with a
public that had already separated its appreciation for Clinton's talents and accomplishments from its skepticism about his honesty and integrity, it only took a short
while for the majority to accept Clinton's compartmentalization as its own in the
Lewinsky affair. More Americans were content to see Clinton, already liberated
from so many of his past political identities, escape this one as well. . . .

In light of Bill Clinton's political successes in every venue since high school, it
should hardly come as a surprise that he was a top student in postmodern politics
while in the White House. Learning how to use the systematic combination of
polling, advertising, and issue repositioning both from his adversaries in the health-
care battle and from his adviser during the Republican revolution, Dick Morris,

Clinton became increasingly adept at dominating the terms of political debate, demonizing his political enemies, and reinventing his own political personae. He was increasingly expert at pleasing the public with his shifting stances on issues large and small and at impressing the public with the skill of his performance on the job. Yet well before the Monica Lewinsky scandal the public had come to distrust Clinton's postmodern character and style. Multiple presidential identities may have allowed Clinton to shift with political fashions and to resurrect his political fortunes, but they also deprived him of the admiration and respect that his successful predecessors in the White House had garnered.

Since each of Bill Clinton's political identities has been ephemeral, perhaps his impact on the public presidency will be similarly short-lived. Although his presidency has been a story of growing sophistication in the courtship of public support, it will leave few political monuments when compared to the administration that set the contemporary standard for the public presidency. The Reagan administration could boast of bringing about powerful transformations in the party system, domestic and foreign policy, and public discourse with the aid of its public-relations strategies. The Clinton administration cannot claim nearly as much. Yet without disputing the conclusion that Reagan was a more successful president than Clinton, it is possible to argue that Clinton will be the more important model for future presidents in the arts of courting the public.

Clinton's attempt to rival Reagan by reshaping the agenda of American politics failed dramatically during his first two years in office, when he had Democratic majorities in the House and Senate. After the Republican takeover of Congress in the 1994 elections, he was pushed into the defensive posture that characterized most of his remaining six years in office. But if our only criterion of presidential success is grand legislative accomplishments, we underestimate the importance of Clinton's education after 1994 in how to win public support. The strategic context that confronted Clinton from the time he assumed office was never suited to policy breakthroughs. An intransigent Republican opposition, a badly divided Democratic following, a fearful and alienated public, above all a conservative rhetoric of politics that was probably Reagan's most profound legacy—all of these combined to block Clinton from the kind of reconstructive politics that we associate with presidential greatness.

If we change the question from one of grand accomplishments and ask instead what Clinton's courtship of the public did gain for him, the list is impressive. It won him reelection in one of the most remarkable comebacks in the history of the presidency. What other president was so thoroughly repudiated in midterm elections after only two years in office and then reemerged to sail easily to electoral triumph? It shielded him during the tawdriest scandal in presidential history. What other president could have survived the taint of sexual impropriety and flagrant dishonesty with his popularity undiminished?

But Clinton's postmodern public talents were more than mere survival skills. The story of the 1990s might have been about a Republican, conservative realignment of American politics, with Newt Gingrich as its central figure. One reason why Clinton has so infuriated Republicans is that he subverted this story. By stealing Republican issues while excoriating conservative extremism, by hollowing out liberal Democratic ideas, by blurring rather than clarifying American political discourse, Clinton played a larger role than anyone else in forestalling a Republican revolution.

By the end of his second term, it was Clinton's brand of centrism that dominated most policy debates in Washington.

The Democratic Party was as deeply affected by Clinton's success with the public as the Republican was. Although congressional Democrats continued to mistrust Clinton, by his second term few could resist the majority of his postmodern issue stances. The party's center of gravity had shifted—to the right? the center? the poll-tested majority position?—as it followed Clinton's path away from its old identity. In the race for the Democratic presidential nomination for 2000, both Vice President Al Gore and former senator Bill Bradley shared Clinton's reputation as being moderate (though both also appealed to liberal constituencies during the party's primaries), and there was a notable absence of candidates to their left who represented the party's liberal tradition.

Although it was Bill Clinton and not Newt Gingrich who left the larger mark on the American political system at century's end, few political figures were eager to claim him as their model or their inspiration. Just as presidential aspirants after Reagan stressed their competence, and presidential aspirants challenging Bush stressed their connectedness to the public, so candidates hoping to replace Clinton stressed their character. Deriding Clinton as immoral and inauthentic, Republicans seeking the presidency claimed to personify the traditional American virtues. Even Clinton's vice president, who had a closer relationship with his chief executive than any of his predecessors had, felt compelled to distance himself in his run for the White House by castigating the president's inexcusable behavior in the Lewinsky affair.

It is possible to imagine a return to a politics of character and conviction after Clinton leaves the White House. Many of the same Americans who have approved of Clinton's policies and performance have doubtless been unhappy with the slick but hollow postmodern style through which he has presented his changing political personae. "Virtue" is a resonant American theme, a reminder of our revolutionary and religious origins, and its appeal has only grown—among communitarian liberals as much as among Christian conservatives—during the Clinton presidency. Nonetheless, the postmodern mood threatens to subvert any reassertion of morals and principles by political leaders; a public schooled in postmodern skepticism by a distrustful press will look for the political payoff every time it hears professions of virtue. Perhaps only a dramatic economic or social issue that galvanizes the public and redraws the map of partisan cleavages will move Americans beyond postmodern detachment and irony.

Thus, while Clinton's approach to the public is unlikely to evoke open expressions of admiration in the short run, his long-run impact on the public presidency is likely to prove substantial. Ronald Reagan has been hard to emulate: What other American politicians possess his professional acting talents, his myth-making resonance, his iconic image? Furthermore, the heroic spectacle of the "Gipper" cannot easily be reenacted in cynical fin-de-siecle America. But Bill Clinton's postmodern techniques can be covertly copied and employed.

Credit (blame?) for developing these techniques should perhaps go to Dick Morris. But it is Bill Clinton who has shown how the shape-shifting politics that Morris prescribes can work. Clinton has repeatedly demonstrated how poll-tested repositioning on the issues can alter and enhance the president's image. Cultivating the appearance of rectitude, future presidents have to be careful to avoid accusations that they are as slick and slippery as Clinton. But especially when they run into difficulties, they will be able to turn to what will be the textbook case of the "Comeback Kid." That a president can reinvent himself to please the public will be the postmodern legacy of Bill Clinton.

The Imperial Presidency Redivivus

MATTHEW A. CRENSON AND BENJAMIN GINSBERG

White House-watchers mark September 11, 2001, as a point of transformation for the Bush presidency. It was only then, the argument goes, that George W. Bush was able to command the support of Congress and the public. A closely divided Supreme Court, not a popular majority, had put him into the Oval Office. Critics initially questioned his claim to the presidency, challenged his leadership, frustrated his initiatives. Only the leveling of the World Trade Center seemed to create a demand for an elevation of executive authority that made Bush president in fact as well as law. Suddenly, he was called upon to *act* as commander in chief and not just to hold the title. Soon he would order an expeditionary force to subdue the Taliban, while the executive branch would extend its powers over our own people in the name of patriotism and homeland security.

September 11 may have represented a lethal landmark for international terrorism, but in fact it was just another milepost in the expansion of presidential power. Since the late 1960s, the misfortunes of presidents have often concealed the magnification of the presidency. From Lyndon Johnson's Vietnamese ordeal to the impeachment of Bill Clinton, the recent history of presidents has been a trial of tribulations and humiliations. But the presidency has grown more exalted even as presidents have fallen. Its essential asset is so obvious as to be invisible: The executive branch is the only arm of government that has the wherewithal to carry out its will. And it has discovered or invented the means to do so with little public attention and without popular support, congressional authorization, or judicial warrant. In this respect, George W. Bush has built upon the claims made and tactics employed by his recent predecessors rather than striking out in new directions of his own design.

The truth is that even before the empowering disasters of September 11, the presidency of George Bush was unchastened by the circumstances of its birth. Bush bullied Congress into a drastic tax reduction slanted toward the wealthy, canceled the regulatory policies of his predecessor, and nullified major international agreements that did not suit his conservative ideology or his oil industry supporters. George Bush seized the political initiative even though he was a minority president, even though his party lost control of the Senate shortly after he took office, even though he was an object of public ridicule. He demonstrated that the presidency need not draw its energy from either legislative or popular mandates or personal stature.

The Framers of the Constitution were wary of presidential power, but even more apprehensive about the authority of Congress. It was the popular branch of government, riding the crest of an advancing wave of egalitarianism and popular democracy. Popular mobilization has now receded and, with it, the authority of Congress. In fact, Congress was a participant in its own disempowerment. Beginning with its creation of the Interstate Commerce Commission in 1887, it delegated a succession of lawmaking powers to the executive branch. And in an attempt to bring those delegated powers under regulation, it passed the Administrative Procedure Act of 1946. The act required federal agencies to open the administrative rule-making process to public participation. Agencies had to give public notice and hold public hearings on pending rules, and the quasi-judicial decisions by which they applied the rules to particular cases could be appealed directly to the federal courts.

The new regulatory regime had two largely unnoticed implications. First, Congress had delegated to the executive branch not only some of its rule-making powers, but a measure of democratic legitimacy as well. Bureaucratic rule-making had now become a participatory process. It was rooted in public consent and could stand on its own. A second consequence was even less noticeable and less immediate. If interest groups were legally guaranteed access to the administrative process, they had less need to mobilize mass constituencies to advance their demands. The gradual progression toward elitist, "stakeholder" policy making was accentuated by the legal right to appeal regulatory decisions to the courts. Litigation did not require democratic mobilization, only lawyers, and the volume of interest-group litigation grew dramatically as subsequent legislation on the environment, civil rights, consumer protection, occupational health and safety, and other public interests made provision for citizen suits to enforce public policy. The population of lobbying organizations inside the Beltway came to include a host of stakeholder and advocacy groups whose only constituents were names on mailing lists. They influenced policy through litigation and administrative adjudication, neither of which required the collective mobilization of a supportive public, both of which represented alternatives to congressional lobbying. The end result of this and other changes in the institutions of American politics was what we have elsewhere called "personal democracy"—the demobilization and privatization of the American public, the reinvention of citizens as mere "customers" of government.

Popular mobilization had been the foundation for the primacy of Congress. Congressional supremacy, in fact, coincided with the peak years of electoral mobilization around the turn of the twentieth century, when appropriations committees specified the amount of money that the Department of Agriculture could spend for the upkeep of horses and magazine subscriptions. Congressional government has generally subsided along with voter turnout.

Though the president is America's chief executive, presidents have never completely controlled the executive branch. For example, independent regulatory agencies like the Interstate Commerce Commission are not completely subject to presidential supervision. But in recent years presidents have worked to subsume the powers of the executive branch. By executive order, President Reagan declared that regulations promulgated by all other federal agencies could go into effect only after they had been reviewed by the Office of Information and Regulatory Affairs in the Office of

Management and Budget, which is itself part of the Executive Office of the President. During the Clinton administration, the clearance powers of the presidency were extended. The president, again by executive order, claimed a measure of control even over the independent regulatory agencies, and instead of just exercising a veto over administrative regulations, the Office of Management and Budget could issue "regulatory prompts" to induce agencies to adopt new regulations at the direction of the president. President Bush has adopted the same practice.

Another Reagan-era innovation calculated to enhance the power of the presidency is the signing statement. The Constitution says that if the president vetoes a bill while Congress is in session, the veto must be accompanied by a presidential statement of objections to the legislation. At the suggestion of Reagan's attorney general, Edwin Meese, the Office of the President began issuing statements even when a bill received executive approval. The signing statement provided the president with the occasion to announce his own interpretation of the statute, indicating the portions that would be enforced by the executive branch and those that would be ignored. Though the president is constitutionally obliged to see that the laws are faithfully executed, he also exercises considerable discretion in deciding what the law is, and sometimes he even keeps these interpretations to himself. In 2004, for example, Congress attached a provision to the appropriation bill for the Justice Department requiring the president to notify Congress concerning the department's non-enforcement of laws on the ground that they are unconstitutional. President Bush's signing statement promised only to provide such information "in a manner consistent with the constitutional authorities of the President to supervise the unitary executive branch and to withhold information the disclosure of which could impair foreign relations, the national security, the deliberative processes of the Executive, or the performance of the Executive's constitutional duties."

The signing statement now becomes part of a statute's legislative history and figures in its interpretation by the courts. Since the 1970s, Congress has repeatedly looked to the federal courts to rein in executive power. The courts have generally told Congress to use its own constitutional powers to fight its own battles. Even when congressional suits have gone against the president, presidential power has sometimes profited. The Supreme Court, for example, compelled President Nixon to surrender his tapes of Oval Office conversations to congressional investigators, but in its written opinion the Court for the first time acknowledged that presidential claims of executive privilege might be valid in some circumstances. Presidents Clinton and George W. Bush have made the most of the judiciary's backhanded grant of executive power. Executive privilege was recently invoked in the case of Dick Cheney's consultations with representatives of the energy industry to protect even the deliberations of the vice president from congressional scrutiny.

This pattern of judicial deference to presidential authority is also manifest in the Supreme Court's recent decisions regarding President Bush's "war on terror." In June 2004, the Supreme Court ruled in three cases involving the president's antiterror initiatives and claims of executive power and in two of the three cases appeared to place some limits upon presidential authority. Indeed, the justices had clearly been influenced by revelations that U.S. troops had abused prisoners in Iraq and sought in these cases to make a statement against the absolute denial of procedural rights to individuals in the custody of American military authorities. But while the Court's decisions were widely hailed as reining in the executive branch, they actually fell far short of stopping presidential power in its tracks.

The most important case decided by the Court was *Hamdi v. Rumsfeld.* Hamdi, apparently a Taliban soldier, was captured by American forces in Afghanistan and brought to the United States, where he was incarcerated at the Norfolk Naval Station. Hamdi was classified as an enemy combatant and denied civil rights, including the right to counsel, despite the fact that he had been born in Louisiana and held American citizenship. A federal district court scheduled a hearing on Hamdi's habeas petition and ordered that he be given unmonitored access to counsel. This ruling, however, was reversed by the Fourth Circuit Court of Appeals. In its opinion the court held that in the national security realm, the president wields "plenary and exclusive power." This power was even greater, said the court, when the president acted with statutory authority from Congress. The court did not indicate which statute, in particular, might have authorized the president's actions, but went on to affirm the president's constitutional power, as supported in many prior rulings, to conduct military operations, to decide who is and who is not an enemy combatant, and to determine the rules governing the treatment of such individuals. In essence, said the court, the president had virtually unfettered discretion to deal with emergencies, and it was inappropriate for the judiciary to saddle presidential decisions with what the court called the "panoply of encumbrances associated with civil litigation."

In June 2004, the Supreme Court ruled that Hamdi was entitled to a lawyer and "a fair opportunity to rebut the government's factual assertions." However, the Supreme Court affirmed that the president possessed the authority to declare a U.S. citizen to be an enemy combatant and order such an individual held in federal detention. Several of the justices intimated that once designated as an enemy combatant, a U.S. citizen might be tried before a military tribunal and the normal presumption of innocence suspended. One government legal adviser indicated that the impact of the Court's decision was minimal. "They are basically upholding the whole enemy combatant status and tweaking the evidence test," he said. Thus, the Supreme Court did assert that presidential actions were subject to judicial scrutiny and placed some constraints on the president's unfettered power. At the same time, though, the Court affirmed the president's single most important claim—the unilateral power to declare individuals, including U.S. citizens, "enemy combatants" who could be detained by federal authorities under adverse legal circumstances. This hardly seems to threaten the foundations of the imperial presidency. Indeed, whatever Hamdi's fate, future presidents are likely to cite the Court's decisions as precedents for rather than limits upon the exercise of executive power.

The courts depend on the executive branch, not Congress, for the enforcement of their decisions. That dependence alone may tilt judicial opinion toward the president. But the president also nominates federal judges. True, Congress must approve the nominations, and the legislature has been able to block some of the president's nominees to the federal bench. But the president controls the pool from which Congress must choose judges, and the composition of the pool has transformed the judiciary. Before 1850, approximately 80 percent of all federal judges had served terms in legislative bodies before reaching the bench. Since 2000, only 4 percent of federal judges have had legislative experience. Most have served as prosecutors or as administrators in the executive branches of state and federal governments. Their careers have not done much to develop their appreciation for the role or authority of legislatures. But they are generally respectful of executive discretion. Federal courts usually confine their judgments to the procedures followed by administrative agencies, not the decisions that result from them.

The judiciary has done more to expand executive power than to restrain it. In one of the most sweeping cases of this kind, the Supreme Court in 1983 invalidated approximately two hundred statutes by which Congress had given itself the power to veto administrative decisions or regulations. The Court held that the legislative veto violated the separation of powers doctrine and did not conform to the process of lawmaking specified by the Constitution, since the veto could be exercised by a simple resolution of either house and could not itself be vetoed by the president. But what happens to the presidential powers that were subject to the legislative veto? So far only the congressional veto has been invalidated. The powers granted to the executive branch appear to remain in force.

Congress tried to regain some of its authority over executive action in the Congressional Review Act of 1996. It allows Congress to overrule administrative regulations. But the resolutions that reverse the executive branch must pass both houses of Congress and stand up to the possibility of a presidential veto—a blunted weapon of legislative authority on the wane.

The executive order is a far more pointed instrument of political authority. Presidents are supposed to use them to implement the constitutional powers of their office, but they and the courts tend to interpret those powers broadly. President Jefferson used an executive order to make the Louisiana Purchase, and Lincoln issued one to free the slaves. Franklin Roosevelt, who generated more executive orders than any president in history, relied on them to steer the country through World War II. For President Clinton, they represented a way to achieve some of his legislative goals in health care and environmental policy in the face of an uncooperative Congress. Especially after Republicans seized control of both houses in 1994, Clinton unilaterally promulgated policies on affirmative action, labor law, and wilderness preservation. President Bush canceled a flurry of executive orders issued at the very end of the Clinton administration, but then proceeded to issue his own.

The executive order has evolved into several different species of presidential directives, some of which are secret because they deal with national security. President Bush's first National Security Directive, issued in 2001, was not secret. It redefined national security to include the defense of the country's economic prosperity. He also invented a new breed of executive order, the Homeland Security Directive, and has continued to act as a one-man legislature in purely domestic policy. He reduced regulatory restrictions on energy companies and prohibited federal agencies from requiring union work crews on government-financed projects. He imposed a twelve-year moratorium on the release of presidential papers and granted former presidents or their representatives conditional rights to restrict access beyond the twelve-year limit. He even came to the defense of some Clinton directives. During the presidential campaign of 2000, he had criticized President Clinton for his decision to declare millions of acres of western wilderness off-limits to mining, drilling, logging, or development. When conservative groups went to court to challenge what they regarded as a presidential landgrab, Bush directed his solicitor general to deny that the courts had any legal basis to overturn the orders. Defending the frontiers of executive power, apparently, took precedence over political consistency.

The full grandeur of presidential power was cranked up for the war in Iraq. One month before the 2002 congressional elections, the White House got legislative authority giving the president complete discretion to determine whether, when, and how to attack Iraq. The president had rejected any language in the resolution that imposed the slightest limitation on his power as commander in chief. In fact, the president's legal advisers were quick to point out that the resolution itself was unnecessary. "We don't want to be in the legal position of asking Congress to authorize the use of force when the president already has that full authority," said one senior administration spokesman. Although the Constitution gives Congress the authority to declare war, presidents have made war without legislative declaration ever since Harry Truman decided not to ask for congressional approval before sending troops to Korea, even though leaders in both houses of Congress assured him that the lawmakers were prepared to pass a resolution empowering him to use force. Truman and his Secretary of State, Dean Acheson, wanted to avoid creating the impression that the president needed to get congressional permission before taking the country to war.

Congress has not exercised its constitutional power to declare war since December 8, 1941. The treaty powers of the Senate seem almost as outdated. Under the Constitution, treaties become binding only when they receive a two-thirds vote of the Senate. But recent presidents have infrequently asked the Senate to approve international agreements. Those that go to Congress at all take the form of "congressional-executive agreements," and they trace the same path that any statute would follow through simple majorities in both houses and on to the president's desk. Increasingly, treaties never reach Congress at all. They are called "executive agreements" rather than treaties, but they amount to the same thing, except that presidents accomplish by signature and handshake what the Framers thought they could do only with the support of a senatorial supermajority. A similar disparity between constitutional prescription and political practices arises when it comes to the abrogation of treaties. President Bush single-handedly declared that the United States was withdrawing from the Anti-Ballistic Missile Treaty, which had been ratified by the Senate in 1972. Bush did not consult the Senate, even though some Senators said that he should do so. At the same time, he and Vladimir Putin agreed to reduce their respective nuclear arsenals. This nation's legislative branch had no more to do with the decision than Russia's did.

In the age of the national security state, when defense and diplomacy stand high among the nation's concerns, perhaps presidential primacy is inevitable. As commander in chief and the personification of the United States in international politics, the president naturally moves ahead of Congress and the courts. But the Bush administration's war on terrorism effectively erases the boundary between domestic and international and empowers the president to declare citizens enemy combatants who can be imprisoned without charges, counsel, or trial. It subjects the rest of us to government surveillance and scrutiny that seem unusual even for wartime. In a sense the president has become commander in chief not just of the American military but of the whole American public. That result, however, is not just the by-product of September 11 and the no-end-in-sight warfare that followed it.

It stems from long-term changes in American political institutions that have made it possible for well-organized interests to get what they want from government by litigation, administrative adjudication, or the politics of access—not the collective mobilization of popular constituencies. The decline in popular activism and the concurrent disintegration of grassroots parties have turned the executive branch into the most fully organized force in American politics and have eroded the under-pinnings of legislative power and legitimacy. Congressional acquiescence in the face of executive initiatives may contribute further to the legislature's loss of public sup-port and the citizens' conviction that participation is a waste of time.

But why should the presidency be so imperialistic? Perhaps the way in which we choose presidents recruits personalities driven to change history. In the days of the early republic, those considered presidential were men who had already changed history by participating in the making of a new nation with a revolutionary form of government. When these "continental characters" were gone, the political parties started filling the White House with dark horses, favorite sons, and largely apolitical generals—men who came to the office unexpectedly in late or middle life. Today's presidents must be self-propelled. Personal organizations, not parties, power their efforts to reach the White House. For some, the presidential quest is a mission that begins relatively early in life. Others attract personal constituencies that chart their paths to presidential greatness and become their traveling companions for the rugged and chancy journey to the Oval Office [and] presidential greatness. Even aspirants who have no personal agendas for the nation come to office motivated by the ambi-tions of the backers who have sacrificed themselves to a vision of their leader's greatness. If they are not driven by their own sense of mission (the "vision thing"), they are driven by the political aspirations of a group whose only immediate goal is to make a president who will build the nation—or the world—of their dreams. No wonder our presidents are driven to grasp all the power they can capture, and are so often doomed to disappoint us.

✦ *F U R T H E R   R E A D I N G*

Alterman, Eric. *Sound and Fury: The Making of the Punditocracy,* Rev. ed. (1999).

Apostolidis, Paul, and Julia A. Williams. *Public Affairs: Politics in the Age of Sex Scandals* (2004).

Bimber, Bruce A., and Richard Davis. *Campaigning Online: The Internet in U.S. Elections* (2003).

Black, Earl, and Merle Black. *The Rise of Southern Republicans* (2002).

Busby, Robert. *Defending the American Presidency: Clinton and the Lewinsky Scandal* (2001).

Chadwick, Andrew. *Internet Politics: States, Citizens, and New Communication Technologies* (2006).

Cornfield, Michael. *Politics Moves Online: Campaigning and the Internet* (2004).

Crenson, Matthew A., and Benjamin Ginsberg. *Downsizing Democracy: How America Sidelined Its Citizens and Privatized Its Public* (2002).

Dionne, E. J. *Why Americans Hate Politics: The Death of the Democratic Process* (1992).

Fiorina, Morris. *Culture War? The Myth of a Polarized America* (2005).

Frank, Thomas. *What's the Matter with Kansas? How Conservatives Won the Heart of America* (2004).

Goldfarb, Jeffrey C. *The Cynical Society: The Culture of Politics and the Politics of Culture in American Life* (1991).

Greider, William. *Who Will Tell the People: The Betrayal of American Democracy* (1992).

Harris, John F. *The Survivor: Bill Clinton in the White House* (2005).

Howard, Philip N. *New Media Campaigns and the Managed Citizen* (2006).

Isikoff, Michael. *Uncovering Clinton: A Reporter's Story* (1999).

Jamieson, Kathleen Hall, and Karlyn Kohrs Campbell. *The Interplay of Influence: News, Advertising, Politics and the Internet,* 6th ed. (2006).

Johnson, Haynes. *The Best of Times: America in the Clinton Years* (2001).

Jones, Jeffrey. *Entertaining Politics: New Political Television and Civic Culture* (2005).

Klein, Joe. *The Natural: The Misunderstood Presidency of Bill Clinton* (2002).

Kohut, Andrew, et al. *The Diminishing Divide: Religion's Changing Role in American Politics* (2000).

Kurtz, Howard. *Spin Cycle: How the White House and the Media Manipulate the News* (1998).

Micklethwait, John, and Adrian Wooldridge. *The Right Nation: Conservative Power in America* (2004).

Patterson, Thomas E. *The Vanishing Voter: Public Involvement in an Age of Uncertainty* (2002).

Putnam, Robert D. *Bowling Alone: The Collapse and Revival of American Community* (2000).

Selnow, Gary W. *Electronic Whistle-Stops: The Impact of the Internet on American Politics* (1998).

Skocpol, Theda. *Boomerang: Health Care Reform and the Turn Against Government* (1997).

———. *Diminished Democracy: From Membership to Management in American Civic Life* (2003).

West, Darrell M. *Air Wars: Television Advertising in Election Campaigns, 1952–2004,* 4th ed. (2005).

Wier, Margaret, ed. *The Social Divide: Political Parties and the Future of Activist Government* (1998).

Zoonen, Liesbet Van. *Entertaining the Citizen: When Politics and Popular Culture Converge* (2005).

CHAPTER
14

New World Order

*The fall of the Berlin Wall, the end of the Cold War, and the sudden and unantici-
pated collapse of the Soviet Union all seemed to signal a new era in American (and
world) history. The old era had been dominated by the Cold War struggle between
the United States and the Soviet Union. The new era was defined by the rise of a
global economy that had begun to transform not only the ways in which business
was conducted but also the ways in which the world's peoples lived, worked, and
governed themselves. Global communication, trade, and capital flow all grew more
rapidly than either national or international political systems could fully comprehend or control. The world's wealth also grew, raising global living standards
while at the same time creating stark new inequalities. Global (mostly American)
culture increasingly penetrated many of the world's most remote localities. Although
none of these developments was entirely new (the late nineteenth and early twentieth
centuries also had been marked by a dramatic increase in international trade and
communication), the speed, scope, and pervasiveness of these trends seemed to define
a new era in international affairs. Most commentators—journalists, politicians,
academics—were euphoric. America had "won" the Cold War. Democracy, freedom,
and capitalism were triumphant. Indeed, writer Francis Fukuyama argued in*
The End of History and the Last Man *(1992) that durable liberal democracy
had defeated its totalitarian rivals because it was without the internal contradictions that brought down communist states.*

*Yet lurking just beneath the surface of the new, post-Cold War era were a host
of problems—some produced by the dynamics of the new globalism, but many deeply
embedded in the history of earlier decades. While the advance of global capitalism
threatened to undermine both nations and nationalism, the end of the Cold War
also released a wave of long-suppressed national and even tribal passions. The same
increasingly porous borders that facilitated the free flow of commerce and people also
increased nations' vulnerability to terrorism, crime, and disease and made the task
of combating environmental pollution all the more difficult. While the United States
was unquestionably the most powerful nation in the post-Cold War world, its power
was not unlimited. Americans themselves seemed unsure about the role their country
should play in the new era: What goals and values should drive U.S. foreign policy?
How should economic and strategic interests be balanced against humanitarian
concerns? What role should force play? Some argued that, as the largest stakeholder
in the new era, the United States must be willing to use economic, political, and
military force to sustain the new global system. "The hidden hand of the market*

will never work without the hidden fist," proclaimed New York Times *columnist Thomas Friedman. "Without America on duty, there will be no America Online." Others sharply disagreed, questioning whether the United States could (or should) play the role of imperial police officer. Some saw increased global integration as a threat to American living standards and national sovereignty. Still others worried that uncontrolled growth posed an irreparable threat to the global environment. The attacks on the World Trade Center and the Pentagon that occurred on September 11, 2001, called into question these and other issues underlying America's role in world affairs. As the documents and essays that follow suggest, those attacks grew out of both the changed circumstances that accompanied the new global era, as well as the long and tangled history of America's involvement in world affairs in general and in the Middle East in particular. History had not ended after all, but it had caught up with America in a most terrifying way.*

◈ D O C U M E N T S

Following World War II, the United States had supplanted Great Britain as the dominant imperial power in the Middle East, repulsing Soviet efforts to penetrate the region and maintaining Western access to its oil reserves. The Iraqi invasion of the tiny, oil-rich monarchy of Kuwait in August 1990 posed the first major post-Cold War challenge to U.S. policy in the region. In Document 1, President George H. W. Bush places U.S. goals and objectives in the Middle East within the larger context of a "new world order." Six months later, a U.S.-led coalition crushed the Iraqi invaders and forced their withdrawal from Kuwait. The idea of a new world order was by no means limited to Republicans, however. In 1994, President Clinton sent U.S. troops on a peacekeeping mission into the former Yugoslavia, where ethnic warfare had claimed more than 200,000 lives. In Document 2, Deputy Secretary of State Strobe Talbott, a Clinton appointee, hails the progress of the new global era while emphasizing America's role as the guarantor of the new international system. The most dramatic challenge to the new, American-led world order came from an unanticipated source—not from historic rivals or allies; not even for that matter from a nation-state; but from small groups of Islamic fundamentalists who began to attack American targets, including the World Trade Center (in 1993), U.S. embassies in Kenya and Tanzania (in 1998), and the U.S.S. *Cole* (in 2000). In 1998, Osama Bin Laden, a wealthy Saudi who had fought against the Soviets in Afghanistan in the 1980s, issued a *fatwa* calling for *jihad* against the United States (Document 3). Three years later, terrorists trained by Bin Laden's al-Qaeda movement crashed airliners into the World Trade Center and the Pentagon, with shocking results. Document 4, compiled by reporters for the *New York Times,* is drawn from e-mail messages and phone conversations during the last, terrifying moments before the collapse of the North Tower. The U.S. response was swift—American-led forces invaded Afghanistan the following month, quickly toppling its Taliban government and killing or capturing many of the al-Qaeda terrorists. The September 11 attacks hastened a major revision of U.S. national security policy in which President George W. Bush announced the new doctrine of "preemption" (Document 5). Six months later, the United States invaded Iraq, justifying the invasion with charges that Saddam Hussein was in league with al-Qaeda and was harboring weapons of mass destruction. Neither charge, it turned out, was true. In the spring of 2003, U.S. troops again easily defeated the ill-equipped Iraqi army and toppled the government of Saddam Hussein. However, while most Iraqis were glad to be done with Hussein, they did not welcome the Americans as liberators, and within months U.S. forces found themselves engaged in a complicated and often deadly struggle to suppress insurgents and create a stable Iraqi government. In Document 6, Senator Robert C. Byrd (D-West Virginia) attacks the Bush administration's policies in Iraq. In Document 7, an Army Reserve civil affairs officer reflects on the difficult situation in which American soldiers now found themselves.

1. President George H. W. Bush Announces a New World Order, 1990

We gather tonight, witness to events in the Persian Gulf as significant as they are tragic. In the early morning hours of August 2nd, following negotiations and promises by Iraq's dictator Saddam Hussein not to use force, a powerful Iraqi army invaded its trusting and much weaker neighbor, Kuwait. Within 3 days, 120,000 Iraqi troops with 850 tanks had poured into Kuwait and moved south to threaten Saudi Arabia. It was then that I decided to check that aggression.

At this moment, our brave servicemen and women stand watch in that distant desert and on distant seas, side-by-side with the forces of more than 20 other nations.

Tonight, I want to talk to you about what's at stake—what we must do together to defend civilized values around the world and maintain our economic strength at home.

The Objectives and Goals

Our objectives in the Persian Gulf are clear; our goals defined and familiar.

*   Iraq must withdraw from Kuwait completely, immediately, and without condition.
*   Kuwait's legitimate government must be restored.
*   The security and stability of the Persian Gulf must be assured.
*   American citizens abroad must be protected.

These goals are not ours alone. They have been endorsed by the UN Security Council five times in as many weeks. Most countries share our concern for principle, and many have a stake in the stability of the Persian Gulf. This is not, as Saddam Hussein would have it, the United States against Iraq. It is Iraq against the world.

We stand today at a unique and extraordinary moment. The crisis in the Persian Gulf, as grave as it is, also offers a rare opportunity to move toward a historic period of cooperation. Out of these troubled times, our fifth objective—a new world order—can emerge; a new era—freer from the threat of terror, stronger in the pursuit of justice, and more secure in the quest for peace, an era in which the nations of the world, East and West, North and South, can prosper and live in harmony.

A hundred generations have searched for this elusive path to peace, while a thousand wars raged across the span of human endeavor. Today, that new world is struggling to be born, a world quite different from the one we have known, a world where the rule of law supplants the rule of the jungle, a world in which nations recognize the shared responsibility for freedom and justice, a world where the strong respect the rights of the weak.

"Address to Congress on Persian Gulf Crisis," 11 September, 1990, *Public Papers of the Presidents of the United States: George Bush, 1990* (Washington, D.C.: GPO, 1991), Book II, 1218–1222.

This is the vision that I shared with President Gorbachev in Helsinki. He and other leaders from Europe, the gulf, and around the world understand that how we manage this crisis today could shape the future for generations to come.

The test we face is great—and so are the stakes. This is the first assault on the new world that we seek, the first test of our mettle. Had we not responded to this first provocation with clarity of purpose, if we do not continue to demonstrate our determination, it would be a signal to actual and potential despots around the world.

America and the world must defend common vital interests. And we will. America and the world must support the rule of law. And we will. America and the world must stand up to aggression. And we will. And one thing more; in the pursuit of these goals, America will not be intimidated.

Vital issues of principles are at stake. Saddam Hussein is literally trying to wipe a country off the face of the earth. We do not exaggerate. Nor do we exaggerate when we say Saddam Hussein will fail.

Vital economic interests are at risk as well. Iraq itself controls some 10% of the world's proven oil reserves. Iraq plus Kuwait controls twice that. An Iraq permitted to swallow Kuwait would have the economic and military power, as well as the arrogance, to intimidate and coerce its neighbors—neighbors that control the lion's share of the world's remaining oil reserves. We cannot permit a resource so vital to be dominated by one so ruthless. And we won't.

Recent events have surely proven that there is no substitute for American leadership. In the face of tyranny, let no one doubt American credibility and reliability. Let no one doubt our staying power. We will stand by our friends. One way or another, the leader of Iraq must learn this fundamental truth.

Our interest, our involvement in the gulf is not transitory. It predated Saddam Hussein's aggression and will survive it. Long after all our troops come home—and we all hope it is soon, very soon—there will be a lasting role for the United States in assisting the nations of the Persian Gulf. Our role then—to deter future aggression. Our role is to help our friends in their own self-defense, and, something else, to curb the proliferation of chemical, biological, ballistic missile, and, above all, nuclear technologies.

Let me also make clear that the United States has no quarrel with the Iraqi people. Our quarrel is with Iraq's dictator and with his aggression. Iraq will not be permitted to annex Kuwait. That is not a threat; that is not a boast; that is just the way it is going to be.

2. One World: An American Diplomat Hails the Opportunities of a New Era, 1995

History and geography have conspired to make [the Balkans] the most explosive powder keg on the continent of Europe. The Drina River, which flows through the now-famous town of Gorazde and along the border between Bosnia and Serbia, traces one of the world's most treacherous fault lines. The three communities that

From "American Eagle or Ostrich? American Engagement in the Post-Cold War World," remarks by Deputy Secretary of State Strobe Talbott, Milwaukee, Wisc., September 12, 1995. Online at gopher:Hdosfan .lib.uic.edu:70/00f..950912%20Talbott%20-%20US%20Policy.

live there—Serbs, Croats and Muslims—bear the legacies of two empires, three re-ligions, and many cultures. That means if the fight among them continues unabated, it might eventually draw in other nations to the south and east, including not only Macedonia and Albania, but also Greece and Turkey, two of our NATO allies that are also regional rivals. Beyond Europe, the entire Islamic world, from Morocco to Indonesia, is watching to see how events unfold in Bosnia. Muslims are waiting to see whether or not their co-religionists in Bosnia will be accorded the same rights and protections as other Europeans.

Moderate and pro-Western leaders throughout the Islamic world . . . are look-ing on with anxiety: Other less friendly forces in the Middle East and Persian Gulf see targets of opportunity. Iran's repeated offers to send "peacemakers" to Bosnia is hardly motivated by altruism.

For all these reasons, it is in the strategic interest of the United States to end the war in the former Yugoslavia—first and foremost so that it does not escalate and spread, but also so that the people of Croatia, Bosnia and Serbia can begin the hard work of building stable, law-abiding market democracies.

For that reason and to that end, Allied warplanes are now delivering a message to the Bosnian Serb Army. That message is clear and simple, and it is the same mes-sage that our diplomats have delivered to all the parties to this conflict: Now is the time to stop killing and start talking about the terms for a political settlement. . . . After four years of brutal war, the United States is committed to helping the people of that region face the responsibility of peace. . . . We will persist in our pursuit of peace in the Balkans, just as we will in the Middle East, in the Transcaucuses, in Central Africa, and everywhere else we can make a difference for the better—and for the sake of our own national interests. . . .

The ongoing conflict in the Balkans and American efforts to restore peace to that troubled region are part of a larger question, which is whether we will, in the months and years to come, be able to promote the cause of security and stability—whether we will be able to advance America's own national interests—around the world.

In the coming months, the American people will face some fundamental choices. We as a nation are just beginning a great national debate. At issue is whether we are prepared to do what it takes—and that means spending what it takes—to have a for-eign policy worthy of our aspirations and our interests as a world leader—indeed, as the world leader.

We're facing these choices and conducting this debate now because we've en-tered a new era. That era might be said to have begun fifteen years ago, on August 14, 1980. That was when an unemployed Polish electrician climbed a dockyard fence in Gdańsk to join the striking workers inside and establish the first free labor union in the Eastern bloc. Since then we've seen Germans tear down the Berlin Wall; we've seen South Africans free Nelson Mandela from prison and elect him their President; and we've seen Cambodians walk across mine fields and defy death threats to vote against the Khmer Rouge.

Over the past decade, nearly two billion people in some 70 nations on five continents—from Brazil to Ghana to Lithuania to Bangladesh to the Philippines—have moved decisively toward democracy and free markets. As Vice President [Albert] Gore noted when he spoke here last year, the ongoing triumph of democracy around the globe "is the story of a century—our century." And it is the story of our global community, marked as it is by increasing integration and interdependence.

A decade ago we routinely, unquestioningly spoke of there being three worlds: the Free World; the Communist World; and the Third World. The organizing principle of international politics back then was an ideological struggle: the heirs of Vladimir Lenin versus those of Thomas Jefferson; the proponents of the ideas of Karl Marx versus those of Adam Smith.

Now, to an extent few of us ever expected to see in our lifetimes, there is one world joined in a loose, imperfect, incomplete but still extraordinary consensus in favor of open societies and open markets. During this dramatic transformation, America has not been a bystander.

Far from it.

From South America to Eastern Europe to Central Asia to the Pacific Rim, our foreign policy has helped nation after nation emerge from totalitarianism—and it has helped them keep moving in the right direction. Thanks in large part to American leadership, the political and economic principles that we have nurtured here in the United States for over 200 years are now ascendant around the globe.

An important moral of the end of the Cold War—a story that is still unfolding and will be for a long time—is that the United States must maintain its position of international leadership.

Only if we do that can we take advantage of historic opportunities, not just to combat threats and enemies, but also to build a world that reflects our ideals and promotes our interests; a world that will be more peaceful and provide better economic opportunities not only for our generation, but for our children's and grandchildren's as well.

The flip side of that proposition is just as important to recognize clearly: If we do not provide international leadership, then there is no other country that can or will step in and lead in our place as a constructive, positive influence.

Make no mistake about that.

And make no mistake that there are plenty of other forces that will fill the vacuum we leave, and they will do so in ways not at all to our liking or to our advantage or in keeping with our interests. For instance, thanks to American leadership, the enemies of the Middle East peace process—in Iran, Iraq, Sudan, and Libya—are now more isolated than ever before. But if we let down our guard, the leaders of those rogue states can still make trouble by menacing their neighbors, sponsoring terrorism, and stockpiling weapons of mass destruction.

Whether deterring threats or seizing opportunities, the United States needs to remain fully engaged in the world. . . .

3. Osama Bin Laden Declares Jihad Against America, 1998

Praise be to God, who revealed the Book, controls the clouds, defeats factionalism, and says in His Book[,] "But when the forbidden months are past, then fight and slay the pagans wherever ye find them, seize them, beleaguer them, and lie in wait for them in every stratagem (of war)"; and peace be upon our Prophet, Muhammad

---

From Osama Bin Laden, Fatwa Urging Jihad Against Americans, 1998, published in *Al-Quds al-'Arabi*, February 23, 1998. Online at http://www.mideastweb.org/osamabinladen1.htm.

Bin-'Abdallah, who said "I have been sent with the sword between my hands to ensure that no one but God is worshipped, God who put my livelihood under the shadow of my spear and who inflicts humiliation and scorn on those who disobey my orders." The Arabian Peninsula has never—since God made it flat, created its desert, and encircled it with seas—been stormed by any forces like the crusader armies now spreading in it like locusts, consuming its riches and destroying its plantations. All this is happening at a time when nations are attacking Muslims like people fighting over a plate of food. In the light of the grave situation and the lack of support, we and you are obliged to discuss current events, and we should all agree on how to settle the matter.

No one argues today about three facts that are known to everyone; we will list them, in order to remind everyone:

First, for over seven years the United States has been occupying the lands of Islam in the holiest of places, the Arabian Peninsula, plundering its riches, dictating to its rulers, humiliating its people, terrorizing its neighbors, and turning its bases in the Peninsula into a spearhead through which to fight the neighboring Muslim peoples.

If some people have formerly debated the fact of the occupation, all the people of the Peninsula have now acknowledged it.

The best proof of this is the Americans' continuing aggression against the Iraqi people using the Peninsula as a staging post, even though all its rulers are against their territories being used to that end, still they are helpless. Second, despite the great devastation inflicted on the Iraqi people by the crusader-Zionist alliance, and despite the huge number of those killed, in excess of 1 million . . . despite all this, the Americans are once [again] trying to repeat the horrific massacres, as though they are not content with the protracted blockade imposed after the ferocious war or the fragmentation and devastation.

So now they come to annihilate what is left of this people and to humiliate their Muslim neighbors.

Third, if the Americans' aims behind these wars are religious and economic, the aim is also to serve the Jews' petty state and divert attention from its occupation of Jerusalem and murder of Muslims there.

The best proof of this is their eagerness to destroy Iraq, the strongest neighboring Arab state, and their endeavor to fragment all the states of the region such as Iraq, Saudi Arabia, Egypt, and Sudan into paper statelets and through their disunion and weakness to guarantee Israel's survival and the continuation of the brutal crusade occupation of the Peninsula.

All these crimes and sins committed by the Americans are a clear declaration of war on God, his messenger, and Muslims. And ulema have throughout Islamic history unanimously agreed that the jihad is an individual duty if the enemy destroys the Muslim countries. This was revealed by Imam Bin-Qadamah in "Al-Mughni," Imam al-Kisa'i in "Al-Bada'i," al-Qurtubi in his interpretation, and the shaykh of al-Islam in his books, where he said[,] "As for the militant struggle, it is aimed at defending sanctity and religion, and it is a duty as agreed. Nothing is more sacred than belief except repulsing an enemy who is attacking religion and life."

On that basis, and in compliance with God's order, we issue the following fatwa to all Muslims[:]

The ruling to kill the Americans and their allies—civilians and military—is an individual duty for every Muslim who can do it in any country in which it is possible to do it, in order to liberate the al-Aqsa Mosque and the holy mosque from their grip, and in order for their armies to move out of all the lands of Islam, defeated and unable to threaten any Muslim. This is in accordance with the words of Almighty God[:] "and fight the pagans all together as they fight you all together," and "fight them until there is no more tumult or oppression, and there prevail justice and faith in God."

This is in addition to the words of Almighty God[:] "And why should ye not fight in the cause of God and of those who, being weak, are ill-treated and oppressed—women and children, whose cry is 'Our Lord, rescue us from this town, whose people are oppressors; and raise for us from thee one who will help!'"

We—with God's help—call on every Muslim who believes in God and wishes to be rewarded to comply with God's order to kill the Americans and plunder their money wherever and whenever they find it. We also call on Muslim ulema, leaders, youths, and soldiers to launch the raid on Satan's U.S. troops and the devil's supporters allying with them, and to displace those who are behind them so that they may learn a lesson.

Almighty God said[:] "O ye who believe, give your response to God and His Apostle, when He calleth you to that which will give you life. And know that God cometh between a man and his heart, and that it is He to whom ye shall all be gathered."

Almighty God also says[:] "O ye who believe, what is the matter with you, that when ye are asked to go forth in the cause of God, ye cling so heavily to the earth! Do ye prefer the life of this world to the hereafter? But little is the comfort of this life, as compared with the hereafter. Unless ye go forth, He will punish you with a grievous penalty, and put others in your place; but Him ye would not harm in the least. For God hath power over all things."

Almighty God also says[:] "So lose no heart, nor fall into despair. For ye must gain mastery if ye are true in faith."

4. The *New York Times* Reports Last Words from the World Trade Center, 2001

The impact came at 8:46:26 a.m. American Airlines Flight 11, a Boeing 767 measuring 156 feet from wingtip to wingtip and carrying 10,000 gallons of fuel, was moving at 470 miles an hour, federal investigators estimated. At that speed, it covered the final two blocks to the north tower in 1.2 seconds.

The plane ripped a path across floors 94 to 98, directly into the office of Marsh & McLennan Companies, shredding steel columns, wallboard, filing cabinets and computer-laden desks. Its fuel ignited and incinerated everything in its way. The plane's landing gear hurtled through the south side of the building, winding up on Rector Street, five blocks away. . . .

Then came the whiplash.

Excerpts from "102 Minutes: Last Words at the Trade Center, Fighting to Live as the Towers Died," *New York Times,* May 26, 2002. Copyright © 2002 by The New York Times Co. Reprinted with permission.

A powerful shock wave quickly radiated up and down from the impact zone. The wave bounced from the top to the bottom of the tower, three or four seconds one way and then back, rocking the building like a huge boat in a storm. . . .

9:00 . . . "What do we do? What do we do?" Doris Eng, the restaurant manager [at Windows on the World on the 106th floor], called the Fire Command Center in the lobby repeatedly with that question, according to officials and co-workers. Just minutes after the plane hit, the restaurant was filling with smoke and she was struggling to direct the 170 people in her charge. Many in the crowd made their living providing information or the equipment that carried it, communications experts taking part in the morning's conference in the ballroom. But with thickening smoke, no power and little sense of what was going on, the restaurant was fast becoming an isolation zone, where people scrambled for bits of news.

"Watch CNN," Stephen Tompsett, a computer scientist at the conference, e-mailed his wife, Dorry, using his BlackBerry communicator. "Need updates."

Videos from two amateur photographers show that the smoke built with terrifying speed at the top of the building, cascading thicker from seams in windows there than from floors closer to the plane. Early on, Rajesh Mirpuri called his company, Data Synapse, coughing, and said he could not see more than 10 feet, his boss, Peter Lee, would remember. Peter Alderman, the Bloomberg salesman, also told his sister about the smoke, using his BlackBerry to send an e-mail message: "I'm scared."

Ms. Eng and the Windows staff, following their emergency training, herded people from the 107th floor down to a corridor on the 106th near the stairs, where they used a special phone to call the Fire Command Center. The building's policy was to immediately evacuate the floor on fire and the one above it. People farther away, like those in Windows on the World, were to leave only when directed by the command center "or when conditions dictate such actions." Conditions were quickly deteriorating, though. Glenn Vogt, the restaurant's general manager, said that 20 minutes after the plane hit, his assistant, Christine Olender, called him at home. She got his wife instead, Mr. Vogt said, because he was on the street outside the trade center. Ms. Olender told Mrs. Vogt that they had heard nothing on how to leave. "The ceilings are falling," she said. "The floors are buckling."

Within 20 minutes of the crash, a police helicopter reported to its base that it could not land on the roof. Still, many put their hopes on a rescue by someone, some way.

"I can't go anywhere because they told us not to move," Ivhan Carpio, a Windows worker, said in a message he left on his cousin's answering machine. "I have to wait for the firefighters."

The firefighters, however, were struggling to respond. No one in New York had ever seen a fire of this size—four and five floors blazing within seconds. Commanders in the lobby had no way of knowing if any stairwells were passable. With most elevators ruined, firefighters were toting heavy gear up stairwells against a tide of evacuees. An hour after the plane crash, they would still be 50 floors below Windows.

Downstairs, the authorities fielded calls from the upper floors. "There's not much you could do other than tell them to go wet a towel and keep it over your face," said Alan Reiss, the former director of the World Trade Department of the Port Authority. But the plane had severed the water line to the upper floors. Mr. Maciejewski, the waiter, told his wife in a cellphone call that he could not find enough [water] to wet a rag, she recalled. He said he would check the flower vases. The room had almost no water and not much air, but there was no shortage of cellphones or BlackBerries. Using them and a few intact phone lines, at least 41 people in the restaurant reached someone outside the building. Peter Mardikian of Imagine Software told his wife, Corine, that he was headed for the roof and that he could not talk long, she recalled. Others were waiting for one of the few working phones.

Garth Feeney called his mother, Judy, in Florida. She began with a breezy hello, she later recalled.

"Mom," Mr. Feeney responded, "I'm not calling to chat. I'm in the World Trade Center and it's been hit by a plane."

The calm manner of the staff could not contain the strain. Laurie Kane, whose husband, Howard, was the restaurant's comptroller, said she could hear someone screaming, "We're trapped," as they finished their final conversation. . . .

9:01 . . . Just two floors below Windows, the disaster marched at an eerily deliberate pace, the sense of emergency muted. The northwest conference room on the 104th floor held just one of many large knots of people in the five floors occupied by Cantor Fitzgerald. There, the smoke did not become overwhelming as quickly as at Windows. And the crash and fires were not as immediately devastating as they had been a few floors below, at Marsh & McLennan.

In fact, Andrew Rosenblum, a Cantor stock trader, thought it would be a good idea to reassure the families. With his wife, Jill, listening on the phone from their home in Rockville Centre, N.Y., he announced to the room: "Give me your home numbers," his wife recounted. "Tim Betterly," Mr. Rosenblum said into his cell-phone, reeling off a phone number. "James Ladley." Another number.

As the list grew, Mr. Rosenblum realized that 40 or 50 colleagues were in the room, having fled the smoke. "Please call their spouses, tell them we're in this conference room and we're fine," he said to his wife. She remembers scribbling the names and numbers on a yellow legal pad in her kitchen, as the burning towers played on a 13-inch television in a cubbyhole near the backdoor.

Mrs. Rosenblum handed pieces of paper with the numbers to friends who had shown up. They went either to the leafy, fenced-in backyard, where the dog wandered among them, or to the front lawn, calling the families on cellphones. . . .

9:35 . . . So urgent was the need for air that people piled four or five high in window after window, their upper bodies hanging out, 1,300 feet above the ground.

They were in an unforgiving place.

Elsewhere, two men, one of them shirtless, stood on the windowsills, leaning their bodies so far outside that they could peer around a big intervening column and see each other, an analysis of photographs and videos reveals.

On the 103rd floor, a man stared straight out a broken window toward the northwest, bracing himself against a window frame with one hand. He wrapped his other arm around a woman, seemingly to keep her from tumbling to the ground.

Behind the unbroken windows, the desperate had assembled. "About five floors from the top you have about 50 people with their faces pressed against the window trying to breathe," a police officer in a helicopter reported.

Now it was unmistakable. The office of Cantor Fitzgerald [on the 104th floor], and just above it, Windows on the World [on the 106th floor], would become the landmark for this doomed moment. Nearly 900 would die on floors 101 through 107.

In the restaurant, at least 70 people crowded near office windows at the northwest corner of the 106th floor, according to accounts they gave relatives and co-workers. "Everywhere else is smoked out," Stuart Lee, a Data Synapse vice president, e-mailed his office in Greenwich Village. "Currently [there is] an argument going on as [to] whether we should break a window," Mr. Lee continued a few moments later. "Consensus is no for the time being."

Soon, though, a dozen people appeared through broken windows along the west face of the restaurant. Mr. Vogt, the general manager of Windows, said he could see them from the ground, silhouetted against the gray smoke that billowed out from his own office and others. By now, the videotapes show, fires were rampaging through the impact floors, darting across the north face of the tower. Coils of smoke lashed the people braced around the broken windows.

In the northwest conference room on the 104th floor, Andrew Rosenblum and 50 other people temporarily managed to ward off the smoke and heat by plugging vents with jackets. "We smashed the computers into the windows to get some air," Mr. Rosenblum reported by cellphone to his golf partner, Barry Kornblum.

But there was no hiding.

As people began falling from above the conference room, Mr. Rosenblum broke his preternatural calm, his wife, Jill, recalled. In the midst of speaking to her, he suddenly interjected, without elaboration, "Oh my God." . . .

10:00 . . . "Mom," asked Jeffrey Nussbaum. "What was that explosion?"

Twenty miles away in Oceanside, N.Y., Arline Nussbaum could see on television what her son could not from 50 yards away. She recalls their last words:

"The other tower just went down," Mrs. Nussbaum said.

"Oh my God," her son said. "I love you."

Then the phone went dead.

The north tower, which had been hit 16 minutes before the south, was still standing. It was dying, more slowly, but just as surely. The calls were dwindling. The number of people falling from windows accelerated. . . .

It was 10:26, two minutes before the tower crumbled. The World Trade Center had fallen silent.

5. President George W. Bush Announces a New National Security Strategy, 2002

The nature of the Cold War threat required the United States—with our allies and friends—to emphasize deterrence of the enemy's use of force, producing a grim strategy of mutual assured destruction. With the collapse of the Soviet Union and the end of the Cold War, our security environment has undergone profound transformation.

Excerpt from *The National Security Strategy of the United States of America,* September 2002. Available online at http://www.whitehouse.gov/nsc/nss.pdf.

Having moved from confrontation to cooperation as the hallmark of our relationship with Russia, the dividends are evident: an end to the balance of terror that divided us; an historic reduction in the nuclear arsenals on both sides; and cooperation in areas such as counterterrorism and missile defense that until recently were inconceivable.

But new deadly challenges have emerged from rogue states and terrorists. None of these contemporary threats rival the sheer destructive power that was arrayed against us by the Soviet Union. However, the nature and motivations of these new adversaries, their determination to obtain destructive powers hitherto available only to the world's strongest states, and the greater likelihood that they will use weapons of mass destruction [WMD] against us, make today's security environment more complex and dangerous.

In the 1990s we witnessed the emergence of a small number of rogue states that, while different in important ways, share a number of attributes. These states:

•   brutalize their own people and squander their national resources for the personal gain of the rulers;

•   display no regard for international law, threaten their neighbors, and callously violate international treaties to which they are party;

•   are determined to acquire weapons of mass destruction, along with other advanced military technology, to be used as threats or offensively to achieve the aggressive designs of these regimes;

•   sponsor terrorism around the globe; and

•   reject basic human values and hate the United States and everything for which it stands.

At the time of the Gulf War, we acquired irrefutable proof that Iraq's designs were not limited to the chemical weapons it had used against Iran and its own people, but also extended to the acquisition of nuclear weapons and biological agents. In the past decade North Korea has become the world's principal purveyor of ballistic missiles, and has tested increasingly capable missiles while developing its own WMD arsenal. Other rogue regimes seek nuclear, biological, and chemical weapons as well. These states' pursuit of, and global trade in, such weapons has become a looming threat to all nations.

We must be prepared to stop rogue states and their terrorist clients before they are able to threaten or use weapons of mass destruction against the United States and our allies and friends. Our response must take full advantage of strengthened alliances, the establishment of new partnerships with former adversaries, innovation in the use of military forces, modern technologies, including the development of an effective missile defense system, and increased emphasis on intelligence collection and analysis.

Our comprehensive strategy to combat WMD includes:

•   *Proactive counterproliferation efforts.* We must deter and defend against the threat before it is unleashed. We must ensure that key capabilities—detection, active and passive defenses, and counterforce capabilities—are integrated into our defense transformation and our homeland security systems. Counterproliferation must also be integrated into the doctrine, training, and equipping of our forces and those of our allies to ensure that we can prevail in any conflict with WMD-armed adversaries.

• *Strengthened nonproliferation efforts to prevent rogue states and terrorists from acquiring the materials, technologies, and expertise necessary for weapons of mass destruction.* We will enhance diplomacy, arms control, multilateral export controls, and threat reduction assistance that impede states and terrorists seeking WMD, and when necessary, interdict enabling technologies and materials. We will continue to build coalitions to support these efforts, encouraging their increased political and financial support for nonproliferation and threat reduction programs. The recent G-8 agreement to commit up to $20 billion to a global partnership against proliferation marks a major step forward.

• *Effective consequence management to respond to the effects of WMD use, whether by terrorists or hostile states.* Minimizing the effects of WMD use against our people will help deter those who possess such weapons and dissuade those who seek to acquire them by persuading enemies that they cannot attain their desired ends. The United States must also be prepared to respond to the effects of WMD use against our forces abroad, and to help friends and allies if they are attacked.

It has taken almost a decade for us to comprehend the true nature of this new threat. Given the goals of rogue states and terrorists, the United States can no longer solely rely on a reactive posture as we have in the past. The inability to deter a potential attacker, the immediacy of today's threats, and the magnitude of potential harm that could be caused by our adversaries' choice of weapons, do not permit that option. We cannot let our enemies strike first.

• In the Cold War, especially following the Cuban missile crisis, we faced a generally status quo, risk-averse adversary. Deterrence was an effective defense. But deterrence based only upon the threat of retaliation is less likely to work against leaders of rogue states more willing to take risks, gambling with the lives of their people, and the wealth of their nations.

• In the Cold War, weapons of mass destruction were considered weapons of last resort whose use risked the destruction of those who used them. Today, our enemies see weapons of mass destruction as weapons of choice. For rogue states these weapons are tools of intimidation and military aggression against their neighbors. These weapons may also allow these states to attempt to blackmail the United States and our allies to prevent us from deterring or repelling the aggressive behavior of rogue states. Such states also see these weapons as their best means of overcoming the conventional superiority of the United States.

• Traditional concepts of deterrence will not work against a terrorist enemy whose avowed tactics are wanton destruction and the targeting of innocents; whose so-called soldiers seek martyrdom in death and whose most potent protection is statelessness. The overlap between states that sponsor terror and those that pursue WMD compels us to action.

For centuries, international law recognized that nations need not suffer an attack before they can lawfully take action to defend themselves against forces that present an imminent danger of attack. Legal scholars and international jurists often conditioned the legitimacy of preemption on the existence of an imminent threat—most often a visible mobilization of armies, navies, and air forces preparing to attack.

We must adapt the concept of imminent threat to the capabilities and objectives of today's adversaries. Rogue states and terrorists do not seek to attack us using conventional means. They know such attacks would fail. Instead, they rely on acts of terror and, potentially, the use of weapons of mass destruction—weapons that can be easily concealed, delivered covertly, and used without warning.

The targets of these attacks are our military forces and our civilian population, in direct violation of one of the principal norms of the law or warfare. As was demonstrated by the losses on September 11, 2001, mass civilian casualties is the specific objective of terrorists and these losses would be exponentially more severe if terrorists acquired and used weapons of mass destruction.

The United States has long maintained the option of preemptive actions to counter a sufficient threat to our national security. The greater the threat, the greater is the risk of inaction—and the more compelling the case for taking anticipatory action to defend ourselves, even if uncertainty remains as to the time and place of the enemy's attack. To forestall or prevent such hostile acts by our adversaries, the United States will, if necessary, act preemptively.

The United States will not use force in all cases to preempt emerging threats, nor should nations use preemption as a pretext for aggression. Yet in an age where the enemies of civilization openly and actively seek the world's most destructive technologies, the United States cannot remain idle while dangers gather.

We will always proceed deliberately, weighing the consequences of our actions. To support preemptive options, we will:
• build better, more integrated intelligence capabilities to provide timely, accurate information on threats, wherever they may emerge;
• coordinate closely with allies to form a common assessment of the most dangerous threats; and
• continue to transform our military forces to ensure our ability to conduct rapid and precise operations to achieve decisive results.

The purpose of our actions will always be to eliminate a specific threat to the United States or our allies and friends. The reasons for our actions will be clear, the force measured, and the cause just.

6. Senator Robert C. Byrd Charges "The Emperor Has No Clothes," 2003

In 1837, Danish author, Hans Christian Andersen, wrote a wonderful fairy tale which he titled *The Emperor's New Clothes*. It may be the very first example of the power of political correctness. It is the story of the Ruler of a distant land who was so enamored of his appearance and his clothing that he had a different suit for every hour of the day. . . .

That tale seems to me very like the way this nation was led to war.

We were told that we were threatened by weapons of mass destruction in Iraq, but they have not been seen.

Excerpt from remarks by U.S. Senator Robert C. Byrd, October 17, 2003. Online at http://byrd.senate.gov/ byrd_speeches/byrd_speeches_2003october/byrd_speeches_2003october_list/byrd_speeches_2003october _list_3.html.

We were told that the throngs of Iraqis would welcome our troops with flowers, but no throngs or flowers appeared.

We were led to believe that Saddam Hussein was connected to the attack on the Twin Towers and the Pentagon, but no evidence has ever been produced.

We were told in 16 words that Saddam Hussein tried to buy "yellow cake" [uranium] from Africa for production of nuclear weapons, but the story has turned into empty air.

We were frightened with visions of mushroom clouds, but they turned out to be only vapors of the mind.

We were told that major combat was over[,] but [as of October 17, 2003,] 101 Americans have died in combat since that proclamation from the deck of an aircraft carrier by our very own Emperor in his new clothes.

Our emperor says that we are not occupiers, yet we show no inclination to relinquish the country of Iraq to its people.

Those who have dared to expose the nakedness of the Administration's policies in Iraq have been subjected to scorn. Those who have noticed the elephant in the room—that is, the fact that this war was based on falsehoods—have had our patriotism questioned. Those who have spoken aloud the thought shared by hundreds of thousands of military families across this country, that our troops should return quickly and safely from the dangers half a world away, have been accused of cowardice. We have then seen the untruths, the dissembling, the fabrication, the misleading inferences surrounding this rush to war in Iraq wrapped quickly in the flag. . . .

The Emperor has no clothes. This entire adventure in Iraq has been based on propaganda and manipulation. Eighty-seven billion dollars is too much to pay for the continuation of a war based on falsehoods.

Taking the nation to war based on misleading rhetoric and hyped intelligence is a travesty and a tragedy. It is the most cynical of all cynical acts. It is dangerous to manipulate the truth. It is dangerous because once having lied, it is difficult to ever be believed again. Having misled the American people and stampeded them to war, this Administration must now attempt to sustain a policy predicated on falsehoods. The President asks for billions from those same citizens who know that they were misled about the need to go to war. We misinformed and insulted our friends and allies[,] and now this Administration is having more than a little trouble getting help from the international community. . . .

I cannot stand by and continue to watch our grandchildren become increasingly burdened by the billions that fly out of the Treasury for a war and a policy based largely on propaganda and prevarication. . . .

I cannot support a President who refuses to authorize the reasonable change in course that would bring traditional allies to our side in Iraq.

I cannot support the politics of zeal and "might makes right" that created the new American arrogance and unilateralism which passes for foreign policy in this Administration.

I cannot support this foolish manifestation of the dangerous and destabilizing doctrine of preemption that changes the image of America into that of a reckless bully.

The emperor has no clothes. . . .

7. An Army Officer Ponders How America Is Losing Hearts and Minds in Iraq, 2004

The General and the Colonel have told us that we are the main effort, at the forefront of helping to rebuild Iraq. But how do you rebuild when all around you destruction and violence continue? Do the facts and figures showing levels of electricity restored, the amount of drinking water available, the number of schools reconstructed or the numbers of police officers hired and trained really convince the Iraqi people that we are here to help? Are we winning their hearts and minds?

Winning hearts and minds is my job, in a nutshell. I'm an Army Reserve civil affairs (CA) officer stationed in Baqubah, 30 miles northeast of Baghdad. In Vietnam, winning hearts and minds was mostly a Special Forces task, but after that they were smart enough to get out of it, and the responsibility has since fallen into the laps of reservists like me who are trained to deal with every conceivable problem that arises when Big Army meets Little Civilian. And that's why CA soldiers are among those most often deployed overseas in the Reserve.

That's how they get you, actually, with promises of foreign travel, foreign language training, Airborne School, Air Assault School . . . and the chance to help others. We're trained in the Army's regimented style to deal with civilians in foreign countries, required to learn a satisfactory number of acronyms, probed, pricked and tested, and then sent overseas to do good.

And here we are, in Iraq, trying to help the Iraqi people as death threats frighten our Iraqi interpreters into quitting to protect their families, and as attacks from mortars, rocket-propelled grenades (RPGs) and improvised explosive devices (IEDs) become daily and nightly occurrences.

We're told by senior officers that most Iraqis are being influenced by "bad guys" and their anti-coalition messages. The latest acronym for these bad guys is AIF, which stands for Anti-Iraqi Forces. The fact that most AIF members are Iraqi in neatly ignored as we try to win the goodwill of the "good" Iraqis.

One day last week we rolled into the town of Zaghniyah to win some of the local hearts and minds. In a country where most people are unemployed, we offer the townspeople $1 for every bag of trash they can collect. Our "docs"—medics, assistants and physicians—set up shop in the local health clinic and we try to "engage local leadership." But most of the local leaders, we are told, are not there. Those people who do speak with us do so only to catalogue their concerns—chiefly unemployment and lack of electricity and water. It's the day after the swearing-in of Iraq's new interim government, and so I explain that their concerns have to be presented to their Governing Council, and that we can fund projects only through that council. An old man waves me off and tells me that they know the Americans control everything and will do so as long as they are here. The rest of the men nod in agreement.

As the day wears on, every ray of sun seems to add weight to my Kevlar helmet and body armor. I am at a loss as to why our efforts aren't recognized or appreciated. But then, as I look at the children collecting trash and the main road clogged with military vehicles, as I watch one of our docs try to help a woman carrying a

From Oscar R. Estrada, "The Military: Losing Hearts and Minds?" *Washington Post,* June 6, 2004, B01. Reprinted by permission of the author.

gaunt and sickly baby in her arms, and as I listen to an old sheik struggle with our demands that he hold American-style town meetings, I realize that Iraqis may see our help as something else. I see how paying them to collect trash may be demeaning and remote from their hopes for prosperity in a new Iraq. I see our good faith efforts to provide medical care lead to disappointment and resentment when we have neither the medicine nor the equipment to cure or heal many ailments. And I see how our efforts to introduce representative democracy can lead to frustration.

Some experiences here have reminded me that our sacrifice for the rebuilding of Iraq is minor compared with that of the average Iraqi. A few weeks ago I was on a patrol in the town of Buhriz, near Baqubah. Our mission: to assess the city's potable water needs. Buhriz is a place where our soldiers are often shot at, so we rolled in with two Bradleys and several Humvees packed with heavily armed troops.

On the way to the water treatment plant, we stop for a psychological operations (psyop) mission. A psyop team walks up and down the market handing out "product," in this case pro-coalition messages in a glossy Arabic-language magazine. Young people take the magazines and seem to enjoy the novelty of the event; some people bombard the team and its interpreter with questions about things the town needs and the whereabouts of detained relatives.

But others return the fancy magazine and pull their kids away from "the occupiers." One man pulls a young boy by the arm and slaps him on the back of the head as he chastises him. I stare at the man and he at me; his hatred is palpable. We're less than five feet apart, but the true separation is far greater. I'm unable to communicate with him without the help of the one interpreter assigned to this patrol of 30 or so soldiers, and the "terp" is with the psyop team. I wish I could ask the man why he hates us, but I doubt anything useful would come of such a conversation. As we drive out of town, a little boy who looks about 3 years old spits at our vehicles as we pass his house.

I flash back to an incident a month earlier when we were returning to our compound by way of "RPG Alley," a route of frequent attacks. A unit ahead of us had reported taking fire and we rushed to the scene. Other patrols and M1 tanks soon arrived and we sat and waited, pointing our weapons into a date palm grove to the north. A small column of Humvees moved down a dirt road toward the grove, and all hell broke loose. I never heard a shot fired from the grove, but someone did, and then everyone was firing.

"Hey, what the hell are we shooting at?" I screamed at my buddy as I continued to squeeze off rounds from my M-16.

"I'm not sure! By that shack. You?"

"I'm just shooting where everybody else is shooting."

But everybody else was shooting all over the place. Small puffs of white erupted in front of us as our own soldiers lobbed grenades at the grove but came up short; tracers from .50-caliber machine guns flew past us, and the smell of cordite filled the air. Then, as suddenly as it had started, the tumult ended. We sat in silence and listened to the crackling radios as a patrol dismounted from a couple of armored Humvees and began to search among the trees.

"Dagger, this is Bravo 6. Do you have anything, over?"

"Roger. We're going to need a terp. We have a guy here who's pretty upset. I think we killed his cow, over."

"Upset how, over?"

"He can't talk; I think he's in shock. He looks scared, over."

"He should be scared. He's the enemy."

"Uhm, ahh, Roger, 6 . . . he's not armed and looks like a farmer or something."

"He was in the grove that we took fire from; he's a [expletive] bad guy!"

"Roger."

From my perch in the Humvee, I listened as the patrol found a suspicious bag hanging from a tree and called in an explosive ordnance disposal unit to examine it. On the other side of the road, in the distance, a horse-drawn cart crept on its way from some unknown village to the piece of road we now controlled. I watched it grow larger until the old man on the cart came face to face with the armed soldier waving him off. He slowly turned the cart around and headed back to where he had come from. I wondered where he was going, whether it was important and how much effort he'd put into the trip. I wondered if we had any chance of winning either his heart or his mind.

As we headed back to our compound, I couldn't stop thinking about the man in the grove, frozen in shock at the sight of his dead livestock. Did his family depend on that cow for its survival? Had he seen his world fall apart? Had we lost both his heart and his mind?

Stop thinking about this, I tell myself as our imposing convoy comes to a stop in front of the water treatment plant that serves Buhriz—it's time, once again, to go about my job of winning those hearts and minds. I spend the next half-hour asking people questions and taking notes that I'll later summarize in a neat and orderly report sprinkled with just the right number of Army acronyms, grid coordinates and date-time groups. I'll detail the gallons-per-day requirements and the inoperable pump and the need for high-capacity filters and all the other bits of information that will help someone somewhere request the thousands of dollars it will take to repair the plant. My work is done, and I feel confident I've done it well. I feel as if I've actually accomplished something worthwhile today.

And then I remember: Security, you forgot to ask about security! So I do, and the treatment plant manager tells me that his biggest threat is coalition soldiers, who shoot up the compound whenever the nearby MP station and government building are attacked. He shows me the bullet holes and asks, "Why?" I give the standard response: We have to defend ourselves, and these problems are caused by the insurgents. And I think the people listening are buying it when the plant's caretaker tugs at my elbow, urging me to come see his house on the corner of the plant grounds. We're running late, but I follow the man before the patrol leader can say no.

An old man, the caretaker's father, comes out of the house and gestures for me to come inside. It's a one-level, three-room concrete building, clean but humble. The old man's grandchildren, his daughter-in-law and his wife stare up at me as he leads me by the arm and points out the bullet holes on the side of the house, the shattered windows and the bullet-riddled living room. He's speaking to me in Arabic. I can't understand a word he's saying, and yet I understand it all. I see the anguish in his face as his eyes start to tear up, I see the sadness as he points to old photographs of safer days under Saddam Hussein. I see the shame as he mimics how our soldiers hit him when he was detained, and I see the disappointment as he asks me "Why?" and I stare at him at a loss for words.

"Why?" I don't even remember what I told him, but I think I apologized. The patrol leader was telling me it was time to go. Everyone, even the old man's family, seemed in a hurry to end the encounter. So we quickly walked out, hoping to somehow outpace the wave of shame that threatened to knock us over.

Only I can't outrun it. I stay up that night thinking of the old man and the young soldiers who fired into the darkness in response to bullets and mortars and RPGs hurled at them from somewhere "out there." I think of the man with the dead cow and of the rush of adrenaline I felt firing from the back of that Humvee at the perceived threat. I think of the old man on the cart, the children who burst into tears when we point our weapons into their cars (just in case), and the countless numbers of people whose vehicles we sideswipe as we try to use speed to survive the IEDs that await us each morning. I think of my fellow soldiers and the reality of being attacked and feeling threatened, and it all makes sense—the need to smash their cars and shoot their cows and point our weapons at them and detain them without concern for notifying their families. But how would I feel in their shoes? Would I be able to offer my own heart and mind?

◈ E S S A Y S

The essays that follow offer sharply divergent views regarding America's role in the new world order. In the first essay, Yale historian John Lewis Gaddis emphasizes the radically new challenge facing the United States in the wake of the September 11 attacks, criticizes the strategic failures of the Clinton administration, and offers a qualified endorsement to the new national security policies of the George W. Bush administration. In the second essay, Michael H. Hunt, a diplomatic historian at the University of North Carolina, places recent events in the broader history of the Middle East, noting the continuities in U.S. policy and offering a critique of the ideas and assumptions undergirding the war on terrorism.

Setting Right a Dangerous World

JOHN LEWIS GADDIS

We've never had a good name for it, and now it's over. The post-cold-war era—let us call it that for want of any better term—began with the collapse of one structure, the Berlin Wall on November 9, 1989, and ended with the collapse of another, the World Trade Center's twin towers on September 11, 2001. No one, apart from the few people who plotted and carried out those events, could have anticipated that they were going to happen. But from the moment they did, everyone acknowledged that everything had changed.

It's characteristic of such turning points that they shed more light on the history that preceded them than on what's to come. The fall of the Berlin Wall didn't tell us much about the post-cold-war world, but it told us a lot about the cold war.

From John Lewis Gaddis, "Setting Right a Dangerous World," *Chronicle of Higher Education,* January 11, 2002. Reprinted by permission of the author.

It suddenly became clear that East Germany, the Warsaw Pact, and the Soviet Union itself had long since lost the authority with which the United States and its NATO allies had continued to credit them right up to the day the wall came down. The whole history of the cold war looked different as a result. Having witnessed the end, historians could never again see the middle, or even the beginning, in the same way they once had.

Something similar seems likely to happen now to the post-cold-war era. For whatever we eventually settle on calling the events of September 11—the Attack on America, Black Tuesday, 9/11—they've already forced a reconsideration, not only of where we are as a nation and where we may be going, but also of where we've been, even of who we are. Our recent past, all at once, has been thrown into sharp relief, even as our future remains obscure. To paraphrase an old prayer, it's obvious now that we have done some things that we ought not to have done, and that we have not done other things that we ought to have done. How much health there is in us will depend, to a considerable degree, on how we sort this out.

But first things first. No acts of commission or omission by the United States can have justified what happened on September 11. Few if any moral standards have deeper roots than the prohibition against taking innocent life in peacetime. Whatever differences may exist in culture, religion, race, class, or any of the other categories by which human beings seek to establish their identities, that rule transcends them.

The September 11 attacks violated it in ways that go well beyond all other terror-ist attacks in the past: first, by the absence of any stated cause to be served; second, by the failure to provide warning; and finally, by the obvious intent to time and configure the attack in such a manner as to take as many lives as possible—even to the point, some have suggested, of the airplanes' angle of approach, which seemed calculated to devastate as many floors of the twin towers as they could. Let there be no mistake: This was evil, and no set of grievances real or imagined, however strongly felt or widely held, can excuse it.

At the same time, though, neither our outrage nor the patriotic unity that is aris-ing from it relieves us of the obligation to think critically. Would anyone claim, in the aftermath of September 11, that the United States can continue the policies it was following with respect to its national defense, or toward the world, before Sep-tember 11? Americans were not responsible for what happened at Pearl Harbor, but they would have been irresponsible in the extreme if they had not, as a consequence of that attack, dramatically altered their policies. Nobody given the opportunity to rerun the events leading up to that catastrophe would have handled things again in just the same way.

It's in that spirit, I think, that we need a reconsideration of how the United States has managed its responsibilities in the decade since the cold war ended, not with a view to assigning blame, indulging in recrimination, or wallowing in self-pity, but rather for the purpose—now urgent—of determining where we go from here. Patriotism demands nothing less.

The clearest conclusion to emerge from the events of September 11 is that *the geographical position and the military power of the United States are no longer suffi-cient to ensure its security.*

Americans have known insecurity before in their homeland, but not in a very long time. Except for Pearl Harbor and a few isolated pinpricks like Japanese attempts to start forest fires with incendiary bombs in the Pacific Northwest in 1944 and 1945, or the Mexican guerrilla leader Pancho Villa's raid on Columbus, N.M., in 1916, the United States has suffered no foreign attack on its soil since British troops captured Washington and burned the White House and the Capitol in 1814. There's a macabre symmetry in the possibility that the fourth plane hijacked on September 11—which crashed presumably after an uprising among the passengers—probably had one of those buildings as its target.

Few other nations have worried so little for so long about what is coming to be called "homeland security." The late Yale historian C. Vann Woodward even went so far as to define this lack of concern as a central feature of the American character. "Free security," he insisted, had done as much to shape Americans' view of themselves as had the availability of free, or almost free, land.

The 20th century, to be sure, eroded that sense of safety, but that happened as a result of the larger role the United States had assigned itself in world affairs, together with ominous shifts in the European balance of power. It did not arise from any sense of domestic insecurity. We entered World War I to ensure that Germany did not wind up dominating Europe, and we were preparing to do the same thing again in World War II when the Japanese attack, followed by Hitler's own declaration of war, removed from us any choice in the matter. . . .

That's why the United States Commission on National Security in the 21st Century—often known, for its co-chairs Gary Hart and Warren Rudman, as the Hart-Rudman Commission—distinguished between "national" and "homeland" security when it warned of our domestic vulnerabilities, with uncanny prescience, in March 2001. In the aftermath of September 11, we have not only adopted the concept of "homeland security"—it has become synonymous with national security. Such is the revolution in our thinking forced upon us by the events of that day. It means that Americans have entered a new stage in their history, in which they can no longer take security for granted: It is no longer free—anywhere, or at any time.

What was striking about September 11 was the success with which the terrorists transformed objects we had never before regarded as dangerous into weapons of lethal potency. There was nothing exotic here like bombs or even firearms. They used instead the objects of everyday life: pocket knives, twine, box cutters and, of course, commercial aircraft. The terrorists also combined what may seem to us to be a primitive belief in the rewards of martyrdom with the most modern methods of planning, coordination, and execution. We confront, therefore, not only a new category of easily available weaponry, but also a new combination of skill and will in using it.

The attacks' cost-effectiveness was equally striking. No previous act of terrorism came close to this one in lives lost and damage inflicted. The dead approximate the number killed in some three decades of violence in Northern Ireland. They are three times the toll on both sides in the most recent round of the Palestinian intifada. They come close, in deaths suffered on a single day, to the most violent battles of the Civil War. The operation required the lives of 19 terrorists and expenditures of about $500,000. The "payoff," if we can use such a term for such a brutal transaction, was approximately 3,300 dead and perhaps as much as $100-billion in recovery costs. Ratios like these—some 174 victims for every terrorist, and $200,000 in damages for every dollar expended—cannot help but set a standard to which future terrorists will aspire.

The whole point of terrorism is leverage: to accomplish a lot with a little. This operation, in that sense, succeeded brilliantly—even allowing for the fact that one of the four planes failed to reach its target, and that more planes may have been in danger of being hijacked. As a consequence, the images of terrified New Yorkers running through the streets of their city to escape great billowing clouds of ash, dust, and building fragments; of the government in Washington forced to seek shelter; of several days of skies devoid of the contrails we have come to expect passenger aircraft to add to the atmosphere over our heads—those memories will remain in our minds just as vividly as the images, from six decades earlier, of American naval vessels aflame, sinking at their own docks within an American naval base on American territory.

Security, therefore, has a new meaning, for which little in our history and even less in our planning has prepared us.

That leads to a second conclusion, which is that *our foreign policy since the cold war ended has insufficiently served our interests.*

National security requires more than just military deployments or intelligence operations. It depends ultimately upon creating an international environment congenial to the nation's interests. That's the role of foreign policy. Despite many mistakes and diversions along the way, the United States managed to build such an environment during the second half of the 20th century. The Soviet Union's collapse stemmed, in no small measure, from its failure to do the same.

As a consequence, the world at the end of the cold war was closer to a consensus in favor of American values—collective security, democracy, capitalism—than it had ever been before. President George H. W. Bush's talk of a "new world order" reflected a convergence of interests among the great powers that, while imperfect, was nonetheless unprecedented. Differences remained with the European Union, Russia, China, and Japan over such issues as international trade, the handling of regional conflicts, the management of national economies, the definition and hence the protection of human rights; but those were minor compared with issues that had produced two world wars and perpetuated the cold war. Americans, it seemed, had finally found a congenial world.

What's happened since, though? Can anyone claim that the world of 2001— even before September 11—was as friendly to American interests as it had been in 1991? It would be silly to blame the United States alone for the disappointments of the past decade. Too many other actors, from Saddam Hussein to Slobodan Milosevic to Osama bin Laden, have helped to bring them about. But the question that haunted Americans after Pearl Harbor is still worth asking: Given the opportunity to rerun the sequence, what would we want to change in our foreign policy, and what would we leave the same?

The question is not at all hypothetical. The administration of George W. Bush has already undertaken, in the wake of September 11, the most sweeping reassessment of foreign-policy priorities since the cold war ended. Its results are not yet clear, but the tilt is far more toward change than continuity. That is an implicit acknowledgment of deficiencies in the American approach to the world during the post-cold-war era that are clearer now than they were then.

One of those, it seems, was unilateralism, an occupational hazard of sole surviving superpowers. With so little countervailing power in sight, such states tend to lead without listening, a habit that can cause resistance even among those otherwise disposed to follow. The United States managed to avoid that outcome after its victory in World War II because we had, in the Soviet Union, a superpower competitor. Our allies, and even our former adversaries, tolerated a certain amount of arrogance on our part because there was always "something worse" out there; we, in turn, fearing their defection or collapse, treated them with greater deference and respect than they might have expected given the power imbalances of the time.

With our victory in the cold war, though, we lost the "something worse." American ideas, institutions, and culture remained as attractive as ever throughout much of the world, but American policies began to come across as overbearing, self-indulgent, and insensitive to the interests of others. Our own domestic politics made things worse: With the White House in the control of one party and the Congress in the hands of another during most of this period, it was difficult to get a consensus on such matters as paying United Nations dues, participating in the International Criminal Court, or ratifying the Comprehensive Test Ban Treaty, the Land Mines Convention, or the Kyoto Protocol on Climate Change. During most of the cold war, knowing what our enemies would make of our failure to do those things, a consensus would have been easy.

A second problem, too, arose largely as a result of unilateralism: We neglected the cultivation of great-power relationships. We seemed to have assumed, perhaps because we were the greatest of the great powers, that we no longer needed the cooperation of the others to promote our interests. We therefore allowed our relations with the Russians and the Chinese to deteriorate to the point that by the end of the 1990s we were barely on speaking terms with Moscow and Beijing. We failed to sustain one of the most remarkable achievements of American foreign policy during the cold war—the success of Richard Nixon and Henry Kissinger in creating a situation in which our adversaries feared each other more than they feared us. It was as if we had switched our source of geopolitical inspiration from Otto von Bismarck to Kaiser Wilhelm II.

That happened chiefly as the result of a third characteristic of our post-cold-war foreign policy: a preference for justice at the expense of order. We had never entirely neglected the demands of justice during the cold war, but we did tend to pursue those goals by working with the powerful to get them to improve their treatment of the powerless. We sought to promote human rights from the inside out rather than from the outside in: Sometimes we succeeded, sometimes we did not.

With the end of the cold war, however, we changed our approach. We enlarged NATO against the wishes of the Russians, not because the Poles, the Czechs, and the Hungarians added significantly to the alliance's military capabilities, but rather because those states had suffered past injustices and therefore "deserved" membership. We then used the expanded alliance to rescue the Kosovars and bomb the Serbs, despite the fact that in doing so we were violating the sovereignty of an internationally recognized state without explicit United Nations approval. Unsurprisingly, that angered not just the Russians but also the Chinese, both of whom had discontented minorities of their own to worry about. Our intentions were praiseworthy in both of those episodes, but our attention to the larger geopolitical implications was not what it might have been.

A fourth aspect of our post-cold-war foreign policy followed from the third: It was the inconsistency with which we pursued regional justice. We were, as it turned out, by no means as adamant in seeking justice for the Chechens or the Tibetans as we were for the Kosovars; Moscow and Beijing, despite their nervousness, had little to fear. But by applying universal principles on a less than universal basis, Washington did open itself to the charge of hypocrisy. It was worse elsewhere, as in Somalia, where our reluctance to take casualties of our own revealed how little we were prepared to sacrifice for the rights of others, or in Rwanda, where we responded to the greatest atrocities of the decade by simply averting our eyes.

Meanwhile, in the Middle East, we tolerated the continuing Israeli dispossession and repression of Palestinians, even as we were seeking to secure the rights of the Palestinians; and we did nothing to adjust policy in response to the fact that an old adversary, Iran, was moving toward free elections and a parliamentary system, even as old allies like Saudi Arabia were shunning such innovations. There was, in short, a gap between our principles and our practices: We proclaimed the former without linking them to the latter, and that invited disillusionment. There are several reasons that the rantings of bin Laden resonate to the extent that they do in so many parts of North Africa, the Middle East, and Asia; surely that is one of them.

A fifth problem was our tendency to regard our economic system as a model to be applied throughout the world, without regard to differences in local conditions and with little sense of the effects it would have in generating inequality. This was particularly evident in Russia, where we too easily assumed a smooth transition to market capitalism. Our efforts to help came nowhere near the scope and the seriousness of the programs we'd launched to rebuild the economies of our defeated adversaries after World War II.

Meanwhile, Washington officials were less sensitive than they should have been to the extent to which American wealth and power were being blamed, throughout much of the world, for the inequities that the globalization of capitalism was generating. Capitalism would have expanded after the cold war regardless of what the United States did. By linking that expansion so explicitly to our foreign-policy objectives, however, we associated ourselves with something abroad that we would never have tolerated at home: the workings of an unregulated market devoid of a social safety net. Adam Smith was right in arguing that the pursuit of self-interest ultimately benefits the collective interest; but Karl Marx was right when he pointed out that wealth is not distributed to everyone equally at the same time, and that alienation arises as a result. The United States and most other advanced societies found ways to reconcile those competing truths with the emergence of the regulatory state during the first half of the 20th century. Capitalism might not have survived had that not happened. No such reconciliation was sought, however, as a foreign-policy priority during the post-cold-war era.

Finally, and largely as a consequence, the United States emphasized the advantages, while neglecting the dangers, of globalization. There was a great deal of talk after the cold war ended of the extent to which that process had blurred the boundary between the domestic and the international: It was held to be a good thing that capital, commodities, ideas, and people could move more freely across boundaries. There was little talk, though, of an alternative possibility: that danger might move just as freely. That's a major lesson of September 11: The very instruments of the new world order—airplanes, liberal policies on immigration and money transfers, multiculturalism itself, in the sense that there seemed nothing odd about the hijackers when they were taking their flight training—can be turned horribly against it. It was as if we had convinced ourselves that the new world of global communications had somehow transformed an old aspect of human nature: the tendency to harbor griev- ances and sometimes to act upon them.

What connects these shortcomings is a failure of strategic vision: the ability to see how the parts of one's policy combine to form the whole, and to avoid the illusion that one can pursue particular policies in particular places without their interacting with one another. It means remembering that actions have consequences: that for every action there will be a reaction, the nature of which won't always be predict- able. It means accepting the fact that there's not always a linear relationship between input and output: that vast efforts can produce minimal results in some situations, and that minimal efforts can produce vast consequences in others. It means thinking about the implications of such asymmetries for the relationship between ends and means, always the central problem of strategy. Leverage is important, and our ad- versaries have so far proved more successful than we in using it. Finally, it requires effective national leadership, a quality for which American foreign policy during the post-cold-war era is unlikely to be remembered.

Where do we go from here? Will the events of September 11 bring our policies back into line with our interests? Can we regain the clarity of strategic vision that served us well during the cold war, and that seemed to desert us during its after- math? Shocks like this do have the advantage of concentrating the mind. Those of us who worried, during the 1990s, about the difficulty of thinking strategically in an age of apparent safety need no longer do so. As was the case with Pearl Harbor, a confusing world has suddenly become less so, even if at horrendous cost.

What's emerging is the prospect, once again, of "something worse" than an American-dominated world—perhaps something much worse. The appalling nature of the attacks on New York and Washington forged a new coalition against terror- ism overnight. The great-power consensus that withered after 1991 is back in place in expanded form: The United States, The European Union, Russia, China and Japan are all on the same side now—at least on the issue of terrorism—and they've been joined by unexpected allies like Pakistan, Uzbekistan, and perhaps even, very discreetly, Iran. Terrorism can hardly flourish without some state support; but Sep- tember 11 brought home the fact that terrorism challenges the authority of all states. Everybody has airplanes, and everything that lies below them must now be consid- ered a potential target. So just as fear of the Soviet Union built and sustained an American coalition during the cold war—and just the prospect of nuclear annihila- tion caused the Soviets themselves ultimately to begin cooperating with it—so the sudden appearance of "something much worse" is a paradoxical but powerful ally in the new war that now confronts us.

Maintaining this coalition, however, will require tolerating diversity within it. That was one of our strengths during the cold war: The United States was far more successful than the Soviet Union in leading while listening, so that those who we led felt that they had an interest in being led. NATO survived, as a consequence, while the Sino-Soviet alliance and the Warsaw Pact did not. If the global coalition against terrorism is to survive, it will demand even greater flexibility on the part of Americans than our cold-war coalition did. We'll have to give up the unilateral- ism we indulged in during the post-cold-war era. The Bush administration, prior to

September 11, had seemed particularly to relish that bad habit. We'll have to define our allies more in terms of shared interests and less in terms of shared values. We'll have to compromise more than we might like in promoting human rights, open markets, and the scrupulous observance of democratic procedures. We'll have to concentrate more than we have in the past on getting whatever help we can in the war against terrorism, wherever we can find it. Our concerns with regional justice may suffer as a result: We're not likely to return soon to rescuing Kosovars, or to condemning oppression against Chechens and Tibetans. The compensation, one hopes, will be to secure justice on a broader scale, for terrorism will offer little justice for anyone.

Even as we pursue that path, we'll need to address the grievances that fuel terrorism in the first place. Once again, there are cold-war precedents: With the rehabilitation of Germany and Japan after World War II, together with the Marshall Plan, we fought the conditions that made the Soviet alternative attractive even as we sought to contain the Soviets themselves. We launched our own form of asymmetrical warfare against Communism. Our "leverage" was to deploy our strengths imaginatively against its weaknesses, and the "payoff" was easily as disproportionate as anything the terrorists achieved on September 11. A relatively small investment of resources and intelligence secured for the United States and its allies, during the second half of the 20th century, a far more congenial world than what they had to live through during its first half. Can we apply the same strategy now against the conditions that breed terrorists in so many parts of what we used to call the "third world"? We'd better try, for some of those regions are at least as much at risk now as Europe and Japan were half a century ago.

The era we've just entered—whatever we decide to call it—is bound to be more painful than the one we've just left. The antiterrorist coalition is sure to undergo strains as its priorities shift from recovery to retaliation. Defections will doubtless occur. Further terrorist attacks are unavoidable, and are certain to produce demoralization as well as greater resolve.

But it does seem likely, even at this early stage in the war they have provoked, that the terrorists have got more than they bargained for. "What kind of a people do they think we are?" Winston Churchill asked of the Japanese in the aftermath of Pearl Harbor. It's worth asking the same of our new enemies, because it can hardly have been their purpose to give the United States yet another chance to lead the world into a new era, together with the opportunity to do it, this time, more wisely.

In the Wake of September 11

MICHAEL H. HUNT

Acute problems attend the interpretive framing of an unfolding foreign policy crisis. Just when perspective is most valuable, it is also hardest for policy makers and commentators alike to find because of the pressure to act and the value of quick and simple ways of understanding. Historians have something important to say at such a

From Michael H. Hunt, "In the Wake of September 11: The Clash of What?" *Journal of American History* (September 2002): 416–425. Copyright © Organization of American Historians. All rights reserved. Reprinted with permission.

moment. Understanding of the past is a useful, perhaps even essential, way of providing orientation in the midst of the press of confusing events. Historical perspective will not make any easier the resolution of the difficulties now facing the United States in the Middle East. On the other hand, it would be reckless to engage ever-more deeply and especially militarily in the region without first considering the possible pitfalls that a historical perspective might reveal.

The argument advanced here is that the nature of the conflict sparked by the horrors of September 11 and represented by the "war on terrorism" has been ill defined historically by those who have declared that war. Their justifications rest on simple binaries, usually couched in terms of defense of civilization and the march of the modern. We need instead a framework that eschews superiority and inevitability and prompts both some degree of self-consciousness among Americans with a voice in the policy debate and a modicum of awareness about those supposedly arrayed against us and ostensibly teetering on the brink of barbarism or trapped in tradition. The pairing proposed here is a bit less neat and a bit less symmetrical. On the one side is a seemingly potent and long-lived but perhaps hollow American nationalism quick to see evil, ready to combat barbarism, devoted to the advance of its way of life, and forgetful of a long record of U.S. intervention in the Middle East. On the other side is something considerably more complex—a multivalent politics in an Islamic key with decades of history behind it and with a striking range of articulations among Muslims in far-flung places. "Fundamentalism" does not begin to do justice to its diversity, and positing some blind hostility to "the West" and "the modern world" misses the genuine, specific grievances varying from country to country and inspiring both intellectual ferment and political action.

Let us begin by considering the two most popular ways of interpretively framing the crisis of September 11. One reading with perhaps the widest currency derives from Samuel Huntington. In 1993 he advanced the view that the United States as the leader of the West was caught in a clash of civilizations. The main challenge, as he saw it, came from Confucian Asia (primarily China) and the Islamic world (Iran seemed at the time of writing the embodiment of militant regional resistance). Huntington's interpretation, with its stark and value-laden delineation of regions in conflict, commanded considerable attention when it appeared and has won fresh converts in the wake of September 11.

This "clash" interpretation has flaws that are troubling but also familiar in American foreign policy thinking. Huntington's notion of civilization is monolithic, static, and essentialist—much like the Cold War–era view of the Communist enemy. Reacting against the revived interest in Huntington's argument after September 11, Edward Said warned of the dangers of making "'civilizations' and 'identities' into what they are not: shut-down, sealed-off entities that have been purged of the myriad currents and countercurrents that animate human history, and that over centuries have made it possible for that history not only to contain wars of religion and imperial conquest but also to be one of exchange, cross-fertilization and sharing." Seen in even longer-term perspective, Huntington is heir to one of the most ethnocentric and aggressive notions in American history. Like nineteenth-century advocates of Manifest Destiny faced by the perceived barbarism of Native Americans, Latin Americans, the Spanish, and the Chinese, he posits U.S. civilizational superiority and on that basis calls for a kind of moral rearmament to promote and defend Western values. In his construction, countries determined to find their own way are not part of a culturally diverse world, but wrong-headed rebels against a preponderant and enlightened West.

The clash of modernity is an alternative, more intellectually refined formulation. But it too is ethnocentric, and it too has a dubious pedigree. The social science modernizers of the 1950s and early 1960s championed the notion that old values and institutions (deemed "traditional") holding back the Third World were to give way to new ones (deemed "modern"). In the new rendition of modernization as in the old, modernity takes at least implicitly American form (for example, in Paul Kennedy's formulation "laissez-faire economics, cultural pluralism and political democracy"), and tradition is embodied by countries cursed with seemingly static and rigid cultures that block development and breed popular dissatisfaction. In its most recent incarnation, modernization appears as part of the popular view of impersonal forces of globalization sweeping around the world and inexorably creating social and cultural as well as economic uniformity—and leaving behind backwaters of failure where tradition either refuses to surrender its hold or collapses into anarchy. The Middle East has figured as one of those backwaters, a natural breeding ground for crazed fanatics given to psychotic behavior. This view has been most widely disseminated in the snappy, enthusiastic writing about the new laissez-faire world by Thomas Friedman, the *New York Times* reporter turned columnist, and by Robert D. Kaplan, a journalist who has painted a dark picture of parts of the world fragmenting under mounting social, demographic, and environmental pressures.

The proponents of the modernization perspective conjure up a tradition-bound world in images of exotic dress and rituals, bizarre theocratic rule, a fanatic faith, inexplicable group identities, and women locked in the harem. While Huntington calls for manning the walls against barbarians at the gate, the modernizers offer the comforting notion that "progress" will inevitably bring most countries into the fold of the modern world, leaving only a few lagging farther and farther behind. In this view, the duty of the United States is to align itself with the forces of history, pushing the reluctant ahead, calling to heel those straying from the designated path, and washing its hands of "failed states" hopelessly trapped in the difficult transition from the traditional to the modern. Relentlessly teleological and culturally tone-deaf, modernizers now as earlier have had difficulty imagining more complicated historical processes by which societies change in idiosyncratic ways involving borrowing, indigenization, localization—all terms meant to suggest a dynamic of cultural amalgamation and accommodation. It is as if China, Japan, India, Iran, and Turkey—all striking examples of indigenous values and institutions interacting with outside social, political, and economic forces to create new forms—did not exist.

The shortcomings of these two influential American interpretations of the Middle East suggest the need for some self-reflection, especially on the nationalist impulses that animate both of them. The events of September 11 jolted U.S. officials and most of the public into an impressive outpouring of nationalist feeling. The heavy, horrifying loss of civilian life was part of the reason. Another was the violation of American soil. Finally, the existence of an easily recognizable "evil other" (the Muslim fanatic retailed widely in public pronouncements and popular culture the last several decades) provided a clear and ready villain. The president went before Congress on September 20, 2001, and in a televised speech that was widely praised vowed to fight back. Liberally sprinkled through the text were the keywords from a century and more of public foreign policy discourse: national mission, the fate of human freedom, world leadership, strength and courage in the face of a dark threat.

> As long as the United States of America is determined and strong, this will not be an age of terror; this will be an age of liberty, here and across the world. (Applause.) . . . [I]n our grief and anger we have found our mission and our moment. Freedom and fear are at war. The advance of human freedom—the great achievement of our time, and the great hope of every time—now depends on us. Our nation—this generation—will lift a dark threat of violence from our people and our future. We will rally the world to this cause by our efforts, by our courage. We will not tire, we will not falter, and we will not fail. (Applause.)

Reading these lines calls at once to mind passages from such classic early Cold War statements as the Truman Doctrine and NSC-68. Once more policy makers proclaim a time of national testing with the fate of the globe hanging in the balance.

The new patriotic consensus expressed itself in a wide variety of ways familiar from previous national trials. The consensus was rapidly evident in proliferating flags on cars, storefronts, and office doors and in heated language on radio talk shows and in official pronouncements. In the name of "civilization" the innocuously named American Council of Trustees and Alumni decried too-free speech, moral relativism, and national self-loathing supposedly evident in critical academic reactions to the "war on terrorism." Muslims around the country came under close official and popular scrutiny and prudently self-censored. Public debate sputtered and died; dissenters fell to the margins of political respectability. The media at once got in step and deferentially made government press conferences, speeches, and press releases the staple of its reporting. The war on terrorism became a compelling story told in familiar nationalist terms of a country rallying and readying to strike back. A corps of instant experts appeared to satisfy the public hunger for information about those big, confusing, overlapping entities—the Middle East, the Arabs, and Islam—suddenly thrust into popular consciousness.

The most remarkable feature of this nationalist upsurge, for a historian at least, has been the ability of policy makers and most pundits to maintain a sense of injured innocence through an audacious repression of a half century of U.S. intervention in the Middle East. That deep entanglement began with the Cold War and the related campaign to promote stable, secular, pro-U.S. regimes that would shore up the anti-communist containment line in the region and assure the flow of oil. A variety of critics—from Arab nationalists to economic nationalists to Marxists to neutralists—challenged the American vision of the Middle East tied politically and economically to the interests of the United States and its European allies. U.S. policy makers soldiered on and in the process made two critical decisions with legacies still playing out today: first, to support Israel, and, second, to overthrow a neutralist, economically nationalist government in Iran in 1953 and replace it with a regime tightly tied to U.S. interests (that of Mohammed Reza Shah Pahlavi).

Since the 1970s, the Middle East has emerged for U.S. policy as the chief zone of conflict, a dubious distinction that East Asia had surrendered after a quarter century of crises and war. Over the last three decades we have remained an active player in the political, military, economic, and cultural life of the region. We have been on both the receiving and giving end of suspicion, misunderstanding, retaliation, and violence. Troubles began with an oil embargo in 1973 and continued with the over-throw of an unpopular, U.S.-backed shah and the taking of American hostages in Iran in 1979, support for Iraq in its long, bloody war with Iran in the 1980s, Ronald Reagan's bombing of Libya, the involvement of marines in fighting in Lebanon in 1983 following the Israeli invasion, the Gulf War of 1990–1991, the residual American military presence in the Persian Gulf, continued containment of Iran, a policy of economic and military pressure against Iraq, and the ongoing diplomatic cover and military and financial support for a territorially expansionist Israel.

Well after September 11, most Americans still do not have the foggiest notion of this pattern of U.S. entanglement. The relevant past has been instead the grand narrative of American confrontation with heterodox ideologies from fascism to totalitarianism to fundamentalism. Or the past simply disappears in timeless con-tests between good and evil or civilization and barbarism. But this U.S. entanglement is widely understood and resented in the Middle East. Americans too need to under-stand it if we are to imagine how our role might, at least among some, generate a resentment that would inspire deadly and indiscriminate retaliation. It has been easy for critics in the region—secular as well as religious—to denounce the official U.S. presence as an obstacle to economic development, social justice, cultural in-tegrity, and democracy. It has also been easy to label as neocolonial the order pro-moted by Washington, in effect linking U.S. policy to the earlier British and French imperial enterprises. Like Britain, the United States has established bases, shored up governments headed by amenable elites (notably in Israel, Jordan, Egypt over the last several decades, and Saudi Arabia), and opposed both openly and covertly governments not responsive to U.S. goals (such as Egypt under Gamal Abdel Nasser, Syria, Iraq, and Iran). By working closely with our British allies in carry-ing out these policies, we have provided a constant reminder of the link between the British era of dominance and the more recent American one.

The post–September 11 nationalist upsurge in the United States with its impres-sive capacity to blank out an inconvenient past has sturdy antecedents. Its immediate antecedents include the popular patriotism of World War I and the early Cold War, the nationalist revitalization project undertaken by neoconservatives in the after-math of the Vietnam War and the seeming loss of moral fortitude in the Nixon years, Reagan's appeal for the country to stand tall in the world, and the celebration fol-lowing a Gulf War victory banishing the specter of national decline. Perhaps the predictions of global theories are wrong—the state is not in steep decline but, to the contrary, remains a potent symbol of popular loyalty and a formidable mobilizing force. Nationalism *seems* still a vital force in American life.

But how seriously should we take this recent explosion of nationalist sentiment? Is it a mile wide and an inch deep? Two general studies of the relation of nationalism to U.S. foreign policy—my own in 1987 and Anders Stephanson's in 1995—diverge on whether this ideology was becoming attenuated at the end of the twentieth cen-tury. The emotional nationwide outpouring immediately after September 11, almost seamlessly tied to the Bush administration response, tends to support my own claim for durability and persistence. But, once beyond shock and grief over the loss of American life, the national response had the feel not of a great crisis or cause whose course would define the life of a generation, but of a sporting event at which the home team sweeps the outclassed opposition from the field or (perhaps more commonly) a quickly satisfied hunger for revenge and a quiet longing for security from future attacks. Every bit as much as the Gulf War, this anti-terrorist war evoked tough talk and soaring aspirations while following a cautious military strategy designed to hold down U.S. losses. Meanwhile, the president called reassuringly for business as usual on the home front, and consumers complied. Stephanson's skeptical appraisal increasingly seems closer to the mark.

This strange disconnect between the epochal issues ostensibly at stake and the minimal sacrifices asked of Americans carries forward a pattern familiar to historians. The public seems as ambivalent today about the direct involvement of Americans in combat as it was during the war in Vietnam or earlier in Korea or even earlier after World War I or earlier still in the course of fighting in the Philippines or still earlier in the war with Mexico. Vietnam and Korea offer especially dramatic illustrations of the public's allergy to protracted or open-ended commitments that result in the heavy loss of American life. Consumer values and the closely related notion of individualism made it difficult for policy makers to elicit significant, sustained popular sacrifice. That public allergy has persisted, confirming its influence following loss of American soldiers serving in Beirut and Somalia and the hesitation over intervention in Bosnia and Kosovo.

The generation of military leaders who had served in Vietnam as junior officers shared the public's aversion and helped to formulate prudential rules to guide decisions on committing U.S. forces to combat. The classic statement by Secretary of Defense Caspar Weinberger, issued in November 1984, included the following almost paralyzing set of preconditions for the use of force: act only in defense of vital national interests, devise clear political and military objectives, commit to win, use the appropriate size and type of force, be sure of the support of the American people and Congress, and seek first nonmilitary solutions to the problem. Secretary of State Colin Powell, himself a Vietnam veteran, called during his tenure as chair of the Joint Chiefs of Staff for a seemingly more flexible if nonetheless cautious rule of thumb: "the use of force should be restricted to occasions where it can do some good and where the good will outweigh the loss of lives and other costs that will surely ensue. Wars kill people." Powell did not make clear how policy makers without the gift of clairvoyance were to tot up the overall costs and benefits of military action.

Even while military leadership passes from one generation to another, the caution remains. The evidence is to be found in the expeditionary model that the armed forces adopted during the 1980s and 1990s. From Beirut to Libya to the Persian Gulf to Somalia to Haiti, American forces undertook variously to punish, order, and feed—but always at a low cost in American lives and with the maximum use of air power. These police and social welfare actions maximized the use of U.S. high-tech weaponry and minimized the exposure of U.S. soldiers to danger. The intervention in Afghanistan neatly fits into this pattern. U.S bombs clear the way for ground forces, preferably allies alongside or in front of U.S. troops. So far it has worked.

But the Bush administration finds itself by virtue of its commitment to a war on terrorism in a familiar—and dangerous—situation. The war's geographical range and vague goals raise the risks; the U.S. public and Congress seem permissive; and so the president may by choice or inadvertence place (or find) his military in a situation that would prove more costly or intractable than anticipated. Then patriotism would receive its true test. Americans would then have to face the serious challenge that lurks behind this foreign policy crisis: whether a country with pretensions to lead and change the world was too self-absorbed even to grasp the dimensions of those gargantuan ambitions or to pay the price in treasure and lives when the bill inevitably comes due. The United States thus hangs suspended between the dominant nationalism that by its very nature constantly risks overreaching and an alternative national identity that is more modest in its goals but less able to supply an emotionally satisfying sense of collective identity and power.

If American nationalism is one side of a new binary, what should we place on the other side? Seen through the prism of that nationalism, "Islamic fundamentalism" (also referred to as "militant Islam") would seem the obvious answer. Here is the most often cited source of evil, darkness, and terror coming out of the Middle East. Buried in that phrase are appealing if vague explanations for such brutal acts as September 11 and for the troubled advance of modern life that makes fanaticism and irrational anger fester in the region. Like all broadly appealing ideological gestures, this one dispenses with considerable complexity. It offers a marvelous economy of explanation at the price of conflating a wide variety of religiously inspired political movements and ignoring the wide variety of ways that religious ideas have assumed a prominence among the countries that are the home of well over a billion Muslims on the planet. In a sweep of territory running from northern Africa to Southeast Asia, there are at least as many public, political expressions of Islam as there are countries, each with its own linguistic, ethnic, and historical profile. The challenge is to understand Islam as among other things a source of political ideas that have taken quite distinct national forms, that are also transnational in their reach, and that thus resist easy categorization or generalization.

Islamic politics, a more useful, complex binary to set against U.S. nationalism, needs to be understood primarily in local terms—as an expression of sharpening disillusionment with secular regimes over the last quarter century. Opposition—sometimes electoral, sometimes violent—appeared in places as widespread and culturally diverse as Iran, Algeria, Egypt, Turkey, Syria, and Iraq. All were states that had sought to build a "modern" society on the basis of socialism, nationalism, capitalism, or liberalism. Those wanting to anchor national life instead in religious values not only attacked the moral bankruptcy of a secular path but also condemned the U.S. government for propping up hated secular leaders divorced from their own people, for guaranteeing the survival of the no less hated state of Israel, and for promoting a soulless materialism. For those critical of the status quo, the American presence has become deeply entangled with national as well as regional problems, and thus solutions to those problems seem to involve unavoidably a confrontation of some sort with the U.S. government. Those wielding the weapon of terror may not elicit much open support in the Middle East or elsewhere in the Islamic world, but their radical critique of present conditions, their potent amalgam of religion and politics, and their determination to act even against the odds enjoys strong popular appeal.

Following this line of argument, the regional past to set September 11 against is not the one favored by critics of the Bush administration—the anti-Soviet war in Afghanistan and the "blowback" from that covert effort that Americans are now experiencing. To be sure, covert U.S. support for the resistance in Afghanistan had unintended, damaging consequences (as virtually all such interventions do). But the blowback thesis flirts with the same ethnocentric notions of U.S. power enter-tained by the Bush administration. They share a tendency, as Francis FitzGerald has phrased it, "to relate the fall of sparrows in distant lands to some fault or virtue of American policy." Just as some policy critics make the United States the main source of evil in the world, so do leading policy makers assume a boundless national capacity to combat evil.

Rather than focusing on Afghanistan and the blowback thesis, we might more fruitfully look to the Iranian revolution of 1978–1979 as a more pertinent past. That revolution was a defining, watershed moment when Islam assumed formidable po-litical proportions with reverberations not only in Iran but also throughout the region. It demonstrated the power of religious ideas and leaders to mobilize the public and effect change. Islamists across the region hailed Ayatollah Ruhollah Khomeini's triumph as a harbinger of cultural and political resurgence that would turn back the inroads of the West and Israel and overthrow secular elites. The revolution's power-ful impact on its neighbors helped almost at once to destabilize the region. Afghani-stan was the first domino to fall when Soviet forces invaded in 1979 to head off what the Kremlin feared would be the spread of Islamic unrest in Central Asia. By throw-ing its protection over the Shi'a majority in Iraq, the Iranian revolutionary regime also helped provoke the Iran-Iraq war of 1980–1988. That war in turn prepared the way for Iraq's invasion of Kuwait in 1990 and the Gulf War of 1991. The war with Iran had drained Saddam Hussein's treasury, created good relations with Washing-ton, and fed his ambitions. Kuwait was tempting and seemingly easy pickings. This string of conflicts ignited by Iran's newfound political faith would set the stage for the current crisis: devastation and civil war within Afghanistan, resentment over the American military presence in Saudi Arabia, and the U.S. dual containment policy directed against Iran and Iraq.

Finally, the Iranian revolution deserves special attention because it throws into sharp relief the very problems that policy makers face today. The run-up to the revo-lution found the Carter administration unable to grasp the appeal of an Islamic politi-cal movement. That administration was also unaware of Iranian resentment over the role of the CIA (Central Intelligence Agency) in overthrowing the government of Mohammed Mossadeq in 1953 and over U.S. support for the shah and his program of secularization, militarization, and ties to Israel over the following decades. Anti-Americanism seemed in 1979, as much as it seems now, an irrational, incomprehen-sible outburst by wild-eyed radicals. The legacy of anger and incomprehension has made it easier for U.S. policy makers, including the current Bush administration, to fixate on Tehran as a sponsor of terror and to ignore a lively political and social experiment that experienced observers invest with considerable promise and that Muslims everywhere watch with great interest.

If the clash unfolding before us involves some sort of fundamentalism, it is tempting to say that it is as much ours as theirs—that there are strong strains of funda-mentalism on both sides. Americans bring to the September 11 crisis a deeply rooted nationalist faith that is universal in its application, ahistorical in its thinking, and reductive in its view of other cultures. The talk from the White House, the Justice Department, and the Pentagon draws from a familiar nationalist repertoire that re-duces complex situations to easily grasped terms familiar from other times of tension and fear. The result is the ethnocentric invocation of a great conspiracy, an axis of evil, a monolith of terror. This is the language of the crusader. Posed against this official American position with broad popular appeal is something more amorphous but demonstrably powerful—a set of values that has come to the fore in Muslim countries, that is preoccupied above all with domestic renovation, and that is in the main opposed to the United States for what it does politically and militarily to sustain a bankrupt old order and obstruct efforts to create something better.

There may be dangers lurking as Americans make their way deeper into the affairs of the region. Taking guidance from convenient simplifications is not likely to prove in practice any wiser today than it has in the past. It may well be now in the Middle East, as earlier in East Asia, that historical perspective will find little if any place in policy decisions and public debate. Ignoring history or embracing a simple, comforting version of it is always an attractive option. U.S. policy makers are likely to plunge heedlessly ahead. A fundamental reconsideration of policy may then have to wait until they encounter resistance that imposes costs higher than the public is willing to pay and that finally creates a kind of education through violence. This is a grim prospect with much uncertainty and much human suffering likely to attend it.

✦ F U R T H E R   R E A D I N G

Albrow, Martin. *The Global Age: State and Society Beyond Modernity* (1996).
Bacevich, Andrew J. *American Empire: The Realities and Consequences of U.S. Diplomacy* (2002).
Barber, Benjamin R. *Jihad vs. McWorld: How Globalism and Tribalism Are Reshaping the World* (1996).
Baudrillard, Jean. *The Spirit of Terrorism* (2002).
Bowden, Mark. *Black Hawk Down: A Story of Modern War* (1999).
Brzezinski, Zbigniew K. *The Choice: Global Domination or Global Leadership?* (2004).
Bush, George H. W., and Brent Scowcroft. *A World Transformed* (1998).
Callahan, David. *Unwinnable Wars: American Power and Ethnic Conflict* (1997).
Clark, Richard A. *Against All Enemies: Inside America's War on Terror* (2004).
Clark, Wesley. *Waging Modern War: Bosnia, Kosovo, and the Future of Combat* (2002).
Coll, Steve. *Ghost Wars: The Secret History of the CIA, Afghanistan, and Bin Laden* (2004).
Daalder, Ivo H., and James M. Lindsay. *America Unbound: The Bush Revolution in Foreign Policy* (2004).
Dudziak, Mary L., ed. *September 11 in History: A Watershed Moment?* (2003).
Eckes, Alfred E., Jr., and Thomas W. Zeiler. *Globalization and the American Century* (2003).
Freedman, Lawrence, and Efraim Karsh. *The Gulf Conflict, 1990–1991: Diplomacy and War in the New World Order* (1995).
Friedman, Thomas L. *The Lexus and the Olive Tree* (1999).
———. *The World Is Flat: A Brief History of the Twenty-first Century* (2005).
Fukuyama, Francis. *The End of History and the Last Man* (1992).
Gaddis, John Lewis. *Surprise, Security, and the American Experience* (2004).
Greider, William. *One World, Ready or Not: The Manic Logic of Global Capitalism* (1997).
Haass, Richard N. *The Reluctant Sheriff: The United States After the Cold War* (1998).
Halberstam, David. *War in a Time of Peace: Bush, Clinton, and the Generals* (2002).
Hardt, Michael, and Antonio Negri. *Empire* (2000).
Hauterwas, Stanley, and Frank Lentricchia, eds. *Dissent from the Homeland* (2003).
Hersh, Seymour M. *Chain of Command: The Road from 9/11 to Abu Ghraib* (2004).
Hoffman, Stanley. *Gulliver Unbound: The Imperial Temptation and the War in Iraq* (2004).
Huntington, Samuel P. *The Clash of Civilizations and the Remaking of World Order* (1996).

Ignatieff, Michael. *Virtual War: Kosovo and Beyond* (2000).

———. *The Warrior's Honor: Ethnic War and the Modern Conscience* (1998).

Johnson, Chalmers. *The Sorrows of Empire: Militarism, Secrecy, and the End of the Republic* (2004).

Keegan, John. *The Iraq War* (2004).

Lebow, Richard Ned, and Janice Gross Stein. *We All Lost the Cold War* (1994).

Lieber, Robert J., ed. *Eagle Rules? Foreign Policy and American Primacy in the Twenty-first Century* (2001).

National Commission on Terrorist Attacks. *The 9/11 Commission Report: Final Report of the National Commission on Terrorist Attacks upon the United States* (2004).

Nye, Joseph S. *Soft Power: The Means to Succeed in World Politics* (2004).

Ohmae, Kenichi. *The Borderless World: Power and Strategy in the Interlocked Economy* (1990).

Prados, John. *Hoodwinked: The Documents That Reveal How Bush Sold Us a War* (2004).

Schrecker, Ellen. *Cold War Triumphalism: The Politics of American History After the Fall of Communism* (2004).

Sellers, Mortimer, ed. *The New World Order: Sovereignty, Human Rights and the Self-Determination of Peoples* (1996).

Stiglitz, Joseph E. *Globalization and Its Discontents* (2002).

Todd, Emmanuel. *After the Empire: The Breakdown of the American Order* (2004).

Tucker, Robert W., and David C. Hendrickson. *The Imperial Temptation: The New World Order and America's Purposes* (1992).

Woodward, Bob. *Bush at War* (2002).

———. *Plan of Attack* (2004).